# SOCIAL ZOOARCHAEOLOGY

This is the first book to provide a systematic overview of social zooarchaeology, which takes a holistic view of human–animal relations in the past. Until recently, archaeological analysis of faunal evidence has primarily focused on the role of animals in the human diet and subsistence economy. This book, however, argues that animals have always played many more roles in human societies: as wealth, companions, spirit helpers, sacrificial victims, totems, centerpieces of feasts, objects of taboos, and more. These social factors are as significant as taphonomic processes in shaping animal bone assemblages. Nerissa Russell uses evidence derived not only from zooarchaeology but also from ethnography, history, and classical studies to suggest the range of human–animal relationships and to examine their importance in human society. Through exploring the significance of animals to ancient humans, this book provides a richer picture of past societies.

**Nerissa Russell** is Associate Professor of Anthropology and Archaeology at Cornell University. Her research focuses on the full range of human–animal relations, with particular emphasis on the social and symbolic roles of animals for ancient people. She has published more than forty book chapters and articles in journals, including *Antiquity*, *Paleorient*, and *Journal of Archaeological Science*.

# SOCIAL ZOOARCHAEOLOGY

## HUMANS AND ANIMALS IN PREHISTORY

**NERISSA RUSSELL**
Cornell University

**CAMBRIDGE**
UNIVERSITY PRESS

CAMBRIDGE UNIVERSITY PRESS
Cambridge, New York, Melbourne, Madrid, Cape Town,
Singapore, São Paulo, Delhi, Tokyo, Mexico City

Cambridge University Press
32 Avenue of the Americas, New York, NY 10013-2473, USA

www.cambridge.org
Information on this title: www.cambridge.org/9780521143110

First published 2012

Printed in the United States of America

*A catalog record for this publication is available from the British Library.*

*Library of Congress Cataloging in Publication data*

Russell, Nerissa, 1957–
Social zooarchaeology : humans and animals in prehistory / Nerissa Russell.
    p.   cm.
Includes bibliographical references and index.
ISBN 978-0-521-76737-8 (hardback) – ISBN 978-0-521-14311-0 (paperback)
1. Animal remains (Archaeology)   2. Human remains (Archaeology)
3. Social archaeology.   4. Human–animal relationships.   I. Title.
CC79.5.A5R87   2012
930.1–dc23       2011020299

ISBN 978-0-521-76737-8 Hardback
ISBN 978-0-521-14311-0 Paperback

*For Marina and Rafael*

# Contents

# List of tables

ix

# Preface

This book has had a long gestation. Its origin lies in a course I taught first as a visiting professor at UCLA some 15 years ago and several times since at Cornell. I had come to feel that zooarchaeology was ignoring many aspects of human–animal relations. In the course I sought to bring ethnography and other disciplines to bear on these issues in a more systematic way than I had begun to do in my research. The first outing of the course convinced me that this material needed to be developed into a book.

At first it seemed like a simple idea to point out the many roles that animals have played in human societies and how they might inform zoo-archaeology. Only as I began writing did I realize that this task involved surveying zooarchaeology from around the world and in all periods, as well as the human–animal literature in other disciplines. Therefore, this book has come together slowly, the more so because although when I started there was very little zooarchaeological literature on these topics, as I was writing, what has come to be called social zooarchaeology flowered, eventually to the point where I could not include it all. What began as a cry in the wilderness has become a synthesis of exciting recent work and an attempt to plot a way forward.

Because this book addresses topics and methods, it is not limited in time and space and ranges widely. It is meant to inspire and to lead the reader to the works referenced; I regret that given the breadth of scope I cannot adequately contextualize the archaeological studies in their own localities. I have tried to use dates sparingly and for orientation, so they are generally approximate and given in calibrated years before present (cal BP).

This book has benefited immensely from innumerable conversations through the years. In particular, I would like to thank the students in the various incarnations of the courses "Beyond Protein and Calories" at UCLA and "Humans and Animals" at Cornell. These students came from a wide range of backgrounds and have enriched my perspective. I have also profited from discussions with my colleagues at Cornell, particularly in relation to an early draft of Chapter 4 presented in a department writing group. Kevin McGowan of the Cornell Laboratory of Ornithology helped me think through evolutionary theory, in addition to being a font of information on everything biological. My many colleagues at Çatalhöyük, notably Louise Martin and Kathy Twiss, have contributed not only to the analysis and interpretation of that assemblage but also to the breadth and depth of my knowledge and thought. I am especially grateful for the most constructive set of comments I received from Jon Driver and two anonymous reviewers. This is a much better book as a result.

1

# Beyond protein and calories

> Our starting point is to recognise that subsistence and economy are not
> synonyms. Subsistence refers to what people live on; economy deals with
> the management and mobilization of resources. This is true, of course, for all
> societies at whatever level of organisational complexity and indicates that if we
> use only palaeoeconomic data to talk of calories and nutrients, an enormous
> amount of potential information is being ignored. The questions that any
> research design should address deal with the links between the management
> of basic resources (plants, animals, raw materials) and people, and with the
> transformation and maintenance of institutions within the process of social
> change and reproduction. (Barker and Gamble 1985:5)

Animals have touched the life of every human. Some of us hunt them,
some raise them for food and other products, and some keep them as
pets. We may take pleasure from watching birds and other wild animals,
and we may struggle to keep some animals, such as mice and rats, away
from our houses. Many of us eat them, some use their meat or other
body parts medicinally, and we make clothing and other products from
their skins and fur. Even if we have little direct contact with animals and
use no animal products (surely a very rare occurrence), they provide a
rich source of symbolism and metaphor: not only food but also food for
thought (Gifford-Gonzalez 2007:10, Lévi-Strauss 1963:89).

The social and symbolic importance of animals stems both from
their pervasiveness in our lives and from their animate nature (Digard
1990:220; Galaty and Johnson 1990; Kent 1989). They move and act,
are like us and yet different. We value and often admire them, and yet we
exploit them. This ambiguity and discomfort permeate human–animal
relations. The sense of guilt that is always present to some degree when
we kill, confine, and control animals adds to the intensity of our feelings
about them (Serpell 1986).

## What is an animal?

In this book, I use the word "animal" as shorthand for nonhuman animals. Of course, the opposition of humans and animals is artificial and anthropocentric. Humans are one animal species among many; like all other species we are by definition unique, but we do not logically form a category opposed to (and above) all other species. There is a long history of attempts to define the essence of humanity in a way that excludes all other species, and these efforts have become increasingly tortured as we learn more about the behavior of other animals. Possession of a soul, consciousness, language, tool use or manufacture, and culture have been favorite distinguishing traits. Yet all of these supposedly human traits have been claimed (if often hotly disputed) for assorted nonhuman animals, leaving the boundary between humans and animals much fuzzier (Corbey 2005; Gowlett 2009; Griffin 2001; Heinrich 1999; Ingold 1988; Kowalski 1991; Pepperberg 1999; Ritvo 1999; Sayers and Lovejoy 2008; Weir and Kacelnik 2006; Whiten and van Schaik 2007).

### ANTHROPOCENTRISM AND ANTHROPOMORPHISM

Dueling tendencies to anthropocentrism and anthropomorphism inform our conceptions of our relations to other animals, although both can be present simultaneously when we uncritically project human traits onto other species (Lockwood 1989). Each carries its own pitfalls. Anthropocentrism inscribes a sharp human–animal boundary and privileges humans strongly, whereas anthropomorphism erases the boundary and risks denying animals their own unique identities. Biologists have long debated the relative dangers of anthropomorphism and anthropocentrism. For much of the 20th century anthropomorphism was reviled in studies of animal behavior. The attribution of any "human" qualities to animals, particularly mental states such as emotions or intentionality, was seen as unwarranted projection that interfered with scientific understanding (e.g., Breland and Breland 1966; Broadhurst 1963; Kennedy 1992). However, anthropomorphism is not applied to all traits shared by humans and other animals, but is only invoked as a critique for those characteristics seen as defining humanity, which themselves have been historically and culturally variable (Asquith 1997; Cartmill 1993; de Waal 2001; Guthrie 1997; Ham and Senior 1997; LaCapra 2009; Milton

2005; Ritvo 1999; Salisbury 1994). More recently, anthropomorphism, in the sense of relying on an empathetic understanding to interpret animal behavior, has been recast in a positive light as increasing the accuracy of scientific knowledge (Bekoff 2004; Cartmill 2000; Crist 1999; Daston and Mitman 2005; de Waal 2001; Goodall 1990; Keeley 2004; Lockwood 1989). Moreover, through its insistence on judging intelligence in other species according to how much it resembles human cognition, anthropocentrism can be seen as at least as great a problem as anthropomorphism in studies of animal intelligence (Barrett et al. 2007; Emery 2006).

In fact, the human–animal boundary, and its patrolling through accusations of anthropomorphism, is less a scientific than a moral phenomenon (Cartmill 2001). Whether we see ourselves as inside or outside of nature, one species among many or set apart from all others, has ethical consequences. The nature of those consequences is not necessarily clear, however. One way to erase the boundary is to treat humans like any other animal, as in human behavioral ecology. Some have argued that this approach risks naturalizing social phenomena such as gender distinctions (Crist 1999; McCaughey 2007). Others see the human–animal divide as enabling the exploitation of women and other groups by likening them to animals (Dunayer 1995; Mullin 1999), although it can also be argued that the denial of biological determinism, hence privileging culture, depends on a sharp human–animal boundary (Birke 1995; Corbey 2005): "[O]ur anthropocentric assumption that humans operate in a distinctly separate and superior sphere to the merely biological one informs the whole of anthropology through the presupposition of the distinction between culture and nature" (Kenrick 2002:193).

Another way to breach the human–animal boundary is to extend the ethical system we apply to humans to other species as well. It is easier to use nonhuman animals (for food, other products, labor, or companionship) if we regard them as belonging to an entirely different category from people. Extending personhood to some or all other animal species renders many of these relations problematic, although those who advocate doing so may see the implications as ranging from treating animals as well as possible while we utilize them, to refraining from killing (and eating) them, to ending the keeping of domestic animals and minimizing contact with wild ones (Fausto 2007; Franklin 1999; LaCapra 2009; Milton 2005; Ryder 2000; Serpell 1986).

These implications depend in large measure on the notion of person-hood, which is also culturally variable. In contemporary western society, personhood tends to be understood in terms of rights and, to some extent, responsibilities (LaCapra 2009). Thus, according personhood to other species would mean extending human rights to them. However, doing so ironically projects an anthropocentric (and indeed Eurocentric) notion of rights and relations onto other species (Corbey 2005; Franklin 1999; Fuentes 2006; Tapper 1988). Many cultures, especially foragers, grant some form of personhood to (some) animals (Brightman 1993; Hugh-Jones 1996b; Kenrick 2002; Morris 1998; Nadasdy 2007; Russell 2010; Willerslev 2007). This personhood is cast not in terms of rights (the terms in which we grant personhood to corporations, for example), but of relations: Persons are entities with which humans enter into social relations. Typically this personhood applies to some but not all animals and not all the time; it is often accorded on an individual rather than a species basis. Crucially, animal personhood is not a barrier to killing and eating animals for these groups; rather, consumption is part of the relationship.

Neither anthropocentrism nor anthropomorphism is limited to mod-ern western society, however, although they take particular forms there. My ethnographic readings indicate that most societies have a term and concept for "animal" in opposition to humans that approximate ours (e.g., V. Anderson 2004; Copet-Rougier 1988). The occasional groups that do not define animals as a category include both foragers (Howell 1996) and farmers (Luxereau 1989). Careful examination of human–animal relations reveals a range of approaches, from anthropomorphic to anthropocentric, relational to exploitive, in any society, which vary situationally (Brightman 1993; Kenrick 2002; Morris 1998).

Some of the most interesting work on anthropomorphism treats it not as an impediment to the scientific understanding of animals, but as a feature of human cognition (Eddy et al. 1993). One can then con-sider why we tend to anthropomorphize and what has resulted from it. As Stewart Guthrie (1997) notes, we behave anthropomorphically with tremendous frequency, talking to plants and inanimate objects as well as animals, imputing motivations to events, and so on. He suggests that we have been selected to anthropomorphize because we are social animals, so it is adaptive to seek intentionally motivated explanations for occur-rences. We are more likely to suffer dire consequences from failing to understand a genuine motivation than from seeing motivation when it does not exist. Guthrie (1993) believes that our inclination to anthropomorphize underlies the origin of religion. Agustín Fuentes (2006) suggests that our anthropomorphic ability to empathize with other species is rooted in our common mammalian heritage, combined with our uniquely human consciousness. Many have attributed it to our hunting heritage, noting that predators benefit from identifying with their prey; certainly human hunters tend to do so (Alger and Alger 2003; Willerslev 2007). Brian Morris (2000:20–1) calls this theriomorphic thinking, but most include it in anthropomorphism. Nurit Bird-David (1993) suggests that foragers conceive of their relation to nature in terms of human relations, although the form varies. James Serpell (2002) argues that anthropomorphism is what enables the pet relationship and what makes it rewarding for humans. In contrast, animals may suffer through being selected to look more humanlike. Because he sees pet keeping as the origin of animal domestication, anthropomorphism is responsible for all our domestic animals in Serpell's view. Steven Mithen (2007) makes a similar argument that both plant and animal domestication result from a misapplication of social intelligence (treating other species like humans and entering into relations with them; in this case caring, parental relations). Mithen believes that this misapplication became possible when the separate modules for social, natural, and technical knowledge became connected in the minds of modern humans, probably in the Upper Paleolithic.

In this book, I self-consciously engage in anthropocentrism in that, as an anthropologist, my interest in animals lies in using them to understand people (Mullin 1999). However, we cannot understand people unless we acknowledge that they have often related to animals in ways we might consider anthropomorphic. Justin Kenrick (2002:194) instead argues that foragers' "understanding is not anthropomorphic, in the sense of a one way projection from an active social sphere onto a passive natural one, it is . . . a process of mutual perception and interaction between species, including humans."

## Animals and zooarchaeology

Zooarchaeology has grown and changed along with its parent discipline of archaeology. When archaeologists first decided it would be useful to know something about the animal bones they excavated as well as the artifacts, they delivered the bones to a friendly zoologist, who obliged with a species list. As some of these zoologists became interested in archaeological collections as a useful record of changes in animal morphology and distribution, they began to measure the bones to document size changes and to consider questions such as when and where domestication occurred and how it might be recognized (e.g., Allen 1920; Bäumler 1921).

This information was of some interest to archaeologists, but as with other related disciplines, they came to feel that zoologists were not asking the questions of greatest relevance to archaeology. Therefore, roughly in the 1970s, archaeologists started to acquire expertise in the arcane skills of identifying scraps of animal bone, and, in line with the concerns of processual archaeology, shifted their focus to how ancient peoples used their animals: hunting and herding strategies, butchering techniques, transport of animal parts, and so on. Methodological discussions focused initially on quantification: What is the most accurate way to determine the relative contribution of different animal species to the diet (e.g., Bökönyi 1970; Casteel 1978; Grayson 1973, 1979; Krantz 1968; Perkins 1973a; Ringrose 1993; Uerpmann 1973; J. Watson 1979; White 1953a; Winder 1991). Later, techniques for determining age at death, needed to construct mortality profiles indicative of different hunting and herding practices, came to the fore (e.g., Chaplin 1969; Cribb 1984; Elder 1965; Higham 1968; Klein 1982; Lyman 1987; O'Connor 1998; Payne 1973; Perkins 1964; Redding 1984; Stiner 1990).

In the last 30 years, zooarchaeologists have come to realize that it is naïve to interpret faunal assemblages recovered from archaeological sites as though they directly reflect human behavior (Binford 1981). It is first necessary to understand the history of the assemblage: how it was created and how carnivores, weathering, fluvial transport, and other agents have modified it. In some cases, the analyst must demonstrate that humans were involved at all. Developing the tools to do this has been a major focus of zooarchaeological research in recent decades and has vastly increased the sophistication of our taphonomic understanding (e.g., Andrews 1990; Behrensmeyer 1978; Behrensmeyer and Hill 1980; Binford 1981; Binford and Bertram 1977; Brain 1969, 1981; Fisher 1995; Gifford 1981; Hanson 1980a; Higham 1968; Hill 1979; Lyman 1984, 1994; Meadow 1980; Shipman 1981; Thomas 1971). It is no longer acceptable to attribute skewed body part distributions, for example, to human choices without first rigorously examining other potential causes.

## Beyond protein and calories, and even attrition

Perhaps because the explosion in taphonomic research was in large measure driven by a debate about whether early hominids were hunters or scavengers (see Chapter 4), although methodological sophistication has increased by leaps and bounds, the questions addressed have remained focused on basic subsistence. Until quite recently, faunal analysts largely limited themselves to the reconstruction of diet and procurement strategies. Implicit in this approach is the assumption that the only role that animals played in prehistoric societies was as a food source: calories and protein. One major challenge to this view is Andrew Sherratt's notion of the Secondary Products Revolution (see Chapter 8), which argues that the (relatively late) use of milk, wool, and animal traction represents a crucial intensification in the exploitation of domestic animals (Sherratt 1982, 1983). Sherratt's shift in focus from meat to the living animal is an important step, but remains narrowly utilitarian.

I will argue that zooarchaeologists have inappropriately narrowed their interpretations by seeing animals only in terms of protein and calories. In every known contemporary society, animals, and indeed meat, are much more than this. They fulfill a variety of roles – as pets, symbols, wealth, objects of feasting and sacrifice, and so on. Hunting and herding do not exhaust human–animal relationships. The social and symbolic functions of animals and meat may often be of equal or even greater importance than their dietary role. Although social and symbolic issues have come to the fore in archaeology in general, not only in postprocessual approaches but across theoretical schools, zooarchaeologists have lagged behind. Of course, there are notable exceptions: Such scholars as Diane Gifford-Gonzalez. Pam Crabtree, Kathleen Ryan, and Richard Meadow were addressing some of these issues in the 1970s–1990s, and in the last decade or so there has been a considerable shift in interpretations. However, the narrow economic focus still predominates.

I do not deny that people must eat, that protein and fat are critical nutrients of which meat is an excellent and frequently used source, nor that the subsistence and utilitarian roles of animals are important. Rather I suggest that the subsistence role of animals has been privileged to the exclusion of all others and that this constitutes a serious problem in interpretation. It is not merely that treating animals solely as sources of protein and calories produces incomplete interpretations that focus on a narrow sphere of human life. Ignoring the importance of other factors in human interactions with animals is likely to yield interpretations that are just plain wrong. If a mortality profile created by bridewealth requirements (see Chapter 8) is interpreted as though it were created by decisions to maximize meat or milk, the subsistence strategy will be obscured rather than elucidated. Therefore, even if the goal is to study subsistence, we must take into account the entire spectrum of human–animal relationships. Just as we must consider the effects of taphonomic forces that have transformed faunal assemblages, so we must consider the full range of human behaviors that may have produced them, or our interpretations will be equally naïve.

In this book, then, I attempt to redress the imbalance in zooarchaeological interpretations. I give short shrift to subsistence not because I devalue it, but because it has been addressed well and thoroughly elsewhere. Likewise, I spend little time on the crucial topic of taphonomy, which has not lacked visibility in recent years. Instead I try to fill in the gaps in modeling ancient human uses of animals and their products by concentrating on the areas that have received less attention in zooarchaeology. Many of these areas revolve around the value and meanings of living animals: animal symbolism, animals as wealth, animals as pets. Although we only see the remains of dead animals, we should remember that in many cases the living animals might have been more important than their meat. Meat itself has significance beyond the merely nutritional, and it tends to be valued out of proportion to its actual contribution to the diet. Hence I also consider the valorization of meat, and specifically the importance of meat sharing, feasting, and sacrifice.

The archaeological literature on these topics is limited, although growing fast. Thus I draw to a large extent on the scholarship of other disciplines: ethnography, history, classics, and religious studies. Although it is beyond the scope of this book to provide detailed zooarchaeological analyses, I outline the ways in which we could incorporate these insights into zooarchaeological studies and interpretations and what changes in method are needed to explore these questions adequately. Primary among these methodological changes are a greater focus on contextual analysis and the integration of information from other materials. I also explore what we can say about human society based on the work done so far, in particular exploring the role of animals and meat in the construction of gender.

I address myself particularly to prehistorians, because those working in periods with documentary evidence have found it harder to ignore these issues. However, most of the discussions here are applicable to later periods as well, which I cover to some extent. My own expertise is in Old World archaeology, so there is no doubt a bias toward concerns and examples from this area. I do not limit myself in geographical scope, however, and New World archaeologists should find much that speaks to their interests as well. I aim both to suggest to zooarchaeologists how they might enrich their interpretations and to inform archaeologists in general of the vast potential of animal remains to illuminate ancient social life. One consequence of the subsistence focus in zooarchaeology is that animals have been given short shrift in archaeological syntheses (see Robb 2007 for a notable exception).

My goal is to place the social at the center of zooarchaeology. I operate from a basis in practice theory (Bourdieu 1977; Giddens 1979; Pauketat 2001; Robb 1999), focusing on the power relations enacted in social life. My primary interest lies in the kind of societies described by Pierre Bourdieu (1977:183–4):

> In societies which have no "self-regulating market" (in Karl Polanyi's sense), no educational system, no juridical apparatus, and no State, relations of domination can be set up and maintained only at the cost of strategies which must be endlessly renewed, because the conditions required for a *mediated, lasting appropriation* of other agents' labour, services, or homage have not been brought together.... [These are] social universes in which relations of domination are made, unmade, and remade in and by the interactions between persons.

In these societies, many of these relations are enacted through animals and their products, and we ignore them at our peril. There is a growing awareness of the importance of social factors in zooarchaeology across theoretical paradigms, as evident, for example, in the recent surge in costly signaling models in human behavioral ecology approaches (e.g., Aldenderfer 2006; Codding et al. 2010; McGuire and Hildebrandt 2005). These models attempt to incorporate what others might call prestige or social capital into evolutionary accounts.

In the chapters that follow I often paint with a broad brush, offering sweeping generalizations and quasi-universal statements about human–animal relations. My excuse is that I am making the case for considering these possibilities in interpreting animal bone assemblages. Ultimately, I hope to stimulate richer, more complete accounts of local prehistories, from which we can build a fuller understanding of the history of human–animal relations.

# 2

# Animal symbols

> Humans use animals in order to draw elaborate pictures of themselves. (Tilley 1999:49)

I have somewhat arbitrarily divided the subject matter of this chapter from that of the next, which treats the ritual use of animals. The symbolic value of animals permeates all spheres in which they participate, but in this chapter I discuss some of the areas where animals act primarily as metaphors. The representation of animals, or animal art, is a huge topic that has received extensive treatment. I do not attempt to cover this field, but I explore it briefly to acknowledge its importance. I then address totem and taboo, classic subjects of anthropological investigation that have received less attention in zooarchaeology. Finally, I consider animal combat.

## Animal metaphors

Animals are universally key metaphors. E. O. Wilson (1984, 1993) even suggests that this special interest in animals is part of our genetic heritage, a phenomenon he terms "biophilia" (see also Kellert 1993). Animals are enough like people to be powerfully evocative, yet different enough to be safely distant. We use animal categories to understand human society and human categories to understand animals: "[T]he construction of principles of metaphoric analogy between the domains of humans and the domains of animals forms a fundamental basis for self-understanding and the construction of meaning in all known societies. Animals are key source domains and target domains of metaphors through which culture is constituted" (Tilley 1999:49–50).

Christopher Tilley goes on to suggest that such metaphors transcend nature/culture dichotomies by linking humans and animals into a single system of meaning and ontology. This is not invariably the case, however. In addition to classifying humans, a prime use of animal metaphors is to impart moral lessons (Descola 1994:96–7; Tapper 1988). These lessons can be conveyed either by attributing human qualities to animals – that is, using animal heroes to stand for humans – or by denigrating animals as the brutish Other that humans must rise above. Most often, we use animal metaphors to label human individuals or groups as inferior. Thus animal metaphors may enforce human–animal boundaries as well as erase them (Dunayer 1995; Mullin 1999; Tapper 1988:51). Moreover, our use of animal metaphors and representations to make sense of people also affects our views and treatment of actual animals. "Culture shapes our reading of animals just as much as animals shape our reading of culture" (Baker 1993:4).

For example, among agropastoral groups in which transhumant herding is practiced by men and farming is practiced largely by women, animal metaphors tend to impute positive traits (strength, courage, intelligence) to the animal species associated with male herding. These are contrasted to species associated with women and farming, or those of lesser importance in herding, which are cast negatively (weak, passive, dirty). These traits are also attributed to the respective genders (Parkes 1987:648–9). This is of course narrated from the male point of view; women in these groups may use animal metaphors differently. As noted in Chapter 8 (in the section, *Animal Wealth and Inequality*), at least some women in East African "cattle complex" societies reject the beauty and importance of cattle. Among the Kalasha of the Hindu Kush studied by Peter Parkes, where men extol the nobility and purity of goats and sacrifice them to male gods, women sacrifice sheep to female deities and feast on them. Although the men apparently regard this use of sheep as making do with a lesser animal because the sacrifice and meat of male goats are forbidden to women, the women quite possibly rank the animals differently. In a midwinter ritual enacting the antagonism between men and women, the women mock male pastoral values. Their own rituals celebrate sexuality and fertility, amounting to an alternative female religion. In any case, both animals and gender are rich sources of metaphor and are frequently linked.

Richard Tapper (1988) suggests that different modes of production have not only their own sets of human–animal relations (see the section in Chapter 6, *Links between Human–Animal and Human–Human Relations*) but also their own corresponding forms of animal metaphors. Among foragers, who construct animals as equals, the metaphors tend to be totemic, with animal species representing human groups. Farmers associate animals with circles of decreasing familiarity radiating from the house, with corresponding degrees of edibility (Leach 1964; Tambiah 1969). Pastoralists' close ties to their flocks make animal metaphors especially powerful, yet they are in a relationship of inequality. Thus their animal metaphors emphasize difference as well as similarity. Ranching metaphors tend to demonstrate human conquest of nature/animals, as in the rodeo. In urban industrial societies most people are distanced from most animals, and animal images become stylized. Animals are idealized as pets or representations of the wild exhibited in zoos, or they are vilified as filthy (such as pigs) or vermin. The only animals with which most people have regular contact are pets, and these are treated like humans. Tapper notes that we tend to give our pets human names, in contrast to the East African Nuer pastoralists who name people after cattle.

## Art

For the sake of convenience, I refer to various types of representation as art, although this term may not be wholly appropriate for all societies because it implies a separation of the artistic sphere that does not always obtain (Conkey 1987). Animal representations occur widely in art, as well as in the less archaeologically accessible folklore. There are many ways to approach the symbolism of animal representations, and I make no attempt at an exhaustive discussion here. Rather, I focus on some of the aspects of animal art that may help us approach the material remains of animals.

Zooarchaeologists have not hesitated to make use of art. At the most practical level, they have drawn on artistic representations to glean information about the appearance of extinct fauna (e.g., Zeuner 1953) or to seek evidence of animal domestication either through depiction of traits such as wooliness in sheep (Bökönyi 1974:160) or through scenes of control of animals (Bökönyi 1969). Because art is stylized, these interpretations are not always unambiguous, as seen in the debate over whether Upper Paleolithic art depicts halters on horses (Bahn 1980, 1984; White 1989). Scenes of activities such as milking, plowing, and riding provide evidence for the ways ancient people used animals. Zooarchaeologists have also attended to animal depictions as indicators of the symbolic importance of certain species and have considered how this importance relates to the bone assemblages they study. I concentrate on this area.

There is no simple relationship between art and subsistence. People depict animals because they are food for thought rather than just food, so the frequencies of animal taxa represented in art rarely match those represented in the faunal assemblages. For example, although tropical forest animals dominate Chavín art in the Early Horizon Andes, camelids form the staple meat source (Miller and Burger 1995). Likewise, the Conte art style from second millennium BP Panama primarily depicts animals that were not eaten (Linares 1976). At Çatalhöyük in Neolithic Anatolia, it was once thought that art and subsistence were in tune, with cattle dominating both (Mellaart 1967; Perkins 1969). However, recent work shows that the faunal remains are in fact mainly sheep/goat, with cattle forming only about 20 percent (Russell and Martin 2005).

The relationship between art and subsistence has probably received the closest scrutiny in connection with the Upper Paleolithic of western Europe, which is famed for its abundant and dramatic art, most of it depicting animals. It has long been noted that the species most abundant in the art are not those most abundant in contemporary faunal assemblages (Leroi-Gourhan 1982:45). This is true both at the global level – with reindeer and red deer dominating animal bone remains, whereas bison and horses appear most frequently in the art (Mithen 1988) – and at the local level. In Cantabria, although both the most commonly depicted and the most commonly hunted taxa vary in different micro-regions, there is always an inverse relation between the two (Altuna 1983).

If hunters are not depicting the animals they normally kill, what motivates the choice of animals portrayed? Some have suggested that the art is directed toward the animals the hunters most want or need to kill, even though they are not the most frequently taken. Mithen (1988) argues that most animal bones at Upper Paleolithic sites come from mass kills resulting from communal game drives. However, he suggests that the outcome of these drives became less predictable in the late Upper

Paleolithic. In the lean times between successful drives, hunters turned to individual stalking of bison and horses. He sees the art as facilitating information flow for these hunts, which required greater skill in tracking and selecting prey. Depictions of tracks and indicators of the condition of the animals served to educate children and refresh the memories of adult hunters. However, Mithen does not explain why bison and horses should have been stalked individually while deer were hunted in drives, given that both are also herd animals, indeed to a much greater extent than are red deer. The recent discovery of animal paintings from earlier in the Paleolithic negates the temporal aspect of the model (Clottes 2003).

Patricia Rice and Ann Paterson (1985, 1986) suggest that animal depictions tend to portray larger species, those with the biggest packages of meat and hence the most desired prey, or perhaps the most feared. Of course, the largest animals – mammoths and wooly rhinos – are only rarely depicted, although mammoths still appear more often in the art than in the faunal assemblages of the Perigord region studied by Rice and Paterson. These species are also rarely hunted (see Chapter 5, *Pleistocene Overkill?*), so one could easily argue that the art concentrates on the largest common game animals. Both Mithen and Rice and Paterson seek to recuperate the "good to eat" motivation for Upper Paleolithic art. However, if the art is directly related to hunting, the depiction of larger animals taken primarily through individual pursuit seems more likely to be related to the prestige value of such prey than to their protein and calories (see Chapter 4).

The purpose of Upper Paleolithic art has been hotly debated since its first discovery, with suggestions ranging from hunting magic, to initiation rituals and other ceremonies, to depictions of shamanistic trances. I do not attempt a full discussion of these issues here (see Bahn and Vertut 1997 for an overview) but instead focus on the meaning of the animal images. As Conkey (1989) summarizes, early interpretations of Paleolithic art generally saw it as sympathetic magic, to be read straightforwardly as depictions of preferred game species. As we have seen, this claim does not accord well with the zooarchaeological evidence. In addition, although the art was to be read directly, the people creating it were not. They were seen as essentially different from us: irrational and pre-religious. André Leroi-Gourhan's (1964, 1965, 1966, 1968) structuralist approach was a radical departure, positing an essential similarity among all human minds and interpreting the animal depictions as symbols.

Leroi-Gourhan attended to the placement of the images in the caves, arguing for a spatial separation between the two main symbols (bison and horses). He initially identified these taxa as male and female symbols, although he later dropped this association. A later study (Delluc and Delluc 1989) concludes that Leroi-Gourhan's spatial scheme applies well to deep caves but does not hold for shallower ones that were lived in as well as painted. Thus there is likely a functional distinction within Upper Paleolithic cave art.

Although ethnographic studies cannot be directly applied to Paleolithic art, they do suggest that animal art produced by foragers is not exclusively about hunting magic. Mathias Guenther (1988) notes that the animals portrayed most carefully in the rock art of the San foragers of southern Africa are not those most frequently hunted. Small antelope, hyrax, and hare are the main game animals, but primarily larger animals (large antelope, elephant, giraffe) are portrayed. The plant foods that form the bulk of the diet do not appear at all. Guenther sees this as partly a matter of esthetic salience: The main game animals are drab, with ordinary shapes, whereas the carefully painted animals are striking for their size, markings, or unusual shape. He suggests that these striking features make them food for thought and hence the protagonists of myths. These animals, especially the frequently depicted eland, are indeed religiously significant (Lewis-Williams 1984, 1988; Parkington 2003; Vinnicombe 1976). They are symbols of group or gendered identity or figures from shamanistic trances.

The notion that the art of hunters can only be about hunting reflects the perception of foragers as closer to nature and less than fully human (see Chapter 4, *The Archaeology of Hunting*). Mithen explicitly states that Upper Paleolithic art may have held both spiritual and ecological meanings and that the two forms of meaning may not have been clearly separated, but he privileges the ecological in explanation. However, ethnography does not indicate that forager art can be read in terms of optimal foraging.

It is surely important to consider the context of the production of the art (Conkey 1989). Who made it and under what circumstances? Many have proposed that the deep caves (where Leroi-Gourhan's spatial distinction holds best) may have been the site of initiation rituals (Owens and Hayden 1997). If so, the art is likely to be in some sense didactic. Although it may convey concrete information about game species as Mithen suggests (which animals to hunt individually, fatter animals are better, etc.), this kind of information seems far better imparted through apprenticeship, with young hunters accompanying experienced ones (Ingold 1996b; Morris 1998:88). The information conveyed during initiation rituals is more likely mythical, relating to cosmology and social roles.

Upper Paleolithic cave art often has many images crowded together, but they rarely form scenes. Images may overlap and are sometimes renewed or transformed (Leroi-Gourhan 1982). This suggests that the purpose of the art is not to decorate the space; rather, the production of the art itself is the point. Creation of the images would be part of a ritual. The same may be true at Çatalhöyük, where wall paintings were plastered over shortly after their creation. Here, however, humans and animals do form real scenes.

Richard Bradley (2001) argues that there is a key distinction between the art of Mesolithic foragers and Neolithic farmers. Therianthropes (creatures blending human and animal traits) appear only in forager art, whereas in the art of early farmers humans and animals are separate, even when the animals depicted are wild. He suggests that foragers do not feel a strong delineation between humans and animals, but this kind of conceptual separation is what makes domestication possible (see Chapter 4, *Hunters' Attitudes to Animals*, and Chapter 6, *Links between Human–Animal and Human–Human Relations*). This is a fascinating insight, although it may not hold universally. Therianthropes certainly appear in both Upper Paleolithic art (the "sorcerer" of Trois Frères is a famous example; Bégouën and Breuil 1958) and in San rock art. However, in both cases they are rare in comparison to naturalistic representations of animals. Therianthropes are far more common in San myth than in their art (Guenther 1988:193). Thus the lack of obvious human features may not mean that the animal is simply an animal. On the other hand, at Neolithic Çatalhöyük, although humans and animals are usually depicted separately, some vultures seem to have human legs (Mellaart 1967:167).

If Bradley's distinction holds in general, it is interesting to note that later, after animal domestication is thoroughly established, some societies are once again able to breach the human–animal boundary in myth and art. The ancient Greeks, for example, were particularly creative in their therianthropic conceptions: satyrs, centaurs, the minotaur, harpies, and medusas among others. And, of course, their gods were given to

changing into animal shapes and to transgressing human–animal boundaries through bestiality. Late Bronze Age and Iron Age imagery in central
Europe also contains frequent therianthropes, often birds with human
heads or feet or stag-men (Briard 1987:145; Green 1992, 1997).

Parkes (1987) suggests that the art of pastoralists tends to focus on
the primary animal species herded, which takes on divine attributes. The
case for mixed farmers is perhaps less clear, but certainly the pervasive
cattle symbolism of Europe and the Near East from the Neolithic on
could be seen in this light. Cattle may have been the primary unit of
wealth (see Chapter 8) and, through sacrifice, the vehicle of communication with deities. They are not always the most frequently herded species,
however. Moreover, the symbolic importance of cattle appears to precede
their domestication and may have motivated it. The first domesticated
herd animals, sheep and goats, inspired much less symbolism. Although
sheep and goats provided the staple meat at Çatalhöyük and other Near
Eastern sites, wild cattle dominate the art. Ian Hodder (1987, 1990) suggests that this art is part of an attempt to domesticate the wild symbolically
by bringing it into the domestic sphere, and that this symbolic domestication preceded herding (see Chapter 6, *Domination*). This seems to
hold for cattle (although other wild animals depicted at Çatalhöyük, such
as onagers and leopards, are not subsequently domesticated), but only
after sheep and goats have already been domesticated. These smaller livestock are not heralded with extensive symbolism prior or subsequent to
their first herding. Thus cattle and sheep/goats may have followed very
different paths to domestication, with the valorization of cattle occurring
well before their herding.

Viewed in this light, the symbolic focus on cattle in the earlier
Neolithic of the Near East cannot really be seen as a metaphorical taming
of the wild that set the stage for animal domestication in general, making
actual control of living animals conceivable. Rather it may have been the
herding of sheep and goats that made the domestication of cattle thinkable. Cattle's symbolic value was tied not to their subsistence role, which
was always minor in the Near East, but more likely to their power and
danger. They would have been the high-prestige game species, the centerpiece of feasts, and possibly the victim of sacrifices. The cattle depicted
are often explicitly marked as male, and males are also favored in ceremonial contexts at Çatalhöyük. Thus the focus is on the larger and more
dangerous bulls.

In some ways this focus on cattle resembles the overrepresentation of bison and horses in Upper Paleolithic cave art. The aurochs (wild cattle) would have been the largest animal in the early Holocene Near East. The timing is probably not coincidental, however. Cattle representations and ritual deposits of cattle body parts (see Chapter 3) begin in the Pre-Pottery Neolithic A (PPNA) on a small scale and take off in the Pre-Pottery Neolithic B (PPNB). That is, they first appear in the context of early farming, prior to animal domestication, and become much more prominent after herding of smaller ungulates begins but probably before cattle domestication. These would surely be times when social roles, including gender roles, were renegotiated. It has often been argued that early farming gave greater importance to female labor. The development of herding would have affected the importance of hunting, likely altering if not undermining traditional male roles.

We now know that hunting played a relatively small role in subsistence at Çatalhöyük (Russell and Martin 2005). Nevertheless, much of the symbolism at the site has often been linked to hunting, and some have suggested the existence of male hunting societies (Hodder 1987; Wright 2000). The symbolic importance of hunting seems to increase through time, with more elaborate projectile points and the appearance of possible hunting scenes in the art (Conolly 1999; Mellaart 1967). However, wild animals are actually less common in the faunal assemblages of the later levels where the "hunting scenes" occur. Although subsistence was based largely on agriculture and herding, these subjects are notably absent from the art: "The main arena for the negotiation of social interests is clearly the symbolism of animals and the wild. Yet part of this negotiation may have been to negate or mask the contribution of agriculture (perhaps linked to women) and domestic production" (Hodder 1987:48).

Çatalhöyük forms the tail end of a larger phenomenon in the late PPNA/PPNB Near East. Although some sites, like Çatalhöyük, are inhabited by mixed farmers and include animal art emphasizing wild taxa, there are at least two special-purpose ritual sites. Kfar HaHoresh in Israel is a small (0.5 hectare) site that may have had some minor domestic occupation but was principally the location of funerary and perhaps other rituals that associate human and animal remains, (see Chapter 3, *Hunting Shrines*). Göbekli Tepe in southeast Anatolia (the early deposits date to at least ca. 11,000–10,500 BP, or late PPNA–early PPNB) has yielded no evidence of domestic occupation, but has multiple public buildings equipped with large T-shaped stone pillars decorated with animals (lions, cattle, foxes, cranes, snakes, etc.) and some human figures. Many of these animals are marked as male, and most or all are wild (a ram could possibly be domestic). At both sites, all the animal bones come from wild taxa (Verhoeven 2002a). These sites have been interpreted as the ritual foci of local foraging groups, reflecting a hunters' ideology (J. Peters and Schmidt 2004). However, it is striking that only these special-purpose ritual sites have exclusively wild fauna and no sign of agriculture. Rather than being a pocket of foragers among farmers, they are more likely the scenes of rituals related to hunting and probably to male gender identity. Marc Verhoeven (2002a:252) suggests that the various ways of linking humans with wild animals "can be regarded as a sort of counteraction to the domestication of society, plants, and animals." Rather than a prelude to domestication, bringing animals under symbolic control, the ritual focus on wild animals is perhaps better seen as resistance to the ideology of herding and agriculture. Ethnographically, hunting is more ritualized among Malawian and some other agriculturalists than among foragers. These rituals are not hunting magic, but link men symbolically to the wild (Morris 1998:23, 152–3).

Jon Morter and John Robb (1998) make a similar argument for the southern Italian Neolithic. There, too, domestic animals predominate in the faunal assemblages of settlements. However, ritual sites removed from these settlements have mostly wild animal remains and feature art portraying men hunting. They suggest, however, that this symbolic stress on hunting is not linked to gendered political roles (i.e., male dominance), for which there is no real evidence. Rather, they see these ritual sites in terms of gender ideology, with hunting being an important part of the construction of male identity. Female figurines, recovered mainly at settlement sites, belong to a similar symbolic sphere for the construction of female identity. Morter and Robb caution against simplistic equations of male and female with wild and domestic or culture and nature: "Such a formulation leaves the female role as an untheorised placeholder filled in with a category from our own society. Moreover, the male role idealised in hunting art is adversarial; rather than, or en route to, being identified with the 'wild', the hunter subdues the wild and brings it into society, where it is integrated into and helps to reproduce society through patterns of feasting, redistribution of meat, and celebration" (Morter and Robb 1998:90–1). Elsewhere in Neolithic and Bronze Age Europe a similar argument might be made on the basis of the prevalence of red deer and hunting themes in the rock art of Neolithic and Chalcolithic Iberia (Fairén 2004) and the extraordinary concentration of engravings at Val Camonica in the Italian Alps (Briard 1987). These are localized occurrences, however. Even many of the other "mountain sanctuaries" with rock art concentrations from these periods lack preponderant hunting/wild animal imagery. Hunting is thus part of the vocabulary that can be deployed in the construction of male identity, but not invariably the major theme.

An analogous situation occurs in the Californian Middle Archaic. In this case, women's subsistence roles are enhanced not by agriculture but by a switch to acorns (which require elaborate processing) as a staple. This shift occurs at a time of population increase and intensified use of resources, which according to optimal foraging theory should lead to a decrease in big game hunting. On the contrary, big game hunting and fishing (for swordfish) increase, and hunting themes come to dominate the Coso rock art. One way to understand this is that the greater contribution of women to the diet freed men to pursue prestige through hunting (Hildebrandt and McGuire 2002; Whitley 1992). Another would be to see the florescence of hunting as part of a renegotiation of gender roles and identities.

ANIMAL DEITIES

Ethnographic studies have shown that animals portrayed in art are often figures from shamanistic trances (Lewis-Williams 1984; Lewis-Williams and Dowson 1988). In some cases, the animals are spirit helpers of the shamans (Balzer 1996; Ingold 1987). This interpretation has been extended to prehistoric art, particularly where animal and human traits are blended into therianthropes, and more recently to purely animal depictions.

Shamans are trendy in archaeology, with the concept applied widely and incorporated into larger schemes such as models of the origins of agriculture (Prentice 1986), of the state (Chang 1983; Thomas and Humphrey 1994), and even of the mind (McClenon 2001; Winkelman 2002). There has also been criticism of the overuse of shamanism, with some preferring to apply the term narrowly to ethnographically documented cultures of Siberia (Kehoe 2000; Klein et al. 2002). For our purposes here, it is not necessary to label ancient individuals as shamans, but we may consider whether some animal depictions represent familiars or spirit helpers.

The shamanistic or trance interpretation of prehistoric rock art has largely stemmed from the work of David Lewis-Williams (e.g., 1984, 2002; Lewis-Williams and Dowson 1988, 1993). Working back from ethnographic research, Lewis-Williams determined that San foragers created much of the rock art of southern Africa. This art contains many images of people and animals, especially elands, that had previously been interpreted as hunting scenes and often as hunting magic. Lewis-Williams was able to establish that these scenes in fact transcribe and interpret the experiences of ritual healers in trances. He identified geometric motifs in the paintings as optical phenomena produced by the neurology of hallucinations, and he suggested that depictions of people pierced with darts or spears or stung by bees are interpretations of the prickling sensations experienced in these altered states of consciousness (Lewis-Williams 1997). Therianthropic blendings of humans and animals likewise commonly occur in hallucinations. John Parkington (2003) has challenged this interpretation, however, arguing that therianthropes in San rock art are instead an expression of the establishment of gender roles in terms of a pervasive metaphor linking women to prey (see Chapter 4, *Motivations for Hunting*). In particular, some of this art may relate to initiation ceremonies, when men's first big kill and women's first menstruation mark them as adults and marriageable (see also Helvenston et al. 2003; McCall 2007).

Lewis-Williams and others have gone on to apply these insights to prehistoric art, notably the cave art of the western European Upper Paleolithic (Clottes and Lewis-Williams 1998; Lewis-Williams 1997, 1998), but also to Neolithic art in the same area and beyond (Dronfield 1995, Lewis-Williams and Dowson 1993; Lewis-Williams and Pearce 2005; Patton 1990), the wall paintings at Çatalhöyük and art at other Anatolian Neolithic sites (Bischoff 2002; Lewis-Williams 2004), and rock art in western North America (Whitley 1998). Geometric motifs attributed to hallucinatory entoptic phenomena are taken as diagnostic of art based on trance experiences. In trance art, the animals are spirit animals and may be either the familiars of the shaman/trancer or this person in animal form.

Others, while not stressing the trance art aspect, have also suggested that animals in art represent the familiars of shamans. This argument is perhaps strongest in areas where the presence of shamans is historically and ethnographically documented, such as northern Eurasia. Hans Bolin (2000) discusses the Neolithic-Bronze Age rock art of northern Sweden in this light. Here the animal most frequently depicted, the elk (*Alces alces*, known as moose in America), is indeed the main game animal of the region. As a result, the art has usually been interpreted as hunting magic. Drawing on the ethnographic description of a shamanistic tradition in northern Eurasia in general and among the Saami of northern Scandinavia in particular, Bolin suggests that this tradition extends back into prehistory, although of course not unchanged through the millennia. Saami cult places with the remains of sacrifice and shamanistic rituals are known archaeologically extending at least 1,000 years into the past (Bradley 2000:3–14). Bolin notes that, in addition to elk, the rock art consists mainly of boats and humans. He reads the boats and the location of the art in inaccessible places near water as related to ethnographically known symbolism of a cosmic river leading to the other world. Some of the human figures merge with those of elk, perhaps depicting shamans in trance, transforming into elk or traveling with their spirit helpers. He further suggests that the rock art portrays a creation story in which elk are the ancestors of humans. Robert Schmidt (2000) pushes this shamanistic continuity back further still, ca. 7500 BP, to the Mesolithic of Karelia and Scandinavia. He interprets burials with special grave goods (including beaver jaws) as the remains of male and female shamans, noting that bear, elk, and waterfowl function as spiritual mediators in this cosmological system. Therianthropic artifacts from Late Dorset (ca. 1500–500 BP) sites in northern Canada have also been interpreted as shamanic paraphernalia, drawing on ethnographic analogy with the modern Inuit (LeMoine et al. 1995).

Shamans are classically associated with animism and with foraging societies, especially those of the far north. However, some have argued for the importance of shamanism in more complex societies in the temperate zone. Miranda Green (1998, 2001) suggests that European Iron Age depictions of therianthropes, often interpreted as gods (e.g., a human figure with antlers identified as the Celtic Cernunnos, the horned god), are better seen as shamans. Rather than link them to Celtic deities known from later myth, they may represent priests related to the historically known Druids, crossing the human–animal boundary in trance and deriving power from this transgression. K. C. Chang (1983:45–80) asserts that shamans' links to heavenly power translated into secular authority when they became the first Chinese kings. He attributes the elaborate drinking vessels of the Chinese Bronze Age to the use of alcohol, in addition to music and dance, to achieve altered states of consciousness to enable communication with spirits. He points to the repeated depiction of humans with their heads in the mouths of animals, interpreting them as a metaphorical rendering of shamans with their animal familiars consuming the shamans' earthly bodies in trance to transport them to the other world.

In more complex societies, animals may become deities, such as bull gods (Rice 1997; Schwabe 1994). The Apis bulls of Egypt are particularly well known, but there are many instances among early civilizations in the Near East and elsewhere of animal gods or gods incarnate in animals. Animals may also be attributes of deities; for example, Athena's owl.

Clearly animals provide much food for thought about the supernatural. Prehistoric art is difficult to interpret with confidence, but strong cases can often be made that the animals depicted are not intended as "real" animals, but as animal spirits or animal deities. Animal art makes it impossible to ignore the symbolic value of animals, and many studies have shown that this symbolic value goes well beyond simply desiring more animals to eat. We need to explore how such value is played out, if at all, in the treatment of real-life animals. For example, Cree hunters achieve communion with their spirit helper by eating a portion of an animal of that species dictated in a dream (Brightman 1993:122). Animals and animal remains may have been involved in rituals of various kinds, and these rituals in turn shape both hunting and herding practices and the faunal remains deposited at archaeological sites.

## Totems

In Claude Lévi-Strauss's (1963) classic definition, totemism is a system of analogies between natural and cultural categories. One common manifestation of totemism is the use of animal (and sometimes plant) species to represent human groups such as clans. As Lévi-Strauss carefully points out, this classificatory use of animals does not necessarily imply a belief that the human group is descended from its totem species, or worship of this species, or taboos on its consumption – although all may occur in some instances. For instance, horticulturalists in Malawi routinely taboo the killing and consumption of their clan totems (Morris 1998:204–7). Although some have suggested that animals become totems because of people's dietary dependence on them, Lévi-Strauss (1963:89) famously observes that "natural species are chosen not because they are 'good to eat' but because they are 'good to think.'" Gifford-Gonzalez (2007:10) has paraphrased this more felicitously in English as "food for thought." Lévi-Strauss also points to the tendency to construct analogies between species of animals and human individuals or groups. That is, animal species are treated as unitary entities rather than groups of individuals. This is generally true of animal analogies and no doubt helps create the category of "animal" as opposed to "human," which seems to exist in almost all languages (see Chapter 1, *What Is an Animal?*).

Tapper (1988:54) suggests that totemic metaphors are primarily associated with foragers (see the earlier section, *Animal Metaphors*). However, this is not exclusively the case, because many farming groups (e.g., the Iroquois) also have animal clan names. It is perhaps more accurate to contrast hunters to herders in this respect. The conception of animal species as unitary corresponds more to a hunter's than a herder's experience, and hunters are more inclined to view animals as the equals of humans (see Chapter 4). Nevertheless, totemic thinking in the sense of using animal species to represent subdivisions of the human species is widespread in all societies, including ours:

> [A]nimals are so heavily used as symbols, not merely because of their formal appropriateness as metaphors for aspects of social structure which they accurately represent, but because, as natural beings with humanlike properties, they are the most suitable symbolic vehicles for the alienation of human (social) consciousness of the social nature of social phenomena through the misrepresentation of those phenomena as natural (Turner 1985:51).

Parkes (1987) suggests that agriculturalists and transhumant agropastoralists have distinctive ways of employing animal species to represent people, neither of which is totemic in the classic sense. Agriculturalists have a complex system of animal symbols radiating from the house and village, as outlined by Leach and Tambiah (see the later discussion of taboos). In contrast, groups with a gendered division of labor in which men do most of the herding, including taking the flocks for extended periods to mountain pastures, and women perform most of the agricultural labor tend to a more dualistic conception. In this system, animal species are opposed as pure and impure, masculine and feminine, with an intermediate species in a more or less neutral position. Parkes believes that the choice of animals that occupy the pure and impure positions depends on local ecological conditions. The species that thrives best becomes the pastoral staple and is labeled as pure not so much because of its economic importance per se, but because this economic centrality associates it with the male sphere.

For many peoples, kinship with animals is expressed not only through totem relations but also through stories of children raised by animals, or animal wife/husband stories. Along with origin myths in which humans and animals are identical, these stories reflect beliefs in the essential sameness of humans and other animals, often expressed (with ironic anthropocentrism) as animals, or spirit animals, being able to take off their skins in some circumstances to reveal the human form beneath (Bahti 1990; Brightman 1993; Harrod 2000).

### THE ARCHAEOLOGY OF TOTEMISM

Anne Bridault (1992) describes an interesting pattern of body part distribution of European elk (moose) in the Mesolithic. In northern Europe, where elk were locally abundant, their bones are common at archaeological sites and represent all body parts. These bones are clearly the remains of game eaten by the Mesolithic foragers. However, elk also had considerable symbolic importance to these groups, as seen in their depiction in rock art, the occurrence of pierced elk teeth in burials, and a deposit of jaws and feet in a ritual pit at Popovo in Karelia. Beyond the apparent range of elk, their bones are scarce, but do appear at many western European Mesolithic sites. These bones are almost entirely teeth (sometimes pierced) and foot bones. Bridault argues that these particular remains, which are certainly not dietary, were acquired through exchange because of their symbolic value. The feet may have symbolic significance in themselves, as Bridault seems to propose, or they may indicate the exchange of hides. Bridault suggests that elk could have been symbols of prestige, associated with shamanistic practices (see also Bolin 2000;

Bradley 2000) or totems of clans. A regional perspective has brought this phenomenon to light, but contextual studies at individual sites are needed to understand the nature of the symbolism.

Approaching totemism in the past requires contextual study of both animal representations and animal remains. If we take totemism to be the use of animal species to mark human groups, then manifestations of these species should be differentially distributed in line with those groups. However, there is no simple, universal formula for such analysis, because as noted earlier, the use of animals as totems may or may not involve taboos on their killing or consumption or, in contrast, use of their parts as talismans. Yet it is still worth examining the pattern of associations of animal representations with houses or burials and exploring whether distributions of animal remains are correlated with them, whether positively or negatively. Special deposits of animal parts that incorporate them into houses, public buildings, or places are of particular interest here. This work is not easy, but it holds the potential not only of identifying totems and totemism in the past but also of shedding light on the kinship system. For example, in principle one might be able to determine how many clans were present at a site and whether a shared clan system linked settlements in a region.

Göbekli Tepe and Nevalı Çori (early–middle PPNB) near Urfa in southeastern Turkey may reward such investigation. Both sites show much evidence of ritual activity, and Göbekli Tepe may be a special-purpose ritual site. Buildings at Göbekli Tepe are outfitted with massive (up to 5 m and at least 10 tons) carved stone pillars. The excavators have named the buildings for the motifs that appear repeatedly on the pillars within them; for example, the Lion Pillar Building (*Löwenpfeilergebäude*) and the Snake Pillar Building (*Schlangenpfeilergebäude*). The associations of animals with buildings that are so evident to the excavators must have been equally clear to the ancient inhabitants, which suggests the association of particular animals with particular human groups. Nevalı Çori has similar animal representations, but so far most have not been found in situ, so it is hard to assess whether the animal imagery is segregated, as it seems to be at Göbekli. Nearby Karahan Tepe, probably dating to the middle PPNB, again has similar snake and other animal imagery on stone pillars (Çelik 2000, 2005; Hauptmann 1999; Helmer et al. 2004; Köksal-Schmidt and Schmidt 2010; Schmidt 1999, 2001, 2003, 2006, 2008; Verhoeven 2002a). Joris Peters and Klaus Schmidt (2004) have proposed a totemic function as one possible interpretation of the site. Following Robert Layton (2000), they argue that totemic motifs should be localized at the regional level, but be diverse within a site. Within-site diversity is evident at Göbekli, but there is as yet insufficient analysis of other contemporary sites to assess the regional variation. Some of the same animals are found at other sites, whereas others so far appear more localized.

Some of the animals depicted prominently at these sites, such as snakes and scorpions, seem to have symbolic salience largely limited to the Urfa/Middle Euphrates region. Others, such as bulls, cranes, and canids, appear over a wider area in roughly this time period. Thus we see repeated symbolic use of animals at two geographic scales. Some form of totemism might explain some or all of these associations. It is certainly also possible that these animals form part of a shared system of myth and ritual, although this suggestion is not incompatible with a totemic function as well. Further work at these sites may throw light on these topics.

Chad Thomas, Christopher Carr, and Cynthia Keller (2005) have shown the potential of this kind of analysis. Drawing on ethnohistorical evidence, they argue that animal parts and effigies from burials and special deposits, as well as animal effigy platform pipes, identify clans in the Ohio Hopewell groups of the Middle Woodland period. Identifying up to 16 clans is only the beginning of their analysis. They then combine this work with other information to investigate how clans structured social and labor organization and to estimate the relative size and distribution of the clans. They are able to argue that leaders of various types were drawn from particular clans. Deeper in prehistory such research would be harder, but it is not unreasonable to imagine this kind of study even without the aid of direct historical analogy. Kristiina Mannermaa (2008) has tentatively suggested that jay wings in three burials from Middle Neolithic Zvejnieki (Latvia) could be totemic markers, although they could also mark shamans or other people of special status.

## Taboos

Marvin Harris (1985:47) asks, "If meat is so nutritious, why are so many animals bad to eat?" Here I explore food taboos, as opposed to incest, sexual, and other taboos, except as they intersect with strictures on food consumption. Whereas totemism uses living animals to construct human identity, food taboos use dead animals, through bans on their consumption, to map identity or cosmology. Although plant foods may also be tabooed, meat is especially subject to such strictures.

Taboo has been defined variously. John Halverson (1976) criticizes Edmund Leach's (1964) classic discussion of the topic for, among other things, lumping together things not eaten for any reason as taboo. Is a cultural or individual belief that a species does not taste good or is disgusting the same as a prohibition on eating it (see Whitehead 2000 for discussion of the relation between prohibitions and disgust reactions)? Interestingly, both Leach's mentalist approach and Eric Ross's (1978, 1987) cultural materialist one share this equation. Such an approach is, perhaps, useful for archaeologists, who can more readily determine whether or not an animal was eaten than the reason for avoiding it. However, for taboo to be a useful concept, it needs to mean more than simply an optimal foraging decision.

Taboo is a general term that includes many types of prohibitions. Taboos may forbid the killing of an animal, the consumption of its meat, the consumption of certain parts of the animal, or its consumption under certain circumstances. Such taboos may apply universally or only to certain people or at certain times. An animal totem or spirit helper may be taboo, but this is not always the case. Some taboos are strictly observed; others have milder force and may often be honored in the breach (e.g., Raharijaona and Kus 2001:61).

There has been considerable debate about the purpose and effect of food taboos. Some have argued that they codify rational decisions about what are the best foods to eat or whether animals are more valuable alive or as meat (Harris 1985; Ross 1978). These decisions include avoiding foods that are potentially toxic or otherwise unhealthy for some or all people. Taboos have also been touted as conservation measures to protect game populations (Ross 1978). Others have stressed their symbolic aspect, arguing that taboos help construct individual or group identity, or that they mark animals considered anomalous in terms of the local classificatory system (Douglas 1966; Leach 1964; Lévi-Strauss 1963; Shell 1986; Tambiah 1969; Taylor 1974). The Amazonian Achuar practice a limited taboo forbidding hunters from eating the first animal they kill of a given species, in order to establish a relationship with that species' spirit mother (Descola 1994:260). No doubt food taboos have served multiple purposes, perhaps simultaneously. Rather than making blanket statements about taboos, we need to analyze their function in each case.

One aspect that merits consideration is whether food prohibitions have positive, negative, or neutral effects in terms of nutrition or reproductive success. Cultural materialists such as Harris and Ross imply that taboos are beneficial by steering effort toward the most productive foods. In a rare attempt to measure the effects of food taboos on reproductive success, Robert Aunger (1994) shows that taboos can be maladaptive, and that they harm mainly women in male-dominated societies. Many have noted what Aunger quantifies: that food restrictions are often differentially targeted at women, particularly pregnant and nursing women (Adams 1990; Brightman 1993; Caplan 1994; Kahn 1986; Morris 1998:195; Parkes 1987; Zvelebil 2000). John Speth and Katherine Spielmann argue that the apparent equality maintained by meat sharing in many foraging societies (see Chapter 9, *Meat Sharing*) is in fact undermined by taboos that deny much meat to certain individuals, especially women (Speth 1990; Spielmann 1989). Food taboos mainly proscribe meat, and pregnant women, arguably in the greatest need of protein and fat, are most likely to be forbidden meat.

Forbidding meat to women helps maintain its overvaluation, supports the association of hunting and sometimes of herding with men, and enforces notions of male purity and status (see Chapter 4). "The foods forbidden to [Cree] women were precisely those conferring honor when served to men" (Brightman 1993:121). In this subarctic group, where plant foods are scarce, food taboos dictate that menstruating and pregnant women should ideally eat no meat (Brightman 1993:123). Among Kalasha agropastoralists, women are forbidden to eat male goat meat (the main herd animal) not because it is anomalous but because it is sacred and closely associated with the male herders, and women are seen as polluting. The meat and milk of cattle are considered impure and avoided by men, but are available to women (Parkes 1987). Thus some taboos are clearly directed not at deriving maximum benefit for all group members but at marking gender differences and gender hierarchy within the group.

Leach (1964) argues that meat taboos parallel and mark sexual taboos: Prohibitions on eating animals according to their degree of familiarity are equivalent to incest rules regulating the availability of women to a male ego. Thus animals closest to humans – pets, the animals we take into our family (corresponding to siblings in terms of incest taboos) – are most strongly tabooed. Leach sees farm animals as an intermediate category: mostly edible, but only when young or castrated; these he equates to cousins and more distant kin. Game animals are more nearby wild animals and are fully edible, corresponding to known non-kin. Remote wild animals are vaguely known and inedible, but strong prohibitions are unnecessary; these wild animals would correspond to distant strangers with whom there are no social relations. He also refers to a fifth category of inedible vermin to which there is no human equivalent, while noting that some animals such as rabbits can be classified as either vermin or game (making them edible). Halverson (1976) has pointed to many of the problems with this classification. Farm animals are close because they are kept for food, rather than being classified as edible because of their intermediate closeness. Those that are not eaten are spared because they are kept for their secondary products. The distinction between game and inedible wild animals is not really based on proximity. It is generally herbivorous mammals that are classified as game, and carnivores and elephants that are not eaten. Some inedible wild animals are in fact nearby. Indeed, Leach notes that foxes are ambiguous in this way, and hence subject to strong taboos. Moreover, game animals can be taboo to some groups or some group members (Reichel-Dolmatoff 1985; Ross 1978). In fact, taboo animals can be found in all of Leach's categories, and pets can be drawn from all the other categories (see Chapter 7).

Stanley Tambiah (1969) describes a similar classificatory system in Thailand, in which animals are grouped in part on the basis of proximity and familiarity. However, it is clear that taboos do not correspond in a simple manner to these degrees of familiarity. Among the "close" animals of the village, dogs are taboo because they are unclean, whereas cats are clean and are not taboo, but are not eaten because they are useful for rodent control. Other domestic animals are eaten, as are most wild species. All domestic animals have a designated wild counterpart, and the rules for the edibility of the wild animal follow those of the domestic species. "Remote" forest animals (large carnivores and elephants) are rarely encountered and are taboo because they exist in a world apart from humans. Anomalous animals that do not fit into the general classifications (e.g., vultures and crows are not considered birds) are not strongly tabooed but are only marginally edible; for instance, they are eaten only by children or for medicinal purposes.

Leach's scheme may not hold up and is certainly not universal, but it is based on a metaphorical link between sex and eating that has been identified in many societies, although it plays out in different ways. In Australia food taboos are analogous to exogamy, based on a principle of avoiding mixing like with like (Lévi-Strauss 1963:42). Northern Thai villagers taboo the eating of one's own cattle or water buffalo because doing so is considered tantamount to incest. These animals are killed chiefly for ceremonies. If for a household ceremony, the animal must come from another household in the village; for a village ceremony it must come from another village (Tambiah 1969:437–8). The Wamirans of New Guinea equate certain foods with men, others with women. Men are responsible for producing taro, and women for producing babies. These gender-associated foods are taboo when people are using their creative energies by planting taro or during pregnancy and nursing. In contrast, certain life-cycle ceremonies pointedly require the eating of both types of food together. Thus food taboos serve to underline gender differences and complementarity (Kahn 1986).

Pets are taboo more or less by definition, although some pet-like relationships end in the consumption of the animal. Given our kin-like relationship with pets, eating them would be like cannibalism (Fiddes 1991:133). Marc Shell (1986) further suggests that all love contains a sexual element, and therefore our relations with pets are inherently incestuous. Whereas Leach sees sexual taboos as analogous to dietary taboos, Shell sees them as synonymous. By this reading, of course, all parental, brotherly, and other forms of love would also be incestuous. Reducing all love to sex may not be particularly useful in understanding relationships. Halverson (1976) points out that animals can only function as pets when they are alive, so that the taboo on eating them results not from their anomalous position (part of the household but not human), but simply from their value as living animals. Nevertheless, the particular role of pets often provokes a strong aversion to killing and eating them that does not usually arise regarding, for example, sheep valued for their wool production. Eating other animals seen as resembling humans, such as bears, or as embodying human essence may also provoke feelings of cannibalism, although this does not always prevent their consumption (Brightman 1993:205; Guenther 1988:193). Indeed, if people do not make a qualitative distinction between humans and animals, all meat consumption amounts to cannibalism (see Chapter 4).

In sum, food prohibitions may arise for a variety of reasons and take a number of forms. Although some reflect particular kinds of human–animal relationships, many more importantly mark human social distinctions. Leach cast taboos in terms of kinship, but for the Sanumá of Venezuela taboos form a completely separate system of classification, based on age and stage of parenting (Taylor 1974:62). Often taboos mark gender differences, age distinctions, and reproductive and productive states (pregnancy, planting taro, etc.). Dietary restrictions would appear to be a particularly powerful way of marking and ranking groups that cross-cut kinship categories. In stratified societies, taboos may take the force of law to restrict certain foods to the elite, as when hunting and game are reserved for the nobility (see Chapter 4, *Sport Hunting*).

## TABOOS AS ETHNIC MARKERS

Two particular taboos have attracted much scholarly attention: India's sacred cows and the Jewish and Islamic prohibition on pork. Because they consist of more or less total bans on the consumption of an entire species by an entire group of people, they are in principle particularly amenable to archaeological study. However, most of the debate has centered around the reasons for the ban on eating cattle or pigs.

### Sacred Cows

The Hindu ban on killing or eating cattle is linked to cow worship. Some have argued that the sacred status of cattle is based on the practical need for their living products (milk, dung, traction) and the inefficiency of beef production in the densely populated Indian countryside (Harris 1966, 1985:48–66; Nair 1987). Yet it is not clear why a taboo is necessary to achieve secondary product goals among Hindus, but not among Indian Muslims or in Pakistan (Diener et al. 1978). Others emphasize the symbolic aspects of cattle, seeing them as inhibiting the practical benefits of herd management through culling (which has to be accomplished indirectly through withholding milk or care from unwanted calves). Hindu attitudes toward cattle and other animals rest on the values of *ahimsa* (nonviolence), which treats all life as sacred and killing as damaging to the soul, and ritual purity, which sees some animals or their products as polluting. Cows are revered as the embodiment of the mother goddess and hence are especially sacred (Robbins 1998; Simoons 1979; Simoons and Lodrick 1981).

Although cow worship is often traced back to the Bronze Age Harappan culture, it has certainly not existed in its present form since that time. Cattle are frequently depicted (along with a number of other animals) on Harappan seals. These are clearly marked as bulls rather than cows, however. The animals and other motifs on the seals may or may not represent deities. Faunal studies show that cattle were eaten during the Harappan, and indeed they form the major meat source (Meadow 1996). Cattle figure prominently in the *Rig Veda*, but as objects of sacrifice rather than worship (*Rig Veda* 1981). Later in the Vedic period cattle consumption became restricted to the elite, and only in the context of sacrifice, conferring sacred status on cattle. Jains and Buddhists later led resistance to the Brahmin monopoly on cattle sacrifice and consumption, with the emerging belief in reincarnation contributing to the notion of sacred cattle (Nair 1987:449–50). This was a period of state formation, and some have argued that the ban on cattle consumption was designed to break down the old redistributive modes of power built on sacrifice and feasting (see Chapter 9). It also helped ensure a supply of pack animals for the army and for the newly important long-distance trade between states, and it facilitated the accumulation of wealth in cattle (Diener et al. 1978). Vegetarianism came to be associated with ritual purity and high caste (although not without exceptions). Recently, the sacredness of cows has become a rallying point for Hindu nationalism, with legislation protecting them from Muslim butchers (Robbins 1998). Thus cattle consumption has long been used to negotiate religious identity and status, although in varying ways.

### Pig taboos

The Jewish and Islamic pig taboo is different in nature from the taboo associated with India's sacred cattle. Pigs are not protected because they are holy, but shunned because they are profoundly unclean. The ban cannot be read as an attempt to maximize living pig populations; rather it seeks to eliminate them. Nor can one make the same argument that Harris and others propose for sacred cattle: that their living products are more valuable than their meat. Pigs do not produce living products other than dung, and although their excrement can be used for fertilizer, it is not suited for burning as fuel because it is not full of undigested grass. Indeed, Harris (1985:67–86) contends that precisely this lack of secondary products, along with the unsuitability of pigs for the arid environments of the Near East, motivates the prohibition. Although pigs are the most efficient converters of feed to meat, their lack of other products makes them less valuable than ruminants. If this is the case, it is hard to see why a taboo is needed. Harris's explanation is that people like pork and would otherwise raise pigs anyway. He even claims that Islam has been restrained from spreading into areas suited to pigs by the strong resistance of pork lovers.

Paul Diener and Eugene Robkin (1978) have challenged Harris's model, arguing that pigs do well in many Near Eastern environments. The Near East is one of the centers of pig domestication (Albarella et al. 2006a), although deforestation may have rendered some areas less suited to pigs by the time of known pig taboos (and eastern Anatolia, rather than the Levant, seems the most likely locus of initial pig domestication). Diener and Robkin suggest that the deforestation resulted from the pig taboo rather than vice versa, however, because sheep and goat overgrazing is a major cause of deforestation. They focus on Islam, suggesting that the pig taboo is political in origin: Pigs are well suited to autonomous household production that helps people resist the centralized state. In turn this threatens the urban elite who need rural farmers to supply them with meat and with grain that they might feed to pigs. They see the pig taboo as only one of a set of Islamic prohibitions designed to limit rural autonomy and force trade through Muslim merchants.

Islam is of course not the only nor the first religion to ban pigs. Early Muslims drew selectively on Jewish dietary law, and some other societies contemporary with the early Israelites also seem to have avoided pigs (Hesse and Wapnish 2002:469). Jewish dietary restrictions divide animals into clean and prohibited categories. Each category contains both wild and domestic animals (Borowski 2002). Pigs are notable as a major domestic animal that is prohibited. Many explanations have been offered for the Jewish pig taboo. In addition to Harris's ecological explanation (building on similar arguments by other scholars), it has been attributed to a desire to avoid trichinosis, a symbolic statement about purity, and an ethnic marker distinguishing pastoralist Hebrews from settled farmers.

Although some have questioned whether ancient people would have made the connection between pork and trichinosis, given that this link was only discovered in Europe in 1860, Michael Ryder (1994) argues that there is textual evidence from the Classical period for the recognition of trichina cysts and their potential to cause disease. He therefore suggests that the taboo is a practical public health measure. This does not, however, explain the patchy and fluctuating pattern of ancient pig use and avoidance.

Mary Douglas (1966) has famously attributed the pig taboo to symbolic dissonance created by the anomalous nature of the pig: It has cloven hooves but does not ruminate. This argument has the advantage of explaining the peculiar intensity of pig loathing. This antipathy seems strongest in Islamic culture, however, whose texts do not emphasize the classificatory difficulties posed by the pig, but simply label it an abomination.

Because many animals are banned by Jewish law (e.g., camel, rabbit, hare, shellfish, eagle, vulture, many other birds, bat, weasel, mouse, lizards; locusts and grasshoppers, in contrast, are explicitly permitted), we might ask why pigs have garnered the lion's share of scholarly and popular attention. Leach (1964:50–1) suggests that the widespread (although not universal) denigration of the pig derives from a particular guilt. We raise pigs only for slaughter (pet pigs excepted), and in small farming situations they are raised close to (or in) the house, fed on the remainders of human food. Pigs are a little too close for comfort. This, however, does not prevent them from being eaten by many groups, nor is revulsion an inevitable correlate of raising pigs. In Oceania, where pigs are even more a part of the household, they are held in high esteem (but guilt is evident in the common prohibitions on eating one's own pigs).

Although pigs can be herded, they are not well suited to pastoralism, particularly in arid regions where pastoralism is most useful. Thus some (e.g., Borowski 2002:411) have suggested that the pig would have been associated with settled farmers and therefore held in contempt by the pastoralist Hebrews. Pig avoidance became an ethnic marker. Richard Lobban (1998) suggests that this marker was acquired during the Hebrews' time in Egypt, arguing that the Egyptian elite in this period had a pig taboo that was absorbed by Moses. He derives the Egyptian taboo, in turn, from a combination of the loss of pig habitat to agriculture and cattle pasture with the rise of the Egyptian state and new prominence for cattle wealth, and the defeat of Lower Egypt whose patron deity, Seth, was associated with the pig. However, this taboo applied only to the nobility, whereas the commoners still raised and ate pigs in considerable numbers.

Zooarchaeology can help evaluate the proposed explanations. Melinda Zeder's (1998) study of the fauna from Tell Halif in southern Israel and a series of sites in the Khabur Basin in northern Syria, covering the Neolithic to Iron Age, reveals patterns in pig abundance germane to this question. Drops in pig abundance do not correlate with drier periods, but they do accompany periods of greater political centralization. At some sites, pigs are more frequent in commoner residential areas than in elite and ceremonial areas. Brian Hesse and Paula Wapnish (1998:126) note that, on a regional level, pig use fluctuates in the Levant through time, with high levels in the Neolithic, Chalcolithic, and Early Bronze Age; dropping to very low levels in the Late Iron Age (the time of the Old Testament); and returning to higher levels again in the Hellenistic, Roman, and Byzantine periods. Like Zeder, they find that in the Middle Bronze Age pigs are associated with commoners rather than the elite and with rural rather than urban contexts (Hesse and Wapnish 2002:469). All of this suggests that in the Levant, climate precludes large-scale pig raising, but household-level sty production, with pigs consuming household waste, provides a useful buffer for common people. At this scale, pigs recycle waste products rather than compete for human food. The household autonomy that this creates may be threatening to governments that seek to control citizens by, among other things, regulating the food supply. Thus Diener and Robkin's (1978) model is best supported by the archaeological evidence for the ancient Levant in general.

Hesse and Wapnish (1998) cast the question as why pig avoidance became a useful marker of ethnic identity for the Hebrews. Noting that previous archaeological approaches have tended to equate the absence of pigs simplistically with the presence of Hebrews based on an essentialized conception of ethnicity, they apply contemporary anthropological understandings of ethnicity to the issue. Viewing ethnic identity as something that is created in interaction with other groups to define boundaries, as much by outsiders as insiders, they ask how the identification of pig avoidance with the Hebrews came about. Although the Hebrews characterized all Philistines as uncircumcised pork lovers, in fact only some Philistine sites have pig bones, and those are limited in their spatial distribution. Moreover, not only the Hebrews but also most other non-Philistine groups in the Iron Age Levant avoided pigs. Hesse and Wapnish examine the Hebrew attitude through time, finding that there are few references to pig taboos before the exile to Babylon. Instead, the taboo arises afterward, when the Hebrews returned to their homeland and needed to reestablish their identity. Whereas before exile their identity had been based primarily on ties to land, the rupture of those ties necessitated other ways of affirming ethnic unity. Religion and dietary rules became central to forging a Hebrew identity at this point. As part of the process, the generalized pig avoidance they had shared with other groups became pig hatred, presumably in specific opposition to their understanding of Philistines as pork eaters. Early Christians may have embraced pork consumption to distinguish themselves from Jews as they were establishing their own separate identity (Vassas 2006). Conversely, the Tharu of Nepal once tabooed the consumption of water buffalo, although they sacrificed them, to distinguish themselves from lower castes. However, as food habits have become less salient as caste markers, this taboo has relaxed (McDonaugh 1997).

### THE ARCHAEOLOGY OF TABOO

Dale Serjeantson (2000) has similarly provided insight into food taboos through her study of the animal bones from medieval Winchester in England. Although eating horseflesh had been forbidden by the Church to distinguish Christians from pagans, some horse bones show clear signs of consumption. Thus this taboo was occasionally broken. She also suggests that named animals, roughly corresponding to pets, are typically not eaten. In this light, it is interesting that medieval dogs and horses rarely show signs of consumption or use, but cat bones frequently exhibit skinning marks. Serjeantson therefore argues that cats were not named or treated as companion animals.

Although archaeology has contributed to our understanding of the history of known taboos, purely archaeological studies of otherwise undocumented taboos are rare. Clearly taboos are one of the more difficult phenomena to study archaeologically. There can be many reasons for the absence of a taxon, including the local environment, seasonality, and hunting technology. Moreover, although cattle and pigs are totally banned for consumption by whole groups (at least more or less), the ethnographic record shows that most taboos are partial: Only some group members are forbidden to eat an animal, perhaps only at some times, or perhaps only some body parts are forbidden. It is challenging to detect such subtle patterning, but not impossible. The effort is worthwhile because, as we have seen, taboos often mark social categories. Whereas total taboos may mark ethnicity, partial taboos mark internal social divisions.

Gustavo Politis and Nicholas Saunders (2002) offer an extremely useful ethnoarchaeological study of the Nukak, foragers and small-scale horticulturalists in the Colombian Amazon, that specifically focuses on how food taboos pattern archaeological assemblages. They find that taboos shape hunting decisions much more powerfully than do cost-benefit utility considerations of the sort often used to model foraging choices. Taboos also structure the bone assemblages in various ways. Crucially, total taboos on the hunting and consumption of some species do not make them invisible in animal bone assemblages. Rather they result in the presence of limited body parts used in special ways. For example, deer and jaguar are never killed or eaten, yet people scavenge deer tibiae and jaguar humeri from carcasses found in the forest to make flutes used at initiations and in other liminal circumstances; jaguar teeth are also collected from these carcasses and used in necklaces that are buried with their owners. Therefore, small numbers of limited body parts used as artifacts or found in special contexts may signal a tabooed and ideologically important animal, rather than one hunted occasionally at a distance from the settlement, as would be a more typical interpretation.

Other species, such as some ducks and piranha, are rarely or never eaten by the Nukak, but are regularly hunted for their feathers or, for the piranha, their sharp-toothed jaws (used as artifacts). Without careful attention to the lack of butchering and burning traces, the remains of these animals would likely be mistaken for food waste. Some animals, such as peccary, are subject to partial taboos; they are often permitted to men but forbidden to women and children. These animals are prepared and consumed on the edge of camp, with only a few bones entering the site. This spatial distribution contrasts with the bones of animals that are freely eaten by all, which are processed and consumed in the household and discarded within the camp. Thus distinctive spatial distributions are a clue to partial taboos. However, in this case the pattern is complicated by the practice of keeping young peccaries as pets within the camp. They often die, and their bones are likely to be spread around by dogs and other forces.

The Nukak build a structure called the House of the Tapir at the edge of their fields. This building is more elaborate and more solidly built than human houses. Although it may be used to some extent for storage, it is primarily a symbolic home for the sacred tapir, intended to keep it from bothering people. "Thus, the most elaborate, time consuming, and substantial Nukak structure, relates not to chiefly or shamanic occupancy (as might be expected), but to a powerful spirit-animal whose natural prototype is a tabooed food resource, and, consequently, is archaeologically invisible" (Politis and Saunders 2002:125). Therefore ideological beliefs about animals even shape the Nukak settlement pattern. Without a direct historical ethnographic analogy, it is hard to imagine how a House of the Tapir could be correctly interpreted archaeologically. It is nevertheless useful to bear in mind that one possible use of a public building, perhaps especially one set apart from the main settlement, is as a spirit dwelling.

Differences between representations of animals suggesting their spiritual importance and animal remains may also be instructive. Perhaps some of the animals in Paleolithic art were actually taboo, for example. Comparing the Nukak to their neighbors, Politis and Saunders concur with Ralph Bulmer's (1976) conclusion based on work in New Guinea that groups using the same technology in similar environments with the same resources available will often make very different hunting choices (producing animal bone assemblages with significantly different proportions of taxa) based on taboos or the ritual value of animal taxa.

Julie Holt (1996) approaches Mississippian belief systems about animals in the American Bottom through a combination of ethnohistory, artistic representations, and faunal remains. Here, too, optimization models do not adequately explain the patterns of species abundance. There is a generally negative correlation between species represented in art and those consumed. The main exception is ducks, but it may be that those depicted are wood ducks, anomalous because of their roosting habits. In the faunal assemblages, fish and deer are the staples, with some other taxa taken opportunistically. Other taxa that could certainly have been taken from time to time are avoided, however. Holt suggests that these animals were taboo because they were either anomalous (Douglas 1990) or metaphorically equivalent to humans. Snakes, spiders, owls, and opossums were likely seen as anomalous, whereas dogs and bears would be human equivalents. As she observes, however, it is tricky to decide what is anomalous, as this depends on a particular classification system, arguably developed to explain why some taxa are avoided. Also in the Mississippian American Bottom, Lucretia Kelly (2001:349) suggests that prairie chickens may have been reserved for the elite at Cahokia, based on contextual patterning.

Serjeantson (2006) and Arkadiusz Marciniak (2005a) have each suggested that the surprising lack of wild animal bones at Neolithic sites in Britain and Poland, respectively, is due to a taboo on these animals. Serjeantson particularly notes the paucity of fish and bird remains, which should have been abundant and easy to take. Although somewhat controversial, stable isotope studies have suggested that the Mesolithic-Neolithic transition in northwest Europe is marked by a shift away from marine resources, which apparently become taboo to early farming groups (Craig et al. 2007; Eriksson et al. 2008; Hedges 2004; Lidén et al. 2004; Milner et al. 2004; Richards, Price, and Koch 2003; Richards and Schulting 2006; Richards, Schulting, and Hedges 2003; Schulting and Richards 2002; Thomas 2003).

### Taboos at Çatalhöyük?

Drawing on these insights, we may examine the faunal remains from Neolithic Çatalhöyük in Turkey for evidence of possible taboos. Here, we can make use of a large body of art and architectural installations (Mellaart 1967; Russell and Meece 2006) in conjunction with a substantial faunal assemblage carefully collected and analyzed with attention to context (Russell and Martin 2005; Russell and McGowan 2005). Patterns suggestive of both total and partial taboos are apparent.

Politis and Saunders' finding that unusual body part patterning can signal taboo animals suggests some candidates at Çatalhöyük. Most notably, leopards feature prominently in the art, appearing in figurines, a stamp seal, reliefs, and, in the form of skins and possibly one unspotted feline, in the paintings. Yet, with more than a million bones recorded, only a single leopard bone has been recovered. This specimen is a third phalanx (claw), perforated to make it into a bead and deposited in a burial along with the only plastered human skull from the site. This is clearly the exception that proves the rule. If indeed skins were worn, as the art suggests, they must have arrived at the site already trimmed of heads and feet, in contrast to some other taxa. But perhaps the people depicted wearing skins are Others: from a primeval time when things were different, from a spirit world with inverted rules, or the like. The faunal remains suggest a strong taboo on killing leopards, whereas the art signals a symbolic importance that may have motivated the taboo.

Bear and wild cat (*Felis silvestris*) are both quite rare in the faunal remains, and they are represented solely by head and foot elements. Bear remains include an articulated paw with skinning cut marks and plaster between the toes, suggesting it may have been set into a wall (to hold a skin in place?); two molar teeth in a burial; and a few other teeth and foot bones from secondary contexts. Wild cat is represented by two articulated paws, a set of articulated mandibles, and a few other foot bones as well as a single humerus fragment. One interpretation is that these animals, perhaps taken in the foothills 15–20 km from the site, were used only for their hides. Other fur-bearers such as badger and fox seem to be used mostly for their skins, but are represented by bones throughout the body. These may have been taken more locally, and both badger and fox lived on the site itself until archaeological activity became too intense. In contrast, the pattern for most hunted animals, even large ones, is to bring the whole body back to the site. It may therefore be that bear and wild cat were permissible to hunt, at least on encounter, but not to consume. Or they may have been altogether taboo, with parts scavenged from found carcasses. Skins will be usable only from a very fresh carcass, an unusual find. Thus the actual heads, teeth, and feet alone may have been brought back. One painting probably depicts a bear, and a stamp seal indicates that a fairly numerous class of reliefs represent bears or bear/human therianthropes (Türkcan 2007), whereas wild cat is not recognizable among the animal representations. Their symbolic role is thus less clear than that of the leopard. Paintings often emphasize the feet of animals, however, and heads and feet are often knocked off the reliefs at the end of their life cycle. These body parts, then, may have particular significance.

Other taxa also exhibit distinctive body part distributions. As noted, all body parts of most hunted animals, such as cattle and equids, were transported back to the site. However, deer and boar differ in this respect. In the earliest deposits, although neither is very abundant, all body parts of these animals are present and show signs of consumption. Later, they are represented mainly by heads and feet. This is particularly true for the deer, whose later remains are largely limited to antler. However, it is not clear whether this is temporal or spatial patterning. The two areas where all body parts are found are in one case off the tell and, in the other, apparently on the edge of the settlement at that point in time. Thus we may be seeing either a developing taboo or a partial taboo of the sort described by Politis and Saunders, in which some people can hunt and consume these animals, but must do so outside the main living area to avoid contact with those for whom the animals are taboo.

The general scarcity of boar in the assemblage, given what would seem to be good habitat (marshy with some riverine forest), could also reflect this partial taboo. Those bones found on site might then be attributed to bringing back skins from these animals. Deer and boar appear in the paintings and there are boar figurines; some of the paintings may be hunting scenes. Although these depictions show that hunting them was not unthinkable, they may indicate that such hunts were particularly ritually charged. Boar mandibles were also mounted on walls in some houses. If consumption or perhaps even contact with boar was forbidden to some segment of the population, these bones may have constituted a particularly strong statement of the identity of the other segment, and would have been dangerous for some people. This may explain why the boar jaws were covered with plaster at the end of their use lives. Ornaments made of boar's tusk, such as pendants, collars, and possibly fishhooks, may also have carried particular connotations, and it is notable that they seem to cluster in particular buildings (Russell 2006). Although the possible hunting scenes might suggest that boars are linked to male identity, an adult female was buried with three boar mandibles (Mellaart 1966a:27). Therefore this taboo may mark something other than gender, or this person may have held a special gender status.

An exception to the deer bone pattern stands out. The remains of two red deer, encompassing all body parts, were spread in a layer beneath a building floor, apparently a foundation deposit including the remains of a ceremonial feast (Russell in press-b). This building also contained more boar than usual, although mostly heads and feet. Like all the buildings so far excavated at Çatalhöyük, this appears to have been lived in as a house, although there are many signs of ritual activity. Did it also function as a locus of ceremonies for a particular group? Or were the inhabitants in some respect ritually distinct from most people?

In general, the bird bones at Çatalhöyük are heavily weighted toward wing elements. This pattern does not appear to be a matter of differential survival. Bustard and coot are the only species with substantial representation of meaty body parts in most areas studied. Despite extensive flotation and dry screening of the deposits, bird bones are also rather rare, although water birds (which do form about 80% of the bird bone assemblage) should have been very abundant near the site, especially during migration. As is also true of boar, bird remains were present in far greater quantities at slightly earlier sites in the vicinity (Baird 2009; Martin, Russell, and Carruthers 2002). Thus most birds seem not to have been eaten, but were probably taken mainly for their feathers (Russell and McGowan 2005). In contrast, eggshell is extremely common (Sidell and Scudder 2005). This selective use of avian resources strongly suggests a taboo on the consumption of most bird species.

Finally, it is likely that dogs carried taboos. Dog bones show signs of consumption only in rare instances, indicating that they were ordinarily deemed inedible (Russell and Martin 2005). In this case, the taboo may reflect a belief that dogs were unclean. There is little sign that dogs were treated as pets. They seem to have been excluded from the interior of houses during occupation, never occur in human burials, and are not buried like humans. Dog feces were collected and dumped in particular locations (Russell and Twiss in press).

Inevitably, lacking historical or ethnohistorical records of the beliefs of the inhabitants of Çatalhöyük, discussions of food taboos at the site are laden with ambiguities. Nevertheless, some of the patterning is highly suggestive, and we may glimpse a complex set of proscriptions at work. Although gender categories are very commonly delineated through meat taboos, it is not clear that gender is the relevant variable here; rather other groups such as sodalities may be indicated. Politis and Saunders' work is extremely useful in showing that not only total absence but also spatial and body part patterning may result from taboos. Contextual analyses have great potential to elucidate this aspect of ancient belief systems.

### Animal combat: Constructing the wild

As discussed in Chapter 6, one consequence of domestication is the creation of a category of the Wild. This concept, and its opposition to the Domestic and the Tame, has proven to be symbolically rich. Although the Wild is often embodied in the forest, the wilderness, the hunt, or wild animals, it is ironically also often created in the midst of domestication. This can be done in many ways, including through feeding practices that are thought to promote wildness (Mullin 2007) or even through breeding to select for "wildness" (Cassidy 2002; Mullin 2007). Here I focus on various forms of animal combat as constructing the Wild, usually to assert human dominion over it. Jean-Pierre Digard (1990:197–9) argues that all animal sports, even races, are really about the opposition of humans and animals and the human triumph over the powerful Wild. In animal combat, he suggests, we reenact domestication, often in a particularly brutal form.

## BULLFIGHTS AND BULL GAMES

Certainly the Spanish bullfight plays out this drama. The bull is generally understood as embodying the Wild and the Male. In the course of the *corrida de toros*, the bull is tamed (brought under the control of the *toreador*). The *toreador* may demonstrate his dominance by swaggering over the dead bull or even stroking its forehead or biting its horn. Many also read the bullfight as an enactment of gender roles, in which the bull gradually becomes more feminine and the *toreador* more masculine through this process of domination (Douglass 1997; Marvin 1994; Pitt-Rivers 1993:14).

There is an obvious difficulty with viewing a domestic animal as wild. This trick is accomplished through a set of beliefs and practices that set fighting bulls apart from other domestic animals. First, the fighting bulls are considered to come from a special breed (*toros bravos*, roughly fierce or wild bulls, applied in the context of a breed to both males and females). Pseudo-scientific discussions of the bullfight derive this breed in some unspecified way more directly from the wild ancestor of cattle, perhaps implying an independent local domestication in Spain (Conrad 1957; I have seen similar claims made for certain horse and dog breeds). The key trait of this breed is an intrinsic fierceness: the desire to charge at humans whenever possible. "Wildness" is here constructed as threat to humanity. This trait of wildness is deliberately bred for, and it is also nurtured through herding practices that minimize contact with humans. The very techniques of domestication – artificial selection and herding practices – are used to negate domestication. There are strict sanctions against exposing bulls to capes before they appear in the ring, because it is feared that a bull familiar with the cape might gore the *toreador*. Thus the "training" happens only during the bullfight, but it is conceived in these terms: teaching the bull to perform properly.

The bullfight in its present form was codified in the 18th and 19th centuries, but many have tried to trace its roots, together with those of other Spanish bull events, much further back in time. Certainly it is derived from medieval pageants and ritual hunts involving bulls, but it has been traced further to Roman gladiatorial combat with animals or to Minoan bull leaping. Some also contend it is a native Iberian development, traceable to Upper Paleolithic bull paintings at Altamira or, less plausibly, to Arab influence during the Muslim occupation. Lola and Arturo Morales Muñiz (1995) evaluate these theories and conclude that the bullfight grew from a long local tradition of special importance of bulls (in fact, one not limited to Iberia but evident over most of prehistoric Europe and beyond) combined with elements of Roman practice, which were in turn derived from a broader eastern Mediterranean tradition of bull rituals such as Mithraism. In origin, then, the bullfight has elements of both sacrifice and public spectacle. They argue that it is still in large measure a sacrifice and rite of purification (see also Pitt-Rivers 1993).

Morales Muñiz and Morales Muñiz are able to bring the techniques and data of zooarchaeology fruitfully to bear on the question of the fighting bull "breed" and its origins. Using withers height, color, horn shape, and so on, they show that there is no breed of *toros bravos*. Rather, there are three separate regional breeding stocks in Navarra, Castile, and Andalusia, each derived from local breeds. The only diagnostic feature of the "breed" is its supposedly inherited fierceness. There is no evidence that this behavioral trait is genetically based, however. Rather, the herding practices used to tame domestic animals are in many ways reversed to produce the "wild" bulls. Large enclosures are crucial, because it has been shown that simply raising bulls in a smaller corral, still with little human contact, substantially reduces their flight distance and hence aggressive behavior. During the *corrida*, aggression is further stimulated by fear, pain, and the use of postures that cattle interpret as aggressive. Much of the pain inflicted is specifically directed at weakening the neck muscles that support the head and horns, so that the bull is rendered less dangerous (Marvin 1994).

Zooarchaeology cannot currently trace the history of bullfighting or fighting bulls. Because the bulls are not morphologically distinct, this task would be difficult. Morales Muñiz and Morales Muñiz suggest that distinctive cut marks on the thoracic vertebrae from the various wounds inflicted might possibly be found archaeologically. In combination with contextual analysis, with attention paid to signs of ritual treatment (although today the dead bull is simply sold for ordinary food), it may in the future be possible to clarify the development of the bullfight. Meanwhile, at least zooarchaeology can help puncture some of the mythology surrounding bullfights and fighting bulls, much of which is repeated uncritically even in serious academic studies of the bullfight.

The bull games of Minoan Crete are among the putative ancestors of the Spanish bullfight (e.g., Marvin 1994:52). These bull games, known from artistic representations, are similarly surrounded with speculation and controversy about their nature and origins. They are most commonly imagined as a spectacle in which scantily clad young men (and perhaps women) grasped the horns of charging bulls and used them to vault onto or over the bulls' backs. A basic area of disagreement is whether such a maneuver is even possible: Bulls tend to toss their heads to the side, not upward (Evans 1963:141; Younger 1976:135; Zeuner 1963:235). Alas, this issue is too dangerous to settle through experimental archaeology! It is difficult to interpret the "snapshots" represented in paintings, seals, and engravings in terms of the motion they represent. Some suggest that the human players are not acrobats leaping over bulls, but sacrifices sent to be gored by them (Pinsent 1983). The bull games have been variously described as a secular sport (Evans 1963), a ritual of regeneration (Serrano Espinosa 1998), propitiation of the bull god responsible for earthquakes (Zeuner 1963:236), an initiation ritual (Arnott 1993; Marinatos 1989), a ritual hunt (Marinatos 1989), a ritual dance (Sipahi 2001), and an elaborate sacrifice (Pinsent 1983). Of course, it is always possible that the bull games never actually took place, but rather the representations depict a myth.

Like the bullfight, there has been much discussion of the origins of the Minoan bull games. There is no sign of a local predecessor in the Cretan Neolithic. However, many have noted similar artistic representations from Anatolia, Syria, the Persian Gulf region, and Egypt, as well as Mycenaean Greece (Bietak 1994; Collon 1994; Rice 1997:45, 178; Serrano Espinosa 1998; Sipahi 2001). Such representations of people interacting with and leaping over bulls or grasping their horns appear slightly earlier in Anatolia and Syria than on Crete. Naturally, the dramatic bull imagery at Neolithic Çatalhöyük has been cited as a progenitor (Collon 1994; Serrano Espinosa 1998; Sipahi 2001). However, although bull imagery

is found in the intervening periods in Anatolia, there is no sign of anything that looks like a bull game. Nor is it clear that the two Çatalhöyük
bull paintings represent bull games of any sort, although bulls are shown
surrounded by people, and some have suggested that a human figure
positioned above the back of one of the bulls is leaping over it (Rice
1997:75; Sipahi 2001).

Also like the bullfight, some have suggested that the bulls were captured from the wild for the Minoan bull games (e.g., Lengerken 1955).
Again, there is little basis for this notion, other than a romantic desire to
cast this as a struggle between civilization and the wild forces of nature.
It is quite clear (cf. Nobis 1996) that aurochsen (wild cattle) are not
native to Crete, but were introduced by the earliest Neolithic settlers
(Broodbank and Strasser 1991:236; de Vos 1996; Jarman 1996; Zeuner
1963:229). It is possible that some of these escaped or were released
to form feral populations, as happened with goats. However, Zeuner
(1963:229) long ago pointed out that the coloring of the bulls shown
in the Minoan paintings could only be found on domestic cattle. Some
writers suggest that, like Spanish fighting bulls, they may have been kept
in a semi-wild state so they would be ferocious (Evans 1963), whereas
others believe they would have needed special training to achieve the
bull-leaping feats (Zeuner 1963:235). The occasional remains of large
cattle falling within the wild size range (Jarman 1996) could be the result
of selective breeding of large bulls for the games. Of course, if the games
have mainland origins, wild bulls could have been used there, but there
is even less information about these events.

Discussions of the Minoan bull games are based almost entirely on the
artistic representations. A few other lines of evidence have been brought
to bear, and they could potentially be applied more fully. Anne Ward
(1968) has marshaled both artistic and archaeological evidence to argue
that the games were probably held in the central courts of Minoan palaces,
contrary to others who ruled these areas out (Pendlebury 1939). Certainly further explorations of the architecture of such areas might be
expected to reveal such spaces as holding pens if they were indeed used
for this purpose. Lawrence Angel (1971:91) interpreted a hip wound in
a male human skeleton at Çatalhöyük as a possible result of goring in
the course of bull games or hunts. One might expect to find numerous
such wounds in Minoan skeletons if these events actually took place on a
regular basis. So far zooarchaeology has had little to contribute beyond

clarifying the domestication status of Cretan cattle. However, we might note that the Minoan herding economy was based on sheep and goats rather than cattle (Greig and Warren 1974; Halstead 1981b; Jarman 1996; Klippel and Snyder 1999; Wilkens 1996). Thus many of the cattle present may have been raised specifically to supply the games, which would be likely to produce a skewed mortality profile, with unusually high proportions of adult males. Although this possibility bears closer investigation, some Minoan faunal assemblages so far reported do note a high proportion of adult cattle (Wilkens 1996).

## OTHER ANIMAL COMBAT

Bullfights and bull games are only some of the better known forms of animal combat. Ethnographically, battles between animals or between animals and humans staged for human amusement or ritual purposes are widespread; they include cockfights, bear baiting, some aspects of rodeo, and dog fights. These fights are not easy to approach archaeologically unless they are elaborate enough to involve special equipment and venues, but it is worth bearing in mind that such animal combat may motivate people to raise domestic animals specifically for the purpose or to capture wild animals and hold them, usually briefly. When domestic animals are involved, regular use in combat could affect mortality profiles, as I have suggested for the bull games. Analysis of pathologies resulting from injury would also help build a case.

Perhaps the most institutionalized example of this practice is the use of animals in the arena during the Roman Empire. Animals were used to execute criminals and heretics, and chiefly to fight each other and be slaughtered in staged "hunts." The emphasis was on spectacle, with the empire demonstrating its power by displaying and destroying exotic animals from the far reaches of its territory. Textual and artistic evidence indicate that the animals used in these spectacles were mostly wild carnivores (lions, leopards, bears), but also included dogs and sometimes wild boar and both wild and domestic cattle (Gilhus 2006). However, zooarchaeology suggests that the wild carnivores, especially the large felids, were in fact very rare in the arena (MacKinnon 2006). They may be depicted so frequently precisely because of their exotic allure.

Rulers of Java and Aceh in the 17th–19th centuries were also fond of staging animal as well as human combat for royal entertainment, including battling tigers, elephants, banteng, cattle, and sheep (Reid

1988:183–9). Yet animal combat is not limited to state societies. The Iban horticulturalists of Sarawak, for example, enjoy cockfights where the roosters are fitted with sharp metal blades and usually fight to the death. Because the spirits also enjoy cockfights, they are performed at sacrifices; indeed before colonial pacification, the Iban conceived of warfare as cockfights staged by the spirits; that is, the warriors were identified with fighting cocks (Beavitt 1989). The losing cock is eaten, so, metal spurs aside, the archaeological visibility of the cockfight would depend on the high proportion of adult males.

Wherever animal combat is popular, people will devote substantial labor and resources to obtaining, maintaining, and training the animals involved. We tend to interpret finds of wild carnivores as the result of hunting or trapping for fur, and sometimes this can be demonstrated (Trolle-Lassen 1987). However, it is also possible that larger carnivores, especially, were captured for use in combat. In the Roman Empire, this use generated a massive infrastructure of acquisition, transport, and keeping of exotic animals (MacKinnon 2006). It can also occur on a smaller and more casual scale. I once witnessed a striped hyena female that had been captured with her young by villagers in Pakistani Baluchistan. They kept the adult in a deep pit and staged combats by throwing in a dog or two periodically. They were attempting to raise the young hyenas for the same purpose, although I rather doubt they survived.

### Animal symbols and zooarchaeology

Juxtaposing zooarchaeological evidence with artistic representations and textual information leads to richer understandings of the symbolic role of animals in past societies. Even in the absence of texts, representations, and ethnohistory, attention to the spatial distribution and context of faunal remains can yield clues to belief systems about animals. These beliefs and associated practices can shape the zooarchaeological assemblage. Therefore, we must be aware of them as potential taphonomic factors even if they are not the objects of study. Body part analysis may be useful in identifying taxa that were brought to sites for special purposes rather than forming part of the diet. In the next chapter, I explore other kinds of special treatment accorded to remains of animals that were eaten.

In addition to the bones themselves, we need to pay attention to animal symbolism that may shape human relations. This requires a critical approach to our commonsense notions of the utilitarian. For instance, among the Kalasha, for whom goats are sacred, the goat stables are places of ritual purity, forbidden to women and inhabited by male ancestor spirits and herding deities. Sacrifices, male initiation ceremonies, and other male rituals occur in them (Parkes 1987). Cattle byres play a similar role among many East African pastoralists, where dung and the places in which it is deposited carry strong gendered symbolism (Moore 1982). To understand animal symbolism, we must draw on many lines of evidence, well beyond animal representations.

3

# Animals in ritual

To assume that a bone deposit has not been affected by ritual activity is to make, somewhat ironically, a major statement about both the ontological status of animals and the spiritual relationships between people and animals in that society. (McNiven and Feldman 2003:189)

In the previous chapter, I considered some aspects of the symbolic value of animals. Because of this value, and the value of meat discussed in Chapter 4, animals and animal products have often played a key role in human rituals. Hunters' rituals often focus on maintaining supplies of game by treating animals and especially animal remains with due respect. Herders may offer sacrifices to influence the course of events. Animal parts, often derived from sacrifice, may be used in divination or as components of costumes. Many of these ritual practices shape the animal remains in the archaeological record.

This is not the place for an exhaustive review of the theory of ritual. I simply note that recent discussions of ritual generally stress its performative aspects, with the power of ritual lying in the sensory experiences it creates (e.g., Bell 1997; Parkin 1992). Bobby Alexander (1997:139) defines ritual as "a performance, planned or improvised, that effects a transition from everyday life to an alternative context within which the everyday is transformed." Catherine Bell (1992), taking a practice theory approach, has introduced the useful concept of "ritualization": the process of marking actions as rituals. Ritualization is accomplished through devices such as formality, traditionalization, invariance, rule governance, and sacral symbolism.

Ritual differs from other performances in that it is meant to have an impact in the world, to effect change. Although ritual is often intended to bolster the status quo, it can also be used to challenge it (Alexander

1997; T. Turner 2006; V. Turner 1969). In any case, the rule-bound nature of ritual means that it is never free from power issues (Parkin 1992). Much of the efficacy of ritual lies in its invocation of tradition, even as that tradition is constantly reinterpreted (Bell 1997).

Recent archaeological considerations of ritual have sounded similar themes (Fogelin 2007). The notion of ritualization and of the marking or framing of ritual action has proven particularly useful for archaeology (e.g., Verhoeven 2002a; Verhoeven 2002b). Even when ritual is not spatially separated from daily life and occurs in domestic contexts, ritualization can be recognized by the special emphasis given to certain items (Bradley 2005; Brück 1999). Archaeologists have also considered issues of power in relation to ritual. Taking a diachronic perspective, some propose that the intensification and elaboration of ritual mark periods of social stress (Hays 1993; Johnson 1982; Wilson 1996). John Barrett (1991) argues that ritual does not serve as a straightforward instrument of domination because of the multiple interpretations that are always possible.

In the classical world and elsewhere where there is textual evidence for sacrifice, zooarchaeologists have long studied the remains of sacrificial rites. At prehistoric sites, however, zooarchaeologists have until recently been reluctant to consider the role of ritual in the formation of faunal assemblages. Happily this situation has changed, and in the last decade or so there has been much greater attention paid to special deposits of animal bones at prehistoric sites. This is a good start, but it treats ritual as something set apart from quotidian life, whereas in fact ritual informs and shapes daily practices. Therefore in addition to analyzing discrete deposits of special remains, we need to consider how rituals, large and small, affect animal bone assemblages. Taking ritual seriously will not only shed light on sacred practices but will also contribute to a better taphonomic understanding of faunal assemblages that is fundamental to any kind of interpretation. In this chapter, I examine animal sacrifice; the ritual treatment of animal remains, both wild and domestic; and some of the uses of animal parts in ritual.

## Ritual treatment of animal remains

The identification of ritual in the archaeological record can be problematic; indeed defining ritual in living societies is not straightforward. Bell's

(1997:81) ritualization approach is useful here: Rather than trying to decide whether a given practice is a ritual or not, she advocates focusing on the extent to which particular practices are ritualized. In this light, we can consider practices that mark animal remains as significant by placing special emphasis on them. Here I examine special disposal practices, trophies, animal parts in apparel and architecture, and animals and animal parts included in burials. All of these practices give animal remains significance beyond consumption waste.

### RESPECTING THE HUNTED

Hunters often conceive of themselves in a relation of reciprocity with their game or with spirit masters of the game species (see Chapter 4, *Hunters' Attitudes to Animals*). Game animals are believed to offer themselves to the hunters, who in turn must treat the animals and their remains with due respect, or the animals will withhold themselves in the future. This respect takes various forms but, crucially for archaeology, often involves specific depositional practices prescribed for the remains of hunted animals. Roberte Hamayon (1990:397–400) argues that these practices transform the killing of wild animals, which are conceived as having souls like humans, from murder to meat acquisition by allowing them to regenerate. Such attitudes and practices are particularly well documented for circumboreal groups, but have been recorded much more widely.

For example, the Navajo place a bead on the head of the first deer killed in a hunt and say a prayer to encourage the deer to return in future hunts, reminding it of its respectful treatment (Nelson 1997:96). Often, such treatment extends to the remains of the animals. The Koyukon of northern Alaska have hundreds of rules for the respectful treatment of game animals, especially bears. These rules include preventing women from having contact with bear meat. Koyukon women hunt and trap but may not kill spiritually powerful animals such as bear, wolf, and otter. Other practices include removing the bear's feet first when butchering to prevent the bear spirit from wandering, and consuming some parts of the bear away from the village at the butchering site in a sort of funeral feast for the bear attended by men and boys (Nelson 1993:202, 212).

Chipewyan and other northern Athapaskans take care to avoid offending game species through contact with menstruating women, the use of improper killing methods or treatment of the carcass, wastage, or letting dogs feed improperly on the remains (Sharp 1988). The Swampy Cree of northern Quebec hang parts of some game species in trees along paths near camp to show them respect and keep them away from dogs. There is some individual variation in which taxa are considered to merit this treatment, but beaver, bear, and usually goose are routinely hung, whereas lynx, otter, and others are more variably included. Not all body parts are hung, but mainly skulls, feet, and skins or ears (Preston 1964).

The Mistassini Cree have similar, but somewhat more elaborate procedures:

> A central attitude in the conduct of hunting is that game animals are persons and that they must be respected. The rules of respect after the killing involve essentially taking care of all elements of the carcass, and not allowing anything to be thoughtlessly discarded. Thus blood and intestines are consumed, buried in the snow or fed to dogs, bones are made into tools, hung in the trees, put on bone platforms, or put in a lake, and all uneaten meat is fed to the dogs or put in the fire (Tanner 1979:130).

The Mistassini hang the most sacred bones (skulls, antlers, large animal scapulae, forelimbs of animals such as bear and beaver) in trees, often with decorations. Other bones, if not used as tools or in divination, are put on platforms if they are from land animals or in bodies of water if from aquatic creatures. The purpose is apparently to prevent dogs from feeding on the bones. Although dogs are given meat scraps, they receive bones only of some young, small animals. "In one particular myth the idea is put forward that animal bones, given the proper treatment, become recovered with flesh as new animals again. The more commonly-held belief is that the inedible remains continue to be part of the species as a whole, and their proper treatment is a way of avoiding giving offence to the master of the species in question, and this enables hunting to continue" (Tanner 1979:180). Before final disposal, the remains of game animals are kept in specific spatial and gendered arrangements, according to who is responsible for their proper treatment:

> [A]ll meat of animals the size of a beaver and smaller are stored on the female section, but the meat of larger animals, i.e. moose, caribou and bear, are stored on the male side. After a meal has been eaten all bones are carefully sorted by the women, and most are stored on the women's side

until they are taken outside for proper disposal. However, certain bones are stored by the men, for example, the skulls (only men are allowed to eat meat from the head). The scapulars of some animals, which are used for divination, may be stored by the women on their side prior to the divination performance, after which they are kept by the men (Tanner 1979:78).

Similarly the Rock Cree feel that it is disrespectful to throw bones on the ground, and they must be kept from contact with dogs and menstruating women. They place meat, bones, and skins on shelves or platforms to maintain this separation. Again, skulls and other bones are hung in trees. Those bones that are crushed and used to make broth are burned or dumped in bodies of water afterward (Brightman 1993). Netsilik Inuit women hang seal mandibles on their drying racks as a sign of respect. Among many Inuit groups, certain individual animals receive special treatment in addition to more general strictures. The first seal, sea lion, or caribou taken in the season or the first killed after the death of a man's wife may be processed and disposed of with special care. This may mean avoiding breaking the bones, keeping them from dogs, placing the bones on the ice away from the camp, or storing them until spring and then burying them with wooden bird images (Murray 2000).

In the Old World boreal zone, bears in particular receive special treatment. The Saami killed bears in their winter lairs and then consumed them at ceremonial feasts. Afterward the bones had to be properly disposed of to show respect to the bear and permit continued successful hunting. It was necessary to include all the bones so the bear could regenerate and to keep the bones from dogs. The bones might be placed in trees, on platforms, or buried. Interestingly, although the ethnohistorical sources all stress that the bones must be left intact, all the archaeological bear burials consist of bones that, apart from the skull and mandibles, have been thoroughly fractured and processed for marrow. In the graves, the bones are piled with foot bones at one end, and the skull and scapulae placed in roughly anatomical position at the other. Although the types of disposal vary, they all parallel local human burial practices, indicating an equivalence between bears and humans (Zachrisson and Iregren 1974).

Such respectful treatment of the remains of game animals extends well beyond the boreal zone. In the American Southwest, the O'odham placed mountain sheep horns near waterholes and kept bones of game animals from dogs, whereas the Tewa returned deer bones to the forest (Szuter 2001:210). Puebloan groups generally laid deer out in the hunter's house and decorated them with corn meal or pollen and other items such as beads, bells, feathers, or blankets before butchery. Some also avoided letting dogs have the bones; in the case of the Papago this was not out of concern about the dogs themselves, but that a dog might carry a bone to the house of a menstruating woman (Muir and Driver 2004:131–3). In South America, the Achuar specifically show respect to the game mothers: guardian spirits who control game species and can exact revenge not only by withholding game but also by causing misfortune such as snakebites. Hunters avoid offending the game mothers by refraining from killing more animals than needed and showing respect to their remains. Such respect includes preventing children from playing with the carcasses, although they are allowed to study them to learn their anatomy. Animal skulls are stored in the roof thatch, not only as trophies but also to keep them from dogs (Descola 1994:257–60). Similarly, the Mundurucú in Brazil keep rows of animal skulls near the men's house and blow tobacco smoke over them to propitiate their mother spirits, and the Chimane of Bolivia hang bones of game animals from the ceiling in baskets to keep the spirits and therefore the living animals in the area (McNiven and Feldman 2003:173).

We also find such ideas and practices in the Pacific. Torres Strait islanders make piles of dugong and turtle bones (their main prey) or hang them in trees as offerings to the spirit masters of these animals. Hunters and shamans hold rituals at these places to ensure good hunting. Dugong body parts are also presented to skulls of the ancestors to gain their help (McNiven and Feldman 2003). Similar beliefs may have motivated a mound carefully constructed of dugong bones in the Neolithic United Arab Emirates (Méry et al. 2009). The Wola of highland New Guinea give some bones to dogs, but maintain hunting success by carefully keeping others from being chewed by dogs or pigs by burning them or pushing them into house walls (Sillitoe 2001:384).

Elsewhere in the New Guinea highlands, bone disposal depends on whether the meat was cooked ritually. Bone from nonritually cooked meals gets no special treatment and is fed to dogs and pigs. The bones of animals cooked at male cult houses must stay in those cult houses, because the war rituals conducted there render them dangerous to humans and domestic pigs. The bones of animals cooked ritually elsewhere are hung in bushes (save the teeth and bones that are used for tools and ornaments). The Kalam give multiple reasons for hanging the bones: to serve as a reminder of the ceremony to the spirits invoked, to prevent pigs from eating things that are dangerous to them or the gardens, and to display the wealth and hunting skill of those hanging them. The danger, however, lies in the traces of flesh and blood rather than the bones themselves. As the bones weather and fall down, they may be replaced in the bushes if someone notices them, but they are no longer a threat (Bulmer 1976:178–9).

In sum, many hunters around the world have believed that continued hunting success and other benefits depend on respectful treatment of the game animals, which often includes special disposal of their remains. One common theme is preventing dogs or pigs from gnawing on them. When examined more closely, these strictures usually only apply or apply most strongly to some animals, typically the larger taxa. They may also apply only to some body parts, often heads and skins. Further, there is often a gendered aspect to these practices. The taxa most closely associated with male hunters usually receive the special treatment, and in some cases preventing contact with women (or menstruating women) is at least as important as keeping the bones from the dogs.

These disposal practices would clearly have a skewing effect on the representation of both taxa and body parts in the archaeological record. Given that they are so widespread in the ethnographic present, such practices surely existed at many times and places in the past. Yet we cannot assume they would always be present in societies with a substantial dependence on hunting. In Malawi, the danger of angry animal spirits (who prevent hunting success and cause illness and misfortune) is counteracted not by respectful treatment of animal remains, but by ritual medicine, often involving animal parts (Morris 1998, 2000).

TROPHIES

Trophies are souvenirs of triumph, classically bloody triumph in war or hunting. War trophies tend to be weapons or sometimes body parts of the enemy; hunting trophies are body parts of the quarry, often the animal's defenses (antlers, horns, tusks) or the whole head or skin. A trophy provides a permanent testament to success in the fleeting hunt, with trophy displays vouching for the hunter's skill and boosting his or her status. Trophy display can shade, on the one hand, into the respectful treatment of the remains of game described earlier and, on the other, into some of the ways of appropriating animal power discussed later in this chapter. Archaeologically it may not be easy to distinguish these motivations nor are they fully distinct in practice (e.g., Roe 1997). The key features that mark the use of animal parts as trophies are their display and the prestige accorded to such displays.

The display of hunting trophies is associated most closely with sport hunting. In fact, in some hunting traditions, the acquisition of trophies is the major motivation for the hunt (Hell 1996). Skulls, especially those with large horns and antlers, are the primary trophies, to be hung on the walls of the hunters' houses. Skins and other body parts may also be displayed, and teeth or other body parts may be made into jewelry to form a portable trophy. The goal of trophy acquisition clearly shapes the range of taxa, ages, and sexes taken. Generally there is a heavy bias toward adult males of larger species, especially those with large horns and antlers. Large carnivores may also be selected.

However, such practices also occur among subsistence hunters, although it is less clear that trophy displays in these contexts shape hunting decisions, beyond perhaps encouraging hunting in general. Trophy displays seem to be most entrenched in the Pacific, particularly New Guinea. The Kalam, for instance, display in their houses the bones, particularly skulls and mandibles, of mammalian prey. They select undamaged bones (thereby ruling out most long bones, which are routinely broken for marrow; damaged skulls are sometimes displayed, however) of the more prestigious game species. Consequently, mandibles are the most frequent body part displayed, followed by skulls, and more distantly by pelves of larger marsupials. The owner may make a separate row of trophies killed by a particularly good hunting dog. These trophy collections are protected from weathering, dogs, pigs, and other agents of attrition. When the house is abandoned, the collection is left in it. Thus although trophy display may not greatly influence hunting decisions, it is likely to have a major effect on the body parts and taxa that survive archaeologically, in this case introducing a strong bias to the mandibles of larger mammals (Bulmer 1976:169–82).

The Wola similarly hang skulls of the larger mammals on their walls, where they are regarded as trophies and souvenirs of the hunt. However, although good hunters are admired, they do not gain high status from either hunting or trophy displays. The size of the trophy displays correlates not with status but with the number of men in the house (Sillitoe 2001:370–7). Another highland group, the Asabano, display both wild and domestic pig mandibles as trophies of hunts and feasts. These mandibles serve as manifestations of the house spirits (Lohmann 2005:200–1). Lowland New Guinea groups also display trophy skulls and mandibles. These trophies and the hunting they represent are important in the construction of male identity (Rosman and Rubel 1989:34). Agta and Ilongot hunters in the Philippines also display wild pig (*Sus barbatus*) mandibles on their houses (Griffin 1998). In the Andaman Islands, animal parts are displayed as trophies, and householders view middens with pride as a sign of hunting success, suggesting a broader definition of "trophy" (Cooper 2001).

Although the trophy displays in Oceania may not significantly affect hunting choices, in some places the value of large carnivores as trophies and emblems of masculinity likely encourages the hunting of animals that might otherwise be avoided. In the New World, there are many examples of the hunting of large felids to appropriate their power and gain status through killing them and displaying their body parts (Gunnerson 1997; Hamell 1997; Roe 1997). Often the meat of these animals is taboo, so they are killed only for protection and for prestige.

The line between respectfully preserving animal remains from dogs and trophy display is often fuzzy. In both North and South America, the bones hung in houses and trees to keep them from being gnawed also serve to advertise hunting success (Descola 1994:257; Preston 1964). Indeed, this symbolism of the good provider is so strong among the Rock Cree that they also hang in trees the cans that held store-bought meat (Brightman 1993:119).

Whereas trophies are usually associated with hunting, similar displays of domestic animal body parts, usually skulls or horns, may commemorate feasts and/or sacrifices. The Dafla and other groups in northeast India display both hunting trophies and the skulls of sacrificed mithan, a large bovine they keep in a loose herding system (Simoons 1968); the Ifugao of the Philippines likewise display heads and mandibles of assorted animals (Griffin 1998).

HUNTING SHRINES

Some have argued that rock art sites such as European Upper Paleolithic painted caves or Chalcolithic/Bronze Age Val Camonica (see Chapter 2,

*Art*) served as hunting shrines: places to carry out hunting magic (e.g., Breuil and Lantier 1951; Briard 1987). As we have seen in Chapter 2, however, there are many competing interpretations of these sites. Here I focus on sites with displays of actual wild animal parts. Although their interpretation is not straightforward, they at least demonstrate a direct link to hunting. Such displays clearly relate to the use of animal parts as trophies, but at shrines they are tied not to the individual hunter but to a collective identity.

On the North American Great Plains, Paleoindians (Pleistocene foragers) often engaged in collective hunts of herd animals such as bison, pronghorn, and mountain sheep. Some of these kill sites have signs of ritual activity probably resulting from hunting ceremonies. They usually involve collections of the skulls of some of the animals killed, which are sometimes decorated and sometimes associated with ritual structures (Bement 1999; Frison 2004).

In Puebloan society, the mountain lion is associated, among other things, with success in hunting and warfare. Directional shrines located a short distance from the villages are known both ethnographically and archaeologically, with the mountain lion linked to the north shrine. The north shrines consisted of piles of rocks, sometimes with carved mountain lion images or skins of actual mountain lions. Offerings of food and the pots containing it are made here to departed souls (Gunnerson 1997).

Linda Brown (2005; Brown and Emery 2008) has drawn on ethnographic, ethnoarchaeological, archaeological, and textual information to build a convincing argument that hunting shrines have been widespread in Mesoamerica from the Classic period to the present. They are associated with a belief in a guardian of animals who must be appeased to maintain hunting success (see the earlier section, *Respecting the Hunted*). Hunters curate certain bones or other body parts in their houses and periodically deposit them in ritual caches at hunting shrines outside the settlements. These shrines are typically associated with rocky features, apparently tied to a belief that the animal guardian spirits live in mountain caves. However, not all skeletal remains are deposited in these shrines. Only medium to large wild animals are represented, and all shrines exhibit a selection of body parts. Although the particular body parts vary somewhat among shrines, cranial remains feature prominently at most. These bones are deposited intact and unburnt to show respect to the animals and to permit them to regenerate. In addition to the bones, hunters would make offerings of items such as food and incense at these shrines before and after each hunt. These practices would shape the taxon and body part profiles of faunal assemblages at both the shrines and the habitation sites.

In the Mediterranean region, structures that can be interpreted as hunting shrines are widespread in the Neolithic and perhaps before. The Hallan Çemi site in eastern Turkey dates to 12,200–11,200 BP and has variously been termed Epipaleolithic or Proto-Neolithic. Although claims have been made for pig domestication (Redding and Rosenberg 1998; Rosenberg et al. 1998; Rosenberg and Redding 1998), in general the fauna and flora at the site are considered to be wild. There are clear signs of ritual use of animal parts in public places: a row of three mouflon (wild sheep) skulls in the plaza and an aurochs skull hanging on the wall opposite the door of a large, probably public, building (Rosenberg et al. 1995).

Later, during the late PPNA and PPNB in the eastern Mediterranean, we see the first sites that can be interpreted as hunting shrines set apart from settlements. The PPNB is generally seen as the period of animal domestication, and most sites in the Levant and southeast Anatolia show evidence of dependence on plant agriculture and herded sheep and goats. Two sites, Kfar HaHoresh in the Galilee Hills and Göbekli Tepe in southeast Anatolia, have no remains of domestic plants and animals and much evidence of ritual activity centered on wild animal imagery. Some see these sites as settlements of foragers contemporary and in interaction with nearby farmers, or as ritual centers for mobile foragers (Peters and Schmidt 2004; Schmidt 2001; see Chapter 2, *Art*). However, Verhoeven (2002a) argues convincingly that they are special-purpose ritual sites used by those farmers to carry out ceremonies focused on hunting and wild animals (see also Bar-Yosef and Bar-Yosef Mayer 2002).

Göbekli Tepe is located on a limestone ridge far from water sources. It is a poor place for a settlement, but has an expansive view over the Harran Plain. No remains of houses have yet been found, but only public buildings with large T-shaped stelae depicting wild animals and, increasingly through time, humans. Fox bones are surprisingly prominent among the faunal remains, and foxes appear on the stone pillars. Fox and gazelle skins may have covered floors, walls, or benches in the structures, given the high proportions of foot bones in the assemblage. The excavators argue that these are not simply hunting shrines, but the locus of shamanistic rituals, perhaps organized according to kin groups (see Chapter 2, *Totems*). As the Puebloan example shows, hunting shrines can serve as the focus for a variety of rituals associating death, hunting, and the wild.

Kfar HaHoresh has human burials (both sexes and all ages), arrangements of animal parts, and what seem to be pictures of animals made of disarticulated human and animal bones. There are remains of structures, but no clear houses, and signs of the preparation and consumption of meals. A plastered human skull was buried above a headless but otherwise complete gazelle. Fox remains, especially mandibles, appear in many graves. It appears to be a special-purpose funerary site, with associated rituals that link humans and wild animals (Horwitz and Goring-Morris 2004).

Somewhat later at Çatalhöyük in central Anatolia (corresponding to late PPNB/PPNC), buildings often called "hunting shrines" are found in the middle of a settlement. The art at the site in general depicts mainly or entirely wild animals (Mellaart 1984; Russell and Meece 2006), although domestic sheep and goats dominate the faunal remains (Russell and Martin 2005). James Mellaart (1966b, 1967) designated as hunting shrines two buildings with paintings on all four walls depicting a range of animal species, each dominated by a huge bull on the north wall. Smaller human figures run or dance around the animals. Some carry what appear to be bows or slings and perhaps leopard-skin quivers.

More recent work at Çatalhöyük rejects the separation of houses from shrines and sees all the buildings as houses (Hodder 1996, 2006). However, ritual clearly played an important role in the lives of the inhabitants, and much of this ritual took place in the houses. Paintings on interior walls were not simply decorative, because they were plastered over quickly, before the interior hearths and ovens could cover them with soot deposits. Thus although it is inappropriate to view the painted buildings as permanent shrines, the paintings likely relate to the performance of rituals in that space.

Katherine Wright (2000) has interpreted the Çatalhöyük "hunting shrines" and the focus on wild animals in the Anatolian Neolithic in general as evidence for male hunting societies. Verhoeven (2002a:252) views Kfar HaHoresh and Göbekli Tepe in a similar fashion (see Chapter 2, *Art*). Hodder (1987, 1990) likewise stresses the identification of men with hunting at Çatalhöyük, but sees the rituals as directed toward control of the wild, particularly the wild within men and women.

The southern Italian Neolithic resembles the PPNB in that separate ritual sites are found on the margins of settled zones, set at a distance from the settlement sites. Although domestic plants and animals provided the majority of the diet, at these ritual sites the faunal remains are mostly wild, including animal skulls placed ceremonially around the walls of underground chambers. Morter and Robb (1998) suggest that this hunting imagery, and its spatial separation from domestic zones, serves primarily to construct male identity.

Clearly some societies that depended on hunting for their subsistence constructed what may be termed "hunting shrines"; for example, North American Paleoindians and perhaps western European Upper Paleolithic groups. These shrines are a more formalized expression of the rites of respect to the hunted discussed earlier. However, it is striking that most of the elaborate hunting shrines are associated with agricultural groups. In these cases, the purpose of the shrines is less to assure a continued supply of a vital food source than to construct masculine identity by asserting a contrast to the domestic, in the double sense of domestic plant and animal use and the household sphere.

FUNERARY RITUAL

I discuss animal burials in Chapter 7 (*Pets in the Past*). Here I focus on the inclusion of animal parts in human burials. Animal parts may play any of a number of roles in burials: food offerings for the afterlife, remains of funerary feasts and sacrifices, and components of dress or paraphernalia, for example. Particularly when burials occur in settlements, where they may be dug through midden deposits, it is sometimes difficult to be sure whether animal remains form part of the burial or are simply present in the fill. However, in many cases animal parts clearly were deliberately placed in the graves. Contextual analysis can aid in interpreting the role of such animal remains.

## Food offerings for the afterlife

Food offerings can be identified when grave goods include meaty animal parts that do not show signs that the meat has already been consumed. Including provisions for the afterlife in burials implies a conception of a life after death that closely resembles life on earth. Such provisioning appears to be largely restricted to relatively complex societies. Clemens Lichter's (2001) thorough study of Neolithic and Chalcolithic burials in southeast Europe finds a few possible cases of food offerings in the Late Neolithic (Salcuța, Iclod, and Lengyel cultures) and clear cases only in the Chalcolithic (Tiszapolgár, Bodrogkeresztúr, and Balaton-Lasinja cultures), along with greater indications of hierarchical social structure. Food offerings, often in pots, are also found in Bronze Age Europe and the Levant (Briard 1987:113–15, Weissbrod and Bar-Oz 2004). In Iron Age Britain, the elite were buried with food offerings of pork, the commoners with mutton (Parker Pearson 1999).

Patrice Méniel's (1989) careful analysis of animal remains in Gallic Iron Age cemeteries distinguishes among nonmeaty pieces included for their symbolic value, remains of funerary feasts (with meat already removed as shown by butchering traces), and food offerings. The food offerings – meaty parts of animals commonly found as food waste at settlement sites – are the most common faunal remains in the graves. The most abundant food offerings are quarters of pigs or halves of young piglets. Forelimbs are more frequent than hindlimbs, and split heads become more common through time, suggesting that the mourners may be keeping the choicest parts for their own consumption. Sheep, goat, cattle, and occasionally poultry are also found. Horses and wild animals appear in other forms, but rarely as food offerings. A similar pattern is apparent in La Tène cemeteries in the Aisne valley, where all bones seem to be meat offerings. Only part of the body is included, however, suggesting that mourners ate the rest (Auxiette 1995). The same may be true for Roman burials in Italy: Food offerings are mainly pig, sheep, and goat, with pig predominating in both settlements and cemeteries. Again, the low-value forelimb predominates (Sorrentino 1989). In the Netherlands, Roman burials frequently include food offerings, mostly chickens and parts of suckling pigs (Lauwerier 2004). At Romano-British Skeleton Green, 36% of the cremation burials include animal bones that are likely to be food offerings, but also serve as gender markers. Cattle remains are found with male burials, birds with females, and sheep with both (Grant 1989). At pagan Anglo-Saxon sites, although sheep are the dominant species at both settlements and cremation cemeteries, cattle are underrepresented in cremations compared to settlements, especially as food offerings. Once again, faunal remains interpreted as food offerings are all from domestic animals (Bond and Worley 2006).

In the Middle Bronze Age Levant, food offerings in tombs are often placed in pots or on wooden plates. Clearly these are meant as meals for the dead in the afterlife, but interestingly the composition diverges from settlement assemblages. Sheep and goat are even more dominant in funerary assemblages, and the sheep/goat and pig tend to be young, whereas the cattle are generally adult. Some have meaty joints, but, as in the Iron Age European burials, many have nonmeaty lower limb segments that may represent meat consumed on behalf of the dead by the mourners. Of those that can be sexed, the sheep are biased toward females, which is antithetical to a viable herding strategy that would preserve the breeding stock (Horwitz 2001).

In sum, the meals of the dead to some extent mirror those of the living. Like those meals during life, the meat consumed may mark gender or status differences. Usually, however, these repasts for the afterlife differ from a typical meal and may provide clues to the relative value of different meats.

### Remains of funerary feasts and sacrifices

Whereas food offerings are intended to provision the dead in the afterlife, other animal remains in burials result from sacrifices or feasts at funerals. It is not easy to distinguish between the remains of feasts and sacrifices, because animals may be sacrificed and then consumed by the mourners. Sacrifice is discussed more fully later in this chapter; here I note that intact animals found in human burials are usually assumed to be funerary sacrifices. Partial, nonmeaty animal remains may also derive from sacrificial animals consumed in funeral feasts. In contrast, meaty animal parts showing signs of consumption are likely to be the remains of feasts; these animals may or may not have been slaughtered in a sacrificial context. Remains of sacrifices and feasts appear in graves of a wider variety of societies than do food offerings, but are largely limited to domestic animals and thus herding groups. The fact that feasting remains placed in graves are primarily from domestic animals perhaps argues that they are ultimately derived from sacrifice, which is also mostly restricted to domestic animals.

Burials tend to include a small selection of bones from animals consumed at funerary feasts, which no doubt are intended to represent the whole feast. For example, a cremation grave at proto-Lengyel Lužiansky includes unburnt animal bones, suggesting that the feast followed the cremation (Lichter 2001: 203). Although most partial animal remains in

Gallic Iron Age graves appear to be food offerings, two cemeteries have many burials with segments of pig spines, with the ribs and vertebral transverse processes, and hence the meat, removed from them. These bones are interpreted as feasting remains (Méniel 1989:90).

Other graves contain nonmeaty, often highly selected animal parts. Rather than being the remains of the meat consumed, these body parts likely are unconsumed portions representing animals sacrificed and eaten by the mourners. Some, however, may be hunting trophies or mementos of feasts acquired by the individual during life. The body parts interred are usually skulls, skulls and feet (probably the remains of skins), mandibles, and sometimes scapulae (Chaix 1989; Crabtree 1995; Davis and Payne 1993; Grigson 1984; Stanc and Bejenaru 2004). For example, skulls of both wild and domestic animals are found in many graves of the Middle Neolithic Hamangia culture of the northeast Balkans. Elsewhere in the Neolithic and Eneolithic Balkans, the skulls or mandibles are of domestic animals: cattle in most cases, but sheep and pig in the Eneolithic Carpathian Basin. Cattle scapulae occur in three graves in the Neolithic/Eneolithic of southeast Europe: at Early Neolithic Golokut, Late Neolithic Iclod, and Eneolithic Jelšovce (Lichter 2001). Although the scapula is a meaty portion, the placement of two of these scapulae by the heads of the deceased and the clear symbolic value of the scapula in the Near Eastern Neolithic suggest that they were probably placed as clean bones.

### Animal remains as symbols

Some partial animal remains in burials have little to do with food or sacrifice, but rather are included for their symbolic value in other realms. In some cases these seem to be amulets or parts of costumes or ritual paraphernalia, to be discussed later. In others, it has been argued that animal parts are included for their symbolism of hunting and the wild or of a particular place.

Many of the possible hunting shrines described earlier include burials or human remains. In addition, many European Neolithic burials contain parts of wild animals that seem to have been included for their symbolic value. Mesolithic Lepenski Vir, in the Iron Gates gorge in the Balkans, has several burials with red deer antlers, and one with a red deer and an aurochs skull (Srejović 1972). In the Middle Chalcolithic Bodrog-keresztúr culture of the Carpathian basin, some burials, nearly always lying on their right sides and therefore probably male, include unworked boars' tusks (Lichter 2001:337). Some southern Italian Neolithic burials contain antlers (Morter and Robb 1998:85). As discussed earlier, most animal remains in Iron Age Gallic graves in France appear to be food offerings. However, horses and wild mammals other than hares (bear and beaver) appear only as teeth, or as a single phalanx in the case of aurochsen (Méniel 1989). Most of these remains are probably hunting trophies, whether belonging to the deceased in life or added to make a statement about the wild.

Andrew Jones (1998) argues that the animal remains in the Late Neolithic communal tomb at Isbister in the Orkney Islands not only represent wild/domestic oppositions but also tie the dead to the landscape. A foundation deposit in the tomb contains human, cattle, sheep, otter, sea eagle, and gull bones. Inside the tomb, human bones are accompanied by cattle and red deer skulls and at least 14 complete sea eagles. The ungulates are represented mainly by meaty parts, fragmented in the same way as food remains in contemporary settlements. In general, bird remains in settlements lack heads, feet, and wings, whereas these parts are differentially represented in tombs. Jones suggests that these are the "birdiest" parts of birds; they are also nonmeaty parts. Sea eagles are found rarely at settlements and mainly in tombs, but only those tombs in coastal or cliffside locations, where these birds are found in life. Two depositional practices appear to be at work: meaty food remains of ungulates that may be remains of funerary feasts, and symbolic depositions of nonmeaty animal parts that are appropriate to the position of the tomb in the landscape, thereby tying their ancestors and themselves to these places. Although the tombs are architecturally similar, the animal deposits mark them as different. This faunal distinction may be tied to the movement of human remains among these different types of tombs in different positions in the landscape. Articulated burials are found in lowland tombs, disarticulated remains at mid-altitudes, and skulls in the highest elevations.

### Animals in funerary ritual

Animals or animal parts sometimes play an active role in funerary ritual, beyond serving as sacrifices, food offerings, or other deposits. Instead of burial, human bodies may be exposed for scavengers to clean the bones. Maasai and other African groups expose their dead to be consumed by hyenas (Kruuk 1972:143). Similarly, the early Zoroastrians exposed

bodies to scavengers, chiefly dogs, who safely removed the highly polluting and ritually dangerous flesh. Their services in corpse disposal were
highly valued and a major motivation for keeping dogs. More recent
Zoroastrians expose bodies to vultures and other birds (mainly members
of the crow family) to clean the bones, although repeated viewings of
the corpse by a dog are an important part of the mortuary ritual (Boyce
1993; Peters and Schmidt 2004; Schüz and König 1983:464).

Tibetans also use vultures to dispose of corpses, although rather
than exposing intact bodies as the Zoroastrians do, a ritual specialist
dissects the body, pounds the bones, and mixes them with the flesh
so that the vultures can consume them completely. This is apparently
a relatively recent practice, dating no earlier than 1000 BP (Wylie
1964–5). Tibetans consider the vultures to be incarnations of *dakini*
(benevolent spirits or angels) and thus appropriate agents for removing
polluting corpses (Ramble 1982). Paintings of vultures flying around
headless human figures at Neolithic Çatalhöyük have been interpreted
as indicating a similar ritual (Cameron 1981; MacQueen 1978; Mellaart
1967). One of the paintings includes an intact human figure next to
a headless one, waving what may be a bow or sling. This figure has
been seen as either warding off or calling the vultures, as Tibetans do
with conch trumpets or sling-like implements swung to make a noise to
which the local vultures have learned to respond (Ramble 1982; Schüz
and König 1983:465–7). However, recent work has shown that human
bodies were buried intact at Çatalhöyük (Andrews et al. 2005), so this
scene is more likely to depict a myth than an actual mortuary practice.
Somewhat earlier representations from southeast Anatolia and northern
Syria also link vultures with either headless humans or disembodied
human heads (Schmidt 2006). Daniel Helmer, Lionel Gourichon and
Danielle Stordeur (2004:158) suggest these scenes indicate a belief
that vultures carried souls to the afterworld, a role they also suggest for
foxes/canids in this same region (see Chapter 7, *Man's Best Friend*).

Scavengers are ordinarily held in contempt (see Chapter 4, *Man the
Scavenger*), but when they serve this cleansing function in mortuary practices, they are usually treated with respect and gratitude.

## OTHER ANIMAL DEPOSITS

In addition to being accorded careful disposal to show respect to hunted
animals, displayed as trophies, and placed in burials or hunting shrines,

animal remains may receive special treatment in perhaps more subtle ways. Here I consider deposits whose purpose may be less clear, but that are marked by context or composition as more than the straightforward dumping of garbage.

### Abandonment deposits

When houses are abandoned, some items that were stored and used there may be left behind, trash from final activities may not be removed, and additional trash from neighboring houses may then be dumped there (Hutson et al. 2007). Here, however, I discuss not this de facto refuse (Schiffer 1972), but rather the remains of rituals associated with abandonment (LaMotta and Schiffer 1999). These may include items deliberately placed at abandonment or the remains of other rituals such as feasts.

The case studies I have been able to locate are all from the Neolithic Near East, with the exception of one site in Mesolithic southeast Europe. I suspect that the practice of placing items including faunal materials at abandonment is not really so restricted in time and space. Rather, this pattern probably results from a combination of my ignorance and a widespread tendency to overlook such deposits, especially in faunal reports.

Vesna Dimitrijević (2000) describes two apparent abandonment deposits in houses at Lepenski Vir. The site was excavated under time pressure in connection with the construction of a dam, so the resolution of the recording is not always what one might desire. In House 40, which contains burials beneath the floor and a stone sculpture in the rear of the building, most or all of a large male wild boar was left on the floor along one wall at abandonment. The boar was not an intact carcass, but had been butchered into large joints of meat. These segments were still articulated, however, and showed no signs of filleting the meat from the bones, so this is probably not butchery waste but a deposit of meaty pieces. Dimitrijević interprets it as a meat offering. House 28 has two stone sculptures in the back and a young red deer skull with a set of intact antlers placed on the floor. These two houses are both located on the periphery of the site, at opposite ends, and unlike most of the houses at the site, later houses were not built over them. Thus they may have a special function or may have been inhabited by special people. However, at least 13 houses had red deer skulls with antlers, although information about them is sketchy, so the placement of antlers at abandonment may have been a more widespread practice. These may have been trophies displayed in the houses during their occupation. Dragoslav Srejović (1972), the site's excavator, stresses the death and regeneration symbolism of antler, which is shed and regrown each year. This raises the possibility that the abandonment of these houses was linked to the death of their occupants.

PPNA Tell 'Abr 3 in the Euphrates valley in Syria has an apparent abandonment deposit in a burnt building consisting of gazelle horns and aurochs skulls in or near clay basins on the floor (Yartah 2005). At PPNB Ghwair I in Jordan four goat and one cattle skull with horns were either placed on the floor of a building or fell from the walls; several stone artifacts were also placed or left there (Simmons and Najjar 2006:83). At early Ceramic Neolithic Ginnig in northern Iraq, a room that has a cattle skull built into the base of the wall as an apparent foundation deposit also has bones placed in a pit in the doorway. These bones stick up into the fill and must have been placed at abandonment, perhaps part of a closing ceremony to mirror the opening one marked by the cattle skull (Campbell and Baird 1990:68). Later, in a Halafian (Ceramic Neolithic) house at Tell Aswad in Syria, a cattle skull was placed across the threshold of an internal doorway of a building, which was tentatively identified as a shrine on the basis of this deposit and of mud pedestals that could be altars (Mallowan 1946:124–5). These deposits suggest that thresholds were symbolically charged at moments of transition, liminal in both time and space. At roughly contemporary early Ceramic Neolithic Tell Sabi Abyad in northern Syria, Verhoeven (2000) suggests that a group of clay objects with embedded bones and horns were placed on the roof of an abandoned house, along with two human bodies, and then later consumed in a probably deliberately set fire. This appears to be a rather different and settlement-wide abandonment ritual. One of the loaf-shaped clay objects contained a wild sheep horn core, whereas most of the sheep at the site are domestic. However, these bones embedded in clay do not seem to have received particularly special treatment: The horn cores did not have their sheaths (suggesting they may have been lying around for a while), and there are dog-gnawing marks on some of the bones (Cavallo 1997). These objects may have been more common than it appears, because the unfired clay masses were only preserved because they were burnt.

At Çatalhöyük abandonment practices are variable, but usually involve more than simply leaving the house and salvaging its lumber. Abandonment behavior includes scouring floors and dismantling architectural installations and often involves the deposition of materials on the floors or in post retrieval pits. There may be a need to replace the posts with some special object, although the specific objects are quite variable, including ground-stone axes, groups of bone tools, human and dog skulls, and other animal parts. Feasting remains are sometimes spread across the floor, and scapulae (mainly of aurochsen) may be placed singly or in groups. Houses may also contain clusters of rapidly deposited and minimally processed remains of meals (in their composition, resembling daily meals more closely than feasts) mixed with dumps of raw materials and collections of items that may well have been stored in the house. These materials are not usually in their original locations or merely fallen from the walls and roof. Instead, they are dumped as though by the armload or basketful so that collections of individual materials (ground stone, astragali, metapodials, equid phalanges, antler; some of the bone material is worked, often as preforms rather than finished tools) are partly mixed in multiple locations, usually around the edges of the floor. Some houses were deliberately burnt after abandonment, and these houses also have remains of plant food stores: cereals, lentils, peas, and acorns (Bogaard et al. 2009; Russell et al. 2008; Twiss et al. 2008, 2009). The reasons for this variation are unclear, but may relate to the status of the occupants, the reason for closing the house, or whether the inhabitants intended to rebuild the house in place (the usual practice). The stored contents may be abandoned as an act of conspicuous consumption or because they are considered unclean (perhaps because an inhabitant died inside the house or was accused of witchcraft).

Abandonment deposits are certainly not universal, although they may be more common than is currently realized. We might expect them where the house carries strong symbolic value, so that its closing is a significant act. Where abandonment deposits have been identified, animal remains play a major role. Some of these remains are the "ceremonial trash" from closing ceremonies, and others are items that were probably stored or displayed in the houses during their occupation and then placed in different positions during abandonment.

*Special deposits*

Some deposits of animal remains are clearly something other than ordinary garbage, but are hard to classify. They no doubt result from a variety of rituals involving animals in one way or another. In some cases these deposits are ceremonial trash derived from these rituals, and in others the deposits may be an integral part of the ceremony themselves. Such deposits have been identified from a wide range of times and places, although they are surely underreported.

At Epipaleolithic Zawi Chemi Shanidar in Iraq a large pile of at least 15 wild goat skulls and large bird bones was located outside the only excavated structure, apparently deposited as a single event. The bird bones are overwhelmingly raptors, and nearly all are wing bones. At least seven white-tailed eagles (*Haliaaetus albicilla*), four smaller eagles, four lammergeiers (*Gypaetus barbatus*), one griffon vulture (*Gyps fulvus*), and one great bustard (*Otis tarda*) contributed to the assemblage. At least some of the wings were articulated, and although they show signs of cuts to remove the wing from the body, there are no indications that they were eaten. Rather, they are probably the remains either of costumes, perhaps including the goat skulls, or of processing for feathers (with the goat skulls perhaps the waste from processing hides for costumes). This is likely a deposit of ceremonial trash from a ritual featuring large, mostly predatory birds (Solecki and McGovern 1980). These birds may symbolize power or death and regeneration as prey and carrion are ingested and carried into the heavens.

The connection between wild goats and birds is not obvious, but is seen again at Çatalhöyük, where a crane wing with cuts suggesting its use as part of a costume (or at any rate as somehow hung from or attached to something) is associated with, among other things, wild goat horns in a deposit of ceremonial trash (Russell and McGowan 2003). Other remains of ceremonies are incorporated directly into houses at Çatalhöyük, with selections of items from rituals buried in small pits beneath house floors. These commemorative deposits generally contain faunal materials. Some seem to be remains of feasts; others are items of ritual paraphernalia (Russell et al. 2009). Perhaps the clay-enclosed bones at Tell Sabi Abyad (see the previous section, *Abandonment Deposits*) are similar but portable mementos of ceremonies past. In both cases, the selected souvenirs surely carry continuing power, which perhaps protects the houses and their inhabitants at Çatalhöyük and travels with the owners of the clay objects at Sabi Abyad. Similar practices of subfloor deposits in houses parallel to intramural burials, although less dominated by animal remains, have been documented in Mesoamerica at Classic El Palmillo (Feinman et al. 2008).

Salima Ikram (2004) describes a deposit in a chamber at the end of a rock-cut passage at Saqqara in Egypt from ca. 4500 BP. A group of pots and a harpoon in a wooden case accompany a group of animal bones; all appear to have been deposited in a single event. The animal bones are primarily cranial and constitute an unusual set of taxa for Egyptian funerary or other ritual contexts: two species of catfish, donkey, pig, hartebeest, jackal, and perhaps dog. Ikram suggests that these animals are all tied to Seth and to wild, chaotic forces. Thus this deposit may be ceremonial trash from a hunting ritual to chase away these forces and establish order.

Special deposits of animal remains appear in some European Neolithic contexts and become more common in later periods. An intact young hare at the bottom of a pit in a Late Neolithic settlement at Murr (Germany) is interpreted as a ritual deposit, although the purpose is unclear (Manhart and Vagedes 1999). In the British Neolithic, cattle skulls and articulated spines were deliberately placed in ditches of cause-wayed camps and long barrows at Windmill Hill, Fussell's Lodge, Maiden Castle (where some of the cattle were wild), Whitesheet Hill, and Beck-hampton Road. Where the domestic cattle can be sexed, all are female and thus valuable breeding animals (Grigson 1984). Such deposits suggest tokens of sacrifices and feasts associated with the monuments.

In Iron Age Britain, both whole and partial animals are found, along with rubbish, in pits originally used for grain storage. The partial remains consist of skulls of horses, dogs, cattle, sheep, and pigs; horse mandibles; and articulated limbs principally of horses but also from cattle and sheep. Because horses and dogs are eaten in the Iron Age, all of these represent potential food that has been deliberately buried. If these animals were considered inedible because they were diseased, their remains should roughly mirror the proportions of taxa raised; in contrast, otherwise rare horses and dogs predominate. At Danebury, horses and dogs are also significantly more likely to be associated with each other than would happen by chance. Where excavated with close attention to context, there are signs not of dumping but of careful placement. A pit at Danebury contains the articulated horse head, neck, and chest with the pelvis and sacrum placed on top of the vertebrae and the rest of the animal missing. Two large flint nodules were placed in the chest cavity, and one complete immature pig lies with its forelimbs embracing the horse's neck, while another young pig has been put on the other side of the pit (Grant 1989:81–3).

Human bog bodies are well known from northwest Europe (Brothwell 1986, Glob 1988, R. Turner and Scaife 1995), but other deposits, including animal remains, are also found in bogs. Sue Stallibrass (1996) describes the Solway Cow, actually the heads and hides of two adult cattle, probably Iron Age or medieval in date. She rejects the possibility that this deposit is ordinary butchery waste, because it would be a lot of trouble to discard it in this remote, difficult-to-access place, nor would people lightly discard the valuable hides. Although she suggests that cattle thieves might have disposed of the identifiable hides in the bog, she argues that a ritual deposit is most likely, in line with accounts of hanging animal heads and hides on poles over sacred pools. Similarly, a deposit of 17 wild boar mandibles from ca. 6100 BP in a Danish bog could be either ordinary butchery waste or a ritual deposit; it is unclear how difficult access was to this location. However, butchery waste would probably include more than just the mandibles. The mandibles show clear signs of butchery and meat removal. If they were the remains of a single meal, it would have been a large feast that required a great deal of hunting effort. Tooth eruption and wear indicate they were all killed at the same time of year, in late fall (Noe-Nygaard and Richter 1990). Thus there is a strong case that the mandibles are a ritual deposit of feasting remains from an autumn ceremony.

On the northwest edge of the Roman Empire there are numerous examples of ritual deposits in pits and wells. In Roman Britain these deposits seem to be a continuation of local pre-Roman Iron Age practices. Votive deposits at Romano-British villas include a pit with an articulated cattle leg accompanied by artifacts; another includes a complete piglet, a lamb skull, pottery, and 34 leather sandals; a third (next to the latter) contains two ducks and two geese, all complete, arranged in clay with the geese facing north and south with wings extended as though flying (Fulford 2001). Cattle skulls and human bones are also found in wells as apparent votive deposits (Scott 1991). Bliesbruck and other Gallo-Roman sites in France have similar deposits in pits and wells, many

showing clearly deliberate placements such as a pitcher surrounded by
goblets and large animal bones. Such pits are always grouped in discrete
areas, but are associated with a variety of site types: urban settlements,
temples, and forts. The deposits include large amounts of trash along
with deliberately placed items such as whole pots, metal artifacts, intact
animals or quarters of meat, and occasionally human remains. Most deliberately placed animal remains are nonmeaty heads, mandibles, horns, and
scapulae, whereas the trash component consists mainly of meaty bones.
Some pits have pots full of food: fruit, mussels, or meat (bones). At Bliesbruck, the pits appear to have been dug specifically to fill them with these
deposits, and they were filled quickly. Thus the pits, often located near
temples, contain a combination of offerings and the ceremonial trash
from feasts, sacrifices, and ceremonies, perhaps part of a chthonic fertility
cult. At all these sites, the animal remains are overwhelmingly those of
domestic animals, mainly food animals – cattle, pig, and sheep – but also
with substantial numbers of dogs among the deliberately placed items
(Petit 1989).

In Mesoamerica, Kitty Emery (2004) has explored the deposits in
Cueva de los Quetzales, a cave that runs below the Maya center of Las
Pacayas with a skylight opening into the main ceremonial area. The faunal materials thrown into this opening may include a component of
ceremonial trash, but Emery argues that most are offerings associated
with cave rituals. Caves play an important role in Maya ritual, particularly in connection with fertility and regeneration ceremonies. Emery
compares the Cueva de los Quetzales assemblage with that from the
nearby residential area of Arroyo de Piedra. Species of ritual importance
are overrepresented at Cueva de los Quetzales, especially those associated with the underworld or regeneration rites: felines, crocodiles, bats,
snakes, opossums, and iguanas. Remains of deer, felids, and turkeys show
an unusually high proportion of immature animals, perhaps a metaphor
for rebirth. Present-day Mayas often place animal heads in ritual deposits,
and there is a slight bias to skulls in the Cueva de los Quetzales assemblage. There is also a bias to the left side among deer and dogs, and
perhaps turkeys, at Cueva de los Quetzales, a pattern seen in other ritual
deposits, because the left represents the underworld and the sacred in
Maya cosmology. Here careful analysis reveals selection in species, age,
and body part that differs from feasting as well as daily discard, indicating
deliberate offerings to this opening into the underworld.

At the Crenshaw site in Arkansas, a Caddoan (Late Woodland/Early Mississippian) ceremonial center, a structure near one of the mounds is located next to a pile of more than 2,000 white-tailed deer antlers. The antlers are attached to the skull and hence are from hunted animals. They show little weathering, so they must have been protected by a roof. With one exception, all are from mature males, and they tend toward particularly robust individuals. Very few other bones or artifacts occur in the pile. Susan Scott and Edwin Jackson (1996) suggest that the structure associated with the pile is a fire temple and the residence of its priest. Ethnographically, Caddoan shamans butchered and distributed the meat of deer, while performing rituals to maintain the deer supply. The antler display may have served as the focus for hunting rituals.

Another ethnographic account of special deposits reflects concerns about the power of the bones. Mongols feel that holes and cavities in bones provide potential homes for demons. Therefore, especially for bones with ritual significance, the holes are plugged with fat, dung, or wood before they are used in protective rituals or discarded (Birtalan 2003).

### Structured deposition

So far I have discussed various sorts of "special" deposits that are set apart as depositionally distinct. Colin Richards and Julian Thomas (1984) have called attention to more subtle indications of the remains of ritual, which they term "structured deposition." They developed this concept in relation to Durrington Walls and other British Neolithic monuments, where apparently "ritual" architecture is accompanied by apparently "utilitarian" trash. They suggest that a closer look reveals signs of ritual in the trash as well. Because ritual is characterized by structured and repetitive action and the use of symbols, it should produce structured waste. Patterns of context and association can therefore reflect ritual, even in the absence of special framing of these deposits. At Durrington Walls, some artifact types are restricted spatially and some types co-occur, whereas others have largely mutually exclusive spatial distributions.

Given the strong symbolic value of animals (see Chapter 2), Richards and Thomas propose that animal remains are particularly good indicators of ritual practices. They posit that consistent associations result from feasts and also examine spatial patterning of body parts to argue that animals moved through the site in a structured series of stages: They were butchered in one area and prepared, consumed, and discarded in others. Associations or spatial distinctions may reveal symbolic distinctions between wild and domestic or other qualities embodied by animals. They argue that the most crucial wild/domestic distinction is within a single taxon and find that wild cattle and pigs (which have domestic counterparts in the British Neolithic) are found only in the outer ditches of several henge sites. This suggests that the wild/domestic distinction is mapped onto an inside/outside contrast and helps define group identity.

Inga Ullén (1994) argues for similar structuring of rubbish in Late Bronze Age Sweden at the Apalle site. In the earlier phase, trash was discarded in a large communal midden, whereas later rubbish accumulations are associated with individual houses. Although the later, individual deposits do not show structure, the communal midden does. The skulls of domestic animals are found only around the edges and in a pit dug into the middle, whereas postcranial remains are not found in these locations, but in the remainder of the midden. Most of the communal midden consists of fire-cracked rock, making it reminiscent of burial mounds with their rounded piles of stones. Given that cemeteries also have piles of fire-cracked rock and that such rocky midden heaps are often used for secondary burials, Ullén proposes that this analogy was felt by the Bronze Age inhabitants and accounts for the symbolic structuring of trash deposition. The midden would thus be a kind of grave for nonhuman, even nonanimate things.

Joseph Kovacik (2000) uses contextual information to define groupings of animals according to social categories at the 29SJ627 site in Chaco Canyon, New Mexico. Rabbits, deer, and bighorn sheep form one group. Their remains are widely distributed across the site, but are concentrated in domestic and cooking areas. Traces of butchery and burning indicate they were routinely consumed. Carnivores and raptors form a second group, found in a limited range of contexts and showing skinning marks but little sign of dismemberment or consumption. Kovacik maps these groups onto an inside/outside distinction, with the socially "outside" carnivores (because they are dangerous, nocturnal, or scavengers) paradoxically found in the internal contexts and vice versa. Interestingly, this distinction disappears in the final phase at the site, when public space is redefined and architecture becomes more formal, evidently rendering these animal groups irrelevant to the construction of space.

Similarly, Robert Muir and Jonathan Driver (2004) identify concentrations of artiodactyls and of carnivore and wild bird remains at larger pueblos in the northern San Juan region of the American Southwest. Drawing on the particular architectural associations and on direct historical analogy, they propose that the artiodactyl and one carnivore/raptor concentration mark the headquarters of war or hunting sodalities, whereas a more disparate wild bird concentration indicates a structure for storage or use of ritual paraphernalia. By examining the occurrence of wild birds through time at the smaller sites in the area, they document an aggregation of ritual activities into the larger pueblos over the course of the Pueblo III period.

As these disparate examples illustrate, it is important for archaeologists to be alert to variations in depositional practices, and for zooarchaeologists to participate in excavations. Much information about ritual and cultural categories has no doubt been lost because special deposits and structured deposition have not been recognized, recorded, or separated for analysis. Yet we should be wary of assigning all unusual deposits to ritual activity. Richards and Thomas (1984) propose that, because ritual is by its nature structured, we can use that structure to detect it in the archaeological record. This is an important insight, but ritual is not the only structured behavior. Bob Wilson (1992) has challenged the general tendency to label unusual deposits as remains of ritual, and in particular the claims for Iron Age pits at Danebury, which he feels could as easily result from ordinary butchery and disposal practices. Some of his objections have been addressed in subsequent work (Hill 1995, 1996), but the general point stands that "unusual" or "structured" does not automatically equate to ritual. Careful contextual analysis is required to make a case not only for the ritual character of unusual deposits but also for their specific nature. In addition, we should be cautious about dichotomizing sacred and secular, ritual and ordinary deposition. In many societies these distinctions are not strongly drawn. Being alert to structured deposition is useful not simply to find ritual but also to provide insight into how prehistoric people organized their world. Animals almost always carry strong symbolic salience, and thus animals and animal remains are quite likely to be used in that structuring.

ANIMALS IN ARCHITECTURE

Some special deposits are directly linked to buildings, which they may protect or decorate. Some of these deposits are placed, visibly or invisibly, at the time of construction, whereas others may be added later, probably marking significant events in the life cycle of the building and its inhabitants.

### Foundation deposits

Foundation deposits are placed before or during the construction of a building, typically under a floor, and sometimes in significant spots such as thresholds. Vesa-Pekka Herva (2005) proposes "building deposit" as a better term, to include items built into walls and other parts of a building as well as the foundation itself. We have seen that the closing of buildings in the Neolithic Near East was often marked with abandonment deposits, so perhaps it is not surprising that their opening frequently includes foundation deposits. Moreover, some of the same items may appear in both kinds of deposits. Cattle skulls or frontlets and scapulae were placed below floors or built invisibly into walls or benches during the Pre-Pottery Neolithic at Mureybet, Tell 'Abr 3, and Tell Halula in northern Syria, Ginnig in northern Iraq, and Çayönü in southeastern Turkey (Campbell and Baird 1990:68; Helmer et al. 2004:151; Yartah 2005). At Çatalhöyük, cattle scapulae and horns are also built into walls. Deposits placed under floors during construction include feasting remains, as well as collections of obsidian and human neonate burials (Carter 2007). These burials are often associated with internal thresholds (entry to houses being from the roof) or hearths, in contrast to other burials placed along the north and east walls, away from the hearths in the south (Moses 2008).

Some Late Neolithic Vinča culture houses in southeast Europe have animal skulls as foundation deposits. The At site in Serbia had a wild boar skull buried beneath a house, and a dog skull with mandibles was placed in a small pit below the foundation of a house at Opovo (Russell 1993). Although some foundation deposits have no doubt been missed or have not been reported given the low priority of faunal remains on many southeast European excavations, it is nevertheless clear that only a few Vinča houses have such foundation deposits. This poses the question of why certain houses are selected: Does the presence of the deposits mark them as particularly important? In this case the "marking" would be invisible during use. Are some houses in particular need of protection because of the history of their inhabitants or because their inhabitants carry special responsibilities? The essentially identical Late Neolithic/Eneolithic

Cucuteni and Tripolye cultures of Romania, Moldavia, and the Ukraine overlap temporally with the Vinča culture of the central Balkans. An apparent foundation deposit under House 1 at Traian in Romania, from the Late Neolithic Cucuteni-Ariuşd culture, contains a pot with ash, clay fragments, snail shells, and sheep/goat bone fragments (Lichter 2001:134). This assemblage suggests a selection of remains from a feast, perhaps part of a ceremony inaugurating the house or connected to its inhabitants. Tripolye A houses often have foundation deposits of cattle skulls or horns, or human skulls. The Tripolye A settlement of Berna-shevka on the Dnieper River in the Ukraine had a domestic cattle skull under every house (a notably different pattern from Vinča sites), and one house also had an aurochs (wild cattle) skull and red deer antlers (Anthony 2007:172). A dog head (skull and mandibles) in a pit in a Middle Neolithic house at Catignano in central Italy appears to be a foundation deposit (Wilkens 2006:136).

At Eneolithic Botai in Kazakhstan, where the faunal remains consist almost entirely of horses, dog remains occur chiefly as special deposits, including foundation deposits and burials in pits just outside buildings. Some are complete, some are partial skeletons, and in some cases the body parts present (heads and feet) suggest skins, possibly used as costumes. In one case a pit with dog remains stood open, filled with water, for some time before being filled in. Another pit has a stone slab surrounded by round stones, on top of which lay a dog skull, the anterior portions of two horse mandibles, and two arrow points (one of them stuck into a piece of ochre). In another house, a foundation pit contains a nearly complete dog with six horse skulls and assorted artifacts. Houses can have as many as six to seven dogs buried in them. Pointing to Indo-European mythological accounts of dogs guarding the underworld, Sandra Olsen (2000) suggests that these deposits were intended to protect the houses and their inhabitants. Similarly, Late Bronze Age Apalle in Sweden has dog bones, mostly skulls and mandibles, buried near the entrances of the houses in the later phase (Ullén 1994:258).

Dogs are also often placed as foundation deposits in Iron Age and Roman Britain, often at thresholds (Smith 2006). Foundation or building deposits of animals or animal parts, often combined with human infants and artifacts, are found at both Romano-British temples and villas. Cattle and horse skulls occur along with infant burials at the temple complex at Springhead in Kent, whereas a lamb was buried next to the entrance of the villa at Kings Weston. Several other villas have similar deposits of animal heads, sometimes with artifacts. In some cases these animal deposits occur near or in the same pit with infant burials. Animal skulls and human infants are also buried in association with grain-processing facilities that served beer production, perhaps related to the symbolism of fertility and transformation linked to fermentation (Scott 1991).

The Middle Kingdom temple of Montuhotep Sankhara at Thebes in Egypt had foundation deposits under each of its four corners (Bartosiewicz 2000a). Although some are disturbed, they each appear to have included saucers, alabaster vessels, ceramic animal figurines, and animal parts. In at least two cases, these animal remains included a salted right cattle forefoot (metacarpal down). As László Bartosiewicz notes, the salting may mean that the animals were killed some time in advance of the laying of the foundation. He suggests that they could be food offerings, with the salted feet kept for soup, or tokens to represent the whole animal. Another possibility is suggested by Calvin Schwabe's (1994:43) discussion of the significance of cattle forelimbs in ancient Egypt, noting that Egyptians saw the constellation Ursa Major as a bull's forelimb. According to Schwabe, the forelimb was the first part removed from a sacrificed bull; because it is possible to make the muscles in the severed foot twitch for a while, it was thought to contain an animating principle, and was touched to the dead pharaoh's mouth in a revivification ceremony. Surely this life-giving power must be involved in these foundation deposits.

Maya sites also have votive deposits that often include animal remains associated with the construction or reconstruction of public buildings and monuments. These deposits are conventionally referred to as caches, a misnomer because they are not intended to be recovered. A wide variety of animal remains, some worked, appear in these deposits, but biased heavily to nonfood species. Brightly colored birds occur in many deposits, and dogs are also a common component (Moholy-Nagy 2004). At Preclassic Colha, stable isotope analysis shows that dogs in caches were fed substantial amounts of maize, whereas dogs in middens were not (White et al. 2001). Later, the Aztecs placed at least 114 "caches" in the Templo Mayor of Tenochtitlan (Mexico City), of which 39 included terrestrial vertebrate remains. These remains include a remarkable array of amphibians, reptiles, birds, and mammals. Felids, particularly cougars, are especially well represented. Many of the offerings contain whole skeletons, whereas others have only limited body parts (Alvarez and Ocaña 1991).

Most foundation or building deposits are probably intended to be apotropaic, serving to protect the building, as well as to forge bonds between people and place (Herva 2005). Brown and Emery (2008) suggest that at least for the Maya these deposits are not so much about protecting the building or "ensouling" it, but rather engaging with and appeasing the forest spirits from whose materials the house is built, so that the house, which is an active agent, will not harm its inhabitants, particularly children. Although the deposits often include other items, human infants and animal remains are strikingly frequent. Perhaps the infants are regarded as messengers to the otherworld from which they have just emerged (Gottlieb 1998, 2004), which raises the possibility that they were sacrificed for that purpose (cf. Borić and Stefanović 2004). In many cases the animals were probably also sacrificed, although some are likely remains of dedicatory feasts and may or may not have been slaughtered in a ritual context. Although a variety of taxa and body parts appear in these deposits, dogs and skulls are prominent in many places and time periods. The choice of dogs, often placed near entrances, confirms the deposits' apotropaic function, with dogs on guard in the spirit world, as they no doubt were in life. The choice of skulls indicates a belief that the essence or power of the animal is lodged in the head, a belief also seen with respect to humans in the various manifestations of the "skull cult" in the Near Eastern Neolithic and elsewhere (Bienert 1991; Bonogofsky 2005; Helmer et al. 2004).

### Installations

Whereas foundation deposits are buried in or below buildings at the time of construction, some animal parts are incorporated visibly into the architecture, set into walls, benches, or other architectural features. Archaeologically, I am aware of this phenomenon chiefly in the Neolithic Near East, perhaps because mudbrick architecture is particularly amenable to this practice. Skulls and horns are the most frequently used parts in architectural installations, and the animals are usually wild although these societies kept domestic herd animals.

Ganj Dareh, in the Kermanshah Valley of Iran, is renowned as the earliest known site of goat domestication (Hesse 1984; Zeder 2001; Zeder and Hesse 2000). Not the herded goats, however, but two wild sheep skulls with their horn cores were attached to the walls of a small niche in a building in Level D, now dated to ca. 10,000 BP (Smith

1990b). About a thousand years later at Zaghe, somewhat to the east in Iran, about 18 wild goat skulls with horn cores were found set in plaster fallen from the walls of a large rectangular building with geometric paintings on some of its interior walls; this is thought to be a public building of some kind, likely with a ritual function (Negahban 1979).

Çatalhöyük is roughly contemporary with Zaghe, and it, too, has horns set into the walls, although here they are wild cattle and occasionally sheep. Additionally, wild boar jaws, vulture heads, a fox skull, and a weasel (badger?) skull were set into walls and later covered with plaster. Cattle horns are also set in benches and on short clay pillars on the edge of platforms; one such pillar has sheep horns. Occasionally, long bone fragments are set into walls, sticking out into the room. Mellaart suggests these fragments were pegs for hanging other installations, but at least one, a wolf ulna, is located too near the floor for anything to hang from it (Mellaart 1962, 1963, 1964, 1966b, 1967; Russell and Meece 2006; Twiss and Russell 2009).

Outside the Near East, architectural installations are known from late Neolithic Skara Brae in the Orkneys, where stone houses have remained remarkably intact. Perhaps the distribution of animal remains as architectural installations is largely a matter of architectural preservation. At Skara Brae cattle and whale skulls were placed over entrances and passages, and cattle long bones were built visibly into exterior walls at both Skara Brae and the outer revetment walls of contemporary tombs (Jones 1998:310).

Like the foundation deposits, architectural installations may be apotropaic in nature. However, their visible, often prominent placement raises other possibilities. The installations may display trophies, totem animals, or the remains of feasts of merit. It is notable that dogs, so prominent in foundation deposits in many parts of the world, do not appear in these installations, which feature cattle and wild animals. These installations, then, may display the wealth or hunting prowess of the inhabitants, or they could be read in terms of controlling the wild and powerful by bringing it into the house (Hodder 1990).

*Other incorporations into architecture*

In addition to foundation deposits and architectural installations, animal remains may be incorporated into architecture either as building materials or as invisible deposits. Using bone as construction material, as in Upper Paleolithic mammoth bone huts or whale ribs and mandibles used as roof beams at Skara Brae, may seem to be simply a practical use of large animal bones in environments where wood is scarce. This is no doubt the case, but it is clear that these bones carry symbolic connotations as well.

Huts made of mammoth bones occur at a number of Gravettian (Upper Paleolithic) sites in the Dnepr River basin in the Ukraine, Belarus, and Russia; they are found in smaller numbers in southern Poland and Moravia. Mezhirich, Mezin, and Gontsy are the best known of these sites. Skulls, mandibles, long bones, and scapulae formed structures probably covered with hides. On the whole, the body parts chosen have high architectural utility but low meat yield; thus they were likely brought to the sites, whether from hunted mammoths or scavenged bone yards, for construction purposes (see Chapter 5, *Old World*). In addition to providing firm support for a tent structure, the mammoth bones were carefully arranged, in patterns that vary from site to site, revealing a visual grammar based on the choice of body parts and their placement (Gladkih et al. 1984; Iakovleva and Djindjian 2001, 2005; Pidoplichko 1998; Soffer et al. 2001). At Skara Brae, Jones (1998) suggests that whales, as the largest marine creature, embody the sea in constructing the sense of place at this island settlement.

Çatalhöyük is perhaps the site where animal remains are most thoroughly integrated with architecture, or at least where this integration has been most thoroughly documented. In addition to the installations and other deposits already described, animal remains are incorporated invisibly in various ways. Cattle horns and scapulae are built into walls or blockings of crawlholes in walls. Perhaps these are conceptually similar to what I term "commemorative deposits" (see the earlier section, *Special Deposits*).

### AMULETS AND RITUAL PARAPHERNALIA

Animal parts often form part of costumes and paraphernalia used on open display in ceremonies, as is discussed later (see *Dancing with Animals*). They may also be carried concealed, singly or as part of a collection, or worn as part of daily attire. Most often we recognize such amulets and paraphernalia in burials, through their association with the human body and their placement on it, although occasionally we may detect them in other contexts.

Amulets are objects felt to hold power, worn, often inconspicuously, to provide luck or protection. Parents often provide infants and young children with protective amulets, perceiving them as especially vulnerable to illness and other misfortune. For example, Mongols use wolf astragali as amulets to protect both children and horses; today Mongolian truckers attach them to their keys for luck (Birtalan 2003). In some cases people collect amulets with personal meaning throughout their lives. Some may take explicitly religious form, invoking the power of deities. Others may have a standardized form, such as the common amulets against the evil eye in the eastern Mediterranean. However, many are seemingly ordinary objects that have power and meaning only in the context of the life of the bearer. This last type is difficult to recognize archaeologically, and identification must rely heavily on context to provide clues. Pendants are often referred to as amulets in the archaeological literature, but here I confine myself to animal remains that are unmodified or not easily interpreted as simple body ornaments.

Hunting always involves an element of chance, and success is both variable and highly desired (see Chapter 4). Thus it is not surprising that hunting charms form one common class of amulets. In Malawi, most hunters carry medicine bags with plant and animal parts, including pangolin scales and hedgehog spines, for protection from the physical and spiritual dangers inherent in hunting. Carnivore teeth and claws were worn as apotropaic amulets (Morris 1998). Similarly, to aid their hunting success, the North American Cree often wear charms, some of them made from animal parts. Such charms are felt to give power to the hunter and show respect to the animal (Tanner 1979:140–1). Netsilik Inuit hunters similarly wear teeth, claws, tails, and mandibles of prey (Murray 2000:59). Moving a bit further from hunting magic per se, in the Amazon jaguar parts are worn to transfer the power, strength, and ferocity of the predator to hunters, warriors, or shamans. However, wearing animal parts also protects people from that animal, so women and children wear jaguar parts for this purpose (Roe 1997; Saunders 1997:25–6). These ethnographic cases suggest that the line between sympathetic magic (hunting charms) and apotropaism is often fuzzy. However, amulets worn by children are likely to be primarily protective.

Several items in burials at the Late Mississippian Toqua site in Tennessee are probably amulets. These include a cougar jaw, cougar canine, wolf mandible, wolf maxilla, and two graves with articulated caudal vertebrae (i.e., tails). There are no further details on the occupants of these graves, but a perforated wolf carnassial was found in an infant burial, suggesting a protective function at least in this case (Bogan 1983:319). At the Anglo-Saxon site of Spong Hill in England, some of the cremation burials include animal remains interpreted as amulets that hold the essence of the animal: antler tines and burr rings, sheep calcanei, and a pierced raptor claw (Bond and Worley 2006:97).

Many Native North American groups have used medicine bundles to access supernatural power for aid in hunting, war, agriculture, healing, or love. Called bundles because they are wrapped when not in use, they contain one or more powerful objects, usually initially revealed during vision quests. These objects are varied, but often include feathers and animal parts. The bundles are associated with songs, rituals, and taboos. When the owner of the bundle dies, in some cases it is passed on to a living person, but in others it is buried with its owner (Hanson 1980b; Harrod 2000; Sidoff 1977). Probable medicine bundles have been identified archaeologically in burials. Medicine bundles were wrapped in bags made of bird and mammal skins or the paws of large mammals; these bags could also simply be stuffed with straw and never opened. Body parts suggestive of such bags (wolf paws; or the toes, tail, and skull of assorted animals) have been recovered from Archaic, Hopewell, and Adena graves (Webb and Baby 1957). A bear paw that seems to have been contained in a bag in a Late Woodland burial in New York is also interpreted as a medicine bundle (Rafferty 2008). At Mississippian Toqua body parts suggest the presence of skin bags made from both birds (hawks, owls) and mustelids (mink, weasel, otter). In one case, a mink-skin bundle contained a sandhill crane skull (Bogan 1983). Numerous burials at protohistoric sites in the Middle Missouri Valley include bird skulls, often with the back cut off, with wing and leg bones. Based on ethnographic examples, these are probably the remains of bird-skin bags that contained medicine bundles. The birds used include whooping crane, raven, crows, hawks, eagles, owls, and ducks. Such bundles are unknown on the Great Plains in the prehistoric period, so may have spread from the eastern woodlands, where, as we have seen, such remains are attested prehistorically (Ubelaker and Wedel 1975). Perhaps body parts suggesting raptor skins in prehistoric Californian burials are also the remains of such bundles (Heizer and Hewes 1940:591). A Danish Middle Bronze Age grave with a copper vessel holding snake vertebrae, a lizard tail, falcon claws, a lynx bone, a bird trachea, a squirrel mandible, pyrite fragments, and pebbles suggests a similar collection of powerful objects (Briard 1987:129).

### Sacrifice and ritual killing

Ethnographically, animal sacrifice is widespread among preindustrial societies that keep domestic animals and even among some that do not. Historically we know that many past societies practiced sacrifice, and we must suspect that many prehistoric groups did as well. One possible motivation for animal domestication is the need for a reliable supply of sacrificial victims (see Chapter 6, *Models of Origins*). Sacrifice is not easy to approach archaeologically, because the difference between slaughter and sacrifice is the intent of the butcher. However, it is of such significance that we must wrestle with how to study it in prehistory.

Complicating this endeavor is the lack of consensus on how to define sacrifice. For some, any offering to deities constitutes sacrifice (Maringer 1960; Ruel 1990), especially, but not limited to, the slaughter of animals. Henri Hubert and Marcel Mauss (1964:13) further specify that offerings are sacrificial only when consecrated: "Sacrifice is a religious act which, through the consecration of a victim, modifies the condition of the moral person who accomplishes it or that of certain objects with which he is concerned." They also stress the destruction of the victim, whether living or not, as does Raymond Firth (1963:13). Others focus on killing as the defining feature of sacrifice, so that only living victims (human or animal) count (Burkert 1983, 1987; Girard 1972; Humphrey and Laidlaw 2007; Jay 1992; Merrifield 1987:22; Meyer 2005; Valeri 1994). Bernard Lempert (2000:120) defines sacrifice as "murder justified by theory."[1] Still others insist that only domestic animals can be sacrificed, because one can only relinquish or offer what one owns (Baal 1976; Bonte 1995; Firth 1963; Ingold 1987, 1994; Smith 1987; Testart 2006). Moreover, sacrifice is seen as intrinsically involving a substitution of victim for the sacrificer, a logic that can only be fulfilled by animals identified with particular people through their care for these animals (Hamayon 1990:419). This last definition has important implications for zooarchaeology, because we could rule out sacrifice (although not necessarily other forms of ritual killing) in the absence of domestic animals.

Scholars also have differing understandings of the motivation for sacrifice. Some see sacrifice as an absolution of guilt or sins (Freud 1918). A variant of this approach stresses the scapegoating of the sacrificial victim as a way to channel violent tendencies (Girard 1972). Walter Burkert

---

[1] "Le sacrifice est un meurtre justifié par de la théorie."

(1983, 1987) similarly sees sacrifice as a way to control male aggression, but does not make the scapegoat aspect central. Others understand the purpose of sacrifice to be the release of the life force to keep the world functioning or allow for the regeneration of life (Frazer 1935; Merrifield 1987:22; Rice 1997). Maurice Bloch (1992) offers perhaps the most developed theorization of this view. He sees sacrifice as one of a class of rituals that seek to achieve transcendence through a three-stage structure in which protagonists first divide themselves internally into what may be characterized as animal and spirit parts, then leave behind the animal part to exist only in the spirit world (thereby expelling their internal vitality), and finally return to this world through the often literal ingestion of external vitality – in the case of sacrifice, the feast that follows slaughter. This third stage involves what Bloch calls "rebounding violence": not only the killing of the sacrificial victim but often also the invocation and sometimes the practice of raids or conquests of other groups.

Many characterize sacrifice as an extension of the gift economy (see Chapter 9, *Feasting*), in which the gods are drawn into relations of reciprocity with humans. The sacrifice is here seen as an offering designed to obtain general goodwill or specific benefits from the deities who receive it (Baal 1976; Firth 1963; Ingold 1987; Tylor 1964). Some counter that sacrifice is not a gift in the usual sense, because the gift is destroyed in the giving and often consists of small and relatively worthless parts, while the givers feast on the rest: "If sacrifice is a gift, it is a strange one, since it consists in taking back with one hand what has been given with the other" (Valeri 1994:104). Jan Van Baal (1976:164) points out, however, that the size of the gift varies with the status or wealth of the giver; humans, being always inferior to the gods, make small gifts. Valerio Valeri suggests that, although sacrifice may involve a relationship between humans and gods, often it is primarily a way to legitimate the killing and consumption of animals, to displace the guilt onto the gods. Hence for many pastoralists slaughter can only occur in the context of sacrifice.

Finally, some emphasize the role of sacrifice in constructing human relationships (e.g., Cole 2001). Jan Heesterman (1993) suggests that Vedic sacrifice is primarily a form of social competition. Nancy Jay (1992, see also Meyer 2005) argues that sacrifice serves to establish patriliny by erasing women's contribution (birth) and constructing corporate groups based on patrilineal kinship. Sacrifice designates and maintains ancestors; the blood of sacrifice is equated with but is superior to the blood of menstruation and childbirth, and sacrifice is cast as a superior form of birth. Susan Sered (2002) notes that animal sacrifice is cross-culturally one of the most consistently gendered practices, being nearly always practiced by men. Women often form the audience for sacrifice; they are absorbed into their husbands' families by participating in the sacrifice and ensuing meal. Although Sered (2002:26) argues that "sacrifice often has to do with the ritual construction, mystification and embodiment of gender and gender hierarchy," she reports that the male association with animal sacrifice holds even in the absence of gender hierarchy in Okinawa, where it is the only explicitly male-only ritual. Here the male predominance in sacrifice is not a matter of outdoing women in birth, but occurs because the association of sacrifice with death would harm women's life-giving powers.

In line with the varying opinions on motivations, there are different ideas about the origins of animal sacrifice. Some of the variation relates to whether animals or humans are seen as the archetypal sacrificial victims. Those who see sacrifice as originally and ultimately about killing humans, with animals as a substitute, tend to place its origins deep in the human past. Sigmund Freud (1918) traces it to an original Oedipal sin: sons who killed and ate their father to obtain his wives, then guiltily commemorated the act – reenacting the murder – by sacrificing to the father, now an ancestor/deity. Few would now accept this as a factual account of prehistory. The greatest disagreement concerns whether sacrifice precedes or follows animal domestication. Johannes Maringer (1960) traces sacrifice to the Middle Paleolithic (although most of the evidence he cites is now disputed). Although Valeri (1994) does not address origins per se, he argues that sacrifice can occur among hunters and that there are many commonalities between hunting rituals and sacrifice. Burkert (1983, 1987) and Adolf Jensen (1963) see sacrifice as postdating animal domestication, but with roots in earlier hunting rituals.

Most who stress that only domestic animals can be sacrificed make a qualitative distinction between hunting rituals and sacrifice, thus locating the origin of sacrifice after animal domestication. Like Freud, Ralph Merrifield (1987:23) sees human sacrifice as the archetype, but relates it to rites of regeneration associated with agriculture (although not necessarily animal domestication). Tim Ingold (1987:243–4) sees sacrifice as an inversion of the relationships among humans, animals, and spirits found in hunting rituals: In hunting, spirit masters give animals to

humans (see Chapter 4, *Hunters' Attitudes to Animals*), whereas in sacrifice, humans give animals to spirits. Reimar Schefold (2002) reports
a perhaps unusual case, among the Sakuddeis in Indonesia, in which
horticulturalists sacrifice domestic animals to spirit masters who reciprocate by supplying wild animals (their livestock) to human hunters, thus
combining both sets of relations. Jonathan Z. Smith (1987) insists most
strongly on limiting animal sacrifice to domestic animals, and he situates
its origin later than most. He argues that animal sacrifice is primarily a
feature of states. Not only are domestic animals the only possible victims
but they are also the essence of sacrifice, which he interprets as "a med-
itation on domestication" (Smith 1987:199). He equates domestication
with selective breeding, although selective breeding probably followed
animal domestication by many millennia (Bökönyi 1969; Clutton-Brock
1992). This definition fits his linkage of sacrifice and the state, because
it is in states that we find selective breeding. Smith sees sacrifice, with
its requirements for specific kinds of animals (sex, age, color, etc.) as an
exaggerated form of artificial selection and thus arising subsequent to it,
although one could equally argue that the selection for sacrifice provides
the model for other kinds of selective breeding. If Smith simply means
that herders tend to cull mainly immature males, however, sacrifice could
easily be present from the beginning of animal domestication.

EVIDENCE FOR SACRIFICE

Much of the theorizing about sacrifice relies heavily on textual evidence
from the classical world, although anthropologists have contributed as
well. It is worth examining some of the empirical evidence from a broader
range of societies before evaluating these theories. Many of the special
deposits described earlier, particularly foundation deposits, are likely to
include the remains of sacrificial animals, but it is hard to establish that
they were dedicated or offered to supernatural beings. A brief consideration of the ethnographic literature demonstrates that we surely severely
underestimate the remains of sacrifice archaeologically.

*Ethnography and history*

The ethnographic literature on sacrifice is vast. I do not attempt a comprehensive review of this voluminous literature here, but it is worth noting
some features of sacrificial practice. Sub-Saharan Africa is surely the most
thoroughly studied region of the world in terms of the anthropology of

sacrifice, including some ethnographic classics, notably Evans-Pritchard's (1940, 1951, 1954, 1956) studies of the Nuer. African sacrifice continues to attract, indeed demand, anthropological attention right up to the present (e.g., Cole 2001, who set out to address other topics but found sacrifice impossible to avoid). No doubt the extensive treatment of African sacrifice reflects the especially large role it plays in African societies, more so than in any other part of the world in the ethnographic present, although arguably comparable in this respect to classical Greece, for example. We should therefore be cautious in applying the African model elsewhere. Although not all African sacrifices involve cattle, and some groups never sacrifice cattle (Shanklin 1983), the prominence of sacrifice is no doubt linked to the centrality of cattle and their valorization as wealth in sub-Saharan Africa (see Chapter 8). Luc de Heusch (1985:212) argues that sacrifice is the only way cattle can be slaughtered when they function as wealth (see also Valeri 1994).

There is tremendous diversity in the form of African sacrifices, the occasions when they are required (initiations, marriages, and especially funerals are frequently marked with sacrifice; house construction may be as well), their organization, their symbolism, and their preferred victims and acceptable substitutes (for an overview, see Heusch 1985). However, it is nearly always domestic animals that are offered, and in most (but not all) places cattle are the preferred, ultimate, or only victims. In West Africa, there is a minor tradition of dog sacrifice in certain circumstances (Copet-Rougier 1988; Ojoade 1990). Both dogs and oxen (castrated cattle) are described as particularly appropriate for some kinds of sacrifice because their ambiguous position (between animal and human spheres, between wild and domestic, between nature and culture, between male and female) makes them particularly suitable for mediating with the divine, while at the same time their particularly close identification with humans makes them an appropriate substitute offered in sacrifice (Beidelman 1966; Copet-Rougier 1988). With rare exceptions, the meat is consumed, either in a feast on the spot or divided for individual consumption at home. Such division is as fraught and laden with rules as is the division of game among hunters (see Chapter 9, *Meat Sharing*; Evans-Pritchard 1951, 1956; Raharijaona and Kus 2001).

The Dinka in Sudan (Lienhardt 1961) and the Merina in Madagascar (Bloch 1985) tease or torment the victim before the sacrifice. In some cases, particularly in Madagascar, the actual killing receives so little ritual-ization that Bloch (1985, 1992) does not consider sacrifice an appropriate term; rather it is the teasing beforehand and the feasting afterward that seem to be the main points (Cole 2001; Parker Pearson 2000; Rahari-jaona and Kus 2001). The blood of the victim figures largely in sacrificial ritual: It may be shed or not; collected; and smeared on sacrificial para-phernalia, people, and other items. In East and southern Africa, another highly charged sacrificial product is the chyme (rumen contents) of cattle or goats, also seen as life-giving and purifying, and likewise smeared on people and objects. Obtaining chyme is sometimes the primary object of the sacrifice (Abbink 2003; Evans-Pritchard 1956; Heusch 1985; Lien-hardt 1961; Ruel 1990).

Sacrificial requirements may shape herding practices and affect age and sex composition of the herds, as noted explicitly for the Hausa (Luxereau 1989) and Maasai (Ryan et al. 2000), but implied by the particular requirements described for many groups. These requirements tend to encourage keeping more male animals to adulthood rather than culling most of them at a young age, but may also affect what taxa are raised, as well as breeding for or retaining particular colors, horn shapes, and the like. However, there is usually a system of acceptable substitutes, at least in some circumstances: a lesser animal or a smaller number of animals, or a nonanimal offering (e.g., Shanklin 1983). In some cases, as with the famous Nuer practice of substituting a wild cucumber for an ox (Evans-Pritchard 1956), the proxy is intended as a temporary device, with the commitment to make the required sacrifice later. In sum, sacrificial needs shape herds, but they are flexible enough to permit the survival of the herd if a prescribed sacrifice would threaten it.

Some of the themes found in ethnographic studies of African sacrifice are echoed in work on South and Southeast Asia. There are numerous instances where animals are kept solely or chiefly because of the need to have them available for sacrifice (although often this ritual may also be the primary source of meat); not surprisingly, herd structure is shaped by sacrificial requirements. This is true of pigs for the Lisu of the highlands of northern Thailand (Durrenberger 1976), pigs and chickens for the Buid of the Philippines (Gibson 1988), goats for the Kalasha of the Hindu Kush (Parkes 1987), and mithan (*Bos frontalis*) for a number of groups in highland Burma and adjacent areas (Simoons 1968). As with cattle on Madagascar, mithan skulls and horns are displayed in, on, or near houses to attest to sacrifices performed. Heesterman (1993:35) observes that there is usually a competitive element, with prestige accruing to the provider of a sacrifice according to its magnificence. As a result, sacrifices are nearly always organized and the victims provided by individuals rather than communities. Ethnography suggests that this is generally the case (e.g., for the Lisu, mithan sacrificers, Malagasy groups), and trophy displays associated with houses are a material manifestation that serves to construct memories of the sacrificer's prestige. However, there are exceptions. The Buid organize sacrifice at the household level, but in this intensely egalitarian society it carries no prestige. Rather, because illness and other misfortunes are the impetus for sacrifices, people are inclined to pity families who sacrifice frequently or on a larger scale (Gibson 1988). The Tamang in Nepal organize sacrifice communally, with the village headman or ritual specialist collecting grain from each household to buy victims to offer to the village divinities and distributing the meat equally afterward (Holmberg 1989:131).

For many Indonesian societies, sacrificed domestic animals are messengers to the deities, carrying human prayers. In return, messages from the spirits – chiefly whether they have accepted the sacrifice and will grant the request – may be read in the entrails of the sacrificed animals. The Iban of Sarawak sacrifice chickens and pigs in a domestic context, consume the victims, and dispose of them along with the usual household trash, which is scavenged by other chickens and pigs (Beavitt 1989). These sacrifices would be difficult to detect archaeologically, but are central to the ritual and social life of the community.

On Sumba, the Kodi cultivate dry rice and raise horses and especially buffalo for exchange and sacrifice. These species act as wealth and are used in bridewealth, to pay fines, and the like. Buffalo are the main sacrificial victim, and none of their potential secondary products (milk, blood, labor) are used: They are used only for meat and only in the context of sacrifice. Large horns are valued, so tough, scrawny old bulls are the preferred sacrificial offering. Most buffalo sacrificed are male, with females offered only after they become sterile. Sacrifices, and the feasts that follow, are held to mark the building of a lineage house or megalithic tomb, for the funeral of an important person, to fulfill ancestral pledges, to celebrate the overcoming of misfortune, or to crush rivals with a grand display of competitive feasting (see Chapter 9).

The horns are displayed in the house of the sacrificer, attesting to the sacrifice and feast for years to come. As a result, there is an incentive for wealthier (older) men to sacrifice buffalo, because they then remain permanently in their possession in the form of the horn display that brings renown; while alive, the buffalo are always subject to claims from others. In contrast, poorer relations might prefer to keep the animals alive and available for needs such as fines and bridewealth. Janet Hoskins (1993) argues that this conflict of interest leads to the violence with which most buffalo are sacrificed, and the laughter at the spectacle. The first buffalo sacrificed belongs to the sacrificer (host), and it is dispatched quickly and with dignity. Others who are indebted to the sacrificer contribute the rest (up to a hundred). Young men who stand in the relationship of wife-takers to the host kill these buffalo, in a slow death by many cuts resembling a bullfight. Later, the heads of the sacrificed buffalo are arranged in a path from the village altar to the gate to carry the message to the spirits, with further ceremony, before they are hung in the sponsor's house.

Across the Pacific, pigs play a major role in social life, often including sacrifice. Feasting on pork is central to these events, to be discussed in Chapter 9. In Melanesia, pigs are an obsession much as cattle are among East African pastoralists, so that some speak of a "pig complex" analogous to the "African cattle complex" (Strathern 1971). The Mafulu of highland New Guinea distinguish between wild (feral) and domestic pigs, although they interbreed and form a single genetic population. They sacrifice both wild and domestic pigs, but in different contexts. While the sacrificer partakes of the wild pigs he has offered, he cannot eat his own domestic pigs, which are given to people from other villages after sacrifice (Rosman and Rubel 1989). Pig sacrifice and the concomitant feasting can secure social position. Hawaiian chiefs built their power by controlling the production of pigs for use in sacrifice and feasting, which was effective because pigs were both a prestige item and the staple meat source (Kolb 1999). For the Tikana of New Ireland, pig sacrifice establishes a new matriline and crucially secures its local land rights (Küchler 2002:43). The victim is a sow specially raised for the purpose and explicitly identified with the woman founding the matriline. It is killed by strangulation, to retain the blood, which is ingested by the members of the landowning clans to represent their incorporation of the new matriline.

The pig complex perhaps reaches its greatest heights in Vanuatu, where life seems to revolve mainly around pigs. Much effort is devoted to their care and the production of crops for fodder, and pigs form the main topic of conversation as well as the focus of rituals. Here, too, certain pigs are closely identified with the individual humans who raise them, substituting for their owners in sacrifice. Men care for these special pigs (while women tend the ordinary ones) and sacrifice them to achieve a series of ranked status grades as well as life after death. Men raise a special boar as a "death pig" that will be sacrificed at their funeral and whose soul will be eaten by the Guardian Ghost of the afterworld in place of their own, allowing their soul to survive. Although all ages and sexes of pigs are sacrificed, to achieve higher grades an increasing proportion must consist of special pigs of two varieties. In northern Vanuatu, the special pigs include hermaphrodites. Throughout the archipelago, men raised tusked boars, or tuskers. Some are castrated, some remain intact, but in both cases the upper canines are knocked out as the permanent canines begin to come into occlusion. Because the canines grow continuously, without the upper tusks to wear against them, the lower tusks curve around until they arc back and pierce through the cheek and jaw and eventually complete a full circle. Some even achieve two or three spirals, increasing in value as they do so. After death, the mandibles with circled tusks are displayed at sanctuaries, but the main value resides in the tusker at sacrifice, not the tusks themselves afterward. Both the hermaphrodites and the tuskers require extra effort and special care to produce. Hermaphrodites are sterile, thus reducing herd productivity, but certain pig lineages are prone to producing them. The tuskers cannot feed normally and must not be allowed to root lest they break the tusks, so are kept in houses and fed a special soft diet (Blackwood 1981; Funabiki 1981; Jolly 1984; Layard 1942).

Across northern Eurasia, sacrifice and ritual killing focus on reindeer and bears. The northern Saami sacrificed domestic reindeer at "shrines": natural places with special significance marked only by offerings. The sacrifices were meant to propitiate spirits, secure good weather, and pro-tect the reindeer. At these shrines the bones of reindeer predominate; sometimes they are reassembled in anatomical order after consumption. However, there are occasional remains of other animals, notably bear, as well as material offerings such as metal items (Bradley 2000:3–10; Zachrisson and Iregren 1974). Here, the bears appear to be the remains of hunted and ritually consumed animals (see the earlier section, *Respecting the Hunted*). Bears occupy a special place in circumboreal cultures and are often consumed in special bear feasts. Usually the feasts feature hunted bears as with the Saami, but in some cases, most famously among the Ainu of Japan but also, for example, among the Gilyak or Nivx of eastern Siberia, bear cubs are captured and raised for months or years as quasi-pets before they are ritually killed and eaten. Before sacrifice, both the Ainu and the Gilyak practice a distancing ritual in which the bear is teased and tormented (Batchelor 1908; de Sales 1980). A 19th-century account describes this ritual for the Ainu:

> In spring occasionally, it appears, they have bear hunts, killing the old bears and capturing the cubs. When the cubs are very small, they are handed over to the men's wives, who either bring them up by hand or suckle them, continuing the latter process until their teeth become disagreeably long. At some of the settlements I visited there were four or five young bears kept in large cages made of hard wood poles. In the autumn these animals are killed and eaten at the feast of bears. (St. John 1873:252)

The Ainu consider the captive bear to be divine in itself, and a messenger to the gods as well as a participant in the feast. Pieces of its own flesh, both cooked and uncooked, are offered to the head of the dead bear before it is hung on an outdoor pole to protect the village (Batchelor 1908). Although, as noted earlier, some scholars limit sacrifice to domestic animals and thus exclude Ainu and Siberian bear feasts (Ingold 1987:260), Hamayon (1990:419) argues that care of the bear permits the identification with it (already an animal seen as very similar to humans) that renders the victim a substitute for the sacrificer, which for her is the key element of sacrifice.

Although indigenous North American societies also held bears in high esteem and often gave their remains special treatment, with bear feasts held especially in the northern part of the continent, only a few, such as the Huron (Trigger 1990:34), raised and sacrificed bears. Dogs and, in the Southwest, turkeys are the only pre-Columbian animal domesticates in North America. These, along with other birds captured and raised for their feathers, supplied the usual sacrificial victims. Ethnographically, dog sacrifice is documented for Iroquoian groups, always with a sense that the dogs substituted for humans. Elisabeth Tooker (1965) presents evidence that the Iroquois white dog sacrifice was a 19th-century invention, perhaps part of the Handsome Lake revitalization movement, in part replacing earlier rituals of torturing and killing prisoners, although it later lost that association. However, dog sacrifice in general was a long-standing tradition in northeastern North America, with prehistoric roots extending to the Archaic (Oberholtzer 2002). Among the Huron, dog sacrifices seem to have substituted for humans within the group, including for the patient in curing rituals (Trigger 1990). The Huron ate the dogs after the sacrifice, whereas the Iroquois white dog sacrifices were burnt.

In the Andean region of South America there are a larger number of native domesticates, primarily llamas, alpacas, and guinea pigs. Modern Aymara llama herders sacrifice and eat a llama or sheep at the important ear marking ceremony, in which the llamas are allocated to family members and marked to indicate their owner. The sacrifice is made to propitiate the spirits that gave the first llamas to humans and that continue to look after their well-being (West 1983). Guinea pigs are sacrificed particularly in healing rituals, where the illness is transferred to the animal (Morales 1995).

Sacrifice persists in mainstream modern western societies as the term scientists use, at least until recently, to refer to the killing of experimental animals. Here animals are sacrificed not to a deity but to science, although Arnold Arluke (1988), based on his ethnography of laboratory practice, suggests that there can be religious overtones and that the use of animals as models for humans connects the two similarly to the substitution aspect of ritual sacrifice. He argues that the term "sacrifice" is more than just a euphemism in this context: "External necessity sees sacrifice as necessary to achieve the higher purpose of advancing the stock of scientific knowledge and medical progress. To accomplish this, the animal must be transformed into an object so that it can have a generalized utility for the scientific community" (Arluke 1988:99). Arluke sees this process as similar to the transformation of the animal into a spirit or life force in a religious sacrifice (cf. Lynch 1988). In discussing the stress that scientific animal sacrifice causes to lab workers, it is striking (and symptomatic of our human–animal relations) that both Arluke and the lab workers see pet or object as the only possible alternative ways to define animals.

Several ethnoarchaeological studies touch on sacrifice and consider the nature of the material remains. In a cautionary tale, Thomas Huffman

(1990) notes that modern Nguni speakers in southern Africa pulverize the bones of sacrificed animals and burn them along with the utensils from the ceremony, then scatter the ash in the byre, or mix it with soil outside the settlement, thereby rendering these animals all but archaeologically invisible. Because most cattle slaughters are sacrifices, cattle would be severely underrepresented in faunal assemblages. He suggests that if this was true in late prehistory, the increasing number of cattle later in the southern African Early Iron Age could be the result of proportionally fewer sacrifices as cattle herds increase as much as the larger herds themselves.

The Tandroy of southern Madagascar value cattle much more highly than sheep and goats, although all three can be sacrificed. However, there would be little sign of this differentiation in village middens, where food waste from all three (and other animals not sacrificed) is deposited with no distinction. In fact, because sacrificed cattle are divided and distributed to non-kin at the ancestral tombs (it is taboo for kin of the host to consume this meat), much of the cattle bone in village middens actually comes from cattle raised in other villages. The only marker of cattle's special value is the display of skulls (bucrania) at the tombs, commemorating sacrifices made there (Parker Pearson 2000). Elsewhere in Madagascar, the Betsileo have similar practices, but here the heads and skins of sacrificed cattle are hung in the northeast corner of the house of the host to commemorate the sacrifice (Raharijaona and Kus 2001).

For the Maasai, almost every cattle slaughter is a sacrifice, and animals are never killed just to provide meat. Mature males (usually castrates) are preferred for sacrifice, so herders tend not to cull young males, and meanwhile bleed them for food. However, the Maasai eat animals that die of natural causes, and disease and drought differentially strike young animals. During the study period, which was a time of extreme stress, 20% of the cattle died from disease or starvation. So for a group following the Maasai's sacrificial regime, a faunal assemblage with high numbers of young animals would indicate not a dairy or meat strategy, but environmental stress (Ryan et al. 2000). The extensive sacrifice practiced by the Talensi of Ghana is archaeologically invisible because, although much of the sacrifice occurs in shrines, the meat is then distributed and consumed in household contexts. After discard, the bones suffer severe attrition from dogs and other scavengers, so that very few are preserved. Skulls and mandibles of sacrificial victims are displayed in the shrines, and potentially would offer evidence of sacrifice, but apparently they do not usually enter the archaeological record (Insoll 2010).

*Archaeology*

We must surely turn to archaeology to understand the origins and development of sacrifice. Maringer (1960) traces its origins to the Middle Paleolithic, where he argues that the so-called bear cult included sacrifice. The evidence for the bear cult is provided by special arrangements of cave bear bones, especially skulls (Lascu et al. 1996). Some have rejected the interpretation of these deposits as deliberate human placement or have suggested that they are the remains of meat caches, and Robert Gargett (1996) has shown that cave bears' own activities can produce spatial patterning of their remains, with larger bones tending to accumulate near the walls of cave bear dens. Nevertheless, some of the arrangements – circles or crosses of skulls, for example – seem compelling, although this does not make them clear evidence of sacrifice. The arrangements could simply be the result of respectful treatment of the remains of hunted bears or even of bear bones found in caves later occupied by humans.

Maringer sees continued evidence of sacrifice in the Upper Paleolithic in special deposits of articulated or partially articulated skeletons, but again, these deposits may result from other rituals. He further cites a scene incised on a pendant from Raymondon cave in the Dordogne: The fleshed head of a bison attached to its defleshed spine, with two legs extended in front, is accompanied by seven human figures arranged on either side of the spine, one carrying a branch; a series of what may be bows is depicted next to the scene (Maringer 1960:92). The attention to animal remains implied by this scene (and a few other depictions of skinned or butchered animals [Bahn and Vertut 1997:175–6]) is fascinating, but not necessarily indicative of sacrifice. Perhaps the most frequently cited evidence for Paleolithic sacrifice is provided by the reindeer carcasses weighted down with stones on a lake bottom at Stellmoor and Meiendorf in Germany. However, careful study shows that these animals are not selected, but are a random sample of a reindeer herd. Some have been partially or fully butchered; others are apparently unused remnants of a mass kill, perhaps stored underwater. Arrow wounds indicate that many of the reindeer were shot in the water, arguing against sacrifice (Bratlund 1991, 1992, 1996; Pohlhausen 1953).

The later component of Stellmoor, which includes sunken reindeer, is Epipaleolithic (Ahrensburgian). Otherwise, few arguments have been made for sacrifice in the Epipaleolithic/Mesolithic of the Old World. A tame bear from Mesolithic France (see Chapter 7, *Neither Wild nor Domestic*) may ultimately have been sacrificed for a bear feast, as among the Ainu and Siberian groups known ethnographically (Chaix et al. 1997). Francesco Fedele (1993) proposes that Mesolithic foragers ventured for the first time into the higher elevations of the Alps to hunt or round up red deer for ceremonies through drives aided by the topography and open landscape at the tree line. Rounding up red deer might imply sacrifice, but there is no osteological or archaeological evidence for this beyond the topographic possibilities. So at present the evidence for sacrifice in the Old World is very thin in foraging cultures, tending to support the idea that it is associated with domestic animals.

In the Near East, the Pre-Pottery Neolithic B (PPNB) is conventionally considered the time of animal domestication, with plant domestication occurring during the preceding PPNA (recent work may push animal domestication back into the late PPNA in northern Syria and southeast Turkey). However, Pierre Ducos (1966), his argument later taken up by Jacques Cauvin (1972:35–9), claims domestic goats at El Khiam in the early PPNA in Jordan. He argues that the high proportion (20%) of neonatal goats, whose intact long bones show they were not eaten, does not make sense in terms of animal husbandry, so must be the result of a first fruits sacrifice. However, Ducos' (1997) later reanalysis of the El Khiam faunal assemblage shows that (a) the neonatal specimens are actually fetal and (b) the goats are actually ibex. Thus these are wild animals, hunted from herds of pregnant females during the late winter or early spring.

There is more suggestive evidence for sacrifice at some sites during the PPNB. At Basta, a large PPNB site in Jordan, a complete cow with an unborn calf is buried near a human burial (adult male). The cow was butchered, presumably the meat was stripped off and consumed, and then the bones were arranged roughly in anatomical position for burial. This certainly indicates consumption and probably slaughter in a ritual context. The body part distribution for the other cattle remains at the site is biased toward horns and scapulae, which perhaps were kept as trophies of hunts, feasts, or sacrifices. The domestication status of the Basta cattle remains uncertain; preliminary analysis suggests that at least some may be herded, but the sample size is small (Becker 2002).

At PPNB Kissonerga-*Mylouthkia* on Cyprus, partial and disarticulated human remains along with the complete, unbutchered carcasses of 9 sheep and 13 goats, most of them immature, were dumped in a well (Croft 2003:51–4). The presence of human remains suggests that this is a ritual context, rather than disposal of diseased or otherwise inedible carcasses. The lack of consumption marks these ritual deaths as sacrifice.

Claims have been made for aurochs and sheep blood residue on a stone slab in the Skull Building at PPNB Çayönü, and for human and aurochs blood on a large flint blade from the building (Loy and Wood 1989). The identification of archaeological blood residues has been controversial, and most now reject Thomas Loy's techniques (Smith and Wilson 2001). However, there is other evidence for the ritual importance of cattle in this building. Cattle horns and skulls occur along with human remains in a pit from the first phase, and on the floor, probably fallen from the wall, in the second phase (Özdoğan 1999:47; Verhoeven 2002a:239). As the name implies, the building also contained a large collection of human skulls. It would therefore be easy to see the cattle remains as tokens of funerary sacrifices.

The symbolic importance of cattle at Çatalhöyük has inspired suggestions of sacrifice. Mellaart (1967:77), the original excavator, points out that there are no obvious architectural correlates of sacrifice: altars, tables, or pits to catch the blood. In addition, the roof entrances would have made on-site slaughter difficult. He therefore suggests that sacrifice occurred off-site, with pieces of meat brought to offer at the hearths in houses. Burkert (1983) interprets the so-called hunting scenes at Çatalhöyük (two paintings of large bulls surrounded by numerous human figures) as dances forming part of a ritual in preparation for the sacrifice of captured wild animals, part of the transition from hunting to classical sacrifice. Based on the earlier claim that cattle were locally domesticated at Çatalhöyük (Perkins 1969), Burkert believes the illusion of the hunt had to be maintained by freeing them for ritual capture before sacrifice. The human figures around the animals in the two paintings have also been seen as teasing or tormenting the animals (deer and boar as well as cattle, all wild). In some cases they seem to be pulling the animals' tails or tongues. This action has been interpreted as either transferring sins to a scapegoat or a distancing device to separate from a lovingly raised animal preparatory to sacrifice (Bloch 1985; Lienhardt 1961; Serpell 1986:148–9). Others (Forest 1993) have rejected the notion that these paintings depict sacrifice.

In contrast to Çayönü, cattle remains at Çatalhöyük are not associated with human remains until the latest levels of the site, where two burials contain cattle horns. Yet the display of cattle horns in houses suggests that they are tokens or trophies of hunts, feasts, and/or sacrifices. The most compelling evidence for sacrifice at Çatalhöyük to date is the intact yearling lamb accompanying a human burial (Russell and Düring 2006). This probably domestic animal was almost surely killed to place in the grave, and thus reasonably interpreted as a sacrifice. However, this animal offering is so far unique among the hundreds of burials at Çatalhöyük; hence it is not a standard funerary practice. In addition, its placement – next to but with the feet carefully held up during the filling of the pit so they would not fall across the human body, from which a mat separates it – indicates ambivalence about its appropriateness in a human burial. The remains of meals placed in houses at their closing (see the earlier section, *Abandonment Deposits*) – and the beginning of construction of the next house – may also derive from sacrifices associated with these key points in the household cycle (Russell in press-a).

From this point on, reasonably persuasive evidence for sacrifice becomes more common. One basis for arguing for animal sacrifice is the presence of animal remains in human funerary contexts, as at Çayönü and Çatalhöyük. This association at least places the animal deaths in a ritual context, although as discussed earlier in the chapter, some may be remains of funerary feasts or be provisioning for the afterlife that do not necessarily derive from sacrifices. Intact animals in human graves, however, provide strong evidence for sacrifice. Complete dogs in human burials of many periods (see Chapter 7, *Man's Best Friend*) were certainly killed in a ritual context, although they may have been intended to accompany their masters in the afterworld rather than to be dedicated to a deity.

Neolithic northern France offers considerable evidence for funerary sacrifice; whether the practice was particularly prevalent in this area or whether it has received unusually careful study is unclear. From the early Neolithic, two cattle were buried in a pit associated with the long tumulus at Er Grah. They were very poorly preserved due to the acidic soil, but fortunately were carefully studied in situ by zooarchaeologists, who were able to determine that they are domestic cattle, one male and one probable female, deposited in articulation, but probably skinned (the third phalanges and tails are missing) and possibly stripped of flesh (given the tight flexion of some joints). However, the position of the ribs and sterna and paleoparasitological analysis indicate that the innards were in place. One has an arrow point between the ribs, but it is not certain that it is in situ (Tresset and Vigne 2006).

In the earlier Middle Neolithic, several human burials at the sites of de Fleury and Rots contain multiple, poorly preserved but apparently intact domestic sheep/goat carcasses. In at least one of these cases at de Fleury, a neat separation is noted between the animal and human bodies, suggesting they were separated by an organic barrier recalling the mat between sheep and human at Çatalhöyük. In the later Middle Neolithic of the region, the intact domestic animals are replaced by jewelry and objects made from wild animal parts. Notably, both wild taxa and sheep/goat are relatively uncommon in the faunal assemblages at habitation sites, which are dominated by cattle and pigs (Arbogast et al. 2002). In the Late Neolithic (Michelsberg and Chasséen cultures), a local tradition exhibits burials of red deer and dogs accompanying human burials and in the shafts of a disused flint mine. In one case, the red deer has grave goods, including a shovel made on a cattle scapula. Such ceremonial interment strongly suggests sacrifice, especially given the similar treatment accorded to the domestic dog, implying that these red deer may have been captured alive and kept for some period before sacrifice. Alternatively, they may result from a ritual hunt. The two complete red deer are both associated with arrow points that may have caused death. Dogs and red deer are a very small part of assemblages at Late Neolithic habitation sites, although marginally more common than in the Early Neolithic (Arbogast et al. 1989).

Elsewhere, we find intact horses in some graves at Middle Bronze Age Sintashta Mogila on the Russian steppe (Anthony 2007:372). At Late Bronze Age Gonur in Turkmenistan, a sacrificial pit accompanying a royal grave contains ten sacrificed humans, a small wagon, an intact dog and camel, and a headless foal. A contemporary pastoralist cemetery nearby has an adult male grave with a complete ram (Anthony 2007:427–31).

European Iron Age and early medieval burials often include animal remains, occasionally of intact animals. Again, these are overwhelmingly domestic animals and most often horses and dogs. These animals may be intended as spirit guides or guardians in the afterlife, or they may be prized possessions included as grave goods (Bond and Worley 2006; Clark 1995; Crabtree 1995; Méniel 1992; Müller 1984; Sîrbu 1993).

In the Classical period, the ancient Greeks apparently sacrificed horses only at funerals (Antikas 2006; Kosmetatou 1993; Reese 1995). Dogs are also more frequent in funerary than other contexts and, in many cases, are clearly not pet burials but offerings (De Grossi Mazzorin and Minniti 2006; De Grossi Mazzorin and Tagliacozzo 1997). The Maussolleion (Mausoleum) at Halikarnassos in modern Turkey, on the border of the Greek and Persian worlds, has a particularly striking funerary sacrifice. The extravagance of the Maussolleion, one of the seven wonders of the ancient world, extended to the sacrifice marking its closure. Outside the sealed entrance lay the remains of at least 5 cattle, 25 sheep and goats as well as 8 lambs and kids, 3 roosters, 10 hens, 1 chick, 26 chicken eggs, and 8 squabs. The animals were left whole or butchered into segments. In most cases the hides were removed, but the meat was not stripped from the bones (Højlund 1981, 1983). The large cattle would have formed a "veritable meat mountain decorated by the smaller sheep, goats and birds" (Aaris-Sørensen 1981:99).

Two cattle burials in an elite area of the Predynastic Hierakonpolis cemetery in Egypt are probably to be understood as funerary sacrifices. At least one is an aurochs (wild cattle) and is deliberately mummified (treated with herbs, wrapped in linen and reeds). The cattle were apparently deposited intact, although later disturbed (Warman 2004). A synthesis of Predynastic animal burials shows that animals buried separately from humans are all domestic (cattle, sheep, goats, dogs). Patterns of predominance of particular taxa vary through time and space within the Predynastic, but there is no indication that these animals were seen as incarnations of deities, as was the case later in Egypt. Many, perhaps all, seem to be offerings to the dead made at later commemorative ceremonies, possibly addressed to the dead in general rather than to particular deceased individuals (Flores 2003). Slightly later, and on the periphery of the Egyptian world, at the cemetery at Early Bronze Age Kerma, capital of the Nubian kingdom of Kush in northern Sudan, several elite tombs are ringed with multiple complete sheep (most are young male lambs) and goats with the occasional dog, placed intact (with skin and stomach contents preserved through desiccation). Beyond those rings are numerous joints of butchered lambs, and then, outside an encircling ditch, are numerous cattle frontlets (bucrania), as many as 400. The cattle skulls were deposited as a single event, and all show the same degree of weathering, so they were probably sacrificed at the funeral rather than being trophies of earlier sacrifices or feasts (Chaix 1989).

Even when the animal is not deposited intact, some funerary contexts suggest sacrifice rather than meat offerings. Frequently animal parts seem intended to represent the whole. The rest may have been eaten at funerary feasts, but placing nonedible pieces in the grave links the animal to the deceased and strongly suggests funerary sacrifice. In Neolithic Britain, cattle heads and hooves often accompany human burials in mounds (barrows). These cattle remains are generally considered to represent the deposition of hides of animals sacrificed and consumed at the funeral (Piggott 1962; Robertson-Mackay 1980). Head-and-hooves or skull deposits of domestic animals (horses, cattle, sheep, goats, and occasionally dogs) in human tombs are also common in the Eneolithic and Bronze Age Eurasian steppe zone, at a time when David Anthony (2007:191) argues power and prestige came to be based in large measure on the performance of public sacrifices and the ensuing provision of feasts. Often multiple animals and sometimes multiple species are represented in a single grave. An Early Bronze Age Catacomb culture grave (4500 BP) at Tsa-Tsa in the Volga region contains particularly dramatic evidence of funerary sacrifice: 3 ram skulls on the grave floor and 40 horse skulls in two rows above the grave. If these skulls represent animals sacrificed and consumed at the funeral, the meat would have fed thousands of people. Sacrificial Complex 1 at Sintashta Mogila includes a pit with the hides of six horses, four cattle, and two rams arranged in facing rows around an overturned pot. Although not on the scale of Tsa-Tsa, this assemblage equates to around 2,700 kg of meat, an impressive funeral feast (Anthony 2007). Beyond the steppe, at Early Bronze Age Alaca Höyük in Anatolia, cattle heads and hooves indicate multiple hides were placed on the roofs of royal tombs, apparently the remains of animals sacrificed and consumed at the funeral (Lloyd 1967:24).

Similarly, a woman's tomb from the Uigur Empire (ca. 1100 BP) in Mongolia contains horse remains. Careful excavation and analysis show that the horse was butchered and then partly reassembled in the grave pit next to the human body. The hind end, the front feet, and the chest are placed in anatomical position on the floor of the pit. The pit fill contains remains of the funerary feast, including more of what is probably the same horse (recognizable because of its subadult age), as well as parts of at least one other horse and at least one sheep/goat. The placement of the skull, mandibles, and hyoids of the young horse next to a post mold at the top of the kurgan indicate the head was mounted on a stake above the grave (Crubézy et al. 1996). Historical accounts describe sacrificial horses being skinned and stuffed and then set up next to the grave at Turkic funerals in Central Asia (Baldick 2000). In this case, as the front feet likely stayed with the skin, the stuffed horse may have been placed in the grave, positioned as though lying on its chest with the legs folded beneath it.

A Late Neolithic Beaker culture round barrow at Irthlingborough in England (ca. 4400 BP) is not a head-and-hooves burial, but has clear evidence for the ritual slaughter of cattle. The single high-status male in the center of the barrow is covered with a stone cairn, within which are included at least 185 skulls, 38 mandibles, 33 scapulae, and 15 pelves of cattle, with few other body parts. The scapulae bear filleting marks, showing the meat was consumed. Most of the anterior teeth are missing from the mandibles, but the teeth show little weathering; this indicates that many of the cattle remains were exposed for a relatively brief period of time (a few months) before deposition. Thus these body parts are not simply the remains of a funeral feast, although some may be. The cattle would have yielded about 40 tons of meat, too much to eat at the funeral in any case. Thus the deposit appears to include the heads of cattle kept as trophies of past feasts and likely sacrifices. Given the smaller number of scapulae and especially pelves, it is possible that these all come from the funerary sacrifices (Davis and Payne 1993). Similarly, at Eneolithic Giurgiuleşti in Romania a pit with burnt animal bones is surrounded by five human graves, at least indicating a funeral feast. Cattle skulls and other bones are also placed over the adult male grave in the group (Anthony 2007:256).

In the Near Eastern Pottery Neolithic human and animal remains are mingled in various ways that may indicate sacrifice. A foundation deposit at Tell 'Ain el-Kerkh in Syria contains the skeletons of a neonatal human infant, a six-month-old piglet, and assorted other cattle and pig bones that appear to be food remains. The human infant is intact, but the piglet has been dismembered and placed in a corner of the pit in several pieces. Akira Tsuneki (2002) rejects human sacrifice as an explanation of the presence of the infant, because there are other subfloor infant burials at the site, but suggests that the piglet may have been sacrificed for the sake of either the infant or the house. The Death Pit at Halafian Domuztepe in southeast Turkey also mixes human and animal remains. There are signs of selection of valuable adult sheep and goat, and cattle are overrepresented compared to the rest of the assemblage. Moreover, the similar treatment of the human and animal bones, all of them showing signs of consumption, is interpreted as evidence of cannibalism (Kansa and Campbell 2004). These circumstances suggest both human and animal sacrifice, followed by feasting. In middle-late Chalcolithic Cyprus, during a time of ritual florescence, funerary sacrifice is suggested by the presence of animal and bird bones in ash deposits in tombs (Keswani 1994:267).

Sacrifice is also strongly implied by burials containing wheeled vehicles (wagons, chariots) along with the horses or donkeys that drew them. These are found in large numbers on the Bronze Age Eurasian steppe and also in the Near East (Anthony 2007; Hesse and Wapnish 2002; Scurlock 2002). Similarly, in the late Chalcolithic (Baden culture) burials of intact cattle appear in Hungary and the roughly contemporary Neolithic (Corded Ware, Globular Amphora) of central Europe (Pollex 1999; Zalai-Gaál 1998). Most are single or double burials, but occasionally as many as 10 cattle are buried together. Some have been interpreted as yoked pairs of draught animals (e.g., Döhle and Stahlhofen 1985), although this interpretation has been challenged on the basis of lack of patterning in the sex of the paired animals and the frequent occurrence of calves as one of the pair (Pollex 1999; Zalai-Gaál 1998). Some of the animal burials accompany or are near human burials, whereas others are isolated. A few of the cattle have double-ended bone points between their ribs, suggesting they may have been killed by arrows or spears, whereas others show axe blows to the forehead. Although the cattle do not appear to have been consumed, they are not necessarily intact. Many were divided into halves or quarters before deposition, skulls are sometimes fragmented with the horns missing, and some lack heads or other body parts. The graves often contain ceramics associated with food and drink, suggesting that feasting formed part of the ceremony associated with the cattle deposits (Zalai-Gaál 1998). This is the time of the Secondary Products Revolution, when cattle start to be used for traction, particularly drawing vehicles (plowing may have started somewhat earlier), and cattle may have taken on value as wealth (see Chapter 8). Thus clear evidence of cattle sacrifice correlates with their enhanced value.

In southern Scandinavia, apparently sacrificed cattle appear as intact skeletons in bogs from ca. 5500 BP, 500 years after domestic cattle enter the region (Noe-Nygaard et al. 2005) and the same time that cattle burials show up across central Europe; hence they are likely part of this larger shift in the valorization of cattle. Bog deposits continue in later periods. Finds of Iron Age human bodies in bogs establish the ideological significance of these wet places. The well-preserved bodies generally show signs of being done to death, sometimes by multiple means. Although some argue these are the remains of executed criminals, disposed of in unhallowed ground, most interpret them as sacrifices to watery deities (Brothwell 1986; Glob 1988; Sanden 1996; R. Turner and Scaife 1995; Williams 2002). Bronze and Iron Age deposits of weapons and pots of food in bogs and other wet places support the notion that these bodies, and also animal deposits, are sacred offerings (Bradley 1990; Glob 1988). Several bogs in Denmark and southern Sweden, in some cases originally lakes that later became bogs, contain remains of animals, often mixed with those of humans. Some of the animal bones are butchered and processed for consumption, interpreted as the remains of sacrificial feasts, whereas others are complete but defleshed skeletons. Horses and to some extent cattle are often represented by heads, feet, and tails, suggesting the deposition of the valuable hides. The structure of many of these deposits shows that they were used repeatedly through time. Nearly all the animal remains are of domestic animals, but the proportions, again favoring horse and dog followed by cattle, differ from contemporary settlements, where sheep/goat predominates, followed by cattle (Boessneck et al. 1967; Hagberg 1967; Jankuhn 1967).

Perhaps a dry-land version of bog deposits has been found in Iron Age Durezza Cave in Austria. During the late Hallstatt and early La Tène periods both human and animal bodies were thrown into this chimney cave. The deposit includes the remains of 138 people, of all ages and both sexes, that may be either sacrifices or secondary burials. The animal remains are nearly all domestic, with the few wild animals probably victims of this natural trap. The domestic animals are primarily dogs, followed by horses with occasional others. The dogs are mostly adult, but the horses and other animals are primarily infantile and juvenile. Butcher marks and articulations show that the animal remains were mostly thrown in as dismembered joints with the meat still on. In contrast, in the nearby settlement, animal bones are much more chopped and fragmented, and dog and horse remains are rare. The ages of the young animals suggest seasonal ceremonies in early spring and early autumn (Galik 2004).

In Africa we also find evidence of sacrifice of cattle (and a few sheep, goat, and dog) through animal burials at Nabta Playa in the Egyptian Western Desert and a considerable cluster in the vicinity of the Aïr Mountains in Niger and nearby in Libya, in the central Sahara. Although some may be natural deaths covered by drifting sand, many are clearly deliberate burials. Preservation in the sandy soil is less than perfect, but one displays cut marks on the fifth cervical vertebra indicative of slitting the throat, and a few have been butchered and then reassembled in the grave. Some are covered with small stone tumuli. The Nabta Playa burials date to ca. 7300 BP, whereas the central Saharan burials begin around 7100 BP and continue through ca. 2500 BP (di Lernia 2006; Paris 2000). These burials might mark the spread of cattle pastoralism across the Sahara, or the origin and spread of a new rite, which di Lernia suggests might be related to rain making in a time of desiccation. He also links these burials to the origin of Herskovits' (1926) "African cattle complex" (see Chapter 8), although the sacrifice here takes a different form, with cattle apparently deposited unconsumed, in contrast to ethnographic "cattle complex" practice. If this linkage is correct, the development of wealth value is implicated at this point, conceivably driven by the demand for sacrificial victims for a rain ceremony. Although sacrifice in sub-Saharan Africa has received extensive ethnographic attention, I know of no reported archaeological evidence. In part, this is due to the generally small number of Holocene African sites excavated, and in part no doubt to practices that render it archaeologically obscure (Insoll 2010), but perhaps more thought needs to be given to investigating the time depth of African sacrifice.

Thanks to the extremely arid conditions in some parts of the Andean region, sacrificial victims are sometimes preserved with their soft parts as natural mummies, providing richer information than usual about the method of slaughter and choice of animals. Apparently only domestic animals were sacrificed. Guinea pigs are found as foundation deposits below floors starting in the earliest urban society at Chavín de Huantar. From the subsequent Early Intermediate period, some of the guinea pigs have slit bellies, which is ethnographically associated with sacrifice for divination. From at least the Late Intermediate period, in the early first millennium BP, llamas and alpacas are also sacrificed, sometimes together with guinea pigs. When the two species are paired, their fur color matches, suggesting that color was significant for the sacrificial purpose. Some of the sacrificial victims have small offerings with them, such as beads or feathers. At Late Intermediate El Yaral, guinea pigs were sacrificed by breaking the necks, cutting the throats, or beheading, with the head placed beside them, but the bellies were not slit (Rofes 2004). During the Inca period, guinea pigs with slit bellies appear again (Sandweiss and Wing 1997), and all communities were required to make regular llama sacrifices that were then consumed (Brotherston 1989:246).

Another strong case for prehistoric sacrifice can be made at Iron Age sanctuaries: ritual sites spatially separated from settlements that are best known from the La Tène of northern France. Méniel (1992) offers a thorough zooarchaeological analysis of these sites, explicitly evaluating the presence and nature of animal sacrifice. Animal remains are deposited in pits and encircling ditches, exhibiting spatial structuring. Some show signs of consumption, and arguably they are feasting remains unrelated to sacrifice. However, their context and special treatment indicate sacrifice, and we know from limited classical accounts of these Gallic groups that, like the Romans, they commonly ate the animals they sacrificed. Contextual analysis shows differing treatment of the various taxa (mainly cattle, horses, pigs, sheep, and dogs) at all the sanctuaries, although the details vary from one site to another. Careful excavation and thoughtful zooarchaeological analysis permit Méniel to establish that dogs at Vertault were buried intact, not gutted to examine the entrails, because partially digested bones attesting stomach contents are found in the abdominal area. Horses found in mass burials at Vertault, however, although apparently complete, were gutted, because large stones and in one case a displaced skull are found in the chest cavity, and the ribs do not lie as they would if the abdominal cavity had been full.

At some sanctuaries sacrificed animals were subjected to more elaborate treatment. Cattle at Gournay were first exposed in a pit, while their skulls were displayed in the sanctuary. Later, perhaps on the occasion of the next sacrifice months or years later, the remains were removed from the pit, leaving behind a few small bones, and deposited partially articulated in the ditch accompanied by large quantities of weapons. The skulls were placed on top still later, just before the next set of cattle remains were moved to the ditch. The balance of taxa varies among the sites, but is always substantially different from that at contemporary habitation sites.

Given classical accounts of spectacular Celtic "wicker man" sacrifices with multiple animals burnt alive inside a massive wicker figure (Green 1992), burnt bones at sanctuaries are of interest. Whereas the ditches at Quimper include burnt remains of apparently complete animals that might derive from such a sacrifice, the pit at the same site and the burnt animal remains from Estrées-Saint-Denis represent limited body parts; at Estrées-Saint-Denis these seem to be butchery waste (Méniel 1992).

Similar practices are still in evidence in the early medieval period at the sanctuary at Arkona in Germany. Arkona lacks the relatively intact animals buried in pits seen at the Gallic sanctuaries. However, the sacred setting makes sacrifice likely, and the mortality profile of the animal remains includes more young animals than in contemporary settlements, with an indication of late summer ceremonies. Almost all remains (98%) are from domestic animals. All body parts are present, showing that they were brought to the sanctuary for sacrifice rather than arriving as joints of meat. Afterward they were processed and eaten as on settlement sites (Müller 1984).

Similarly, deposits of skulls, articulated spines, and butchered bones in the ditches of causewayed enclosures in Neolithic Britain are also likely to be the remains of ceremonial feasts and perhaps sacrifices (Grigson 1984). Where they can be sexed, all are female (Grigson 1984:215). Generally females are considered more valuable than males; hence they are a significant sacrifice. However, with cattle used for traction, adult males and especially castrates also carry great value, so the calculus is less clear. Further support for the importance of sacrifice at this period comes from a recent reinterpretation of the stone and metal daggers of the Late Neolithic-Bronze Age in Scandinavia and adjacent areas that are such a strong marker of male identity (although occasionally found with women) not as weapons of war, but instruments of sacrifice (Skak-Nielsen 2009).

As discussed earlier, there is ethnohistorical evidence for dog sacrifice in Native North America, especially the northeast. Contextual zooarchaeology has identified some likely prehistoric instances, although differing somewhat from the ethnographic descriptions. In several cases dogs were butchered and probably consumed, with the bones subsequently bundled together and buried. One is from the Terminal Woodland near

Lake Superior, ca. 600–800 BP, at a special-purpose site that otherwise has mainly beaver bones (Clark 1990). At least six bundles from the 9th century BP on Lake Huron were placed individually on the ground surface at the Frank Bay site, and soil was then mounded over them. Some have red ochre and quartz crystals, typically human grave goods, and several show cut marks on the cervical vertebrae that testify to the slitting of their throats. Again, beaver and muskrat dominate the Frank Bay faunal assemblage apart from these burials (Brizinski and Savage 1983). Puppy remains at the Rhoads site, a protohistoric Kickapoo settlement in Illinois, may reflect the historically known Kickapoo practice of raising specially fed puppies for sacrifice (Parmalee and Klippel 1983).

In the American Southwest, signs of deliberate killing and special deposition indicate dog sacrifice. Dog burials predate other animal interments in the region, starting ca. 2500 BP, although they become more common and elaborate after 1000 BP. Apparent dog sacrifices often mark the closing of both pithouses and kivas, providing ritual evidence of continuity between these structures. In the Southwest, earlier groups lived in semi-subterranean pithouses, whereas later people built pueblos with rectangular rooms for residence and storage. However, the ceremonial structures, kivas, are round and sunken, and they are generally seen as a survival of the pithouses in the ritual sphere. Humans were also used as deconsecration sacrifices for kivas, so dogs may have once again served as substitutes for humans (Hill 2000). Possible dog sacrifice is also reported from southern California, where a double dog burial is dated to ca. 700 BP (Vellanoweth et al. 2008).

In addition to dogs, bird sacrifice was widespread in the later Southwest. All the birds sacrificed seem to have been raised in the villages; they include domestic turkeys, two species of macaws and three species of parrots imported from the south and in some cases bred locally, and raptors captured as chicks. Ethnography and art indicate that feather acquisition was a major motivation for raising these birds. The macaws were typically sacrificed as soon as they grew adult feathers. However, because the feathers could have been plucked without killing the birds (indeed, macaws can potentially live for decades and provide multiple feather harvests), sacrifice may have been ritually necessary to the process of feather acquisition. After plucking, and often removal of the head, which might be buried separately, the birds were buried as ceremonial trash, in one case wrapped in strings of beads (Creel and McKusick 1994; Hill 2000).

In California, there is also both ethnographic and archaeological evidence that young raptors were captured to raise for their feathers. Some were eventually released, but sacrifice is also documented, for example at the funerals of Chumash chiefs. Bird burials, including condors, are probably remains of such practices (Simons 1983).

In Mesoamerica, there is ethnohistorical evidence of dog and turkey sacrifice, and also that women raised captive deer and peccaries for sacrifice, in particular at calendrical festivals (Masson 1999; Pohl and Feldman 1982; White et al. 2001). Archaeologically, stable isotope analysis shows that dogs, but not deer, from ceremonial contexts at Preclassic Colha were fed a special diet of maize, whereas other dogs scavenged the remains of human meals (White et al. 2001). This suggests that at this point dogs, but not captive wild animals, were specially raised for sacrifice. However, at Late Classic Lagartero, not only some dogs but also a few deer must have been fed maize, and hence were captive most of their lives. Recovered from a feasting context, these animals were very likely victims of sacrifice (White et al. 2004).

Classical archaeology has a long, if uneven, tradition of paying attention to sacrifice, because it is so clearly attested in texts and artistic representations. Moreover, until recently classical archaeology's focus has been on public buildings such as temples and palaces, where sacrifice is likely to have occurred. Some analyses have simply assumed that any animal bones found in or near temples are the remains of sacrifices, whereas more recent analyses usually include more sophisticated contextual and taphonomic studies to establish the link to temple use. Newer studies are also more likely to compare these assemblages to those found in secular contexts to illuminate the place of sacrificial practice in the economy. So far, these comparisons seem much more common in Roman archaeology than in that of ancient Greece. However, a study of the animal bone assemblage from the sanctuary at Mycenaean Phylakopi on Melos, comparing it to residential areas, indicates that the faunal remains at the sanctuary are probably unrelated to its use and do not constitute the remains of sacrifices (Gamble 1985). Only recently has it become routine for classical archaeologists to collect animal bones or to use screening to collect them systematically, impairing the ability of zooarchaeology to provide insights into sacrifice as well as other animal-related issues (Reese 1994). This is a pity, because zooarchaeologists have contributed significant insights where they have been able to study sacrifice effectively.

Paintings of people leaping over bulls and architectural embellishment with stylized bull horns (horns of consecration) indicate the importance of cattle in the Minoan (see Chapter 2, *Bullfights and Bull Games*). However, there has been considerable debate about whether the bull games were part of a sacrificial ritual and about the nature and even existence of Minoan sacrifice in general. Martin Nilsson (1927) and John D. Evans (1963) assumed the bulls used in games were then sacrificed, with their skulls (bucrania) displayed as trophies and inspiring the horns of consecration. Depictions of sacrifice show animals being stabbed with daggers, but Nilsson thought the labrys (double axe), another pervasive Minoan symbol, was used as a poleax to stun the cattle first (cf. Cromarty 2008:13).

Edmund Bloedow (1996) challenges the existence of Minoan sacrifice. He suggests that bucrania and other horns are actually hunting trophies, in some cases offered at what amount to hunting shrines (see the earlier section, *Hunting Shrines*). Because many of these horns derive from wild (actually feral, see Chapter 7, *Island Introductions*) animals, and most of the animals depicted on Minoan seals are also feral (notably the agrimi, or feral goat), he rejects the possibility that they were sacrificed; instead he interprets the association of these animals with weapons on the seals as hunting scenes. However, one of the seals – depicting an agrimi kneeling at an altar with a dagger poised at its throat – is hard not to read as sacrifice. This raises the intriguing question of whether Minoan sacrifice is exceptional in focusing on wild animals. In addition to the depictions of agrimi with daggers on seals, cattle remains from ritual contexts have been identified as wild (i.e., feral; Nobis 1988, 1990, 1993; Sakellarakis 1971). However, sheep/goat, not cattle, predominate in Minoan faunal assemblages from ritual contexts (Cromarty 2008). Nanno Marinatos (1988) has interpreted the evidence from depictions to indicate that Minoan sacrifice was a ritualized form of hunting, in line with Burkert's theories, whereas later Greek sacrifice was more about offerings to the gods.

A further point of discussion concerns the antiquity of burnt offerings in the Greek tradition. Such offerings are mentioned in Homer, but could be an anachronism introduced later. Birgitta Bergquist (1988) argues there is no archaeological evidence for burnt sacrifice in the Bronze Age Greek world, but ample such evidence for the Iron Age. So far, this seems to hold true for the Minoan (Bronze Age Crete), in which Marinatos (1988) believes sacrifice emphasized blood libations rather than burnt offerings (both present in later classical sacrifice). However, on mainland Greece at roughly contemporary Mycenaean sites, recent work has clearly demonstrated the occurrence of burnt offerings. At the Palace of Nestor at Pylos most of the faunal remains appear to be ordinary postconsumption waste, but there are six concentrations of burnt bone with a distinctive character. Five of these were found in discrete deposits on the periphery of the palace, and one was found in Room 7. All six are made up almost entirely of burnt cattle bones. One of the groups was too small to quantify meaningfully in terms of body parts; mandibles, humeri, and femora dominate the remaining five (including Room 7). The groups contain remains of 5–11 individual cattle each; two of them also have the same body parts from a red deer. Where age can be determined, the animals are all subadult or adult, and most or all are male. The groups found peripheral to the palace are all deposited in unburnt matrix, so the burning occurred elsewhere and the remains were gathered up for disposal, raising the possibility that these result from discrete events in which multiple cattle and the occasional red deer were sacrificed. Butcher marks show that the animals were dismembered and defleshed; the meat was presumably consumed in an associated feast, and the selected bones were burnt complete (not broken for marrow). The group found in Room 7 is particularly important in establishing that these bones are the remains of sacrifice. Along with the remains of 10 cattle, the room contained a giant pithos and 20–22 miniature cups (kylikes), a sword, a spearhead, and more than 200 Linear B tablets. The room is interpreted as belonging to an archivist or accountant, who monitored tablets before storage in the archive in adjacent Room 8. These items were all found on the floor, covered by the final destruction layer of the palace. Therefore they are interpreted as selected items serving as vouchers of a sacrifice and feast, with the weapons probably used in the sacrifice, and all being verified by the accountant before archiving the records (Isaakidou et al. 2002; Stocker and Davis 2004). Given that this process was still in progress at the time of the destruction of the palace, perhaps the sacrificial event was part of rallying warriors for battle. In any case, it seems clear that periodic sacrifices at the palace offered bulls or oxen, and sometimes also wild (or tame?) red deer, and that selected body parts were burnt as offerings after the meat was stripped from them.

Further recent evidence for Mycenaean burnt sacrifice comes from a sanctuary at Ayios Konstantinos in the northeast Peleponnesos. Yannis

Hamilakis and Eleni Konsolaki (2004) compare the faunal assemblages from three rooms in this sanctuary; based on the artifactual assemblages, the fill of Rooms B and C is ordinary waste, whereas Room A had a ritual function. The faunal assemblages also differ. The mostly unburnt bone from Rooms B and C is 75% sheep/goat with 7% pig; there are a few juvenile animals but most are adults. In Room A, most of the bone is burnt, and although 34% is sheep/goat, most is from neonatal piglets. A few cut marks indicate dismemberment and filleting, thus implying that at least some of the meat was removed and consumed before burning the entire skeleton of the piglets. Burnt sacrifice is clearly attested here, although with a different focus and on a smaller scale than at Pylos; Hamilakis suggests this difference in scale and content reflects a contextual distinction between sanctuaries and palaces.

In Iron Age classical Greece (here defined broadly to include the Geometric, Archaic, Classical, and Hellenistic periods), the presence and nature of burnt offerings are attested much more clearly. Literary references describe the offering of thigh bones (femora) wrapped in fat, and this is supported by archaeological evidence. However, there had been more disagreement about which body part a thin curly object in artistic depictions of sacrifice represented. Zooarchaeology has settled the question: It is the tail or, rather, the upper part of the tail bones (caudal vertebrae) attached to the sacrum. Many sites associated with temples and sanctuaries in Greece and Asia Minor (Anatolia) contain deposits of burnt femora, patellae (evidently left attached to the femora), sacra, and caudal vertebrae, or else unburnt deposits missing these parts (Benecke 2006; Bergquist 1988; Chenal-Vélardé and Studer 2003; Durand 1987; Forstenpointner 2003; Forstenpointner et al. 1999; Peters 1993; Reese 1989; Van Straten 1988, 1995; Vila 2000).

Texts and artistic depictions indicate that the fleeting sacrificial ceremony was often commemorated with an inscription or a votive offering, or by hanging the skull of the sacrificial victim on the wall of the temple or of the house in the case of domestic sacrifices (Van Straten 1995). This practice is remarkably rarely attested archaeologically. The Artemision at Ephesos in Asia Minor has concentrations of goat horn cores with a few from cattle and sheep along with some fallow deer antlers, in addition to the remains of burnt offerings, but the horns are chopped off and the rest of the skull seems to have left with the hide (Bammer et al. 1978; Forstenpointner et al. 1999). Simon Davis (1996) notes a different pattern of body part selection at the Archaic sanctuary of Apollo Hylates at Kourion, in southern Cyprus: the faunal remains are nearly all sheep/goat and are heavily biased to the right hindlimb. However, the right hindlimb is not just the thigh, but runs from the hip joint (detached from the pelvis) to the ankle (astragalus and calcaneus). Davis suggests this body part selection may be a Cypriot practice; certainly it would be instructive to pay attention to preferences for side as well as body part in other such deposits.

Ancient Greek literature suggests that specific taxa were sacrificed to particular deities. We need more well-studied assemblages to assess the extent to which this actually happened. My survey of published studies covers a range of deities, but only a few have had more than one temple assemblage analyzed. In all cases, sheep, goat, cattle, and pig form the vast majority of the offerings, with small amounts of other domestic animals and often a few wild taxa as well (Bammer et al. 1978; Davis 1996; Forstenpointner et al. 1999; Jarman 1973; Nobis 1997; Reese 1989; Vila 2000; Villari 1991). Sheep/goat is almost always the most frequent taxon. The main hint of taxon selection for a particular deity involves pigs for Demeter. Pig remains are somewhat more frequent than cattle and sheep/goat during the Archaic and Classical periods at the temple of the Heroes and Demeter at Messene in the Peloponnesos, and equally frequent in the Hellenistic period (Nobis 1997). Pig also forms 80% or more of the faunal remains from the Classical period at the temple of Demeter at Knossos on Crete (Jarman 1973). Although dogs do not form part of the usual set of sacrificial animals, there are signs of occasional dog and especially puppy sacrifice in several places in the ancient Greek world. Literary evidence indicates that dogs were sacrificed only to chthonic deities and never eaten (i.e., burnt or otherwise destroyed in a holocaust), but archaeological evidence shows they were (infrequently) offered to a wide range of deities and sometimes eaten (Roy 2007).

Based on literary evidence, Marcel Detienne (1979) proposes that all meat in classical Greece was derived from sacrifice. Most scholars have accepted this view, with the exception of wild game, which formed a very small part of the ancient Greek diet (Jameson 1988:87–8). According to this view, all meat from domestic animals was either consumed at the temple in the feast following the sacrifice, or bought from butchers who in turn purchased surplus sacrificial meat from the temples. If this were true, archaeologists would be justified in treating faunal assemblages from temples as an accurate record of the Greek pastoral economy, as indeed many have. Of course, the indications of at least partial selection of particular kinds of animals for different gods mean that no single temple assemblage should be taken as representative. Yet surely it is possible that slaughter outside the sacred sphere was simply not mentioned in the texts, or that every Greek slaughter was a sacrifice, but some (many?) animals were sacrificed at a household level. These home sacrifices might be selected quite differently from the animals offered in public ceremonies.

Greek temple sacrifice occurred at such a scale that it would have both shaped herding practices to supply the required animals and reflected the realities of herding practices necessary to sustain a viable flock. Yet was the temple economy in fact equivalent to the entire Greek herding economy? Zooarchaeology is well suited to answer this question. Unfortunately, there is a dearth of studies of faunal assemblages from secular contexts in the Classical period, perhaps because archaeologists are convinced that all slaughter took place at temples. Although it is very instructive to compare sacred and secular assemblages from the same site or from contemporary sites in the same region, I have been able to find no such matched comparisons in Greece proper during the Classical period. Indeed, I have located only three assemblages from residential contexts, two of them rather small. At Nichoria, near Kalamata in the Peloponnese, the Geometric assemblage is dominated by cattle (40% by number of identified specimens [NISP] ), with substantial amounts of sheep/goat (25%) and pig (24%). Given the limited sample size (140 NISP), body part distribution appears even, suggesting that this assemblage does not represent limited cuts of meat bought from a butcher. Sheep and goats tend to be slaughtered during the first two years, but all ages are present, indicating a mixed meat/milk/wool herding strategy (Sloan and Duncan 1978). At Lerna, in the Argolid, the Classical deposits are small and mostly from wells, which may contain ritual deposits. More than half the bones are from two articulated dog skeletons; whether these are offerings or disposal of natural deaths, they are not food remains. If we exclude the dog and the small amount of nonmammalian remains, we are left with 50 identified specimens, of which 42% are sheep/goat (all identified to species are goat), 38% cattle, 18% pig, and 4% donkey (Gejvall 1969). Kassope in Epirus is the only substantial sample, with ca. 36,000 specimens. It is from the Hellenistic period, however, so it may not be an appropriate model for Classical period economies, narrowly defined. Here it is clear that the faunal assemblage is secular postconsumption waste. Although there are some birds (mostly chicken), fish, tortoise, and shellfish, mammals overwhelmingly dominate the assemblage. The majority (82%) of the mammals are domestic; of these, 45% are sheep/goat, 31% pig, 21% cattle, 3% equid, and 1% dog. The wild animals are 81% red deer, 11% wild boar, 6% roe deer, and 2% hare (all percentages based on NISP). The sheep/goat and cattle are mostly adults, suggesting a herding strategy oriented to secondary products: dairy and traction from the cattle, wool from the sheep, dairy from the goats and perhaps also sheep. The pigs, used only for meat, were killed younger, but not as infants; perhaps they were a complement to the suckling pigs often found in sacrificial assemblages (Boessneck 1994).

These few scattered residential assemblages are insufficient to provide a meaningful comparison to temple deposits. Intriguingly, they raise the possibility that cattle are under- rather than overrepresented in sacrificial assemblages, despite the belief that cattle were the ideal sacrificial animal (Jameson 1988). There was a general prohibition on the sacrifice of working cattle, however, and the Kassope evidence suggests that working cattle may have included a substantial part of the cattle population.

Beyond Greece proper, there is somewhat more evidence indicating that sacrifice was not the exclusive source of domestic meat. James Roy (2007) argues that the ancient Greeks did eat meat not derived from sacrifice, which was sold in a special area of the market, but was considered inferior. Donkey and dog meat largely fell in this category; neither was raised for meat, but could be consumed. Peters (1993) provides an all too rare example of a direct comparison of associated residential and temple assemblages, from Archaic Milet in Asia Minor (Turkey). Kalabak Tepe is a settlement, and the adjacent Zeytin Tepe is its associated sanctuary to Aphrodite. At Kalabak Tepe, nearly all the animal bones derive from domestic sheep/goat (64%), cattle (23%), and pig (11%). Butchering marks show that horse and dog were also occasionally eaten, along with a very small amount of game and fish. Sheep and goat were mostly slaughtered in the late juvenile–early adult range, whereas most cattle were subadults and adults; pigs were killed in the infantile–juvenile stages. This finding suggests that sheep/goat were kept primarily for secondary products (Milet was famous for its wool in slightly later times), and the cattle for traction. At Zeytin Tepe, the animal bones were found together with votive offerings. Sheep/goat is still more dominant (90%), with cattle accounting for virtually all of the remaining 10%. Pig may be lacking because it was not considered a suitable sacrifice to Aphrodite. The animals in the temple assemblage are generally younger than those in the town, with the sheep/goat mostly early juveniles and the cattle infantile–juvenile. It may be that all the domestic animals at Kalabak Tepe were sacrificed in a household context, but it is certainly not the case that the residents were obtaining all their meat from sacrifices at the sanctuary.

This study suggests that we should be very cautious in reading pastoral economy directly from temple assemblages alone, and that there is a crying need for the excavation and faunal analysis of more residential areas from the classical Greek world. Temple assemblages show a variety of mortality profiles, with cattle tending to the older age ranges, sheep/goat to juvenile–subadult, and pigs to younger ages, but with considerable variability (Bammer et al. 1978; Davis 1996; Forstenpointner et al. 1999; Nobis 1997; Reese 1989; Vila 2000; Villari 1991). It is likely that there is some degree of selection for sacrifice in most cases, according to the deity involved and local custom. We should not assume that these assemblages represent the entire herding strategy of these areas, although sacrificial requirements will surely have affected herding strategies as well as responding to availability.

The situation is considerably different for the Romans. First, it is agreed that, although sacrifice was important in Roman society and sacrificial meat remained more highly valued, there also existed a secular market for meat (Gilhus 2006:17, 115–16). Second, there has been considerably more zooarchaeological study of Roman assemblages, if somewhat unevenly distributed across the territory of the Roman Empire, and there are numerous comparisons of sacred and residential faunal assemblages.

Roman sacrificial practice appears to be a blend of Greek and local Italian traditions. The *suovitaurilia* – sacrifice of a pig, sheep, and cow – was an important Roman ceremony, particularly as a rite of purification in various contexts. Archaeologists have traced its roots, in the form of votive deposits of sacrificial remains with this combination of animals, back to the Chalcolithic in Italy. In the Roman period, adult male animals were chosen, but this was not always the case earlier. Goats and dogs also appear in small numbers in many of these pre-Roman deposits (Prummel and Bouma 1997; Wilkens 2004). Dog sacrifice was a widespread if minor

Greek practice, and the same is true of the Romans. Local Italian pre-Roman Iron Age societies also sacrificed dogs and frequently consumed them afterward (De Grossi Mazzorin and Minniti 2006; Wilkens 1997). However, there is not complete continuity from earlier Italian societies to the Romans. Graeme Barker (1989) documents changes in the selection of sacrificial victims among the Samnites of south central Italy in the third millennium BP. In the earlier period, sheep and goat dominate faunal assemblages in settlements, whereas sacrificial assemblages are biased toward pigs. After the Romans conquered the Samnites, the balance of taxa does not differ between residential and sacrificial assemblages.

Textual sources indicate there was some degree of selection of taxa for specific deities, although cattle, sheep, and goat were suitable for all gods, and pigs for most. It is less clear whether other attributes such as sex and color were prescribed (Kadletz 1976). The *suovitaurilia* is in evidence beyond Italy, with a foundation deposit of skulls from a pig, sheep, and cow at a Roman temple at Elst in the Netherlands. Here and elsewhere nearby, young cattle are selected for sacrifice; otherwise they were rarely killed before a long life of labor (Lauwerier 2004). Demeter continues to receive pigs disproportionately: At Roman Cyrene in Libya pigs (most of them young) form 78% of the sacrificial remains from the sanctuary of Demeter and Persephone, with sheep/goat 17% and cattle 3%. In the nearby settlement of Berenice, sheep/goat strongly predominates. A discrete deposit of pelves and femora with ash is interpreted as the remains of portions offered to the gods, whereas the rest of the pigs were consumed in feasts at the sanctuary (Crabtree and Monge 1987). In contrast, at two Romano-British temples in Essex (Harlow and Great Chesterford), almost solely lambs were sacrificed. The age distributions indicate autumn sacrifice at Harlow, and spring and autumn at Great Chesterford, revealing a seasonal sacrificial calendar. Moreover, at Great Chesterford the body parts are mainly heads, feet, and right forelimbs. Phalanges, however, are lacking and probably stayed with the hide, which was removed. At the temple we may be seeing the primary butchery waste along with the priests' portion, consisting of the right foreleg, with the rest taken for consumption elsewhere (Legge et al. 2000). The thousands of lambs sacrificed at Great Chesterford, probably bought from local farmers, must have exerted a significant influence on regional herding strategies. In particular, the neonatal lambs sacrificed in the spring at Great Chesterford would have enabled dairy production. Anthony Legge

suggests that indeed these sacrifices would have pushed local sheep farmers to dairy, as the only viable strategy with that kill-off pattern. My
childhood neighbors in New Hampshire raised sheep largely to supply
the local Greek community with Easter lambs, however, although they
also harvested some wool (but they milked only their goats). Thus the
lambs may themselves have been the major product in such a situation,
dampening wool production.

In the later Near East, most of our knowledge of sacrifice comes
from texts. Archaeological evidence provides general support for textual descriptions, but as in the Classical world it also shows a somewhat
broader range of sacrificial practice. Throughout the area in the Bronze
and Iron Ages, sheep and goats dominate faunal assemblages in general
and also form the primary sacrificial victims, although particular deities
have special requirements (Borowski 2002; Scurlock 2002).

In Mesopotamia, the meat from sacrifices was offered to the gods on
temple tables for their symbolic consumption and then distributed to
be eaten by humans elsewhere. As a result, temples tend to be empty of
animal remains. A notable exception is the Seleucid (late third millennium
BP) temple to Śamas at Larsa (Iraq), which was destroyed while still in
use, preserving the offerings in place. Here we find jars full of bones that
apparently represent meat for distribution, the axial bones (spine and ribs)
already largely removed and discarded. The bones are mainly sheep, with
a little camel. There are also a few donkey bones, including a skull with a
fracture on the forehead showing it was poleaxed; therefore equids were
occasionally sacrificed outside funerary contexts, at least here (Mashkour
et al. 1998). Another such case is the sacrifice of several donkeys and
three humans as part of the closing ritual for a monumental building at
Tell Brak, Syria (Oates et al. 2008).

In the Levant we see evidence for a sacrifice that was not consumed
in the form of seven to nine sheep and two goats – complete but with
cut marks on the atlas showing their throats were cut – in a pit at Middle
Bronze Age Kamid el-Loz in Lebanon. There are no other butcher marks,
so they were not eaten (Bökönyi 1993). In the Jordan Valley, sheep
and goats are even more common in the sacrificial assemblage at Tell
el-Hayyat than in settlements. At Tell Haror in the Negev, however,
they form only 62% of the assemblage at a temple complex, with dog
contributing an unusually high 5%. In the courtyard were votive deposits
consisting of puppies and birds buried with votive vessels (Nakhai 2001).

Although the Book of Leviticus specifies the right thigh as the priests'
portion of the sacrifice (Borowski 2002), some Late Bronze and Iron
Age Levantine sites have accumulations of right sheep/goat metacarpals
(a meatless portion), suggesting they were left as offerings to represent
the animal (Nakhai 2001). Alternatively, perhaps these bones are related
to beliefs about the powers of cattle forelimbs in Egypt (see the earlier
section, *Foundation Deposits*, and note that the foundation deposits at
Thebes also contained right forefeet). At a Phoenician temple on Malta
the sacrifices (96% sheep and goat, most of the rest cattle) were consumed
on the spot in a feast for the worshippers, as in the Classical world
(Corrado et al. 2004).

Sacrifice has a long history in China, with complete skeletons of one-
year-old pigs buried in pits at Early Neolithic Cishan (ca. 9000 BP),
sometimes covered by large amounts of millet (Jing and Flad 2002). Pig
and dog burials interpreted as sacrifice are found at later Neolithic sites,
with cattle appearing at the Late Neolithic Longshan culture site of Shan-
taisi. The Early Bronze Age Shang Dynasty is known for its spectacular
funerary sacrifices of animals and humans. With the earliest Chinese texts,
written on oracle bones (see the later section, *Divination*), we know that
the Shang court practiced animal sacrifice much more broadly: "For the
Shang, animal sacrifice was a critical aspect of the cosmological system
and was also an activity that increasingly served to create and strengthen
the power of the Shang royalty by emphasizing the ritual significance of
animals that were disproportionately controlled by the elite. In this way,
the control of sacrificial activity seems to have been a crucial aspect of the
emergence of the state in China" (Yuan and Flad 2005:253). Although
the texts indicate that wild animals were occasionally sacrificed, most victims were domestic pigs, cattle, sheep, or dogs; human sacrifice is also
frequent. The occasional wild animals in sacrificial contexts may have been
tamed individuals owned by royalty. Cattle were the preferred Shang sacrificial victim, and requirements for age, sex, color, and the like probably
shaped herding practices (Li 2007).

Archaeological evidence from Shang sites shows more pig burials,
in some cases apparently trussed up and buried alive; however, more
commonly they were deposited after death, most often complete but
sometimes missing the head or split lengthwise. Other pits contain dogs
(again, some apparently trussed up and buried alive) or complete cattle
or cattle skulls, and some combine segments of cattle, pig, and sheep, and

sometimes humans. At Anyang there are also chariot burials with teams of two or four horses and other horse deposits, as well as pits with deer, monkeys, turtles, fish, and birds, although most sacrificial deposits contain domestic animals. Generally pigs and to a lesser extent dogs are the foci of sacrifice in earlier periods, shifting later to cattle and finally horses in the late Shang Dynasty. The combinations of animals found in archaeological sacrificial deposits do not wholly correspond to those prescribed for various purposes in the texts, suggesting there may have been greater flexibility than the textual evidence would indicate. Archaeologically, sacrifices are related to the foundation, construction, and completion of buildings, as well as to funerals (Fiskesjö 2001; Yuan and Flad 2005).

EVALUATING SACRIFICE

This incomplete survey of sacrificial practice around the world and through time permits us to evaluate some aspects of the theories of sacrifice reviewed earlier, most of which are based on restricted geographic and temporal evidence. One point of contention is whether only domestic animals can be sacrificed. The archaeological, ethnographic, and historical records clearly show that it is overwhelmingly domestic animals that are sacrificed. However, there are occasional but persistent (although not universal) exceptions. In some cases, these exceptions could easily be seen as a secondary application of sacrificial logic, developed around domestic animals, to their wild counterparts to make a symbolic statement. This might apply to the low level of wild animal sacrifice in the Classical world, for example. The limited archaeological evidence so far available would also support such an interpretation for Mesoamerica, with sacrifice first applied to dogs and later extended to deer and peccaries. However, there are a few cases, such as Ainu and Siberian bear ceremonies, in which the ritual killing of wild bears exhibits all the hallmarks of sacrifice. However, these bears are captured as cubs and raised for an extended period in preparation for sacrifice. This practice indicates that the reason domestic animals are generally favored is not so much because they are property and therefore constitute a genuine loss (sacrifice), but that they are sufficiently identified with the sacrificer to serve as a substitute in communications with the divine (Hamayon 1990).

This substitution means that the sacrificial victim can take on a scapegoat role, embodying human illness, sins, or misfortune so that they can be destroyed with the animal. Such a role seems to be sporadic rather than universal, however, and often figures in only some ceremonies within the sacrificial practice of particular societies. It is therefore unlikely to represent the essence or archetype of sacrifice, as Freud (1918) and René Girard (1972) argue. There is considerable variation in the degree to which the killing itself and the violent aspects of sacrifice are emphasized within the larger ritual. In some cases the killing is so blasé and unmarked that ethnographers have hesitated to label the ceremony a sacrifice (e.g., Bloch 1985; Humphrey and Laidlaw 2007), although teasing and tormenting the animal may precede its routine slaughter. Archaeologically, this disinterest in the violent aspect may be seen in representations of sacrifice that focus on moments other than the killing. In other cases the killing is dramatic. Theories of sacrifice that characterize it as channeling violent impulses into acceptable behavior thus do not appear universally applicable. The surprise some feel at the lack of focus on the slaughter itself may say more about the nature of the modern west, where animal slaughter is hidden and its ritualization therefore dramatic, than societies where slaughter is a familiar part of meat production that does not seem out of the ordinary.

Our survey of sacrificial practice reveals that sacrifice is embedded in larger social relations. It is most often linked to feasting, and the sharing out of sacrificial meat resembles the careful division and distribution of game (see Chapter 9). Often the preferred sacrificial victim is the animal that serves as wealth and mediates most human relations, as with cattle in Africa, although the main sacrificial animal is not always symbolically laden in other contexts (e.g., Shanklin 1983). Generally, however, use in sacrifice tends to valorize animal taxa or categories (of age, sex, color, etc.) and may provide a major motivation for raising them (Gibson 1988). In the ethnographic literature we have encountered several clear cases of herding strategies shaped by sacrificial requirements, and this is likely to happen wherever sacrifice is practiced to a significant extent. In those cases where every slaughter is a sacrifice, the culling strategy and sacrificial requirements are identical and must serve to supply suitable victims while maintaining the herd.

The Kalasha consider the wild markhor (*Capra falconeri*) the most sacred animal of all. Therefore they prefer domestic goats with twisted horns resembling the markhor, favoring such animals for sacrifice (Parkes 1987). Although sacrificial preferences for animals of particular colors, as documented among many groups (Heusch 1985), would not ordinarily be visible in the archaeological record, we do recover horn cores. A preference such as that of the Kalasha has at least two archaeological implications: Sacrificed animals may differ from those slaughtered for everyday use in terms of horn size and shape, and selection for such animals may influence the horn shape in the population. Breeding animals to resemble their wild form would complicate the identification of domestication and the separation of wild and domestic forms. Moreover, the Kalasha are trying to breed their goats to resemble the markhor, a wild goat they consider ancestral to their domestic goats, although in fact the wild ancestor is the bezoar goat (*Capra aegagrus*). Thus to the degree they are successful, they are creating a convergent evolution that may hamper distinguishing the two species osteologically.

We have seen many instances around the world of the display of a "trophy" to commemorate a sacrifice, often the head or horns of the victim. Although there are other reasons to curate and display animal heads and other parts, those trophies derived from domestic animals are quite likely to result from sacrifice. Perhaps more surprising is the recurring theme of reassembly, in which sacrificial victims are butchered and usually consumed, after which the bones are reassembled in approximate anatomical position. As we have seen earlier (in the section, *Respecting the Hunted*), such reassembly may also mark hunted animals consumed in a ritual context. However, finding such reassembled skeletons should at least raise the possibility of sacrifice.

In sum, zooarchaeology has a substantial contribution to make in the study of sacrifice, so far only partly realized. In later societies with documentary evidence of sacrifice, zooarchaeology can reveal the degree of variability in practice that may not be evident from written prescriptions. It can also resolve questions raised by the texts and depictions, such as whether all meat consumed derives from centralized sacrifice. Zooarchaeology can trace the origins of sacrifice in prehistory (already providing sufficient evidence to reject Smith's theory that sacrifice is limited to states), and it can test some of the competing theories of origins and motivations. We have much to contribute to religious studies.

## Divination

Sacrifice is closely linked to divination. In those cases in which animals are offered or sent as messengers to deities, sacrificers are usually concerned that the sacrifice will be accepted and effective. This may mean that the animal should indicate its consent, for instance by nodding, and that it should die in the right way. Afterward, it is very common for parts of the animal to be used for divination. The question may simply be whether the deities have accepted the sacrifice, or the main purpose of the sacrifice may be divination, to answer other pressing questions. Although such divination usually happens immediately after the sacrifice and may be the climax of the ceremony, some more durable animal parts may continue in use for divination long afterward. The contact with the divine that occurs during sacrifice gives its material remains special power (Hubert and Mauss 1964:97). Divination can be seen as the other direction of the flow of communication with deities that sacrifice opens. The timing of the link may also be reversed: Divination may determine that a sacrifice is necessary to solve a problem, often to cure illness but also to ameliorate other kinds of misfortune (Shanklin 1983). It may also be used to select the particular victim (Heusch 1985:184).

Of course, divination is not limited to sacrificial contexts. Given the human desire to know the future and understand the present and past, divination is probably universal (Gadd 1966; Tedlock 2001). In a sense, it is a form of proto-science, a careful observation of the natural world and an exploration of cause and effect, in which cause is attributed to supernatural forces (Dobkin 1969; Durkheim and Mauss 1963; Harwood 1970). However, it persists in the margins even of societies ruled by modern science; consider the prevalence in contemporary America of plucking daisy petals to determine whether one is loved. Because of the complexities of interpreting divine will in the signs of the natural world, divination perhaps more than sacrifice per se tends to produce ritual specialists (Tedlock 2001), although it is certainly not limited to specialists. In the absence of specialists, in important cases divination is often performed by committee, through consultation among wise and experienced men and women (e.g., Abbink 1993; Hoskins 1993). Divination may be performed in many ways and with many kinds of aids and paraphernalia (insights gained in altered states, reading signs in the sky or in the appearance and sounds of animals). In this section the focus is on methods based on animal parts, which may affect human–animal relations and archaeological remains.

ENTRAILS

Probably the most widespread use of animal parts in divination is extispicy, or the examination of entrails, usually following sacrifice but occasionally in conjunction with animals slaughtered for special feasts. Extispicy is well known from the ancient Mediterranean world, where it was particularly elaborately developed in Mesopotamia and Etruria. However, it is also documented from Africa, Indonesia, and the Andes (Beal 2002; Beavitt 1989; Collins 2008; Heeßel 2010; Richardson 2010; Rofes 2004; Sandweiss and Wing 1997; Schneider 1957; Scurlock 2002). Like sacrifice, it is largely or entirely limited to domestic animals. As the Me'en of Ethiopia say, it would make no sense to read the entrails of wild animals: Because they lack relationships with people they would bear no message (Abbink 1993:709).

Although various internal organs may be examined, the focus is usually on the intestines and the pattern of their bends, and especially on the liver (Heeßel 2010). The practice of reading the liver may have spread around the ancient eastern Mediterranean from Mesopotamia, although the systems of interpretation vary regionally. However, Indonesian groups are unlikely to have learned to read livers from this source. Rather, the use of livers is probably due to their sensitivity to environmental influences and their inherent variability. William Halliday (1913) believes the practice began as a confirmation of the soundness of the animal offered, and eventually it was elaborated into systems of augury. He notes that it is associated with a belief that the liver is the seat of the soul, thought, or emotions (see also Hoskins 1993) and that this gives it special meaning. However, it does seem possible that this belief derives from the communication via the liver in extispicy rather than the other way around.

Archaeologists rarely find evidence of extispicy, because it is based on soft parts. However, in cases of extraordinary preservation, traces of the practice may be directly observable (Sandweiss and Wing 1997). In both Mesopotamia and Etruria archaeologists have recovered models of livers labeling the significance of their zones, although the systems differ (Finet 1966; Halliday 1913). Despite the elaboration, usually the final determination was simply a yes or no answer. It is likely, however, that extispicy was practiced very frequently in the past, perhaps wherever we find sacrifice. History and ethnography show that one of the commonest occasions for divination in general and extispicy in particular is the preparation for warfare, whether a tribal raid or the movement of imperial armies.

The earlier discussions of ritual treatment of bones show that scapulae often have special significance. This value might derive from their use in divination (scapulimancy), although the archaeological evidence for this practice is limited. Ethnography and history reveal it to be extremely widespread, however, and often linked to special treatment of scapulae, so archaeologists would do well to be more alert to the possibility. More than a century ago, Richard Andree (1906) undertook a survey of scapulimancy, concluding that it had spread across Eurasia from a Central Asian and particularly Mongolian origin, but failed to reach the New World. He is wrong about the lack of scapulimancy in the New World, and probably wrong about a single origin in Central Asia. Halliday (1913:198) argues that the scapula, with its thin blade, simply lends itself to divination; hence it developed independently in many places. The varying techniques used to read scapulae tend to support independent invention, and Andree's survey provides useful documentation of this variation.

Scapulimancy is indeed particularly prevalent and prominent in Central Asia. Andree reasonably attributes this prevalence to the presence of many groups of nomadic pastoralists, most of them with large herds of sheep and goats, whose scapulae are the most commonly read. However, he notes that the Kalmyk also use scapulae from saiga, roe deer, and reindeer. They use scapulae from wild animals in more limited circumstances: Hare scapulae can only predict one day into the future, whereas wild boar scapulae only predict the outcome of a boar hunt. The Kalmyk use what seems to be the most common technique of scapulimancy: They cook the shoulder, remove the meat from the scapula (they use a knife and not gnawing for scapulae to be read; some groups make the opposite requirement), lay it on hot coals until the thin blade cracks, and interpret the pattern of the cracks. They can learn about good or bad luck, the impending deaths of various categories of persons, or a good or bad hunt. Other Central Asian groups use similar techniques, but with differing interpretive systems. Among the Kirghiz, at least, scapulae must be broken afterward to avoid bad luck (Andree 1906).

The Koryak of northeastern Siberia, in addition to treating reindeer scapulae in a similar manner, have a different technique for seal scapulae, which they use to predict the outcome of whaling expeditions. While one elder holds the scapula, another shakes hot coals onto it, and the prediction is based on the way the coals bounce off. Yet another way to read scapulae is to hold the blade to the light and interpret the pattern of the light and dark areas of the blade resulting from variations in thickness. This would probably not work with animals larger than sheep, because the blade would be too thick for much light to pass through. This technique is practiced in parts of Pakistan, the Caucasus, and the Balkans; I have witnessed it in Albania. Early twentieth-century Macedonian bandits used a variant to decide whether to kill their captives or hold them for ransom: A hole in the blade stood for the grave and meant death for the captives, a longitudinal line indicated they would receive ransom, and a transverse one meant they would be pursued and captured.

Most interpretative techniques involve designating zones of the scapula with particular meanings, much as with the liver in Mesopotamia. Sometimes these zones are mapped onto astrological signs, but the systems are quite various. The scapulae generally come from animals that have been sacrificed or consumed at feasts, and there are usually rules about their treatment, often involving not using metal tools to clean them. The right or left scapula may be specified, or the two sides may have different meanings. A particular kind of animal may be required, in terms of species, age, sex, and color. In different places the scapulae may answer a wide variety of questions, the most general concerning good or bad luck to come (for individuals, households, herds). As well as hunts, they may also indicate the outcome of battles or the impending death or illness of individuals. Scapulimancy may also reveal information about the personal character of the sacrificer, wives' fidelity, or the onset of winter weather. Sometimes ritual specialists practice scapulimancy, but often ordinary people read the scapulae of animals they slaughter (Andree 1906; Baldick 2000). Andree argues that scapulimancy is absent in classical Greece and Rome, but although it played a minor role in comparison to extispicy, the scapulae of sacrificed animals were sometimes used for divination (Gilhus 2006:26; Halliday 1913).

Scapulimancy is also ethnographically attested among the Athapaskan peoples of the North American Boreal zone. Here the scapulae of wild animals are used, and the predictions are about hunting. The scapulae are heated and the cracks read. Omar Khayyam Moore (1957) suggests that for the Montaignais-Naskapi, who mainly use scapulimancy to determine the direction to set out on hunting trips, the practice acts as a random-izing device to vary the parts of the landscape used and thus promote conservation. However, he did not actually test this claim. The Cree also heat scapulae, and sometimes pelves and bird sterna, on the coals to read the cracks and char marks. All present collaborate in the interpretation. The scapulae of different taxa have different meanings and are appropri-ate to different occasions, with size the key variable. Large ones, from moose and caribou, are hard to read, and few now know how to do so, although the Cree believe that they were used more frequently in the past. Characteristics of the species also come into play: Predictions from the slow porcupine's scapulae will take a while to come to pass, but pre-dictions from hare scapulae will happen soon. Scapulae used in divination are afterward hung for a while on the wall by the head of a sleeping per-son, in the hope that they will provoke prophetic dreams about hunting. The Cree give scapulae special treatment by hanging them in trees or the like along with skulls, even when not used in divination (Tanner 1979; see the earlier section, *Respecting the Hunted*).

Archaeologically, I am aware of only two areas where scapulimancy has been identified or proposed. In the eastern Mediterranean, scapulae with incised notches have been recovered from many sites, from the Mousterian (Middle Paleolithic) through the Iron Age. They have been variously interpreted as tallies, musical rasps, or divinatory tools, and they may not all have the same function. Occasionally other bones bear similar notches. There are two cases from Late Bronze Age Cyprus in which notched scapulae have been found together with worked astragali (knucklebones, see later discussion) in sanctuaries, which provides some support for their use in divination there (Reese 2002; Zeuner 1958).

The "oracle bones" of ancient China constitute the best known and earliest clear instance of scapulimancy. Beginning in 5300 BP, herbivore scapulae, as well as the occasional turtle plastron, bear signs of the appli-cation of hot coals to cause cracking. Later, in the Bronze Age Shang dynasty, inscriptions on the bones record the interpretation of these cracks. Some have derived the origins of Chinese writing from the cracks themselves and the meaning attributed to them, although this claim has been disputed (Postgate et al. 1995). There is greater consensus that scapulimancy was central to the power of the Shang rulers, who used divination to allay anxiety and legitimate their authority (Chang 1983; Fiskesjö 2001; Flad 2008; Nelson 2002). Perhaps supporting Andree's placement of the origin of scapulimancy, the earliest known scapula with traces of divinatory burning (multiple deliberately placed marks on the blade) is a sheep or deer scapula from Late Neolithic Fuhegoumen in Inner Mongolia. A few other approximately contemporary but less well-dated examples are known from elsewhere in Inner Mongolia and northern China. Such burnt scapulae become common about a thousand years later during the Chalcolithic Longshan culture (a time of growing political complexity), using scapulae of cattle, sheep, deer, and pig (Flad 2008). The burn marks are scattered, and Rowan Flad suggests that divination was practiced by independent, perhaps itinerant ritual specialists, as seen ethnographically in the region. In the Bronze Age (a time of state formation), the system becomes more standardized, with scapulae pretreated by drilling hollows in the blade before burning to guide the cracks; oracle bones also become more common. By the Late Shang dynasty, scapulae from cattle become the primary medium, along with turtle plastra that eventually predominate. Inscriptions recording the interpretation were applied afterward, and the bones were stored as an archive, chiefly in Anyang, the Shang capital. After the Shang Dynasty, scapulimancy and plastromancy continue and spread, but at lower intensity (Flad 2008). Deer were used earlier, but in the Shang dynasty only the scapulae of domestic animals were used, and it is possible that turtles were raised for their shells. Although the preference for domestic animals and especially cattle mirrors the choice of sacrificial animals (see earlier discussion), animals in sacrificial deposits always have their scapulae (Fiskesjö 2001). It is likely that oracle bones derived from sacrifice, but in a different context that did not produce deposits readily identified as sacrificial.

Even without the inscriptions, scapulae with drilled hollows or regular patterns of burn marks are easily recognized as the remains of divination. These practices appear to be limited to China, and largely in the context of complex societies with institutionalized divination. Less systematic burning by placing the scapula on hot coals until it cracks, as commonly attested ethnographically, is harder to detect; divination from unburnt scapulae still more so. Therefore we need to be alert to burning on scapulae that are disposed of in distinctive ways.

KNUCKLEBONES

Ruminant astragali have a distinctive form that lends itself to their use as dice: They have four more or less flat surfaces on which they can fall, each one recognizably different. This property suits astragali to use in games of chance, gambling, and divination. They are used in one or more of these ways in many places around the world, sometimes referred to as knucklebones or hucklebones (actually the astragalus is part of the ankle). They may be used without modification, or they may be enhanced by grinding one or more of the sides to flatten them or by drilling holes that are sometimes filled with lead to weight the bones. Where they occur, sheep/goat astragali are the most frequently used, being a convenient size that is slightly larger than modern dice. However, from the Neolithic on, the astragali of other animals are also used, including cattle, deer of all sizes, antelope, and even pig on occasion (pigs have astragali similar to ruminants but more angled, so that they are only likely to land on two faces).

A children's game in modern western Iran uses two knucklebones that are both thrown like dice and shot against each other like marbles. Some are ground on baked bricks to flatten two of the sides and carefully curated (Watson 1979b:199). In Turkey children play a more elaborate game. Players arrange knucklebones in rows, and then they take turns throwing a larger and heavier, sometimes leaded, astragalus at one of the rows in an attempt to turn over the knucklebones. Depending on the faces turned up on the thrown and hit knucklebones, the player may win all the knucklebones on the ground (Brewster 1960:16). There are many variants on this game, including one with a phase in which the knucklebones are thrown like jacks. Both men and boys (but not women and girls) play these games; there is also a boys-only game played with a single knucklebone. The four sides are assigned ranked titles: sultan, vizier, servant, and slave. After initially throwing the knucklebone to determine who will play the sultan and vizier, the other players take turns throwing. If it comes up with the servant face, nothing happens. If it comes up with the slave side, the sultan dictates a punishment for the slave (thrower), administered by the vizier. If the knucklebone comes up as sultan or vizier, the thrower replaces the boy in that role. Similar names for the faces of the knucklebone elsewhere in the Near East and in Europe indicate that variants of this game are or were widespread (Dandoy 1996; Lovett et al. 1901). This mirroring of (now archaic) social structure is also seen in the use of knucklebones for divination by the Thonga of Mozambique. Astragali from sacrificial animals are retained for divination: Sheep astragali represent the chief and his family; goat astragali represent commoners. Sets contain astragali from male and female animals of different ages to represent male and female humans in five age stages: child, adolescent, adult, mature adult, and elder. The ancestors communicate to the living through these knucklebones when they are cast before taking ritual action (Heusch 1985:72). The Buryat and Kirghiz use single, apparently unmodified sheep astragali for divination to determine the sex of the next child after the birth of a baby. Most Buryat keep sets of knucklebones for everyday divination, with one side signifying good fortune. At the lunar New Year they play more elaborate divinatory games, one of them involving 108 painted knucklebones. Men throw a single knucklebone, and the value thrown permits them to take a certain number of the painted knucklebones. The one who ends up with the most will have good fortune for his flock in the coming year (Birtalan 2003).

Knucklebones may be significant for the development of mathematics. However they are used, the different values assigned to the faces imply a notion of counting and even a rudimentary awareness of probability, because the values tend to be related to the frequency with which the faces come up. These values mean that knucklebones could potentially be used as accounting aids where mathematical notation was lacking (David 1962:2–3). On the whole, the archaeological contexts in which they are found do not support this use, with the exception of Iron Age Tel Beer-Sheba and Tel Ta'anach in Israel, where caches of knucklebones are found in storerooms (Sasson 2007). Their use in accounting, and indeed numerical values for the faces, is probably a later development from earlier use in games and divination.

In some cases, knucklebones held power or received special care beyond their actual use. Genghis Khan reportedly entered into a sworn "brother" relationship through the exchange of several items, starting with sets of knucklebones (Baldick 2000:94). Painted and pierced knucklebones at Gordion, the capital of ancient Phrygia, may have been worn as ornaments, evoking the game pieces (Dandoy 2006). The same is probably true of the golden astragalus from Eneolithic Varna in Bulgaria and the many later renditions of knucklebones in other materials (Amandry 1984), as well as astragalus-shaped pots in the Classical world (Gilmour 1997). The Buryat bury an astragalus with the placenta to protect a child, whereas the Kirghiz put one under the child's pillow for the same purpose

(Birtalan 2003:42–3). Similarly, foundation deposits of groups of astragali in the Iron Age Near East suggest an apotropaic function, perhaps linked to sacrifice (Venturi 2006).

Archaeologically, knucklebones go back at least to the Neolithic in Anatolia (Marinelli 1995; Mellaart 1970; Russell 2006), Iraq (P. Watson 1979), and Europe (Russell 1990; Séfériadès 1992), recognized by abraded surfaces and sometimes drilled holes. A small bovid astragalus with three abraded sides is attributed to the late Upper Paleolithic at Remouchamps, Belgium, but from a somewhat questionable context (Dewez 1974). The Neolithic knucklebones are found in domestic contexts. In the Bronze Age eastern Mediterranean a few still occur in settlements, but most are found, sometimes in concentrations, in burials or in temples or sanctuaries (Gilmour 1997; Joukowsky 1986; Reese 1985, 1989; Schliemann 1884; Steel 2004; Zeuner 1958). This pattern is even stronger in the Iron Age, and many are plugged with lead or other metals, painted, or inscribed with the names of gods or heroes (Bammer et al. 1978; Bar-Oz 2001; Forstenpointner et al. 1999; Gilmour 1997; Mellink 1956; Sasson 2007; Venturi 2006). Typically those in burials are interpreted as toys; those in sacred contexts as votive offerings or tools for divination. However, the distinction may not be so neat, with divination merging into gaming and gambling and practiced in both private and public contexts. At Classical Kition on Cyprus knucklebones occur in a sanctuary along with cone shells (*Conus mediterraneus*), some of which are filled with lead or abraded and drilled, which may have been used similarly in divination (Reese 1985). The Corycian Cave on Mt. Parnassus in Greece also has many seashells deposited as votive offerings along with nearly 23,000 knucklebones, many of the astragali leaded or decorated (Amandry 1984, Poplin 1984). Several instances of groups of burnt astragali in Classical-Hellenistic Greece, some with signs of use, suggest either a different form of divination involving fire, or destruction of the residual power in knucklebones after divination (Prummel 2003:158–9).

Elsewhere, knucklebones have been reported from the pre-Harappan and Harappan levels at Mehrgarh and Sibri in Pakistan (Russell 1995). Two perforated duiker astragali from Iron Age Simunye in Swaziland, South Africa, are interpreted as remains of a diviner's set (Badenhorst and Plug 2002), as are a number of worked astragali found with crocodile remains at the Schroda site in the Transvaal (Voigt 1984). At least two sets

(16 and 14) of sheep astragali were found in Anglo-Saxon adult human cremations in England (Crabtree 1995:23). Although there has been some question as to whether knucklebones occurred in pre-Columbian North America, numerous instances attest to the presence of abraded astragali, whereas ethnographic references suggest that astragali may frequently have been used unmodified as well (Eisenberg 1989; Koerper and Whitney-Desautels 1999; Lewis 1988; Lovett et al. 1901).

Astragali tend to be overrepresented in archaeological faunal assemblages. Taphonomic factors are partly responsible: Astragali are very dense and lack marrow, so are rarely deliberately broken. However, they may also be curated and used as knucklebones, with or without modification (David 1962; Ducos 1988; Koerper and Whitney-Desautels 1999). Distinguishing knucklebones from butchery waste, and gaming pieces from divination tools, requires attention both to microwear on the astragali and to context. Finds in ritual contexts suggest divination, and perhaps general power accruing to the knucklebones as a result. Knucklebones in burials are ambiguous: personal divination sets or favorite toys? History and ethnography provide examples of both. At Neolithic Çatalhöyük in Turkey, concentrations of astragali, both modified and intact, show that they were collected in some cases after they had been burnt or even after they had been swallowed by dogs and emerged in the feces. This suggests not the curation of a key part of sacrificial victims, but foraging for suitable bones in the middens, making child's play more plausible.

OTHER BODY PARTS

Although the scapula and astragalus are by far the most frequently used bones for divination, others sometimes play a role. The Cree use pelves, tibiae, and beaver tails as well as scapulae in making hunting predictions (Tanner 1979). Mongols use assorted bones in particular circumstances, but especially tibiae (Birtalan 2003; Szynkiewicz 1990). On the basis of a pit with more than a hundred cattle mandibles and another with more than a thousand cattle incisors that may have fallen out of mandibles that were later removed at Anyang in China, Yuan and Flad (2005) suggest that mandibles may also have been used in divination, as well as the scapulae and turtle plastra.

Although they will rarely be preserved, historical and ethnographic accounts also mention the use of hides in divination (Piggott 1962).

Stallibrass (1996) suggests that this might account for the Iron Age disposal of a cattle hide in a British bog.

SUMMARY

The ethnographic and historical literature shows that divination is a pervasive, if not universal, practice. There are myriad divinatory methods, many involving animal parts. We should therefore assume that we are likely to find the remains of divination in virtually any archaeological context. We probably cannot rule out the use of any body part a priori, but scapulae and ruminant astragali are particularly likely to be used. Their curation may affect body part distributions, so this is a concern even for those uninterested in divination for its own sake.

The details of the method and the questions asked will be hard to recover in prehistoric contexts. However, in addition to its frequent link to sacrifice and a desire to be sure the offering has been accepted, divination with animal parts is very often associated with warfare. When wild animal parts are used, it is often to inquire about hunting. Healing and concerns for the welfare of the herds can also be involved.

## Dancing with animals

Rituals often involve costumes and frequently dancing. Animal parts are common ritual costume elements, especially in shamanic or dance contexts. Shamans may use dance to achieve altered states and communicate with the divine, and wearing animal costumes not only adds to their presence but also may help them become one with their animal familiar (Chang 1983; Harrod 2000). Ritual dances are found in nearly every society, but Yosef Garfinkel (2003) argues they are particularly important in village societies, where larger populations and the isolation created by permanent houses (Wilson 1988) require compelling group rituals and activities to forge communal identity. In urban societies, performances are co-opted by the elite, and dance becomes less central.

Animal costumes are particularly likely to figure in hunting rituals and initiations (Morris 2000:100, 123). In such rituals, masked dancers or performers impersonate animals, spirits in animal form, or animals' spirit masters. As with the shamans, such dancers take on the identity and power of the entity they represent. Masks and costumes are typically carefully made and curated, often in the context of secret societies that hold the right to make and wear them. As so often in ritual contexts, the dancing animals are nearly always wild.

Among groups on the North American Great Plains, dancers dressed as bison are ritually hunted in a major ceremony at the start of the hunting season (Harrod 2000:86–99). Other Native American dances feature carnivores such as foxes, jaguars, and condors, where the aim is more to capture the power of the animals than to ensure a successful hunt (Collins 1991b; Saunders 1997; Simons 1983). Ironically, in Africa, ceremonies with masked performers embodying wild animals and rituals focused on wild animals in general are more elaborate in agricultural than foraging societies. In contrast, in pastoralist societies, these ceremonies are absent, with ritual life instead focused on domestic animals and sacrifice (Morris 2000). If this opposition between sacrifice and masked dances about wild animals can be generalized, it has considerable archaeological implications. On the one hand, evidence for one practice renders the presence of the other unlikely. On the other, as domestic animals are adopted and gain more importance, archaeology has the potential to illuminate the transition from one system to the other. This is clearly a major ideological shift that is likely to have been contested and negotiated as it occurred. We have seen that sacrifice serves to construct gender relations. In ethnographic accounts of masked performers it is men who wear the animal masks, although women may participate in communal dances and even be equated with animals. Therefore these two ritual systems may mark a distinction between constructing masculinity through hunting and the wild and constructing it through livestock and wealth.

Archaeologically, there has been more discussion of shamans' costumes and paraphernalia than the costumes of masked dancers, perhaps because the latter are less likely to be buried with the wearer. An unusual Natufian grave in Israel (Epipaleolithic, ca. 12,000 BP) may belong to a shaman: An elderly and disabled woman was buried with 50 complete tortoise shells (which might have been rattles) and parts of a wild boar, eagle, aurochs, leopard, two martens, and a complete human foot (Grosman et al. 2008). The same has been suggested for another female burial in Germany from the Late Mesolithic (ca. 8500 BP). Excavated in the 1930s but recently restudied, there is less information than we would like on the placement of the items in the grave. These items include many tortoise shells and mussel shells; a crane bone container filled with microliths; 50 drilled incisors of aurochs, bison, and red and roe deer that presumably formed a necklace or were sewn onto clothing; a ground-stone axe; two roe deer frontlets and a set of wild boar canines that might have been part of headgear; and what may be painting tools. Moreover, the woman suffered from a deformation of the juncture of the skull and spinal column that may have created neurological symptoms interpreted as spirit possession (Porr and Alt 2006). Julie Bond and Fay Worley (2006) suggest that wild animal remains in Anglo-Saxon cremations, particularly antler and bear skins/claws, are remains of shamanic paraphernalia, in contrast to the more common meat offerings from domestic animals.

Some elements of shamanic costumes seem to be extremely widespread and to have great time depth. The turtle or tortoise shell rattles that appear in the Epipaleolithic and Mesolithic burials described earlier are also attested in North American shamans' graves as well as described ethnographically (Bogan 1983). The same is true of beaver and sometimes other large rodent mandibles, found on ethnographic shamans' costumes in Siberia and putative shamans' graves in Mesolithic Russia and prehistoric North America (Heizer and Hewes 1940; Schmidt 2000). Bear claws or skins are reported from North American shamanic burials as well as Anglo-Saxon England (Heizer and Hewes 1940; Webb and Baby 1957).

Adena and Hopewell shamans in the North American Midwest had particularly elaborate costumes. In addition to remnants of animal skins, bear claws, and headdresses with copper antlers in graves, there are several instances of wolf and cougar mandibles and maxillae modified as part of costumes, probably attached to the animals' skins. Their use is illuminated by one grave in which such a modified wolf maxilla, retaining the front teeth and canines and a long tab of the palatine bone, was found in place in the mouth of an adult male human whose upper incisors had been knocked out in life to permit the substitution of the wolf teeth (Parmalee and Stephens 1972; Webb and Baby 1957). Although such dental inserts seem to be limited to the Adena and Hopewell cultures, worked carnivore mandibles from a wide range of species are found from the Archaic through the Hopewell periods in the Midwest and were probably elements of masks (Parmalee 1959).

Garfinkel (2003) bases his analysis of prehistoric dance on artistic representations. Although he mentions costumes as a frequent component of dance, he devotes little attention to adornment, identifying dance scenes on the basis of the posture and arrangement of the human figures. Some scholars have suggested that costumed figures in art may be dancers, for example in the American West (Simons 1983) or at Neolithic Çatalhöyük in Anatolia (Mellaart 1962:64–5; Sipahi 2001). Others have rejected this interpretation of the group scenes in the "hunting shrines" at Çatalhöyük (Forest 1993; Garfinkel 2003:60), although Garfinkel sees other motifs at the site as representing dance.

In addition to artistic representations, archaeological evidence of costume elements potentially provides traces of dance. A deposit of vulture and other raptor wings and wild goat skulls at Zawi Chemi Shanidar is clearly a dump of ritual paraphernalia and quite likely dance costumes (see the earlier section, *Special Deposits*). I have argued that a crane wing from a special deposit at Çatalhöyük is most likely part of a costume, quite possibly for a crane dance, various forms of which are widely attested ethnographically (Russell and McGowan 2003). Condor remains in a grave at the Windmiller site in California may also be part of a dance costume (Simons 1983). Combining archaeological and ethnographic evidence, Paul Collins (1991b) builds a strong case that people brought foxes to the Channel Islands off southern California due to the centrality of the fox dance in their religious life. It is possible that some heads-and-hooves deposits in burials (see the earlier section, *Sacrifice*) represent not merely skins but costumes.

Ethnographically, feathers are probably the animal part most frequently used in costumes (Furst 1991; Hesse 1986; Zarur 1991). These may be bird costumes such as the crane and condor costumes referenced earlier, but they may also be used to ornament costumes and headdresses more generally. Only occasionally are feathers preserved archaeologically, but the Andean region, for example, has produced spectacular ancient feather work. Elsewhere it may sometimes be possible to recognize people wearing feathers in depictions (Hill 2000; Mellaart 1966b), or the body part representation of bird remains may indicate a bias toward wings and hence feathers. Wing fans and other bird remains in Mississippian and Caddoan burials in North America have been interpreted as ritual paraphernalia (Bogan 1983; Potter 1997; Scott and Jackson 1996). Body part representation has provided the basis for arguments for feather use as early as the Upper Paleolithic and in many areas (Bouchud 1953; Rodríguez Loredo de March 1993).

## The zooarchaeology of ritual

Ritual is ubiquitous in human societies and takes a multiplicity of forms. At prehistoric sites we can assume that the inhabitants had a ritual life, but it is challenging to trace ancient rituals from material remains. We all know the joke about archaeologists designating anything they cannot identify as a ritual object. In my experience archaeologists more often refuse to admit the possibility of ritual significance if any other explanation can be found. Certainly rigor is as necessary to the study of ritual as to the study of any other realm of human behavior. The most promising work on the archaeological study of ritual builds on Bell's (1992, 1997) practice theory approach, and it seeks the "framing" that sets ritual apart by constructing times, places, costumes, and so on, or by overemphasis (Bradley 2005; Verhoeven 2002a).

Therefore, a contextual approach is essential to finding and understanding ancient ritual (Grant 1989, 1991). Because zooarchaeologists are not always on site during excavation and are not always archaeologically trained or interested in questions of context or the social significance of animals, special deposits of animal bones are often overlooked or ignored in analysis. I have found that when I describe to colleagues the special deposits we have documented at Çatalhöyük, they often recall similar deposits at sites they have studied, but on which they have never commented in print. At sites that are rich in other signs of ritual, notably art, such as Çatalhöyük or Lepenski Vir, archaeologists are more inclined to notice special faunal deposits. However, they are surely much more widespread and may constitute one of the best sources for the study of prehistoric ritual at less spectacular sites. Both excavators and analysts need to become more sensitized to the context of animal remains.

In addition to special deposits, it is worth examining spatial patterning in bone distribution. Priscilla Renouf (2000) argues that marine and terrestrial taxa (seals and caribou) are kept ritually and spatially separate in otherwise unremarkable garbage dumps at Port au Choix, Newfoundland. Ian McNiven and Richard Feldman's (2003) ethnoarchaeological study of ceremonial middens in the Torres Strait reminds us that there is no strict dichotomy between garbage and ritual remains.

Even if the zooarchaeologist is not interested in ritual for its own sake, it is important to be aware of the taphonomic and selective effects of ritual practices on the assemblages we study to analyze hunting and herding practices. Hanging selected body parts in trees, where they will weather away, or dumping them in lakes and rivers will affect the composition of assemblages, as will placing them at hunting shrines (Brown 2005; Szuter 2001). Curating trophies will also affect taxon and body part representation, as well as providing clues to the values placed on different animal species and on hunting or sacrifice. Phenomena such as hunting shrines indicate that hunting acts to construct male identity and is therefore likely to involve the targeting of high-prestige taxa, rather than following the dictates of optimal foraging theory.

4

# Hunting and humanity

> Because hunting takes place at the boundary between the human domain
> and the wilderness, the hunter stands with one foot on each side of the
> boundary, and swears no perpetual allegiance to either side. He is a liminal
> and ambiguous figure, who can be seen either as a fighter against wildness or
> as a half-animal participant in it. (Cartmill 1993:31)

The original human–animal relationships were between humans (at whatever point in our evolutionary history we wish to start calling our ancestors human) and wild animals. These relations of course continue to the
present. We, and our ancestors, have interacted with wild animals in many
ways: watching and studying them, driving them away, depicting them,
imitating them, invoking them in myths and rituals, worshipping them,
and collecting feathers and other items from living animals. Arguably the
most significant interaction, and certainly the most visible archaeologically, is killing them.

## Hunters or scavengers?

> [T]heories about human evolution . . . may be significant as much for
> what they say about contemporary definitions of what it is to be human,
> as for anything they tell of the past (Fiddes 1991:59).

From World War II until the 1970s, the dominant model of human
evolution was encapsulated in the phrase "Man the Hunter" (Dart 1957;
Morris 1967; Washburn and Avis 1958; Washburn and Lancaster 1968).
Although "Man" was supposed to mean human beings, the masculine
form is no accident, for women are largely invisible and passive in this
model. According to this view, it was hunting, the killing of animals,

that made us human. This was the crucial change that set us apart from apes and created new mating patterns, new forms of social organization, big brains, tools (actually weapons), and language. The killing of animals was also linked to the killing of other humans, so that the very thing that defined our humanity also condemned us to murder, rape, and wage war. Another epithet for this model is the "killer ape" theory.

Matt Cartmill (1993, 1999) has examined the historical context of this model and why it held such appeal despite the stunning lack of evidence to support it. The killer ape theory is a dark, pessimistic view of ourselves, and it is odd that most people were so eager to embrace it. Cartmill relates this acceptance on the one hand to postwar pessimism in the wake of the Holocaust and on the other to views of nature in opposition to culture that have developed through the centuries in western thought.

In the 1970s, the Man the Hunter model began to come under fire on three fronts. First, it was discovered that other primates, notably chimpanzees and baboons, also hunt. Although this observation bolsters the probability that early hominids hunted as well, it removes the uniquely human quality of hunting. Indeed, we may have been slow to acknowledge hunting by other primates precisely because hunting and eating meat were two of the ways that we set ourselves apart from them and from nature (Fiddes 1991:55). Second, feminists took issue with the androcentrism of the model, and they countered with "Woman the Gatherer" and other more balanced views of human evolution (e.g., Ehrenberg 1989; Falk 1997; Fedigan 1986; Hager 1997; Hrdy 1999; McBrearty and Moniz 1991; McGrew 1981; McKell 1998; Morgan 1972; Power and Aiello 1997; Skybreak 1984; Tanner 1981; Willoughby 1991; Zihlman 1981; Zihlman and Tanner 1978). Finally, Lewis Binford (1981, 1984b, 1985, 1987; Binford et al. 1988; Binford and Stone 1986) led an attack on the notion that early hominids hunted, arguing that the evidence better supported scavenging until very late in human evolution, and perhaps hunting did not occur until the advent of anatomically modern humans (*Homo sapiens sapiens*). This assertion has stimulated a tremendous amount of research aimed at finding ways to distinguish hunting from scavenging in the zooarchaeological record, assessing the opportunities for hominid scavengers in various environments, and modeling the nutritional benefits of scavenging animal products (e.g., Blumenschine 1986a, 1986b, 1987, 1989, 1991c; Bunn et al. 1988; Domínguez-Rodrigo 2002; Grayson and Delpech 1994; Hasegawa et al. 1983; O'Connell et al. 1988, 2002; Outram 2000; Selvaggio 1998b; Shipman 1986a; Stiner 1990, 1991a; Stiner and Kuhn 1992; Tappen 1995).

Currently, the pendulum seems to be swinging back, with some scholars making a strong case for hunting by early hominids (Bunn 2001; Domínguez-Rodrigo 2002; Stanford 1999, 2001). The question is now reframed as when hominids started hunting large game. Even the Man the Hunter paradigm has been resurrected with a twist. Craig Stanford (1999) argues that both human intelligence and male dominance ("patriarchy") are derived from hunting or, more precisely, from the social relations created by sharing meat (see also Wrangham and Peterson 1996).

### MAN THE SCAVENGER

Oddly, the implications of scavenging for human behavior have received little attention (cf. Blumenschine and Cavallo 1992; Fedigan 1986:36; Patou-Mathis 2009). If Man the Hunter condemned us to a tragic life of violence, how have we been shaped by our putative past as Man the Scavenger? Scavenging has not been perceived as a romantic way of life (Fiddes 1991:84). In farming we nurture life and produce food. In hunting we take life, and its long association with virility and the aristocracy has given it an air of nobility. In scavenging, we live off the deaths and kills of others.

We hold scavengers in contempt, characterizing them as cowardly, dishonest, and lazy. Surely this is an unfair portrait of creatures such as hyenas or perhaps our ancestors who face down lions (which are not above scavenging themselves) to claim a carcass (Glickman 1999). Is it really nobler to attack an antelope? Leaving such questionable moral judgments aside, how might scavenging have shaped our destiny by exerting particular selective pressures? Did scavenging make us human?

To begin with, we can state with confidence that our early ancestors (*Homo habilis*) did consume meat by about 2 million years ago (mya). There are two lines of evidence: (1) studies of our closest living relatives and (2) archaeological remains. Primatologists have repeatedly observed limited meat eating among chimpanzees, as well as baboons, which inhabit the savanna as our hominid ancestors are generally thought to have done (de Waal 1989; Goodall 1971; Stanford 1996, 1999). This meat comes primarily from hunting, not scavenging, although chimps occasionally scavenge carrion or steal prey from baboons, and baboons sometimes scavenge (Hasegawa et al. 1983; Rose and Marshall 1996; Stanford 1999:121–3). Because both modern humans and chimps, our closest relatives, eat meat, it is plausible that our common ancestor and the intervening hominid forms did so as well. Archaeologists have found cut marks on bones and traces of blows from breaking them for marrow (Blumenschine 1995; Bunn 1981, 1982, 1983, 1989; Bunn et al. 1980; Bunn and Kroll 1986; Potts and Shipman 1981; Shipman 1983, 1986b, 1989). They have also found microwear traces on stone tools resulting from use on meat and bone (Keeley and Toth 1981). We do not know how much meat early hominids consumed, but it is generally seen as an important source of concentrated nutrients tied to the shift from arboreal to terrestrial life, partly replacing fruits as our ancestors moved onto the savanna. The compact protein and fat content of meat has also been considered crucial for the development of larger brains (Foley 2001), although insects might provide as good or better a source than large game (Morris 2004).

If we accept that early hominids consumed perhaps small but significant quantities of meat, that this was a crucial part of their subsistence, and that this meat was scavenged rather than hunted, what are the implications for hominid behavior? In this connection, paleoanthropologists often distinguish between active scavenging (or power scavenging), in which predators are driven away from the kill, and passive scavenging, where the scavengers wait until the predators leave to consume whatever is left unchallenged (Bunn 2001; Bunn and Ezzo 1993; O'Connell et al. 1988; Rose and Marshall 1996). This is somewhat odd terminology, given that both involve active effort, and it can only be understood as carrying barely concealed gendered implications. Passive scavenging is likened to the female-associated gathering, whose difficulty and dangers tend to be played down (Kent 1989:7), whereas active scavenging is almost like the noble male pursuit of hunting. In practice the separation is not so neat. "Active" scavengers will surely seize any "passive" scavenging opportunities they come across, and the arrival of other predators/scavengers can quickly convert passive scavenging to active. Studies of scavenging opportunities in Africa have shown that it is a dangerous activity, and without the ability to drive away competitors it would have been rather unproductive on the open savanna (Blumenschine 1986b, 1987, 1989; Blumenschine et al. 1994; Brantingham 1998;

Kortlandt 1980; Lupo 1998; Stiner 1993a). Even hyenas hunt more than they scavenge, and many vulture species kill some of their own prey, because there are not enough scavenging opportunities to support them (Houston 1983; Kruuk 1972:109). This has led some to propose that hominids concentrated their scavenging activities in the closed environment of riverine forests, where they would be less subject to competition (Blumenschine 1987; Marean 1989, 1997; Tappen 1995); however, carcasses would be much harder to find in such areas, especially with our deficient sense of smell, and stable isotope studies indicate a grassland-based diet for early hominids (Lee-Thorp et al. 2003; Sponheimer et al. 2006).

What are the requirements for successful scavenging? A scavenger needs to locate dead animals, process them in whatever way is necessary to consume the available nutrients, and protect itself from competitors. Scavenging animals use two techniques for locating carcasses: smell and vision. Mammalian scavengers such as hyenas and dogs tend to rely primarily on smell (Butler 1998:75); birds such as vultures and crows use their sharp vision, although some species of vulture also rely on scent (Houston 1983; Mundy et al. 1992; Stevenson and Anderson 1994:91). Hyenas also listen for the sounds of other hyenas feeding (Kruuk 1972). Humans and other primates tend to depend more on vision than smell in general, and our sense of smell is not particularly developed. Neither is our vision as good as that of vultures and, without wings, we lack their ability to get a panoramic view of the landscape if suitable hills or trees are absent. In his study of scavenging opportunities in the Serengeti, Robert Blumenschine (1986b) found that by far the most effective way to locate carcasses was by watching for vultures and following them to the carcass, a technique also used by lions and hyenas (Houston 1983:143; Kruuk 1972; Mundy et al. 1992) and by Hadza hunters in Tanzania, who acquire a significant amount of meat through active scavenging; the Hadza also listen for mammalian predators (O'Connell et al. 1988). We do not seem to have developed any extraordinary ability to locate carcasses on our own. Our sense of smell is probably less good than our primate ancestors, and our vision no better. Following vultures is thus likely to have been the usual method used by early hominids as well, which guarantees that there would always be competition at least from vultures for the carcass. Given the efficiency of vultures at locating carcasses, such competition would be difficult to avoid in any case.

Having found a carcass, the hominids would need to gain access to its nutrients in a digestible form. If the carcass were intact, this would mean penetrating the hide to reach the meat. If it were largely stripped of meat, it would mean breaking the bones to get at the marrow and brain. Unlike hyenas, hominids lack the built-in equipment to perform either of these tasks (sharp teeth to tear open hides, bone-crushing teeth to reach marrow). Like many vultures, unequipped hominids would need to wait until the hide of large animals was breached by other predators or by rotting (König 1983; Mundy et al. 1992; Rabenold 1983). Even if the hominids managed to arrive after the skin was breached but before the meat was gone, removing the meat would be difficult, without shearing teeth or sharp claws. Clearly, scavenging hominids would require tools. Simple ones would suffice: sharp edges for cutting through the hide and removing meat, hammer stones or more likely anvils (requiring no modification) for breaking bones for marrow. Oldowan tools (the earliest known) are much better suited to these purposes than for use as weapons, and microwear supports meat cutting as one of their functions (Keeley and Toth 1981). One of the few recorded uses of tools by nonhuman animals is Egyptian vultures throwing stones at ostrich eggs to break the shell (Lawick-Goodall and Lawick 1966); scavenging can thus plausibly stimulate tool use.

Moreover, if the carcass were not so fresh, the scavengers would need to be able to digest rotting meat. Here there is some support for a physiological adaptation to scavenging. Some predators prefer fresh meat to the point that they will not eat anything they have not killed themselves, although all mammalian carnivores with the possible exception of cheetahs scavenge on occasion (Kruuk 1972:108). Humans are among those, like dogs and wolves (Mech et al. 1970), that are not only willing to eat an animal that is not freshly killed, but actually prefer it slightly aged (hung). There are limits, however. Unlike vultures and hyenas, modern humans cannot handle raw, putrid meat; early hominids probably could not do much better. In this case (and in the African savanna, it would not take long for meat to become distinctly high), the hominids could eat the meat only if it were cooked. In contrast, vultures appear to enjoy meat much more rotten than humans can stomach (Dennett 1999, Rabenold 1983). Hence our tastes in meat suggest that, although our ancestors are unlikely to have been specialized scavengers, they probably incorporated some found meat in their diet.

Archaeologists disagree over when hominids began to control fire
and cook food. Most would concur that fire was in use by 500,000 BP
(Goren-Inbar et al. 2004), considerably later than the first evidence for
meat consumption. Some have suggested that fire was in use from 1.6 mya
(Bellomo 1994), but others have dismissed these as naturally occurring
bush fires. There is good evidence for the use of fire at Swartkrans in
South Africa from at least 1 mya (Brain and Sillen 1988). Fire would
also be necessary to make effective use of many of the plant resources
of the savanna, particularly tubers (Carmody and Wrangham 2009; Stahl
1984). Control of fire and the concept of cooking may have been applied
first to tubers and later extended to meat, or vice versa (Wrangham et al.
1999).

Finally, the most challenging aspect of scavenging is probably the
competition for the carcass. The African savanna contains some highly
specialized and well-equipped scavengers, such as hyenas and vultures.
Most predators, and all social carnivores, will also gladly appropriate any
carcasses they encounter (Schaller 1972; Schaller and Lowther 1969;
Stiner 1993a:65). Confrontations between lions and hyenas are often
fatal (Schaller 1972:188). Hominids could plausibly drive away vultures,
at least to the extent that they could share in the carcass. Protecting
the carcass from lions or hyenas would be another matter, even with
weapons, although cooperation among a group of hunters would help.
Again, fire might be the only way that hominids would have a chance.
Given these difficulties, along with the challenges of finding carcasses
before other scavengers have stripped most of the flesh from it, Blumenschine (Blumenschine 1986b, 1987, 1989, 1991a, 1991b; Blumenschine
and Cavallo 1992; Blumenschine et al. 1994; Blumenschine and Madrigal 1993) has suggested that the only viable scavenging niche for early
hominids would be seeking carcasses no longer of interest to other scavengers: skeletons stripped of flesh, but retaining marrow and the brain.
Even so, they would still face competition from hyenas and lammergeiers,
which have adapted to make use of these within-bone nutrients that are
inaccessible to most predators. It is here that cognitive and behavioral
adaptations would have been most necessary.

Clearly, then, scavenging cannot be seen as a less challenging occupation than hunting. It is both difficult and dangerous, and wherever there
is a substantial potential for scavenged carcasses, there will also be serious
competition for them.

How do the requirements of scavenging differ from those of hunting? The last two elements of scavenging, processing the carcass and defending it from competitors, also apply to hunting, although perhaps with somewhat less force. With a freshly killed carcass, hunters still need to breach the hide and remove the meat, but have less need to break the bones. Moreover, killing the animal themselves gives hunters a head start on scavengers and a better chance to extract a significant amount of meat before more powerful animals drive them away. Still, hunters face these same problems to a large degree. They do not have to locate dead animals, but they do have to locate live ones. This may be easier, especially in an open environment, or one with features like waterholes that reliably draw animals to them. Then, of course, they have to pursue and kill the animal. This aspect has received the most attention.

Humans have not adapted to hunting or scavenging primarily through bodily change (Trinkaus 1987). Indeed, we seem to have lost speed and strength and reduced our sharp canine teeth, in comparison to our ancestors. It has been argued that our naked skins are an adaptation to hunting, because they permit rapid cooling after the heat of pursuit (Montagna 1965; Morris 1967). However, not only would this be a unique adaptation among predators but also it seems odd that women have less body hair than men, when it is assumed that men were the primary large game hunters. It has even been suggested that our large brains were initially a cooling mechanism for the hunt (Fiałkowski 1986).

For the most part, the proponents of the Man the Hunter model envisioned our adaptations to the hunt as occurring in the brain and the behaviors it permitted: larger brains to enable tool use and language, and changes in reproductive patterns and social organization. Weapons are our substitutes for teeth and claws. Language supposedly arose to facilitate communication during the hunt (a strange argument; surely gabbing is the last thing hunters should be doing while stalking their prey) or to communicate information about game (Laughlin 1968). Again, this hypothesis does not fit especially well with the greater verbal abilities of women than men (Falk 1997). The notion that hunting meant male provisioning of their mates and offspring at home bases, with the resulting female dependence on males leading to concealed estrus and monogamy (Lovejoy 1981), has been extensively critiqued (Falk 1997; Fedigan 1986; McBrearty and Moniz 1991; Morgan 1972,

1982; O'Connell et al. 2002; Tanner 1981; Willoughby 1991; Zihlman 1991, 1997; Zihlman and Tanner 1978).

Scavenging, perhaps still less than hunting, seems unlikely to have directly fostered the development of language. It is hard to see what communication would be required beyond pointing to a circling vulture or giving an alarm signal at the approach of a competing scavenger. The origins of language must be sought elsewhere – in sharing information about plant resources or, more likely, in the realm of interaction among social, conscious beings. The need to fight off competitors at carcasses, as well as for protection from predators in an open environment, would have been a powerful inducement to sociality, however (Rose and Marshall 1996). Our closest relatives – chimps, bonobos, and gorillas – are social in the forest, and it is highly likely that our common ancestor was as well. Life on the savanna would have required more frequent cooperation in defense, however, as seen in baboons (DeVore and Washburn 1968; Kummer and Kurt 1968).

Scavenging would require cooperation in subsistence, at least in the defensive aspect. Because a hominid would need brethren for defense while consuming a carcass, he or she would be wise to inform them of any carcasses located and to share the meat or marrow with them. This defensive support is especially important because, unlike most scavengers, humans cannot bolt down large amounts of raw meat before competitors arrive (Mundy et al. 1992). Additionally, a large carcass creates ideal conditions for tolerated scrounging (Blurton-Jones 1984; Gurven 2004): It is more than an individual can consume, and hence not worth defending from others. In the long run, given the difficulty of locating carcasses, the individual is likely to benefit more from the reciprocal sharing of information about carcass location than he or she loses through sharing the meat and marrow. This is no doubt why most vultures have communal roosts (Rabenold 1983). Thus whereas chimps and gorillas essentially forage independently alongside each other (except for mother/infant pairs), scavenging would require closer coordination and cooperation.

So we can see scavenging, at least as much as hunting, as encouraging some of the traits we consider important in the development of human beings (Patou-Mathis 2009). Yet I think it is a mistake to focus narrowly on hunting or scavenging, and indeed this emphasis on the animal portion of the hominid diet is a symptom of the general overvaluation of meat discussed later (Fedigan 1986; Isaac and Crader 1981; Tanner 1981; Zihlman and Tanner 1978). The more significant factor is what might be termed the original "Broad Spectrum Revolution," with apologies to Kent Flannery (1969). To a diet largely consisting of fruits and leaves (although with a certain amount of insects and a little meat), early hominids most likely added both carrion and hunted meat in increased amounts along with seeds and roots. Stable isotope studies indicate that *Paranthropus robustus, Australopithecus africanus*, and *Homo* cf. *ergaster* had omnivorous (and isotopically indistinguishable) diets (Lee-Thorp et al. 2000, 2003; C. Peters and Vogel 2005; Sponheimer et al. 2005).

Through the years, various animal analogies, including chimps, bonobos, baboons, and wolves (Fox 1978), have been proposed to elucidate aspects of human evolution. Indeed, using animals to think about people is one kind of human–animal relationship (see Chapter 2). I offer yet another analogy that is instructive in this context: crows. Like humans, crows have a generalist, opportunistic dietary strategy that varies seasonally and includes small but significant quantities of scavenged meat (this is still more true of ravens). Crows also are among the most intelligent birds; are social; recognize individual crows and humans; and have a strong family structure built around extended families in which members cooperate in subsistence, reproduction, and defense. The form of crow sociality is not unlike the classic hunter-gatherer pattern: dispersing into small, extended-family units for part of the year (nesting season) and aggregating in large groups at other times (Baglione et al. 2006; Canestrari et al. 2008; Emery 2006; Heinrich 1999; Holzhaider et al. 2011; Hunt et al. 2006a; Hunt et al. 2006b; Kenward et al. 2006; Marzluff and Angell 2005; McGowan 1996; Rutledge and Hunt 2004; Schloegl et al. 2007; Schwab et al. 2008; Taylor et al. 2009; Tebbich et al. 2007; Weir et al. 2002; Weir and Kacelnik 2006; Yorzinski et al. 2006). Moreover, the crow's ability to recognize individuals suggests some degree of consciousness and that crow social life, like that of hominoids, is based on interactions among individuals, not just undifferentiated members of the flock (Emery 2006). Reasonably high intelligence is a prerequisite for this kind of sociality, but such a social system will also tend to select for intelligence, which is needed to navigate social interactions successfully (Dunbar 1996; Gamble et al. 2011). Perhaps not coincidentally, crows are not forest birds, but prefer a relatively open habitat, with some trees in which to nest, keep watch, and retreat from danger. Similar habits (even nesting) have been suggested for early hominids (Sept 1992).

Although a generalized dietary strategy is sometimes associated with relatively high intelligence (hominids, crows, raccoons), this is not invariably the case (opossums, armadillos). A generalist strategy may reinforce intelligence, but only when intelligence is already a significant part of the adaptation, based on complex sociality. When our hominid ancestors moved into a new niche on the savanna, they were already both social and reasonably intelligent, judging from our closest relatives. There seems not to have been a single open niche available, or not one that they were suited to exploit. So they adopted a broad-based, opportunistic strategy. This flexible approach is still seen in the modern human diet, which in worldwide perspective is more variable than that of most mammals. Such a catch-as-catch-can strategy favors quick thinking and ingenuity. It may also favor pooling of resources among group members, because the acquisition of many foods will be unpredictable, whereas other foods will be predictable but only seasonally available. A flexible rather than obligate approach to diet and food acquisition favors learned over innate behavior, and hence extended periods of juvenile dependency. Juvenile dependency further encourages close-knit social ties along kinship lines and the pooling of resources within these groups. It is not scavenging in the narrow sense of appropriating carrion that is important, but scavenging in the broader sense of an opportunistic use of a wide range of food sources.

In this light, the question of whether early hominids were hunting or scavenging their meat becomes less important. Given chimpanzee hunting, it is very likely they were doing some of each. The weight of the evidence currently suggests that hominids did not regularly practice hunting of large animals until the Middle Paleolithic, and somewhat variably then (Baryshnikov et al. 1996; Binford 1984b, 1985, 1987; Binford and Stone 1986; Blumenschine 1991c; Bunn and Ezzo 1993; Grayson and Delpech 1994; Lieberman 1993; Lieberman and Shea 1994; Milo 1998; Outram 2000; Selvaggio 1998a; Shea 1993, 1998; Stiner 1990, 1991a, 1994; Stiner and Kuhn 1992). Even now, foragers will happily scavenge meat when they have the opportunity (Gifford-Gonzalez 1989:183; O'Connell et al. 1988), and many a denizen of modern western civilization has dined on scavenged road-kill venison. It is not the noble, tragic, and brutal act of hunting that has defined humanity, but the flexible, clever, and inventive pursuit of scavenging in the broad sense: Humans the Improvisers.

Certainly by the advent of anatomically modern humans, meat had become a regular component of the diet, to a greater or lesser degree. Before animal domestication, anatomically modern humans acquired most of their meat by hunting. Even after domestication, hunting continued and continues to be practiced in virtually all societies. Hunting is about more than simply acquiring food.

## The prestige of hunting and meat

Hunting and meat tend in all cultures to be valued far beyond their actual contribution to the diet (Adams 1990; Biesele 1993; Brightman 1993:233; Descola 1994:250; Fiddes 1991; Kent 1989; Morris 1998:63–4; Russell 1999; Woodburn 1968). Indeed, it is essentially this attitude among zooarchaeologists – the overwhelming focus on past animals as meat sources to the exclusion of all other roles – that has motivated me to write this book. The existence of vegetarians shows that we do not actually require meat to survive. Yet I know of no wholly vegetarian societies (as opposed to individuals or categories of people within a society who do not eat meat), either in the present or in the past. In many cases, the symbolic statement people make by giving up meat rests precisely on the high value accorded to it (Fiddes 1991).

"[A]ll over the world ... people honor and crave animal foods more than plant foods and are willing to lavish a disproportionate share of their energy and wealth on producing them" (Harris 1985:22). Many groups who acquire their meat through hunting have a special term for "meat hunger," and people may pressure hunters to provide meat when they have been too long without (Descola 1994:250; Gross 1975; Harris 1985:27; Hugh-Jones 1996b; Kensinger 1989; Morris 1998:63–4; Pollock 1998; Woodburn 1968). Among those with domestic animals, eating meat is a sign of prosperity, and feasts are almost always marked by large amounts of meat. Meat is an excellent source of protein and sometimes of fat, is a compact source of calories, and contains other valuable nutrients such as iron and vitamin B12 (Harris 1985:31–6). There are good reasons to regard it as an important food.

Still, the value placed on meat exceeds its nutritional importance, which may be overrated. True carnivores eat raw flesh, bone, and innards to acquire a fuller range of nutrients than is available in cooked muscle alone (Fiddes 1991:177). The symbolic significance of meat probably derives from the highly charged act of killing animate beings not so different from us. Nick Fiddes (1991) sees killing and eating animals as a way of demonstrating human superiority over nature, whereas Brian Morris (1998:186) argues that for subsistence hunters killing animals is not about exercising power *over* nature, but incorporating the powers *of* nature, the life force of the animals.

Similarly, the prestige accorded to hunters is quite out of proportion to the protein and calories that they provide (Kensinger 1989; O'Connell et al. 2002). This skewed valuation distorted our perception of foragers (hence the Man the Hunter model of human evolution), so that it was not until ethnographers started measuring actual food intake that they realized that meat is in fact a rather minor component of most forager diets, and often not even the main protein source (Kelly 1995; Lee 1968; McCarthy and McArthur 1960). Ironically, the first such evidence was presented at the 1966 Man the Hunter conference, later published in the book by that name (Lee and DeVore 1968). Both the overvaluation of meat and the focus on hunting to the exclusion of gathering are clearly related to scxist attitudes that value men's activities over women's (e.g., Brightman 1993:8–9, 1996; Conkey and Spector 1984; Fedigan 1986; Kensinger 1989; Zihlman 1981).

This prestige is attached primarily to hunting larger mammals, but sometimes extends to the killing of large aquatic turtles and pelagic fish such as tuna. These exceptions seem to occur mainly in Pacific island societies, where large wild mammals are scarce or absent. These creatures are taken individually at some risk, no doubt adding to the prestige of the hunter/fisher. Recent studies of contemporary Meriam turtle hunting and archaeological tuna remains from a number of sites in the Pacific suggest that in both cases these resources are sought for their prestige rather than their nutritive value (Bliege Bird and Bird 1997; Fraser 2001). Swordfish may fill a similar role in the California Middle Archaic (Hildebrandt and McGuire 2002). Kristen Hawkes (2001:231) links hunting to language in a novel way, proposing that if big game hunting is motivated by prestige ("reputation"), such reputations are dependent on storytelling. Thus big game hunting will only arise among hominids with language: Language causes big game hunting, rather than vice versa.

## WHAT IS HUNTING?

Hunting is more than just killing animals to acquire food.

> [T]he delineation of a separate category called "hunting" seems to be a gender-valued distinction, rather than a designation of a particular kind of activity. For example, women do "hunt" small animals in the course of foraging, yet somehow this is seen as "collecting"; and men are always hunters, no matter what proportion of their subsistence activities is the pursuit of game. Thus, the existence of a separate activity category "hunting" seems predicated on the existence of the gender division of labor (Cucchiari 1981:42).

As Cartmill has pointed out, only a very limited kind of killing counts as hunting in the western tradition (see also Poplin 1990):

> The symbolic meaning that hunting has for us has a lot to do with our definition of the term, which is a curiously restricted one.... A successful hunt ends in the killing of an animal, but it must be a special sort of animal that is killed in a specific way for a particular reason.
>
> Above all, the quarry must be a *wild* animal. The word "wild" can mean many things; but for the hunter's purposes, a wild animal is one that is not *docile* – that is, not friendly toward people or submissive to their authority.... Such an animal is part of the human domain, and killing it is just animal-killing, like shooting a cow in the dairy barn.
>
> The hunted animal must also be *free* – that is, able to flee (and to strike back at) its human assailant....
>
> The methods and motives of the hunter are also important in defining hunting. Hunting has to involve *violence*.... The fatal violence must be inflicted *directly*, not mediated by a snare or a trap. The hunter's assault on the quarry must be *premeditated*, which usually entails a period of chasing, stalking, or lying in ambush. (Running over wild animals on the highway does not count as hunting, even if you do it on purpose.) Finally, the killing must be undertaken at the hunter's initiative [not in self-defense].... Animal-killing that does not meet all these criteria is not hunting but something else: fishing, trapping, slaughter, vandalism, religious sacrifice, self-defence, pest control, or a road kill (Cartmill 1993:29–30).

This definition shows that the symbolic aspects of hunting are at least as important as the subsistence aspects. For us, at any rate, hunting is tied to notions of the wild and to oppositions between nature and culture. Foragers may not feel these oppositions, but they, too, define hunting as more than just acquiring animal protein (Sharp 1988:187). The acquisition of smaller and slower animals that can be collected fairly easily is generally not counted as hunting: The element of pursuit is critical. The Cree, for example, applied their verb "to hunt" only to moose, caribou, and bear, although they killed and ate many other wild species (Brightman 1993:8). The San count as hunting only the killing of large game animals with the bow and arrow, a masculine undertaking, whereas women procure meat in other ways (Parkington 2003:140). The Achuar distinguish between hunting (a male activity) and gathering animal foods (an activity of women and children) on the basis of whether the prey can defend itself or run away. Thus land tortoises are gathered, whereas water turtles are hunted (Descola 1994:251–6). In contrast, in Malawi, where most hunts are collective drives carried out by men and boys capturing a broad range of game in nets, and small mammals are a significant source of protein, "hunting" refers to small as well as large animals, even digging mice out of burrows (Morris 1998:76).

Szuter (2001) has tried to redefine hunting more comprehensively to reflect more accurately the contributions of both genders: "Hunting is not merely the pursuit and killing of large animals; it involves more than merely a group of men heading out to kill an animal; and it is not restricted to the use of a bow and arrow in active pursuit of a large animal. 'Hunting' glosses all of the activities that take place before, during, and after the hunt that make the kill possible" (Szuter 2001:199). She therefore includes in hunting such activities as raising birds for feathers to fletch arrows, butchering and distributing the meat, and cooking and serving it. Thus defined, hunting becomes an endeavor that typically involves many people of varied ages and genders. She also includes small game hunting, which carries less prestige but in some cases provides more meat. She recognizes, however, that the prehistoric and ethnographically known cultures of the American Southwest that she studies used a restricted definition that associates hunting and its prestige with men.

## Motivations for hunting

Hunting can be difficult and dangerous. In most places, it is not the easiest way to get food and often not even the easiest way to get protein. Why, then, do hunters hunt? Why do they continue to hunt when they have domestic animals and plants, so that subsistence is no longer an issue? And, although women often do hunt (Brightman 1993:126–7; Bronner 2008; Brumbach and Jarvenpa 1997; Estioko-Griffin and Griffin 1981), why are hunters mostly men?

SUBSISTENCE HUNTING

In the Arctic and subarctic, few plant foods are available to humans, so hunting and fishing must supply the bulk of the diet. This is rarely true elsewhere. Nevertheless, plant sources of protein and fat may be hard to find in some environments, notably the tropical forest (Good 1987; Gross 1975). The common craving for meat, like those for sugar and fat, must reflect the status of meat as a critical resource – important and often in short supply, but not necessarily the major component of the diet – in our evolutionary past (Abrams 1987). Hence the fundamental motivation for subsistence hunting is nutritional: the acquisition of a concentrated source of protein. Often the fat may be even more important (Brink 1997; Cachel 1997, 2000; Speth and Spielmann 1983).

Nevertheless, the meat itself is neither the only nor necessarily the primary motivation for hunting, even among foragers. For one thing, hunting is not the only way for foragers to obtain meat. Scavenging aside, the imperative to share, and especially to share meat, that characterizes most forager societies means that in theory any individual hunter could more easily get meat by waiting for someone else to hunt than by hunting him- or herself. Obviously this should rapidly end hunting altogether, yet this is not the case. The prestige accorded to successful hunters is a sufficient motivation, even if hunters and their families end up with less meat than other members of the group (Altman and Peterson 1988; Dowling 1968; Hawkes 1993; Wood and Hill 2000), and even when there are strong cultural measures to counter this prestige, as in the San practice of "insulting the meat" (see Chapter 9, *Meat Sharing*). Indeed, the need to institute such leveling mechanisms testifies to the amount of prestige that hunting carries.

Moreover, supplying meat is often tied to reproduction. Young men may need to prove themselves as hunters before they can marry or become sexually active (McCabe 1982; Parkington 2003; Tanner 1979:279). Even married men may need or be able to trade meat for sex with their wives or other women (Hugh-Jones 1996b; Kensinger 1989). Studies have shown that better hunters have more offspring (Hawkes and Bliege Bird 2002; Kaplan and Hill 1985; Smith 2004), although in fact it may be very hard to tell who is a good hunter (Hill and Kintigh 2009).

Bringing home a supply of nuts, or usually even of fish, does not normally bestow the same kind of prestige and benefits, although these are also good sources of protein and sometimes of fat and are generally valued foods. The special prestige attached to hunting is tied to the overvaluation of meat. The only other product carrying this status among foragers is honey, also highly valued and difficult to obtain in the wild. Yet although honey is valued and its obtainers celebrated, there does not seem to be the same kind of obligation to provide honey to prove one's manhood or secure one's place in society. The Okiek foragers of Kenya share meat but not honey (Marshall 1993, 1994).

Some of the particular power of hunting to confer prestige and mark masculinity surely lies in the sexual imagery in which it seems invariably to be couched. Killing a wild animal is frequently likened to sexual intercourse (e.g., Biesele 1993:2; Brightman 1996; Fiddes 1991:145; Hugh-Jones 1996b; Ingold 1987:251; Kensinger 1989; Leroi-Gourhan 1968; Morris 1998:73; Parkington 2003; Poplin 1990:46; Roe 1997:180; Tanner 1979). "From the point of view of male hunters, sex is a metaphor for hunting, and women are metaphors for animals" (Brightman 1993:127). Slaughtering a domestic animal or other forms of killing that do not count as hunting fail to carry this sexual connotation (although it does occur in the context of the bullfight, which can be seen as a ritualized hunt, with a constructed "wild" animal used to enact the drama of human/male conquest of nature; see Chapter 2). This is particularly interesting given the usual identification, at least in the West, of male with the wild and female with the tame and domestic (e.g., Hodder 1990). Hunting, then, converts the male to the female, the wild to the tame, and it establishes male domination over both: "[M]eat is almost ubiquitously put to use as a medium through which men express their 'natural' control, of women as well as animals" (Fiddes 1991:146). Cartmill (1993:240) points out that the language and imagery associated with hunting evoke less war than rape (cf. Morris 1998).

This glorification of male dominance over both women and the wild seems out of place in the generally nonpatriarchal foraging societies, yet they, too, link hunting and sex. One could argue that here the imagery is less of rape than of consensual sex, given the attitude that prey are equals of the hunter and willingly offer themselves to (or even seduce) the hunter so long as the hunter treats them with proper respect. Yet one could equally see this as mystification, an attempt to assuage the guilt of killing animals with a justification eerily similar to "she asked for it."

In any case, the link between hunting and sexuality, in particular of men doing it to women, may explain why hunters are primarily men in all cultures. This association is unlikely to have the same appeal to women, and it may make it seem inappropriate for them to participate in the kinds of killing that are defined as hunting. Alain Testart (1986) argues that women are forbidden to hunt with weapons that draw blood because it is necessary to keep separate the blood of wounds and menstrual blood that flows without a wound. Fear of menstrual blood, and especially concern that it be kept away from hunters and warriors, is also widespread cross-culturally (Brightman 1993:129, 1996; Galloway 1997; Grahn 1993; Hugh-Jones 1996a; Kensinger 1989; Sacks 1975; Sharp 1988), and there is evidence that game animals are in fact frightened by the smell of human menses, or blood in general (Brightman 1996; March 1980). Robert Brightman (1996:708) suggests the ban on women using penetrating weapons is less about the blood than the incongruity of women using such phallic weapons, given the sexual imagery of hunting. Scavenging, although it may be equally or more dangerous than hunting, does not lend itself to the same kind of imagery, perhaps explaining why we view it with such derision. Defending a carcass against predators and other would-be scavengers may require strength and fortitude, but it does not involve taking an animal against its will or even with its tacit consent (Fiddes 1991:84).

Hunting is thus tied to male fears of female sexuality and attempts to control it, although in more egalitarian societies it is cloaked in a language of equality and willing participation. The need to treat hunted animals with respect and to construct them as gladly offering themselves to the hunter betrays an underlying discomfort with the act of hunting. In an egalitarian society, animals cannot be exploited without guilt (Morris 1998:73, 108). The obvious injustice of taking one life to sustain another must be explained away (Brightman 1993:202–3; Harrod 2000:46; Hugh-Jones 1996b:132). Sexuality is a particularly powerful metaphor to help overcome the reluctance to kill. Has its use to make hunting more palatable to the hunter unintentionally facilitated male domination of women? If animals are like women, then women are also like animals. Among the San, origin myths portray a reversal from an earlier time when animals were people and people were animals. Women, however, are not fully reversed and retain more animality (Guenther 1988:193). Particularly when animals sink to a lower status with domestication (see Chapter 6), women may as well. If one accepts Fiddes' view that hunting was about domination from the beginning, the equation of women and prey implies female inferiority as soon as animals are hunted: "The evidence rather suggests that domination of the natural world, as represented in the meat system, antecedes sexual domination, providing both a model and a metaphor for men's control" (Fiddes 1991:161).

Whereas men overcome the guilt of hunting through sexual metaphor, Digard (1990:229) proposes that women in foraging societies overcome it through caring for pets (see Chapter 7). Hunters often bring back the young of female animals that they kill. However, not the hunters but their wives usually raise these animals. Digard views this as reparations for the men's actions.

Recent work in primatology suggests that hunting in chimpanzees is tied not to dietary need (hunting occurs in times of plenty, not scarcity) nor to reproductive success through giving meat to females in exchange for sex. Instead, hunting, which is primarily a male activity, is related to male bonding. Meat is exchanged among males to build coalitions (Mitani and Watts 1999, 2001). Anthropoid hunting is thus political in its very origins (see also Stanford 1999, 2001). This explains, in part, the association of hunting with males in anthropoids, which is not the case in carnivores. Although it may seem natural to us because we are so accustomed to it in our own species, it is not obvious why hunting, rather than other activities, should promote male bonding in chimps. In animals that are now often believed to have some degree of consciousness (Bickerton 2000; Corbey 2005; Gallup et al. 1977; Gomes et al. 2009; Winkelman 2010), the symbolic statement of domination over others may be the key appeal of hunting for chimpanzee males. Moreover, this domination is achieved through cooperation. The sense of guilt perhaps came later with the further development of consciousness.

### RITUAL HUNTING

Hunting is often ritualized in various ways, particularly in the observation of proper behavior before and during the hunt and the proper treatment of the prey (see Chapter 3, *Respecting the Hunted*). Yet sometimes the hunt itself is a ritual. All the cases of ritual hunting I have located in the ethnographic and historical literature are from societies with domestic animals and staple plant crops. Only when hunting stands apart from the usual method of obtaining meat can it become a ritual in itself. The closest to an exception are the ritual hunts annually organized by Bemba and Ndembu headmen in Malawi, where farming provides the staple food and domestic animals are few. Hunting also occurs in other contexts aimed mainly at subsistence, but these annual communal hunts, with animals driven by burning the bush, confer prosperity on the village. The meat is shared and consumed in a ritual context (Morris 1998:67). Southern Bantu groups, who do keep substantial flocks, also hold large ritual hunts at key times: initiations, preparations for war, accession of rulers, or times of drought (Kuper 1982:13). The Gauls are reported to have held a ritual hunt in the spring, in which they killed a stag to mark the renewal of the vegetation (Briard 1987:58). The stag may be chosen here because its antlers regenerate annually; they would just be starting to grow in the spring.

Marinatos (1989) argues, based on artistic evidence, that hunting of wild bulls on Minoan Crete was part of an initiation rite for elite youth. She thinks the repeated depictions of hunters grasping the bulls by the horns as they use nets or spears to hunt them do not portray a rational hunting technique. Rather these must be ceremonial hunts bringing the young men into confrontation with the wild, embodied in Crete's most dangerous animal. On the basis of paintings at Çatalhöyük, Mellaart (1984) makes a similar argument for hunting of bulls and other wild animals.

Again working from artistic evidence, in this case paintings on Moche pots from Peru, Christopher Donnan (1997) and Steve Bourget (2001) interpret scenes of hunting deer, foxes, and sea lions as ritual hunts to obtain victims for sacrifice, based on similarities in the hunters' weapons and dress to warriors in other scenes. The symbolic parallel seems clear, but although Moche warfare aimed to capture victims for human sacrifice, the deer (and apparently also the foxes) in these scenes are pierced through the throat with spears, whereas the sea lions are hit over the head with clubs, blood spraying from their mouths. These animals are not being captured alive for sacrifice, although perhaps the hunt itself was seen as an offering to the deities.

In early historic southern Arabia (roughly corresponding to modern Yemen, third to mid-second millennia BP), historical and artistic evidence indicates that ritual hunts were reserved for the elite. Kings and tribal leaders would join in multiday hunts annually and to mark special events such as coronations. Feasts and often sacrifices followed the hunts. Although other animals, including large carnivores, might be hunted, the primary game species was the ibex, sacred to the main deity, Athtar. Ibex symbolized water and fertility, and a successful ritual hunt was considered essential for a good harvest (Lewis 2007).

Emmanuelle Vila and Anne-Sophie Dalix (2004) make a rare argument for ritual hunting based, in part, on faunal remains. In the Late Bronze Age Near East, many groups did not eat pork (see Chapter 2, *Pig Taboos*). At Ugarit (Ras Shamra) in Syria, domestic pig remains are absent, but wild boar is found in small numbers, with clear signs of butchery and consumption. Pointing to artistic representations and textual references to wild boar in myths, Vila and Dalix suggest that the hunting and/or consumption of wild boar formed part of an elite ritual. The size of the boar remains indicates that only males were hunted: dangerous and therefore prestigious prey whose hunting enacted masculinity and power. They associate this (possibly ritual) hunt with the elite and consider the site as a whole to have been an elite center. Their case would be strengthened by contextual analysis of the boar remains.

In sum, these ritual hunts in agricultural and urban societies seem related to agricultural fertility and to power. The tie to agriculture is ironic, and worth bearing in mind as an alternative interpretation to hunting as a means to supplement domestic foods when small amounts of wild animal remains are found at farming sites.

SPORT HUNTING

Once domestic animals become the major source of meat (which may occur quite a long time after animal domestication, as herders seek to conserve their flocks by acquiring meat elsewhere), hunting can be seen as a sport. The ideology created to justify the killing of wild animals becomes a reason to continue killing them when the hunt is no longer necessary to acquire meat. Because of that ideology, game is valued more highly than the meat of domestic animals, and hunting often becomes the privilege of the elite (Salisbury 1994; Sykes 2005).

The line between subsistence hunting and sport hunting is fuzzy. Because prestige and the construction of male identity are involved in most hunting (Morris 1998:64), it is rarely just about subsistence. After an initial decline with the inception of herding, hunting often increases again, frequently accompanied by more elaborate ritual and symbolism (Halstead 1987:73; Wright 2000). Such effects may occur even in foraging populations. Although optimal foraging would predict that population growth and intensification of resource use would lead to a shift to smaller game, in fact under such circumstances in the Middle Archaic of the North American west coast big game hunting increases. William Hildebrandt and Kelly McGuire (2002) suggest this increased hunting is motivated by a desire for male prestige. The development of a more female-centered subsistence system based on acorns permitted men to indulge in prestige hunting. This show-off hunting may also be part of a renegotiation of gender roles accompanying these changes. Hunting themes come to dominate rock art at this period, further emphasizing the symbolic importance of hunting.

Elite hunting carries strong symbolic value and is generally quite ritualized (e.g., Green 1992:62), so that the distinction between ritual and sport hunting, especially in the premodern period, may be slight. Drawing on faunal remains and oracle bone texts, Magnus Fiskesjö argues that royal hunting is particularly prominent during periods of state formation and consolidation such as the Shang dynasty, and it plays a significant role in that process: "[T]he royal hunt, as a form of dangerous leisure, served as an intentionally conspicuous, grandiose risk-taking, simultaneously used to build and cultivate an image of control and physically incorporating the surrounding wilderness, thus expanding the domain and the charge of the Shang king and his archaic state in a dynamic process of 'domestication' that is central to state formation" (Fiskesjö 2001:51). Although royal hunting provided meat for the royal household and training in the military arts, Fiskesjö sees its primary role as establishing the legitimacy of the king. Shang rulers also sometimes hunted "wild" (non-Shang) people, who were explicitly equated to wild game. Fiskesjö argues that the Shang, as well as other early rulers elsewhere in the world, used the hunt to enact their domination of the wild: wild animals, wild people, wild land: "The hunting of wild animals – and of those people that the archaic kings chose to designate as 'wild' people, or barbarians – served as the means of incorporation and domestication of the entire range of living things, using the wild as a lever of state formation" (Fiskesjö 2001:166). Later, once the state is firmly established, royal hunting wanes. The wilderness and the kingdom's subjects have been tamed, so it no longer carries the same symbolic weight. Similar considerations seem to have obtained in the royal hunts in early historic southern Arabia, described in the previous section. Rulers tried to extend their territorial influence by inviting leaders of surrounding tribes to participate; inscribed memorials of such hunts indicate that they served to lay claim to territory and domesticate the landscape much as in the Shang dynasty (Lewis 2007).

Shang royal hunting was an elaborate affair, with beaters to drive the game, horse-drawn chariots, and probably dogs. Other royal hunts and elite classical and medieval hunts were similar, typically using horses and often specialized breeds of dogs (Salisbury 1994). Plato defines the ideal hunt as the pursuit of quadrupeds from horseback with the aid of dogs (Poplin 1990:45). François Poplin considers the element of pursuit essential to a "real" hunt. The horses and dogs extend human capabilities while leaving the actual kill to the human hunter. Quadrupedal mammals make the most satisfying prey because they can move quickly, heightening the pursuit. Dangerous animals such as boar or large carnivores, or those with large trophy horns and antlers, are the main targets of elite hunts (Green 1992; Salisbury 1994).

Falconry is another widespread form of elite hunting, in which power and wealth are enacted through the capture, keeping, and training of various kinds of raptors. Falconry involves special equipment, often the aid of dogs and horses, and, most crucially, labor-intensive training and maintenance of the hawks (Chun 2005; Dobney et al. 1999; Dobney and Jaques 2002; Forde 1963:343; Michell 1900; Pegge 1773; Prummel 1997). It is presently practiced particularly in the Middle East and Central Asia with a wide variety of birds and is often thought to have originated in the prehistoric Eurasian steppe zone, although there is not much evidence for this claim (Dobney 2002; Müller 1993).

Wietske Prummel (1997) outlines several lines of evidence for the archaeological detection of falconry: falconers' equipment, raptor burials, raptor remains in garbage deposits (especially goshawk, sparrow hawk, and falcons, the main species used), predominance of females among the goshawk and sparrow hawk remains (preferred for falconry because in these taxa females are larger than males and thus can take larger prey), and the remains of prey of these hawks (although Prummel notes that the balance of taxa taken is quite different between modern wild and trained birds). Of course, all but the distinctive equipment of falconry (of which the potentially most ancient elements are made of perishable materials) could result from other behaviors. Prummel notes the occurrence of raptors of the appropriate species in human burials in early medieval central and northern Europe as likely reflections of falconry (Tyrberg 2002), but raptors in burial contexts in prehistoric North America are not interpreted in this manner, given the lack of ethnohistorical evidence for Native American falconry and the abundance of such evidence for keeping raptors for their feathers or other ritual uses (see Chapter 3). Prummel finds support for the practice of falconry at Slavonic Oldenburg in northern Germany (1250–850 BP) in the presence of raptor species suitable for falconry, remains of their prey, and a bias to females in the hawks. Others have primarily relied on the presence of suitable raptors and their potential prey to argue for falconry in medieval contexts, often specifically associated with the elite (Cherryson 2002; Dobney and Jaques 2002; Hamilton-Dyer 2002; Heinrich 1997; Müller 1993; Müller and Prilloff 2006).

Using these same criteria, Keith Dobney (2002) argues that falconry may be very ancient, with suggestive associations of raptors and their prey in sites as early as the Epipaleolithic in the Near East and with artistic evidence dating back to the Bronze Age. Dobney even suggests that keeping tame birds for falconry may have provided, along with the dog, a model for the domestication of herd animals. This would cast falconry in a very different light – as a subsistence strategy rather than an elite pastime. If so, it would parallel the transformation of hunting in general. Yet would the substantial effort involved in keeping and training hawks be justified by the amount of small prey that they provide? He does not directly address this issue (although he presents anecdotal evidence of the effectiveness of tame raptors as hunters), but Dobney intriguingly links possible falconry to the Broad-Spectrum Revolution (Flannery 1969) in the early Holocene, when there is a shift toward greater quantities of small game of various types. The broad-spectrum phenomenon is not limited to the Near East, but occurs in many places around the world; perhaps we should be looking more closely at these bird assemblages as well. Dobney also notes the evidence for the symbolic significance of raptors in the early Neolithic of the Near East (e.g., Dobrowolski 1990;

Solecki and McGovern 1980), and suggests that tame hawks might have a religious function (as shamans' familiars) as well as a practical one.

Bertrand Hell (1996) notes a longstanding dual hunting tradition in Europe, contrasting an elite tradition involving stalking and centered on the acquisition of trophies, and a commoners' tradition (also geographically distinct, mainly in France and the Mediterranean zone) that employs beating and is meant to acquire food and protect crops. Similar distinctions could probably be made elsewhere. The lower/middle-class, rural tradition of hunting strongly resembles hunting in prehistoric agricultural societies: sometimes providing useful nutritional supplementation, but perhaps more importantly enacting identity through rural tradition. Both elite and commoner traditions strongly invoke specifically masculine identity (Bronner 2008; Kalof et al. 2004; Song 2010), although the elite version also stresses domination over nature and the wild within (Hell 1996; Morris 1998:119). In contrast, the commoner hunting tradition tends to view hunting as a way to rejoin nature (Cartmill 1999).

Sport hunting, then, retains many of the features of subsistence hunting and is not always easily separated from it. However, the elite can appropriate the prestige inherent in hunting, especially large game hunting, for the new purposes of laying claim to territory and sovereignty. Where hunting is an important display of elite power, the nobility often try to forbid commoners from hunting. Zooarchaeology can potentially provide an indication of how successful they were in preventing poaching, as in the classic study of Fort Ligonier, Pennsylvania, where despite historically documented orders forbidding the garrison's soldiers from hunting, a considerable amount of wild faunal remains were recovered (Guilday 1977).

### Hunters' attitudes to animals

Hunters' views of wild animals tend to be quite different from people's perceptions of domestic animals. In both sport and subsistence hunting, hunters generally construct the prey as equals, although they are really not (Cartmill 1993:29–31; Tapper 1988:52). Among foragers, however, the equality comes closer to being genuine. In these societies, the boundary between humans and animals is less marked and more permeable (see Chapter 1, *Anthropocentrism and Anthropomorphism*). Morris (2000:21) argues that this is because "empathy and identification is built into the act of hunting itself, which requires that a hunter to be successful must ask himself what he would do if he were an animal." Foragers may consider people to be descended from animals; animals may take on human form, and so on. Souls may inhabit different kinds of bodies. People who both hunt and herd may categorize wild animals together with humans as sentient beings, as opposed to the nonsentient domestic animals (Kent 1989:15).

Guenther (1988) believes hunters ponder ontological questions concerning how animals are distinct from humans. They generally reach an ambiguous answer. Among the San, at least, similarity with humans is emphasized in myth and art, whereas difference is emphasized in hunting, thereby permitting hunting and meat eating not to be murder and cannibalism. Nevertheless, like the Cree, the San identify with their prey, which Guenther thinks encourages conservation.

Ingold (1994) argues that foragers see their environment, and the animals in it, not as resources to exploit but as something alive and powerful, with which they must maintain relationships to survive (see also Bird-David 1999). The animals' side of the relationship is to offer themselves to hunters to feed people. The human obligation is to treat the animals and their remains properly: kill them only as necessary and in an appropriate fashion, share out the meat correctly (see Chapter 9, *Meat Sharing*), dispose of the bones and other waste appropriately, and behave respectfully (see Chapter 3, *Respecting the Hunted*). This behavior is an investment in future hunts, for if the relationship is broken, the animals will not offer themselves.

As I have suggested earlier, however, this attitude is to some extent a mystification. Hunters do not really have an equal relationship with their prey: The predator–prey relationship is inherently unequal. Moreover, hunters do not really have relationships with animals in the same way they do with human beings. They relate to humans as individuals, but to animals as species. It could hardly be otherwise with wild animals. An animal that is known individually is very close to being a pet. Indeed hunters may actually cultivate a relationship with spirits that own or are embodied in all animals or a particular species (Brightman 1993; Descola 1994:257–60; Harrod 2000:47–9; Ingold 1987:245–55; Schefold 2002; Tanner 1979; Willerslev 2007). This master or mother of animals offers them individual animals, and they offer the spirit their grateful respect.

Much of this attitude is maintained in sport hunting, where animals must be constructed as equals or near-equals to be worthy prey (Bronner 2008). Only in commercial hunting, when the animals become commodities, is this attitude (and with it any conservation ethic) wholly lost (Morris 1998:117). Pastoralists, however, for whom domestic animal wealth is paramount (see Chapter 8), may regard hunting, and perhaps wild animals, with "condescension" (Evans-Pritchard 1940:73).

### The call of the wild

Hunting, particularly in an agrarian or pastoral society, is intimately bound up with notions of the wild. This association relates to conceptions of nature and culture, which are historically contingent (Arnold 1996; Barry 1999; Cartmill 1993; Clutton-Brock 1999; Cronon 1995; Dwyer 1996; Escobar 1999; Evernden 1992; Harris 1996; Horigan 1988; Ingold 1994; Merchant 1980; Mullin 1999; Oelschlaeger 1991; Thomas 1983). There can be no conception of the wild without a conception of the domestic. The idea of wild animals thus largely postdates animal domestication. In contrast, there can be a notion of the domestic in the sense of a household sphere without animal domestication (Hodder 1990). We create nature when we create culture.

Because human bodies are ill equipped for killing animals, significant hunting, especially of larger animals, became possible only with the development of weapons. The use of weapons rather than teeth and claws to kill animals in itself creates a distancing not experienced by other predators (Cartmill 1993:12; Hodder 1990:283). This has implications for how we relate both to animals and to other humans: "Because our weapons were abruptly invented, not slowly evolved, we have not had time to acquire the inhibiting instincts that ought to go with our killing ability. When a defeated wolf goes belly up, the victor turns away with instinctive chivalry; when a defeated man goes belly up, the victor spears him in the belly" (Cartmill 1993:12). The sexual metaphor for hunting (and hunting/warfare as a metaphor for sex) also depends on the use of weapons. Biting and clawing an animal to death do not lend themselves so readily to phallic imagery. Thus with the first tools and especially with the first weapons we began to create nature and the wild by separating ourselves from it, and perhaps at this point we also created gender.

"[K]illing and eating are irreducibly political acts. . . . Humans kill and eat animals, while animals, by and large, do not kill and eat humans, and this is the visible measure of human hegemony. When men or women kill animals, the event indexes the hunters' superior power" (Brightman 1993:198). Fiddes argues that human hunting originated not from a need to supplement protein and calories on the savanna, but as a consequence of the emergence of culture: "[E]mbryonic culture, perceiving itself in a new light to be different from, or superior to, the rest of nature, found in hunting a way to *express* that vanity" (Fiddes 1991:60). How then does one deal with chimpanzee or baboon hunting? Because some argue that chimpanzees have a form of culture (Boesch and Tomasello 1998; Gibson 2002; Horner et al. 2006), one could simply push this symbolic statement back to prehominid ancestors. Baboons are harder to accommodate. Either we must adopt a more inclusive definition of culture than is normally used or attribute hunting to different motivations.

The notion of hunting as domination is intriguing and seems to be deeply embedded in human culture (although Morris [1998:170] would argue that subsistence hunters are interested in control over nature and animals, not dominion). It is not clear, however, whether our cultural sense of separation from and superiority to other animals led to hunting or whether hunting led to or reinforced this sense. Is predation invariably equivalent to domination? Do nonhuman predators feel superior to their prey? Certainly we feel that they would if they were conscious, as exemplified in such concepts as the lion as the "King of Beasts." Lions, jaguars and other carnivores are symbols of royalty precisely because the metaphor of predation to represent hierarchy is so compelling. It is also important that they are wild, uncontrolled by humans.

Paul Semonin (2000) suggests that our fascination with carnivorous dinosaurs as well as the readiness of 18th-century scholars to embrace the implausible notion that the mastodon was a ferocious carnivore derive from a modern western view of nature as wild and separate from us. To view prehistoric or contemporary animals in terms of "dominance," where the predators at the top of the food chain are dominant, and to model the natural world in terms of a war among species is inappropriate, he argues. One could just as easily emphasize interdependence and our place in nature rather than apart from it:

> Imagine for a moment that nature is not wild – that the original state of all living beings consists of a natural system characterized by interdependence, in which conflict and competition exist but no species is dominant and war is a profoundly unnatural act. Look at *Tyrannosaurus rex* as a minority species, an isolated meat eater living precariously at the top of

a pyramidal food chain inhabited by millions of other life-forms that are not subordinate species but living creatures, many of whom will outlive the so-called ruling species (Semonin 2000:411).

This view of nature as wild, in terms of strife and domination, is largely a product of hierarchical, and agricultural, societies. However, there are elements of it even in foraging societies. Brightman (1993) sees among the Cree a tension between views of humans as equal or even subordinate to the animals that willingly offer themselves to the hunter, and humans as dominating their animal prey by the act of killing them. In a society such as the Cree where survival depends on killing animals, this tension can never be fully resolved:

> Animals are beings like the self, but they must be killed and eaten, each death jeopardizing anew the relationship on which life depends – for who is to say that the animal is really reconciled to its death – and indicting the hunter as a murderer and cannibal. The paradox is moral and, like the Judeo-Christian theodicy, ultimately beyond solution. Since the human-animal categories are themselves continuous rather than discrete, it is unsurprising that no single representation of the hunter-prey relationship can be articulated (Brightman 1993:203).

Our very ability to empathize with our prey renders it impossible not to see hunting to some extent as domination. This does not mean, however, that we must necessarily see ourselves as outside nature; that is, see nature as wild. Such a concept can only follow the domestication of plants and animals, and it is linked to notions of control not only of other species but also of other people.

At various times and places, the wild sphere has been regarded with fear, contempt, or admiration (Cartmill 1993; Evernden 1992; Merchant 1980; Oelschlaeger 1991). The current western tendency to see the wild as noble, the domestic as mundane, is reflected in scientific attitudes to animals. Zoologists rarely study domestic animals, which are regarded as unnatural; higher status is granted to the more autonomous wild animals and those who study them (Clutton-Brock 1994:23; Coppinger and Coppinger 2001:24; Digard 1990:33; Ingold 1994:10). The reluctance to study domestic animals may also be motivated by fear of anthropomorphism (see Chapter 1, *Anthropocentrism and Anthropomorphism*): Because humans have closer contact with domestic animals, they are more prone to projecting human traits onto them (Lockwood 1989:53).

Domestic animals could be admitted to the reference collection in the Cornell University Museum of Vertebrates only by labeling them as "captive," a rather inadequate description of the domesticatory relationship (see Chapter 6).

## The archaeology of hunting

My purpose in this chapter has been somewhat different from that in most of the others. Hunting, scavenging, and how to distinguish them have already received a great deal of attention in zooarchaeology. I am not proposing new methods to study them nor arguing that they have been left out of zooarchaeological interpretation. Rather I am suggesting that we explore the implications of hunting and scavenging further in terms of human–animal and human–human relations. We might also consider whether we as zooarchaeologists have participated in the overvaluation of both hunting and meat.

Archaeological studies of hunting, even more than those of herding, have focused on issues of protein and calories, subsistence, and optimal foraging. These studies are based on the assumption that foragers are closer to nature than food producers (Brightman 1993:326; Ingold 1994:4; Mullin 1999:203–6), more like animals, and ecological models are thus sufficient to explain their behavior. Yet from the start human hunting has involved more than just the need to obtain high-quality food in an efficient manner. Like anyone else, hunters need to work within the ecological parameters of their environment to survive. However, there are many choices possible within these parameters.

> Cree hunting strategies are not now and have never been in the past determined by material forces. The relevant ecosystem is itself a social construction, albeit one with maximal "resistance". . . . No foragers forage indiscriminately, none know or act upon all the characteristics of proximal fauna potentially relevant to the provisioning of human populations. Diet breadths and foraging strategies do not passively encode universally recognized material properties. There is always "selection" between alternative possible designs for provisioning society (Brightman 1993:34–5).
>
> [T]he production process is, throughout, dominated by conceptions of edibility, gender, prestige, and labor that are themselves irreducible to it or to the technological and environmental context (Brightman 1993:340).

We cannot ignore the social and symbolic aspects of hunting if we seek to explain hunting strategies. These variables enter into hunters' decisions as much as ecological factors. The very concept of hunting strategies, and indeed of optimal foraging, implies that human hunters do not simply opportunistically kill any animal they encounter, but rather make choices of what to seek and what to kill. These choices are not shaped solely by considerations of maximizing meat yield or maintaining a sustainable yield. In interpreting faunal remains, we must consider that hunters may have gained prestige by killing certain (often large) animals and that hunting may have been pursued because it bolstered notions of humanity and masculinity, even when it was not the optimal way to obtain nutrients.

Mary Stiner (1990, 1991a, 1991b, 1993a, 1993c) has drawn attention to what appears to be a uniquely human hunting strategy (emerging relatively late in human evolution, ca. 40,000 BP): the prime-oriented mortality profile. Whereas most predators pick off the old and the young, which are more easily captured, humans tend to concentrate on prime adults, with the greatest fat reserves. This strategy is unlikely to be the most efficient way to obtain meat. Although obtaining fat may have been one incentive (Speth 1983; Speth and Spielmann 1983), the hunters were probably largely motivated by prestige, just as in modern trophy hunting. Likewise, killing a mammoth, with far more meat than a small band could utilize without extensive storage capabilities, is surely not the easiest nor the most profitable way to obtain meat. Nevertheless, people did at least occasionally hunt mammoths and other huge and dangerous megafauna (see Chapter 5). In modeling hunting strategies, we need to include not just caloric input and output but also the prestige value of the animals pursued (Brightman 1993; Dwyer 1985). Some studies suggest that this may be especially true of young, unmarried male hunters (Bliege Bird and Bird 1997; Wood and Hill 2000).

In contrast, people may choose not to hunt or eat certain animals because of food taboos (see Chapter 2), mythological associations, or personal relationships with that species or category (spirit helpers, etc.). Some animal species may be seen as antagonistic to each other and thus may not be hunted or consumed at the same time, potentially producing a seasonal pattern not solely related to the presence or prime condition of the animals nor to pragmatic scheduling concerns of the hunters (Renouf 2000).

In short, although most hunters no doubt strive for a strategy that optimizes their goals, including obtaining what they consider to be an adequate amount of meat, they do not necessarily conceive these goals in the narrow terms of protein and calories. Such least effort models rather reflect the concerns of contemporary capitalist society, where time is money and profit is paramount. The aim of capitalism is to reduce costs to maximize profit, but this logic does not apply in other kinds of societies (Bourdieu 1977; Godelier 1999; Gregory 1980, 1982, 1997; Hyde 1983; Weiner 1992). It is ethnocentric and inappropriate to apply capitalist models to non-market-based economies. Ingold (1996b) argues that optimal foraging models do not work as evolutionary explanations, either.

It may be that prestige and taboos are harder to represent quantitatively than protein and calories. However, the rigor of caloric models is somewhat deceptive. First, human nutritional needs are complex, flexible, and remarkably difficult to specify with precision (Jerome 1980). It is difficult to set a minimum requirement for any given nutrient that is not violated by some thriving population somewhere in the world. Second, in archaeology we typically have to make so many assumptions and approximations that such models have margins of error of a magnitude that renders them of limited value. Finally, even if we could build accurate nutritional and energetic models, if the people to whom we apply them are operating according to a different logic, the models will not adequately account for their behavior. "The efficiency of hunting may have been measured in terms of the relative spiritual power of the hunter and his prey or the quality of the relations between a hunter and the spirits that controlled animal behaviour" (Trigger 1995:451). If hunters are seeking to maximize prestige or spiritual power rather than to minimize effort, optimal foraging models will not be particularly useful.

In the real world, hunters normally balance multiple and often conflicting goals. In seeking to understand ancient hunting, we must strive to take all of these goals into account. This means considering both ecology and society. Costly signaling models are a step in this direction.

5

# Extinctions

> The account of the ways along which this animal world has gradually suc-
> cumbed to our species would involve the whole history of civilization.... By
> and by they turned the artillery of Nature on herself. The dog raised a flag
> of truce and came in to join the hosts of man against the rest. The mountain
> sheep and the wild goat descended from their rocky fortresses, gave up the
> contest, and surrendered skins and fleece and flesh and milk to clothe and
> feed the inventor of the fatal arrow.... Those that refused to enter in any way
> into these stipulations are doomed sooner or later to extinction, and many
> species have already disappeared or withdrawn to the waste places of earth in
> despair. (Mason 1966[1895]:259–60)

Driving animal species into extinction may be the most brutal kind of
human–animal relationship. People have been responsible for the disappearance of many animal species, most of them in the last two hundred years. In this chapter we are concerned with prehistoric extinctions
and the role that humans may have played in them. We can take some
lessons from more recent extinctions. The anthropogenic factors that
can contribute to animal extinctions include overhunting or persecution,
pollution, the introduction of exotic predators or competitors, and habitat destruction (Eldredge 1999; Halliday 1978; MacPhee and Flemming
1999). In general, habitat destruction is the most insidious (Fuller 2001).
All of these factors are exacerbated by human population growth.

## Island extinctions

The clearest evidence for humanly caused prehistoric animal extinctions
comes from islands around the world. Islands are often described as natural laboratories that act as models for mainland areas or for the earth as
a whole (Halliday 1978:170; Kirch 1997). Although it may be useful to

view the earth itself as an island, we should be cautious in drawing analogies between island events and those on the mainland (Walter 2004). As outlined in the theory of island biogeography (MacArthur and Wilson 1967), the bounded, small-scale ecosystems of islands are particularly fragile. Not only are there fewer opportunities for restocking from other regions but island floras and faunas also are typically impoverished in their number of species, creating simpler and more vulnerable ecosystems. Where islands lack large predators, animals lose their bodily and behavioral defense mechanisms. This is frequently the case because the small landmass of islands does not provide territories of sufficient size for larger predators. For similar reasons, large herbivores on islands often become dwarfed. In contrast, small animals may become larger to avoid the small predators that remain. Island animals that care for their young tend to develop lower birth rates, because the population is limited not by predation but by the availability of food (Alcover et al. 1998; Schüle 1993:403). This vulnerability has led to high rates of extinctions following human contact. At least 27% of all mammals or 35% of nonflying mammals and more than 60% of bird species have been lost from islands worldwide; mammals weighing more than 5 kg are more likely to become extinct than smaller ones (Alcover et al. 1998).

## OCEANIA

These features of island faunas are well illustrated in Oceania, where species of flightless birds developed on many islands. A similar bird on Mauritius in the Indian Ocean, the dodo (*Raphus cuculatus*, a flightless pigeon), survived long enough to become both an icon of extinction and a symbol of stupidity because it did not have the good sense to fear humans (Halliday 1978:56–67). Most of the extinct birds of the Pacific are known to western science only through fossils, not having long survived the arrival of humans on their islands. Only recent archaeological and paleontological work in the Pacific has made the scale of these losses apparent (Steadman 2006). For example, 40% of the bird species of New Caledonia became extinct shortly after its colonization by humans (Spriggs 1996:530). Although flightless birds experienced particularly heavy losses, land birds in general suffered extensive extinctions; seabirds were much less affected. The total loss in the Pacific is on the order of 2,000 species of birds, most of them flightless rails. Most of these extinctions have occurred in the last 3,000 years, associated with the spread of the agricultural Lapita culture through the Pacific (Steadman 1995). Exploitation of this easy prey may have substantially aided the colonization of the Pacific islands, and their extinction may have triggered the abandonment of some formerly inhabited islands (Anderson 2001; Steadman 1989).

The loss of the New Zealand moas is the most thoroughly studied of these many extinctions. The moas were 10 species of large flightless birds that became extinct some time after the arrival of humans, along with 33 other species of endemic land birds, a bat, and some reptiles and amphibians (Anderson 1989b; Holdaway 1999; Martin and Steadman 1999:32; Steadman 1995:1124; Worthy and Holdaway 2002). The current chronology indicates that humans arrived about 700 BP and drove the moas to extinction over 100–200 years (Holdaway and Jacomb 2000; Nagaoka 2005; Wilmshurst et al. 2008). Most agree that the extinction of the moas was caused by a combination of factors linked to human activities. In addition to overhunting this easy prey, people contributed to their demise by clearing forests and by introducing dogs and rats, which also preyed on the birds and their eggs (Anderson 1989a; Davidson 1985; Kirch 1982:76). Atholl Anderson (1989a) adds that not only the moas but also the humans were naïve about hunting. The settlers of New Zealand came from places where they had no experience with large terrestrial game, and thus were culturally unequipped with conservation strategies.

Similar processes have been documented for Hawai'i (Olson and James 1982), the Marqesas (Rolett 1992, Steadman and Rolett 1996), the Pitcairns (Wragg and Weisler 1994), and many other islands across the Pacific (Flannery and Roberts 1999; Steadman 1989, 1995). Where the faunal records are sufficient, these extinctions seem to have occurred over several centuries or longer, rather than being a process of immediate extermination. There is general agreement that a similar set of factors led to these extinctions: deforestation and other habitat alteration, introduced predators, and overhunting. David Steadman (1989) suggests that introduced avian diseases, carried initially by domestic chickens brought by Polynesian settlers, and more recently by mynahs and other imported birds brought by Europeans, may also have played a role. Giant tortoises were likely also wiped out by human activities on many of these islands, as were horned turtles on Vanuatu (Schüle 1993; White et al. 2010).

Extinction or local extirpation of at least 12 species of birds has been recorded on New Ireland, close to New Guinea. Here the sequence of events is less well known. Faunal remains have been studied only from periods postdating human colonization ca. 35,000 BP. Thus we cannot judge whether initial human settlement caused the extinction of any local taxa. The time of disappearance of the birds is also not known, although several species become considerably less common in later, Holocene deposits. We know that all 12 species survived at least 20,000 years of contact with human foragers, and most of them considerably longer, including two species of flightless rails that are last recorded ca. 2000 BP. Although the extinction process is not fully understood on New Ireland, it is suspected that, in addition to human hunting, agricultural practices and animals introduced to the island by humans both before and after the advent of agriculture played a role (Steadman et al. 1999).

The prehistoric extinctions in Oceania raise two key points. First, most scholars think that overhunting alone was insufficient to wipe out these species, although it certainly contributed to the process (cf. Duncan et al. 2002). The extinctions also required significant alterations of the ecosystem, in addition to the relatively small populations, bounded habitats, and specialized adaptations that characterize island faunas. Introduction of exotic species, especially rats, appears to be particularly important (Blackburn et al. 2004; Green and Weisler 2004; Hunt 2007). Second, most or all of these extinctions were caused by agriculturalists (the Lapita culture and its descendants) whose staples were domesticated plants and animals. Agricultural practices and these domestic/commensal animals were responsible for most of the alterations to the island ecosystems. Because they did not depend on the wild fauna for their survival (or perhaps did not realize this in time in the cases of islands marginal for agriculture that were later abandoned), the settlers were not impelled to implement conservation measures (Tudge 1999). Matthew Spriggs (1996) terms this a pioneer attitude, noting that earlier, nonfarming settlers of Pacific islands did not cause these dramatic and disastrous ecological effects. Moreover, the severe degradation of island ecosystems mostly happened in the initial period of settlement, after which people adopted a more conservation-minded approach.

There is at least one exception, however. Recent work shows that the local population of elephant seals on Tasmania was extirpated by overhunting during prehistoric times (Bryden et al. 1999); some terrestrial megafaunal species may also have been killed off by early settlers (Turney et al. 2008). The Tasmanians did not practice agriculture, so this presents quite a different scenario. Seals and sea lions are particularly vulnerable in their rookeries and thus far more sensitive to overhunting than most land mammals. Seals became extinct in New Zealand along with the moas (Nagaoka 2001). Recent work along the west coast of North America has demonstrated that fur seals, which now breed only on islands, once had mainland rookeries and that prehistoric hunters targeted both mainland and offshore rookeries of seals and sea lions (Burton et al. 2001; Porcasi et al. 2000). This hunting pressure appears to have depressed local pinniped populations and is probably responsible for the loss of mainland fur seal rookeries.

MEDITERRANEAN

The Mediterranean islands have also received considerable study, but although the extinctions that occurred on them are clear, the human role in them is not. Like the Pacific islands, many in the Mediterranean had impoverished faunas in the Pleistocene and early Holocene as a result of their separation from the mainland (Schüle 1993). A number of endemic species had adapted to island conditions, including the lack of large predators. Along with a lagomorph and several rodents, some of them giant forms, and giant tortoises on most islands, there were dwarf bison and boar on Sicily; a species of "Irish elk" (*Megaloceros cazioti*) on Sardinia and Corsica; the small bovid *Myotragus balearicus* on Mallorca and Menorca; flightless swans on Sicily, Sardinia, and Malta; endemic owls on Sardinia and Corsica; pygmy elephants on Cyprus, Rhodes, Crete, Sicily, Malta, Sardinia, and several smaller islands; and pygmy hippopotami on Cyprus, Crete, Sicily, and Malta (Alcover et al. 1999; Johnson 1980; Schüle 1993). The larger taxa become extinct in the early Holocene, at roughly the same time that humans reach the islands. A number of bird species were also locally extirpated at this time. This is one in a series of extinction events on these islands, with the earlier ones attributed to faunal turnover as new species colonized the islands or to volcanic eruptions (Alcover et al. 1999).

There are claims for Lower Paleolithic occupation of Sardinia, but these are disputed (Schüle 1993; Vigne 1988). Thus the pygmy elephants most likely became extinct before human contact, and in any case there is no actual evidence of hominid involvement in their extinction. This was a period of low sea levels when the island was colonized by several new species, so it would have been a time of general ecological upheaval (Alcover et al. 1999:177). The Sardinian elk must have become very rare in the early Holocene because it does not appear at Mesolithic sites (Sondaar and van der Geer 2000; Vigne 1996), although a few apparently survived until 7500 BP (Benzi et al. 2007). Extinction due to climatic change thus seems most likely, particularly because the continental *Megaloceros* species also disappears at the end of the Pleistocene and with no sign of human intervention. In addition, the "dwarf wolf" (*Cynotherium sardous*) disappears at the end of the Pleistocene before the arrival of humans. However, the giant pika (*Prolagus sardus*) survived into the historical period, when it disappeared primarily due to habitat destruction and introduced competitors, although people did eat it from their first settlement of the island (Masseti and De Marinis 2008; Schüle 1993; Sondaar and van der Geer 2000; Vigne 1988).

The suite of mammals on Corsica in the Upper Pleistocene was essentially the same as that on Sardinia. On Corsica all the larger mammals disappear before the arrival of humans (Vigne 1988). The small mammals fared better, surviving 8,000 years of human contact until they were apparently done in by the introduction of the black rat (*Rattus rattus*) during the Roman period; perhaps agricultural intensification at this time also contributed (Vigne 1992:93).

The extinction of the pygmy hippos of Cyprus has been surrounded by still greater controversy. Until recently there was no evidence for human occupation on the island until after the extinction had occurred. The careful study of the site of Akrotiri *Aetokremnos* by Alan Simmons and his colleagues has now convinced most archaeologists that people were present while the hippos were still extant, and that they hunted them (Reese 1996, 2001; Simmons 1988, 1991a, b, 1996, 1999, 2001; Strasser 1996; cf. Bunimovitz and Barkai 1996; Vigne 1996). So far, however, this remains a single, rather ephemeral occupation, and the early agriculturalists who visited and settled the island not long afterward seem to postdate the hippos. Did people stay just long enough to wipe out the hippos and then abandon the island, as on the "mystery islands" of the Pacific? Or was this in fact a one-time, brief stop by passing sailors, with little lasting impact on the island fauna? On many Pacific islands there are sequences in which endemic species appear early in the human occupation and then fade out through time. The Tasmanian elephant seals show a changing demographic profile indicative of overhunting before they disappear. We do not as yet have this kind of clear record implicating humans on Cyprus.

The principal islands of the Balearics, Mallorca and Menorca, were once home to an odd species of endemic ruminant, sometimes termed the cave goat or island-goat (*Myotragus balearicus*). This goat-like animal had adapted to island conditions (no predators, limited food) in several dramatic ways. It exhibited an extreme shortening of the lower limb to promote rock-climbing ability at the expense of speed; it could manage no more than a slow walk. Its eyes rotated to face front, sacrificing a broader field of vision useful for predator detection to achieve binocular vision to aid in climbing. It developed beaver-like incisors to peel bark (Köhler and Moyà-Solà 2001). This distinctive creature was once thought to have died out at the end of the Pleistocene, before humans arrived on the islands ca. 7000 BP (Alcover 2008; Andrews 1915; Bate 1909; Bover et al. 2008; Schüle 1993). However, archaeological work, backed up by a radiocarbon date on one of the *Myotragus* bones, shows that they survived until 4700 BP, into the Neolithic period (Burleigh and Clutton-Brock 1980). Indeed, William Waldren (1974, 1982) suggests that they were actually herded by Neolithic Mallorcans, although this claim has recently been challenged (Ramis and Bover 2001). There is general agreement that humans are responsible for their ultimate demise, although in fact there is little direct evidence for this claim. In any case, *Myotragus* extinction followed more than 2,000 years of coexistence and cannot be characterized as the rapid slaughter of slow, naïve animals. It should be noted that only a single *Myotragus* specimen has so far been dated in the Holocene, so possibly the population was already dwindling. Factors such as habitat alteration and competition with herds of domestic sheep and goat (attested in the earliest human occupation remains) may have pushed it over the edge at least as much as hunting. The other two terrestrial mammals of Mallorca, a rodent and a shrew, seem also to have become extinct in the period following human colonization (Alcover et al. 1999:178; Bover and Alcover 2008).

Thus the Mediterranean case is less clear-cut than the Pacific one. Many of the large mammals became extinct at the Pleistocene-Holocene boundary, a time of climatic change. Of course, this change is an alternative candidate for the cause of these extinctions. It required a great deal of careful work to establish the contemporaneity of humans and endemic large mammals on Cyprus and Mallorca; more such work is needed on the Mediterranean islands to clarify the role that humans played in extinctions there.

## MADAGASCAR

In the early Holocene, the fauna of Madagascar included pygmy hippos, giant tortoises, at least 16 species of giant lemurs ranging up to the size of gorillas, and 7 species of flightless elephantbirds weighing up to 500 kg. All of these species, as well as eight smaller birds, are now extinct, leaving the crocodile as the only large native animal. Thus at least 33 species of mammals, birds, and tortoises became extinct, and most or all of these extinctions follow the arrival of humans ca. 2000 BP. These settlers were Iron Age farmers, herders, and merchants. Climatic changes may have played some role, as late Holocene desiccation affected the island.

However, most scientists have concluded that the extinctions were caused by human activity, involving some combination of overhunting, habitat alteration, and the introduction of competing animal species and exotic predators. At least some of the extinct species survived for a millennium after human occupation of the island. There is only limited direct evidence of human hunting in the form of kill sites or historical accounts, although there is somewhat more evidence for the collection of elephant-bird eggs. In contrast, anthropogenic alterations of the landscape, such as deforestation and erosion, are well attested by palynological and sedimentological studies. The greatest factor is likely to have been introduced domestic ungulates (cattle, sheep, and goat), including feral herds that may have extended well beyond the apparently sparse early settlements (Burney 1997, 1999; Burney et al. 1997; Burney et al. 2003; Dewar 1997; Godfrey et al. 1997; Goodman and Rakotozafy 1997; MacPhee and Marx 1997; Perez et al. 2005; Wells and Andriamihaja 1997). The various anthropogenic factors may have been the last straw for endemic species already stressed by climatic change (Burney 1997; Crowley 2010; Virah-Sawmy et al. 2010).

## CARIBBEAN

A number of Holocene extinctions (total or local) occurred on Caribbean islands after their colonization by humans. On Antigua in the Lesser Antilles, 10 species of vertebrates (birds, reptiles, bats, and rodents)

disappeared during the prehistoric period subsequent to the arrival of
humans ca. 4000 BP; three more have become extinct in historic times.
Most of these are small animals, and most are unlikely to have been
hunted by people. Thus their demise appears to result from habitat
destruction as a result of agricultural practices. Although the rice rat
(Oryzomyini sp.) may well have been eaten, as it was elsewhere in the
Caribbean, it seems to have survived until the introduction of Old World
rats in the historic period. Human hunting may have caused the local
extermination of Audubon's shearwater (*Puffinus lherminieri*), although
introduced predators such as rats may also have played a role. Further extinctions took place in the historic period, following much more
severe environmental disturbances associated with deforestation to establish sugar and cotton plantations and the introduction of rats, cats, dogs,
goats, mongooses, and other animals. Some of the animals attested in prehistoric Holocene archaeological and paleontological sites may actually
have become extinct during the historic period without being recorded
(Morgan and Woods 1986; Steadman et al. 1984).

NORTH ATLANTIC

Serjeantson's (2001) study of the great auk (*Alca impennis*) provides
insight into an anthropogenic extinction of a non-endemic species. The
great auk was a goose-sized, penguin-like flightless seabird of the North
Atlantic that came ashore only to breed; it became extinct in the mid-
19th century. Archaeological finds indicate that the great auk once bred
quite widely around the shores of the northern Atlantic, even into the
Mediterranean during the Pleistocene. These birds were easily caught in
the shoreline breeding colonies, but much harder to take at sea. Although
Mesolithic foragers had little impact on British auks, when Neolithic
farmers settled near a breeding colony, they rapidly wiped out the local
population. The sporadic later finds may represent occasional birds taken
at sea.

Several factors appear to have contributed to the great auk's demise.
Its flightlessness of course made it easier to catch and restricted it to
shoreline, rather than cliff-top, breeding colonies. It would also leave it
vulnerable to introduced predators. The great auk laid single eggs and did
not replace them if lost. It never learned to fear humans. Nevertheless,
human foragers did not overhunt the auks, whether because the human
populations were simply too small or because of conservation measures.

As in the Pacific, however, the expanding Neolithic farmers may have had an exploitive, frontier mentality that lacked a tradition of restraint in harvesting wild resources. On the other side of the Atlantic, local Beothuk foragers harvested auks sustainably from their major breeding ground on Funk Island. European cod fishers entered the area in the 14th century and killed the auks to sell for food and feathers, salting them like the cod. They treated the birds like the fish, as an unlimited resource owned by no one. This unrestrained killing by commercial fishers on both sides of the Atlantic finally drove the great auk to extinction. Similar exploitation limited the population of the gannet (*Sula bassana*) and eliminated many of its local breeding grounds. It was able to survive because it flies, nests on top of cliffs, and in many places received protection through conservation strategies imposed by the state or adopted by local communities (Serjeantson 2001).

SUMMARY

Humans have decimated the fauna (and flora) on many islands around the world. The loss, especially of birds in the Pacific, has been a major blow to global biodiversity. We should be cautious in regarding islands as miniature models of continents, because island faunas have special vulnerabilities. What broader lessons can be learned, then, from island extinctions?

Supporters of the Pleistocene overkill model (see the later discussion) take the lesson that, when people colonize new lands, they wipe out a substantial portion of the native fauna. A closer examination of island experiences produces a more nuanced view, however. Those outside anthropology and archaeology tend to attribute extinctions to a unitary human influence without distinguishing among different kinds of human societies. Thus they believe that any human group entering a new territory will cause devastation. However, what the island record shows is that, speaking grossly, foragers rarely cause extinctions, whereas farmers, with a very different relation to the natural world, often have a severe ecological impact. Some farming practices are no doubt more harmful than others, with herding likely to be particularly damaging to island ecosystems.

Current data on island extinctions show that overhunting alone rarely drives species to extinction, even naïve endemic species in limited island environments. Rather, destruction of vegetation (usually associated with agricultural practices) and the introduction of exotic animal species seem to be the key factors. Where it is possible to assess the timing of extinctions, they usually occur after centuries or even millennia of contact.

### Pleistocene overkill?

For decades, a fierce debate has raged over whether the first set of extinctions caused by people is the disappearance of megafauna in the New World and Australia in the late Pleistocene. The term "megafauna" has been variously defined, but in this context typically refers to mammals >44 kg. About half of the genera of such animals have disappeared within the last 40,000 years. To a greater extent than the island cases, large mammals were differentially affected. Some small vertebrates also disappeared, but these are explained as commensals of the megafauna. The focus on megafauna differs from earlier mass extinction events, as does the fact that extinctions are largely limited to terrestrial species (P. Martin and Steadman 1999).

In the 1960s, Paul Martin attributed this phenomenon to human hunting of naïve fauna as people entered previously unpopulated continents. Arguing that the extinctions were closely coincident with the arrival of humans, he outlined the Pleistocene overkill or blitzkrieg model, in which profligate hunters swept through Australia and later North and South America, slaughtering naïve megafauna in their wake. In this model, rapid human population growth and high mobility permitted the colonization and elimination of megafauna of the entire New World within two millennia; local populations of megafauna were wiped out in less than a decade (P. Martin 1967; P. Martin and Steadman 1999).

This model has been hotly debated ever since. The two extreme positions can be characterized as Martin's blitzkrieg on the one hand and attribution of the extinctions solely to climatic change on the other. In between are those who argue for a combination of climate and human hunting, or those who think that overhunting is the main factor but that it operated more slowly. Additionally, there is a position positing rapid extinction ultimately caused by human entry into new areas, but through the introduction of epidemic disease rather than overhunting; there is also a recent argument for a meteor impact. In this section I briefly summarize the evidence for Pleistocene extinctions in Australia and the New World, with a look at the Old World, before evaluating these explanations.

## AUSTRALIA

In Australia most of the extinctions occur well before the end of the Pleistocene, with some further losses in the Holocene. During the Pleistocene 28 genera and about 55 species of vertebrates became extinct, including 15 of the 16 megafaunal mammalian genera. Other taxa include giant reptiles (snakes, lizards, crocodiles, and horned turtles) and flightless or nearly flightless birds. Most of the extinctions happened ca. 46,000 BP or earlier. Human presence is likely from 45,000–42,000 BP, but the timing of both the extinctions and human arrival is disputed (Cupper and Duncan 2006; Flannery and Roberts 1999; Gillespie 2008; Grün et al. 2010; Johnson 2005; MacPhee and Marx 1997; P. Martin and Steadman 1999; Miller et al. 1999; O'Connell and Allen 1998, 2004; Roberts et al. 2001; Wroe and Field 2006). The latest chronological study, which appears methodologically sound, suggests that extinctions happened over a long period, largely before human arrival (Price et al. 2011).

Archaeological remains associated with extinct megafauna are claimed at Nombe rockshelter in New Guinea and Cuddie Springs (36,000–30,000 BP) in Australia (Field et al. 2001; Trueman et al. 2005). However, the most recent analyses of Cuddie Springs argue that there is no real association: The megafaunal remains are earlier and redeposited (Fillios et al. 2010; Grün et al. 2010). Extinctions in Tasmania seem to predate human arrival on the island (Cosgrove et al. 2010), save the local extirpation of elephant seals mentioned earlier.

Proponents of overkill point to the Australian case as demonstrating that extinctions coincide with the arrival of humans rather than the end of the Pleistocene, so that they cannot be attributed to climatic change. However, there are climatic changes during the Pleistocene, with a trend to greater aridity. The uncertainties of the dating of extinctions make it hard to evaluate the climatic role. There is evidence for an increase in brush fires from around the Last Glacial Maximum, which have been variously attributed to the effects of increased aridity, human action, and the increased fuel load following the extinction of the megafauna; these fires are seen as limiting food for browsers, which went extinct at a greater rate than grazers (Bowman et al. 2010; Field et al. 2001; Flannery and Roberts 1999; Miller et al. 2005; Owen-Smith 1999; Prideaux et al. 2010). One model combines climatic and human factors in the extinction of the last megafauna, suggesting that Last Glacial Maximum drying stressed both megafauna and humans and concentrated them around waterholes. The people shifted first to a greater reliance on megafauna and later to the use of seeds (Field et al. 2001).

There are also Holocene extinctions in Australia and New Guinea. These are more clearly linked to human activity and are apparently part of the Lapita phenomenon. The timing is late, ca. 3000–2000 BP. Although agriculture was not introduced to Australia, dogs were. Their introduction appears to have led to the disappearance of the larger predators, the Tasmanian devil (*Sarcophilus harrisii*) and the thylacine (*Thylacinus cynocephalus*), as well as the flightless Tasmanian native hen (*Gallinula mortierii*). These three species survived at least until European contact on Tasmania, where there were no dogs. In New Guinea both dogs and pigs were introduced through contact with Lapita peoples, and although agriculture may already have been practiced, it was intensified at this time and new crops were added. This led to the loss of the thylacine in Papua New Guinea and two species of wallaby (*Thylogale*) in Irian Jaya (Flannery and Roberts 1999; Holdaway 1999).

### NEW WORLD

Most of the debate over Pleistocene extinctions has centered on the New World, primarily North America. Most megafaunal species became extinct in the late Pleistocene: 34 genera of megafaunal mammals in North America (and 3 genera of smaller mammals), and 51 genera of megafaunal mammals in South America (and no smaller mammals). There is some overlap among genera lost in the two continents, but altogether 74 megafaunal genera became extinct (P. Martin and Steadman 1999). In contrast to the island cases, birds were much less affected. Many of these extinctions are not well dated, but the latest dates are ca. 13,000 BP on the mainland. There are a few later survivals on islands, such as the pygmy mammoths of the Channel Islands, which eventually became extinct without human intervention, probably as a result of habitat reduction caused by Holocene rising sea levels (Agenbroad 2001). Proponents of overkill see the island survivals as evidence that climatic change was not responsible for the extinctions, but the more buffered maritime climate and indeed the dwarfing may have mitigated the effects of climatic change. There is evidence for severe climatic change in western North America at the Pleistocene-Holocene boundary, which included not only rising temperatures but also increased seasonality (Broughton et al. 2008; Elias 1995; Neck 1995; Pinter et al. 2011).

The discovery of Paleoindian artifacts in clear association with extinct fauna was crucial in establishing the antiquity of human occupation in the New World. However, such sites are few, are primarily located in western North America, and chiefly involve mammoths and bison, with rarer associations with horse (Fox et al. 1992; Frison and Todd 1986, 2001; Grayson and Meltzer 2002; Haynes and Eiselt 1999:75; Hofman 2001; Kenady et al. 2011; P. Martin and Steadman 1999; Meltzer 2006; Meltzer et al. 2002; Miller 1983; Surovell and Waguespack 2008; Todd et al. 1990; Webb and Hemmings 2006; Webb et al. 1984; Wheat 1972). Similar claims for associations with mastodons are less well supported, but some may be valid (Breitburg et al. 1996; Crabtree 1939; Eiseley 1945; Fisher 1984a, 1984b, 1987; Haynes 1990, 1995; Laub and Haynes 1998; Norton et al. 1998; Tankersley et al. 2009; Webb 2006).

In South America one recent study shows that the giant ground sloth became extinct before humans arrived in Patagonia (Borrero 1999). Elsewhere there is evidence of overlap, with finds of mastodon (*Cuvieronius*), horse (*Equus* and *Hippidium*), ground sloth (*Mylodon* and *Megatherium*), giant armadillo (*Doedicurus*), and camelids (*Paleolama*) at archaeological sites. Here, too, the extinct megafauna seem to have disappeared by ca. 13,000–12,000 BP, although some argue for survivals into the early Holocene (Barnosky and Lindsey 2010; Borrero 1995; Borrero and Martin 2008; Bryan et al. 1978; Dillehay et al. 1992:156; Politis and Messineo 2008; Politis et al. 1995; Steadman et al. 2005). Although it is clear that humans hunted some megafaunal species, they form a minor part of the diet, with guanaco as the staple game animal. Plant use is attested by the contents of a human coprolite from Las Buitreras in the Patagonian region of Argentina, and the evidence points to a generalized subsistence strategy in this area rather than specialized hunting of megafauna (Borrero 1995:211). The same is true at Monte Verde in Chile (Dillehay 1989; Dillehay et al. 2008).

We are left, then, with occasional but clear associations of humans and some species of extinct megafauna. There is also clear evidence of human hunting of megafauna in the form of the occasional projectile point between the ribs. The question is whether this hunting was the sole cause of extinction and whether so many species were rapidly wiped out on initial human contact, as in the blitzkrieg model; or whether hunting was a major or minor contributing factor as in the compromise scenarios; or indeed whether the levels of hunting were so low that they had no real effect at all on the megafaunal populations.

Humans and extinct megafauna clearly overlapped in the New World, but dates are still sparse enough to create uncertainty about the timing both of the extinction of many species and the arrival of humans. Donald Grayson (1987, 1989, 1991, 2001; Grayson and Meltzer 2003) has argued that North American megafaunal extinctions are in fact spread over a long period through the Pleistocene. However, a recent statistical analysis (Beck 1996) of the last dates of occurrence of megafauna does support an extinction event in the terminal Pleistocene. This same analysis casts doubt on the blitzkrieg model, because the spatial patterning through time does not radiate from northwest to southeast, tracking human progress through the continent, but if anything moves in the opposite direction, which would support a major role for climatic change.

The peopling of the New World is itself a topic of fierce debate. The blitzkrieg model depends on the Clovis First version of the peopling of the New World, with the Paleoindian Clovis culture arriving very shortly before the megafaunal extinctions. If humans entered the Americas earlier, then the slaughter of the megafauna must at least have proceeded more slowly. There are no widely accepted pre-Clovis mammoth kill sites in North America (Haynes 1995). There is general agreement that humans had entered the New World by the Clovis phase of the Paleoindian period, ca. 13,000 BP. Claims for very early settlement of the New World, at 100,000 BP or more, have not withstood scrutiny. However, several sites in both North and South America date to 2,000–3,000 years before Clovis. Although these dates are not universally accepted, they are not easily dismissed. There is less support for claims of sites, mainly in South America, dating to 20,000–40,000 BP or earlier, but these have not yet been soundly refuted (Gilbert et al. 2008; Hamilton and Buchanan 2007; Meltzer 1995; Scheinsohn 2003; Waters et al. 2011; Waters and Stafford 2007).

Particularly in South America, evidence is strong for human occupation of the southern cone from at least 14,500 BP. Monte Verde is the best known and most closely examined site, but there are others (Fiedel

1999; Meltzer et al. 1997). Thus there may have been an overlap of several millennia between humans and extinct megafauna. Most who work in this region view climate as the primary cause of megafaunal extinctions, with human hunting a minor additional factor, perhaps mainly for horses and mastodons (Dillehay et al. 1992; Politis et al. 1995).

Of course, one could salvage a version of the blitzkrieg model by arguing that the Clovis and allied cultures were not the first humans to enter the New World, but were a later adaptation to big game hunting that subsequently spread rapidly and eradicated megafauna: thus, delayed blitzkrieg. This claim sacrifices the notion that humans will inevitably wipe out megafauna on their first entry to a new landmass, and it raises doubts as to whether New World megafauna would still have been naïve about humans after some millennia of contact.

### OLD WORLD

The Pleistocene overkill debate has focused heavily on the New World, indeed mostly on North America, with relatively little attention to the important comparative case of Eurasia. Martin notes that the pattern there is different, with fewer and more gradual extinctions, but he still attributes them to human hunting despite the paucity of kill sites or archaeological remains of extinct megafauna (P. Martin and Steadman 1999). Northern Eurasian megafaunal extinctions were actually quite extensive, however (Stuart 1999). All animals weighing more than 1,000 kg were lost, surviving only in Africa and South Asia. One-quarter of the species >40 kg also disappeared. Most of these extinctions occurred between 50,000 and 10,000 BP, at a much higher rate than during the preceding 700,000 years.

These extinctions happened more gradually, are regionally variable, and do not correspond to entries of hominids into Eurasia. Although the extinctions were spread across 40,000 years, they can be roughly divided into two sets: warm-adapted fauna disappearing earlier, ca. 50,000–40,000 BP, and cold-adapted later, ca. 14,000–10,000 BP at the end of the Pleistocene. The pattern of retreat to northern Siberia and the northern Russian Plain at the end of the Pleistocene strongly implicates climatic change (Stuart 2005; Ugan and Byers 2008). Perhaps human hunting on top of the late Pleistocene climatic changes pushed mammoths over the edge, or perhaps there is some other factor we do not yet understand. In any case it can scarcely be modeled as a blitzkrieg. *Homo erectus* arrived in southern Eurasia by at least 800,000 BP and about 500,000 BP in the north. Anatomically modern humans arrive around 40,000 BP (Stuart 1999).

There are complex interactions among animals and their habitat. European Holocene forests may have been denser than in Pleistocene interglacials because of the loss of megabrowsers, but the role of extinct fauna in modifying the landscape is not well understood (Stuart 1999). A similar argument has been made for the "mammoth steppe" of the New World, but has been challenged (Guthrie 2001). If Holocene forests were thicker for whatever reason, this may have shut out fallow deer and lions north of the Mediterranean zone, where they had previously spread during warmer conditions. The same may apply to the extinct Irish elk (*Megaloceros giganteus*). Although overhunting may have contributed to the extinction of *Megaloceros* (Stuart 1999), this seems unlikely. *Megaloceros* remains have never been found in an archaeological context. There is no evidence that they were hunted at all, and they were certainly not a major game species. Indeed it is rather a mystery why they were not hunted. They may always have been quite rare.

A third minor set of extirpations and extinctions occurs later in the Holocene of Europe, when the lion and musk ox disappear locally and the European wild ass (*Equus hydruntinus*) becomes extinct (Stuart 1999). Recent evidence also indicates that wild horses survived into the Holocene in parts of Europe, including Iberia and the alpine forelands, as well as in Anatolia (Clutton-Brock and Burleigh 1991; Döhle 1999; Martin and Russell 2006; Steppan 2006; Uerpmann 1990). Little is known about these extinctions, but they are probably due largely to human activities, perhaps more to habitat destruction than hunting. Much has also been made of the apparent survival of woolly mammoths on Wrangel Island off northeastern Siberia until ca. 4000 BP. Martin interprets this as evidence that mammoths would have survived elsewhere if they had been protected from human influence, and he suggests they were finally exterminated here when people reached the island (P. Martin and Steadman 1999). However, we do not know when humans arrived on Wrangel Island, and a recent study attributes the mammoths' eventual extinction to climatic factors (Stuart 1999; Vartanyan et al. 2008). Mid-Holocene mammoths have also been found in the Pribilofs (Veltre et al. 2008). Similarly, Irish elk survived in a refugium in western Siberia until 7700 BP (Stuart et al. 2004).

Of the extinct megafauna, the clearest human associations are with mammoths. Mammoths were occasionally hunted, and in some areas their bones were extensively scavenged for the construction of impressive huts (Gladkih et al. 1984; Haynes 1989; Pidoplichko 1998; Soffer et al. 2001). Mammoth ivory appears to have been a prized raw material, and it was probably obtained through both hunting and scavenging (Bellier et al. 1999; Christensen 1999; Patou-Mathis 2009; Soffer et al. 2001). Along with other extinct megafauna such as the woolly rhinoceros, mammoths were depicted in Upper Paleolithic art (Bahn and Vertut 1997; Bellier et al. 1999; Chauvet et al. 1996; Clottes 1995; Clottes and Courtin 1996; Leroi-Gourhan 1982), but artistic representations do not correlate with hunting frequency (see Chapter 2, *Art*).

The faunal evidence suggests that killing mammoths was a very rare event. The one area where mammoths may have been hunted, or at least scavenged for food, with some regularity is the steppe zone of Moravia and the Ukraine in the Gravettian period. It is generally agreed that much of the mammoth bone used to construct huts in this area was scavenged from bone beds, but whether mammoth was a significant part of the diet remains unresolved (Iakovleva and Djindjian 2001, 2005; Kozłowski and Montet-White 2001; Soffer et al. 2001; Svoboda 2001; West 2001; Wojtal and Sobczyk 2005). A simulation study suggests that mammoth herds could not have withstood the kind of harvesting levels necessary to subsist on them as a staple (Mithen 1993, 1997). If this is correct, hunting must have been only occasional. With this possible exception, it seems unlikely that human hunting placed serious stress on mammoth populations. Mithen's simulation, as well as studies of modern elephants, do suggest that even low levels of predation may drive proboscidean populations to extinction. However, even the relatively low levels that he models may be too high, and clearly African elephants have withstood low-level hunting for many millennia. There is even less sign of human predation on other extinct megafauna.

In sum, although the Eurasian pattern differs somewhat from the New World, there were substantial late Pleistocene extinctions there as well; however, the Eurasian evidence does not support an inevitable blitzkrieg whenever humans enter a new landmass (cf. Surovell et al. 2005). Similar megafaunal extinctions occurred here as in the New World during the later Pleistocene. That they involved a smaller number of species probably results from a more impoverished megafauna, to begin with

(McFarlane 1999). Humans clearly did hunt at least some of the extinct species, notably mammoth, as attested by occasional kill sites with embedded projectile points and the identification of mammoth blood residues on tools from the mammoth bone hut site of Mezhirich (Soffer et al. 2001). Mammoths seem only to have been a major resource during the Gravettian of the east European steppe, around the Last Glacial Maximum, although the extent of dependence on mammoths is disputed. Nevertheless, the Gravettian of this region is the closest thing we have to specialized mammoth hunters, and apparently at population densities rather higher than those of American Paleoindians. Yet Gravettian hunting did not wipe out the mammoths, which survived another 10,000 years.

However, the main megafaunal prey of Neanderthals and modern humans in Paleolithic Europe were reindeer and red deer and, to a lesser extent, bison, ibex, and horses (Altuna 1983; Aura Tortosa et al. 2002; Bratlund 1996; Burke 1993; Chase et al. 1994; Davis 2002; Gaudzinski 2000; Grayson and Delpech 2002, 2003, 2008; Grayson et al. 2001; Hoffecker and Cleghorn 2000; Krasnokutsky 1996; Mellars 2004; Miracle 2005; Olsen 1995; Patou-Mathis 2000; Pike-Tay 1991; Pushkina and Raia 2008; Rendu 2010; Spiess 1979; Stiner and Kuhn 1992; Weinstock 2002; West 1997, 2006). In the Near East humans hunted primarily small bovids (gazelle, sheep, and goat) and fallow deer (Evins 1982; Hesse 1989; Marín Arroyo 2011; Rabinovich 1998; Speth and Tchernov 2001; Stiner et al. 2009). These species altered their range at the end of the Pleistocene, but did not become extinct. In Southeast Asia, megafaunal extinctions are primarily linked to sea-level changes, not the entry of humans (Louys et al. 2007).

PLEISTOCENE KILLERS

Having briefly surveyed the evidence, let us consider the arguments for and against the Pleistocene overkill model. The key elements are (1) that mass extinctions occur shortly after the entry of humans to a previously uninhabited landmass; (2) that these extinctions are differentially targeted to megafauna, in contrast to other extinction events; (3) that animals outside of Africa and especially in Australia and the Americas were naïve with respect to human hunters and thus easily killed; (4) that Paleoindians and presumably other pioneer settlers were mobile, specialized big game hunters; and (5) that unrestrained hunting is the primary cause of extinction.

*Timing of extinctions*

Extinctions are difficult to date precisely, and future work will no doubt clarify the somewhat murky picture at present. On current evidence, the correlation of megafaunal extinctions with human entry is not as tight as the blitzkrieg model would predict. Particularly in Australia, most megafaunal extinctions may have happened before the arrival of humans. Eurasian extinctions do not correlate with human immigration. New World extinctions may be more concentrated near the time of human arrival, although probably not as tightly as once seemed the case. Statistical analyses of the available dates disagree, some showing strong correlations between human arrivals and extinctions (Beck 1996; Gillespie 2008) and others rejecting such correlations (McFarlane 1999; Ugan and Byers 2008). However, Michael Beck's analysis does not support blitzkrieg, because the geographic pattern of last dates does not follow the path of human entry. The presence of pre-Clovis people in the New World would eliminate the tight correlation between human arrival and final megafaunal extinctions. It also begs an explanation for why these people initially ignored megafaunal prey and then shifted to focus on it. If the Clovis technology of large projectile points and spear-throwers is what permitted big game hunting and brought about overkill, why did the advent of similar technology in Europe ca. 35,000 BP not cause extinctions there (McFarlane 1999; Stuart 1999)?

In many places, there appears to be an overlap of millennia rather than centuries between humans and doomed megafauna. This has also been demonstrated for a flightless duck in North America (Jones et al. 2008). In an examination of several extinction events, Jared Diamond (1989a) concludes that sitzkrieg, a long, drawn-out period of reduction, is much more common than blitzkrieg. Sitzkrieg extinctions are not caused by overhunting alone, but by a variety of factors, as we have seen in the island cases. This seems a better model for most, if not all, human interactions with megafauna. It is hard to argue that climate did not play a role in many of these extinctions, because they occur at the end of the Pleistocene after extended periods of human interaction.

*Differential extinction of large animals*

Advocates of the overkill model point to the overrepresentation of large animals among the vanished species as an anomaly compared to other extinction events, which they suggest is best explained by human hunting. There are two reasons why hunting might produce this effect: the preference of hunters for large game and the greater vulnerability of large animals. By and large, optimal foraging theory predicts that hunters will tend to target larger prey, because it comes in bigger packages and thus usually provides a bigger payoff in relation to caloric costs (as large animals become rarer, search costs increase and hunters should switch to smaller prey). For small bands lacking extensive storage, however, there is a point of diminishing returns. If one can only use a small portion of a mammoth, for instance, the payoff is only that portion, so that the reward may be no greater than an elk (Outram 2001). Megafauna hunters might have been able to dry some of the meat or, in some cases, to store it by freezing or underwater caching, but the high mobility that characterizes most of these groups would limit their ability to use such stored meat. We do not see signs of encampments around New World mammoth kills. Rather, these sites are characterized by very limited signs of human activity. Paleoindian sites in general are small and ephemeral, as are early Australian sites. Only in parts of the European Upper Paleolithic are there longer term, substantial sites in association with extinct megafauna, and these hunters did not quickly wipe out the mammoths, but coexisted with them for tens of thousands of years.

If the costs were low enough, hunters would still be expected to target megafauna even if they could use only a small part of the meat. Gary Haynes and Sunday Eiselt (1999) suggest climatic change at the end of the Pleistocene restricted North American mammoths to easily identified refugia, so that search costs were low even as the mammoth population was dwindling. There are other costs, however. Even if mammoths and mastodons were so naïve as to permit human hunters to approach them with ease, they surely offered resistance when wounded. Prehistoric hunters lacked the means to kill a proboscidean instantly. Living elephants, especially the matriarch, are known for protecting herd members. Thus a mammoth hunt must have been a dangerous undertaking under the best of circumstances. The loss of a hunter is a substantial cost for a small band, especially if the band depends on big game hunting. Mammoth and mastodon hunts were more likely undertaken out of bravado and a desire for prestige than as a result of rational calculations of caloric value.

Large animals are more vulnerable to any kind of stress because they typically have slower maturation and lower rates of reproduction than smaller animals (Godfrey et al. 1997; Owen-Smith 1999). As a result, large animals are overrepresented in all major extinction events, regardless of cause. There is disagreement about whether late Pleistocene extinctions exhibit a greater degree of differential disappearance of large taxa (Alroy 1999; Brook and Bowman 2004; P. Martin and Steadman 1999; McFarlane 1999). In part this depends on whether one restricts consideration to mammals, where this size bias is more evident, or includes other animals such as birds, where it is not, at least in North America (Grayson 1977, 1991).

## Naïveté

Larger herbivores isolated on islands without large predators often lose both bodily and behavioral defenses against predation (see the earlier section, *Island Extinctions*). Martin (2005) suggests that behavioral naïveté toward human hunters is a contributing factor to New World and Australian megafaunal extinctions. Naïveté cannot explain Pleistocene extinctions in Europe, although its lack could be invoked to account for the extended time lapse between human entry and megafaunal extinction. However, naïve island fauna can often withstand human hunting pressure for thousands of years, even in relatively restricted areas.

How naïve were the New World and Australian megafauna? We should distinguish between two kinds of naïveté here. Animals outside of Africa lacked knowledge of human hunters before human entry into the other continents. They would probably not at first have recognized humans as a threat (Alroy 1999). A similar situation exists where animals are protected from human hunting, or with tame animals. This is primarily a matter of learned behavior, and research suggests that aversion to previously unknown predators can be acquired within a single generation (Berger et al. 2001). A more extreme form of naïveté results from the long-term isolation of animal populations from *all* predators, as on many islands. If all behavioral responses to predation have been lost, the animals will have difficulty learning to flee from newly introduced predators.

Most of the Australian and New World megafauna were not free from predators and thus would not have exhibited this more extreme form of naïveté (McFarlane 1999:101). The size of mammoths and mastodons might have protected them from predation. Yet even in this case, although adults were large enough to be more or less invulnerable, juveniles were subject to predation by the largest predators and may even have been the major food source of sabertooth cats (Marean and

Ehrhardt 1995; Martin et al. 2001). It is thus unlikely that they lacked behavioral defenses against predators, so naïveté cannot have played a significant role in their extinction.

### Big game hunters

Pleistocene foragers, particularly Paleoindians and the peoples of Upper Paleolithic Europe, have traditionally been represented as specialized big game hunters, subsisting largely on a diet of megafauna with little plant food or smaller game. However, this picture has recently been challenged in many areas. In South America, evidence for big game hunting is confined to the open regions of the pampas and the puna. Elsewhere Paleoindian subsistence resembles that associated with the later Archaic period, a broad-spectrum strategy using a wide range of resources (Dillehay et al. 1992, 2008). In North America, both Clovis and Folsom groups may have been less mobile than generally thought, and there is considerable variability in subsistence and settlement strategies (Bamforth 2002; Byers and Ugan 2005; Cannon and Meltzer 2008; Hill 2007, 2008; Powell and Steele 1994). In Europe, the Upper Paleolithic covers a much longer period of time, so it is not surprising that there is much variation in subsistence strategies. In some times and places, notably the Magdalenian of western Europe, there is clear evidence for specialized hunting of reindeer (Altuna et al. 1991; Grayson et al. 2001). Elsewhere there is more variability in prey, including small game such as rabbits and probably plant foods (Adán et al. 2009; Bar-El and Tchernov 2001; Bicho et al. 2000; Bocheński et al. 2009; Hockett and Bicho 2000; Hockett and Haws 2009; Kornfeld 1996; Laroulandie 2005; Patou 1987; Rendu 2010; Speth and Tchernov 2002; Stiner 1993b, 1999, 2009; Stiner and Munro 2002; Stiner et al. 2000; Surovell 1999).

The image of late Pleistocene foragers as mobile, specialized big game hunters is based partly on a preservational bias for big game hunting sites and equipment (Dillehay et al. 1992). In Europe, the striking depictions of animals in cave art have no doubt helped create this impression. To a large extent, however, it derives from an overemphasis on projectile points and other weapons at the expense of the rest of the tool assemblage. When the assemblages are considered as a whole, a different picture emerges, not only of activities but also of mobility (Bamforth 2002). Joan Gero (1991) argues that the focus on projectile points derives from gender bias that values activities perceived as male above those associated with women. It is certainly an example of the closely related overvaluation of hunting by archaeologists (see Chapter 4). This distortion becomes very clear in the frequent depiction of Pleistocene foragers as hunters not simply of big game, but of the biggest: as specialized hunters of mammoths and mastodons. Given the paucity of evidence for human hunting of these animals, this portrayal is based on nothing more than romantic fantasy. The evidence clearly shows that Pleistocene hunters depended primarily on mid-range animals such as bison, reindeer, and guanaco. These species have survived, although their ranges changed at the end of the Pleistocene. Proboscideans are a poor choice for a staple, because the package size is too large for a band of hunters to use, their reproductive rate is slow, and they are dangerous to hunt.

*Hunting as the cause of extinction*

The crux of the overkill hypothesis is that human hunting was the primary cause of megafaunal extinctions. The main alternative explanations are climatic change, hyperdisease, and meteor impact. Simulation studies have suggested that human hunting could have led to megafaunal extinctions in North America (Alroy 2001; Brook and Bowman 2004; Mithen 1997), although another simulation rejects this possibility in Australia (Choquenot and Bowman 1998). There is relatively little evidence to support the overhunting of megafauna, however. Kill sites exist but are very rare, and remains of extinct megafauna with clear indications that they were killed and eaten by humans are also sparse. Martin has tried to interpret this lack of evidence as support for the rapid nature of the extermination of the megafauna, but this is a weak argument. A slaughter on this scale – on the order of 100,000,000–10,000,000,000 animals in the New World (MacPhee and Marx 1997) – should leave a substantial amount of evidence. The sites would simply be compressed into a very narrow time range.

Certainly some sites have been lost, many remain undiscovered, and some may be ambiguous with respect to the degree of human involvement. We have little trouble detecting such sites in Eurasia, however, and North America does not suffer from a lack of archaeological work. We do find evidence for Paleoindian hunting of mid-range megafauna such as bison and camelids, as well as occasional use of mammoths and mastodons. However, there is little support for the massive slaughter of the largest megafauna.

There are some genuine taphonomic issues for proboscideans. If one imagines a scenario in which portions of the prey are brought back to a base camp, for animals the size of mammoths these portions may not contain bones. The bones themselves are weighty, so that butchery may involve less dismemberment, as in smaller taxa, than flensing as in whales: The meat is likely to be filleted off the bones at the kill site. An ethnoarchaeological study of Efe elephant butchery suggests that some bones are transported to temporary processing camps nearby, however, and even to the more permanent village if it is close. Long bones, ribs, and vertebrae are often taken and processed for their marrow and fat. Feet are nearly always removed from the kill site, because the fatty footpad is a great delicacy, whereas the skull, mandible, pelvis, and scapula are left behind (Fisher 2001). Thus kill sites should differ in body part representation from the remains of natural deaths. The presence or absence of foot bones should be particularly diagnostic, because these dense bones are likely to survive.

Butcher marks may be less apparent on proboscidean bones than on those of smaller taxa, due to the thick cartilage of the joint capsule (Frison 1989; Frison and Todd 2001; Haynes 1991, Soffer et al. 2001). Nevertheless, the need to cut through the hide should ensure that stone tools or at least resharpening flakes would be present at butchery sites. Thus although the consumption of mammoths and mastodons may be manifested differently at kill and habitation sites compared to other prey, it should not be archaeologically invisible. The meager evidence for hunting mammoths and mastodons is therefore probably a genuine indication that they played a very small role in human subsistence.

If Paleoindians were indeed specialized big game (megafauna) hunters, and if they drove much of this megafauna rapidly to extinction, they were not practicing a very stable subsistence strategy. In most predators such behavior would lead to their own extinction. Because humans are not biologically specialized, they can escape this fate by shifting their food sources. Our omnivory enables humans to extirpate their prey (Owen-Smith 1999; Tudge 1999). However, humans are unlikely to wipe out their staple food sources (Haynes and Eiselt 1999:72). As noted earlier, there are very few if any later instances of overhunting alone causing extinction, either in prehistory or in the more recent past (MacPhee and Flemming 1999:364).

For hunting to cause extinction, predation must exceed births and immigration of the prey species. Most critically, it must be maintained at these levels even when the prey becomes very scarce (when optimal foraging theory would predict switching to other food sources), and there must be no refuges free from predation that can shelter relic populations (Owen-Smith 1999). We must picture the relatively small Paleoindian population spreading rapidly through the New World, but taking the time to hunt out virtually every last mammoth, mastodon, and members of other extinct species as they went, even in marginal areas. If Paleoindians were in fact opportunistic hunters of big game, it is much more plausible that they would have left an area as soon as game populations began to drop, given that there were other areas still rich in game and no human competition for territory. This scenario would suggest the settlement and rapid abandonment of hunted-out territories until the hunters finally reached Tierra del Fuego, at which point they would be forced to change their subsistence strategy. However, the actual history of the peopling of the New World does not fit well with this model. Setting aside for the moment the possibility of pre-Clovis settlement of the New World, in fact early Paleoindian settlers established populations over wide areas of North and South America and continued to develop locally. This suggests that they must have begun quite early to use a broad and sustainable range of resources.

Ross MacPhee's (MacPhee and Flemming 1999; MacPhee and Marx 1997) hyperdisease hypothesis recognizes these problems and suggests a mechanism other than overhunting through which the arrival of humans could cause megafaunal extinctions. He proposes that humans carried with them a virulent disease that infected a wide range of mammals, leading to the extinction of many before the remainder developed immunity. This has the advantage of explaining how a small number of humans could kill such a large number of animals, and why there have been few subsequent megafaunal extinctions after the era of first contact in Australia and the New World. At present, however, there is no evidence to support this idea beyond the pattern of extinctions, despite attempts to find traces of the killer microbe in frozen Siberian mammoths (Stone 2001). Demographic studies of the latest megafauna might also indicate whether epidemic disease was a major factor.

Despite its appeal, the hyperdisease model has a number of drawbacks. It is modeled on the disastrous effect of Old World diseases on New World human populations after European contact. Native Americans, although decimated, were not wiped out, however. Rather, after initial serious losses, populations rebounded as resistance developed

(Ramenofsky et al. 2003). This is the usual response to a new virulent disease. MacPhee offers only one case in which disease may have played a significant role in extinction – the New Zealand quail (*Coturnix novaezelandiae*) – and this is not certain. This model posits that humans carried some disease to which they had developed resistance but which was deadly to a wide range of other mammals. This disease may still be with us, but now that humans have spread around the world all surviving animal populations have developed resistance, so it is no longer so virulent. This disease must have been carried by virtually all human populations from at least prior to the settlement of Australia, 40,000 or more years ago. This model seems at odds with the European evidence, however, where megafauna survived human contact until the late Pleistocene and where extinctions are spread across thousands of years (Stuart 1999). Nor does it fit with the evidence in many areas for extended coexistence of humans and megafauna, because to cause extinction it would have had to wipe out populations very quickly, before they could develop resistance.

Richard Holdaway (1999) has evaluated the hyperdisease hypothesis for New Zealand and finds it lacking. Here the size effect in extinctions is clearly related to the introduction of specific predators, starting with humans and Pacific rats. Unrelated species become extinct, whereas closely related ones survive. Species survive on smaller islands where rats were not introduced, although one would expect a disease to spread to them. Although in New Zealand the extinct taxa are mostly birds, similar arguments could be applied to mammals in other regions. Moreover, the species that survive or become extinct do not make demographic sense. Epidemic disease should pose the greatest danger to species that live in large herds. Yet caribou, for example, survive, whereas solitary predators such as sabertooths are wiped out.

The hyperdisease hypothesis cannot be dismissed, but at this point is not convincing. Supporters of the overkill hypothesis dismiss climatic change as a cause by pointing out that megafauna survived many earlier climatic fluctuations of comparable magnitude (P. Martin and Steadman 1999). Yet were these fluctuations truly comparable? Recent work is building a picture of the Pleistocene-Holocene transition as rapid and violent (Chebykin et al. 2002; Haynes and Eiselt 1999; MacPhee et al. 2002; McFarlane 1999:102). Warming and increased precipitation transformed much of North America from a mosaic environment to more uniform large tracts of evergreen forest, deciduous forest, and prairie. Forests expanded in tropical and subtropical zones of the New World and Africa (Owen-Smith 1999). Temperate forest also expanded in Europe and, as in North America, was apparently more dense and continuous than in previous warmer intervals (Denèfle et al. 2000; Stuart 1999). In northern Eurasia and North America the vegetation community that has been labeled the "mammoth steppe" disappeared (Chebykin et al. 2002; Guthrie 2001). Seasonality increased, with potentially profound effects on vegetation and fauna (Axelrod 1967; Byrne 1987; Haynes and Eiselt 1999:75; Lewis et al. 2000; Lundelius 1989).

Thus for the New World the current evidence supports climatic changes at the Pleistocene-Holocene transition as the primary cause of megafaunal extinctions, with human hunting perhaps playing some role in pushing some taxa over the edge. In Eurasia the same is true for mammoths, but it is less clear what caused extinctions earlier in the late Pleistocene. Most of these animals were not major human prey. The animals lost in Australia were primarily browsers, and the proximate cause would appear to be the loss of rainforest, which was replaced by open woodland and savanna. This change is tied to dramatically increased burning at ca. 38,000 BP, whether anthropogenic or the result of increased aridity (Kershaw 1986; Miller et al. 1999; Owen-Smith 1999; Roberts et al. 2001). In any case, overhunting does not seem to be the primary cause. One intriguing hypothesis that combines climatic and anthropogenic effects suggests that large Australian predators and herbivores stressed by climatic change were pushed over the edge not by direct human hunting, but by human competition for their plant and animal foods (Webb 1998).

Recently, a meteor impact has been posited as the cause of the extinction of North American megafauna and the end of the Clovis culture (Firestone et al. 2007). So far the existence of the impact remains controversial (Buchanan et al. 2008; Haynes et al. 2010; Surovell et al. 2009), however, and because it is supposed to have caused the Younger Dryas cold period, it should have helped rather than harmed the cold-adapted Pleistocene fauna.

## The rhetoric of extinction

There is little evidence that overhunting alone has ever caused extinctions. Introduced predators have caused or at least made major contributions to extinctions, especially on islands. As humans spread around the world, we were of course also introduced predators. Humans certainly altered ecosystems as they entered them. Yet perhaps our dietary flexibility is so great that human hunters are more likely to switch to other prey before extirpation occurs.

Where there is clear evidence of a major human role in extinctions, the humans in question are not foragers but agriculturalists. Ingold (1994:11–12) attributes this to a fundamental difference in worldview. Whereas foragers see humans and animals as part of a single world of which people are an insignificant part, agriculturalists see humanity and nature as separate, leading to an exploitive approach to the natural world that is at the root of extinctions and other environmental degradation. Agriculturalists see humans as responsible for the survival or extinction of wild animals. In contrast, foragers see their environment as responsible for human survival or extinction.

Although the distinction between foragers and agriculturalists is useful, we should recognize it as crude. Human conceptions of nature and their relation to it need to be explored in each particular instance. In fact, some horticulturalists have attitudes and practices that are not very different from those of foragers (Descola 1994). Animal domestication (as opposed to plant cultivation) might be particularly important in changing attitudes of humility and respect to those of exploitation (see Chapter 6, *Implications*).

Although contemporary extinctions are attributed primarily to habitat loss and secondarily to introduced exotic taxa, with only a minor role for overhunting, "[i]nterestingly, when Late Quaternary extinctions are under discussion, the relative ranking of causes is essentially inverted. Overkill is often identified as the chief, if not the only, cause of these extinctions, especially those that took place on continents and large islands" (MacPhee and Flemming 1999:363). As we have seen, there is very little evidence for overhunting as the cause of these extinctions. Grayson (2001:35) claims, perhaps with slight exaggeration, that no archaeologist or paleontologist specializing in this period in North America subscribes to this view. And yet not only have many archaeologists accepted this explanation but it is also the account invariably presented in popular media.

Why is Pleistocene overkill so compelling? Why do we so want to castigate ourselves for the loss of Pleistocene megafauna? In popular and often in archaeological discussions, Pleistocene overkill is treated as a morality tale: The corrupting influence of greedy humans destroys pristine nature. It is no accident that the Pleistocene overkill hypothesis was put forward in the late 1960s, a time of dawning environmental consciousness. In the early 19th century the moral of megafaunal extinction was different. The passing of mastodons and mammoths served as a metaphor and justification for the inevitable extinction of Native Americans, replaced by superior Europeans through manifest destiny (Semonin 2000:365, 375). Changing characterizations of nature and the wild are also reflected in descriptions of megafauna. In the late 18th century mastodons were actually believed to be terrifying carnivores, symbolizing the threat of the wilderness that must be tamed by human action (Semonin 2000). Now we depict these creatures as naïve and vulnerable.

The myth of Pleistocene overkill is deployed in three particular ways. Non-anthropologists especially use it to demonstrate the inevitable environmental destruction caused by humans (Diamond 1989b; P. Martin and Steadman 1999; Schüle 1993). They lump all humans together, without distinguishing different types of societies or different practices. As we have seen, it is primarily agricultural societies, and perhaps really only certain types of agriculture, that cause environmental degradation. Pleistocene overkill is also one of the primary pieces of evidence used to counter the romantic notion of the "ecological Indian" (Krech 1999; Redman 1999). Some have also linked Pleistocene overkill or, at any rate, megafaunal extinctions to the origins of agriculture by invoking the need to turn to other resources after the disappearance of the megafauna (Diamond 1997:110; Piperno and Pearsall 1998:237; Ross 1987:12). As we have seen, however, the extinct species were hardly dietary staples.

These stories, particularly the first one, are based on the modern western notion of humans as apart from and opposed to nature. What has changed over the last two centuries or so is that the narrative has moved from one of the glorious human conquest of savage nature to the tragic human desecration of helpless nature. This belief is also manifest in the re-wilding movement (Caro and Sherman 2009; Foreman 2004; Martin 2005), which seeks to restore America to its pristine, Pleistocene state by introducing animals as closely related to extinct forms as possible (elephants for mammoths, lions for sabertooths, etc.). The history of damage caused by well-meaning introductions of exotic species should give us pause, and if climate was in fact responsible for megafaunal extinctions, these animals do not belong in Holocene North America (Caro and Sherman 2009; Oliveira-Santos and Fernandez 2010; Wolverton 2010).

I certainly do not seek to erase or excuse human responsibility for the many well-documented extinctions that we have caused, nor to deny the need for conservation measures, which I heartily support. However, it is crucial that we understand the causes of extinctions as clearly as possible in order to prevent them. It is actually dangerous to believe that humans inevitably cause extinctions, because it suggests there is little we can do to stop them. An understanding of humans as part of nature rather than opposed to it might help. Taking seriously the approaches of societies that do not set humans apart from nature may be productive (Nadasdy 2003). Rather than pursuing simplistic arguments at a global level, zooarchaeology has a more important contribution to make when it can offer detailed studies of the history of extinctions in particular times and places. Zooarchaeologists are uniquely positioned to explore the ecological and social conditions leading to the loss of animal species under many different circumstances; the social component, however, has tended to be lacking. This kind of sophisticated understanding may actually help prevent further extinctions.

# 6

# Domestication as a human–animal relationship

> Just as humans have a history of their relations with animals, so also animals have a history of their relations with humans. Only humans, however, construct narratives of this history. Such narratives range from what we might regard as myths of totemic origin to supposedly "scientific" accounts of the origins of domestication. And however we might choose to distinguish between myth and science, they have in common that they tell us as much about how the narrators view their own humanity as they do about their attitudes and relations to non-human animals. (Ingold 1994:1)

Domestication is another topic that has received extensive attention in zooarchaeology. Much of this work has centered on techniques to recognize domestic animals and discussions of when and where the first such animals are found. However, there has also been considerable discussion of how and why domestication came about and of its significance for humans and animals. In this chapter I focus on the latter issues: on domestication as a human–animal relationship. Domestication is surely the most important transformation in human-animal relations, with far-reaching consequences for both partners.

For reference, I provide in Table 6.1 my interpretation of the current best guesses for when and where the main domestic animals were domesticated. There are better data for some animals than others, and many dates will likely be pushed back (or occasionally moved forward) in the future. In cases where there is clear evidence for independent domestication in more than one region, I give the earlier date. As will be clear from the following discussion, there can be disagreement and uncertainty about what counts as "domesticated"; this is particularly problematic for cats, which have a long history of at least occasional commensal and perhaps pet relationships with humans, but are only morphologically domesticated rather late.

Table 6.1. *Approximate dates and regions of domestication of major domestic animals*

| Taxon | Region | Date |
|---|---|---|
| Dog (*Canis familiaris*) | Central Europe | 32,000 BP |
| Sheep (*Ovis aries*) | Near East, South Asia | 10,500+ BP |
| Goat (*Capra hircus*) | Near East | 10,500+ BP |
| Cattle (*Bos taurus*) | Near East, South Asia, (North Africa?) | 10,500 BP |
| Pig (*Sus scrofa*) | Near East, East Asia | 10,500 BP |
| Water buffalo (*Bubalus bubalis*) | East or South Asia | ?5000 BP |
| Chicken (*Gallus gallus*) | Southeast Asia/East Asia | 8000 BP |
| Horse (*Equus caballus*) | Central Asia | 5500 BP |
| Bactrian camel (*Camelus bactrianus*) | Central Asia | 5000 BP |
| Dromedary (*Camelus dromedarius*) | Arabian peninsula | 4500 BP |
| Cat (*Felis catus*) | Near East | 4000 BP |
| Llama (*Lama glama*) | Andes | 5000 BP |
| Alpaca (*Lama pacos*) | Andes | 5000 BP |
| Guinea pig (*Cavia porcellus*) | Andes | 1000 BP |
| Turkey (*Meleagris gallopavo*) | Mesoamerica/Southwest | 2000 BP |
| Muscovy duck (*Cairina moschata*) | Northern South America | ?1000 BP |

## Definitions

Domestication, and what constitutes a domesticated animal, is surprisingly difficult to define. Our ties to free-range cattle, barnyard pigs, battery hens, race horses, lap dogs, barn cats, laboratory rats, trained elephants, honeybees, and house mice encompass a wide range of human–animal relationships. Yet most people would consider all of these animals, save perhaps the mice, to be domesticated. And what of zoo animals, farm-raised game, aquacultured fish and shrimp, and "wild" animals that are heavily managed, even bred in captivity? Faced with these difficulties, those who would define domestication must either do so in terms so broad that the term becomes essentially meaningless, or choose just some of these relationships, leaving the others in an ambiguous zone between the wild and the domestic. I return to this fascinating gray area in Chapter 7; here, I consider the various ways of defining domestication.

Part of the difficulty in pinning down domestication is that it combines biological and social aspects (Crabtree 1993:205; Meadow 1989:81). Domestication involves both an alteration in human–animal relations and behavioral and morphological changes in the domesticated animal. Roughly speaking, definitions of domestication can be divided into those that emphasize the biological side and those that emphasize the social, although many versions include aspects of both. I arrange them according to which factor predominates.

Many scholars distinguish between taming and domestication. Generally, taming is seen as an alteration in the human–animal relationship with a particular animal that does not have lasting effects through succeeding generations, whereas domestication involves a long-term change in relations beyond the lifetime of a single animal that often results in morphological and behavioral change (Bökönyi 1969, 1989; Clutton-Brock 1994; Harris 1996; Hesse 1984; Ingold 1980:82, 1984; Reitz and Wing 1999:279–305). Thus raising the young of hunted animals as pets, a frequent practice of contemporary hunters (Bulmer 1976:182; Reed 1977; Serpell 1986:48–56) and no doubt past ones as well, does not constitute domestication. Although the relationship between humans and tamed animals is clearly different from that between humans and wild animals, and worthy of our consideration (see Chapter 7), the distinction is a valid one. Keeping the occasional pet does not fundamentally alter the relationship with wild animals, nor does it transform human–human social relationships in the way that domestication does.

## BIOLOGICAL DEFINITIONS

Definitions of domestication that emphasize the biological aspect tend either to emphasize human control of breeding or to see domestication as a type of symbiotic relationship between two species, not unique to humans. Clearly, these involve quite different roles for human intentionality and agency.

### Control of breeding

Sándor Bökönyi (1969:219) offers one of the classic definitions of animal domestication: "the capture and taming by man of animals of a species with particular behavioural characteristics, their removal from their natural living area and breeding community, and their maintenance under controlled breeding conditions for profit." The key elements are thus the control of the animals' movement and of their breeding, effecting their separation from the wild breeding population. This separation permits the changes in size, behavior, and morphology through which we can recognize domestic animals. Bökönyi's rather curious inclusion of the phrase "for profit" in his definition is presumably intended specifically to exclude pets, which represent a rather different human–animal relationship (see Chapter 7). Bökönyi (1969:219–20) distinguishes two stages in animal domestication: animal keeping, which controls animals' movement and breeding but without deliberate selection or control of feeding, and animal breeding, with controlled feeding and artificial selection for particular traits. Animal keeping characterizes the earliest domestication in the Neolithic, whereas animal breeding does not appear until the Classical period in the Old World.

Juliet Clutton-Brock (1994:26) similarly defines a domesticated animal as "one that has been bred in captivity, for purposes of subsistence or profit, in a human community that maintains complete mastery over its breeding, organization of territory, and food supply." She retains the notion that domestic animals must be kept for profit (here with the addition of "subsistence" to remove the capitalist implications of "profit") and places still greater emphasis on control of breeding, movement, and feeding. She regards domestication as a process culminating in the establishment of distinct breeds (Clutton-Brock 1994:27), analogous to Bökönyi's animal breeding. Presumably animals kept under conditions of less than complete mastery arc only partly domesticated, so that domestication was a process lasting several millennia.

Clutton-Brock (1994:28–30) argues that domestication involves behavioral perhaps more than genetic modification, with humans taking control of cultural transmission in animals, although this requires an unusual definition of culture: "[A] culture is a way of life imposed over successive generations on a society of humans or animals by its elders" (Clutton-Brock 1994:29). By usurping the position of the alpha animal in the dominance hierarchy, humans become "elders" to the animals and alter the behaviors transmitted.

Thus what can be viewed as the standard definition of animal domestication emphasizes human control of animals, especially of their breeding. These definitions have generally been offered by scholars with backgrounds in biology and animal science, whose concern is to explain how domestic animals come to look and act differently from their wild counterparts. Although they do not dwell on this aspect, such definitions clearly imply that domestication was deliberately undertaken by humans motivated by subsistence or profit. Bökönyi (1969:219) and

Clutton-Brock (1994:26) both believe that people first domesticated animals (other than dogs) to ensure a steady meat supply. Humans are active agents and animals are passively shaped by human control.

### Symbiosis

Those emphasizing control of breeding are concerned with how domestic animal populations are isolated from the rest of the species so that changes can occur. Despite the focus on the biological effects of domestication, they see the cause in cultural terms: deliberate human behavior. Another school of thought conceives the domesticatory relationship itself in biological terms, as what may loosely be termed "symbiosis."

This approach was pioneered by Frederick Zeuner (1963), who explicitly denied human intentionality a role in domestication. Rather, he argued, human domestication of animals is just one instance of a class of mutualistic relationships among species, as for instance between ants and aphids (see also Morey 2010). Domestication developed from tolerated scavenging around human settlements (dogs, pigs, ducks), or from human social parasitism on herd animals (reindeer, sheep, goat). Later attempts to control crop robbers (cattle, water buffalo, elephant, rabbit, goose) led to their domestication. Only after domestic animals were already well established in human society did people deliberately domesticate some taxa, such as chickens, cats, horses, and camels (Zeuner 1963:56).

Terence O'Connor (1997) expands on this model, arguing that seeing domestication as the human exploitation of animals is inappropriate; animals benefit as well through increased populations. Relationships between humans and various domestic animals can be characterized in terms of the mutual benefits or lack thereof as either mutualism (benefiting both species) or commensalism (benefiting one, neutral to the other).

This kind of definition deemphasizes human intentionality and gives a greater role to the animals. As O'Connor (1997:154) suggests, it poses the question of why humans became attractive to other species at particular points in time, rather than why they decided to control other species. This approach eliminates the need to include phrases such as "for profit" in definitions of domestication, and it more easily accommodates a wider range of human–animal relationships, including pets. Indeed, domestication as such becomes a nonissue. Rather there are a variety of human–animal relationships to which both parties adapt to varying degrees.

Of course, it is possible to characterize domestication and other human–animal relationships in this way, and it is useful to be reminded that animals play an active role. From the human point of view, however, it is also productive to consider the social aspects of domestication.

## SOCIAL DEFINITIONS

Other definitions of domestication focus on the changes in relationships among humans and animals, and between humans. These approaches emphasize not symbiosis, but bringing animals into the human social sphere.

### Property

Ducos recognizes the difficulties of the variability in human–animal relationships that O'Connor underscores: "It is not obvious, however, that there does exist a single common criterion for all the man/animal relationships we call domestication. In fact it is possible that our intuition of what is domestication corresponds to modern situations, not to ancient ones" (Ducos 1978:53). However, he rejects symbiosis as an adequate explanation of domestication, arguing that domestication is an unnatural, asymmetrical relationship entered into willingly by humans, but not by animals (Ducos 1989). Rather than focusing on the biological aspect of these relationships, he calls for a social definition: "[D]omestication can be said to exist when living animals are integrated as objects into the socioeconomic organization of the human group, in the sense that, while living, those animals are objects for ownership, inheritance, exchange, trade, etc." (Ducos 1978:54). In other words, animals are domesticated when they become property. Ducos (1978:56) distinguishes between the social and biological aspects of domestication, suggesting that we call animals that are socially integrated "domesticated" and those that show morphological signs of domestication "domestic." He further notes that, although domestication may or may not involve control of animals, it generally does mean a shift from relating to animals as species to relating to them as individuals.

Ingold (1980:82) also distinguishes between social and biological domestication, although unfortunately he uses the opposite terminology from Ducos ("domestic" for animals incorporated into the household, "domesticated" for those exhibiting morphological change). Ingold identifies three elements of domestication that may occur together or separately: taming, herding, and breeding. Taming involves the social incorporation of the animal into the household (not necessarily as property). Herding refers to keeping flocks of animals as property; the animals may or may not be either domestic or domesticated. Breeding entails control of reproduction, but, as in ranching, such animals, although morphologically domesticated, may be allowed to run wild (hence not socially domestic).

For Ingold (1984:4), domestication is a change in human social relations that involves "the social incorporation or appropriation of successive generations of animals." Although living wild animals are not directly engaged in human social relations, tame ones have personal relations with individual humans, and domestic ones are the objects or vehicles of relations between individual people and households. The key change in animal domestication lies not in animals' bodies, nor even in human–animal relations, but in the social definition of animals as a resource. Wild animals are shared, whereas domestic animals are husbanded by their owners (see also Hamayon 1990:325–7). This is essentially the same as Ducos' definition of domestication as the transformation of animals into property.

Digard (1990) likewise takes a broad view of domestication and seeks a definition encompassing all the taxa we perceive as domestic. He also sees possession by humans as the key trait that distinguishes domestic from wild animals, although he does not make the distinction between domestic and domesticated animals. Rather, he views domestication as an ongoing process that is essentially the same in all cases, but varies in degree according to the suitability of the animal taxa and the features of human societies. He argues that we should not think in terms of a state of domestication, but of domesticatory action that people exert on animals, within a particular, culturally variable domesticatory system. There is thus no particular threshold at which animals become domesticated or fully domesticated.

QUESTIONING DOMESTICATION

Some examine the range of human–animal relationships and challenge the validity of domestication as a concept. Indeed, the members of the Palaeoeconomy school offered the concept of human–animal relationships (or "man–animal relationships" in their parlance) as an alternative to a simple wild/domestic dichotomy (Higgs and Jarman 1972; Jarman 1972, 1977; Jarman and Wilkinson 1972). The Palaeoeconomists saw domestication as a biological concept focused on the morphological changes in the animal. They preferred to study "animal husbandry" referring to the human–animal relationship, and admitting of many degrees of intensity. For them, human–animal relationships form a continuum from random hunting to factory farming, with husbandry (control) gradually intensifying along this spectrum. The point at which domestication is recognizable through morphological change is meaningless in terms of these relations (Jarman 1977).

Howard Hecker (1982) similarly rejects the utility of the concept of domestication, as based on a false wild/domestic dichotomy. He also focuses on the human–animal relationship by substituting the term "cultural control" for domestication. Again, the problem is that morphological domestication does not necessarily correspond with the key behavioral changes that are of interest to anthropologists. In fact, the elements of cultural control are quite similar to those that Bökönyi and Clutton-Brock propose as defining domestication: deliberate interference with movement, breeding, or population structure that is of long enough duration to require active care, affecting a whole group of animals (not just individual "pets"), and rendering this group more accessible for future human use (Hecker 1982:219). Intentionality is explicitly a key element.

Thus to a large extent those who reject the notion of domestication are not really objecting to the standard definitions, but to the way domestication is recognized. Instead of morphological change, they rely primarily on mortality profiles to detect the changes in the human–animal relationship that they term husbandry or cultural control. In contrast to the symbiotic view, they stress human intentionality, but their concern is with its effect on the structure of animal populations and the organization of human subsistence, rather than with the incorporation of animals into human society and its effect on human social relations.

The notion of a spectrum of human–animal relationships is a salutary one. I am not convinced, however, that domestication is a useless and arbitrary concept. The transformation of animals from shared resource to property is a critical transition, and not one that people are likely to slide into imperceptibly. There is a real difference between "managing" wild animals by practicing conservation measures and appropriating domestic animals as property. The difference lies less in the practices of animal control than in the human social relations. Herding represents a quantum shift in human–animal relations that is eminently worthy of study. However, this change in relations is unlikely to correspond with the appearance of morphological change in animals, so we must rely on other lines of evidence to detect it (see the later section, *Studying Domestication*).

## Models of origins

A thorough treatment of the origins of animal domestication would include consideration of the emergence of agriculture and other important social and economic changes that provide the context for at least most animal domestication. In this section, however, I give short shrift to this larger context and instead focus on the human–animal relationship, reviewing the major models that seek to explain how and why people domesticated animals. Naturally, these models are to some degree dependent on how domestication is defined, but all seek to explain how humans came eventually to control the breeding and movements of some animals to the extent that the animals changed physically and behaviorally.

### COEVOLUTION

Coevolutionary models are linked to symbiotic definitions of animal domestication, because coevolution is the process through which organisms adapt to symbiotic relationships. Because symbiosis benefits both partners in the relationship, changes in morphology and behavior that enhance the relationship will be selected for in both species. This selection happens unconsciously at the level of the gene, so that intentionality is completely absent in this model.

In this view, humans did not undertake domestication deliberately, nor were they pushed into it by population pressure or climatic change. Rather, it happened by itself: People and animals just slid into it. Following this model, domestication is not about control or domination. It is rather a harmonious relationship of mutual benefit. Adherents of this position see animals benefiting from domestication at least as much as people (O'Connor 1997; Rindos 1984, 1989). Others have objected to this view, arguing that many changes wrought by domestication are maladaptive (Clutton-Brock 1994:27; Shepard 1993:286–7). This disagreement stems from different understandings of what is meant by "benefit."

Domestication has indeed led to wider dispersal and greater numbers of the domesticates (as well as the domesticators). Yet it has not made them better adapted to life in the wild (not surprisingly, given that they are adapted to domestic conditions) nor has it enhanced their quality of life in most cases. However, symbiosis is not concerned with the quality of life, only with how many copies of a gene get into the next generation. In this sense, domestication can certainly be seen as symbiotic. However, does this mean that it is unintentional or inevitable?

A good case for a coevolutionary development of domestication can be made for some animals, but not, in my opinion, for those of greatest social and economic significance. First, some animals that are sometimes considered domestic have clearly not been deliberately domesticated and are not even symbiotic but commensal. These include the house mouse (*Mus musculus*), common and black rats (*Rattus norvegicus* and *R. rattus*), and house sparrow (*Passer domesticus*). Leaving aside recent breeds developed for laboratory use and sometimes kept as pets, these animals were not deliberately domesticated nor even deliberately kept. Rather, they moved into niches created by human settlement, and their adaptations to these niches produced changes sufficient for speciation (Armitage 1994; Boursot et al. 1993; Brothwell 1981; Cucchi and Vigne 2006; Ericson 1997; Tchernov 1984, 1991). These unwelcome guests can be considered domestic only under the broadest definition that considers domestication as equivalent to mutualism.

Second, some animals may have domesticated themselves by moving into a symbiotic relationship that humans welcomed and actively encouraged, but did not initiate. Dogs, the first domesticate, may well have arisen in this way from wolves scavenging on the margins of human occupations. People may have decided they were worth having around, perhaps initially as watchdogs, later for their help in hunting (Budiansky 1992; Coppinger and Coppinger 2001; Crockford 2000; Morey 1994; O'Connor 1997; Uerpmann 1996). Once the dogs were tolerated, their role as companions would also have arisen. Other uses (food, traction, herding) are probably later developments. Alternative views would derive dogs from pet wolves or from wolves deliberately domesticated as hunting aids (see Chapter 7, *Man's Best Friend*).

The coevolutionary case for cats is even stronger. Little is known about cat domestication. Morphologically wild cats occur in small numbers at many Near Eastern and European sites. These animals were transported by humans to Cyprus (along with a range of other conventionally wild and domestic species such as sheep and fallow deer; see Chapter 7, *Island Introductions*), where one was buried near a human at Neolithic Shillourokambos (Vigne and Guilaine 2004). Domesticated cats are securely known only from around 4000 BP in Egypt (Faure and Kitchener 2009). Cats are atypical domesticates in that they are not social in the wild, so deliberate domestication would be difficult (Clutton-Brock 1994:26; Zeuner 1963:37). Cats were probably attracted to human settlements when grain stores began to attract mice and other rodents, and they were tolerated or encouraged because of their pest control abilities (Armitage 1986:15; Faure and Kitchener 2009; Zeuner 1963:56). Some individuals, such as the Shillourokambos cat, became pets or held other special relationships with people.

André Haudricourt (1977) makes the novel proposal that human excrement was a major factor in domestication. Dogs and pigs eagerly consume human feces, and reindeer, and perhaps other herbivores, crave human urine for its salt content. Haudricourt suggests that human excrement would have attracted animals to human camps and familiarized them with human odors. If this attraction were enough for domestication, however, these animals should have become domesticated wherever their range overlapped with human occupation, and shortly after coming into contact. On the contrary, animal domestication occurred in relatively few areas and followed very long periods of human–animal interaction.

Although a coevolutionary model may be appropriate for some animals, notably dogs and cats, I do not find it plausible for herd and farm animals such as sheep, goats, cattle, pigs, and llamas. The changes in property relations involved in the transition from hunting to herding are so profound that they could not happen without people noticing or caring. Hunting and herding operate according to very different logics (see Chapter 8, *Difficulties of the Transition to Herding*). Sharing until nothing is left is the standard approach of immediate-return foragers (Woodburn 1982). This creates obvious problems in maintaining a breeding population.

Crucially, the inhabitants of the Near East at the time of the origin of agriculture were delayed-return rather than immediate-return foragers (Woodburn 1982). The people of the Epipaleolithic Natufian culture, for instance, stored wild grain and probably other foods (Belfer-Cohen and

Bar-Yosef 2000), and this private storage clearly set the stage for saving rather than sharing the seeds of cultivated plants. Nevertheless, even horticulturalists view wild animals as a shared resource. The sanctions on farmers who failed to share animals might not be as strong as on foragers (and this is probably why animal domestication occurs in the context of plant cultivation), but they would still be present. Keeping private herds is a real change from hunting wild animals, and it could not have happened unconsciously or without substantial renegotiations of social interactions.

Moreover, whereas dogs can scavenge around human settlements and largely take care of themselves with relatively little impact on the human organization of labor, maintaining a viable herd of sheep, for example, requires considerable labor input. People herding sheep are not doing whatever they had been doing previously, so roles would have to shift to accommodate this new activity. The movements of at least some group members and the seasonal schedule would have to adjust to the needs of sheep for fodder. Such changes do not happen imperceptibly, but must be negotiated. At some point people must decide, and convince their neighbors, that the benefits of owning animals outweigh the added labor and disruption, not to mention the potential crop damage and other costs of keeping animals.

## THE PET THEORY

The keeping of pets is a widespread practice that I explore further in Chapter 7. Because pet keeping brings tame animals into human communities, some have seen it as the basis for animal domestication (Reed 1977; Serpell 1986, 1989; Uerpmann 1996). Hunters often bring back the infants of their prey to raise as pets. Charles Reed (1977:563) specifically identifies little girls as the likely pet keepers, reasoning that their maternal instinct and female hormones would incline them to care for infant animals, while adult women would be inured to killing them, as would boys, who would already be learning to hunt. David Rindos (1984:10–11) takes exception to the gendered aspect of this model, "since I am a man who played with dolls as a child, cried when his guinea pig died, and has recently discovered his paternal 'instincts.'" In any case, the model proposes that, although most such pets would not have survived or would have run away or been driven away as adults, a few stayed and bred in the settlements. The elders of the group realized that these animals breeding in the village provided a handy meat supply and encouraged it.

In my view, this model suffers from an inadequate conception of domestication. The presence of tamed pets no doubt provided useful knowledge about animals and the techniques of controlling and interacting with them. This knowledge surely smoothed the way to domestication. The transition to herding, however, is more complicated than simply deciding that having domestic animals around is a good idea. In the same way that the coevolutionary approach does not explain the social aspect of domestication, the pet theory fails to provide an account of why people would be willing to alter their lives so profoundly.

Carl Sauer (1969) recognizes this problem and proposes that what he calls the "household animals" (dog, pig, chicken) had their origin as pets, but the domestication of herd animals (sheep, goat, cattle) must be explained differently (see the later section, *Religion and Feasting*). There is much to be said for this distinction. Dogs, pigs, and chickens can all forage for themselves within human settlements and can survive in small numbers with little human intervention. The distinction here between the pet theory and the coevolutionary view is slight: Were they tolerated because they were treasured as pets or because they offered some more concrete benefit (hunting aid, guard service, sanitation) to the human partners in the relationship? For pets to provide the origins of herds, however, at some point there must be a transition from companion animal to resource. One does not eat one's pets. And who but the pet's owner has the right to kill it and eat it? Thus issues of property and the organization of labor do eventually intrude, but perhaps at a later point in the process.

## THE WALKING LARDER

If domestication of herd and farm animals was a conscious choice, why would people make it? Animal domestication involves a conceptual shift from seeing animals as a shared resource to seeing them as property, and from a focus on the dead animal to a focus on the living animal and its offspring (Meadow 1989:81). It also involves more work than hunting, as well as considerable social upheaval. What would make all this seem worthwhile?

The classic answer is that domestic animals provided a convenient and reliable meat supply: a walking larder (e.g., Armitage 1986; Bökönyi

1969; Chaplin 1969; Clutton-Brock 1994; Davis 1991; Flannery 1969; Hecker 1984; Hole 1996; Rosenberg et al. 1998). In early versions of this hypothesis, domestication was simply a good idea that happened to present itself and was adopted because of its intrinsic superiority to hunting (Carter 1977; Wilson 1862:vol. 2, 464). More recent variants recognize that herding is more laborious than hunting, and they tend to stress "push" effects that would reduce game populations. Some have favored the regional process of climatic change (Hole 1996), whereas others have blamed local game depletion due to overhunting resulting from population growth (Rosenberg et al. 1998) or increased sedentism (Bar-Yosef and Meadow 1995:91; Chaplin 1969:239; Hecker 1984; Meadow 1989; Tchernov 1993). Some also note the "pull" effect of the integration of animal and plant domestication, in that surplus agricultural produce can be "banked" by feeding it to animals (Clutton-Brock 1994:26; Flannery 1969:74), and both animal and plant production are enhanced by grazing the flocks on the stubble of the crops, which they fertilize with their manure.

It is uncertain, however, whether early herding was more stable, reliable, or productive than hunting. Indeed, given that it involved restricted movement and hence a limitation of the foraging ability of the animals, it is far more likely to have been both less productive and riskier. This may explain, in part, the size reduction seen in many early domesticates. Ingold (1980) regards pastoralism as inherently unstable. Whereas predation by wolves, for example, tends to maintain the prey population at a sustainable level by removing the maximum sustainable yield, herding removes the minimum possible number of animals to sustain the human population, maximizing the herd population. This permits the herd to expand beyond its food base, a recipe for disaster. Herding animals for meat alone ("carnivorous pastoralism" in Ingold's parlance) thus does not increase but actually reduces the productivity of the land compared to hunting; it is not an intensification of hunting as cultivation is an intensification of gathering.

Of course, Ingold is referring to pure pastoralism and pure hunting, in which hunter and herder are entirely or at least primarily reliant on animals for their subsistence. If people are getting the bulk of their diet from plant foods, they can overhunt and reduce the local game population. In this case herding might be more productive than hunting, but only because herding would involve a smaller harvest of animals. The same result could be accomplished with greater yields and less labor, not to mention less social upheaval, by instituting conservation measures that reduce the number of animals killed or change the age/sex composition of animals hunted. Overhunting by definition means that the ecosystem cannot produce enough animals to support that level of offtake; herding will not change the carrying capacity without substantial added labor to produce fodder. Protection of the flocks may reduce competition from other predators, but this again could be accomplished more easily by hunting out those predators. In fact, if overhunting has severely reduced prey populations, the competing predators will probably have largely disappeared.

SECONDARY PRODUCTS

If animal domestication was not a plausible way to increase or stabilize meat supplies, might it have been aimed at some other subsistence goal? Some have argued that the only way domestic animal production can be superior to hunting in economic terms is through the use of secondary products (renewable products of the living animal, such as milk, wool, and labor), and that only the use of these products would supply a rational economic motivation for animal domestication (Ingold 1980:100; Vigne and Helmer 2007).

The conventional wisdom is that domestic animals were originally used for meat, and only later for secondary products (Bökönyi 1969; Childe 1951; Greenfield 1988; Hesse 1993; Perkins 1973b). Indeed, Sherratt (1981, 1982, 1983) proposes a Secondary Products Revolution that transformed human–animal relationships several millennia after animal domestication (see Chapter 8).

The question of whether secondary products were used from the beginning of animal domestication, and hence may have motivated it, or only much later is at least potentially amenable to empirical resolution. At this point we cannot claim a definitive answer, but there is a certain amount of evidence to consider.

*Wool*

At this time, the question of whether a secondary product motivated domestication seems clearest for wool. Wild sheep are not woolly but hairy, with a slight woolly undercoat. Hence it is unlikely that people domesticated them for their wool. In any case, there is no sign of wool in the archaeological record until ca. 5000 BP (Armitage 1986; McCorriston 1997; Ryder 1973, 1984). Although textile remains only occasionally survive from early sites, we do have preserved textiles going back to the Upper Paleolithic (Adovasio et al. 1996; Kehoe 1991; Kvavadze et al. 2009; Nadel et al. 1994; Soffer et al. 2000) and a number of examples of impressions or actual textiles from the Neolithic (Adovasio and Illingworth 2003; Adovasio and Maslowski 1988; Barber 1994; Makkay 2001; Médard 2006; Moulherat et al. 2002; SAPPO 2007; Tringham et al. 1992). As yet, all of these are vegetal fibers, mostly flax (linen). There was some controversy about the identification of the textiles from the 1960s excavations at Çatalhöyük. Hans Helbaek (1963) described these fibers as wool; Harold Burnham (1965) was noncommittal but inclined toward wool. However, a careful study by Ryder (1965; Ryder and Gabra-Sanders 1985), the acknowledged authority on ancient wool, clearly demonstrates, on both morphological and chemical grounds, that the fibers are flax. Bökönyi (1974:159–60) cites a figurine from Tepe Sarab in Iran ca. 8000 BP as depicting a woolly sheep, but this may not be what it actually represents. Ryder (1984) sees it as a hairy sheep in the early stages of developing wool. Thus present evidence strongly suggests that wool use was not a factor in the domestication of sheep, but a considerably later development.

### Dairy

The evidence for the first use of dairy and traction is less clear-cut. The recent development of a technique to detect chemical traces of milk on pottery should help clarify the dairy issue (Dudd and Evershed 1998). Milk residues have now been found as early as the 9th millennium BP in the Near East and southeast Europe (Evershed et al. 2008). However, animal domestication occurred in the Pre-Pottery Neolithic, so this technique will not resolve the question of whether milk was used from the beginning of herding unless we can find other materials that bear milk residues.

The major alternative approach is the use of mortality profiles: age and sex patterning in the remains of animals slaughtered. Sebastian Payne's (1973) seminal work points out that optimizing for meat, milk, or wool production will produce differing mortality profiles. For meat, one would seek to slaughter most animals at the late juvenile–early subadult stage, when they have reached nearly full size and growth slows, such that additional feed yields a diminishing payback in weight gain. One would tend to slaughter more males than females to preserve the breeding stock. Because it is generally only possible to sex the bones of adult animals, this strategy would create an assemblage with a large number of late juvenile–early subadult remains, and the relatively few adults would be biased toward females. For milk, one needs to eliminate the calves that compete for the milk. Because one also needs to preserve adult females as the milk producers, male calves would be differentially slaughtered. Thus the assemblage should reflect peak mortality in the infantile stage and an adult sex ratio that is heavily female. Both sexes produce wool, so to optimize for wool production one would let most animals reach the adult stage. Thus the mortality peak would be in adults, even in quite old adults, and the adult sex ratio should be roughly even.

Payne's model was based on herders producing for a market economy, and it represents extreme strategies unlikely to be practiced in a subsistence economy. Nevertheless, the general principles reflect the realities of herding. If one wants to produce substantial quantities of milk, for instance, one must keep adult females and deal with competition from the calves either by eliminating them or by weaning early. Those who have applied Payne's model have generally found that a dairy mortality profile does not appear until ca. 7000 BP in the Near East (Davis 1984b; Gilbert and Steinfeld 1977; Whitcher et al. 1998) and ca. 6000 BP in Europe (Greenfield 1984, 1988, 1989, 2005, 2010; Legge 1989; Sakellaridis 1979), although some have suggested earlier dairy use (Halstead 1987; Rowley-Conwy 2000).

Several complicating factors render the straightforward application of Payne's model problematic, however. First, as with any use of mortality profiles, there are taphonomic issues. The more delicate bones of younger animals are more prone to destruction, particularly by dogs, thus producing a skewed age profile. Underrepresentation of infantile bone clearly has an especially strong effect on the recognition of dairy mortality profiles. The usual solution has been to base age estimates on mandibles, which are relatively solid as well as easily aged (Higham 1968). However, experimental and ethnoarchaeological work has shown that even the mandibles of infantile sheep and goats are significantly more likely to be destroyed by dogs than adult mandibles, producing severe distortion of the mortality profile (Munson 2000; Munson and Garniewicz 2003).

Second, the dairy mortality profile itself may not be applicable to early herds. Lactating female mammals let down their milk in response to the suckling and nuzzling of their infants. This let-down response is partially voluntary, and it requires a certain degree of relaxation and willing participation on the part of the mother (Amoroso and Jewell 1963). Modern dairy goats and cattle usually let down their milk in response to bumping and tugging by a human or mechanical milker. Less specialized animals, however, may not let down without the presence of their own infant. Many artistic representations from relatively late in the use of dairy depict a calf or other young animal held next to its mother while she is being milked (Amoroso and Jewell 1963; Cranstone 1969:256; McCormick 1992). Abundant documentary evidence from medieval Ireland indicates that cattle were kept primarily for dairy and that calves needed to be present to milk the cows (McCormick 1992). This would result in few animals slaughtered at less than 9–12 months of age, and indeed the Irish faunal assemblages have mortality profiles that peak at 1–2 years of age. This kind of age profile could easily be mistaken for meat rather than dairy production, especially if the analysis lumps specimens into infantile/juvenile/subadult/adult age categories, because the distinction then becomes one between early rather than late juvenile slaughter peaks. For example, when viewed in this light, the cattle from Opovo, a Late Neolithic site in Yugoslavia, appear to fit a dairy profile, when otherwise they would be seen as being raised for meat (Russell 1993).

The ability to let down the milk in the absence of a calf seems to be acquired relatively late and of variable date in cattle. It may well be earlier for sheep and goat, but nevertheless the first domesticates would most likely need the stimulus of the presence of their young. Thus we should expect mortality profiles more like those from medieval Ireland than Payne's model if dairy were the main use of the first domesticates. Early domesticates, or animals in the early stages of dairy use, would also not produce much milk beyond the needs of their offspring. If the offspring had to be kept alive to maintain milk production, the amount of milk available to humans would be relatively small. However, the infant can be shorted to some degree, and it can be weaned early. These compromises enable the extraction of a certain amount of milk for human consumption at the cost of less vigorous animals, perhaps contributing to the size diminution that often marks domestication (Meadow 1989).

A further problem with applying Payne's herding strategies to early societies is that subsistence production is unlikely to be so specialized. Even if milk was a major goal, early herders probably sought to strike a balance between meat and dairy production. Moreover, they were most likely equally concerned with minimizing the risk of loss of a large part of the herds on which they depended, which would entail raising "extra" animals as insurance (Cribb 1987; Redding 1984; Stein 1989). The wealth value of animals may also have encouraged the maximization of herd size at the cost of optimal production (see Chapter 8). Hence it is quite likely that even an early herding strategy centered on dairy might not conform to Payne's classic profile, because the herders raised many more animals than expected to provide insurance against animal loss and to increase their flocks. An additional practical problem is that if herds were moved seasonally, as is likely to be the case if they were of significant size, a single site assemblage would not reflect the entire mortality profile of the herding system. It may completely lack the infantile portion of the kill-off if it is not the location where lambing took place, for example (Vigne and Helmer 2007).

Roger Cribb (1984, 1985, 1987) points out that herds are rarely static, but rather dynamic. That is, herders nearly always try to increase their flocks in anticipation of catastrophic losses from disease, predation, bad weather, and raiding (Cribb 1987:384–6). He has tried to address this dynamic aspect with computer simulation of sheep/goat herding strategies, which has yielded some unexpected results. Most strikingly, it is impossible to optimize for a single product. Maximizing milk production also increases meat and wool yields; maximizing for wool decreases total productivity. The relation between milk and meat production is particularly strong. This should be no surprise to anyone familiar with the dairy industry, who will realize that a byproduct of dairy production is veal calves. Cribb suggests that a herd structure that would at least permit dairy production is thus likely to have arisen quite early, whereas wool production is more likely to occur only after the advent of more specialized economies.

Using his simulations to test some of the herding strategies reconstructed by zooarchaeologists from the age and sex structure of their assemblages, Cribb (1987:402–10) finds that many of these strategies are not viable: The herd would die off over several generations. In particular, infantile remains are seriously underrepresented in archaeological assemblages, no doubt due to a combination of taphonomic processes affecting their survival, seasonal movement of flocks, and a failure to bring the remains of neonatal animals lost to natural causes back to the site. These factors are unfortunately too complex to enable a standard correction factor for archaeological mortality profiles, but we need to remember in modeling that we are very likely to be missing a substantial amount of the infantile mortality.

An alternative approach to detecting dairy production in ancient herds uses x-rays to assess the thickness of cortical bone, with extended lactation causing thinning due to calcium loss. In a number of Israeli assemblages spanning the PPNB to the Late Bronze Age, this thinning appears only in the Chalcolithic (or in one case the Early Bronze Age), and it becomes more pronounced in the Late Bronze Age (Horwitz and Smith 1990, 1991; Smith and Horwitz 1984). Another technique based on the same principle measures the size of the osteons themselves within the bone (Chamberlain and Forbes 2005).

At the moment, then, the evidence tends to support a gradual, patchy adoption of milking at some time after the domestication of sheep, goats, and cattle, rather than as the motivating force in their domestication. Jean-Denis Vigne and Daniel Helmer (Helmer et al. 2007; Vigne and Helmer 2007), however, have recently argued on the basis of mortality profiles refined from Payne's that milk was used from very early in the domestication process and may have been at least a partial motivation for domestication. Hesse (1993), who tested this claim with mortality profiles in the Kermanshah Valley in Iran, rejects significant dairy use by early herders. On theoretical grounds, arguments can be made both ways. Dairy is a more efficient use of domestic animals than meat and is the most productive use of uncultivable pasture land (Ingold 1980:176; Russell 1988). For example, Paul Halstead (1981a:314) has calculated for Neolithic Greece that a village of 40–240 people would need 2,400–14,400 sheep to subsist on meat alone, but only 1,000–6,000 if they used both meat and milk. Moreover, the use of the living animal provides an obvious incentive for keeping it around.

However, would it occur to a hunter to use an animal for dairy? Drinking milk beyond infancy must have seemed like a strange notion, and presumably the first use of dairy was to feed infants who had lost their mothers or whose mothers had lost their milk (Köhler-Rollefson and Rollefson 2002). This use would require the presence of tame, lactating female animals; there would not be time to tame one for the purpose. Ingold (1980:100) suggests that, other than pets, animals may first have been tamed and kept as decoys for hunting others of their species. This would not require breeding animals; it would be easier to tame captured wild animals. However, a female in heat would be the best lure, which could well lead to having a tame, lactating female around the settlement. Thus use as decoys might provide the motivation for taming, and dairy the motivation for domestication.

Still, the let-down issues discussed earlier would limit the amount of milk available from early domesticates, and lactose intolerance would limit its utility. Although it might be useful to have a supply of milk for infants, adult mammals, including most humans, stop manufacturing lactase, the enzyme that breaks down lactose (milk sugar) and permits the full digestion of milk. Thus people over five or six years of age would benefit little from drinking milk, bringing the value of dairy production into question.

Of course, populations with a history of dairy use have adapted by maintaining lactase production in most adults. In these cases, primarily in central and northern Europe and east Africa, there must have been sufficient benefit from drinking milk as adults to create selective pressure for this mutation (McCracken 1971). Lactose intolerance has not been suppressed in the Near East, where dairy products are consumed mainly as yogurt and cheese, which breaks down the lactose into a more digestible form. Fresh milk may have been drunk by adults only where components not preserved in cheese and yogurt – high water content in arid east Africa, and the lactose itself for temperate Europe – were needed. Lactose enhances calcium absorption, a valuable property where vitamin D from fish or sunlight is scarce (Harris 1985:143–8; Sherratt 1983:94–5). Yogurt and cheese could not be invented until animals were already being milked, whether as a source of infant food or as a fertility offering. So the question remains open, and at this point we should simply bear in mind that dairy use may not initially have been of substantial nutritional benefit except to infants. A recent study of European Mesolithic and Early Neolithic human remains found all lacked the gene for lactose tolerance (Burger et al. 2007). Only after lactose tolerance became widespread or cultured dairy products were developed would dairy use enable a significant intensification of herd animals compared to use for meat alone.

*Labor*

Animal labor can be useful to humans in many ways. Carnivores may aid in hunting, protection, vermin control, and herding, among other tasks. Game animals can lure others of their kind. Some animals can be ridden, many can carry burdens, and some can be used in traction: pulling plows or vehicles. The use of animals in traction and transport has been seen as particularly significant, forming part of the Secondary Products Revolution (Sherratt 1981, 1983). This is also the easiest kind of animal labor to detect archaeologically, although such detection is far from straightforward.

The use of animals to pull wheeled vehicles occurs far later than the beginnings of animal domestication (ca. 5500 BP at the earliest), so although there is considerable debate about exactly when and where it began, I do not pursue it here (Anthony 1986, 1998, 2007; Anthony and Vinogradov 1995; Bakker et al. 1999; Hanks 2010; Kuznetsov 2006; Pétrequin et al. 2006; Piggott 1979, 1983; Sherratt 2003). The use of the plow, as evidenced by pathologies and biomechanical alterations in cattle skeletons (Baker 1984; Bartosiewicz 1993; Bartosiewicz et al. 1997; Bogucki 1993; Halstead 1987; Mateescu 1975; Milisauskas and Kruk 1991; Sherratt 1981, 1982, 1983), may occur somewhat earlier, but probably does not predate the Late Neolithic, although it was possibly used on a small scale from the Early Neolithic on Crete, ca. 7500 BP (Isaakidou 2006).

Zooarchaeological work on the skeletal alterations resulting from use as pack animals has so far been limited. Bearing excess weight should cause diagnostic remodeling and pathologies just as traction does. Pathological alterations similar to those associated with riding (Bartosiewicz and Bartosiewicz 2002; Daugnora and Thomas 2005; Pluskowski et al. 2010) have been interpreted as evidence of pack bearing in Egyptian donkeys from Abydos, ca. 5000 BP (Rossel et al. 2008), and patterns of osteoarthritis in dogs from the North American Archaic have been seen as evidence for pack use (Warren 2000).

Given the simplicity of the technology involved and the easy conceptual extension of human burden-bearing to animals, pack use could have been practiced from very early times. Larger animals such as cattle, horses, and camels are the most likely candidates, although dogs have been used as pack animals (Crabtree and Campana 1987; Sharp 1976; Warren 2000). Horses and camels were domesticated fairly late, and cattle, although earlier, seem not to have been the first animals to be domesticated (see Table 6.1). Rather, the first herd animals domesticated in the Old World were sheep and goats, an unlikely choice if use as pack animals was the primary goal. The situation may be different in the Andes, where llamas are important beasts of burden. This function, along with wool, might in theory have been an important motivating factor in their domestication. The size increase with domestication in llamas supports this argument (Mengoni-Goñalons 2008). However, extensive use of animals for either traction or carrying burdens should create a mortality profile dominated by adults. This profile appears only later in Andean prehistory for llamas (Browman 1989) and is quite different from the juvenile-dominated mortality profiles of early Old World domesticates. Thus although animals may have occasionally borne burdens from very early times, it does not become a major factor until much later.

Ancient foragers may often have tamed animals for use as hunting decoys as Ingold suggests. This is an important precursor to domestication in that it provided a supply of tame animals and a model for using live animals. However, taming in itself is unlikely to lead to domestication. If we see domestication in biological terms as alterations to the bodies of animals, there is no need to control the breeding of such decoy animals or to separate them from the wild breeding population. Most likely only females would be used for such purposes. If we take domestication to be a social phenomenon involving the conversion of animals to property, taming for decoys may be a better model. Someone would have to be responsible for the care of decoy animals, and this might lead to notions of ownership, just as with pets. In the absence of other factors, however, this practice is unlikely to grow beyond the keeping of occasional animals with minimal social impact.

So far I have been discussing the initial domestication of livestock. If we consider secondary domestication, the addition of new domesticates where some animals have already been kept for a long time, labor may have played a greater role. In particular, camels may have been domesticated as beasts of burden, although their milk may have been equally important. They are also eaten and raced, and their hair is used for textiles, but these are subsidiary uses (Bulliet 1990; Gauthier-Pilters and Dagg 1981; Hakker-Orion 1984; Knauer 1998; Köhler 1984; Köhler-Rollefson 1996).

Horse domestication most likely began by taming some individuals to ride as an aid in hunting other horses (Anthony 1986, 1991, 1994, 1995, 1997; Anthony and Brown 1989, 1991, 2000; Anthony et al. 1991; Benecke and Driesch 2003; Brown and Anthony 1998; Olsen 2003, 2006); milking of mares also occurred early in the process (Outram et al. 2009). Once mounted, a new range of possibilities opened up for the riders: enhanced battle capabilities, more effective utilization of the steppe, easier movement (Anthony 1986, 1995, 1998; Anthony and Brown 2000; Anthony and Vinogradov 1995). Ancient riders seized these opportunities in short order. Thus labor, in the form of riding, probably motivated horse domestication, initially to enhance the ability to use horses for meat.

In summary, although milk and labor cannot be eliminated as motivations for domestication, nor can wool for llamas and alpacas, the weight of the present evidence suggests that they were not a factor in the primary domestication of livestock (i.e., in cases where there were no other animal domesticates aside from dogs). Rather, the use of secondary products seems to be a later intensification of the domesticatory relationship, although perhaps not very much later in some cases.

### RELIGION AND FEASTING

If the motivation for the transition to herding cannot be found in the need or desire for a steady supply of meat or for products of the living animal, what then might have impelled people to reorganize their societies and take on the additional labor of animal husbandry? Some believe this social change had a social motivation, in religion or status competition.

### *Sacrifice*

Eduard Hahn (1896) proposed that animals were domesticated for their religious significance, noting that the early domesticates (sheep, goats, and cattle) all have curving horns evoking the crescent moon. The motivation for domestication, in his view, was to provide sacrificial victims for the moon goddess. Hahn connected many domesticatory techniques to religious worship. Thus traction originated in pulling sacred carts in religious processions, and plowing was a symbol of male insemination of the female earth. Castration and milking were likewise practices related to fertility cults, with the milk offered to the goddess.

Hahn based his model largely on early texts from Mesopotamia and Egypt. Given the short chronology of this time before the advent of radiocarbon and other absolute dating techniques or the excavation of Neolithic sites in the Near East, he believed that these texts were written shortly after the inception of plant and animal domestication. After more than a century of research and improvement in dating techniques, we now know that Near Eastern peoples had practiced agriculture and animal husbandry for several thousand years and through major social changes before these texts were written (see Table 6.1). As a result, more recent archaeologists have tended to dismiss Hahn's ideas. Some geographers (Isaac 1971; Sauer 1969:chapter 5; Walsh 1989) have continued to advocate these views in relatively recent times, however, and it is worth considering whether they might apply to the Neolithic societies that did domesticate animals.

As we have seen, plowing and wheeled vehicles appear well after the beginning of herding. Although artistic depictions of plowing by ithyphallic men and furrows under burial mounds in Late Neolithic and Bronze Age Europe render a religious, phallic interpretation quite plausible, it cannot be seen as an impetus to early domestication. Present evidence does not support a major role for milking in early domesticates, although small amounts of milk may have been extracted for offerings. Whether or not this use of milk was an incentive for domestication in the first place, it could well have initiated dairy use whenever it occurred. After all, initial milk yields would be too small to be of substantial nutritional value, particularly given lactose intolerance (Sauer 1969:86–7). Yet milk, as the stuff of life, has strong symbolic value. It is offered to deities and used in rituals in many African societies, Mongolia, and in the Vedic tradition (Baldick 2000:98; Heesterman 1993; Heusch 1985; Ruel 1990), so this symbolism has certainly been apparent to many societies that use dairy products. The origins of dairy practice surely lie in some combination of this symbolic value and the use of animal milk to sustain human infants whose mothers are unable to nurse them (which would certainly enhance the life-giving symbolism of animal milk).

Nor should we dismiss the symbolic appeal of crescent-shaped horns. Cattle horns had strong symbolic value for many Neolithic cultures in the Near East and Europe (see Chapter 3). Cattle heads and horns were displayed on walls and included in burials. Whether they are phallic symbols, moon symbols, both, or neither, they definitely carried great significance and may well have provided part of the incentive for cattle domestication. Contemporary South Asian societies keep cattle or mithan (*Bos frontalis*) primarily for sacrifice (Fürer-Haimendorf 1963; Simoons 1968); the same is true for water buffalo among the Kodi (Hoskins 1993). However, cattle do not appear to be the earliest domesticates (see Table 6.1). Sheep and goat horns are sometimes depicted in the Neolithic, but are much less prominent. Indeed, prior to the first evidence of animal domestication, gazelles predominate in Near Eastern animal depictions (Cauvin 1972).

All of this discussion is centered on the Near East. Although this appears to be the area of the earliest animal domestication, there is at least one other center of independent animal (and plant) domestication in the New World, and there is likely another one in East Asia as well. Could this model apply to these cases? It does not work in a straightforward fashion for the New World, where animals were not used for dairy and animal-drawn plows and wheeled vehicles are totally lacking. Moreover, the native faunas of South America and Mesoamerica (the areas with domesticated animals other than dogs) lack animals with crescent-shaped horns. In East Asia, the pig is the first animal domesticate other than the dog, with chickens perhaps domesticated at around the same time (see Table 6.1). These animals lack horns and are not used for dairy or traction.

However, a less literal version of the model, positing that animals were domesticated for religious rather than subsistence reasons, is tenable. Eggs are an even more obvious fertility symbol than milk and have served as such in many societies, including our Easter eggs. Because traction and perhaps dairy postdate domestication in the Old World, their lack elsewhere is not terribly significant, and the lack of horns does not preclude the use of llamas and pigs in sacrifice. The crux of the religious argument is that the reason for raising animals was to ensure a reliable supply not of meat, but of appropriate sacrificial victims (Heusch 1985:212).

This model solves the problem of why people might wish to take on the burden of raising animals when the payoff nutritionally, at the start, is probably less than that of hunting. It has its own difficulties, however, in addition to the methodological issue of how to recognize sacrifice archaeologically. How is this demand for animal victims created in a hunting context? Ethnographic evidence suggests that this is not impossible. There are numerous examples of the capture of wild animals specifically for the purpose of sacrifice or ritual killing, with the animals kept for varying lengths of time before they are killed (see Chapter 3, *Sacrifice and Ritual Killing*). Although these instances have not led to domestication, one could certainly argue that they could do so in cases in which the animal taxon was more suitable and the human social organization was appropriate (in most cases this would mean sedentism and/or agriculture).

As discussed in Chapter 3, many argue that only domestic animals can be sacrificed, but some hunters' rites approach sacrifice very closely. The bear feasts of Siberia and the Ainu, as well as the eat-all feasts of the North American Cree (Brightman 1993; Tanner 1979), involve a ritual consumption of animals intended to assure the future availability of game and even to coerce the animal spirits or their spirit master into providing more game (Brightman 1993:236–43). This is not so different from sacrificing an animal to evoke the generosity of a deity, and both involve the notion of releasing the life force of the animal.

Thus although the details of Hahn's model do not hold up very well in the light of subsequent research, the general notion that domestication may have been motivated by the need for sacrificial animals deserves reconsideration. Sacrifice is a widespread practice in societies with domestic animals, and some practices of ethnographically known foragers resemble it. Ceremonies such as the Ainu bear feast, in which a ritual killing of an animal is tied to a particular occasion and the animal is kept for some time before being killed, seem most likely to lead to animal husbandry.

### Feasting

When the sacrificial animal is eaten, as it usually is, sacrifice will be associated with feasting. Feasting thus often plays a religious role, but it has social purposes as well. Whether or not they involve sacrifice, feasts are occasions for negotiating social relationships and for increasing the status of successful hosts (Blanton and Taylor 1995; Gregory 1982; Sherratt 1995; and see the section *Feasting* in Chapter 9).

Brian Hayden (1990, 1992, 1995a, 1996a, 2001a, 2009) has suggested that feasting provided the impetus for plant and animal domestication. Briefly, he argues that, rather than being pushed into cultivation and later herding by environmental or population pressures, people developed agriculture in areas of abundance. The motivation for the increased labor input that was required lay in prestige competition as enacted through feasting by ambitious aggrandizers/accumulators/acquisitors ("triple-A personalities"; Hayden 1996a:131). This personality type is found in all cultures and is expressed through competitive feasting whenever the environment supports it. "Where desirable plants and animals were amenable to controlled production, this situation should have led to domestication" (Hayden 1990:37).

Hayden (1995a:294) attempts to account for the fact that dogs are the first, and in many places the only, domesticated animal with an analogy to plant domestication. Just as the first plants to be domesticated were not staples but condiments or those with nonfood products (e.g., bottle gourd), so the first domesticate of all is not a farm animal. Rather, he suggests, people domesticated dogs for consumption at feasts. Their value as feasting food rested on both their rarity and the labor investment in raising them. "As with all kept animals, the number of animals raised at any one time must have been very limited, time consuming, and labor intensive" (Hayden 1990:41). Yet this hardly seems an apt description of dogs/wolves. Indeed, as we have seen, it can plausibly be argued that dogs domesticated themselves precisely because they survive so easily as scavengers on the margins of human settlements with minimal care or none at all. If one wished to make a statement about labor investment, other animals would be much more suitable. If wolves were indeed deliberately domesticated for use in feasts, and perhaps for general display value, their value was probably based more on the power implied by the control of a dangerous animal (see the later section, *Domination*).

Dogs have often been consumed at feasts, usually in conjunction with sacrifice (Adams 2004; Clutton-Brock and Hammond 1994; Comba 1991; Fenton 1978; Gilmore 1933; Heusch 1985; Kirch 2001; Masson 1999; Ojoade 1990; Pohl and Feldman 1982; Powers and Powers 1984; Schwartz 1997; Tooker 1965; Trigger 1990; Wing 1978, 1984). This is especially true of, but not limited to, areas where dogs are the only domestic animal. However, dog meat is not the only meat used in North American feasts, and its role in feasts is probably a secondary use rather than the motivation for domestication. Hayden implies that animal domestication is solely about food, so that the choices are either that dogs and other domestic animals were staples of daily meat consumption or they were special feasting food. However, dogs played many roles in early societies (see Chapter 7) and were only occasionally eaten. For that matter, wolves were rarely eaten. They are scarce in archaeological faunal assemblages, and although some are consumed, they seem more often to be killed for their fur or their symbolic value (and after the domestication of other animals, probably to protect the flocks). It is perhaps more likely that the gradual incorporation of already domestic dogs into feasting suggested possibilities that could be applied to other animals.

Hayden's model works better for other domesticated animals. "[Dogs in the Pacific Northwest] were unlikely to be used for daily subsistence needs. The use of any domesticated animals as a daily meat staple would require enormous herds.... Thus, the use of meat from domesticated animals as a staple food during the early phases of domestication seems unlikely. Domesticated animals appear much more likely to have been eaten only on special occasions" (Hayden 1990:41). I have already noted that domestication is not a particularly good way to maintain a steady meat supply. Use in feasts and sacrifices (often hard to separate) provides a plausible alternative to the use of secondary products as a motivation for keeping animals. This is particularly true of competitive feasts, where the host seeks to maximize labor input to create an impressive display (Gregory 1982; Hayden 1995a:289). Thus the greater labor requirements of herding as opposed to hunting become a positive feature that is desirable in itself.

Hayden suggests that animals were domesticated primarily for their high fat content in contrast to the meat of wild animals: "Only by keeping animals and intentionally feeding them to increase their fat content could individuals achieve this goal" (Hayden 1990:42). Fat is indeed a coveted delicacy, and it is often in short supply in wild foods. Many plants may have been domesticated for their oily seeds (Hayden 1990). However, if the first domestic animals were fed so abundantly, it is surprising that domestication is marked by a decrease in size. Thus the fattening of animals is probably a later development. The intensive processing of animal bones for marrow and bone grease seen in most Neolithic assemblages also suggests that fat was not abundant.

The perceived need for animals to be consumed in special contexts thus offers one of the more satisfying explanations for why people would take on the difficulties of raising animals. Whether it is a religious requirement to have particular animals to sacrifice on particular occasions or a desire to provide special delicacies for competitive feasts, the extra labor can seem not only worthwhile but also a welcome addition to the value of the offering. This explanation also fits better with current evidence that early domesticates were used primarily for their meat. It would therefore behoove us to devote serious attention to the recognition and study of feasting remains at prehistoric sites (see Chapter 9). However, where Neolithic feasting has been identified, it is usually based on animals other than sheep and goats, the first domesticated livestock.

### Shamanism

Although shamanism is associated with foraging societies, some have also placed it in the Neolithic. Lewis-Williams (2004; Lewis-Williams and Pearce 2005) specifically links these beliefs to animal domestication. Present-day shamanistic religions often include a notion of spirit masters/mistresses of each animal species, who may be considered to own and certainly to care for these animals (Harrod 2000; Ingold 1987:245–55). If this is an ancient belief rather than one inspired by knowledge of domestic animals (including dogs), it could make human ownership of animals thinkable. Shamans often have animal familiars (see Chapter 2, *Animal Deities*) and sometimes have tamed animals that embody this role and help the shaman control wild animals of that species (Hamayon 1990). This control is used both to enhance hunting success and to impress other people and build the status and power of the shaman. Lewis-Williams argues that this use of tamed animals could lead to herding, probably in connection with keeping animals corralled for sacrifice and feasting. Hamayon (1990), however, sees this practice as unrelated to domestication, because the animals are not raised for food.

Lewis-Williams specifically bases this model on the art from Çatalhöyük, suggesting that shamans domesticated cattle at the site to bolster their power. He sees the art and architecture of Çatalhöyük as embodying a shamanistic worldview and providing the setting for shamanic rituals. His argument is based essentially on the earlier work at the site by Mellaart (1967), much of which is now out of date, raising problems with Lewis-Williams's model. Çatalhöyük can no longer be seen as existing in glorious isolation as the first farming site in Anatolia, but instead is heir to a long tradition in eastern and central Anatolia stretching back more than 1,000 years before the beginning of its occupation. Is it then appropriate to assign a foraging worldview to people who were farmers and herders of sheep and goats? The art, too, although distinctive, grows from a set of shared motifs found for more than a millennium in Anatolia. Current evidence suggests that cattle domestication first occurred not at Çatalhöyük, but slightly earlier in the middle Euphrates valley to the east (Helmer et al. 2005).

If broadened in time and space, the model has much to recommend it, but some difficulties remain. If domestication is a result of shamans asserting their power over animals in order to gain power over people, and shamanism is classically a religion of foragers, why is it that animal domestication (dogs aside) occurs only in the context of plant agriculture? One would have to make either a technological argument (architectural structures associated with settled communities were needed to control herds sufficiently to domesticate them, for example) or propose that shamanism experienced a last desperate florescence as its basis in a foraging way of life was lost. This might explain the puzzling emphasis on hunting or, at least, on wild animals in the art of Çatalhöyük and other Anatolian Neolithic sites (Russell and Meece 2006; Verhoeven 2002a).

Lewis-Williams suggests that shamans first, at sites east of Çatalhöyük, sought power through the control of sheep, goats, and pigs. However, after a while these herded animals became ordinary and lost their ability to inspire awe. So the shamans then turned to cattle, which eventually also lost their dramatic power, spelling the end of shamanism. However, sheep and goat domestication is not attended by extensive art and symbolism, nor much sign of sacrifice and feasting. The process and motivation seem rather different from cattle. And cattle already hold symbolic power and are found in art and special deposits at the time of early sheep/goat herding, well before evidence of cattle domestication. Moreover, cattle retain strong symbolic significance for thousands of years after domestication. The situation appears somewhat more complicated.

## DOMINATION

Models of domestication depend partly on its definition. Having cast his net broadly in his definition (see the earlier section, *Social Definitions*), Digard seeks the factor that unites the domestication of the dog, sheep, silkworm, canary, carp, and so forth, concluding that the common thread is domination (see also Ingold 1994). As he defines it (including pets, among other relationships), animal domestication is probably a human universal. Although he fully acknowledges the various useful products and services derived from domestic animals, he feels that the extraordinary amount of energy we devote to domesticatory action, which is often not economically justifiable, can only be explained as an end in itself. People domesticate animals because they crave the sense of power over life and other beings that this gives them: "[I]t is the desire for the appropriation and domination of nature and of beings that constitutes their constant and profound motivation (both proximate and ultimate)"[1] (Digard 1990:249–50). Regardless of whether domination motivated domestication, it is a piece of it.

As we have seen in Chapter 4, it can be argued that hunting is fundamentally about domination as well. How then is domestication different, and why does it arise in some cases and not others? Digard's answer to the second question is that domestication occurs everywhere in some form; the variations lie in the intensity and the characteristics of the particular domesticatory relationship, which are shaped by the environment and the structure of the individual society. In response to the first question, clearly domestication differs in that hunting exerts domination by killing the animal, whereas domestication involves control of the living animal. We find many useful things to do with animal bodies, but it all starts with the desire to manipulate them. Humans thus appear as obsessed with control of their surroundings. Has this compulsion for control and domination in fact made us human?

Domestication is a very particular kind of domination. Many animals have dominance relations that facilitate social interactions. These relations tend to involve dominant animals driving subordinates away from food and mates, and depend on stylized behaviors that establish who is dominant and demonstrate that submissive animals will not challenge dominant ones. These kinds of behaviors are very much present in our relationships with domestic animals, particularly pets (Serpell 1986; Tuan 1984). Yet these interactions are not about controlling access to food and mates: Mates are not at issue because these relationships cross species, and indeed we offer food to domestic animals (although we may need to keep them away from unauthorized food). From the animal's point of view, we invoke dominance behaviors with which they are familiar. However, from the human point of view, we are mostly acting from a different model. Here the Latin root of domestication (*domus*, house,

---

[1] "...c'est le désir d'appropriation et de domination de la nature et des êtres qui constitue sa motivation profonde et constante (première et ultime à la fois)." My translation.

home, family) is most appropriate: We bring animals into the household, and the idiom that we use is that of family relationships.

Ingold suggests that both the gendered concept of domination in hunting (see Chapter 4, *Hunters' Attitudes to Animals*) and the domesticatory relationship take their model from the human family. Animal domestication is an extension of gender relations to animals, continuing the association of women and animals and their subordinate position to men: "[T]he relation of domination entailed in 'domestication' originally comes about through the substitution of animals for subordinate humans within the domestic division of labour of the hunting economy" (Ingold 1987:254). However, as we have seen, one can argue that women are made subordinate because they are equated to animals, not vice versa.

The more plausible family role occupied by domestic animals is that of permanent children. This fits much better with observations that it is often women who care for animals. And of course taming would have to precede domestication, and it usually occurs by raising animal infants, so they would start out with that status. (Although this familial model applies well to pets and farmyard animals such as pigs, it may not work as well for herd animals.) Treating animals as children implies nurturing, but does it also imply domination? Human societies vary in the degree to which parents are considered to own, rule, or control their children. However, young children, if only because of their lesser physical and mental capacities, have a lesser degree of autonomy than adults. Likewise, caring for animals implies that they cannot or are not allowed to care for themselves. Keeping adult animals within human society usually requires continued care, hence placing even fully grown animals in the position of children.

Cauvin's (1972, 1994, 2000b) answer to why plant and animal domestication occurred at a particular time in the Near East is that it stems from a symbolic revolution, a new religion that fundamentally changed the relationship of humans to nature. Whereas the symbolism of the Epipaleolithic Natufian period in the Levant centers on animals, mostly gazelles (their main prey), in the Khiamian period that immediately predates the first appearance of plant domestication, the animal symbolism disappears and is replaced with images of human females. Although animals are no longer depicted, actual body parts (skulls/horns and scapulae) of aurochsen are buried in houses and walls; later they appear in human burials, mounted on walls, and carefully placed in houses at abandonment. Aurochsen form an insignificant part of Khiamian faunal assemblages, so evidently they play a primarily symbolic role.

Cauvin interprets the female representations (mostly figurines) as indications of a new goddess cult centered on a supreme deity. Cattle/aurochsen appear in this same religious complex as the male principle, but in animal form and subordinate to the female. Cauvin bases his argument for the subordination of bull to goddess on the (later) reliefs at Çatalhöyük, where Mellaart (1967:122) has interpreted bucrania beneath plaster reliefs of possibly female figures as the goddess giving birth to bulls. It is by no means certain that this is actually what is being depicted, but human (most often female when marked) and cattle (most often male when marked) depictions do characterize the Neolithic of the Near East and southeast Europe from this point onward.

For Cauvin, this symbolic revolution brings about an ideological shift enabling the control of plant and animal reproduction: "Thus, in surreal assemblages which bring evidence of the world of the imagination, there are ideas of fertility, of maternity, of royalty and of being the mistress of wild animals. Here are all the traits of the Mother-Goddess who dominates the oriental pantheon right up to the time of the male-dominated monotheism of Israel" (Cauvin 2000a:29–31). Crucially, Cauvin insists that this symbolic nexus appears *before* the beginnings of agriculture:

> This change, whose historical importance has been underlined because of the germ of all the later constructions of mythic thought of the Near East and the east Mediterranean that it contained, occurs at this initial stage as a purely mental development. It is out of the question to seek to derive it from some transformation of the material infrastructure, following a line of reasoning that has become too classical. The strategies of subsistence were in no way agricultural, and the bull can be defined as economically insignificant, since that species, which was present sporadically among the hunted fauna, was not yet preferred to other game. That only became the case at Mureybet after 9000 BC, some time before the species was finally domesticated (Cauvin 2000a:32–3).

This symbolic change involves not merely a new deity, but one that is for the first time set above humans (as inferred from the famous Çatalhöyük figurine of a female figure seated on what could be described as a throne, and from praying/adoring figures that sometimes surround those interpreted as the Goddess). This creates a chasm between the human and the divine, and between humans and their natural environment, enabling a domination of the environment that would previously have been literally unthinkable (Cauvin 1994:98–101). Cauvin reads the subordination of the bull to the goddess through the metaphor of descent as an attempt to control the beast in humans, hence humans themselves. He sees a further symbolic transformation in the PPNB, at which point bulls are controlled by humans in depictions that he reads as bull games (again at Çatalhöyük), and male human figures begin to appear – sometimes controlling bulls as in the figurine of a man riding a bull (perhaps better described as an ungendered person sitting on a quadruped) – yet again from Çatalhöyük. The notion of self-control of the inner beast becomes dominant specifically in this distinctively male symbolism, and Cauvin sees this concept as providing both the model for animal domestication and an expansionary ideology responsible for the spread of the Neolithic (Cauvin 1994:166–71). Although plant agriculture occurred both literally and symbolically in the female sphere, men performed animal domestication, based on masculine ideas and symbols (Cauvin 1994:176).

Reading symbols is always fraught with difficulty. Marija Gimbutas and her followers read these same depictions as representations of harmony both within society and between humans and nature (e.g., Baring and Cashford 1991; Barstow 1978; Eisler 1987; Gimbutas 1982, 1989, 1991, 1999; Starhawk 1989). Putting this aside, one could make other objections to Cauvin's interpretation. Should we really read "thrones" and "adoration" as indications of domination and hierarchy? They hold this meaning for us because of their much later association with royalty. Cauvin argues that these later rulers borrowed the symbols from the gods. Yet would they carry this sense in an egalitarian society? Cauvin does not explain why people suddenly felt the need to subordinate themselves to an omnipotent deity.

There are also questions about the timing. Cauvin relies heavily on the imagery of Çatalhöyük, which overlaps with the later PPNB and which has both domestic plants and animals, to interpret the earlier Khiamian and PPNA symbols. Clearly there is some continuity in woman and bull imagery, but it is only at Çatalhöyük that Cauvin can build a strong case that the woman is a Goddess (Cauvin 1994:49), and it is only here and at later sites that female figures are seated and surrounded by adoring followers. In fact at Çatalhöyük the adoring gestures seem directed more at bulls and other animals than at the female figures, which form minor parts of these compositions.

Cauvin likewise derives the subordination through descent of the bull to the Goddess solely from the representations at Çatalhöyük, based on reliefs of splayed humanoid figures in what Mellaart (1967:122) labels a birth position, with arms and legs extended and upturned. In two instances, these reliefs appear over the plastered heads of a bull and a ram, equipped with real horns. Mellaart and Cauvin interpret these reliefs as depicting the Goddess giving birth to these animals. Yet it is not certain that these reliefs are human, female, or giving birth. The excavators of Nevalı Çori describe an extremely similar figure in the same attitude on a stela there as an animal (Hauptmann 1999). The heads, hands, and feet were knocked off the Çatalhöyük reliefs in antiquity, complicating identification. Traces of ears (or a horned hairdo, according to Mellaart) suggest they may represent animals or a human–animal hybrid, and a recent find of a stamp seal in the same position but with head and feet intact depicts a bear (Türkcan 2007). The frequent attention to the navel on both seal and reliefs might mean that these are in fact therianthropes; although all placental mammals have navels, most are inconspicuous. These reliefs do not resemble the depictions of human females in the paintings or figurines. There is no indication of gender, although rounded bellies with bulls-eye designs painted on some might be intended to represent pregnancy and are the strongest argument that these may be depictions of birth. However, not all have heads beneath, and sheep do not otherwise form a major part of the symbolic sphere. There are bucrania and the occasional ram's head elsewhere on these walls and others with no association with female imagery; it is not clear that their proximity to the splayed reliefs in these two cases indicates a relationship.

However one wishes to interpret the Çatalhöyük imagery, it is much later than the symbolic revolution that Cauvin describes. The shift in symbolism marked by the sudden appearance of women and bulls is real. Yet even if one reads the Çatalhöyük imagery as representing an all-powerful Goddess and a subordinate bull-god, it is dangerous to project this interpretation back to the Levantine Khiamian. The earlier imagery, in concert with the various forms of "skull cult" first seen in the late Natufian (Bar-Yosef and Belfer-Cohen 1989:473), is seen more reasonably as related to ancestor worship. If one or more of these ancestor figures is being transformed into a supreme deity at Çatalhöyük, this may constitute a second symbolic revolution.

Another issue of timing relates to Cauvin's assertion, critical to his model, that these symbolic and ideological changes *preceded* plant and animal domestication. This is correct in terms of detectable morphological changes in the plant and animal taxa. However, it is debatable whether the appearance of human female symbolism predates cultivation, and surely this is the relevant development. Cauvin himself is ambiguous about this timing. Although at some points, as quoted earlier, he insists that the symbolic transformation preceded agriculture, elsewhere he states that they occurred simultaneously. As he points out, most of the earliest PPNA settlements are suddenly located on the alluvial soils that are best for agriculture, a change from the Natufian and Khiamian. This change, he reasonably says, would only happen if the people were already farming (Cauvin 1994:83), implying that agriculture began no later than the Khiamian, at the same time as the symbolic changes. Or, one could argue, it may have begun even earlier, and the symbolism follows it.

For animal domestication the situation is more complicated. It appears to follow plant cultivation in the Near East, based on all means of detection (see the later section, *Studying Domestication*). If, as Cauvin sees it, the domination of wild nature is symbolized through animal representations, it is puzzling that plants are brought under practical control before animals. Domesticated animals appear in the PPNB, at the time that the bull symbolism comes to the fore. So again the symbolic change may be simultaneous with or perhaps follows the earliest herding. However, bull symbolism, although more muted, is present from the Khiamian, in the form of special deposits of body parts rather than figurines or other representations. Although these deposits certainly testify to the symbolic importance of cattle, its significance may have been linked more to feasting than to the animal itself.

As Cauvin notes, the symbolism centers on cattle, whereas the first herd animals to be domesticated were sheep and goats. This suggests that the symbolism may not have followed from the practice of domestication, although it is unclear why the symbolic control of cattle would lead in the first instance to the actual control of sheep and goats. The symbolic dominance of cattle may be exaggerated, however. Just as the proportion of female human figurines in the Neolithic tends to be overstated, because some are male and most are not visibly gendered, so the majority of animal figurines are not clearly identifiable as anything other than quadrupeds. Of those that can be identified, cattle are indeed the most frequent, but other animals such as pigs and sheep also occur. In addition, although cattle heads and horns predominate as architectural installations at Çatalhöyük, sheep heads and horns, the jaws of boar and weasels, and the beaks of vultures also occur. The famous bull painting from Mellaart's building F.V.1 is reproduced so often that one has the impression that herds of cattle cavort across the walls of Çatalhöyük. In fact, there are only three certain and two possible (fragmentary) paintings of cattle, most of which are not clearly marked as bulls (Ducos 1988; Mellaart 1962, 1963, 1964, 1966b, 1967; Russell and Meece 2006). In contrast, in the same room as the F.V.1 bull painting, there are paintings of 3 red deer, one fallow deer, 4 boars, at least 12 equids, a bear, a putative wolf, 4 quadrupeds that may be dogs, an animal Mellaart calls a lion, and 2 cranes (Mellaart 1966b:184–91). There are other paintings of deer in different houses, as well as painted goats. Although not all these animals are central figures in the paintings as the bulls usually seem to be, they demonstrate that bulls are not the only animal with symbolic importance. Deer and perhaps boar are treated in much the same way as the bulls in the paintings, surrounded by human figures who seem to tease and torment them (see Chapter 3, *Evidence for Sacrifice*).

The sudden cessation of animal (gazelle) symbolism in the Khiamian and its resumption in the PPN with different animals is clearly significant, as is the appearance of human female symbolism just as the gazelles disappear. The timing better supports a reading that plant cultivation shifted the focus away from hunting and toward either fertility, as Cauvin argues, or ancestor worship related to the increased importance of inheritance. Animal symbolism may have returned through another route (hence the shift in taxa), initially gaining importance as the central components of feasts that, among other things, may have marked the conversion of group members into ancestors. Cattle, as the largest species available, would make a particularly impressive centerpiece. The Çatalhöyük depictions indicate that by ca. 9000 BP this feasting role had been elaborated into myths and rituals surrounding the capture and consumption of animals for special events, especially cattle but including other animals as well.

Thus Cauvin has pinpointed an important ideological shift related to the origins of agriculture, although it is uncertain whether this shift in fact precedes the economic and social changes, proceeds in tandem, or even follows them. Indeed, in a postscript added to the English translation of his book, Cauvin (2000a:220) backs off from the position that the symbolic revolution preceded the economic one, now casting them as occurring simultaneously and being of equal importance. Nor am I convinced that this shift involves the creation of a supreme deity, as opposed to a new emphasis on lineage and ancestors, on ties to house and land. It would be rewarding to examine other parts of the world where agriculture has arisen independently in search of similar symbolic transformations. Unfortunately, there is probably no other area where we yet have tight enough dating of plant and animal domestication even to attempt to address the question of whether ideological changes preceded or followed domestication.

Cauvin's case is stronger in arguing that ideology was critical to the spread of agriculture. Although settled farmers most likely had higher rates of population growth than mobile foragers, most (Bogucki and Grygiel 1993; Haak et al. 2005; Morelli et al. 2010; Pluciennik 1996; Price et al. 1995; Robb and Miracle 2007; Sampietro et al. 2007; Thomas 1996; Tsonev 1996; van Andel and Runnels 1995; Willis and Bennett 1994; Zvelebil 1986) think the spread of agriculture through the Near East and across Europe is too rapid to be explained by demography alone (cf. Ammerman and Cavalli-Sforza 1971, 1984; Cavalli-Sforza 1996; Chikhi et al. 2002; Diamond 1997; Pinhasi and von Cramon-Taubadel 2009). Cauvin argues that it is rather the allure of the idea embodied in the Bull: the power derived from mastering the beast within (see also Rice 1997) and the way that the new religion and the new economy were firmly linked to each other. Given its increased labor requirements and the need for substantial social reorganization, farming would not be intrinsically appealing to foraging groups:

> Just imagine, by contrast, what was the effect on hunter-gatherers from time immemorial of the arrival of human groups, even rather scattered groups, driving before them docile goats and sheep, where the exotic nature of the species would add to their surprise at the mastery of the herdsmen. We should ask ourselves if this strange power would not have had a much more considerable impact than the simple perspective of a controlled reproduction of their subsistence resources (Cauvin 2000a:205–6).

Thomas (1991, 1996, 1999) has made a somewhat similar argument for the spread of the Neolithic into northwest Europe. He sees it as primarily an adoption of a religion or ideology, although he contrasts this ideological Neolithic to a more economically defined Neolithic in southeast and central Europe. Certainly the meaning of the Neolithic ideology was transformed and reinterpreted as it spread and developed in Europe. Drawing on Cauvin's work, Hodder (1990) has embraced the notion that the symbolism at Çatalhöyük and elsewhere is about controlling the wild as a metaphor for controlling people. Specifically, he sees the inside/outside distinction created by the house as central: The wild is tamed and controlled, literally domesticated, by bringing it into the house. Like Cauvin, he suggests that symbolic domestication of animals by bringing their representations and body parts into the house preceded their domestication in the usual sense of physical control. The concept of "inside" was gradually extended such that by the time the Neolithic reached northwest Europe, the original inside/outside dichotomy – which Hodder terms "domus/agrios" – in which the home is contrasted with the wild, has become a "domus/foris" distinction that opposes the community to the foreign beyond.

Cauvin himself was not entirely happy with Hodder's interpretation. If symbolic domestication merely involves bringing the wild/outside into the house, then it would occur wherever there were houses. Cauvin on the contrary sees a symbolic revolution that happens at a specific and restricted time and place; the Neolithic does not develop as soon as there are houses in, for example, the Upper Paleolithic of Central Europe or the Natufian in the Near East. Moreover, the intimate notion of home does not seem to Cauvin to provide the expansionary dynamic he associates with the Neolithic, especially from the PPNB, and which he attributes to the bull metaphor (Cauvin 1994:274).

Others have also argued that Hodder may place too much weight on the domus/agrios distinction (Davis 1992; Morter and Robb 1998). Halstead (1996:306) suggests that ancient people may have been less obsessed with domestication and control of the wild than are archaeologists and that the tensions between household and community may have been more important in the Neolithic.

Hodder's notion that animals are symbolically tamed by bringing them into the house before they are physically domesticated has an obvious appeal. If animal domestication involves bringing animals into the household, there is a connection with this symbolism. However, not only does this model fail to address why the Neolithic did not develop everywhere as soon as there were dwellings but also animals were almost surely being brought into the household as pets on a regular basis even before there were substantial houses (see Chapter 7).

More fundamentally, what is the role of domination in human–animal relationships? As we have seen here and in Chapter 4, it is possible to read virtually every human–animal relationship as domination; the same is true of human relationships. Yet is domination really what all of them are fundamentally about, or is it just a contemporary western and perhaps male obsession? If relationships among living beings are composed of some combination of domination and cooperation, altruism and exploitation, do we explain them adequately by focusing solely on the power relations (Haraway 1991)? "We do not feel forced in the social world – for example in the field of our relations with kin – to choose between either exploiting others for personal profit or avoiding all direct contact. Yet in the context of relations with animals, this is precisely the choice that is forced on us by the conventional dichotomy between wildness and domestication" (Ingold 1994:11–12).

In human relations, Deborah Tannen (1990) has argued that, in western societies at least, men tend to focus on the dominance relations in interactions, whereas women concentrate on the cooperative and affective components. Both are present in all interactions, so focusing exclusively on either one provides an incomplete picture. It is worth examining human–animal relationships in terms of domination, but this does not tell the whole story. Moreover, because domination is a component of all relationships, it is not enough to say that hunting or domestication is based on domination. We need to consider the role that domination plays, the form that it takes in particular instances, and why it may sometimes lead to killing animals, other times to caring for them as virtual family members, and yet other times to treating them as commodities. In relation to animal domestication, did the perceived need to control the beast within lead to control of the beasts themselves?

## Implications

Although the debate over how animals were domesticated is fascinating, in some sense it does not matter a great deal how domestication occurred.

What matters most is that it did, with profound implications for both people and animals. The effects on animals have been rather thoroughly treated elsewhere (e.g., Armitage 1986; Clutton-Brock 1992; Dobney and Larson 2006; Groves 1989; Hemmer 1990; Meadow 1989; Mignon-Grasteau et al. 2005; Morey 1992; Price 2002; Ryder 1973; Tani 1996; Trut 1999; Zohary et al. 1998), and I only briefly sketch some of them here. The most obvious are probably the physical changes: size reduction in many species; changes in fur and horns; alterations in the shape of the head, often involving a neotenous reduction of face and jaw; changes in body proportions; less developed muscles and bones; and smaller brains. Behavioral changes are perhaps even more important, most obviously the loss of fear of humans. Other changes include a reduction in flight distance, greater docility, and retention of juvenile dependency. Some of these changes are the result of deliberate selection and training by people; most are probably adaptations of the animals to the domestic niche. As a result of these changes, domestic animals have spread virtually throughout the world, often at the expense of wild animals.

## TRANSFORMATIONS IN HUMAN SOCIETY

As an archaeologist, my primary interest is in the effects of animal domestication on people. Here we must distinguish among different kinds of domestic relationships. The more symbiotic relationships with, for example, cats and dogs may have been personally rewarding for many people in the past as they are in the present. However, such relationships may not have had a significant effect on human social relations. In contrast, the domestication of herd and farm animals has had profound implications for human society, human–animal relationships, and human conceptions of the natural world.

With Ingold (1980, 1984) and Ducos (1978), I see the key quality of domestication as social: Domestic animals have owners. This is a fundamentally different relationship from that with wild animals, and it creates a fundamentally different set of human social relations. Wild animals can be appropriated only by killing them. Their meat is generally regarded as a common resource to which all members of the group have a claim. Although the hunter usually has special rights over the kill, they are primarily rights of prestige and distribution; the hunter is obliged to share the meat widely (see Chapter 9).

Domestic animals have owners while they are alive; these owners have rights in them that other people do not, including the right to decide if and when to slaughter the animal. Moreover, while a hunter will usually be motivated to kill animals whenever meat is short in the group, a herder always has a strong motivation *not* to kill her or his animals, because every slaughter diminishes the herd. Indeed, herders do not remain herders for long if they kill too many animals and fail to maintain the breeding population and allow a buffer for losses to disease, predators, and so on. Thus people depend less on other members of the group, who are no longer obligated to share all major resources with each other, and more on the resources of the household (Ingold 1980:168). Clearly, this shift bolsters the household as an institution. Storing plant foods would create a similar effect, and indeed it may have enabled the change in social relations that underlies herding by weakening the imperative to share and by strengthening the household.

Domestic animals also bring new responsibilities. Hunters often feel a responsibility to treat wild animals with due respect (see Chapter 4, *Hunters' Attitudes to Animals*), but herders bear the daily burden of ensuring that their animals have food and water and protecting them from predators and human raiders. These necessities of herding demand considerable work, so the division and scheduling of labor would have to be substantially reworked when people started to keep animals (Bonte and Galaty 1991). This implies changes in household organization and perhaps shifts in power within as well as between households. I discuss some of the further implications of owning animals in Chapter 8.

### LINKS BETWEEN HUMAN–ANIMAL AND HUMAN–HUMAN RELATIONS

Whereas people tend to regard wild animals as something like equals and admire their autonomy, domestic animals are clearly in a subordinate relation. Behaviorally, humans usually accomplish control of animals by usurping the place of the alpha animal in the dominance hierarchy. Indeed, possession of a dominance hierarchy may be a prerequisite for domestication (Armitage 1986; Clutton-Brock 1994; Garrard 1984). From the human point of view, this relationship tends to be described either in kinship terms, emphasizing domestication as the act of bringing animals into the household, or in political terms, emphasizing the inequality. At best, we care for domestic animals tenderly and direct their

lives in what we perceive as their best interests; at worst, we exploit them
and treat them cruelly.

Although the analogy with children (see the earlier section, *Domination*) fits some domestic animals, notably pets, the political metaphors
are perhaps more apt for farm and herd animals. Those who raise animals
for meat must to some degree overcome the intimacy of the relationship
in order to eat their livestock. Politically, domestic animals can be seen
as slaves, whom we control and exploit for our profit, benefiting them
only insofar as it is useful to us (Clutton-Brock 1994; Dunayer 2001;
Kent 1989; Shepard 1993; Tani 1996; Tapper 1988). One could even
see pets as analogous to the relatively pampered, often genuinely loved
house slaves, whose subordination to the masters is nevertheless clearly
maintained. The difference is largely one of emphasis: Slaves are also
treated as permanent children, and there are strong elements of caring in
most nonindustrial herding relations.

If slaves are like animals and domestic animals are like slaves, is there
a relationship between animal domestication and human inequality? Did
one provide the model for the other in a concrete sense, not merely as a
source of metaphors? Was the subordination of other humans unthinkable until people had had the experience of controlling animals (Serpell
1986:179)? Or was animal domestication, at least for herd and farm animals with owners who control them, impossible until there existed a
concept of control of subordinate persons?

In the Old World, and probably in South America, one could make a
good argument that animal domestication provided a model for human
exploitation. In the Near East, animal domestication appears in the PPNB
(see Table 6.1). Although the degree of inequality in the Epipaleolithic
Natufian culture and the PPNA (with the first signs of plant domestication) are debated (Bar-Yosef and Meadow 1995; Belfer-Cohen 1995;
Byrd and Monahan 1995; Henry 1989; Kuijt 1994, 1996; Wright 1978),
real social stratification, as opposed to competition for prestige, is not
apparent until the later Ceramic Neolithic (Halafian, Yarmoukian; Nissen 1988; Singh 1974; Steadman 2000). Likewise, the spread of domestic plants and animals precedes the development of stratified societies in
Europe, Asia, and Africa. East Asia was an independent center of plant and
animal domestication. Recent work shows that rice and millet domestication and likely that of domestic pigs precede substantial human hierarchy
here as well (Barton et al. 2009; Cucchi et al. 2011; Fuller et al. 2007;

Fuller and Qin 2010; Jiang and Liu 2006; Jing and Flad 2002; Larson et al. 2010; Wang et al. 2010; Yuan et al. 2008).

In South America, the beginnings of camelid (llama, alpaca) and guinea pig domestication are poorly understood (Mengoni-Goñalons 2008; Spotorno et al. 2006). Domestic llamas, at least, precede the Early Horizon, which represents the first states in the Andes. In contrast, the turkey was the only "farm" animal domesticated in Meso- and North America. Turkey domestication was probably fairly late, around 2000 BP (Rawlings and Driver 2010; Speller et al. 2010), yet clearly hierarchical societies in Mesoamerica date at least from 3500 BP. Hierarchical societies also developed in North America (e.g., the chiefdoms of the Mississippian culture of the Southeast and Midwest, ca. 1000–500 BP). Perhaps the strongest counterexample is the stratified hunter-fisher-gatherer societies of the Pacific Northwest, the famous exception to the general rule that complex societies are based on agriculture (Rosman and Rubel 1971).

Nevertheless, although these groups lacked herd or farm animals, they did have dogs. Indeed, every known hierarchical society has possessed dogs or some other domestic animal. Wolfgang Schleidt (1999) intriguingly argues that wolves/dogs made us human by teaching our ancestors how to cooperate and establish friendships with non-kin (altruism, roughly speaking), in the course of establishing a symbiotic relationship as hunters of wild herd animals. There are some difficulties with this proposal. Why would early humans (apparently Neanderthals) enter into such a symbiotic relationship if they were not already cooperative hunters? Nor is it obvious that the result of such a relationship would be to pattern human society on the structure of wolf (or wolf-becoming-dog) society. Moreover, it is a highly Eurocentric model and one that does not fit especially well with current evidence that anatomically and behaviorally modern humans originated in sub-Saharan Africa (d'Errico et al. 2008; Marean et al. 2007; McBrearty and Brooks 2000; Mellars 2006), where there are no wolves. Although Africa does have wild dogs and other cooperative predators, none of these were domesticated.

One could make a somewhat stronger if less cheerful argument that dogs, as the first domesticate, provided the model both for the domestication of other species and for the exploitation of other humans. Humans and dogs may have slipped into a domesticatory relationship through a coevolutionary process, but once fully established, the dogs assumed a subordinate position. Dog trainers know that it is essential to maintain this hierarchy, mirroring that of the wolf pack, for the human–dog relationship to work (Monks of New Skete 2002). Dogs were thus the first inferior group in human society, for the essence of domestication is to bring animals into society. Dog domestication might provide a means for people to move from regarding animals as equals to considering the possibility that they could be controlled or enslaved. Ingold (1987:254–5) notes that Arctic/subarctic foragers often conceptualize the relationship between the master/mistress of animals and the animals he or she is associated with as like that between human masters and their dogs: one of care and control. This might ease the transfer of care and control of other animals from spirits to humans. It is not such a big step to extend this control to other humans as well.

Hodder (1990) argues that the symbolic taming of the wild by bringing it into the house (domesticating it) is in the first instance about controlling people (see the earlier section, *Domination*). Rather than the presence of dogs, he sees this symbolic control as paving the way for both animal domestication and the domination of other people. Of course, the people engaged in this symbolic domestication kept dogs, and the example of dogs may have made the idea of taming the wild more plausible. As discussed in Chapter 4, there can be no conception of the wild until there is a notion of the domestic. Referring to dogs, Fiddes (1991:59) argues that "[t]he point at which we increased our power by using animals to control other animals indeed seems significant, but the importance of such (anthropocentric) improvements is ideological as well as practical, demonstrative as well as enabling, affirmative just as it is effective. Domestication of animals, bringing them into the human fold as part of our stable of resources, serves as a signal of human superiority."

At least in recent times, the wild/domestic divide has been used to justify oppression of people linked to the wild; this is also true of ancient China (Fiskesjö 2001). The more extreme versions of the separation of nature from culture have been traced to the 16th–18th centuries in Europe. Not coincidentally, this was a time of colonial expansion. If culture is superior to nature, and humans are superior to animals, then "civilized" people are superior to people who are closer to "nature." Foragers in particular have been labeled as living like animals because they use only wild resources. Certain races and ethnicities, women, poor people, and the insane have also been designated as more wild and less cultured than those in power, and thus in need of control (Dunayer 1995; Ingold 1994, 1996a; Mullin 1999). Interestingly, this strategy has been at least partially reversed in the last 50 years, when the trend has been to naturalize gender and racial hierarchies, and inequality itself, through invoking our foraging and animal past (Ardrey 1966; Beteille 1981; Dawkins 1976; Lorenz 1966; Storr 1968; Wilson 1975).

Beyond the general question of whether the presence of domesticated animals inspired the domination of other humans, has the particular form of human–animal relations shaped human societies? Haudricourt (1962) first made this argument, suggesting that the total control of the shepherd over the life of the sheep inclined Mediterranean societies to paternalism and hierarchy, so that it is only in this area that the slave state developed fully. In contrast, he feels that East Asian domesticates (pig and chicken) were less closely controlled and that people who were primarily gardeners as in East Asia tended to view animals more as equals. This view, he suggests, produced an ideology of harmony and cooperation, exemplified in the Chinese state. Unfortunately, this does not seem an especially good characterization of Chinese or other Asian states, which are conventionally represented precisely as highly paternalistic and rigidly hierarchical.

In a similar vein, Gordon Brotherston (1989) argues that the Inca, and presumably earlier Andean states, drew on the social relations of herding as the ideological model for the state. The result was a much more centralized and hierarchical society than elsewhere in the New World. Andean religion exhibits these same characters, with a supreme deity and metaphors parallel to those in the Judeo-Christian tradition of the ruler as shepherd and worshippers as flock.

There is a better argument for religion following the form of herding relations than there is for the state doing so. In a crude way, monotheistic religions do seem to have originated in areas with domestic herd animals. Yet this relationship was certainly not inevitable. Marx (Hobsbawm 1964) considered ancient Greece and Rome to be the classic exemplars of slave states, yet despite arising in the Mediterranean and relying on herd animals, their religions were highly polytheistic (although hierarchical), as were those of the earlier states in the eastern Mediterranean.

Guillermo Algaze (2001) explicitly argues that a key conceptual shift enabling the emergence of the world's first states in southern

Mesopotamia, which he terms the "Labor Revolution," involved coming to regard subordinate humans as domestic animals to be exploited:

> Southern elites came to view and use fully encumbered laborers in the same exploitative way that human societies, over the immediately preceding millennia, had viewed and used the labor of domestic animals. This represents a new paradigm of the nature of social relations in human societies.... Scribal summaries detailing the composition of groups of foreign and native-born captives used as laborers describe them with age and sex categories identical to those used to describe state-owned cattle.... [T]he two classes of labor (captive "others" and domestic animals) were considered equivalent in the minds of Uruk scribes and in the eyes of the institutions that employed them. Early Near Eastern villagers domesticated plants and animals. Uruk urban institutions, in turn, domesticated humans (Algaze 2001:212).

Similarly, Sanskrit uses the same word for domestic animals and serfs or slaves (Tani 1996:404), and more recently, the French term for feral animals, *marron*, was first used for fugitive slaves (Digard 1990:166). Algaze implies that not merely the domestication of animals but also their use for labor provide a model for human exploitation (see Chapter 8, *The Secondary Products Revolution*). However, this human exploitation arises in a society that already exhibits substantial inequalities. Might these inequalities also have their roots in the human domination of animals?

More specifically, Yutaka Tani (1996) argues for a link between the use of bellwethers (castrated rams) and human eunuchs. The bellwether has a special relationship with the shepherd; it is trained to lead and help control the flock. Tani likens this to the use of eunuchs to guard the harem and demonstrates a striking overlap in the geographical distribution of these practices. Tani concludes it is more likely that the bellwether inspired the use of eunuchs than the other way around.

Providing a mental template for domination is not the only way that animal and plant domestication contributed to human inequality. By permitting more intensified food production (particularly of plants), domestication supplied a resource base to support complex societies and the higher population densities needed to achieve them. Only rarely are wild resources able to provide this foundation, and then only to a lesser extent. This capacity, along with the profound changes in social relationships described earlier, is what led Gordon Childe (1951) to label the transformations brought about by plant and animal domestication the Neolithic Revolution, which in turn provides the underpinning for the Urban Revolution. The use of domestic animals in feasting (see Chapter 9) and as wealth (see Chapter 8) can also create and enhance human inequality.

Ingold (1980, 1994) argues that the form of human–animal relations is closely tied to the form of human social relations, both ideologically and materially. Carrying this argument further, Tapper (1988:52–3), perhaps somewhat playfully, suggests that we can use human–animal relations of production to define modes of production analogous to those that Marx (Hobsbawm 1964) set forth for humans. Thus foragers, who tend to construct their relations with animals in terms of equality and reciprocity, correspond to Marx's Germanic mode of production. Domestic animals used for their labor (i.e., not pets) are like slaves, hence recalling slave states. Pastoralists herd animals as communities (flocks). They dominate and control them, but leave individual animals a large degree of autonomy in foraging. This Tapper sees as similar to a contract in which the masters protect the herd in exchange for "rent," like the feudal system. Ranching, although a development of the capitalist system, resembles the Asiatic mode of production in its human–animal relations: Control is not through contract but force. In contrast, factory farming, which reduces animals to machines manipulated for profit, exemplifies capitalist relations.

Tapper strains a bit to make human–animal relations fit neatly into Marx's modes of production. For example, as discussed earlier (Chapter 4, *Hunters' Attitudes to Animals*), one could easily argue that foragers' construction of animals as equals is a mystification of underlying relations of exploitation. He also perhaps glosses over peasants' relations with their animals, in which the animal is treated not only as a commodity but also as a member of the household to some extent. Certainly such animals have little autonomy compared to those of pastoralists. However, Tapper's point is important: There are many forms of human–animal relations, and these are intimately related to human social structure (see also Digard 1990).

The connections between human–animal relationships and human social relationships are complex. The two have interacted with each other in various ways in different kinds of societies, and these interactions have helped produce these different social formations. In addition to simply supplying a ready source of meat and other animal products, animal domestication has played an active role in the transformation of human societies and has had profound effects on both wild and domestic animal populations.

## Studying domestication

The way one defines animal domestication influences the criteria used to identify it archaeologically (Crabtree 1993:202). For those who see domestication as primarily a biological change, alterations in the bodies of the animals are the primary or only signs of true domestication. These alterations include morphological changes such as horn core shape, and especially size reduction (e.g., Armitage 1986; Bökönyi 1969; Clutton-Brock 1992; Crabtree 1993; Grigson 1969; Meadow 1989; Reitz and Wing 1999; Tchernov and Horwitz 1991; Uerpmann 1979; Zeder and Hesse 2000). Such changes take time to occur; the time may be short or long depending on how closely the herders control the breeding of their animals and whether there is conscious selection. Another approach to detect the earliest stages of herding is the analysis of mortality profiles: the age/sex structure of animals killed. It is expected that a domestic herd will be characterized by slaughter of most males at an early age, producing an assemblage with many immature animals and an adult sex ratio (usually sex can only be determined in mature animals) heavily biased toward females (e.g., Bökönyi 1969; Chaplin 1969; Collier and White 1976; Ducos 1978, 1993; Hesse 1982; Legge 1972; Perkins 1964; Rosenberg and Redding 1998; Zeder and Hesse 2000). Other evidence for domestication includes artistic representations and artifacts or features associated with herding (e.g., Bökönyi 1969). However, these usually appear only long after other evidence indicates that domestication has taken place.

If the essence of domestication for the archaeologist is a change in property relations such that animals have owners, clearly this shift will not always coincide with morphological change in the animals. Thus although changes in size, horn core shape, and so on are useful in demonstrating that domestication has occurred, they neither mark the earliest appearance of domestication nor are present in all cases in which the domesticatory relationship arises. The other common method of identifying domestication, the analysis of mortality profiles, holds more promise because it focuses on herd management. It is not foolproof, however, because herding strategies can vary for many reasons (see Chapter 8) and some hunting strategies or seasonal slices thereof may mimic a herding profile. Approaching domestication as a social relationship suggests other lines of supporting evidence. They may not be definitive in themselves, but can help build a picture suggesting that domestication may have occurred. They are particularly useful in pinpointing the likely beginnings of domestication identified morphologically later in a sequence.

Digard (1990) suggests that domestication is best conceptualized as domesticatory action or as a set of domesticatory practices. Although herding requires few tools, it demands extensive knowledge, hence specialists such as shepherds. Tani (1996) discusses some of these essential practices, noting differences between wild and domestic herds of sheep and goats. Whereas the wild animals are dispersed much of the year and, even when together, are spread out in small clumps, the domestic herd must be denser and more cohesive to permit control by a small number of herders. A wild herd is characterized by what Tani calls strong vertical ties between mother and offspring, and weak horizontal ties among these units or with mature males. These ties are reflected in the dispersal patterns and the ease with which individual animals move from one flock to another. The breaking down of vertical ties and the establishment of horizontal ties do not happen automatically. Rather, the domestic flock must be created through specific practices, which include separating lambs from their mothers for much of the day and keeping them together so that they bond as a group. Such practices, involving a strict limitation of when lambs can nurse, might lead to higher infant mortality, especially in the beginning. This could account for the high percentage of early infantile sheep in the Aşıklı Höyük assemblage in early Neolithic Anatolia, for example, where the sheep remain morphologically wild (Buitenhuis 2002). These domesticatory practices apply not only to the beginning of domestication but throughout the process (Digard 1990:172, Tani 1996). Virtually all domestic animals easily become feral. Continued domesticatory practices are necessary to maintain a domestic state or domestic behaviors.

Because domestic animals are owned individually rather than forming a shared resource, it is likely that domestication will bring changes in the way animals are butchered (relating to the distribution of meat, see Chapter 9) and the contexts of consumption. Patterns of sharing are likely to change as the ideology shifts from one in which all households or group members have equal rights to one in which rights depend on ownership. There may arise a greater distinction between the butchering pattern for animals up to approximately the size of a sheep, which can be consumed by a single household and so may no longer be shared beyond it, and larger animals that are still apt to be shared given the difficulties of storing meat. This is likely to be accompanied by a greater distinction between "ordinary," within-household consumption and larger scale consumption (i.e., feasting; see Chapter 9).

7

# Pets and other human–animal relationships

How, if at all, do we own our pets? (Shell 1986:142)

In the previous three chapters I have discussed human relations with wild and domestic animals. However, many human–animal relationships do not fit neatly into these two categories. I now consider some of these other relationships and their implications for people, animals, and the archaeological record.

## The spectrum of human–animal relationships

As discussed in Chapter 6, some have rejected the distinction between wild and domestic in favor of a continuum of human–animal relations (see also Harris 1996). Although they are right to insist that human–animal relations cannot be adequately expressed by a simple dichotomy, neither is a smooth continuum that places human–animal relations somewhere between two poles (random hunting to factory farming) a satisfactory description. Not only is there a quantum distinction, rather than just a difference of degree, between the domestication of herd animals and other human–animal relationships but many human–animal relationships are also of a different kind from hunting or herding: More than just the intensity of the relationship varies. I therefore find it preferable to think in terms of a spectrum, rather than a continuum, of various types of human–animal relationships. Alternatively, one could conceptualize human–animal relationships in three or more dimensions, with multiple axes of variation rather than a single continuum.

Thomas Sebeok (1988:68–71) has offered one of the most thorough attempts to characterize the full range of human–animal relationships,

which is also notable for being cast largely from the animal's point of
view. It may be summarized as follows:

1) humans as predators of animals
2) humans as prey of animals
3) humans as partners of animals
   a) guest–host relationship, as with aquarium fish
   b) nexus of mutual dependence, as with bee-keeping or work animals
   c) sexual partners, as with bestiality
4) sport and entertainment, as with races, animal combat, or bird watching
5) parasitism of humans on animals or vice versa
6) insentience, in which an animal mistakes a human for an inanimate
   object, as with a bird perching on a human head
7) taming, a necessary precondition for training and domestication
8) training, which may be either
   a) apprentissage, as with scientific or laboratory training, which min-
      imizes the human–animal bond
   b) dressage, as with circus training, which maximizes it

In this chapter I do not examine all these types of relationships in detail,
but it is useful to bear in mind the variety of human–animal relationships
that exist. Here, I consider relations that can be characterized as pet
keeping, as well as some that do not fall neatly into wild or domestic
categories.

## Pets

Some include pet keeping in the definition of domestication, whereas
others purposely exclude it (as Bökönyi does with his qualification, "for
profit"; see Chapter 6, *Control of Breeding*). In fact, the reason pets are so
difficult to classify is that this relationship is separate from domestication
(O'Connor 1992a:109). In terms of both morphology and control of
breeding, pets can be either wild or domestic. There is no doubt that a
Pekinese, for instance, is domesticated in both these senses. However, a
young animal adopted from the wild can also be a pet. Pet keepers often
restrict their pets' movements, but this is not always the case. Nor is it
clear that all pets are owned as property in the way that herd animals are,
although pets usually do "belong" to a single person or household.

"Pet" is an intuitively familiar concept, but hard to define at its boundaries. We tend to feel, for example, that when the caretakers of an animal raised for meat, dairy, or other products name and feel bonds of affection with that individual animal, the animal verges on being a pet. Wilbur the pig in *Charlotte's Web* (White 1952) nicely illustrates both this attitude and the conflict it is seen to create between utilitarian and affectionate human–animal relationships. What makes an animal a pet? For some it is the personal relationship implied in giving an animal a name, but many work and meat animals are named (e.g., MacIntyre 1984). For others it is the decision not to eat the animal (Kent 1989:17), yet on the one hand there are other reasons to refrain from eating animals generally considered edible (see Chapter 2, *Taboos*), and on the other hand animals that appear very much like pets are sometimes eaten, as in the Ainu bear feast (see Chapter 3, *Sacrifice and Ritual Killing*, and other examples in Harris 1985:176–7). For these same reasons, affection toward the animal is an insufficient criterion. A pet must be tamed: The flight distance must be reduced, it must be habituated to humans, and so on. This is also a necessary step for domestication and herding, of course, so the other component of pet keeping is that the animal is not kept "for profit," for the tangible products it yields, but for the joy of sharing one's life with another creature. Pets are companions rather than slaves.

Although only some animal species can be domesticated successfully, virtually any animal can be a pet, at least while it is young. Harris (1985) suggests that animals can only achieve full pet status (be treated with affection *and* not be eaten) when that species is not highly ranked as a food source. Similarly, Digard (1990) notes that both cats and horses begin to be kept as pets (or for pleasure) precisely when they become economically useless. This point is marked for horses with the advent of motorized transport, and for cats with the introduction into Europe of the Norway rat, against which they are ineffective predators. However, this is not universally the case. Among foragers, it is precisely those species they eat that are primarily kept as pets, through capture of the young when hunters kill the mother.

Pets are tame, but in some ways they are more like wild than domestic animals. As with wild animals, people generally view and treat pets as something close to equals. Just as with hunted animals, however, this is something of a mystification. Although many people expend considerable effort and modify their lives in significant ways for the benefit of pets, nevertheless the people are still in control. (For this reason I use the term "pet" rather than the currently more fashionable "companion animal." The latter erases the power relation inherent in pet keeping.) The relationship generally does not work well (at least from the human point of view) unless the pet keeper is dominant over the pet. Pets stand in a position of permanent childhood (Serpell 1986:63). They are loved and cared for, but usually not fully autonomous. They are domesticated in the sense that they are brought into the household and often the house. They are adopted into the family, but if they grow up and leave (as some do), they cease to be pets.

Because pets become quasi-humans, eating them seems tantamount to cannibalism. Indeed, part of the reason that pets form a problematic category is that they blur the boundaries between kin and non-kin and between humans and animals, implicitly calling these distinctions into question. They do not clearly belong to nature or to culture (Fiddes 1991:133–43; Leach 1964; Shell 1986).

Pets are found in a wide range of societies, but are most prevalent among hunter-gatherers and horticulturalists who lack domestic farm animals, on the one hand, and urban dwellers on the other. Those who make their living directly from domestic animals tend to take a more utilitarian attitude toward animals. It is a common practice for foragers to bring back the young of animals they have killed and raise them as pets (Bulmer 1976:182; Harris 1985:189; Serpell 1986:chapter 4). Like modern westerners, they are often willing to put up with considerable inconvenience to keep these pets, and to go to a good bit of trouble to provide them with food.[1] All this effort for an animal that, had it grown up in the wild, they would have killed and eaten without a second thought.

---

[1] I witnessed such a situation among the Barí of Venezuela. An adolescent boy was developing considerable skill with the sling, which he exercised on orange-chinned parakeets. However, his sling stones only stunned the hard-skulled birds. Had he killed them, his family would happily have eaten them. However, because he brought them back alive, they became pets. His increasing prowess with the sling soon led to a large colony of parakeets in the house. These birds eat the fruit of a particular palm, and soon the children of the house were spending all their time collecting these fruits to feed the parakeets. Although the situation was clearly getting out of hand, once brought into the house the birds were never killed and eaten. Rather, they began "mysteriously" to escape at night.

This practice cannot be justified in economic or subsistence terms. Pet keepers simply like having animals around. The greater prevalence of pet keeping in societies without domestic herd animals suggests that it is to some degree related to the higher esteem in which wild animals are held (see Chapter 4). When one regards animals as equals or near-equals, it is easier to conceive of bringing one into the family. Of course, domestication can also be seen as bringing animals into the domestic sphere, as implied in the term itself (and the German *Haustier*), but herd and farm animals are brought in as slaves or servants rather than children (see Chapter 6); the degree of inequality is greater.

Pet keeping becomes frequent again in industrialized societies. Here it forms part of a more compartmentalized approach to animals. We separate wild animals, utilitarian domestic farm animals, and pets, and we do so primarily at the level of the species or at least the breed. Although foragers' pets belong to the same species that they hunt and eat, and indeed are usually acquired in the process of the hunt, we usually classify whole species as inedible (taboo) because they are pets. Clearly there are exceptions. We classify some dogs as working animals; we may keep some pigs as pets while eating others. However, it is primarily pot-bellied pigs that are kept as pets in America, where this breed is not used for food. Although sheepdogs or police dogs may be filling a practical role, we do not eat them, and we are horrified at the thought of eating dogs or other "pet" species. We tend to see the occasional pets belonging to species and breeds that we do raise for food as problematic and inappropriate.

This approach is in line with the general western tendency to compartmentalize aspects of life, separating the political from the economic from the ritual, for instance. For societies with a more integrated approach to life, it is not a problem to blur categories that are less distinct to begin with. Even western categories can shift, however, as with pot-bellied pigs moving from food to pet. The animal rights movement can be seen as an attempt to extend the compartmentalized relations and attitudes we have toward pets to all animals; in essence, to redefine all species as pet species.

## PETS IN THE PAST

Given the apparent strength of the human inclination to share our lives with animals, as well as the wide range of contemporary societies in which pets are common, surely many, indeed most, past societies kept pets as well. Hence some of the animal remains from archaeological sites should be the remains of pets. Because most of the societies we study, especially in prehistory, lacked the compartmentalization of contemporary western society, pethood is likely to have been conferred on individuals rather than whole species in most cases. This means that we will not usually be able to recognize pets from the differing treatment given to a taxon as a whole; rather we will have to look for special treatment of certain individuals.

How might we recognize prehistoric pets? One defining feature of pets is that they are not eaten, so we can look for animal bones that have not been processed for food. There are, however, reasons other than being kept as a pet why an animal might not be eaten. It could be an offering, it may have been considered inedible because it was diseased or unclean (although this last is likely to operate at the level of the taxon rather than the individual), or it may have been killed for products other than meat (fur, feathers, etc.). Another defining feature of pets is that they are brought into the human family, treated as quasi-kin. This status may be reflected in the treatment of dead pets as though they were people, with similar burials, for example (Ojoade 1990:217).

Archaeologists have found such burials of dogs (Arbogast et al. 1989; Bartelle et al. 2010; Clark 1990, 1995; Collins 1991b; Day 1984; Detry and Cardoso 2010; Grigson 2006; Hill 2000; Hogue 2006; Horard-Herbin 2000; Morey 2006, 2010; Morey and Wiant 1992; Olsen 2000; Paris 2000; Shigehara and Hongo 2000; Smith 2006; Szuter 2001; Wapnish and Hesse 1993; Warren 2000; Yohe and Pavesic 2000), foxes (Collins 1991b), coyotes (Heizer and Hewes 1940), bears (Heizer and Hewes 1940), badgers (Heizer and Hewes 1940), deer (Arbogast et al. 1989; Heizer and Hewes 1940), pronghorns (Heizer and Hewes 1940), cattle (Luff 1996; Paris 1998, 2000; Pollex 1999; Warman 2004), horses (Daugnora and Thomas 2005; Lucy 2000; MacEachern et al. 2001; O'Connor 1994), donkeys (Clutton-Brock 2001), camels (Meadow 1984), eagles (Heizer and Hewes 1940), hawks (Martinez-Lira et al. 2005), ravens (Driver 1999; Serjeantson and Morris 2011), and turtles (Heizer and Hewes 1940). Complete animals are also sometimes found in human graves: dogs (Chapman 1997:139; Clutton-Brock 1995; Currie 2001; Davis and Valla 1978; Lichter 2001; MacEachern et al. 2001; MacKinnon and Belanger 2006; Prummel 2006; Trantalidou 2006; Wing 1984), foxes (Collins 1991b; Maher et al. 2011), raccoons (Wing 1984), sheep and goats (Arbogast et al. 2002; Lechevallier et al. 1982; Russell and Düring 2006), horses (Antikas 2006; Argent 2010; Manaseryan 2006), and donkeys (Zarins 1986). In addition, animal bones may be jumbled together with human bones in communal graves (Bond and Worley 2006; Chaix 1989; Jones 1998). Of course, not all animal burials are the remains of pets (see Chapter 3). When only parts of an animal are buried, it is better seen as a funerary offering. Draft animals buried with carts or chariots are more likely to be sacrifices. When a complete animal is buried in other circumstances, it requires careful contextual analysis to sort out whether it might be a pet. Whole animals buried with people could also be sacrifices or spirit guides. Smaller animals could even be mummified components of medicine kits. At best, an animal buried with a person was most likely killed to accompany its owner: the animal equivalent of suttee (wives killed or committing suicide to accompany their dead husbands) if this is indeed a pet. Whole animals buried alone might again be sacrifices or animals that died from disease. The South African Venda bury animals in cenotaphs as a symbolic substitute when a person dies far from home (Hutten 2008).

The most convincing arguments for identifying animal burials as remains of pets are based on detailed analyses of the burials themselves and of the larger cultural context, often drawing on historical or ethnographic knowledge of the society (Collins 1991b; MacKinnon and Belanger 2006; Smith 2006; Thomas 2005; Wapnish and Hesse 1993). Similar studies have led to the conclusion that other burials do not contain pets, but sacrifices (Hill 2000; Olsen 2000; Pollex 1999; Smith 2006) or spirit guides (Currie 2001; Wing 1984). Erica Hill's (2000) careful analysis of animal interments (not all are buried in pits) in the American Southwest draws in part on ethnographic sources from the region, but chiefly relies on the nature and context of the interments themselves. She distinguishes at least two kinds of animal interment: the remains of sacrificial animals that are then disposed of as "ceremonial trash," their uselife having ended; and animal offerings intended to continue to exert influence, which are placed in connection with the closing of abandoned buildings. Bird interments are treated as ceremonial trash, whereas dogs fall into both categories. She does not identify any of these burials as pets, but does suggest that dogs are treated as analogous to humans, perhaps even subject to execution as witches.

It is always important to build the most plausible interpretations possible through the thorough investigation of multiple lines of evidence. Yet given the emotional bonds that define the pet relationship, people will often honor pets with formal burial. Thus deliberately interred, intact animal skeletons are quite likely to be the remains of ancient companion animals.

## Neither wild nor domestic

There are some forms of human–animal relationships that not only fail to fit comfortably into the categories of wild (hunted) or domestic animals but are also not necessarily transitional between them. These relationships may share some of the characteristics of domestication, yet the animals are defined as wild. Although I argued in Chapter 6 that domestication is a useful concept because of its profound social implications, here I call into question a simplistic distinction between wild and domestic. We have already seen that pets do not fit neatly into wild or domestic categories, and other examples of animals that are neither wild nor domestic have been discussed in earlier chapters, particularly in relation to symbolic uses of animals. The cases explored here further illustrate that the dichotomy between wild and domestic, nature and culture, is essentially false. We would do better to regard domestication as a special and significant kind of human–animal relationship, but one of many such relationships. There are more than two choices.

### TAMING

Most who study domestication distinguish between truly domesticated animals and those that are only tamed (see Chapter 6, *Definitions*): Whereas domesticated animals breed in the human sphere, merely tamed animals spend only part of their lives there. Domesticated animals are usually tamed; so are pets. Virtually any animal brought into human society for whatever reason must be tamed to some degree. Usually we think of taming as an active human practice directed at animals. However, we also speak of wild animals that approach humans closely of their own volition as being tame: the suburban deer calmly browsing under our windows, for example. Taming is in essence a deliberate act of habituation, which reduces fear to permit close interactions. It is usually accomplished by handling, feeding, and grooming the animal. The human thus takes on a parental role, and it is often easier to tame young animals, which are more receptive to parenting. As with domestication, taming is at least partly about control. We hold tame animals in a certain degree of contempt compared to wild animals, as can be seen in the other usages of the word "tame."

In addition to taming pets and domesticated animals in the usual sense, people may tame animals for use in hunting other animals. A tame animal, often a female in heat, may serve as a decoy to lure animals to the hunters (Digard 1990:109; Ingold 1980). Paul Bahn (1980) suggests that the horses he believes were confined by humans in the Upper Paleolithic of France may have been used as decoys for hunting their conspecifics (although many question his evidence for human control of horses, e.g., Rowley-Conwy 1990; White 1989). The raptors used in falconry are captured young and tamed (see Chapter 4, *Sport Hunting*). Similarly, tame cormorants and herons are used in fishing, with a ring around their necks to prevent them from swallowing the fish (Digard 1990:129). Tame birds may also be kept for their feathers (Bulmer 1976:171; Szuter 2001:214–16).

People may also capture and keep animals for varying lengths of time before sacrificing them (see Chapter 3). A bear from Mesolithic France with pathological alterations to the mandible indicating it was captured young and restrained for several years may be a prehistoric example of such a practice (Chaix et al. 1997). Ethnohistorical and archaeological evidence suggest the Maya also captured, penned, and sacrificed deer and perhaps other species such as peccary (Masson 1999; Pohl 1991).

Such captive animals are usually tamed at least to some degree, but some cases are better viewed as simple restraint. For example, the Kalam of New Guinea capture and store live eels in baskets in the river for up to four months; eels are considered a great delicacy and feasting food (Bulmer 1976). Bogucki (Bogucki and Grygiel 1983) has proposed similar storage of live freshwater mussels in damp pits at European Neolithic sites. Prehistoric and ethnographically known groups in the American Southwest kept snakes for use in snake-handling ceremonies (Szuter 2001:216).

MANAGEMENT

Many human–animal relationships falling into the gray area between or outside of wild and domestic in the contemporary world can be classed as the management of "wild" animals. For example, how would we classify tuna that are captured as they migrate and "penned" in areas of the ocean off Gibraltar delimited by nets, fattened up on wild-caught mackerel and herring imported from the North Sea, and harvested months later (Bestor 2001)? What about endangered species, most or all of whose reproduction takes place under carefully controlled circumstances, in order to be able to return them to "the wild" (where their every move may be tracked by radio collars)? And what of suburban deer, whose behavior we minimally attempt to control with fences and repellents, and now sometimes through the more direct intervention of contraception? Even rural deer and other game species are managed through selective hunting in designated seasons. In some cases we culturally define animals as wild that clearly have a domestic character. The "wild game" served in American restaurants must be farm-raised according to law. We raise fish and game birds to stock the wilderness, so fishers and hunters can have the thrill of killing a "wild" animal. Some of these animals, such as the ring-necked pheasant, are exotic species that have been introduced specifically for this purpose. The very phrase "wildlife management" is something of an oxymoron.

Is this obsession with control and manipulation of the wild simply a capitalist phenomenon? Or did prehistoric peoples also manage "wild" populations, as often suggested? First we must consider what "management" means. Some construe it very liberally to include any demographic impact that hunters have on their prey (Tudge 1999). However, because any predation will have such an impact, this is not a particularly useful approach. More typically, management is taken to mean deliberate human practices that act to maintain or increase game populations, including selective hunting, hunting taboos for conservation purposes, and the use of fire and other environmental manipulations to improve game habitat.

The use of fire to improve both plant and animal habitat has been documented ethnographically (Bliege Bird et al. 2008; Hallam 1979; Metailie 1981; Rodríguez 2007), and paleoenvironmental evidence has been interpreted as indicating such practices in the past (Bennett et al. 1990; Bogucki 1988:38–47; Dods 2002; Fletcher and Thomas 2010; Kershaw 1986; Lewis 1972; Mason 2000; McCorriston and Hole 1991; Mellars 1976; Pinter et al. 2011; Roberts 2002). Although this use of fire affects game species, it is perhaps better seen in Yen's (1989) terms as domiculture, a manipulation of the environment, rather than as a human–animal relationship per se.

Selective hunting and hunting taboos for conservation/herd management purposes (there are of course other reasons for hunting taboos; see Chapter 2) are really two sides of the same coin: They are a means to regulate hunting to achieve some end, usually conservation of the herd or increased herd productivity. Just as in contemporary wildlife management, there may be seasonal taboos on hunting certain game, taboos on hunting certain animals (usually females), or selective targeting of other animals (usually males). The Gunwinggu of Australia use such hunting taboos during the breeding season to protect game species; if these animals are killed by mistake, only the senior men are allowed to eat them (Altman and Peterson 1988).

The extent to which pre-contact Native Americans practiced selective hunting for conservation is controversial. Calvin Martin (1978) has championed the notion of the "ecological Indian," arguing that Native American notions of respect for wild animals included a ban on overkilling that broke down only after European contact. Others assert that such notions of game management are a western projection; Native Americans managed game animals by killing them so they could regenerate (Brightman 1993; Krech 1981, 1999; see Chapter 4, *Hunters' Attitudes to Animals*). The Cree did practice deliberate conservation measures for fur-bearers in the 19th century, however (Brightman 1993). Thus ethnographic evidence indicates that hunters in foraging societies may in some cases practice deliberate game conservation, but this is by no means universal.

Paul Sillitoe (2001) also suggests that the Wola and perhaps some other highland New Guinea groups effectively practice conservation, even though there is no conscious conservation ethic. Although game is highly valued and can be used in prestige-generating exchanges, which would seem to promote overhunting, in fact hunting is occasional and has not wiped out local game populations. This is apparently because the economic and political system is based on transaction rather than production. It is unseemly to use game one has killed oneself in prestige exchanges, so hunters usually sell their catch to others in need of material for a prestation. Because hunting return rates are low, the economic benefit to the hunter is small and the political benefit nil, not justifying the missed opportunities for political interaction caused by spending a lot of time away hunting. This system seems to be structured more to prevent entrenched inequality among humans than to conserve game populations, but it does have a conservation effect.

Members of the Palaeoeconomy school proposed similar kinds of management in the context of following reindeer herds in the European Upper Paleolithic, with herd following seen as a close human–animal relationship that in many ways approximates herding (Bahn 1977; Jarman 1977; Sturdy 1975). The feasibility of herd following has been challenged, however (Burch 1972; White 1989).

Michael Jarman's (1972) "red deer economies" is perhaps the classic argument for intensive prehistoric management. Jarman argues that red deer were actively managed at many sites in Mesolithic Europe. To optimize meat yield, one should cull most of the young males and preserve the adult females for breeding (Chaplin 1975; Clutton-Brock and Albon 1989; Mitchell et al. 1977). In contrast, to optimize the number of mature stags and maximize their body (and antler) size, one needs to cull females as well to keep the female density low (Clutton-Brock and Albon 1989). Jarman apparently envisages the former strategy, for he argues that males are being culled to maintain the herd.

Jarman's argument has some flaws, however. In terms of sex ratios, it rests on two sites – Star Carr and Seeberg Burgäschisee-Süd – both of which are reported to have about 70% male red deer. The original analysis of the Star Carr fauna included antler fragments when calculating the sex ratio (Fraser and King 1954). Because any antler fragment is automatically attributable to a male (except in reindeer), and there is no comparable female structure, this practice tends to produce a serious bias toward males. A reanalysis of the Star Carr fauna shows that without the antler (much of which was shed and/or worked, thus unlikely to represent animals killed at the site) the sex ratio is essentially even, based on a careful metrical analysis of the postcranial remains, and that subadults and adults predominate (Legge and Rowley-Conwy 1988). At Seeberg Burgäschisee-Süd, Jean-Pierre Jéquier (Boessneck et al. 1963) reports an *adult* sex ratio of seven males to three females. Jarman then applies this ratio to all age groups, in fact distributing the males somewhat preferentially among the lower age classes because this fits his model! Of course, in a managed herd, culling young males will lead to an adult sex ratio that is biased toward *females*. Selective *hunting* intended to conserve the stock might well focus on adult males (Elder 1965), but although this is good conservation practice, it hardly represents herd management and certainly does not optimize meat production. The only production scheme likely to create such a pattern would be rearing the deer for traction (valuing mature males), although the sex ratio would probably be more balanced, because females would be needed for breeding.

At Seeberg Burgäschisee-Süd and also at Neolithic Opovo (Russell 1993, 1999), the adult sex ratio and the age structure, which is heavily weighted to adults in the red deer, suggest not herding, but selective hunting. Whether deliberately or not, adult males were killed at a rate far beyond their representation in the living population. Studies of present-day red and roe deer indicate that adult sex ratios are generally at least slightly biased toward females. This bias is not always the result of selective trophy hunting; male–male combat during the rut and the amount of energy invested in the rut in general seem also to be contributing factors (Andersen 1953; Bubenik 1982; Clutton-Brock et al. 1982; Ellenberg 1978; Farkas and Csányi 1990; Geist 1982; Jarman 1972; Nahlik 1987; Nikolandić 1968). There are a number of possible reasons for the skewed sex ratio, which may arise unintentionally as a result of hunting practices or may involve the deliberate targeting of adult males.

Red deer spend most of the year in sexually segregated groups (Chaplin 1975; Jarman 1972; Maxwell 1967; Mitchell et al. 1977), which would facilitate selective hunting by making it possible to seek out male herds, and could conceivably lead to unintentional bias toward males if human hunters tended to encounter male herds more often. Hunting deer selectively is easy, because the sexual dimorphism in size is reflected in their tracks (Tegner 1951). Selectively hunting adult males is a low-intensity exploitive strategy that promotes conservation of the herd and thus tends to reduce risk of game depletion. Alternatively, hunters may actively seek adult males because they are needed or preferred. One factor could be fat, a nutrient of some importance, particularly when most meat comes from relatively lean wild animals. The fat content of wild animals varies seasonally and by sex. Generally, young and very old animals, breeding females, and rutting males have low fat reserves, whereas prime adult males apart from the rut and females that did not reproduce that year have higher reserves (Mitchell et al. 1981; Speth 1983, 1991). Although the sex ratio of animals selected for fat content should tend to even out through the year, this selection might lead to somewhat of a bias toward prime males.

Desire for antler as a raw material might also motivate hunters to seek male deer in the appropriate seasons (Choyke 1987), and deer may be hunted in part or even primarily for their hides (McCabe 1982). The hides of animals of different ages and sexes may be preferred depending on their intended use. Because of their larger size, mature males may have been sought out to make a more impressive showing at feasts, as at Opovo (Bulmer 1976; Russell 1993, 1999). And of course the hunter who bagged a large male may have gained more prestige.

Thus herd management to maximize meat production would not produce the mortality profiles seen at Seeberg and Opovo. Practicing conservation of the herd by sparing females might do so, but there are many other factors that could also incline hunters to target adult males.

As these examples show, arguments for herd management must be built on a careful and thorough examination of many lines of evidence. Many factors, including hunting pressure without any deliberate changes in hunting strategy (Choyke and Bartosiewicz 1984; Elder 1965), can produce mortality profiles resembling those of managed herds. Along with age and sex patterns, we can consider seasonality, pathologies, and paleoenvironmental data. Do the hunters refrain from killing animals, especially adult females, during the seasons of birth and lactation? Do pathologies indicate the restraint or use of some animals? Are there signs of burning or other anthropogenic alterations to the environment that would encourage game species? How do mortality profiles of the poten-tially managed species compare with others less likely to be managed? In addition, the social behavior of the animals must be considered. How easy is it to target particular age and sex groups? Does the behavior of certain age/sex groups make them more or less likely to encounter hunters?

Medieval deer parks show that deer can be managed to a point that at least approaches domestication. In the early medieval period, deer were fenced to provide food and sport for the nobility, presumably because they were otherwise under threat from habitat loss to farmers. In addition, some stags were captured, branded, and shackled. These stags were referred to as "domesticated," although we would probably refer to them as tamed. They were used in hunting, most likely as decoys. Rare references to deer's milk cheese implies that does were milked on occasion. By the later Middle Ages, these park deer were foddered in the winter, and domestic cattle were used as wet nurses for fawns (Salisbury 1994:50–1; Vigne 1993). As a result, the fallow deer in parks showed physical signs of domestication, notably variable color.

Although fallow deer, at least, are obviously amenable to a loose form of herding, the implications for the feasibility of prehistoric management are unclear. The maintenance of park deer relies heavily on fencing. Deer parks were a creation of the elite designed to preserve a bit of the wild for their enjoyment, ironically by taming it. Although the park deer provided food, it is unlikely that their productivity was comparable to that of domestic herds or cultivated land. Rather, they supported conceptions of nobility that were linked to the "noble" pursuit of the hunt (Salisbury 1994:28; see Chapter 4, *Sport Hunting*).

### ISLAND INTRODUCTIONS

Because of their bounded nature, islands provide particularly useful windows on human–animal relationships. Both subtractions (see Chapter 5, *Island Extinctions*) and additions to island fauna are more obvious than they are on the mainland and are more easily related to human activity. There are many documented cases of human transport of animals to islands around the world. Although some animals may be unintended hitchhikers, most must have been brought deliberately. Some are clearly domestic animals brought by colonists to raise for food in their new homes, but many are animals usually considered wild, which appear to have been brought to stock islands with desired game. In some cases it is less clear whether wild animals were stocked or tame/domestic animals became feral.

In perhaps the most straightforward cases, people carried domestic animals in boats as part of a colonization effort. Early European settlers in North America, for example, brought their familiar domestic animals with them. So, apparently, did the Lapita culture and Polynesian settlers of the Pacific, who brought dogs, pigs, and chickens in their outrigger canoes and raised them on most of the islands they settled. They also brought Pacific rats (*Rattus exulans*), although it is less clear whether this transport was deliberate. The rats were apparently raised for food or at least became a major food source on some islands (Anderson 1989a; Coutts and Jurisich 1973; Davidson 1985; Kirch 1982; Rainbird 1993; Spriggs 1996; Steadman 1989; Van Tilburg 1994). Although the domestic animals were raised under human control, they often established feral populations as well, to the detriment of the local faunas. In addition to the animals brought deliberately, there seem to have been some hitchhikers (Austin 1999). Similarly, Clutton-Brock (1995:8) has suggested that people carried the now-extinct Falkland Islands "wolf" (*Dusicyon australis*, a different species from the wolf) to the islands from South

America in tamed form, where it established feral populations. Likewise, dingoes are feral descendants of domestic dogs brought to Australia by around 3500 BP.

The wild/domestic distinction is more blurred in the numerous cases in which European colonizers stocked the new lands with feral populations of animals they thought useful to have around (Mullin 1999:205). The house or English sparrow, for example, was deliberately imported to North America several times in the mid-19th century both because some people mistakenly thought it would eat insects and because recent European immigrants missed having them around (Skinner 1904).

The prehistoric introduction of animals on the Mediterranean islands, particularly Cyprus, has been especially well studied. From the Neolithic on, people have brought a remarkable variety of animals to these islands: some "wild," some domestic, some as hitchhikers (see Table 7.1). These animals are not found on the islands before human settlement, and they replace endemic island faunas that disappeared before or after the arrival of humans (see Chapter 5, *Island Extinctions*). The species and subspecies found on the islands are not always those from the nearest mainland area, further indicating that they arrived by boat rather than swimming (Groves 1989). Vigne (1992:92–3) points out that virtually all of these taxa are in some way associated with humans: Some are domestic, some are favored game, and some are commensal. The islands lack noncommensal species that people tend to regard as pests, such as moles, or most carnivores and rodents.

Some species, such as cattle and dog, were clearly brought as domesticates and raised by humans. Others were brought as domesticates but established feral populations (Albarella et al. 2006b; Horwitz and Kahila Bar-Gal 2006; Kahila Bar-Gal et al. 2002; Poplin 1979; Schüle 1993; Vigne et al. 2000). In some cases feral animals escaped very early in the domestication process, as with the Mediterranean "mouflon," which is descended from early domestic sheep from the mainland. Colin Groves (1989) uses a clever technique to trace this process. Domestication often leads to reduced brain size, presumably related to selection for docility and the lessened need for the animals to fend for themselves. In island situations, at least, without major predators, this brain size reduction can persist in feral animals for thousands of years. By examining brain sizes, Groves confirms that the mouflons are feral, and he argues that those on Corsica and Sardinia are descended from very primitive domestic sheep,

Table 7.1. *Animals believed to have been transported by humans to Mediterranean islands*

| | | |
|---|---|---|
| Balearic Frog | *Rana parezi* | Balearics |
| Balearic Toad | *Bufo viridis* | Balearics |
| Garden Dormouse | *Eliomys quercinus* | Crete, Corsica, Sardinia, Balearics |
| Fat Dormouse | *Glis glis* | Crete, Corsica, Sardinia |
| Cretan Spiny Mouse | *Acomys minous* | Crete |
| Spiny Mouse | *Acomys cahirinus* | Cyprus |
| Rock Mouse | *Apodemus mystacinus* | Crete |
| Wood Mouse | *Apodemus sylvaticus* | Crete, Corsica, Sardinia, Balearics |
| House Mouse | *Mus musculus* | Cyprus, Crete, Corsica, Sardinia, Balearics |
| Algerian Mouse | *Mus spretus* | Balearics |
| Norway Rat | *Rattus norvegicus* | Crete, Corsica, Sardinia, Balearics |
| Black Rat | *Rattus rattus* | Cyprus, Crete, Corsica, Sardinia |
| European Hare | *Lepus europaeus* | Crete |
| Brown Hare | *Lepus capensis* | Cyprus, Crete |
| Granada Hare | *Lepus granatensis* | Sardinia, Balearics |
| Corsican Hare | *Lepus corsicanus* | Corsica |
| Rabbit | *Oryctolagus cuniculus* | Crete, Corsica, Sardinia, Balearics |
| North African Hedgehog | *Atelerix agirus* | Balearics |
| Eastern European Hedgehog | *Erinaceus concolor* | Crete |
| Western Hedgehog | *Erinaceus europaeus* | Cyprus, Corsica, Sardinia |
| Long-Eared Hedgehog | *Hemiechinus auritus* | Cyprus |
| White-Toothed Shrew | *Crocidura russula* | Sardinia |
| Lesser White-Toothed Shrew | *Crocidura suaveolens* | Cyprus, Crete, Corsica |
| Pygmy White-Toothed Shrew | *Suncus etruscus* | Cyprus, Crete, Corsica, Sardinia |
| Wild Cat | *Felis silvestris* | Cyprus, Crete, Corsica, Sardinia, Balearics |
| Small-Spotted Genet | *Genetta genetta* | Balearics |
| Genet | *Genetta plesictoides* | Cyprus |
| Red Fox | *Vulpes vulpes* | Cyprus, Crete. Corsica, Sardinia |
| Dog | *Canis familiaris* | Cyprus, Crete, Corsica, Sardinia, Balearics |
| European Polecat | *Mustela putorius* | Sardinia |
| Weasel | *Mustela nivalis* | Cyprus, Corsica, Sardinia, Balearics |
| Beech Marten | *Martes foina* | Crete |
| Pine Marten | *Martes martes* | Corsica, Sardinia, Balearics |
| Badger | *Meles meles* | Crete |
| Brown Bear | *Ursus arctos* | Corsica |
| Horse | *Equus caballus* | Cyprus, Crete, Corsica, Sardinia, Balearics |
| Donkey | *Equus asinus* | Cyprus, Crete, Corsica, Sardinia, Balearics |
| Pig | *Sus scrofa* | Cyprus, Crete, Corsica, Sardinia, Balearics |
| Cattle | *Bos taurus* | Cyprus, Crete, Corsica, Sardinia, Balearics |
| Goat | *Capra hircus* | Cyprus, Crete, Aegean Islands, Corsica, Sardinia, Balearics |
| Mouflon/Sheep | *Ovis musimon/aries* | Cyprus, Crete, Corsica, Sardinia, Balearics |
| Red Deer | *Cervus elaphus* | Crete, Corsica, Sardinia, Balearics |
| Fallow Deer | *Dama dama* | Cyprus, Crete, Aegean islands, Sardinia, Balearics, Rhodes |

*Sources:* Albarella et al. 2006b; Cherry 1990; Cucchi et al. 2002; Davis 1984a, 1989, 1995, 2004; Groves 1989; Halstead 1987; Kahila Bar-Gal et al. 2002; Masseti 2009; Masseti et al. 2006; Masseti and De Marinis 2008; Payne 1995; Poplin 1979; Schüle 1993; Schwartz 1973; Steensma and Reese 1999; Suchentrunk et al. 2006; Vigne 1988, 1992, 1999, 2001, Vigne et al., 2000, 2004a, 2004b, 2009; taxonomic designations follow Wilson and Reeder (2005).

whereas those on Cyprus had more fully domesticated ancestors. Likewise, the "wild" goats of Crete and the Aegean islands are derived from
animals very early in the domesticatory process. Mediterranean boar are
descended from the wild form, as are the wild cats of Sardinia and Corsica,
which derive from North Africa. The cats of the Balearics and probably
Crete are feral, however. Genetic studies have confirmed some of these
results (Horwitz and Kahila Bar-Gal 2006; Kahila Bar-Gal et al. 2002;
Suchentrunk et al. 2006).

Domestic animals going feral, and commensal species such as mice
and shrews stowing away to reach the islands are easily understood. More
puzzling, and particularly fascinating in terms of human–animal relationships, is the apparent stocking of the islands with "wild" species. Some of
these introductions are documented, such as the establishment of hares
brought from southern Italy on Corsica in the late 15th century or of
rabbits in the 1950s. Although not actually documented, bears appear
to have been introduced to Corsica, probably as tame animals, in the
medieval period. They then established a feral population that was later
hunted to extinction (Vigne 1992:92). However, humans must deliberately have brought deer, wild boar, hedgehogs, and wild cats with them
in small boats during the Neolithic. These animals were almost surely
tame and possibly young. Their transporters do not seem to have bred
them in captivity on arrival, however, but rather set them loose and then
hunted their descendants. Moreover, models indicate that importing a
single breeding pair is not enough; several animals are required to establish a population, and even then it will be decades before it can sustain
hunting pressure (Ducos 2000). This suggests that, back on the mainland, people regularly captured wild animals (for pets or other purposes),
although such practices are usually archaeologically invisible. It also shows
that they felt a need to have these animals around in addition to their
domestic herds. Were wild deer necessary for certain ceremonies? Was
prestige attached to hunting them? Was killing a wild boar a requirement
for attaining manhood?

The Mediterranean islands are not the only ones to which prehistoric people intentionally transported apparently "wild" animals. The
transport of the gray cuscus (*Phalanger orientalis*) from New Guinea to
New Ireland at ca. 20,000 BP, followed by its intensive hunting, was
just the first of a series of introductions of plant and animal species to
Melanesian islands (Gosden 1995). Later another species of phalanger

(*Spilocuscus maculatus*) and a wallaby (*Thylogale brunii*) were also introduced to New Ireland, in addition to domestic pigs and dogs and domestic/commensal rats (Steadman et al. 1999:2564). Like the fallow deer of the Mediterranean, humans may have transported the Malayan deer (*Cervus rusa*) from Java and Bali to Flores, Timor, and Komodo (Schüle 1993:403), and red deer (*Cervus elaphus*) along with domestic animals to the Hebrides in the Neolithic (Serjeantson 1990). Groves (1984) has identified 20 species in island Southeast Asia transported by humans from the mainland to islands or from one island to another. Many were probably accidental stowaways, often associated with agriculture and in several cases specifically wet rice cultivation. However, some were surely deliberately translocated as pets or sources of meat or, for two species of civet, perfume. People may have brought bush pigs (*Potamochoerus larvatus*) to Madagascar (MacPhee and Marx 1997:187).

Elizabeth Wing (1993) attributes the presence of several large rodents in the West Indies to human activity. Rice rats may have been commensal hitchhikers that were spread unintentionally. In contrast, two species of hutia (*Geocapromys*, ca. 1 kg) appeared on distant islands they could not have reached on their own, and the agouti (*Dasyprocta*, ca. 2 kg) must have been brought deliberately from the South American mainland. An extinct native rodent, *Isolobodon portoricensis* (ca. 1 kg), may have been domesticated at one point, because there is a smaller size variant. The hutias were heavily used over a long period. Because they developed in an island environment free from mammalian predators, Wing argues that their population levels could only have been maintained after human colonization through active management practices. She suggests that the frequent finds of dogs with their lower fourth premolars broken out may indicate that dogs were muzzled to protect the hutias. Humans may also have transported parrots and boa constrictors from island to island within the West Indies (Steadman et al. 1984).

Collins (1991a, 1991b; Rick et al. 2009) has made an exemplary study of island foxes (*Urocyon littoralis*) on the Channel Islands off the coast of southern California. He draws on osteological, archaeological, and ethnographic evidence to determine how and why foxes spread through the islands. He is able to establish that the foxes might have reached the northern Channel Islands on their own but were more likely brought by humans, whereas humans must have transported them to the southern islands. He makes a strong case that people transported foxes for use both as pets and in ceremonies such as the Fox Dance. Both motivations may be related to the existence of a fox totem, because some California Native American groups are known to have kept living examples of their totems as pets, to have been buried with them, and to carry parts of the totem animal's bodies. Collins also suggests that the foxes may have acted as spirit helpers. Foxes and parts of foxes are found in human burials on the Channel Islands and are also buried separately. There is no sign that they were eaten or their bones used for tools. Here we have a clear case of deliberate human stocking not of a food species, but of a species that was ritually necessary.

What can we learn from these various island cases? There are enough of them to suggest that people have with some regularity brought animals with them in their travels, including animals that are not herded or domesticated by most definitions. The same is probably true on the mainland, but it is much harder to detect there. Do these cases inform us about the motivations for animal domestication? At least some of them suggest that people will often go to considerable lengths to ensure the supply of animals that are ritually required. They lend plausibility to the notion that people might in some instances have been willing to rearrange their lives and invest extra labor in raising animals to have a supply of the right animals or animal products for sacrifices, feasts, and ceremonies. However, these cases also point up the variety of human–animal relationships that are neither domestication nor the simple hunting of wild animals. People may encourage or manage animal populations without actually controlling breeding or movement. The motivations for such behavior may include the need for a steady supply of meat, but at least in some cases the symbolic value of animals is more important.

Modern wildlife management practices are not so different. Consider, for example, the widespread practice of raising Asian pheasants on American game farms for release into the wild for hunters to shoot. Although they are classified as wild game, few of the pheasants will survive the winter if they are not shot. They are incapable of maintaining their populations in the wild and so fit a classic definition of domestication. If food were the goal, it would be much easier simply to slaughter the pheasants on the farms. Although the pheasants are eaten, the real point is the hunt itself. Not only do hunters want the thrill of shooting a "wild" animal but they also want to be able to shoot this particular species. They are willing to support with their hunting fees this species' raising and stocking and to participate in the charade of defining a farmed species as wild.

The fallow deer of the Mediterranean islands should perhaps be seen in much the same light. Mortality profiles indicate they were left to run wild and be hunted, rather than herded (Vigne et al. 2000), but their introduction and perhaps their management show that hunting wild deer was so important that Neolithic people would go to considerable trouble to provide deer for the purpose. This same species later became park deer in Europe (see previous section).

## Man's best friend

Dogs may be considered the most thoroughly domesticated animal. They were the first animal to be domesticated (see Table 6.1), and are one of the few species with a completely different common name from its wild ancestor (the wolf) in every language that I know of. Although most domestic animals revert to wild type when they establish feral populations, feral dogs do not become wolflike, but more closely resemble jackals[2] (although jackals have been ruled out as their wild ancestor through studies of fossils, genetics, and behavior). There are more breeds of dog than any other animal species (Morris 2002), and dogs embody a remarkable range of variation in size and form, from the Chihuahua to the Newfoundland, that is unknown in any other species (Drake and Klingenberg 2010). Distinct breeds of dog can be detected earlier than those of any other species as well, at 3000–5000 BP, and dog breeds proliferate in the Roman period (Bartosiewicz 2000b; Baxter 2006; Clark 2000; Clutton-Brock 1995; Cram 2000; De Grossi Mazzorin and Tagliacozzo 2000; Handley 2000; MacKinnon 2010; Parker et al. 2004; Rice 2006).

Zooarchaeologists have capitalized on the close association between humans and dogs by using dogs as a proxy for humans in isotopic studies of diet (Burleigh and Brothwell 1978; Cannon et al. 1999; Clutton-Brock and Noe-Nygaard 1990; Day 1996; Hogue 2006). The assumption is that dogs are fed or scavenge leftovers of human food, so that their diet reflects that of humans. It is probably unwarranted to assume that dogs consume foods in the same proportions as people in all cases. However,

---

[2] I am indebted to Kevin McGowan for pointing out this anomaly to me.

where dog bones are more readily available than human, isotopic studies on dogs may produce useful results on a gross scale, such as determining whether maize formed part of the diet (Burleigh and Brothwell 1978; Hogue 2006) or whether inland groups spent part of their time on the coast (Clutton-Brock and Noe-Nygaard 1990, but cf. Day 1996).

Yet although dogs are highly domesticated and may have provided the template for the domestication of other animals (see Chapter 6, *Links between Human–Animal and Human–Human Relations*), they also stand as a special case in comparison to other domesticates. Dogs are not herd animals, and they have only occasionally, and probably only late in prehistory, been raised for meat. Perhaps because they did not start as food animals and have had a longer domesticatory relationship with humans than any other animal, dogs have filled virtually every role in the whole spectrum of human–animal relationships. Dogs have been pets, guard animals, hunting aids, herders, sources of traction and other labor, racers, military aids, participants in animal combat, status symbols, spirit guides, sacrificial offerings, island introductions that have some-times gone feral (on the mainland as well), sources of fur, objects of worship, pariahs, sources of medicine and raw material for witchcraft, and indeed sources of food for both daily consumption and special feasts. They have often played many of these roles simultaneously within a single society. Their close ties to humans, the similarities to humans in their diet and social structure, and their scavenging habits have frequently placed dogs in a liminal or ambiguous position. They are like us but different, of the human world but animals; they exemplify both nature and culture. This ambiguity has led to both veneration and contempt.

The varied roles and ambiguous position of dogs are particularly clear for Australian dingoes. Humans brought these dogs to Australia, already domesticated, about 3,500 years ago (Clutton-Brock 1995). They were thus introduced into a longstanding foraging mode of subsis-tence, remaining the only domesticate on the continent until European contact. Some of the dingoes stayed in the human sphere; others estab-lished feral populations. Australians threw bones to the dogs, but did not otherwise feed them, although the dingoes often managed to steal food meant for humans. As a result the feral dingoes were consistently in better condition than the domestic ones, somewhat calling into question the notion of dog domestication through symbiosis. Australians were willing to put up with the nuisance of hungry dogs constantly after human food supplies because of their value as watchdogs, their companionship, and their warmth at night; while occasionally used in hunting they seem to have provided limited benefit in that capacity. They treated the dingoes affectionately while expending little effort in their care and no control over their reproduction, and only occasionally ate them (Clutton-Brock 1995:15; Hamilton 1972; Harris 1985:186–9; Hayden 1975; Manwell and Baker 1984; Meggitt 1965).

In Australia, dingoes were the only domesticates. In Nigeria, where a wider range of plant and animal domesticates is used, dogs play even more varied roles. Mythology presents dogs as allies of humans against other animals. Dogs symbolize male sexuality. They guard houses not only against human strangers but also against witches and spirits. They serve as nursemaids, capitalizing on their tendency to eat excrement to keep human infants clean. They help in hunting and even in warfare. Many Nigerians consider dog a delicacy, and dog meat and fat are thought to have medicinal and aphrodisiac properties. There may be some discomfort about eating an animal so closely linked to humans, however, which is manifested in the terminology for cuts of dog meat that describe the dog body parts by analogy to a Peugeot 404 station wagon. Dogs are also sacrificed, being considered a substitute for humans. Some groups worship dogs or beings with some dog characteristics. And dogs are pets. Some dogs, especially good hunting dogs, may receive burials as elaborate as those of humans (Ojoade 1990).

Dogs straddle symbolic boundaries even more than other domestic animals. In the Amazon, the Achuar value dogs for hunting, but also esteem them beyond this role. Dogs that do not hunt may also be highly valued, because they are part of the household, domestic but not raised for meat, at the intersection of nature and culture. Although many wild animals are kept as pets, their socialization is individual, whereas it is part of the essence of dogs. They also exist at the intersection of male and female. Their main use is in hunting, a male activity, but they are raised and exchanged by women. Because an Achuar household often has 20 dogs, a considerable portion of women's garden production is devoted to them. Dogs occupy a quasi-human position in the household. They are cared for much like children and fed mostly cooked food. Sick dogs are treated with herbs and healing rituals. Like people, dogs must observe dietary taboos (Descola 1994:230–5; see also Kohn 2007). Dogs likely played such varied roles in the past as well. It is not unusual to find that some dogs at a site are eaten, some buried, and others are neither buried nor eaten.

## COMPANION

Most modern western people would probably consider the primary role of dogs to be as pets or companion animals (Serpell 1986, 1995). There are good indications that dogs have often been regarded as companions in the past as well. Some would argue that this goes back to the very beginning of the human–dog relationship, that it was their position as pets that led to dog domestication (see Chapter 6, *The Pet Theory*). As we have seen (the earlier section, *Pets*), the definition of pet, and therefore the recognition of pets in the past, is not completely straightforward. At many sites, dogs are rarely or never eaten, but this could be a sign of either affection or contempt. Ethnographically, dogs have often been viewed in both these ways. It is not only western societies who keep dogs primarily as pets; this may be true for some Australian Aboriginal groups as well, where dogs act as substitute children (Hamilton 1972).

Dogs are the most frequently buried animal (Morey 2006, 2010). Minimally, dog burials have been reported from the Epipaleolithic and later periods of the Near East (Clutton-Brock 2001; Davis and Valla 1978; Grigson 2006; Onar et al. 2002; Wapnish and Hesse 1993), the Mesolithic and later periods of Europe (Antikas 2006, Arbogast et al. 1989; Barber and Bowsher 2000; Benecke 1994; Bökönyi 1984; Bond and Worley 2006; Chapman 1997; Day 1984; Detry and Cardoso 2010; Facciolo and Tagliacozzo 2006; Horard-Herbin 2000; Jones 1998; Lichter 2001; MacKinnon and Belanger 2006; Petrasch 2004; Prummel 2006; Smith 2006), the Chalcolithic of Central Asia (Olsen 2000), the Bronze Age in China (Fiskesjö 2001), the Jomon in Japan (Shigehara and Hongo 2000), the Neolithic and later in Africa (MacEachern et al. 2001; Paris 2000), the Archaic and later periods in North America (Bartelle et al. 2010; Collins 1991b; Hill 2000; Hogue 2006; Morey and Wiant 1992; Oberholtzer 2002; Szuter 2001; Vellanoweth et al. 2008; Warren 2000; Yohe and Pavesic 2000), and Mayan Mesoamerica (Wing 1984). In some cases the dogs are buried alone; in others they accompany humans. As noted earlier (*Pets in the Past*), although burial of an intact animal indicates that it was not eaten, dog burials do not necessarily mean the animal was a pet. In some cases, however, it seems likely that the dog was a valued companion.

HUNTER

One popular explanation for dog domestication is that people valued dogs for their aid in hunting (Clutton-Brock 1995; Downs 1960; Mason 1966[1895]:259; Musil 2000). At least in some circumstances, the use of dogs can substantially increase the human hunter's take, although of course there is some cost in feeding and caring for the dogs (Bulmer 1976:172; Marshall 1994:71; Salisbury 1994). Dogs can follow the scent of game animals, flush prey, pursue it, help the hunter follow with their barking, and bring animals to bay. Many of these canine skills may be especially useful to human hunters in dense forests (Perri 2010). Based on a large sample of European and Near Eastern Neolithic faunal assemblages, Bartosiewicz (1990:291) concludes that the proportion of dogs is positively correlated with the proportion of wild fauna, suggesting that hunting was one important function of Neolithic dogs. The relatively large number of dogs (3%) associated with the high proportion of wild fauna at Opovo further supports this conclusion (Russell 1993:184).

According to Raymond Chaplin (1969:237), dogs are particularly helpful in hunting herd animals of moderate size such as reindeer, saiga, sheep, and goat; they are less useful for cattle, boar, and deer. However, it is precisely cattle, boar, and deer that form the bulk of the wild fauna from the sites studied by Bartosiewicz, so even in this case they must be of considerable use. In contrast, dogs do not appear among the reindeer hunters of the Upper Paleolithic; rather Rudolf Musil (2000) suggests they were used to hunt horses. One imagines that the dogs would have helped drive the horse herds into the range of waiting hunters. However, dogs are apparently not always tremendously useful as hunting aids; Australian dingoes seem to have been of very limited use in many cases, although effective in others (Hamilton 1972; Hayden 1975; Manwell and Baker 1984; Meggitt 1965).

Clutton-Brock (1994:25) suggests that wolves and humans were major competitors for game in the Paleolithic. In her view the natural response would be to form an alliance, in which tame wolves were used as hunting aids. When two species compete for the same resource, however, the more usual results are either that one species outcompetes the other, which goes extinct, or that they specialize in different segments of the resource. While the first dogs appear in the late Upper Paleolithic, they do not become common until the Epipaleolithic and Mesolithic in Europe and the Near East, when the bow and arrow comes into use.

Clutton-Brock (1995) suggests that dogs are more useful in this type of hunting for tracking animals and bringing them to bay. The coincidence of dogs and bow hunting is intriguing, but I am not convinced that dogs are particularly helpful hunting aids in this context. The main advantages of the bow and arrow are stealth (the bow is quiet and it is hard for the animal to tell where the arrows are coming from, so the hunter is often able to get off several shots) and the ability to attack from a distance. Spear hunting would seem to benefit more from having animals tracked and brought to bay. Certainly this is how the use of hunting dogs is portrayed in classical and medieval art (Manaseryan and Antonian 2000). Dogs can still be useful in this way with bow hunting, as they are now in hunting with firearms (Brightman 1993:9), but there seems no reason to think that the bow would make them more useful than before.

Dogs and wolves are hunting carnivores, and their group hunting strategy may facilitate the development of a cooperative hunting relationship with humans. Clearly hunting has been a role frequently played by dogs in many human societies. This role is developed in its most elaborate form in the Middle Ages, when separate breeds of hunting dogs were developed for virtually every prey species (Clutton-Brock 1995:18; Salisbury 1994). This elaboration, of course, was in the context of sport hunting by the nobility rather than subsistence hunting. Only in sport hunting can the hunter afford to maintain such specialized hunting aids. It remains unclear whether aid in hunting was the sole or primary motivation for the domestication of dogs, but once domesticated, they have often been put to this use.

Archaeologically, it is often the case that some but not all dogs are buried. This might indicate that some are cherished pets and others are not. It may also indicate the value placed on especially good hunting dogs. Both in Nigeria (Ojoade 1990:217) and among the Kalam of highland New Guinea (Bulmer 1976:177), distinguished hunting dogs may be given funerary treatment analogous to that of a human warrior. The Kalam also honor extraordinary hunting dogs by creating a separate area in their display of trophy skulls for those killed by that particular dog (Bulmer 1967:180).

### HERDER

Although most authors have seen hunting aid as a prime motivation for dog domestication, Frederick Zeuner (1963:62) has suggested that dogs were domesticated as sheepdogs, or at least that they distinguished themselves as such early in the human–dog relationship, which began as tolerated scavenging. He points out that wolves engage in the same sort of behaviors, driving and separating sheep or other animals from the herd. Indeed, he sees this as the mechanism of sheep domestication, so that dogs in effect domesticated sheep.

The tasks of sheepdogs build on natural canine behaviors with, of course, the key difference that sheepdogs do not attack and kill the members of their flock. There is little evidence for the antiquity of sheepdogs and the use of dogs in herding, however. Certainly sheepdogs do not appear among the first specialized breeds, which are instead hunting dogs used by the elite (Clutton-Brock 1995:16–18).

Sheepdogs perform two main functions. One is that referred to by Zeuner, to help the shepherd control the flock; breeds such as collies are specialized in this task. This is a very late (medieval) development, beginning in Iceland (Planhol 1969). The other is to protect the flock from predators, especially wolves, and also human thieves (Digard 1980). Breeds specializing in this task, such as the Pyrenean sheepdog and the Komondor, have often been bred to resemble sheep themselves, leaping out to attack unsuspecting predators. Clearly this degree of specialization would not have been present among early dogs, but large, fierce dogs would be useful in protecting herds, among other things (Digard 1980; Planhol 1969).

Herding as performed by modern sheepdogs requires careful training and tight control by the shepherd. The demonstration and testing of these skills in sheep trials show that they are not simple and straightforward to achieve. In the absence of such careful training, it is not clear that the herding proclivities of dogs would have been especially useful. Wolves "herd" flocks to make them run and separate out the slow and weak animals; this is not usually the shepherd's goal. Thus herding sheep is more likely a later development, following on the notion of training dogs, rather than something that would have arisen unconsciously through symbiosis. In contrast, protecting flocks from predators requires far less training. The dog need only be taught not to harm the sheep and to treat them as its pack. This function may have greater antiquity, because once sheep and other herd animals were domesticated, the dogs in the community would in any case need to be taught not to harm them. Still, the association of Neolithic dogs with wild rather than

domestic fauna suggests that this was not the major role played by early
dogs (Bartosiewicz 1990). Nor could it have been the first role, because
dog domestication considerably precedes that of sheep and other herd
animals. By the Bronze Age, however, there is artistic evidence of the use
of dogs in herding as well as hunting (Manaseryan and Antonian 2000).

GUARD

The use of dogs as guards or watch animals may be underrated in early
human–dog relationships. This function requires little training: Once a
dog adopts a human group, it will defend it against outsiders – human
and animal. Their warnings of approaching predators or human raiders
may have been a major factor in making dogs seem worth having around
the camps of Paleolithic foragers. Later, as some people settled down
and acquired more possessions, dogs could guard against thieves as well.
Digard (1980) describes how Bakhtiari dogs mirror human segmentary
social structure: The dogs each defend their master's own tent, but when
strangers come into the camp, they band together against them. Jankuntjara dogs in Australia behave in the same way (Hamilton 1972). Harris
(1985:188) notes that dingoes, which do not serve many other purposes,
are highly valued as watchdogs. Guarding is the main function of dogs in
indigenous Andean societies (Wing 1977) and in villages in Zimbabwe
(Butler and Bingham 2000). For the Jankuntjara, "[t]his sentinel function of dogs is one of the main reasons given for keeping them – not only
against unwelcome strangers, or members of secret revenge expeditions,
but against all varieties of *mamu*, which are invisible to people but can
be seen by dogs" (Hamilton 1972:289).

   Tibetan nomads also keep dogs primarily as guardians of their possessions, from both outsiders and neighbors. Robert Ekvall (1963) describes
less explicit but equally important functions that the large numbers of
fierce guard dogs fulfill. By impeding movement around the otherwise
very open camps, they afford a degree of privacy, because no one can
approach another tent without one of the owners calling off their dogs.
The constant danger posed by the dogs isolates children from each other,
tending to encourage independent, individualistic personalities, and it
leaves the family dogs as the child's chief playmates, habituating the children to work with other species.

   Avraham Ronen (2004) argues that dogs were domesticated as guards.
Focusing on the sedentary Natufian foragers of the Levant as exhibiting

the earliest truly reliable evidence for dog domestication, he points out that hunting practices do not seem to have changed with the advent of dogs, and this is a period of broad-spectrum foraging rather than big game hunting in any case. Sedentism would have increased territoriality and concerns for property, however, making guards more desirable. He argues that barking would be an advantage for guarding, but a disadvantage for hunting. (Although surely this depends on the type of hunting; barking permits hunters to follow their dogs more easily as they bring an animal to bay.) Wolves and other wild canids do not bark as adults, limiting their utility as watch animals. The fox farm experiments, however, have shown that adult barking is likely to have occurred early in the domestication process (Trut 1999). Still, the first tame wolves would not have barked, so either there was another reason for taming them (or allowing them to tame themselves), or they were able to provide some guarding help even without the auditory alarm.

## SCAVENGER

Zooarchaeologists are acutely aware of the scavenging tendencies of dogs, as we encounter gnawed and digested bones and ponder what has been lost to canine activity. The scavenging opportunities provided by human settlements are often seen as a potential attraction to wolves that led to their habituation to humans and eventually their domestication (Isaac 1971; O'Connor 1997; Zeuner 1963). Scavenging may benefit the humans as well as the dogs. People may value the waste removal performed by scavengers at the same time that they hold the scavengers themselves in contempt (Bulmer 1976; Butler and Bingham 2000; Butler and du Toit 2002; Butler et al. 2004; Digard 1990:117; Leach 1964; Poplin 1986; Russell and Twiss in press; Tambiah 1969). As people become more settled, this scavenging becomes more important as a sanitary service. (Indeed, garbage collection companies often include the word "scavenger" in their name, and of course, our attitude toward garbage collectors carries the same ambivalence.) Pigs have often performed this function as well, and they have occupied a similarly ambiguous position.

## LABORER

In addition to hunting, herding, and guarding, dogs have performed various other kinds of labor in many societies. The sled dogs of the Arctic

are famous, and the use of dogs to pull travois in the North American
Plains is also reasonably well known (Brasser 1982; Morey 2010:92–4).
Saint Bernards are renowned for their mountain rescue work (Morris
2002:642–3). In the contemporary world, dogs are used to detect drugs
and other contraband, to locate people buried in collapsed structures or
hidden and buried human remains, to guide the blind and aid the deaf,
and for many other tasks. Where the labor of dogs is important, they tend
not to be eaten, like horses (Harris 1985:184, although cf. Park 1987).

Most of these uses are relatively late developments. Some of these
jobs depend on particular characteristics of dogs, especially their sense
of smell. The use of dogs for traction occurs, not surprisingly, in the
New World, where other suitable domesticates are lacking. Still, at least
in the case of Arctic sled dogs, this is not because there are no suitable
domesticable animals. In the Old World, reindeer are used to pull sleds
and sledges; caribou could have been domesticated in the same way, but
were not, leaving dogs to do the work. Given their relatively small size,
dogs are unlikely to be the first choice for draft animals when others are
available. They are also more expensive to keep, being higher on the food
chain than the ungulates more frequently used as pack and draft animals.
Although their omnivorous diet similar to that of humans means that
many dogs can survive at low cost to their masters, working dogs have
much reduced opportunities to scavenge and forage for themselves and
need to be fed. Pathologies suggest dogs may have been used for traction
in southeastern North America as early as the Archaic, however (Warren
2000). In contrast, the use of sled dogs in the Arctic is surprisingly late
(Morey 2010:chapter 6).

#### FOOD AND FUR SOURCE

Dogs were clearly not domesticated as a meat source. Again, their position high on the food chain makes them relatively expensive to feed
(Harris 1985:179). Although wolves were occasionally eaten in the past,
they were never a main game species, and they were probably hunted
mostly for their fur or, later, to protect domestic flocks. Likewise, early
dogs around the world have been eaten from time to time (e.g., Grant
1984:221; Halstead 1987:77; Tarcan et al. 2000), but in contrast to the
other early domesticates, most dogs were not eaten. Raising dogs for consumption appears to be a late development that occurs in places lacking
other meat sources, notably Mesoamerica, the Caribbean, and the Pacific

islands (Clutton-Brock and Hammond 1994; Harris 1985:179–82, 186; Rainbird 1993; Wing 1978, 1984). Lynn Snyder (1991) marshals considerable ethnographic evidence for frequent dog consumption by many Native North American groups, arguing from cut mark evidence that this was also true at the protohistoric Gray site and the prehistoric (ca. 1000 BP) Packei site, both in Nebraska. She suggests that dogs would have been a valuable source of meat and fat during the lean period in the late winter and early spring. At these sites and at Late Bronze Age Hauterive-Champréveyres in Switzerland (Studer 1988) dog bones are treated identically to those of consumed ungulates, indicating that at least some dogs were raised specifically for meat. We should not assume that in those places where dog was eaten occasionally it was a famine food. In contemporary Nigeria some consider it a delicacy (Ojoade 1990). The situation may have been similar in Iron Age Europe, where dogs were sometimes eaten and occasionally placed in human graves as food offerings (Galik 2000; Green 1992:111–13).

Not only have dogs been eaten in many places but they have also formed the centerpiece of feasts. This has occurred both where they are reared as a significant meat source and where they are eaten only occasionally, perhaps solely or primarily in the context of feasts and sacrifices. Ethnographically, dog feasts are known from North America (Comba 1991; Fenton 1978; Gilmore 1933; Hayden 1990; Snyder 1991), Mesoamerica (Pohl and Feldman 1982; Wing 1984), Indonesia (Adams 2004), and Polynesia (Kirch 2001; Kolb 1999). For the most part, archaeological evidence of feasting on dogs has been sought only where there is ethnographic or historical attestation of this practice. Most of the work has been in Mesoamerica (Guillén 1998:281; Masson 1999; Pohl 1991; Wing 1984). Mary Pohl (1991; Pohl and Feldman 1982) has combined ethnohistorical and archaeological evidence to argue that raising dogs (and tame deer) was an important part of Mayan women's work and that this labor and the feasts it enabled served to underwrite power relations in the Formative period, although the power was largely appropriated by men.

Hayden (1990, 1995a), drawing heavily on ethnographic accounts of societies on the Northwest coast of North America, argues that dogs were domesticated as a meat source not for daily consumption, but specifically for feasts (see Chapter 6, *Models of Origins*). On the whole, it seems more plausible that one would initially domesticate valued food species – that is, herbivores – for feasting. In the beginning, raising and fattening these animals would be a sufficient intensification of labor to add value. It is more likely later, after domestic animals became a common food source, that raising dogs for feasts would make a stronger statement of added value through labor investment.

In fact, however, dogs seem to have been used as feasting food, and especially to have been raised specifically for feasts, primarily in areas where they were the only domestic animal. Fiddes (1991:138–41) notes that if value had only to do with scarcity and labor investment, then carnivore meat would be the most highly valued. Yet it is distinctly avoided, and often tabooed, in many societies. He suggests that this is because carnivores occupy a position in the food chain too similar to ours. They are seen as being too close to us, so that eating them smacks of cannibalism. Clearly, however, this is not a universal perception, because not only dogs but also certain other carnivores such as raccoons have been eaten with some frequency.

Although we do not think of dog fur or dog hides as particularly valuable, these have been used and highly esteemed in some cases. Wolf fur is prized, so the first dogs would have had desirable fur. An Iron Age human burial in France contained, among other things, a complete but skinned (as indicated by cut marks) young dog (Green 1992:113). In this case, the skin may have been displayed over the grave or elsewhere. In contrast, a Romano-British child burial at Asthall is wrapped in a dog-skin shroud, as evidenced by the articulated paws (Booth et al. 1996). Similarly, in the American Southwest at least two dog burials lack tails, perhaps a result of skinning, and several lack heads, which may have been used in ritual contexts elsewhere (Hill 2000:379–86).

I have often found skinning cuts on Neolithic dog bones from refuse deposits. At Opovo, dogs have more skinning cut marks than any other taxon, accounting for 26% of skinning cuts although they form only about 3% of the identified mammals. Dog heads have been found carefully placed in pits and as foundation deposits under houses (Russell 1993:166–7, 359). It is thus possible that dog skins were used in rituals. This may also have been the case at Krasno-Samarskoe, a Late Bronze Age settlement on the edge of the Russian steppe zone, where the assemblage has an extraordinarily high proportion of dogs. The body part distribution of the Krasno-Samarskoe dogs is heavily skewed toward heads and feet, which suggests that these are chiefly dog skins. Only part of the site has been excavated, because most of it is now under an artificial lake, so this is very likely an area of the site where dog skins were processed or stored. Either dog skins were valued for their fur or leather, apparently above other animals available, or there is again a substantial amount of ritual activity involving dog skins. Because there is also evidence of dog sacrifice and ritual feasting, ritual use seems quite likely (Anthony et al. 2005).

Thus although not primarily a food animal, in some places dogs have been a major meat source. In others, people have occasionally eaten them as famine food, as delicacies, or as ritual feasts. Dog hides have also been valued at times, in some cases probably as ritual paraphernalia, but in others perhaps for their fur. Dog fur may have been a cheap substitute for other pelts, or possibly it was prized for certain purposes. I do not know of any breeds developed for their pelts, but in cases such as Krasno-Samarskoe, such selection should be considered a possibility. A breed of woolly dogs whose fur was shorn to make precious blankets once existed on the North American Northwest Coast, however (Barsh et al. 2006).

## SYMBOL

Man's best friend has long been a potent symbol. The position of the dog as a tame carnivore; a domestic animal not raised for food; an omnivore that eats human food and scavenges human waste, including feces; and a conspirator with humans in the killing and control of other animals has rendered it symbolically ambiguous. This ambiguity may be expressed in terms of liminal roles, mediating between life and death, for instance. Or it may be manifested in both positive and negative symbolism associated with dogs, often within the same culture. This is the case in the English-speaking world, for example, where we can speak of dogged determination, man's best friend, bitchiness, a dogsbody, dog-eat-dog worlds, a dog's life, going to the dogs, a top dog, to treat someone like a dog, and to be in the doghouse.

A Nigerian myth depicts dogs as allying themselves with humans against the other animals (Ojoade 1990:215). In their classic works on animal symbolism, Leach (1964) and Tambiah (1969) both emphasize that dogs tend to be tabooed as food because they are in an ambiguous, intermediate position between human and animal, wild and tame. Leach makes an analogy between consumption taboos and incest taboos, where dogs are like siblings: too close to marry or to eat. Tambiah notes some manifestations of this status among Thai villagers. Because dogs are perceived as ignoring age distinctions and committing incest themselves, a ritual that corrects the deficiency when the husband is not, as required, the classificatory older brother of the wife involves the couple eating rice together from a tortoise shell (symbolizing the vagina) "like dogs." The Thai do not eat dogs because of their close position in the house and because they are considered unclean. They also do not eat wolves, which are seen as the wild counterpart of dogs.

Dogs are often associated with death, and particularly with mediating between life and death. Cerberus is an obvious example from the western tradition. Schwabe (1994:47–8) suggests that in the ancient Near East this association originated in a fear of being eaten by dogs after death, which evolved into the notion that dogs can ward off or even reverse death. This concept is most developed among the Zoroastrians, who believed that the body must be eaten by a dog to free the soul. Through time, this belief gradually became attenuated such that it sufficed merely for the body to be breached by a dog, and later simply for a dog to look at the corpse. As a result, Persians, in contrast to most Near Eastern peoples, held dogs in high esteem, and dogs became associated with healing. In Nigeria dogs and dog meat have medicinal and magical value – partly curative, partly aphrodisiac (connected to the association of dogs with male sexuality, and female dogs with female fertility). Because they can see spirits invisible to people, dogs can also signal a person's impending death (Ojoade 1990).

Archaeologically, dogs often appear in connection with human death. Wing (1984:228) proposes that the presence of dogs and dog figurines in human burials in Colima, Mexico, indicates that dogs played the role of spirit guide, ushering people into the afterlife. Collins (1991b:217) makes a similar suggestion for the Channel Islands. Dogs dominate the animal figurines at middle Preclassic Chalcatzingo (Guillén 1998:280). At this period, animal and human figurines have moved from their earlier mortuary context to what Ann Guillén believes is use in life-cycle rituals, followed by discard in middens. This might mean that the spirit guide role of dogs was extended from death to life. Jones (1998) notes that the various animal remains found in Neolithic communal tombs on Orkney are treated in different ways. Dog remains are explicitly associated with human remains and get special treatment; they are not simply offerings of meat. He suggests that dogs were equated with people in these burials.

Dogs and horses are found in human burials in the Eurasian steppe zone in numerous Bronze and Iron Age kurgans (Anthony 2007).

In Europe, dog remains are also found in various kinds of "special deposits" apart from burials. I have already noted the foundation deposits at Neolithic Opovo. In Anatolia, there is also some evidence that dog heads, complete with mandibles, were kept or displayed in houses at Çatalhöyük (Russell and Martin 2005:81–2). Dog bones, and especially heads, are similarly placed uneaten in pits at Late Bronze Age Apalle in Sweden. At first, these deposits are on the edge of the settlement, perhaps guarding the village. In the later phases they are buried near the doorways of individual houses, part of a changing use of space that locates more activities inside or directly associated with individual houses rather than in shared public space (Ullén 1994:257–8, and see Chapter 3, *Foundation Deposits*, for a discussion of similar burials at Botai in Kazakhstan).

Dog bones play a minor role in what Richards and Thomas (1984) have termed "structured deposition" in the British Neolithic (see Chapter 3, *Ritual Treatment of Animal Remains*). Along with horses and most wild fauna, they are spatially segregated at Durrington Walls in opposition to deposits of cattle and wild boar (Richards and Thomas 1984:214). The association of dogs and horses in special deposits is more pronounced in the British Iron Age. At sites such as Danebury, pits used initially for grain storage are filled with special deposits, including whole or partial animals. Horses and dogs figure prominently among these, often together. These remains have been interpreted as offerings to chthonic deities in whose care the precious seed grain is placed, suggesting a particular association of dogs with the earth (Cunliffe 1992; Grant 1984; Green 1992:100–3; Hill 1996). This recurrent association of offerings of horses and dogs probably indicates that killing these animals, which held special status among domestic animals in that they were not usually eaten and were perhaps regarded as companions, made a strong symbolic statement in a way that slaughtering a food animal would not. These symbolically charged dog slaughters would often occur in the context of sacrifice, as discussed in Chapter 3 (*Sacrifice and Ritual Killing*).

The multiple roles of dogs enable a wide range of dog symbolism. The ethnographic record reveals the breadth of these possibilities. Many of these meanings, such as the medicinal and aphrodisiac uses of dog products, would be difficult to approach archaeologically except, perhaps, in conditions of direct historical continuity (but see Chapter 9, *Medicinal*

*Uses*). One recurring theme, however, is the equivalence of dogs and humans that results from their close companionship and the similarities in diet and social system. This is expressed on the one hand in sacrifice, where dogs may constitute a substitute for a (potential) human victim, and on the other hand in taboos, where the closeness of dogs to humans is signified through the metaphors of incest and cannibalism. There do seem to be manifestations of these attitudes in archaeological remains (e.g., Holt 1996).

### PARIAH

For some cultures, dogs are strongly identified as unclean, as a result of their enthusiasm for eating garbage and excrement, and perhaps also because of their uncomfortable resemblance to humans; this can be expressed as taboos on eating dogs (Brightman 1993:133; Tambiah 1969). For instance, the Kalam do not eat dogs because they eat garbage and occasionally break into graves, and because their blood and bones are harmful to taro (Bulmer 1976:172).

Archaeologically, we can see whether or not dogs were eaten. When they are not, it is harder to determine why, but the larger picture of the treatment of dogs may provide some illumination. Burials and special treatment of dog remains may indicate an attitude more of closeness than of impurity, although the two are not necessarily completely separate. There may be other clues as well. At Çatalhöyük, dog gnawing is absent on bones from indoor deposits that are associated with the use phase of the houses (Russell and Martin 2005:41–2). Dogs were apparently not permitted in houses while they were occupied; conversely, carnivore ravaging of faunal remains is most pronounced in midden deposits on the edge of the settlement, where dogs were less disturbed. This does not necessarily mean that dogs were considered unclean, but does suggest that their status was closer to pariah than pet.

There are other ways in which dogs are marked as unclean. Some ethnographically known groups feel that it is disrespectful to game animals to allow their remains, especially the bones, to be eaten by dogs (see Chapter 3, *Respecting the Hunted*). Thus lack of gnawing, especially on bones of the primary game species, might indicate a view of dogs as polluting, as might the absence of key body parts that were disposed of elsewhere to keep them from the dogs.

Beyond the symbolic denigration of being labeled as unclean, dogs have often been physically abused. Robert Park (1987) documents extensive evidence of trauma resulting from blows to the head among Thule culture dogs from Canada's Devon Island, and relates this to ethnographic evidence for disciplining dogs by beating them. In my experience such facial trauma, although rare in other taxa, is relatively common in prehistoric dogs (Bartelle et al. 2010; Hill 2000; Russell 1993:167–8, 372–7; Warren 2000). Although some of these injuries may have been received during their service in hunting large animals, most are probably the result of human violence. At Colima in Mexico, human burials contain a number of dogs and raccoons, many of which suffered broken canines and incisors in life (Wing 1984:231–2). It is unclear whether this is a deliberate mutilation for some unknown purpose or the result of frequent kicks in the teeth.

Thus despite the picture of harmony and cooperation painted by symbiotic models of dog domestication, in many places in the past, as in the present, a dog's life was not easy. Some dogs may have been well-loved companions or treasured hunting fellows, but many lurked on the edges of human settlements and were greeted with a hurled stone or a kick in the teeth when they ventured too close to people.

SPECIAL CASE

Dogs stand out as a special case in human–animal relations for several reasons. First, although other animals have filled each of the roles played by dogs, none has filled all of them. With the exception of riding (and young children sometimes ride large dogs) and dairy, it is hard to think of an animal role in human society that dogs have not occupied. Second, our current western tendency to think of dogs as pets leads to puzzlement and horror when confronted with some aspects of human–dog relations in other times and places. Third, the very closeness of the human–dog relationship has often been uncomfortable. There is a deep ambivalence toward an animal that threatens to blur or cross the human–animal boundary by living like a quasi-human.

This ambivalence is clear in the ethnographic record. For example, the Kalam bury the best hunting dogs like human warriors, but the only care afforded to the bodies of ordinary dogs is to make sure their polluting influence does not come in contact with gardens (Bulmer 1976). Among the Cree, dogs were once the center of feasts and sacrifice, but became inedible in the 19th century. This is related to the beginning of their use as draft animals, but builds on preexisting notions. Although dogs were seen as the most socialized animal, they were also regarded as dirty because they eat excrement and insult the bones of game animals. As elsewhere, dogs were invoked in insulting epithets applied to people. Thus, the potential to define dogs as polluting and therefore inedible was already present, and their new value as living labor merely tipped the balance (Brightman 1993:184).

Archaeologically, too, this ambivalence is apparent. It is quite common to find some dogs carefully buried, others disposed of carelessly, and a few eaten, all at the same site. This situation is rarely encountered with other taxa. Thus contextual analysis is particularly necessary in assessing the roles of dogs, which are likely to be multiple even within a single society. Indeed, dogs and the wolves from which they were domesticated come close to embodying the entire spectrum of human–animal relationships.

8

# Animal wealth

> Everywhere you look, in villages or the wilds of New Guinea, you see pigs (*Sus scrofa papuensis*). Alive, they clean up village garbage, work the soil of abandoned gardens and constitute a "food reserve on the hoof" (Vayda et al. 1961). They are exchanged by families or groups to acquire wives, dependents and prestige, but also to compensate for a death or to vie in peaceful gift-giving contests. Once killed, their meat becomes the ceremonial meal *par excellence*. Far from being a mere source of food, then, pigs are a universal, highly charged symbolic object that stands at the heart of a complex web of social relations. (Lemonnier 1993:126)

The circumstances of zooarchaeology, in which we study the remains of dead animals, indeed most often the remains of animals that have been eaten, tend to blind us to the value of living animals (Bogucki 1993:492). We see animals as only protein and calories, whereas in some cases their meat may have been their least important contribution to human society. In many ethnographically and historically known societies, domestic animals have functioned as wealth, and sometimes as the principal form of wealth. Pastoral societies are built around this animal wealth, and relationships are expressed in the medium of animals. Animal wealth often plays an important role in agricultural societies as well.

Animal wealth has played a large role in archaeological interpretation where ethnohistorical evidence attests to its importance, as in southern Africa. Elsewhere, it is only beginning to figure into archaeological models, which for the most part treat animals only as packages of meat. This approach reflects a larger tendency in archaeology to conflate "economy" with "subsistence" (Bogucki 1993:493). In this chapter I argue that the value of live animals as wealth must be considered anywhere there are domestic animals. Animal wealth may have been of crucial importance in the spread of agriculture and the emergence of inequality. Nowhere is it more critical to put flesh on the bones.

## The emergence of animal wealth

Is animal property necessarily animal wealth? Can we assume that as soon as animals are domesticated they act as wealth? In some sense, any property is a form of wealth. Yet domestic animals, even domestic herd animals, do not invariably form the central repository of wealth and the idiom of exchange and social relationships. In modern western society, for example, livestock are just one more form of commodity. Money, based until recently on precious metals, is the fundamental form of wealth for us. Because wild animals are not property and therefore do not function as wealth, it is unlikely that animal wealth was the original motivation for animal domestication (Bökönyi 1989:24). Thus the first domestic animals would not have formed wealth, and we must explore the process through which they took on this value.

### THE VALORIZATION OF ANIMAL WEALTH

Pierre Lemonnier (1993:136) defines wealth as things that can be reexchanged. Thus food consumed in a feast may create debts and build relationships (see Chapter 9, *Feasting*), but it does not constitute wealth. In contrast, live pigs exchanged at such events do, if they are widely valued such that they can be exchanged again elsewhere. To function as wealth, animals must have a value in themselves beyond their nutritional benefit. Sherratt (1982:20) argues that this happens when herders expand into new areas and have a great need for livestock to establish their herds. This demand, ultimately based in food value, transforms domestic animals into commodities. Well-established herders who can export livestock thus acquire substantial wealth in exchange. Once herds become established in the new settlements, demand will drop and livestock will cease to have special value.

In this model, livestock are just another commodity, exchanged primarily for other goods. In ethnographically known examples of animal wealth, certain animals have special value distinct from other goods, and they are primarily exchanged for each other or for rights to human labor and reproduction. Although these animals are used for subsistence, their primary value is as a store of wealth, which actually interferes with the maximization of nutritional value (Kelly 1985; Schneider 1979, 1980).

It is more useful to think in terms of farmers seeking utility – that is, a wide range of benefits – from animals rather than simply seeking food (Schneider 1979:65).

Ingold (1980:224–7) argues that in societies characterized by the domestic mode of production – which in its classic formulation involves the organization of production and the accumulation of wealth at the household level, and chronic underproduction (Sahlins 1972) – forms of wealth must conform to the following principles:

1) They must provide subsistence or produce commodities exchangeable for subsistence items.
2) They must reproduce themselves (i.e., they must be living plants or animals); otherwise it would require the production of surplus to accumulate them.
3) To allocate this natural increase, the owners must be able to trace the parentage of the offspring. This criterion rules out plants and lower animals, and it necessitates relatively close observation and control of an animal herd.
4) They must be K-selected (few offspring with large parental investment) rather than r-selected (many offspring with low parental investment) species, because in r-selected species population increase is limited chiefly by the environment. Plants do not function well as wealth because even if land is freely available and one can achieve a large increase through planting more, this is at the cost of a proportional increase in labor input. Once one reaches the limits of available labor, further expansion is impossible.
5) To work as wealth, animals must tolerate crowding; that is, they must be social, thereby effectively limiting animal wealth to certain ungulate species.
6) They must not compete directly for human food. This eliminates pigs, and any barnyard animal (whether or not the same species can work as wealth in a herding situation), because people must raise or gather fodder for them, again creating limitations due to the availability of labor.
7) They must be mobile so that they can move to new pastures, or the herd size will be limited by the local grazing.

One could probably challenge the necessity of some of these criteria, but they do demonstrate why certain animals have functioned so well as wealth. For Ingold, as for Sherratt, the value of animal wealth is ultimately based on subsistence, even if this valorization causes conflicts with the optimal subsistence use of the animals. "The fact that cattle are valued for other than subsistence reasons, and that this valuation is associated with a variety of nonsubsistence uses, does not exclude their use to support life" (Schneider 1957:297).

Two aspects of Ingold's model need to be addressed. First, he specifically excludes pigs from functioning as wealth, but others have argued that pigs do form wealth in parts of New Guinea (Kahn 1986; Lemonnier 1993; Wiessner 2001). New Guinea pig wealth works somewhat differently from, for example, cattle wealth, however. The value of the pigs is related much more to their use in feasting (see Chapter 9, *Feasting*), so that large populations of pigs are built up only to be consumed. As we see later, this is a rather different attitude from that held by the owners of cattle wealth. Nevertheless, cattle that form wealth are also sacrificed and provide the center of feasts, and New Guinea pigs are exchanged when alive, with patron–client relations similar to those associated with cattle. Live pigs are used as bridewealth, to pay fines, and to cement social relations. So pigs can be wealth, but pig wealth is more limited than wealth in herd animals.

The valorization of New Guinean pigs is tied to their ability to control human female reproduction, and this depends on a symbolic linkage with women. Wamiran women raise pigs and men exchange them, mostly with members of their wives' lineages. This is not bridewealth because the Wamirans are matrilineal, so the husbands do not have rights to their children. It does, however, mitigate the inherent imbalance between wife-givers and wife-takers. Pigs are regarded as surrogate women: Like women, they possess natural fertility and supply food, qualities on which men depend. Through the exchange of pigs, men can symbolically control the reproductive powers of women, which in actuality are beyond their possession (Kahn 1986:75–81). Likewise for the Great Man societies of southern New Guinea, domestic pigs only work as wealth that can be used for bridewealth and blood money because they are perceived as an embodiment of life force as a result of their intense socialization through the labor of women: "In this way, an animal that, in its wild state, symbolizes strength and maleness is transformed into an item of wealth, and above all wealth recognized as a life-substitute, or 'token of life,' suitable for compensation and exchange, when domesticated by female labor – and particularly when it reproduces in captivity" (Lemonnier 1993:144).

Ingold also invokes the inherent underproduction of the domestic mode of production (DMP). As Marshall Sahlins (1972) framed the DMP, self-sufficient households have little incentive to produce a surplus, so they tend to underproduce in capitalist terms. However, when animals become wealth, this wealth is in itself a motivation to produce a surplus and can thus overcome the underproduction of the DMP. The desire for animal wealth impels not only pastoralists to increase their herds but also farmers to grow more grain to exchange for cattle: "If cattle are convertible into most other things of value . . . and if grain is not so easily convertible, then it follows that the prudent farmer, when he can, will convert his grain into livestock. And it also follows that the farmer, to some extent at least, is not producing grain to feed himself and his family but for the purpose of obtaining livestock, which in turn are not produced for food" (Schneider 1979:65). Similarly, in New Guinea, where there is a wide range of intensity in both agricultural and pig-rearing practices, in those areas where pigs are more important as wealth, not only pig husbandry but also plant cultivation are more intense than elsewhere (Lemonnier 1993; Rosman and Rubel 1989).

The workings of animal wealth have been studied most thoroughly in eastern and southern Africa, where the "cattle complex" (Herskovits 1926) is one of the classic objects of anthropology. The cattle complex attracted attention because the peoples of much of sub-Saharan Africa treated cattle in a way that European colonial settlers and administrators found irrational: They did not maximize protein and calorie production, they overgrazed pasture, and they were emotionally bonded with their cattle. One of the major contributions of anthropology has been to explain how this behavior is in fact completely rational given the valorization of cattle in these societies.

To maximize sustained meat production, the best approach is a selective cull that keeps the herd size relatively small while maintaining a high offtake: the "rational" course in the eyes of the beef-eating European colonists. However, this is not the goal for African herders, because for pastoralists food production is wealth destruction (Ingold 1980:87). Rather, they aim to maximize the size of the herd, because living cattle have a social as well as a subsistence value (Comaroff and Comaroff 1991; Kelly 1985:112). Cattle are central to the social and economic functioning of these societies. They are used to pay fines, including blood money that prevents feuds. They are used to create and maintain non-kin relations (stock associateships) that provide crucial ties beyond the family and often beyond the local community. In hard times, they can be exchanged for grain and other necessities. Most importantly, they are required for bridewealth (see the later discussion), and hence the very reproduction of individuals and society (Bonte 1995; Comaroff and Comaroff 1991; Galaty 1989; Hakansson 1994; Ingold 1980; Kelly 1985; Schneider 1957, 1979, 1980). In southern Africa particularly, cattle exchanges were also important vehicles of hierarchical relations (Kuper 1982). Thus for African herders to adopt what Europeans consider "rational" practices, they "would have to stop thinking of animals as repositories of value and think of them only as so much hamburger on the hoof" (Schneider 1980:217).

Cattle are important not only as stores of value for the current generation but also as property that can be passed to the next: "Cattle are . . . the major goods handed down through inheritance from the ancestors, and a man's herd is regarded as the property of the family ancestors" (Kuper 1982:15). They enable the continuation of the lineage both through bridewealth and through inheritance.

Cattle build connections among people: among contemporaries through marriage and stock associateships, across generations, and between the living and dead through inheritance. In turn people feel connected to cattle as well as through them. Although this love of cattle may vaguely resemble our caricature of the miser fondling his or her bags of money, clearly the fact that cattle are both wealth and sentient beings enables a much stronger emotional tie. African herders speak of their cattle as beautiful, they take pleasure in counting them, and they may name people after cattle (Abbink 2003; Bonte 1995; Evans-Pritchard 1940; Galaty 1989; Herskovits 1926; Schneider 1957).

Large stock such as cattle carry the primary wealth value. Smaller stock such as sheep and goats may be kept as insurance, for meat, and as a vehicle for trading up to large stock, but do not hold the same value, either economically or symbolically and emotionally. To some extent they may be able to substitute for cattle, but small stock are always second best (Ingold 1980:186; Kuper 1982:12; Schneider 1957). Thus small stock are regarded in a more utilitarian manner that more closely resembles western, market-driven attitudes.

Animal wealth has received the most study among pastoralists, whose entire socioeconomic system is centered on it. However, wealth in animals is not limited to pastoralists. In much of Africa, cattle are important in agricultural societies precisely for their wealth value, although they have little dietary significance (Bloch 1985; Schneider 1957:298). Groups such as the Kipsigis keep many cattle in prime farmland. "It cannot simply be argued that these people kept cattle because this is nutritionally the maximizing course, especially when it is considered that the cost of producing a hundred calories of beef is much higher than an equivalent amount of calories from crops" (Schneider 1979:63).

> As in most other eastern and southern African societies, [among the Gusii] cattle (and to a lesser extent goats and sheep) played a central social and economic role. Cattle served as prestige goods which were used to establish social relationships, primarily as bridewealth in marriage, but also to create clientage and to compensate for crimes. In the establishment of kinship and affinal ties, cattle were also exchangeable for persons and for rights in persons. In addition, cattle were repositories of wealth, a form of capital which grew through proper husbandry, and a medium of exchange for most other goods from goats to grain and craft products. Although used in exchange for food at times of famine, cattle among the Gusii and other agricultural peoples in the Kenya highlands were marginal to subsistence (Hakansson 1994:258).

Although they are unimportant as sources of milk or meat, the social value of cattle has major implications for the Gusii economy. The need for cattle as wealth has necessitated higher agricultural production (and higher labor input) to acquire them, which in turn has had a major effect on the settlement pattern and the demographic structure. Thus the socially defined need for animal wealth can be a significant stimulus to intensification of production and production for exchange (Hakansson 1994:270–1).

Although the African cattle complex may be an extreme case of the importance of animal wealth, it is certainly not unique. In many parts of both the Old and New Worlds, ethnography, ethnohistory, and history describe the similar operation of animal wealth systems, based on cattle, water buffalo, camels, horses, reindeer, pigs, sheep, goats, or llamas (e.g., Brotherston 1989; Forde 1963; Green 1992; Hoskins 1993; Ingold 1980; Lemonnier 1993; Mace and Houston 1989; Parkes 1987). Again, the animal wealth belongs in some cases to pastoralists, in others to mixed farmers. It is apparently very common for domestic animals to function as wealth. Not only are they well suited to it, as Ingold points out, but also the presence of property that can reproduce itself may render wealth and its accumulation a relevant concept where it has not been before. That is, domestic animals may create wealth not only in the particular sense for their individual owners but also may in large measure create the idea of Wealth. Clearly the differentiation between rich and poor constitutes a revolution in social relations and the organization of production.

Of course, animal wealth is not the only possible kind of wealth, and animal domestication does not mark the beginning of social differentiation. Earlier societies possessed prestige goods that no doubt served as status markers. Societies in Mesoamerica and North America developed substantial wealth differentiation with few or no animal domesticates other than dogs. Still, domestic animals seem to have played a large role in the development of inequality in many cases. In the Near East, we begin to see differentiation in household wealth in the PPNB, the time of animal domestication (Bar-Yosef and Bar-Yosef Mayer 2002; Garfinkel 1987).

Before money and before metals, the primary competing form of wealth would be land. Although foragers may defend territories and particular resources, for the most part land becomes wealth only with the advent of agriculture. Given that plant domestication precedes the domestication of herd animals, it might seem that wealth in land would precede animal wealth and be more fundamental for farming communities. However, in the circumstances in which most early farmers found themselves, where labor rather than land was the limiting factor in agricultural production, wealth in land may be less important (Bogucki 1988). When animals function as bridewealth, however, they address the shortage of labor.

### Animals as money and capital

The analogy between pastoral wealth and capital has been made often, mainly for the sake of endowing capital with that property of natural increase found in living things. This naturalization of a social phenomenon has, with an irony that Marx would have relished, been turned on its head by anthropologists who profess to apply the stereotypes of modern capitalism to an illumination of pastoral production (Hart and Sperling 1987:330–1).

If animals are wealth, are they therefore a form of money, and are herders capitalists? Certainly there are points of resemblance. Herd animals accumulate "interest" when they are not "spent"; indeed the term for interest on loans and for animal offspring was the same in classical Greek, just as Latin had the same word for money and herd, and "cattle" is etymologically related to "capital" (Hart and Sperling 1987:327; Ingold 1980:229). In contrast to grain agriculture, this increase in herd size does not require the investment of substantially more labor (Schneider 1979:102). Rich pastoralists tend to get richer (it takes money to make money) not only because they can afford not to eat or trade away a large proportion of their cattle but also because they can afford to invest more milk in calves (Grandin 1988). The "profit" derived from the increase of herds and the value placed on the accumulation of individual animal wealth have convinced some (e.g., Paine 1971) that herders are capitalists.

Whether this is the case depends on the definition of capital. If capital is anything that is set aside from immediate consumption, acts as a means of production, and can increase when not expended, then cattle used as wealth surely qualify. However, if we view capital in Marxist terms as tied to particular social relations of exploitation, in which the fetishization of the commodity conceals the appropriation of other people's labor (Marx 1936[1890]), cattle wealth cannot be considered capital. Herders (apart from truly capitalist modern ranchers) do not behave as capitalists in all respects. Pastoralists who are involved in market economies sell animals to support their families; that is, to bring in a set amount of income with minimal diminution of their herds. This means that they sell more animals when prices are low and fewer when prices are high, or they may refrain from selling off their herds in the face of a devastating epidemic or drought; clearly they are not motivated primarily by capitalist profit (Ferguson 1985; Ingold 1980:231–4). The patron–client relations often associated with animal wealth (see the later discussion) are unequal, but differ from capitalist wage exploitation in that they occur within the household and kin (or fictive kin) relations, not between classes. Thus although animal wealth may be capital, herders are not capitalists.

Similarly, whether African cattle and other animal wealth can be viewed as a form of money depends on one's definition. Harold Schneider (1957, 1979, 1980), who has argued this position most strongly, sees money as something that acts as a medium of exchange, a store of value, and a unit of account (Schneider 1980:213). The value of a monetary unit, in this case cattle, is standardized through exchange, and other values fluctuate against it (Schneider 1979:99). Others have argued that animals are too inherently variable (by age, sex, etc.) to serve as such a standardized unit and that the noncapitalistic logic of herders invalidates the construction of cattle as money (Hart and Sperling 1987:335). However, it is worth exploring how herding practices are transformed when animals take on monetary/wealth value.

In Schneider's (1980:213) view, African cattle become money because they are the commodity for which there is the broadest demand and so become the standard for all other commodities: "When a good is valued sufficiently to take on monetary characteristics . . . managers of that wealth will conduct management strategies differently than if it were merely a commodity, if the return for managing it as a financial asset is greater than managing it for other, subsistence, reasons" (Schneider 1979:226). People will try to accumulate as much money/cattle as possible; they will invest cattle by loaning them to others with interest, usually paid in calves. A key point is that "[c]attle used as money are less useful as food or milk producers" (Schneider 1979:101). That is, the decisions made on the basis of investing cattle as money are not the same as the decisions made to maximize meat or milk production. Hence the apparent irrationality of African herders: They are proceeding from a different set of premises from western farmers.

If cattle or other large stock are money, small stock such as sheep and goat tend to function as small change (Schneider 1957, 1979). Whereas cattle (or camels, horses, etc.) are the real repository of value, small stock can be used for lesser transactions, and several goats can be exchanged for a cow.

Although thinking of African cattle as money is useful in understanding the actions of their herders, there are limits to this analogy. Cattle are usually not exchangeable in all contexts and for all goods; indeed, their role as bridewealth is enhanced by the difficulty of acquiring them in other ways (Goody 1973:5). This does not necessarily invalidate viewing cattle as money. After all, even in our highly monetized society, some things cannot or should not be bought and sold for money, such as human beings. However, cattle serve as money in a more limited fashion than cash or metals. Herders may behave more as though cattle were money than as though they were food sources, but are not driven solely by the profit motive. Cattle in fact reproduce fairly slowly, with one cow producing three female offspring over its roughly 12-year lifespan in the best of circumstances (Hart and Sperling 1987:334). If herders really wanted to increase their herd size as much as possible, they would be better off with the more quickly reproducing small stock. They recognize this by shifting the balance toward small stock when their herds of large stock have become dangerously small. Yet small stock do not carry the same value, even though they can be exchanged for large stock. Cattle and other large stock have value in themselves. Moreover, despite their wealth value, cattle remain sources of food, and the herders cannot ignore this subsistence value. It is thus better to speak of cattle as wealth rather than money.

### *Implications for herding strategies*

When cattle or other animals are used as wealth, herding decisions are made differently from when they are simply a source of food. First, if one wishes to optimize meat production, one will select for large animals, and hence fewer animals on any given amount of pasture land. Yet animals used as wealth are valued as units, "just as Westerners value a dollar as a unit and ignore whether it is wrinkled or torn" (Schneider 1980:217). Because the object is not to maximize beef but to maximize the number of animals, the cattle are likely to become smaller and may not be in prime condition due to overstocking (Cranstone 1969; Hesse 1984; Isaac 1971; Schneider 1980). For example, although the Nuer population was not food-limited, at least before the advent of rinderpest, their cattle population was always at the limit of available pasture. They could easily have brought this situation into balance by slaughtering cattle for beef, but they did not do so because the cattle had social value for bridewealth and other payments (Kelly 1985:103–12).

Second, when cattle are wealth, their owners are reluctant to slaughter them. Thus people may keep large numbers of cattle but rarely kill and eat them, as Tacitus indicates for the Celts (Green 1992:14). When an animal with this kind of value is killed, it is likely to be a major event – the center of a feast and probably regarded as a sacrifice.

Third, animals may not be killed or sold at the optimum time for meat or milk production, because there are other more important considerations: "[C]attle used as money will not be sold when they reach optimal feeder weight but will be kept to full maturity and until they can be used to effect an optimal exchange for grain, a wife, or political gain"

(Schneider 1980:217). Generally speaking, this means culling animals at a later age than would be predicted on the basis of optimization for meat or milk. In addition, large horns or tusks may add to the value of the animal, so that old, tough animals are preferred so these impressive structures can be displayed at the feast and often for years afterward (Hoskins 1993; Jolly 1984; Layard 1942).

## Wealth as a motivation for herding

Wealth is unlikely to have been a motivation for the original domestication of animals, because animals can only become wealth after they are domesticated. However, once they have become so for some people, the wealth value of animals may induce others to herd. We have already seen that some agricultural groups keep cattle primarily for their wealth value, and boost their agricultural production to do so (see earlier section, *The Valorization of Animal Wealth*).

In most of southern and eastern Africa, agriculture plays a more important role in subsistence, but cattle herding carries greater prestige and symbolic value. Moreover, there is a strong gender link, with cattle and herding associated with men, agriculture with women. This is also true of the Kalasha and other agropastoralists in South and Central Asia (Parkes 1987). Where this gendered division of labor is less strong and men participate more fully in agriculture, cattle carry less prestige value. This has obvious parallels to the association of hunting with men and gathering with women among foragers (see Chapter 4, *Motivations for Hunting*), and this linkage is made explicit in these agropastoral societies. Gathering of wild foods is considered a female activity, and wild plant foods are devalued as pauper's fare. Hunting is considered male and contributes little to the diet, but is ritually marked and plays a part in major ceremonial events (Kuper 1982:11–13). Just as meat is overvalued, so too are living cattle, and it is this social and symbolic value rather than the need for meat and milk that impels people to keep cattle in many instances. Even those groups that approach pure pastoralism – that is, those whose subsistence is largely derived from cattle or other livestock – do so primarily by choice rather than necessity. For instance, "Nuer reliance on cattle products is due as much to cultural preferences as to inherent environmental limitations affecting agriculture" (Kelly 1985:99). There are many ways that the Nuer could increase their grain production, some of which are practiced by their neighbors, but they choose to maximize cattle herds instead.

### DIFFICULTIES OF THE TRANSITION TO HERDING

Although the lure of wealth may be an inducement to invest labor in herding, there are also considerable obstacles to switching from hunting to herding. The logics of the hunting and herding ways of life are sharply opposed. Hunters share a wild resource, whereas herders husband domestic animals as individual property. Hunters ensure the continuation of game supplies by killing and consuming as many animals as they can, whereas herders ensure the continuation of their herds by refraining from killing them as much as possible. This is often framed as a greater orientation to the future on the part of herders, but in fact it is more a matter of a different kind of future orientation. The apparent profligacy of killing more game than needed and immediately consuming food when it is abundant comes not from a lack of concern for the future, but from a belief that the future food supply is best guaranteed by honoring the animals or spirits who have given food in the present by expressing proper appreciation of this gift, so that they will be inclined to give more in the future (see Chapter 4, *Hunters' Attitudes to Animals*, and Chapter 3, *Respecting the Hunted*). As discussed in Chapter 6, then, there is a major transition in both human–animal and human–human relationships with the adoption of herding.

The difficulties of this transition are illustrated by the experiences of three Ju/'hoansi (formerly known as !Kung) men in southern Africa who attempted to become herders. Debe attempted to build up a flock of goats and cattle, but his relatives would visit when they had low hunting success and he was obliged to share meat with them, resulting in the slaughter of most of his flock. Eventually he was forced to abandon herding. Bo tried to avoid this problem by feeding visiting friends and relatives a good meal and then sending them off. In this way he maintained his herd, but he became a social outcast. He was branded as stingy, the cardinal sin in Ju/'hoansi society, and accused of witchcraft. His life made untenable, in the end he sold off his flock and left the area (Lee 1993:143–4). Rakudu was another herder shunned as "stingy," and as a result his son was unable to marry (Hesse 1984:245).

There may be difficulties in the human–animal relationship as well. Domestic animals were introduced to the Koyukon as part of a development scheme. Some families successfully raised animals, but when it came time to slaughter them, they found it difficult to kill and eat animals with which they had been so intimate. Beautifully expressing domestication as a process of bringing animals into the household, the Koyukon said that it would be like eating their children; they preferred the anonymity of the hunt (Nelson 1997:328). Many urban dwellers who take up farming share this difficulty, but it is striking that, in this instance at least, it is also felt by people who have no hesitation about killing wild animals. For them, domestic farm animals uncomfortably blurred the boundaries between pets and prey.

The possession of herds can also make groups more vulnerable to attack. The Sandawe foragers of East Africa seem to have acquired and lost cattle at least twice (ten Raa 1986). Their method of avoiding extermination by larger pastoral groups in the region was to fade away and hide when warriors made incursions into their territory, but cattle complicated this strategy: "As soon as they had acquired only one single head of cattle they needed to construct a kraal to defend it against animal predators. Nor could they defend it against human raiders: it is impossible to hide an ox in a rock crevice or behind a tree, and it is also impossible to silence it. The acquisition of even one single animal cost them, therefore, their mobility as well as their invisibility" (ten Raa 1986:373).

These examples, of course, relate to the adoption of herding by foragers. It may have been less difficult for farmers to begin herding. The transition from gathering to cultivation may have been less traumatic, although no less profound in its consequences. Because there is usually a lesser imperative to share plant foods beyond the household, it may have been easier to retain seed supplies and stored plant foods. Once storage had undermined universal sharing, husbanding animals may have become less unthinkable. It is probably for this reason that the domestication of herd animals occurred in the context of plant agriculture, even though the reverse order might seem more logical (as it did to 19th-century theorists). Pastoralists could maintain the mobility of foragers, and herding, at least at low levels, might interfere less with gathering wild plant foods than farming interferes with hunting. Property relations stood in the way of pre-agricultural animal domestication.

For farmers, already accustomed to saving things for the future, animal wealth may have great appeal. On a practical level, animal wealth provides insurance against bad harvests. Archaeologically, this has usually been envisioned in terms of the walking larder model (see Chapter 6, *Models of Origins*): Farmers feed surplus grain to livestock, which can be slaughtered in time of need. However, as indicated by ethnographic studies, the exchange value of the livestock may be more important. The grain that a household can obtain in exchange for a cow will sustain it far longer (six months in one example) than the meat from the animal would (Hakansson 1994; Kelly 1985:98; Schneider 1957, 1979). Small stock, with their more rapid reproduction, function better as insurance (Bogucki 1993:497). However, the large stock carry the primary wealth value. This is no doubt in part because the use of animals as a walking larder requires slaughtering them as needed, which is antithetical to the accumulation of wealth.

Equally important is the opportunity to enhance status through the prestige value of animal wealth. This appears to have been a major factor in the adoption of horses by the residents of the North American Great Plains, many of whom were horticulturalists to begin with (Ewers 1955; Ingold 1980:162–5; Oliver 1962).

The appeal of domestic animals as wealth is a double-edged sword, and it would not straightforwardly lead to the adoption of herding by all societies. For those to whom status differentiation by wealth was already a valid concept, even if in a limited fashion, animal wealth is likely to seem highly attractive and may form a major motivation for reallocating labor to herding. For the most part these will be agricultural societies, although sedentary foragers practicing storage might also fall in this category. In contrast, mobile foragers who do not store food and who value sharing and abhor hoarding would have a very difficult time keeping herd animals.

## Bridewealth

Where animals function as wealth, often their primary and defining value is as bridewealth. Transfers of wealth at marriage can be roughly divided into bridewealth and dowry. Although they are structurally opposed, bridewealth and dowry are not mirror images of each other. Dowry consists of wealth bestowed on the bride by her family to endow her or the new household formed by the couple. Husbands' rights to access their wives' dowry vary, but in essence the dowry stays with the bride. In contrast, bridewealth is paid by the groom's family to the bride's family and is distributed among the bride's father and other relatives. It does not accompany the groom or the new couple (Evans-Pritchard 1931; Goody 1973; Kuper 1982; Ryan et al. 2000; Tambiah 1973; Turton 1980).

Bridewealth replaced the earlier term "bride price" (Dalton 1966; Evans-Pritchard 1931) to clarify that it is not about buying women. Rather, bridewealth is usually conceptualized as compensation to the kin group of the wife for the loss of her labor, and particularly her reproductive potential. In most cases, what bridewealth secures is the transfer of the children of the marriage from the lineage or other kin group of the wife to that of the husband. In some societies one may choose to marry either with or without bridewealth, the difference being that without bridewealth the children remain affiliated with the wife's lineage (Barnes 1980; Hagen 1999; Hakansson 1994; Kuper 1982; Lindström 1988; Schneider 1979; Tambiah 1973). Given this, it is not surprising that bridewealth is generally associated with unilineal systems of descent, and especially with patriliny. Indeed, a recent study suggests that cattle herding tends to convert matrilineal societies to patriliny, and even more strongly to maintain them as patrilineal (Holden and Mace 2003). This association is not invariable, however. In some cases, the more important aspect of bridewealth is that of exchange, and the relationships thus created (Barnes 1980; Hagen 1999; Peters 1980; Strathern 1980).

Dowry can consist of many kinds of goods such as textiles, furniture, and money, and it may include land (Goody 1973; Rheubottom 1980; Tambiah 1973). Bridewealth does not include land and is always made up of movable items. Although bridewealth can be composed of other things such as beehives, hoes, and imported prestige items (Barnes 1980; Cronk 1989; Goody 1973; Hagen 1999; Kuper 1982), it is classically made up of livestock. Animals only occasionally form part of dowry, and when they do, they are not payments to the kin of the groom, but serve as a nucleus of the herd of the new household and the basis for future exchanges with the bride's kin (Strathern 1980; West 1983). Increasingly, money is being offered as part or all of the bridewealth, but there is a sense that this is not as good as livestock and that it marks a breakdown of the system (Hagen 1999; Parkin 1980). Money seems more appropriate as dowry, aimed at starting the new couple off on a good footing.

The reason that money does not work well as bridewealth but cattle do is precisely because cattle are limited in their monetary function. Their exchange occurs primarily in the context of bridewealth, making it easier for them to maintain a constant value (Goody 1973:5). Adam Kuper

(1982:167) points out that if cattle derived their value as bridewealth from their productive value, the value of cattle and thus the amount of bridewealth would be expected to fluctuate with the market; bridewealth would be a rational investment in the capitalist sense. In fact, this is not the case. Bridewealth has been very stable throughout southern Africa at about 10 cattle for commoners, more for nobility. Similarly, in East Africa the rights obtained in the wife and her offspring per the number of cattle offered are quite standardized across groups (Schneider 1979:98).

Although there are varying rules about the amount and composition of bridewealth, and often they are partially negotiable, the bridewealth payment is typically quite high in relation to the average household herd size. Even the wealthiest herders cannot usually pay bridewealth by themselves, but must draw on kin and other relationships to make it up. Often bridewealth is so high that a man can only marry after receiving bridewealth for his sister or daughter (Dombrowski 1993; Goody 1973:6; Kuper 1982:167). In some southern African societies, the amount of bridewealth is dependent on the status of the bride (Kuper 1982). However, more commonly it is based on the ability of the groom (or the groom's family) to pay (Hakansson 1994; Kelly 1985). The higher the bridewealth, the greater the network of people called on to assemble it, and the greater the number of people to whom it is distributed. The bride's father cannot simply keep it for himself, because he has to compensate kin and others for their contributions to earlier marriages. As a result, a bridewealth system can operate with relatively few cattle (Dombrowski 1993; Huffman 1990). In fact, the amount of bridewealth has more to do with the value of female labor than with the size of cattle herds. In southern Africa, bridewealth is higher where agriculture is important, because it is a female activity, even though groups with lesser dependence on agriculture have more cattle (Kuper 1982:157–8). Both among and within societies, where people have many cattle, the father tends to provide his sons' bridewealth, whereas those poor in cattle depend on the receipt of bridewealth for the marriage of a sister to be able to marry themselves (Kuper 1982:158).

The effect of bridewealth is to distribute cattle widely and, in the long run, fairly evenly within a society. Because of the reproductive capacity of cattle, however, families can benefit from bridewealth by manipulating the timing to take advantage of the float time. Families poor in cattle are likely to delay their sons' marriages while they use their daughters' bridewealth to build up their herds (Kelly 1985:114). Because the larger the bridewealth payment, the more widely the cattle are spread through different herds, and the wider the area from which they will be drawn, bridewealth acts in part as a risk-reduction mechanism (de Vries et al. 2006; Dombrowski 1993).

For our purposes, one of the most important aspects of bridewealth is that it has a significant impact on herding practices and on the composition of herds. Kirk Dombrowski (1993:27) considers bridewealth on a par with aging, predation, and disease in determining herd populations in East Africa. Herders keep more animals to meet bridewealth needs, because one must be prepared to give these animals away and still be left with a viable herd. Because over the long term bridewealth paid is balanced by that received, this would be a stable system (although at a higher level than dictated by subsistence alone), except that polygyny creates an essentially unlimited demand. This is especially true where the amount of bridewealth is elastic; there may be a minimum payment, but no maximum. In this case those rich in cattle are inclined to pay as much as they can. Not only does this boost their status by demonstrating their wealth but it also relieves them of the burden of caring for excess cattle, while setting the stage for future reciprocity. Meanwhile, they gain a wife who will add both directly and indirectly, through her offspring, to the pool of household labor. Thus with no upper limit on bridewealth, the only upper limit on the cattle population is the Malthusian one set by the environment, which indeed seems to be what limits cattle populations at least among the Nuer. If the use of animals as wealth in general tends to overcome the underproduction of the DMP, bridewealth requirements are particularly apt to do so, with their unlimited demand for surplus production (Kelly 1985). Moreover, to the extent that grain or other products can be exchanged for cattle, it will stimulate surplus production of these goods as well as the cattle herds themselves (Hakansson 1994).

The effect of bridewealth goes beyond the size of the herds, however, as demonstrated by Kelly's (1985) incisive analysis of the Nuer expansion. Over the course of 70 years, the Nuer expanded their territory (at the expense of their neighbors, the Dinka) to four times its previous size. When expansion was halted by introduced cattle diseases, their territory had grown to 35,000 square miles. In Kelly's view, this remarkable expansion, and much else about Nuer and Dinka society, is ultimately due to differences in bridewealth practices between these two groups. Because custom prescribes not only the number but also the age and sex composition of the cattle offered as bridewealth payments, the need for bridewealth rather than milk or meat determined the composition and size of the herds.

Differences in the specifications of bridewealth payments rendered the Nuer far more expansionary than the Dinka. Not only were Nuer bridewealth payments larger but they were also one-way payments from the groom's to the bride's family. In contrast, the Dinka practice an unusual version of bridewealth in which the groom's payment is roughly equivalent to Nuer bridewealth, but about half is immediately paid back to the groom's side by the bride's family. Both Nuer and Dinka pay more than the minimum required amount if they are able, but the proportion returned to the groom's side among the Dinka actually grows as the bridewealth rises above the minimum, so that effective bridewealth size grows much more slowly than among the Nuer.

The composition of Nuer and Dinka bridewealth is also different. Dinka bridewealth is composed chiefly of female cattle, permitting them to slaughter most males when they are young. This leads to a more productive system in terms of meat and milk. The Nuer bridewealth formula includes many male cattle, requiring them to maintain these animals despite their lack of contribution to subsistence. As noted earlier, the competition to pay the highest bridewealth creates an inflationary tendency that is limited only by pasture. Having reached this limit, there were still ways for the Nuer to continue to expand their payments. One was to acquire more cattle by raiding the Dinka. This provided more cattle for individuals to offer as bridewealth, but added to the overpopulation of cattle. Another was to seize Dinka territory. These tactics were aided by differences in the kinship systems that also were ultimately dependent on bridewealth. The Nuer were able to assemble larger forces because of stronger ties among patrilateral kin created by bridewealth payments, whereas Dinka bridewealth gives a larger role to matrilateral kin:

> The Nuer-Dinka divergence with respect to the reciprocal payment therefore did not simply "reflect" a change in the relative significance of matrilateral relations but indeed constituted such a change in and of itself. In short, cultural valuations of the relative importance of matrilateral and patrilateral relations in the fabric of social life were transformed by changes in the bridewealth system, since the bridewealth system represents a primary context in which kinship valuations are both encoded and experienced (Kelly 1985:188).

Thus it was ultimately bridewealth and the details of its specific form among the Nuer and the Dinka that both motivated and enabled the Nuer expansion. Dinka captured in this process were incorporated into Nuer society through adoption and marriage, adding to the labor pool and, in the case of girls, providing an additional source of bridewealth for their adoptive fathers (Evans-Pritchard 1951). Not only did Nuer bridewealth power this expansion but it also interfered with their subsistence goals. As with many pastoralists, the Nuer ideal is to live entirely off one's own flock, subsisting purely on meat, milk, and blood. However, only the richest households ever achieve this ideal, and then for only a limited time (Kelly 1985:230). It is less ecological limitations than the demands of bridewealth that prevent the Nuer from living off their flocks; wealth is more important than subsistence in shaping herding strategies:

> Economic and social goals were partially consistent with respect to the accumulation of cattle, but diverged at the point when cattle were deployed in bridewealth or other social transactions. . . . [T]he same cows designated for eventual inclusion in a son's bridewealth payment also facilitated reduced agricultural production in the interim. However, the accumulation of bullocks and oxen for bridewealth purposes did not contribute to the Nuer objective of reducing their reliance on grain, since male animals held in reserve for future exchange provided neither milk nor meat. It is evident that bridewealth effectively organizes economic production and that objectives inconsistent with bridewealth requirements are of secondary importance (Kelly 1985:232).

The expansion of the Nuer was not based on ecological adaptation. In fact, the Dinka system is better adapted to the environment. Their smaller group size and hence herd size permit the use of lesser water sources, thus opening up areas effectively closed to Nuer herds. Their more productive herd structure permits higher densities of human population on the same land. The Nuer system was expansionary not because it was more productive, but because it was less so. Nor does this fit with simplistic notions of cultural evolution, in which more hierarchical societies vanquish more egalitarian ones. Nuer bridewealth and society are in fact more egalitarian than those of the Dinka, where the lack of a minimum payment enables the poor to marry each other so that they remain poor and reinforces wealth differences. Unlike the Nuer, Dinka bridewealth payments above the ideal amount are based on the status of the bride's family, not the wealth of the groom's, which tends to restrict large bridewealth payments to wealthier families rather than evening out cattle wealth (Kelly 1985:249).

## THE ORIGINS OF BRIDEWEALTH

Clearly it is not the intrinsic value of livestock that leads to their use as bridewealth, but rather their use as bridewealth gives them much of their value (Evans-Pritchard 1951:90). This raises the question of how livestock become bridewealth.

Because bridewealth is so important in shaping herding practices as well as other aspects of society, it is crucial to understand when and how it originated. Can we assume that any society with domestic animals will rapidly develop bridewealth? Or does it occur only under specific circumstances? These questions are difficult to answer in a satisfying manner. Archaeologists have paid scant attention to bridewealth (but cf. Bogucki 1988; Huffman 1990; Smith 2000; Wengrow 1998), and sociocultural anthropologists have carefully studied its workings but devoted little thought to its origins. An exception is G. A. Wilken (1883:26–8, cited in Barnes 1980), who situated the origin of bridewealth in the transition from matriarchy to patriarchy. In his view, bridewealth (bride price) began as compensation to the family of an abducted bride; with the full establishment of patriarchy it evolved into outright purchase of the bride. As noted earlier, however, closer ethnographic study has shown that bridewealth is rarely a matter of purchasing a bride, and of course the notion of primitive matriarchy has been rejected within anthropology.

Anthropologists since Wilken have seldom discussed the origins of bridewealth, but they have noted some associations that may aid in a consideration of its derivation. Ethnographically, bridewealth is extremely common in mixed farming societies, especially those in which women perform much of the agricultural labor. It may help balance agricultural and pastoral risks by exchanging cattle for women (Bogucki 1988; Kuper 1982:169). Thus bridewealth is not limited to pastoralists. Moreover, pure pastoralists are rare, and even those who do not cultivate their own cereals acquire them through exchange or other means, including the exchange of livestock (Hakansson 1994; Hjort 1980). So it is unlikely that bridewealth originated only with pastoralism. On the contrary, bridewealth may have played a major role in creating pastoralism by valorizing livestock. Not ecological constraints on agriculture but the high cultural value on cattle impels those classic pastoralists, the Nuer, to attempt to live off their flocks, and as we have seen, that high value is due largely to their use as bridewealth (Kelly 1985:99).

As noted earlier, bridewealth is particularly associated with lineage systems, but not exclusively so. Rather bridewealth tends to create exogamous lineages, because it is often felt that one should not both contribute to and receive a share in the bridewealth of the same bride (Evans-Pritchard 1951). In any case, bridewealth is all about legitimacy and inheritance, so it is likely to appear when they become an issue. It tends to be found when the main factor limiting production is labor, whereas dowry is more common when the main limiting factor is land (Goody 1973).

Bridewealth is concerned with securing labor and inheritance within the household and perhaps lineage, so it should be associated with the appearance of the domestic mode of production (Sahlins 1972) The DMP is itself linked to the transformation of food sources into private property, of which domestic animals are an important part. Whereas in hard times foragers rely on carefully maintained sharing relationships, the owners of domestic animals (or crops) can consume their own surplus. Because this surplus is private property rather than a shared resource like game, it is not necessary to share it beyond the household. Households then must rely primarily on their own herds and crops, causing a fragmentation into autonomous household units: hence, the DMP (Ingold 1980:168).

Some foraging groups do use bridewealth on a small scale, although obviously not with livestock. This practice would clearly facilitate a transition to bridewealth in livestock, but it is not clear whether it reflects the origins of bridewealth or a secondary occurrence. The cases that I know of are in East Africa (Cronk 1989; ten Raa 1986), where both individuals and groups may shift through time among foraging, agriculture, and pastoralism (Mace 1993; Sobania 1991). Thus it may be a remnant of bridewealth practices from pastoral or agropastoral periods, a way to facilitate intermarriage with other groups, or perhaps on the contrary a way to head off the flow of women to other groups.

In summary, then, bridewealth seems likely to arise in the context of the DMP when labor, especially female labor, is the key limiting factor in production. It implies a gendered division of labor and is most probable in the context of mixed farming, at least on a regional scale. Reindeer herders, who do not practice agriculture, have dowry rather than bridewealth (Ingold 1980:165). Similarly, bridewealth does not occur

ethnographically in the New World, where domestic animals are largely
lacking. In the Andes, where both agriculture and herding are present,
production is limited more by land or by animals than by labor. Moreover, women provide the herding labor. Thus the emphasis is on endowing children and especially women with flocks, rather than exchanging
livestock for women (West 1983). In Melanesia, where agricultural labor
is largely male and pig raising is largely a female task, bridewealth when it
occurs is paid in durable goods or pork rather than livestock (Kahn 1986;
Strathern 1980). Thus tentatively we can expect bridewealth in livestock
to originate with early mixed farming if the organization of labor is based
on female cultivation and male herding. Domestic animals alone are not
enough, nor even the combination of herding and agriculture.

BRIDEWEALTH IN THE TRANSITION TO HERDING

Although mixed farming with a gendered division of labor in which
men herd and women cultivate and there is a relative abundance of
land may provide the conditions for the origins of bridewealth, it does
not make it inevitable. However, like farming itself, once established
bridewealth tends to be an expansionary system. Indeed, bridewealth may
have contributed to the expansion of both mixed farming and pastoralism.

   Bridewealth is a system potentially open to anyone with marriageable daughters, even if they do not initially have herds (Kelly 1985:246;
Mace 1993:370). Thus for foragers who wish to do so, it is an easy way
to acquire livestock, although as we have seen, the subsequent maintenance of these herds may be quite problematic. Lee Cronk's (1989,
1991, 2004) study of the Mukogodo in Kenya during the early 20th
century provides a vivid illustration of how this process can take place.
The Mukogodo were foragers at the beginning of the 20th century,
who practiced endogamous marriage with bridewealth consisting of a
few beehives. British colonization pushed Maasai pastoralists into Mukogodo territory. The Maasai began to marry Mukogodo women, offering
livestock as bridewealth. Mukogodo fathers accepted livestock instead
of beehives, perhaps because they had a higher exchange value, perhaps
for their wealth and prestige value, perhaps because they found herding
easier than hunting. As foragers, the men provided most of the food, but
women and children performed most of the herding labor. Once large
numbers of Mukogodo fathers began to accept bridewealth in livestock,
it became necessary for the Mukogodo to maintain herds. Mukogodo

women were marrying out, and Maasai would accept only livestock as bridewealth. There was a period when no Mukogodo men could marry. This kind of very real social pressure may impel foragers to alter their cultural values so as to support herding. Because the values and organization of herding are so different, for the Mukogodo this change meant their absorption into Maasai culture, adopting Maasai language and customs as well as intermarrying.

The Mukogodo's existing practice of bridewealth in beehives clearly made it easier for the Maasai to marry Mukogodo women with bridewealth in livestock. However, the same thing might happen without preexisting bridewealth among the foragers. If the herders were desired exchange partners, and livestock was their favored medium of exchange, foragers might be eager to build alliances through marriage, and bridewealth in livestock might appeal to fathers for the same reasons it did among the Mukogodo. We should recall, too, Cauvin's observation that flocks of tame animals would make a powerful impression on foragers, and there might well be prestige value in emulating the herders. The Mukogodo case demonstrates that acquiring livestock through bridewealth is a particularly powerful inducement to become herders. Once a substantial number of marriages are brokered in this way, having livestock becomes not simply a matter of wealth and prestige, but essential for the continued survival of families. Men without livestock are doomed to die unwed and childless.

## Animal wealth and inequality

The transformation of animals into wealth in itself implies some degree of inequality. Those with more animals are richer than those with fewer; those with none are shut out of the primary exchange system and, if the animals also act as bridewealth, excluded from marriage or at least marriage with full rights. There are also other ways that animal wealth can act to promote inequality.

If plant and animal domestication tend to lead to the domestic mode of production (see the earlier section, *The Valorization of Animal Wealth*), this creates a new set of problems for the now more autonomous households. The households must develop means to deal with the risk of crop failure or herd loss, as well as with the fluctuations in labor availability through the household cycle. The accumulation of wealth and the social relations maintained through wealth are important solutions (Bender 1978; Bogucki 1993; Gebre Mariam 1980).

Animal wealth is particularly suited to maintaining social relationships because of the productive and reproductive powers of livestock. "Ownership of stock is often not clear-cut. The local culture may, for example, in theory or practice differentiate between the rights to sell and dispose of stock; the rights to milk cattle and slaughter their offspring; and the rights to make decisions over the care and herding of stock" (Dahl 1980:207). As Ingold (1980:173) puts it, foragers share out meat, whereas herders own shares in animals. When an animal is slaughtered, the meat is likely to be distributed according to the past transactions involving that animal and its ancestors. "Exchange and transfers of [animal wealth] create and reproduce social relationships in general, as well as relationships of dependency and subordination through marriage, descent, and indebtedness. The strategic manipulation of prestige goods enables individuals to access others' labor, which in turn can be used to build power" (Hakansson 1994:251). Accumulated wealth can also be inherited, maintaining household differences through the generations (Bogucki 1993).

Lemonnier (1993:130) pinpoints the use of wealth (in pigs as well as other valuables) as the key difference between the Great-Men and the more hierarchical Big-Men societies of New Guinea. In his analysis, Great-Men societies are based on direct equivalence of people. Homicides are resolved by blood feud, marriages are ideally exchanges of sisters without bridewealth, and so on. The Big-Men societies, however, use wealth as equivalents for people, as blood money and bridewealth, for example. In marriage, this creates a tendency to exogamy and a wider and more open circle of affines, who are also exchange partners. This broader network enhances the ability of the successful Big Man to put together prestige-enhancing feasts (see Chapter 9) and to assemble war parties.

Animal wealth is perhaps associated most closely with societies in the middle range of complexity, and in these relations defined through livestock are likely to be of supreme importance. However, animal wealth can play an important role in more highly stratified societies as well, and may encourage increasing centralization. This seems to occur in the context of societies that are primarily agricultural but use livestock as wealth. "[B]y allowing successful farmers to convert crop surpluses to livestock, prestige, obligations of labour, or political support, such exchanges may ultimately have undermined domestic economic and political autonomy"

(Halstead 1992:55). Thus animal property initially promotes household autonomy, but to the extent that it creates and perpetuates substantial wealth differences among households, it may eventually contribute to their subordination to larger institutions.

In southern Africa, cattle were an important power base for rulers of stratified societies. Chiefs and kings tended to have some rights over all cattle herded by their subjects, in some cases actually owning all the cattle (Reid 1996; Segobye 1998). Cattle wealth was also crucial for the rulers of early states in Mesopotamia and Egypt, and it has been implicated in the rise of these states (Rice 1997; Schwabe 1994). This suggests that in some cases, the accumulation of animal wealth and the power built from it can be converted into broader and more durable forms of power. For a time, the familiar currency of livestock will continue in use as a component of state wealth and power, as well as a potent source of symbolism. Just as wealthy and influential Nuer men are called "bulls" (Evans-Pritchard 1940), so bulls and bull-gods were associated with royalty in Mesopotamia and Egypt.

## PATRON–CLIENT RELATIONS

In addition to the natural increase of the herds, there are mechanisms through which herders can enhance their wealth and convert it to power, creating greater inequality than that based simply on accumulation. Among these are the various forms of patron–client relations that are so common among herders. Wealthier herders lend out livestock to those who lack them. In compensation for their herding labor, the clients have rights to some portion of the animals' production. This is likely to include some or all of the milk and other secondary products yielded by these animals, as well as some of the offspring.

There are obvious benefits for both patron and client. Patrons can maintain larger herds than would be possible with the labor of their households alone and minimize risk by spreading their animals across the landscape. Clients can build their own herds gradually from the offspring received. However, this sets up relations of dependency that would not occur among foragers who share wild animals as a common resource. If all goes well, this is a temporary dependency that provides a way back into herding and the accumulation of wealth for those who have lost their herds. But if through bad luck or ineptitude the client fails to build a new herd, the dependency will be extended and may become permanent.

Lemonnier (1993, see also Oliver 1955) describes the workings of such patron–client relations in the Big-Men societies of New Guinea. To put on a feast with impressive prestations at a wedding, funeral, or other event, the Big Man must manage a large network of people over a period of years. The Big Man distributes pigs to these people to raise; in compensation they receive one piglet from each litter the pigs produce. "The Big Man thus compensates his dependants for their labor by leaving them a portion of the product and by sharing with them some of his own prestige. Such painless generosity, which shows the first signs of exploitation, is a salient feature of Big-Men societies" (Lemonnier 1993:127).

In addition to long-term loans, where animals are used for labor their owners may lend them out for short-term use in hunting, plowing, and transport. Naturally the owners receive some payment in exchange for the use of their animals, as well as the prestige of being wealthy and generous enough to have animal labor to spare (Bogucki 1993; Ingold 1980:164).

Many herders dampen risk by actively maintaining non-kin as well as kin-based exchange relationships, on which they can draw in times of need. These "stock-friendships" are based on the exchange of various items, but especially livestock. Such exchanges take the form not of direct barter, but of delayed reciprocity through the bestowal of gifts or long-term loans. Although the debt thus created causes an imbalance between giver and receiver, in the long run these stock-friendships are conceived as relationships between equals. However, only those already wealthy in animals can afford to build the most and strongest stock-friendships, and they are thus more likely to maintain their position (Dahl 1980; Gebre Mariam 1980; Ingold 1980:170; Oliver 1955; Schneider 1957, 1979).

Although patron–client relations among herders can benefit both parties despite the difference in wealth and status, and with luck may lead to the eventual wealth of the erstwhile client, the exploitive element is heightened in relations between herders and foragers. Because the property relations of herding are so foreign to the sharing ethic of most foragers, foragers may not want to build their own herds (see the earlier section, *Difficulties of the Transition to Herding*). So rather than receive payment in livestock, foragers often become clients of herders in exchange for food, typically in a shorter term relationship. However, the grazing competition of the herds tends to reduce game and may make it unfeasible to continue hunting for a living. Thus the foragers may be pushed into a relationship of permanent dependency, with absorption as the only alternative (Smith 1990a).

### Wealth differences and herding strategies

Patron–client relations, stock-friendships, and bridewealth are all ways that wealthy herders can reduce risk by spreading their livestock around and that those poor in livestock can begin to build a herd. Another way to accomplish these goals is through trading up or trading down between large and small stock. Most herders keep a mix of large (cattle, horses, camels) and small (sheep, goat) stock. The small stock provide small change when wealth is measured primarily in large stock. They may also provide a meat supply, when herders try to avoid slaughtering the more valuable large stock. Moreover, a mix of large and small stock reduces risk, both because the same wealth value is spread across a larger number of animals and because the different species have differing tolerances for drought, disease, and other stress factors (Dahl 1980).

There is no single ideal ratio of large to small stock even within a particular environment. Rather, the optimal ratio depends on the wealth of the household as well as the severity of the risk factors. Generally, wealthier households do better by investing in a higher proportion of large stock. They are often more resistant to drought, but the same amount of livestock value comes in a smaller number of larger units with large stock, so the loss of a single animal is a greater setback, one that the poorer households may not be able to afford. Smaller stock also reproduce more rapidly, so it is easier to build up a herd under favorable conditions (Grandin 1988; Mace and Houston 1989). Of course, drought, epidemic, raiding, or other disasters may quickly render a wealthy household into a poor one, and poorer households with good planning and good fortune may build up their herds and become wealthy. So herders will adjust their stock ratio by trading up to large stock when things are going well and trading down to small stock when they are going badly. For example, among the Gisu in East Africa, 12 field rats may be exchanged for a hen, 6 hens for a goat, and 3 or 4 goats for a cow (Schneider 1979:100).

Thus the fortunes of households rise and fall with the disasters that beset them and the success of their management practices, and household success may be roughly measured not only in the number of animals but also the ratio of large to small stock. The stock ratio is not the only way in which herding strategies differ between rich and poor, however. Where animals are used for dairy, the human consumers of dairy products are always in competition with the calves. The rich are able to give a higher proportion of the milk to the calves, because with a larger total number of animals they can still meet their own needs. Needless to say, these calves are more likely to survive and thrive, so that the rich get richer and the poor get poorer. Not only do the rich and poor tend to follow different milking strategies but there are also conflicting interests within the household. The women, who are the milkers among the Maasai and many other African groups, tend to favor the interests of their family, especially their children, in milk allocation. Their husbands, who own the cattle and depend on them as bridewealth, are likely to urge that more milk be given to the calves (Grandin 1988).

Similar considerations ought to apply to age and sex ratios in a herd. The poor are constrained to manage their herds so as to encourage growth and production of subsistence products (although these two goals are partially in conflict and have to be balanced). Wealthier households are better able to maintain "unproductive" animals that may be required for bridewealth, sacrifice, or feasts.

## ALIENABILITY

A key difference between wealth in land and wealth in animals is the ease with which animal wealth can be separated from its owners. This counterbalances the ability of the rich to get richer through herding strategies as outlined earlier, a check that does not operate with land wealth (Schneider 1979). This alienability enables sudden gains as well as sudden losses in wealth and is likely to encourage warfare and militarism.

Although crops are always subject to the threat of bad weather, pests, and plant diseases, herds are considerably riskier. "The distribution of animal wealth over the population is not static but changes constantly with stochastic luck in breeding a good proportion of female calves, with managerial skills, with the social demands for stock, and with the vicissitudes of theft and disease" (Dahl 1980:207). Whereas crop losses do not generally affect the chances of producing a good crop in the following season, animal losses reduce the capacity of the herd to reproduce. Thus just as animal wealth can grow more dramatically than land wealth, so can it shrink more drastically.

## Cattle raids and warfare

The vulnerability of animal wealth to theft and raiding is of particular interest, because although most other risks serve mainly to reduce herds, cattle raids reduce the herds of some while building the herds of others. To seize land by force requires a sustained campaign resulting in conquest or driving the owners from their homeland. Animal wealth, however, can be appropriated in a swift clandestine raid. Given the vicissitudes of herding, which often leave some households without viable herds, the attractions of livestock raiding as a get-rich-quick scheme are considerable. It is thus not surprising that livestock raiding and a glorification of the warrior are a frequent concomitant of animal wealth (Cranstone 1969; Gebre Mariam 1980; Ingold 1980). The use of livestock as bridewealth heightens this effect. Young men are particularly likely to resort to raiding, because if they have not inherited a sufficient flock they need animals both to marry and to establish a herd to maintain the household thus created, especially if they lack sisters (Fleisher and Holloway 2004; Kelly 1985). Schneider (1979:89) asserts that the higher the ratio of cattle to people, the more cattle raiding there is. This is probably because bridewealth tends to be higher when there are more cattle, and thus the stakes are generally raised. Of course, the vulnerability of animal wealth to raiding means that herders must be prepared to defend their flocks, so warriors gain importance in both offensive and defensive capacities.

Raiding is also an important way for foragers and horticulturalists to acquire livestock. If domestic animals become desirable among people lacking them, surging demand may far outstrip the supply available through exchange. As with the Blackfoot adoption of horses, raiding may become the principal means of acquisition. However, where the sharing ethic of hunting still prevails, raiding may not lead to instant wealth for the warriors. Among the Blackfoot, raiding was treated like hunting for live animals: The horses thus acquired were distributed according to the same rules as hunted meat. Like hunters, successful horse raiders were rewarded with prestige and positions of leadership in recognition of their bravery and generosity. Meanwhile, the horses they gave away could be used to build animal wealth by their new owners. Raiding brought prestige, but only breeding brought wealth (Ingold 1980:163).

### THE LIMITS OF ANIMAL-BASED INEQUALITY

Although animal wealth presents opportunities for social differentiation not available to foragers, in comparison to land wealth there are limits to the degree of inequality that can be achieved. The vulnerability of livestock to theft, drought, hard winters, and disease makes it difficult to maintain a high degree of animal wealth through time. Bridewealth and to a lesser extent stock-friendships and other livestock exchanges have also been seen as important leveling mechanisms. Bridewealth is particularly effective because one does not have to have cattle initially to join the system (Goody 1973; Kelly 1985; Peters 1980; Schneider 1957).

There has been considerable debate as to whether pastoralists are egalitarian and whether animal wealth promotes or counteracts inequality (e.g., Salzman 1999; Schneider 1957, 1979; Sutter 1987). Part of the dispute rests on the definition of "egalitarian." Those who see pastoralists as egalitarian emphasize the ideology of equality, in which wealth in animals brings prestige but not power. They stress the leveling mechanisms inherent in the risks of herding, as well as the openness of the system to those without herds through bridewealth or clientage. Others have focused on the quite substantial differences in wealth and the dependency in patron–client relations, and they see the leveling mechanisms as only partial antidotes. In other words, it is a matter of political versus economic inequality or, as we think of it in the United States, equality of opportunity as opposed to equality of outcome.

It also depends on which societies one examines. Roughly speaking, East African pastoralists tend to be egalitarian at least in ideology and opportunity, whereas South African societies centered on cattle wealth are more hierarchical and include actual states. Pastoralists elsewhere seem to be more mixed. Schneider (1979) argues that it is not animal wealth in itself that promotes egalitarianism, but rather a substantial subsistence reliance on herding in addition. That is, animal wealth must be the only or by far the predominant form of wealth for the leveling mechanisms to be effective. Schneider's rule of thumb is that egalitarian societies will occur when there is one or more cattle or other large livestock per person. Societies with a lower ratio are primarily agricultural, permitting monopolization of land and other resources by nobility. These rulers may then be able to monopolize animal wealth as well (Kuper 1982).

Kelly (1985) notes that whether bridewealth acts as a leveling mechanism or supports inequality depends on the form that it takes. In his example, Nuer bridewealth, with a strict minimum and essentially no maximum payment, is more egalitarian in its effect than that of the Dinka, who have no minimum and rarely exceed the ideal payment. The Nuer system ensures that all bridegrooms are impoverished when they marry, with a greater redistribution of cattle. The Dinka system, while stemming the loss of brides marrying out of the group when cattle are short, encourages cattle-poor people to marry each other and stay poor. As Schneider puts it, egalitarian systems are inflationary, whereas hierarchical systems are deflationary (Schneider 1979:10).

Thus animal wealth by itself is a shaky foundation for substantial power, although it will inevitably lead to wealth differentials. However, when animal wealth is combined with and to some degree is convertible to more stable forms of wealth, it can support and validate strong and permanent hierarchies.

### GENDER ISSUES

Although the degree of inequality created among men by animal wealth may be debated, there is much more general agreement that animal wealth has a deleterious effect on women's status (e.g., Schneider 1979; Smith 1990a). Frederick Engels (1972) considered animal domestication to be the basis of female exploitation. He viewed domestic animals as the first private property, and its possession provided men with a power base from which women were excluded. The need to control property and its inheritance led to the desire to control women's reproduction. Although this model is based on the outdated belief that animal domestication preceded plant domestication, it still has much to recommend it. With land plentiful in early agriculture, domestic animals may often have been among the first forms of substantial private property (Sacks 1975). Engels assumed that men owned the livestock, forcing women into a position of dependency. This is often but not always the case. Where it is not, as among the Aymara (West 1983), women have higher status. However, because owning property raises the issue of inheritance, its presence is likely to lead to a concern with controlling women's reproduction and hence some degree of gender hierarchy even if women can own, bequeath, and inherit livestock and other property. If the alienability of livestock leads to raiding and heightened warfare, the concomitant glorification of the warrior is also likely to act to the detriment of women's status.

There is a strong, although not invariable, association of pastoralism with patriliny and patriarchy. In Africa, at least, matriliny is common where land is the main form of wealth. This is no doubt linked to women's position as the main cultivators. Where mobile, usually animal, wealth is substantial, however, matriliny shifts to patriliny (Holden and Mace 2003; Schneider 1979).

Tapper (1988:55) offers an alternative, mentalist explanation for the association of animal wealth and patriliny. Among the Nuer, for instance, both cattle and humans have names and lineages, but they are mirror images of each other. The requirements of herding, as well as the behavior of cattle and most other herd animals, produce an animal society that is matrilineal and uxorilocal. To differentiate themselves, Tapper suggests, their owners must organize themselves as patrilineal, virilocal lineages. Although the Nuer and others may well find this symmetry pleasing, and it may reinforce their marital system, the mere possession of animal wealth does not seem to be enough to create patriliny. Nor is patriliny limited to those who are largely dependent on herd animals for their subsistence. Rather, it is the use of animals as bridewealth that is most strongly (although not invariably) associated with patriliny.

Bridewealth is particularly implicated in the development of gender hierarchies. As we have seen, it is often the payment of bridewealth that assigns the offspring to the bridegroom's lineage. Bridewealth converts matriliny to patriliny in each instance. Although it is rare that women are bought and sold as commodities, the practice of bridewealth does make women into some kind of property, in a way that men are not (Hyde 1983:94–101). It also creates an equivalency between women and livestock. I have suggested (Chapter 4) that women are already widely equated with animals in hunting societies, and also that the domestication of animals provided a model for human exploitation (Chapter 6). Bridewealth is the logical outcome of these two tendencies. If for hunters animals are like women and hunting is like sex, for herders women are like animals and animals are property, and one can be exchanged for the other.

This is not to say that bridewealth treats women as mere chattel or that brides have no say in their marriages. On the contrary, in general women have higher status in societies practicing bridewealth than in those practicing dowry (Goody 1973). The bride may have considerable say in the choice of her husband. Although her family will exert strong pressure on her to choose a bridegroom with adequate livestock (else it will not be a full marriage), the possibility that she will abandon a husband she dislikes, thus requiring the return of her bridewealth, restrains the bride's family from forcing her into an unwanted marriage (Evans-Pritchard 1951).

In contrast, although bridewealth may put women in a better position than dowry, it leaves them in some ways worse off than in marriages with no transfer of property. First, it does somewhat limit their choice of partner. Second, although there is some dispute about the degree to which this operates, bridewealth tends to stabilize marriages (Evans-Pritchard 1951; Gluckman 1950, 1953; Goody 1973; Leach 1953; Peters 1980). Because bridewealth generally has to be refunded if the marriage fails, certainly if the failure is deemed the wife's fault, the wife's family is likely to pressure her to stay in a marriage she would rather abandon. Third, the payment of bridewealth purchases rights to various aspects of the wife's labor and reproduction, which she is then expected to provide to the husband. The tension inherent in such marriages is illustrated by Edward E. Evans-Pritchard's (1951) puzzled observation that, although Nuer marriages mostly seemed happy and harmonious to him, the men privately confessed that they rather hoped their wives would die after they had produced several children (because they did not wish their wives to survive them and remarry, potentially giving another man access to their children and their cattle), and that they believed that wives secretly wished their husbands would die as well. Evans-Pritchard believed that the reason for the "harmony" of Nuer marriages lay in the unquestioned authority of the husband and his right to beat his wife with a stick if she transgressed this authority (see also Llewelyn-Davies 1981).

Even without bridewealth there can be a link between domestic animals and women. The matrilineal Wamirans do not practice bridewealth. However, men exchange pigs (by gifts of piglets, reciprocated at a later date) and pork primarily with the families of their wives, thereby symbolically controlling women's reproductive powers, on which they depend. Women raise pigs, whereas men raise taro (reversing the classic association of women with plants and men with animals). Men regard both pigs and women as economic and social extensions of themselves. Both are sources of food and fertility; both pig exchanges and marital exchanges maintain links between men. So pigs are seen as surrogate women and as symbols of controllable female sexuality. Women's role is felt as fundamental, producing food and children, whereas men are more peripheral and insecure, and thus they seek to control women and pigs, as well as taro (Kahn 1986).

It is not surprising that women may regard livestock differently from men under these circumstances. "It is a striking fact that Pakot women do not place as high a valuation upon cattle as do the men. One woman said that she did not think cattle were beautiful at all, but that grain was beautiful" (Schneider 1957:293). Even when women perform some or even most of the labor of herding and when the valorization of livestock rests mainly on their use as bridewealth, livestock are of value primarily to men. As a result, tensions often arise within the household around herding decisions, with men wanting to maximize the herd size and women more concerned with feeding their families or gaining status by sacrificing a magnificent animal (Cribb 1987; Grandin 1988; Payne 1973).

## The archaeology of animal wealth

Judging from the ethnographic record, it is very common for herd animals to act as wealth. We should therefore expect that this occurred in the past, and we should include it in our archaeological models. Indeed, an important question that can only be answered archaeologically is at what point in the domestication process animals became wealth. We have seen that the use of animals as wealth affects herding practices. Zooarchaeologists have already developed a set of tools to study ancient herding practices, including age and sex mortality profiles, balance of taxa, pathologies, and seasonal slaughter patterns. It is simply a matter of adjusting our models to take into account wealth as well as subsistence uses of herd animals. As we have seen, the two can operate simultaneously and are only in partial conflict. Nevertheless, subsistence and wealth goals are sufficiently different that the operation of animal wealth leads to different herding decisions from those based on subsistence alone.

Zooarchaeologists have modeled strategies that optimize for meat, milk, and wool production, as well as risk reduction (Payne 1973; Redding 1984). What would a strategy maximizing wealth look like? One of the key features of animal wealth is that each animal carries value as a unit.

Thus to maximize wealth, the herder minimizes slaughter and maintains as many animals as possible. This would lead to a higher proportion of adults and a sex ratio with a larger percentage of males than in meat and milk strategies. Indeed, it would mimic a wool strategy, in which adult animals of both sexes are valued for their productive capabilities. It might also result in size reduction through time, because herders are more concerned with having as many animals as possible than with the size and condition of those animals. This overstocking could also lead to pathologies resulting from overcrowding and malnutrition. We can also expect that herders would be trading up and down according to their changing circumstances. These are household strategies, and only rarely will we be able to attribute animal bones to particular households. When we can, we should of course take full advantage and examine differing household strategies. On a larger scale, however, if conditions in an area are generally good for a time, we should see a shift toward large stock as most herders trade up. Long-term droughts or major epidemics or serious damage to pasture from overgrazing is likely to lead to a general trading down to small stock. Combining fine-grained climatic and environmental information with faunal data will thus be rewarding.

In particular, we should consider the effects of bridewealth on herding strategies. Kelly's (1985) study of the Nuer and the Dinka makes it clear that these effects can be profound and that they depend not only on the presence of bridewealth but also on its particular form. We have seen that much of the valorization of livestock, particularly the value of various demographic categories (adult males, white calves, etc.), derives from bridewealth requirements and that these requirements shape the herds. Because there are many ways that bridewealth might be specified, one cannot create a unitary model of a bridewealth signature in mortality profiles. However, we can be aware that bridewealth is likely to be a major factor shaping these profiles, and we can look for correlations between mortality profiles and population expansion or contraction. More generally, Keith Ray and Julian Thomas have suggested that the use of cattle in social exchanges constructs both kin and other relations among humans and the herd structure of the cattle (as a result of these exchanges): "This record would have made each herd literally a living history, the population structure of the herd providing a parallel for that of the human group, each herd/group characterised by genealogies and lines of descent" (Ray and Thomas 2003:41).

In addition to the animal bones themselves, there may be other signs that animals are acting as wealth. The "cattle complex" label was applied to African herders because not only did they raise cattle and use them as wealth but they also based their esthetic on them, named themselves after them, and so on. Thus artistic renditions of the large stock of the area may indicate that these animals have wealth value. If they depict age and sex characteristics, these depictions may give clues as to which are the most highly valued animals. Renditions of livestock in materials such as precious metals may show the transfer of valorization from one form of wealth to another.

When livestock act as wealth, there is a great temptation to build herds quickly by raiding. Hence increased warfare and the glorification of the warrior may be associated with animal wealth. We might also expect to see renegotiation of gender roles as livestock become wealth, particularly as they come to be used as bridewealth.

Although much work remains to be done, animal wealth has begun to receive some archaeological attention in recent years, chiefly in southern Africa, where ethnographic and ethnohistorical evidence attest the importance of cattle wealth in later periods, and in Europe. Drawing on this work and my own, I consider four broad topics in Old World archaeology where it may be useful to examine animal wealth: early agricultural societies in the Near East, the spread of mixed farming into Europe, the Secondary Products Revolution in Europe and the Near East, and the southern African Iron Age.

## ANIMAL WEALTH AND EARLY AGRICULTURE

It is hard to imagine that animals were domesticated in order to become wealth. However, because in my view the essence of domestication is the conversion of animals to property, once domesticated, livestock have the potential to function as wealth. In a limited sense, of course, livestock would be wealth from the start, simply because they are property. Yet how and when did they take on the special value that is so common ethnographically? And how and when can we recognize the appearance of bridewealth in the archaeological record? I begin by examining the archaeology of the southwest Asian region in the period during which the domestication of herd animals seems to have occurred, the Pre-Pottery Neolithic B, and the analogous cultures in Anatolia.

Although there is not complete consensus, most see plant domestication beginning during the Pre-Pottery Neolithic A (PPNA) and animal domestication during the Pre-Pottery Neolithic B (PPNB) in the Fertile Crescent (Bar-Yosef and Meadow 1995; Belfer-Cohen and Bar-Yosef 2000; Byrd 2005; Cauvin 2000a; Conolly et al. 2011; Crabtree 1993; Harris 1998; Helmer et al. 2005; Horwitz et al. 1999; Kislev 1999; Legge 1996; Lev-Yadun et al. 2000; Melamed et al. 2008; Verhoeven 2004; Vigne 2008; Willcox et al. 2008; Zeder 2008; Zeder and Hesse 2000; Zohary 1999; Zohary and Hopf 2000; but cf. Nesbitt 2002; Rosenberg and Redding 1998). The PPNB is also the period of the first substantial expansion of farming within and beyond the Fertile Crescent, and it is marked by the appearance of large, aggregated settlements (e.g., Basta, 'Ain Ghazal, Çatalhöyük) with rectangular buildings. Thus at the beginning of the PPNB or perhaps slightly before, sheep and goats are appropriated as property. Slightly later (probably) cattle and pigs are added to the livestock (see Table 6.1).

One of the classic criteria for recognizing animal domestication is size diminution. Many domestic animals become smaller than their wild counterparts. As we have seen, treating animals as wealth leads to privileging quantity over quality, and hence often to size reduction. Might this be the cause of the size diminution associated with domestication? The causes of size diminution with domestication are poorly understood and much debated. Possibilities include poor nutrition; restricted movement; deliberate selection for smaller and more easily managed animals; the 'island effect' of a restricted gene pool; and natural selection under conditions of protection from predation, controlled breeding, and higher intraspecific competition for food (Armitage 1986; Bökönyi 1969; Clutton-Brock 1992; Crabtree 1993; Legge 1996; Meadow 1989; Tchernov and Horwitz 1991). The issue is further complicated by a general size reduction in wild species in the early Holocene, presumably conforming to Bergmann's rule as the climate warmed (Chaplin 1969; Davis 1981). Nevertheless, the size reduction in some domestic animals is clearly greater than the climatically induced change in wild mammals. None of these causes is inconsistent with the influence of wealth considerations. The desire for as many animals as possible would simply mean that herders would be more likely to push nutrition and crowding to the limits, and they would be less likely to take steps, including selective breeding, to counteract size diminution.

It is likely that the valorization of animals as wealth contributed to their size reduction at some point. However, we cannot simply take size reduction as an indication of such valorization. First, not all animals become smaller when they are domesticated, including some such as horses and camels that are known to have operated as wealth. In addition, some species less likely to have been primary forms of animal wealth do show size diminution with domestication, such as cats and dogs. Second, recent work suggests that the apparent size reduction in goats in the early stages of domestication is really a change in sex ratios (Zeder 2001; Zeder and Hesse 2000; see also Köhler-Rollefson and Rollefson 2002). With herding, most males are killed off before adulthood, leaving mostly the smaller females to be measured. Thus the size range of the population is unchanged, but the mean size of measured adult bones is reduced.

Although the initial size reduction may be more apparent than real, there is no doubt that many domestic animals eventually become genuinely smaller. If diminution is to be taken as a sign of valuing quantity over quality, this is the point of interest. We need more careful studies of measurements region by region (because environmental factors also affect size) that examine the entire range of measurements, rather than simply comparing the means. For cattle, recent work shows that initial size reduction is seen mainly in males, reducing sexual dimorphism, and probably as an adaptation to the conditions of herding (Helmer et al. 2005). The relatively low proportions of cattle in Near Eastern Neolithic assemblages unfortunately creates sample size issues in trying to assess sex ratios and mortality profiles.

We have seen that herding practices that build wealth often rest on strategic trading up and down between small and large stock. However, our current understanding of early herding in the Near East is that only small stock (sheep and/or goats) were available initially. (This understanding may change as cattle and pig domestication dates are pushed back.) Somewhat similar situations would have applied for longer periods in China and South America, where there would have been effectively only large stock (pigs and camelids, respectively), unless one counts chickens in China and guinea pigs and (probably later) muscovy ducks in South America. The lack of opportunity to trade up and down would not prevent livestock from functioning as wealth (as demonstrated

ethnohistorically in the Andes). However, it would inhibit the accumulation of animal wealth to some degree, enhancing the risks of herding
and promoting other methods of risk reduction (such as integration with
plant agriculture).

The Near Eastern case is particularly interesting, however, in its lack of
large stock. Ethnographically, large stock have formed the main animal
wealth, with small stock acting as small change and generally being treated
in a much more utilitarian fashion. If people have only small stock, does
this prevent them from developing animal wealth? Or do the small stock
function as large stock in miniature until they are supplanted by larger
domestic animals? This is not an easy question, because the roles of small
and large stock are related partly to relative and partly to absolute size.
Small stock are obviously relatively smaller units of investment, and thus
it is less of a loss to slaughter one for consumption or exchange it for
other goods. However, they also lend themselves to routine slaughter
for subsistence because their absolute size is such that a single family
can consume the whole animal, whereas a larger carcass requires storage
or sharing among a larger group. It is therefore likely that small stock
function as wealth to a lesser degree than large stock. Indeed, where we
see small-stock-based pastoralism ethnographically, it tends to be tied
to production for exchange to provision cities (Khazanov 1994). These
animals are more commodities than wealth, and such societies do not
develop a "sheep complex" that puts small stock at the symbolic center
of the culture. It is worth noting that, although sheep and goats are
occasionally depicted in the PPN, they do not form a central image
in the way that cattle do in the PPNB and later in the Near East and
beyond.

Plant agriculture and sheep/goat herding spread from the Fertile Crescent into central Anatolia and the margins of South Asia without domestic
cattle. In both the upper Euphrates region and South Asia, we see signs of
local domestication of cattle (Helmer et al. 2005; Meadow 1993). Some
have interpreted the cattle imagery of this period as reflecting a bull cult
that may well have included sacrifice (Cauvin 1994, 2000b; Rice 1997).
Cattle domestication may have been motivated by the need to supply
sacrificial victims, or both domestication and the sacrifice of cattle may
have been expressions of a desire to control nature, the wild, and the
wild within. It is also possible that cattle were deliberately domesticated
to form a superior kind of animal wealth. Even if this were not the original

motivation, the raising of cattle for sacrifice and the prestige associated with this would likely lead to the valorization of cattle, as well as something resembling the cattle complex as reflected in the extensive cattle imagery in figurines and wall paintings and the placement or architectural installation of cattle body parts.

The PPNB shows signs of household differences in wealth not evident previously (Bar-Yosef and Meadow 1995; Garfinkel 1987). These are expressed in architectural and other media and are not archaeologically visible (as yet, at least) in terms of animal wealth. Yet the coincidence in time with animal domestication at least raises the possibility that animal wealth may in part have underwritten these differentials. Even if animal wealth did not drive the initial accumulations, it is likely to have been drawn into the wealth system.

The PPNB is also a period when art and, it is usually believed, ritual take on new prominence. This phenomenon is best known from the dramatic wall paintings, reliefs, and animal part installations at Çatalhöyük, but is also evident at slightly earlier sites such as Nevalı Çori and Bouqras (Clason 1989/90; Hauptmann 1999; Mellaart 1967; Russell and Meece 2006; Verhoeven 2002a). It really appears first in the late PPNA in southeastern Anatolia and northern Syria, most famously at Göbekli Tepe (Helmer et al. 2004; Peters and Schmidt 2004). Animals figure prominently in this art and probably also in the rituals (Russell and McGowan 2003), but it is chiefly wild animals that are depicted (Russell and Meece 2006). Although cattle (of uncertain domestication status) are included, this art cannot be seen as a simple celebration of wealth, animal or otherwise. Rather, the increase in art and ritual may reflect tensions as changes in social roles are contested (Hays 1993; Johnson 1982). At least in its most dramatic form, this art follows rather than precedes animal domestication. Thus it may be less about symbolically domesticating the wild (cf. Cauvin 1994; Hodder 1987, 1990) than about negotiating the conversion of animal property to animal wealth or about the emergence of wealth differentials in general. Building wealth requires a reallocation of labor, hence a redefinition of the division of labor. The would-be wealthy must induce others in their households and beyond to devote their efforts to production on the wealth-seeker's behalf. Gender and age roles are likely to be renegotiated, and new relations of clientship and subordination to be introduced. Some would benefit more than others, and such changes would be resisted.

During the PPNB, farming settlements begin to spread within and beyond the Levantine area in the first significant expansion of the Neolithic. Is this expansion simply a matter of the consolidation of farming, the mastery of agricultural techniques, and the growth of populations? There is probably some increase in population, but the substantially larger settlements that appear at this time seem to be more a matter of aggregation than population explosion. It does not appear that farmers are forced to seek new territory because of a land shortage at this point. Cauvin (1994) argues that instead the PPNB sees the genesis of an expansionary new ideology, what could probably be called a new religion. To the ideology of control of and separation from nature mediated by a female deity is added an explicitly male component of violent control and conquest symbolized by the bull and bull games. Although weapons are elaborated and take on new symbolic value, Cauvin does not see the expansion of the PPNB as military conquest. Rather it is the ideas that conquer, with northern Levantine people (missionaries?) blending and intermarrying with local populations.

Cauvin offers his mentalist model in reaction to the vulgar materialism of most explanations of the development of the Neolithic, based on factors such as population growth and climatic change. We might, however, link these ideological changes to social transformations resulting from the conversion of animals to property. After all, it is striking that the masculine symbol that develops as a counterpart to the supposed Goddess is not a humanoid god, but a bull. Some of the expansionary tendencies of the PPNB may derive from the new demands of animal wealth.

In particular, we should consider whether some of the expansion of the PPNB from the northern Levantine area and of the intermarriage with local people (both farmers in the southern Levant and foragers elsewhere) was driven by the operation of bridewealth. If so, then herd animals became both wealth and bridewealth virtually immediately on domestication, which perhaps suggests that some form of bridewealth in other media (such as the Mukogodo's beehives, for example) already existed. David Wengrow (1998) has suggested that the human female and cattle figurines that are common in the Neolithic of the Near East and southeast Europe are tokens of marriage exchanges of women for cattle. The advantage of this interpretation is that it explains why these two symbols rise to prominence at this time, something that others have not adequately accounted for. If these represent deities, the Goddess and the Bull God, why should the female principle be human and the male be animal so consistently, and why is it cattle in particular that represent the male god? Even if these are not deities but more general symbols of femaleness and maleness, the question remains. Wengrow is building on the argument of Denise Schmandt-Besserat (1983, 1992, 1996) that cuneiform writing originated from pressing clay tokens representing different kinds of goods into clay bullae. Earlier, the tokens themselves were exchanged to keep track of exchanges. She traces these tokens back to the beginning of the PPNB.

There are some difficulties with this argument, however. First, although Schmandt-Besserat's argument is convincing for later periods, the objects she identifies as the earliest tokens are not representational, but geometric objects such as cones and spheres. At Çatalhöyük, at any rate, the contexts in which they are found suggest use in cooking or pyrotechnology rather than exchange (Atalay 2006). Wengrow extends her definition of tokens to include what are conventionally termed figurines: relatively realistic depictions of humans and animals as opposed to the more schematic representations of Schmandt-Besserat's tokens. The notion of figurines as tokens of marriage exchanges, however, rests on the stereotype that all Neolithic human figurines are female. In fact, some are male, and the majority are not gendered. Moreover, if these were tokens of bridewealth exchanges, the number of cattle figurines should at least equal, and probably considerably exceed, that of human figurines. If they were actually used to keep track of transactions or contracts, one would expect several cattle for every woman, and probably that categories of cattle by age and sex would be clearly indicated. However, the number of human figurines generally exceeds the number of cattle or other animal figurines, and age and sex are rarely indicated on the cattle figurines. The bridewealth token interpretation also does not explain why human female and cattle imagery appears in other media (paintings, reliefs, architectural installations) that lend themselves less well to acting as records of exchanges. Yet it does explain why the figurines are so often found broken, in ways that appear deliberate; this might indicate the fulfillment of the contract and cancellation of the debt.

In sum, the lack of a sheep or goat complex and the burgeoning of cattle symbolism in the PPNB might suggest that animals did not become fully valorized as wealth until the domestication of large stock. However, the spread of the PPNB, which seems to involve a mixture of movement

by farmers and adoption by local foragers and farmers, apparently begins
before cattle domestication. It is tempting to see this spread as driven in
part by the need for more grazing land to expand herds, not necessarily
for subsistence but based on the desire for wealth; by the attractions of
animal wealth for those who did not yet possess it; and perhaps by the
need to acquire livestock to participate in bridewealth exchanges.

### ANIMAL WEALTH AND THE SPREAD OF AGRICULTURE

As we have seen, agricultural systems began to spread within southwest
Asia at about the time that herd animals were domesticated. Cattle symbolism, which existed at a low level even before cattle domestication,
blossoms during this period and comes to predominate among animal
symbols in the Neolithic. In particular, cattle are the only one of the
domestic animals represented with any frequency, although sheep and
goats usually supply the staple meat. Thus Neolithic animal symbolism is
more about cattle being food for thought than beef being good to eat.
Cattle clearly carried value beyond their subsistence contribution, and
domestic cattle may have functioned as wealth at least to some extent.
Subsequently, mixed farming (cereals, legumes, sheep, goat, cattle, and
pigs) continued to spread, ultimately across most of the Old World. In
this section I examine the spread of agriculture through Europe, where
it has been particularly well studied.

There is little doubt that the Neolithic agricultural system in Europe
derives from the Near East (although some have tried to argue for local
domestication of some taxa). Although some of the wild ancestors of
domesticated plants are found in Greece, and aurochsen and wild boar
were present throughout Europe, the wild ancestors of sheep and goats
did not occur in Europe. The spread of agriculture across Europe has most
often been modeled as a spread of Near Eastern farmers, with native foragers fading away in their wake. This is epitomized in the wave-of-advance
model, which postulates population growth pushing the inexorable and
steady spread of farmers from southeast to northwest (Ammerman and
Cavalli-Sforza 1971, 1984; Barbujani and Bertorelle 2001; Cavalli-Sforza
1996; Chikhi et al. 2002; Hazelwood and Steele 2004; Pinhasi and von
Cramon-Taubadel 2009; Renfrew 1996). In recent years, the smooth
wave has come to be seen as much more of a process of fits and starts,
and native foragers have been given a larger role (Bocquet-Appel et al.
2009; Bogucki 1996; Bogucki and Grygiel 1993; Morelli et al. 2010;

Pluciennik 1996; Price et al. 1995; Robb and Miracle 2007; Sampietro et al. 2007; Thomas 1996; Tsonev 1996; van Andel and Runnels 1995; Willis and Bennett 1994; Zvelebil 1986). Positions vary from those who see the spread of farming solely in terms of adoption by local foragers to those who see a more complex and regionally variable process, with the participation of foragers varying in kind and degree, as well as speed, in different parts of Europe.

Although agricultural populations were clearly larger than those of native foragers, it now seems that Neolithic population growth was not rapid enough to explain the rate of spread of farming communities (Richards 2003; Robb and Miracle 2007; Willis and Bennett 1994). Those parts of Europe that exhibit long-term frontiers between farmers and foragers also argue against an inexorable demographic expansion (Price et al. 1995). Thus, at least for some parts of Europe, notably in the central, northern, and western regions, we must ask why foragers chose to adopt farming and in many cases to blend and intermarry with immigrating farmers.

Although it was once thought that the advantages of agriculture were self-evident and sufficient motivation in themselves, few archaeologists now hold this view. In comparison to foraging, agriculture is more work, carries more risk, and usually leads to deterioration in health (Armelagos et al. 1991; Bowles 2011; Larsen 2006; Smith 1976). Some believe that the larger populations of farmers allowed them to overwhelm native foragers, perhaps aided by epidemic diseases (Diamond 1997). In these early stages of agriculture, however, with the small communities that typify Neolithic Europe, populations may not have been large and dense enough to support epidemic diseases. We should not discount coercion altogether; there is evidence of violent interactions between farmers and foragers in some areas of Europe. This violence seems to have occured primarily in those regions where long-term frontiers were maintained; that is, where foragers resisted the adoption of agriculture. However, the level of violence does not appear sufficient to support a model in which incoming farmers routinely slaughtered and enslaved native foragers. The European colonization of the New World is not a particularly good model for the spread of agriculture through Europe, because the differential in technology, political organization, and population size was much less in Neolithic Europe. There must surely have been tensions between immigrant farmers and native foragers, although they may have been eased by the tendency for these groups to settle in different segments of the landscape. For the most part, however, foragers' incorporation into farming societies must have been a matter of their active choice.

If farming was not a clearly superior mode of subsistence, why should foragers choose it? Recent answers have focused on the attraction of the wealth of farmers, the various material possessions that a more sedentary lifestyle and the increased productivity per unit of land associated with farming made possible, and the possibilities for aggregation and feasting (Bender 1985; Bogucki 2000; Dennell 1992; Fischer 1982; Price et al. 1995; Robb and Miracle 2007; Thomas 1996; Voytek and Tringham 1988; Zvelebil and Lillie 2000). Early peaceful interactions between farmers and foragers seem to have centered on the exchange of prestige goods, mainly flowing from farmers to foragers. These goods include pottery, stone axes, and later metal, all of which were introduced by the farming groups. It is likely that, as in so many parts of the world, farmers and foragers exchanged agricultural for forest products, such as game and honey. Livestock may have formed a part of these exchanges, as subsistence products, or wealth, or both.

The degree and kind of interaction between farmers and foragers varied locally through Europe. At a gross level, we can summarize them as follows. The initial immigrant farmers to Europe, who seem to have come across the Aegean from Anatolia, perhaps following established exchange routes, targeted alluvial soils in eastern Greece (Bogucki 1996; van Andel and Runnels 1995). Local forager populations appear to have been sparse and concentrated on the southern and western coasts, so that initially there would have been little interaction. As farmers expanded into these areas, there are indications of gradual adoption of domesticates and Neolithic technology by the foragers. As farming communities spread north through the Balkans, the main area of forager occupation was the rather densely populated Iron Gates region of the Danube, with rich fishing grounds. Here exchange with incoming farmers stimulated a florescence of material culture, best known from Lepenski Vir with its fish-faced stone sculptures, before the foragers either disappear or are absorbed into farming groups (Jovanović 1972; Radovanović 2000, 2006; Srejović 1972; Voytek and Tringham 1988). At roughly the same time that farmers began to expand through the Balkans, farming groups also moved west along the northern Mediterranean coast as far as southern France. Here they entered into sustained relations with local foragers, who acquired a few sheep and eventually developed their own pottery style, La Hoguette (Barnett 2000; Bernabeu Auban et al. 2001; Binder 2000; Bogucki and Grygiel 1993:406–7; Geddes 1985).

As farmers moved north and west from the Balkans, they encountered somewhat denser populations of foragers. In Central Europe, once again there often seems to have been a spatial partitioning of the landscape that may have reduced initial frictions, with farmers in the valleys and foragers in the upland interfluves. In some cases, at least, this pattern was sustained for many centuries, with foragers gradually and selectively adopting Neolithic artifacts and practices (Bogucki 2000; Nowak 2001; Zvelebil 1986). On the northern and western fringes of Central Europe, the situation was less one of interdigitation than of longstanding frontiers between foragers and farmers. Exchange clearly occurred across these boundaries, but violent interactions are more evident here than elsewhere. The impression is that local foragers resisted farming settlements in their regions, which perhaps did not lend themselves to complementary utilization as in Central Europe (Price 2000; Zvelebil 1996).

The Neolithic of the Atlantic fringe and northwest Europe, including Britain, has a somewhat different character from that of Central Europe. It is characterized by megalithic monuments, ephemeral settlements (in contrast to the substantial and symbolically salient houses of the Central and southeast European Neolithic), and perhaps a lesser reliance on agriculture. Many have seen these features in terms of native foragers selectively adopting certain, mainly ideological, features of the Neolithic, with little if any role for colonizing farmers (Arias 1999; Armit and Finlayson 1992; Thomas 1999). Recent work, especially stable isotope studies, suggests that the transition is marked by a sharp dietary shift, however, and there may be some role for migrating farmers (Collard et al. 2010; Milner 2002; Richards et al. 2003a, 2003b; Rowley-Conwy 2004; Schulting and Richards 2002; Thomas 2003). Nevertheless, local foragers probably played a larger role here than elsewhere in Europe.

What, then, is the place of domestic animals in the decisions made by foragers about whether and how to participate in farming? Ethnography has shown that the transition from hunting to herding is a difficult one, and it cannot occur without profound social transformations because of the very different property relations of herding. It has also shown that the lure of animal wealth can draw people into herding and that bridewealth is particularly powerful in this regard. Younger people, especially those shut out of alternative routes to prestige, are likely to be most attracted to herding, and young men may feel pushed into it in order to marry if their fathers begin accepting bridewealth in livestock. If the foragers recognize the value of the farmers' wealth, young women and their families may be interested in marrying into these groups. Farmers may seek such marriages to increase their labor pool and to maintain ties with foraging groups, with whom they exchange agricultural for forest products. If foragers will accept less bridewealth, it may also be a way for less wealthy farmers to marry.

All of this depends on the valorization of livestock as wealth, and perhaps on its use as bridewealth. In Europe the prime candidate for animal wealth is cattle. Sheep and goats play a relatively small subsistence role in the Neolithic outside of the Mediterranean zone. Even in Mediterranean areas, cattle have much greater symbolic importance than small stock or pigs. Cattle clearly carry value beyond their production of beef, and this value seems to intensify through time. As in the Near East, cattle figurines occur frequently in the European Neolithic. In the Late Neolithic of southeast Europe, we find stylized cattle horns, not unlike the later Minoan "horns of consecration," inside or on houses and house models (Gimbutas 1982; Raduncheva et al. 2002; Tringham et al. 1992). The only building from the Neolithic of the northern Balkans that can convincingly be described as a shrine, at the late Vinča site of Parţa in Romania, has cattle skulls placed on a clay platform, along with large clay humanoid figures (Lazarovici 1989). The valorization of cattle is particularly evident in their transfer to another medium of wealth at the Eneolithic cemetery of Varna, where numerous gold-sheet appliqués in the shape of cattle and cattle horns were recovered (Gimbutas 1977; Renfrew 1986). This is some of the earliest gold in Europe, a new form of wealth. We can thus see the gold bulls as the translation of cattle wealth into metallic wealth.

The earlier Neolithic of Central Europe exhibits less cattle symbolism. This is no doubt partly a matter of preservation: Houses here use much less clay in their construction, and they are not burnt at the end of their life cycle as those of southeast Europe often were. Figurines are less common here in general, but those that occur are more heavily weighted toward animal than human representations. Herding may play a larger role in these societies, however, so cattle were surely important.

The symbolic role of cattle becomes more obvious in the later Neolithic and Chalcolithic of Central Europe, but by then, as in the earlier Neolithic of northwest Europe, we are into the period of the Secondary Products Revolution, which is discussed in the next section.

Throughout the European Neolithic, the size of livestock, but especially cattle, continues to diminish. Indeed, this trend is not reversed until selective breeding counteracts it during the Roman period. After the fall of Rome, cattle again become smaller until the renewal of selective breeding in the Renaissance. Is this the result of wealth considerations stressing quantity over quality? Or is it simply poor animal husbandry technique? Although even before the Romans other kinds of wealth, notably coins and other forms of precious metals, were available, cattle wealth retained some importance. This can be seen even in early Roman society through etymology: The word *pecunia* (money) is derived from *pecus* (cattle, herd). As other forms of wealth became established, cattle wealth may have been largely symbolic, as it is today for the elite of Latin America and of Texas. With the fall of the Roman Empire, cattle wealth may have taken on more importance again. Certainly cattle wealth and cattle raiding figure prominently in Irish epics dating to the early medieval period (Faraday 1904). Early European herders did not deliberately select for smaller animals. Rather, their interest in maintaining the maximum number of animals as opposed to producing the greatest quantity of meat and milk both provided no incentive to select for larger animals and created conditions that would favor smaller animals. Only when other forms of wealth are secure can herders afford to treat their animals as commodities.

We have seen that, when animals are wealth, herders will pursue strategies of trading up and down between large and small stock according to their fortunes. There are some situations in which household strategies may coalesce to produce a general trend toward trading up through time. This may happen when herding is first established in a region or when a new settlement is founded by the emigration of primarily young and unestablished households. We need to look more closely at local sequences with this in mind, but there are some suggestive cases. For example, Halstead (1981a:322) notes a decrease in sheep and goats relative to cattle during the Greek Neolithic. He interprets this drop as the result of vegetational change caused by cultivation, but might it instead reflect the ability of larger numbers of households to trade up as herds become more established? On a smaller scale, there is a slight shift from small to large stock within the 100–200 years of occupation at Opovo (Russell 1999). This could represent trading up as the new households establish themselves.

Some have recognized that the wealth value of cattle played an important role in European Neolithic economies, perhaps contributing to their spread (Barker 1992; Davis and Payne 1993; Halstead 1981a; Marciniak 2005a; Orton 2010a; Ray and Thomas 2003; Runnels and van Andel 1988). Sherratt (1982) has specifically argued that the exchange of livestock, especially cattle, underpinned the large settlements and rich material culture that we see in certain areas during the Neolithic: Çatalhöyük in central Anatolia, Thessaly in Greece, the Maritsa basin in Thrace, the lower Danube valley, and the Carpathian basin (although he discusses only the first and especially the last in detail). He sees these areas as islands of good grazing surrounded by heavier forest, thus able to produce live cattle for export to new settlements established in the surrounding areas. Once these settlements cleared enough land for cattle grazing and built their herds, the cattle-exporting regions lost their advantage and suffered economic collapse. This model does not work well for Çatalhöyük given our present understanding of cattle domestication at the site. We see the beginning of this process only roughly two-thirds of the way through the occupation, when it was already large and rich, so cattle wealth cannot be the basis of its success. Yet the Neolithic settlers of the other regions clearly did have domestic cattle and may well have used them to build wealth.

I have argued earlier (see the section, *The Origins of Bridewealth*) that bridewealth is likely to operate in mixed farming societies in which women perform most of the agricultural and men most of the herding labor, and in which labor rather than land is the limiting factor. Most of this certainly applies to the European Neolithic, although the gendered division of labor is uncertain. Many have seen these societies, especially those of southeast Europe, as prime examples of the domestic mode of production. We have seen that in the European Neolithic cattle were valued beyond their subsistence contribution. Thus it is distinctly likely that bridewealth in cattle was practiced in many of these societies. Sherratt suggests that bridewealth may have been the context of much of the cattle exchange in the Carpathian basin and his other cattle-exporting zones. Douglas Price (1995:145) argues that bridewealth, along with competitive feasting, may have been a strategy practiced by Neolithic farmers to draw others into debt relationships, motivate their kin and associates to produce a surplus, and gain prestige.

If prestige items such as livestock, decorated pottery, and stone and metal axes were mutually regarded as such by both farmers and foragers, then the farmers, with their ability to accumulate more possessions, would generally hold higher status than the foragers. Only in a few places where sedentary or semi-sedentary foragers harvested rich aquatic resources, as in the Iron Gates and coastal northwest Europe, could the foragers compete on something like an equal footing. It is precisely those places where stable frontiers persisted for centuries. In most cases foragers would be at a disadvantage in the exchange of prestige goods, and thus we might expect not simply intermarriage but hypergyny, with women tending to marry into higher status families to gain access for themselves, their families, and their offspring to this status and wealth (Zvelebil 1996). Hypergyny may be motivated simply by the desire for access to prestige and wealth, but would operate more powerfully if bridewealth were offered. Then, as with the Mukogodo, the forager men might have to adopt herding just to be able to marry.

A recent strontium isotope study provides support for hypergyny in the upper Rhine valley in Germany (Price et al. 2001). Strontium isotopes derive from the soil and are deposited in the skeleton. Because teeth do not change after they erupt, but bones are continuously renewed and remodeled through life, if people move to a different area the strontium isotope signatures in their teeth and bones will differ. In this region, the earliest Neolithic culture is the Linear Pottery (LBK). An early LBK cemetery held a high proportion of immigrants, both male and female. This is interpreted as the arrival of a whole group, with their children born after their arrival showing the local strontium signature. At a later LBK site, the immigrants are mostly women. This is seen as the result of intermarriage into an established group. Although the origin of the immigrating women cannot yet be established with certainty, their isotopic signatures are consistent with those of adjacent foraging groups. It is to be hoped that future isotope and DNA studies will shed further light on this process, which surely varied locally across Europe. A combination of stable isotope analysis and ancient DNA has identified at least one case of a woman marrying into a later Neolithic village in Germany, for example (Haak et al. 2008). Recent ancient DNA work has shown that early farmers in Central Europe have Near Eastern ancestry

(Bramanti et al. 2009; Haak et al. 2010), so that it should be possible to identify local foragers who intermarried with them.

Foragers who found it necessary or desirable to acquire livestock would be faced with a limited number of options. They could capture and tame feral animals that had escaped from the herders (Bogucki 1995). For cattle and pigs in Europe, they could also capture and tame local wild animals. However, it may be that domestic pigs and cattle were by this time sufficiently changed that wild forms would not be accepted as bridewealth payments. Bridewealth requirements are often specific and might demand a color or horn shape not found in morphologically wild animals. Another option was to raid the herds of the farmers. They could acquire livestock through exchange, but this might be difficult if there was a limited set of goods exchangeable with cattle and foragers did not have easy access to such goods. If grain were among these exchangeable goods, it would provide an incentive for plant agriculture as well as herding. Or they could marry their daughters and sisters to those who would pay bridewealth in cattle. No doubt all of these strategies were used to varying degrees, but bridewealth would likely soon come to predominate. Because one of the major motivations for acquiring cattle was probably to enable the payment of bridewealth so forager men could marry, they would soon, if successful, be drawn into the reciprocal system.

THE SECONDARY PRODUCTS REVOLUTION

In analogy to the Neolithic Revolution (Childe 1951) of which animal domestication forms a part, Sherratt (1981, 1982, 1983) has proposed a later Secondary Products Revolution (SPR) in the use of domestic animals in the Old World. Although Sherratt and others believe that early domestic animals were used only for their meat, the use of living products such as milk, wool, and traction made herding more productive, dramatically so, in Sherratt's view. Sherratt argues that dairy, wool, and traction (both plows and wheeled vehicles) all appear at about the same time, around 5500 BP in the Near East, and spread very rapidly over much of the Old World as part of an integrated system that had far-reaching effects. Plows increased production by permitting the cultivation of both larger areas and heavier soils. The cart and other animal transport aided agriculture and permitted cities to draw on a larger area, integrating regions. Transport animals such as horses, donkeys, and camels are domesticated around this time. Wool textiles provided a product suitable for exchange from agriculturally marginal areas, permitting the development of specialized pastoralism. Dairy provided an alternative food source so that domestic animals need not be slaughtered for meat, but could be kept alive for wool and labor. Keeping animals for their living products might promote larger herds, and it increases the value of animals and encourages raiding and warfare. These changes reinforced each other and had major social consequences.

Plow agriculture means a greater investment in a particular plot of land, so land tenure and inheritance became more important. Following Jack Goody (1976), Sherratt associates hoe agriculture with female labor and plow agriculture with male labor. Bronze Age European rock art depicting men plowing (Briard 1987) tends to support this association, although finds of ards in bog hoards of female-associated artifacts (based on burials) may indicate that Late Bronze Age women in Denmark also plowed (Gibbs 1987). Thus the SPR involves a major shift in the gendered division of labor and in gender relations, because hoe agriculture is also associated with matriliny and plow agriculture with patriliny. Sherratt suggests that men's assumption of most of the agricultural labor freed women to devote substantial time to textile manufacture, thereby bolstering trade. "The secondary products revolution produced an economy dominated by men, who played a dominant role in handling large livestock either as herds or in ploughing. Women became increasingly relegated to the domestic sphere" (Sherratt 1981:299). One could, however, see their role in textile and perhaps dairy production as giving women an important new economic power base (Chapman 1997:137). The increased value of land creates opportunities for building inequality based on land wealth. Sherratt argues that this rising inequality, along with the increased productivity of the SPR and its economic integration of larger areas, led to urbanization in the Near East. Ultimately, he sees the plow and cart, exemplifying the first use of nonhuman power to mechanize agriculture, as leading to further mechanization. He suggests that industrialization occurred in the Old World and not in the New because only Old World societies used animal traction. Bökönyi (1969:222) credits the use of secondary products in the late Neolithic of southeast Europe with stimulating a "fever of domestication," in which cattle herds in the Carpathian basin were supplemented by the capture and taming of local aurochsen. This is the same intensive cattle herding that Sherratt (1982) attributes to breeding cattle for export to surrounding communities (see previous section).

Just as with the Neolithic Revolution, many have questioned how revolutionary the SPR was in the sense of being a sudden shift or a package of new traits arriving in Europe ca. 5500 BP. In particular, there is considerable evidence for the use of milk in temperate Europe well before the SPR. Mortality profiles of cattle, sheep, and goat at some sites suggest combined meat and milk strategies, for instance in early Neolithic northern Italy (Rowley-Conwy 2000). Bogucki (1984, 1989) has argued convincingly that the ceramic sieves of the Central European LBK were used to process dairy products such as cheese. New techniques for detecting traces of milk on ancient pottery have pushed dairy use back to the 9th millennium BP in the Near East (Craig et al. 2000; Dudd and Evershed 1998; Evershed et al. 2008). The plow may also have appeared somewhat sooner, around 7000–6500 BP in southeast Europe (Chapman 1981, Mateescu 1975). The timing of the first use of cattle for traction, too, may soon be clarified by new methods of detecting the effects of traction on cattle bones, so far applied mainly in Roman and medieval contexts (Bartosiewicz 1993; Bartosiewicz et al. 1997; de Cupere et al. 2000). The only Neolithic study that identifies the use of cattle for traction is from a Scandinavian site dating from the time of the SPR (Johannsen 2005).

Although some use of secondary products seems to have occurred before the SPR, signs of intensive dairy and wool use do not show up in mortality profiles in Europe and the Near East until this time, which is roughly the Early Bronze Age in the Near East, the Copper Age in southeast Europe, the late Neolithic in Central Europe, and the early Neolithic in northwest Europe (Davis 1984b; Greenfield 1988; 1989, 1999, 2005; Grigson 2000; Halstead 1981a, 1992; Legge 1989, 2005; Miracle and Forenbaher 2005; Sakellaridis 1979; Whitcher et al. 1998; but cf. Arbuckle et al. 2009; Makarewicz 2009; Vigne and Helmer 2007). Therefore many regard the SPR not as a sudden innovation in herding strategies, but as an intensification (Barker and Gamble 1985; Bogucki 1993; Chapman 1997; Grigson 2000; Lev-Tov 2000).

Whether innovation or intensification, the SPR is an interesting and important phenomenon. This intensified use of animals and associated technology such as the plow and wheeled vehicles appears to have spread rapidly across Europe so as to form a near-synchronous horizon. Bronze metallurgy, developed at about the same time in the Near East, spread more slowly. The SPR is associated with increasing inequality, although more so in some regions than others. Graeme Barker and Clive Gamble (1985:18) call the SPR an "essential component in the development of social ranks and classes," not only because it broadens the subsistence base but also because they associate it with the keeping of live animals for prestige purposes; that is, as wealth. The value of animals, or rather of cattle and later of horses, seems to increase at this time.

Again, this valorization takes somewhat different forms in various parts of Europe. It is perhaps seen least clearly in the southeast, where there is little symbolic celebration of cattle or traction at this period. Only on the borderlands of southeast and Central Europe, in the late Chalcolithic Baden culture of Central Europe and the northern Balkans, do we find such manifestations. Cups in the form of wheeled carts appear in Baden burials and continue into the Early Bronze Age. These cups are models of carts alone, with no depiction of the animals that drew them. Later, in the Bronze and Iron Ages, cart models are found here and elsewhere in Europe drawn sometimes by cattle, sometimes by birds such as ducks and geese. Depictions of cattle-drawn carts are found on pottery from the late Funnel Beaker (TRB) culture of Poland, immediately preceding the Baden culture. Burials of pairs of cattle, alone or accompanying human burials, appear in the Baden culture as well and in the contemporary Globular Amphora culture of Poland and Germany (Milisauskas and Kruk 1991; Sherratt 1981:265). These burials are usually interpreted as yoked pairs of traction animals that would have drawn the carts or plows, presumably sacrificed at their owners' funerals or on other occasions.

In west and northwest Europe, we see more attention to the plow than the cart, and to cattle as objects of wealth in themselves. Furrows from actual plows (or more properly ards) are found beneath burial mounds (barrows) in northwest Europe. There is some disagreement as to whether the furrows simply represent fortuitous preservation of field surfaces or whether plowing was part of the funerary ritual (Rowley-Conwy 1987). It is hard to be sure, but it seems unlikely that people would choose to construct a burial mound in the middle of a plowed field. Given the numerous Neolithic and Bronze Age depictions of plows in rock art (Briard 1987:25–26), it is more plausible that the plowing held ritual significance. Plowing is often linked to the male contribution to fertility, as inseminating the earth, and hence might well be associated with death and rebirth. This association is bolstered by the rock art plowing scenes, which generally include clearly male human figures. Some interpret the erect phalluses in these scenes as references to fertility, although they may simply be intended to mark the figures as male. In any case, it seems clear that plows and plowing carried strong symbolic significance in addition to their more purely agricultural role. Evidence that Bronze Age women may have plowed (Gibbs 1987) suggests the plowing scenes may be more about male ideology than subsistence practice.

In many parts of Europe, archaeologists have argued for a more pastoral way of life at this period. This means a larger role for domestic animals in the subsistence economy, and often more mobility and more ephemeral settlements. In the Balkans, this period may see the beginning of transhumant pastoralism, still practiced by groups such as the Aroumani and Vlahs (Greenfield 1999). There are surely complex reasons for this change in settlement pattern (e.g., Tringham and Krstić 1990), but the increased value of cattle may be one factor.

Other changes occur at the time of the SPR. Although earlier Neolithic ceramics often featured elaborate serving ware likely to have been used in contexts of feasting and hospitality, roughly at the time of the SPR there is a new emphasis on drinking paraphernalia, probably also used in ceremonial contexts. These are usually associated with some kind of alcoholic beverage, whether wine, beer, mead, or kumiss (fermented milk), suggesting that drinking assumed a larger role in hospitality at this point. Is this because, as Sherratt (1981:280–2) suggests, the advent of dairy production enabled kumiss manufacture at this point? It seems more likely that a variety of beverages were consumed; with grain readily available, the Neolithic and Bronze Age peoples of Europe need not have been limited to kumiss, traditionally a drink of pastoralists. Traces of wine have been found even earlier in and near the Caucasus (McGovern 2003). Indeed, Sherratt (1986) later argued for mead or mixed honey, fruit, and grain beverages of the type that Patrick McGovern (2003) has called "grog" rather than kumiss, as indicated by residue from a Danish Bronze Age birchbark container.

Future studies of residues from these drinking vessels may clarify what people were tippling during and after the SPR. More importantly, this period marks a shift in which drinking assumes a larger role than eating in feasting and hospitality. Grain, fruit, honey, and other raw materials for alcoholic beverages had been available for a long time and were very likely used to make beer, wine, mead, or grog. The SPR may or may not coincide with increased consumption of alcohol, but drinking moves to center stage and takes on new ceremonial significance. Is liquor a replacement for copious meat as cattle become too valuable to slaughter for all but the most important occasions? Or is this simply the spread of a new rite and perhaps a new, male-linked ideology (Hodder 1990:93)?

Another key change at this period is a shift from female to male imagery in human representations. Although this change should not be overstated – earlier figurines and other representations include some men and usually the majority are not clearly gendered, and female images do appear after the SPR – the change is real and striking. Moreover, it is not simply men who now dominate human representations, but male warriors: men with weapons or the weapons alone. Weapons such as daggers also appear in burials as an apparent mark of masculinity. Warfare seems to become more important in both practical and ideological terms. Among other things, this militarization may be related to the increased value of cattle, which stimulates cattle raids and necessitates their defense.

Clearly gender roles were being renegotiated, and the art no doubt forms part of these negotiations (just as the predominantly female representations may have done earlier in the Neolithic). The nature of these changes has been much debated (e.g., Chapman 1997; Gimbutas 1991; Hodder 1991; Sherratt 1981), and this is not the place for a thorough discussion of these issues. However, we might consider the double impact on women's lives of the increased value of cattle through their use in bridewealth and the rise of a warrior elite. At the same time we should recognize that the increased importance of textiles, dairy, and brewing, all traditional female activities, might have bolstered women's position. Yet as John Chapman (1997:137) notes, "[T]he onset of secondary products created new opportunities for the consolidation of economic power, but in spatially differentiated and gender-contrasting sectors – the *domus* and the *agrios*."

Farming reached the Atlantic fringe of Europe with the SPR already in progress. Moreover, at least in part of this area, this represented the breaching of a long-term, stable frontier between farmers and foragers (Price 2000). In southern Scandinavia, the transition from Mesolithic to Neolithic seems to involve the adoption of pottery and prestige goods before farming. The populous, sedentary Mesolithic foragers of this coastal region apparently needed agriculture only after rising elites, based on the exchange of these prestige goods, created a "need" for increased productivity to support their bids for power through competitive feasting and similar stratagems (Price 1995). The enhanced value of cattle at this time may have been one major incentive to adopt farming; obtaining grain for beer may have been another. This may partially explain the special character of the Neolithic of northwest Europe: focused on monument rather than house, apparently more mobile and pastoral. The high value of cattle encouraged investment in herds rather than cereal agriculture and sturdy houses, although plant agriculture was practiced at least on a small scale.

In sum, although the SPR probably does not mark the first use of secondary products, their use became much more intensive and was accompanied by other striking social changes. Many of these changes are directly or indirectly linked to the increased valorization of cattle. Some have argued that this is the point at which cattle take on value as wealth and bridewealth (Bogucki 1993). As I have outlined in previous sections, I believe there is evidence of the wealth value of cattle, and more tentatively of their use as bridewealth, earlier in the Neolithic. However, just like the secondary products, the wealth value of cattle clearly intensifies sharply with the SPR. I would suggest, however, that it is not simply the increased subsistence value of living adult animals that is responsible for this greater value. Rather, secondary products *enable* people to live off their herds while slaughtering fewer of them, so that they can more effectively build cattle wealth. That is, cattle did not take on wealth value because they made a more important contribution to subsistence; the ability to live off secondary products allowed their preexisting wealth value to be realized with fewer constraints. So we should perhaps see the SPR not as a response to population growth, necessitating higher food production, as Sherratt argues, but as a strategy to build more wealth.

CATTLE WEALTH IN THE SOUTHERN AFRICAN IRON AGE
Southern Africa is the one area where cattle wealth has received substantial archaeological attention, given the direct continuities with ethnographically known cultures for which cattle wealth was central. Huffman (1990) has broadened the interpretations of cattle remains by drawing on both ethnography and a wider range of archaeological remains than the

animal bones themselves. A rhetorical device often used in faunal reports equates the percentage of bones (or minimum number of individuals or some other measure of abundance) of a species with the "importance" of that species in the economy. Huffman (1990:5–6) challenges this narrow view of the economy: "[T]he economic importance of a resource is dependent upon inter-related cultural factors such as supply and demand and the complexity of use, not numerical abundance. For example, wild fruits frequently eaten by herdboys are not as important as cattle that are exchanged for wives, given as tribute, sacrificed to the ancestors and consumed by guests." Because bridewealth is important in contemporary southern African societies, Huffman considers when cattle became bridewealth in this region and how this might be recognized archaeologically. He points to non-osteological evidence of cattle's importance, such as thick dung deposits marking kraals where cattle were enclosed, and settlement layouts that center on byres.

In the Early Iron Age (EIA) cattle bones are relatively scarce, but other evidence, such as storage facilities, shows that people had definitively switched from the foraging values of sharing to the agropastoral values of accumulation. Moreover, the dung deposits represented by phytoliths indicate a larger number of cattle were kept than implied by the faunal remains. Ethnographically, most eastern Bantu groups that practice bridewealth have settlements that center on livestock byres and communal storage controlled by the ruling elite. This area also contains high-status burials. Low-status burials, huts, and private granaries ring this public area. All known eastern Bantu societies with this settlement layout practice bridewealth. Huffman traces this pattern to at least EIA 2 (ca. 1200 BP) and probably EIA 1 (cf. Greenfield and van Schalkwyk 2006). Huffman suggests that, in addition to the disinclination to slaughter valuable cattle, the deceptively low proportion of cattle bones may result from differential discard practices. Contemporary Nguni speakers pulverize and burn the bones of sacrificed animals and scatter the ash in the byre or on the fields. If a high proportion of slaughtered cattle were sacrifices, such a practice would make them zooarchaeologically invisible. Elizabeth Arnold (2008) challenges this view, however, at least for the Thukela Valley, where she observes that not only are cattle few in number in the Early Iron Age (sheep and goats predominate) but also none of the livestock are managed to maximize herd size. Mortality profiles do not show a predominance of adults, which would indicate a reluctance to slaughter livestock. Only at the end of the Early Iron Age is such a pattern evident, and only for the sheep and goats.

This situation changed later in the Iron Age, at least in some areas. In southern Africa, cattle wealth became a basis for chiefly power. Here, and also in some East African kingdoms, the chief or king held some rights to all cattle belonging to his followers; in some cases he owned all of them (Barker 1992; Reid 1996). Although other valuables such as metals were also important, much of elite power rested on cattle wealth. On the one hand, kings could lend out or allocate cattle to their followers, or they could extract cattle as fines or taxes. On the other, they were expected to use their cattle to provision urban workers. Thus Iron Age centers show cattle mortality patterns reflecting an emphasis on meat production, with slaughter targeting animals, probably mostly males, at the late juvenile–subadult stage when they near full size. This pattern has been seen as elite privilege and the wasteful consumption of tender meat, but it is better interpreted as large-scale provisioning of lower classes (Reid 1996); a similar process may be observed in early Near Eastern states (Zeder 1991). Shaw Badenhorst and Ina Plug (2002) tentatively attribute size reduction in Late Iron Age cattle to overstocking due to their wealth value. Livestock remains are abundant at Iron Age sites of the Toutswe tradition in Botswana, but a stable isotope study shows that they contributed little to the diet, so cattle probably served mainly as wealth (Murphy 2010).

Scholars may wrangle over when cattle became an important source of wealth in southern Africa and how this wealth functioned, but few would dispute that at least by the later Iron Age cattle held wealth value. Many see this as central to the emergence of complex societies in this region. The area holds great potential for understanding the process of the valorization of cattle. Cattle wealth is hard to ignore here because the societies in question are relatively recent and clearly linked to ethnographically known groups for which cattle wealth is crucial and well documented. Deeper in prehistory we do not have the advantage of this direct historical linkage, so we must work to build methods to study animal wealth on the basis of archaeological evidence alone.

## APPROACHES TO ANIMAL WEALTH

These case studies have operated at a gross scale and serve to sketch the possibilities of considering wealth as a factor in herding practices.

Much work remains to be done at a finer level. Although we can see some of the effects of wealth at the regional and site scales, wealth interactions and strategies operate at the level of the household. Thus where possible it is important to employ the techniques of household archaeology. We will not always be able to trace the herding strategies of individual households, but we can often look at the faunal evidence together with other signs of household wealth and difference, such as architectural variation, depictions of animals, and isotopic studies of diet (Halstead 1992). We must draw on many lines of evidence, but the key is to include wealth value in our models of herding. We have long been willing to view metals in prehistory as having value beyond their ability to hold a cutting edge. We now need to recognize that live animals had value beyond protein, calories, and fiber.

9

# Meat beyond diet

> [F]ood selection is imbued with social rules and meaning, and it is clear from the extent of its association with cultural rituals, both religious and secular, that meat is a medium particularly rich in social meaning.... Our attitudes toward meat, I suggest, are a reflection of our world view, and changing habits in meat consumption may well indicate a changing perception of the world we inhabit. (Fiddes 1991:5)

The bulk of zooarchaeological work has concerned itself with meat, but meat as protein and calories. Here I consider meat as food; that is to say, the social aspects of meat. Recently archaeologists have devoted substantial attention to the social facets of food and commensality (e.g., Halstead and Barrett 2004; Jones 2007; Twiss 2007), building on a long tradition of such work in sociocultural anthropology (e.g., Douglas 1984; Goody 1982; Harris 1985; Kahn 1986; Lévi-Strauss 1988). As noted in Chapter 4, meat in particular carries value well beyond its nutritional contribution. It is therefore especially suited to enacting social relationships. Sharing meat, offering it to guests, and conspicuously consuming it make powerful statements about identity and status.

## Cooking and consumption

Until recently, cooking and consumption of meat received short shrift in zooarchaeological analysis. Gifford-Gonzales (1993) argues convincingly that in a field then dominated by men, zooarchaeologists, perhaps unconsciously, relegated food preparation to the female sphere, and hence regarded it as unimportant. Consumption in general was of little interest, both because of its domestic, feminine associations and because Marx and others privileged production. For example, Binford (1981:136),

in his seminal work on the importance of taphonomy in zooarchaeological interpretation, presents ample detail and discussion of butchering
techniques and their traces. However, he dismisses the traces of cooking
and consumption in a single sentence, even though he notes that they are
more numerous than butcher marks and often obscure them. Butchery,
typically perceived as a masculine task, has been extensively studied. In
fact, women often participate in butchery or even play a larger role in it
than men (Szuter 2001). Cooking has only recently received archaeological attention.

In contrast, sociocultural anthropologists have long seen cooking as
significant. Nutritionally, cooking enhances some nutrients and destroys
others, and it makes many foods, including meat, more easily digestible
(Jones 2007; Wrangham 2009). Symbolically, in most cultures it is a mark
of humanity that sets us apart from other animals (Brightman 1993:157;
Fiddes 1991:114; Lévi-Strauss 1965; Salisbury 1994:64). However, a
recent study (Wobber et al. 2008) shows that great apes prefer cooked
foods to raw in most cases, so that the taste for cooking, if not the ability
to perform it, may predate hominids.

Goody (1982) famously distinguishes everyday cooking from the "cuisine" found initially in elite circles in state societies. He emphasizes cuisine's use of rare, exotic, or costly ingredients; elaborate recipes requiring
specialized personnel and equipment; and value added by extra labor
input. Valasia Isaakidou (2007) draws on multiple lines of evidence,
including texts and ceramic cooking wares, to argue for the development
of cuisine in Goody's sense at Minoan Knossos. Among the meats, Isaakidou stresses the presence of rare, imported fallow deer, as well as a shift
to more mature domestic animals (perhaps the sign of costly fattening of
adult animals, although there are other ways to interpret this move, as
she notes). The number and distribution of cut marks also indicate that
meat is butchered into smaller portions during the palatial period, permitting a wider variety of cooking methods and, in contrast to roasting
large joints, enabling dishes that combine meat with other ingredients in
more elaborate recipes.

Even societies lacking cuisine, however, can make strong statements
by cooking special foods. Druze families precede business negotiations,
including contracting marriages, with dinners prominently featuring
meat, eaten only on special occasions. The importance of the occasion
and the status of the guest are marked by the choice of taxon (lamb

or mutton being the most highly valued) and body part. Rather than the tender, meaty portions that we might consider high quality (Binford 1981), the best cuts are the head and sternum, which verify the species offered (Grantham 1995). More ordinary food preparation can also be laden with meaning. Chipewyan women derive satisfaction and construct their gender identity through the skillful drying of meat (Sharp 1988).

Meat consumption can define status boundaries. Exotic foods carry prestige and are often a feature of stratified societies, particularly empires (Jones 2007; Sherratt 1995). Plant foods lend themselves more readily than animals or meat to the long-distance transport that renders them exotic, but some meat products, particularly various forms of preserved fish, may travel long distances (Arndt et al. 2003; James Barrett et al. 2008; Van Neer et al. 2004). Wild game is often a local "exotic" product reserved for nobility (Allsen 2006; Betzig 2008; Fiskesjö 2001; Ikram 2004; Lion and Michel 2006; Salisbury 1994). When meat is expensive, the simple act of eating it regularly marks wealth and power. Thus in late medieval Europe meat was scarce and costly, so that ordinary people rarely ate it; in contrast, the nobility gorged on it, eating 2–3 pounds of meat and fish per person per day (Salisbury 1994:57–8).

Cooking methods may also mark distinctions. In addition to the elaborate cuisine of the elite, simply roasting meat carries status because it requires young animals; tougher animals and cuts need slow stewing (Lévi-Strauss 1965; Salisbury 1994:59). In Greek sacrificial practice, cooking methods differentiate the inner circle of participants, who eat the roasted innards, from the broader group, who partake of stewed meat (Detienne 1979).

## Meat sharing

Sharing food, especially meat, plays a large role in many accounts of human evolution. Food sharing is not unique to humans, however. As we have seen in Chapter 4, members of the crow family resemble humans in their flexible, broad-based subsistence strategy and their sociality. They also resemble us in their food sharing, which occurs both within and beyond the family unit. At least in some species, this sharing goes beyond the simple co-feeding seen in many species. Young ravens will direct each other to food sources, even in lean times and even though most of the ravens are unrelated. They apparently benefit from having large groups of young ravens to fend off the local adults who control territories and to defend carcasses occurring within them (Heinrich and Marzluff 1995). Rooks offer food to each other in patterns that reflect and construct social relationships within the flock (Scheid et al. 2008). In what may be an illuminating parallel to early humans, a recent simulation suggests that wolves may hunt in groups and share food to minimize losses from raven scavenging (Vucetich et al. 2004). Cape hunting dogs (a wild African canid) practice ritualized food sharing in which one animal swallows meat regurgitated by another, apparently reinforcing group bonds (Fox 1978:21).

Other primates also share meat and, to a lesser extent, concentrated, high-value plant foods. As discussed in Chapter 4 (*Subsistence Hunting*), chimpanzees share the meat they hunt. Primatologists debate the reasons for this sharing, much of which does not follow lines of relatedness. Although some have argued that this sharing amounts to tolerated theft, in which it is less costly to share with persistent beggars than to fend them off, most see it as crucial to building and maintaining social relationships, whether between males and females in consortships or among males (de Waal 1989; Gilby 2006; McGrew 1996; Mitani and Watts 1999, 2001). Recent laboratory experiments suggest that chimpanzees will not give food to group members when they suffer virtually no cost either way (Vonk et al. 2008). In sum, chimpanzees will not share unless prompted by begging, but when confronted by beggars they take other, social factors into account in the decision to hoard or share. Bonobos hunt less than chimpanzees, so they share meat less often than plant foods. For bonobos, female–female relations are stronger than male coalitions, and food sharing constructs these relationships (Hohmann and Fruth 1996). In contrast, Capuchin monkeys hunt about as much as chimpanzees, but do not hunt cooperatively or share meat except with infants; the same is true of baboons (Stanford 1999:188–95).

Food sharing is one of the contenders for a universal human behavior, although as with other primates some foods are more likely to be shared than others, with meat primary among them. James Enloe (2003) notes that sharing rules are variable among human societies, and he stresses that sharing usually occurs in multiple stages with differing sets of rules – which typically become less formal as sharing moves from primary division at the kill site or first arrival at the habitation site to secondary and often tertiary sharing as the initial shares are subdivided and passed on to relatives, friends, and neighbors (e.g., Bahuchet 1990; Bodenhorn 2000; Gould 1967; Kitanishi 2000; Whitehead 2000; Woodburn 1998:52). Martin Jones (2007) sees the unique features of human food sharing as the sharing beyond kin and even residence groups, the typically low tension around food sharing, and the conversation and pleasant social interaction that accompany meals. He argues that this combination is fully formed in the Upper Paleolithic, at which time conversation is added to the meal and the hearth for the first time becomes a social focus point. In fact there is often considerable tension around primary sharing divisions, but generally much less during actual consumption.

Many have given food sharing a major role in human evolution. Washburn (Washburn and Avis 1958) suggested that hunting led to male food sharing among early hominids, because carnivores share meat but male primates do not share plant food. More recent work has shown that chimpanzees and bonobos do share plant foods, but has also stressed the importance of meat sharing among males. Glynn Isaac (1978) elaborated this observation to argue that food sharing and delayed consumption at a home base are fundamental to the development of human society. This sharing builds on the gendered division of labor, with men hunting and women gathering plant foods. However, this model has been widely critiqued, particularly with respect to the roles of hunting and home bases occupied by nuclear families (e.g., Binford 1981 Sept 1992; Zihlman 1991). Whereas the original Man the Hunter model of human evolution credited hunting with making us human (see Chapter 4), its more recent incarnation stresses not hunting per se but the social manipulation of meat (Kuhn and Sarther 2000; Stanford 1999). Stanford argues that navigating reciprocity and the associated social relationships requires high intelligence, more so than hunting: "When meat becomes a resource that is not only a food but also a social currency – a way to help you obtain what you want in the group – we are seeing the emergence of barter, currency-based human social systems. In human and some other primate societies, meat eating is about politics as well as nutrition" (Stanford 1999:201). Specifically, Stanford suggests that meat sharing is at the roots of patriarchy, with the males who obtain most of the meat using it to create male alliances and to manipulate females.

In fact, two kinds of food sharing are at issue in evolutionary models: sharing between mates that may create the nuclear family, and broader sharing including non-kin that requires well-developed social intelligence. Steven Kuhn and Catherine Sarther (2000) suggest that the first kind is expressed archaeologically in the remarkably stable tool types of the Lower and Middle Paleolithic, whereas the dramatically more rapid rate of stylistic change and the elaboration of technology seen in the Upper Paleolithic mark the second. They argue that as long as sharing stays within the family or a small, defined group, there is little incentive to invest effort in changing or elaborating a technology that produces sufficient food. However, sharing with non-kin is open-ended, creating a more or less unlimited demand for food, and it is rewarded by prestige and social relations that carry many benefits. Incidentally, this would place food sharing beyond immediate kin, rather than agriculture, at the root of the overexploitation that threatens to destroy the world's environment (cf. Quinn 1999).

Sharing beyond the nuclear family, even with non-kin, has been the focus of more recent theorizing on the subject. The evolutionary benefits of sharing with offspring and other close kin are clear, but it is more challenging to understand why people would give away food more broadly. An obvious answer is that sharing smooths out uneven food acquisition: When one family has a surplus, it benefits by sharing in the expectation that other families will return the favor when they have surpluses, so that everyone has enough to eat most of the time (Gould 1967; Winterhalder 1986). This model of generalized reciprocity (Sahlins 1972:193–4) fits well with the observation that meat, especially that of large animals, is the food shared most frequently. A single family cannot consume a large animal without using preservation techniques such as drying or smoking for storage, and large animal hunting is variable and unpredictable in yield. Careful ethnographic work, however, has shown that, although there are often elements of generalized reciprocity in meat sharing, this kind of risk pooling does not adequately explain sharing patterns (e.g., Bird-David 1990; Hovelsrud-Broda 2000; Speth 1990; Whitehead 2000; Woodburn 1998).

Much of this work takes a human behavioral ecology approach, in parallel to discussions of hunting and meat sharing among other primates and using the same terminology, some of which becomes a bit strained when applied to humans. The debate has stimulated a number of painstaking studies that attempt to quantify the actual flow of meat in various foraging groups. The main models debated by this school to explain the patterning of targeting large game, which is then shared beyond the nuclear family, are kin selection, reciprocal altruism, tolerated scrounging, and costly signaling. Kin selection theory focuses on the benefits to those who share genes with the donor, so that holders of the same gene benefit overall, despite a cost to the donor. Members of hunting bands are typically related to varying degrees, and kinship is the basis for social structure (although kinship imperfectly reflects biological relatedness). This model would predict that meat would be given differentially to relatives, with closer relatives receiving more. Reciprocal altruism predicts that gifts will be returned in the future to the ultimate benefit of the donor. It depends on stable social relationships, but genetic relatedness is not necessary. In the context of sharing, it is roughly equivalent to generalized reciprocity. Tolerated scrounging (also known as tolerated theft), often posited as the basis for chimpanzee meat sharing, focuses not on the benefits of sharing but the costs of not doing so. If it would be more costly to defend food from others than to share it, hunters may prefer to be generous. Ethnographers have often documented that others will demand shares from successful hunters, and sometimes hunters will try to conceal meat from others to avoid sharing, suggesting that tolerated scrounging may play a role among humans. Costly signaling posits that features such as peacock tails that handicap an individual demonstrate to others that an individual who can nevertheless survive and thrive must be especially fit. This is usually a male strategy, so the tendency for big game hunting to be a male endeavor that brings prestige has led some to suggest that it should be seen as costly signaling (Feinman 1979; Gurven 2004).

Some support can be found for each of these models in ethnographic accounts. The Micronesian Ifaluk, who are fisher/horticulturalist/copra workers, share most surplus food, although some is stored. Relatives are favored in the distribution of shares, followed by neighbors. Some asymmetrical sharing is also directed to chiefly households, and people are more likely to give to households with many dependents and hence greater need (Betzig and Turke 1986). Kinship is also one of several factors shaping sharing patterns among the Pilagá in Argentina (Henry 1951), and kin are heavily favored in meat distribution among the Huaulu of Seram, Indonesia (Valeri 1994:122). However, in many groups relatives are not favored, at least in the early stages of sharing (Bird-David 1990; Kaplan et al. 1984; Kitanishi 2000; Tanner 1979; Woodburn 1998).

When chimpanzees hunt successfully, other group members gather around and beg forcefully for meat. Some have suggested that meat sharing among chimps is more a matter of permitting onlookers to take some meat because it is not worth the trouble and risk of defending it than of gifting (Gilby 2006; Stevens 2004), although as we have seen in Chapter 4 (*Motivations for Hunting*), this interpretation is disputed. The argument for extending such a tolerated scrounging model to humans is based on widespread ethnographic observations that humans likewise tend to gather and demand shares after a hunt, often quite stridently (Bliege Bird and Bird 1997; Blurton-Jones 1984; Hames 1990; Peterson 1993; Willerslev 2007; Woodburn 1998). However, in other cases such demands are lacking; rather there is simply a general expectation of sharing, often based in a perception that animals or their spirit masters have shared themselves with humans in offering themselves to the hunter (Bodenhorn 2000; Brightman 1993; Gibson 1988; Tanner 1979). This perception can only apply to wild animals, and it is wild game that is shared most widely among humans.

Although reciprocal altruism is similar to the anthropological concept of generalized reciprocity, many have observed that sharing frequently appears to be distinct from reciprocity or any form of exchange, in that no return is expected (no debt is created) and gifts of food do not even out over time (Alvard 2001; Bird-David 1990; Bodenhorn 2000; Gibson 1988; Hovelsrud-Broda 2000; Price 1975; Whitehead 2000; Woodburn 1998). Observers have sometimes noted that being well liked trumps the potential to give back: Disabled or impaired people who are generally regarded with affection receive more meat than good hunters (Kent 1993b:352; Marshall 1994:72). Yet there is often a sense that return is expected, and certainly that people who have meat or other valued items should share them (Endicott 1988; Henry 1951). Part of the problem is that the return may not be in the same currency (meat for meat), but may come in the form of other goods, labor, political support, and so on (Dowling 1968; Gurven 2004). These alternative currencies are harder to measure.

Characterizing sharing as a risk-reduction strategy approximates a reciprocal altruism model. Given the unpredictability of large game hunting, it is not surprising that risk reduction plays a role in meat sharing, but it does not seem to explain sharing patterns completely (Hames 1990; Hegmon 1991). Because hunters could often reduce risk more effectively by targeting small game (or plant foods), yet frequently persist in seeking large game, some have argued that meat sharing is less a subsistence than a mating strategy, with success in hunting large game serving as an honest signal of male quality. Hawkes (1993, 2001) suggests that large game hunters are rewarded in another currency: favorable attention (i.e., prestige). This prestige leads to more mating opportunities and also more male allies (Bliege Bird and Bird 2008; Dowling 1968; Kaplan and Hill 1985). That men benefit more from extra mating opportunities than women explains why it is primarily men who hunt large game, whereas women tend to target the less flashy resources that support their families. Moreover, some studies have shown that young, unmarried men particularly target the high-risk, high-visibility large animals, whereas married men or those with children pursue a lower risk strategy (Bliege Bird 1999; Bliege Bird and Bird 1997; Wood and Hill 2000). Kim Hill and Keith Kintigh (2009) intriguingly propose a different reason for rewarding hunters with prestige. Armed with long-term data on the Aché in Paraguay, they suggest that given the variability in hunting success not only is it very difficult for ethnographers to distinguish who are the best hunters with relatively short-term information (for a few months or a year or two), but in fluid forager bands it would also be equally difficult for the foragers to do so. So rather than rewarding good hunters materially to encourage production, they are better served by enforcing sharing and according prestige to successful hunters.

The mixed support for these four models in the ethnographic record suggests either that multiple factors drive human meat sharing or that all these models are inadequate. Some comparative studies of quantitative research on sharing among foragers worldwide conclude that there is no single strategy underlying human sharing, but rather a balance of multiple strategies (Gurven 2004; Gurven and Hill 2009; Hill and Kaplan 1993). Raymond Hames (1990) comes to a similar conclusion for the Yanomamö. So perhaps the goal should not be to discover a single explanation for meat sharing, but to understand its workings in each case. Even if we limit ourselves to foraging groups there is considerable variation in meat-sharing patterns, but some recurring themes do emerge (Kelly 1995). Susan Kent (1993a) distinguishes between highly egalitarian foragers, where sharing works to integrate societies and maintain equality (Price 1975), and other societies where egalitarianism is less central and sharing may serve to create inequality. At least for these strongly egalitarian groups, Kent argues that a social explanation for sharing is better supported than the models from behavioral ecology, because there would be better ways to reduce risk, benefit kin, or show off. "[W]ithout [formal] sharing, a family can survive and even thrive economically" (Kent 1993a:483), but it suffers socially by having fewer friends and visitors. The Basarwa at Kutse in Botswana share even when it is economically unnecessary (when everyone has enough meat) because of the social ties it creates; an extreme case is two hunters who exchanged shoulders of the steenboks they each bagged on the same day. Basarwa sharing networks often link unrelated people, arguing against kin selection. Kent objects to applying the term "tolerated theft" to egalitarian sharing, preferring "demand sharing" to describe the insistence on extensive sharing in such groups. Whereas "theft" suggests an illicit act, demand sharing on the contrary does not break but actively enforces social rules (see also Endicott 1988 for the Batek of Malaysia).

GAME AS PROPERTY

A successful hunt nearly always converts the dead animal into the property of the hunter. However, game is a special kind of property, whose ownership mainly consists of the right to distribute it (even in modern America, hunters can give away but not sell wild game). Such ownership is straightforward for a solitary hunt, but when more than one hunter participates, it is not always obvious who should own the animal. And yet ownership is necessary for the meat to be shared out. Various groups have developed mechanisms to assign ownership in these cases; sometimes they also serve to assign ownership to someone other than the solitary hunter (Dowling 1968). Thus ownership may devolve to the first to see the animal, the first to wound it, the one who delivers the fatal wound, the owner or maker of the weapon that deals the crucial wound (who may not even be present on the hunt), or the owner of the dog credited with the kill (Bahuchet 1990; Gould 1967; Hames 1990; Valeri 1994:121; Wiessner 1983). Hunters may also give their game to other hunters to display and distribute (Bird-David 1990; Tanner 1979:158–9). It is ironic that so much concern is given to the ownership of a carcass that will be shared out, in many cases with the owner receiving less or even none of it. John Dowling (1968) concludes that owners are rewarded with prestige, which serves to motivate hunting.

However, there is a further paradox in that, although in some cases good hunters are rewarded with renown and perhaps materially, in many societies hunters are discouraged from boasting or claiming any special esteem as strongly as they are enjoined to share. This may be enforced by leveling devices such as insulting the catch of successful hunters to prevent them from putting on airs (Brightman 1993:234; Lee 1993: 54–6, 183–8; Tanner 1979:153; Wiessner 1996; Willerslev 2007:37; Woodburn 1998:59). Testart (1987) makes a fundamental distinction between groups where the hunters own, and share out, their own game and those where ownership and distribution are transferred to others. Testart includes cases where the ownership of the game belongs to the maker or owner of the weapon (not necessarily its user) in the first set, because the hunter chooses which weapon to use; he notes that the initial distribution in these groups is always within the hunting group, if any. In the second system, limited to Australia, the game is handed over to others outside the hunting party for distribution (variously the elders, a designated official, or the hunter's father-in-law). Furthermore, Testart links these sharing patterns to kinship systems, with hunter-controlled sharing systems associated with Eskimo-type kinship in which kin are defined in concentric circles around ego. Surrendering game to others for distribution is analogous to exogamy, creating relationships not between individuals but between categories of persons, as in the elaborate Australian kinship systems.

Regardless of who distributes the meat, the act of sharing always attracts much attention and concern, and it is hedged about with rules and expectations. In the pre-Soviet period, Siberian Yukaghir hunters gave large game to the wife of an elder to distribute, helped by the hunter's wife. The shares were meant to be equal among those present, except for the addition of the head (and the right to pitch his tent first) to the hunter's share. Other than the head, no particular body parts are designated for any individual (Willerslev 2007:36). The Nayaka foragers of India also divide the meat evenly:

> The butcher places the pieces in piles, each of which will be distributed to a household in the hamlet, the pile received being proportionate to the household's size. Children are given almost the same share as adults. People stand around the butcher while he works and help to assess the quality and volume of the growing piles. They constantly make suggestions as to where the butcher should place each piece of meat. Mere presence in the hamlet entitles a person to a share, and this includes the old and the infirm, who can never reciprocate. The hunter receives a share just like anyone else's, though he also usually gets the skin (Bird-David 1990:192).

Among the Cree, there are up to three stages of meat sharing. The hunter may give the carcass to an unsuccessful companion before the hunting party returns to camp. Once the party enters camp, game animals become women's property: Women butcher and cook the carcasses. After quietly admiring the kill, the owner's family distributes the meat evenly among all families (unless some families already have a surplus); the owner retains the hide. If a family runs out of meat later, others will share with them. Some body parts are more highly valued than others and show respect to the recipient. In particular, some body parts of beaver and bear are designated for men or women, and the higher prestige male-designated portions are further ranked according to the age or status of the recipient (Brightman 1993; Tanner 1979).

In other cases, there are more or less set portions into which animals are divided in the initial stage of sharing, varying for each taxon (Gould 1967). The definitions of the portions also vary among different ethnic groups for the same taxon (Murray 2000). Theodore White (1952, 1953b, 1954, 1955) tried to address this phenomenon in early zooarchaeological work that was unfortunately hobbled by a lack of taphonomic sensibility; it is worth making a renewed attempt to detect such variation. For the Gunwinggu, distribution is often modified by taboos applying to certain taxa for some people (Altman and Peterson 1988:80). The Pilagá also modulate sharing according to taboos, as well as kinship, proximity, and need. Moreover, shamans tend to receive far more than they give because others fear their sorcery (Henry 1951). Mullu Kurumbu horticulturalists in India assign set body parts according to participants' role in the hunt (Bird-David 1990:192). Many foraging groups have practices such as snacking in the field and selective taboos that tend to reserve more meat and especially marrow for adult men than women, despite an ethic of sharing (Speth 1990; Zvelebil 2000). However, this is not the case for the Kutse Basarwa, where male hunters' snacking on marrow in the bush is balanced by preferential access to marrow for women and children in camp (Kent 1993a). Similarly, the Malaysian Batek tend to give slightly larger meat shares to women to compensate for the taboo that prevents them from eating meat during menstruation (Endicott 1988:117).

Meat sharing among foragers for the most part enforces egalitarian relations, although as is evident from the examples just discussed, certain segments of society may be somewhat favored (men, elders): "[T]he acts of giving and receiving meat that mean and create equality and community may also engender hierarchy and distance" (Brightman 1993:234). Because givers establish a position of superiority over receivers, "paradoxically, a demand in the context of an egalitarian society can also be a gift: it freely creates a status asymmetry, albeit of varying duration and significance" (Peterson 1993: 871).

Where relations are less egalitarian, meat sharing is usually asymmetrical. The Barrow Inupiat value generosity highly, but although wealthier people make a show of generosity, they receive more than they give and are perceived as generous because of their higher status more than receiving prestige because of their generosity (Bodenhorn 2000). After hunts by small groups, the horticulturalist Bemba and Ndembu of Malawi give the hind leg of larger animals to the chief; the Ndembu then divide the rest of the meat among the married men of the lineage. Malawians also periodically conduct communal hunts, using beaters and fire to flush animals. After such hunts the killers keep animals up to the size of hares, while the organizer of the hunt (often the village headman) divides the larger prey. Designated portions go to this organizer, the chief, and the landowner, as well as the hunters who delivered the initial and the fatal blows. The rest is distributed according to roles in the hunt and social status. Solitary hunters must also give a leg of larger game animals to the village chief and then distribute the rest according to kin relations (Morris 1998). In general, however, although some sharing occurs in any society, strong emphasis on sharing is associated with egalitarian societies and indeed is an important mechanism for maintaining equality (Dowling 1968; Knauft 1991; Woodburn 1998).

Whereas meat sharing serves to dampen social difference based on hunting ability (or success) and is often seen as encouraging underproduction, the value placed on generosity means that the desire to share can motivate hunting. The Etolo of the New Guinea highlands may hunt in order to make gifts for social or political purposes (Dwyer 1985). Likewise, the amount of fish acquired does not determine sharing patterns for the Kubo of lowland New Guinea, but rather spear-fishing effort is adjusted to produce enough to share with those due to receive part of the catch (Minnegal 1997).

The high value on generosity does not render sharing unproblematic: Selfishness and envy surround meat sharing. Many ethnographic studies reveal that hunters will consume game or portions of game themselves when unobserved. Sometimes hunters eat innards or other parts in the bush before bringing the game back, a permitted practice (Gould 1967). In other cases, concealing game is regarded as cheating, but may nevertheless occur (Altman and Peterson 1988; Bird-David 1990; Dowling 1968; Kelly 1995; Marshall 1994; Sillitoe 2001; Willerslev 2007). Still more prevalent is a general air of tension around meat distributions, and people may complain and bear grudges over perceived inequities in sharing (Altman and Peterson 1988; Brightman 1993; Hagen 1999; Henry 1951; Morris 2000:64; Whitehead 2000; Woodburn 1998). Although ownership of game among foragers primarily confers the right to distribute it, people are not necessarily eager to perform the distribution, in light of the pressure to share out appropriately. They may delegate the task to others, sometimes individuals recognized as skilled in making equitable distributions (Whitehead 2000:137–8). Those present typically monitor the sharing out closely, with extensive commentary. Among the Kutse Basarwa, "[t]he person who butchered the animal distributed the meat with the advice of the hunter and often his wife. Husband and wife commonly had long discussions concerning who should get which piece and how much" (Kent 1993b:339). Two young Gunwinggu men concealed their large catch of fish outside camp until their mother could retrieve and distribute them, because they were daunted by the delicate and fraught task of sharing them out (Altman and Peterson 1988:89).

THE ARCHAEOLOGY OF MEAT SHARING

Because meat sharing is so central to the social relations of foragers and, to a lesser extent, in other societies, tracing it archaeologically is imperative. Fortunately this is a particularly well-developed area of social zooarchaeology. The need to identify material signatures of meat sharing has stimulated considerable ethnoarchaeology. However, archaeological detection is complicated by the multistage sharing that typically spreads the meat and bones of a single animal widely and relatively evenly, obscuring patterning that may be present in the earlier stages (Binford 1984a). Dogs and children can also move and destroy bones to the extent that such patterning is no longer evident (Jarvenpa and Brumbach 1983). Yet the dispersal of the remains of individual animals around a site may be good evidence of the presence of sharing (Yellen 1977). Among the Kutse Basarwa, animal bone assemblages associated with huts did not vary in terms of the amount of bone or estimated meat weight, nor the number of animals represented (measured by MNI), according to whether or not the hut dwellers participated in formal sharing networks (suggesting that formal sharing did not provide benefits in terms of extra food). However, faunal assemblages associated with those who shared formally exhibited higher taxonomic richness (more species), an indication that meat travels farther in formal than informal sharing (between camps rather than only within them). This study also reminds us that calculating the minimum number of individuals (MNI) for each hut area independently would yield a substantial overestimate of the number of animals consumed in the camp. The households of better hunters do not have remains of more or better meat (Kent 1993a:494).

Faunal assemblages at Okiek settlements, where homesteads are scattered across ridges, exhibit body part patterning because of sharing that would typically be interpreted as the result of transport decisions (leaving low-value portions of the carcass at the kill site, bringing meatier parts to base camps or settlements). In fact, the Okiek almost never leave bones behind at kill sites, in part because they want the marrow. In what is probably a typical pattern of meat sharing, the remains of larger animals are spread more widely, and hence they are less complete at any one location than the remains of smaller ones. In contrast to the more egalitarian Basarwa, the dwellings of successful Okiek hunters are marked by more bones and a wider range of body parts; because the hunter is entitled to at least one hindlimb, these meaty portions are better represented. However, hunting success is not the only factor affecting assemblages (and household meat consumption): A particularly well-liked old man accumulated the remains of more animals and a wider range of body parts than did other unsuccessful hunters (Marshall 1994).

Binford (1984a) suggests that it is easier to detect body part patterning resulting from sharing if relatively few animals are involved, so that there is less of a palimpsest effect; therefore sharing may be more visible archaeologically for rare taxa. Because many of the foraging groups for whom sharing is likely to be central are mobile, however, their short-term settlements may retain sufficiently high resolution to trace sharing. Karen Lupo (2001) similarly finds that body part patterning resulting from transport decisions among the Hadza is visible only in smaller assemblages, contrary to our usual valorization of larger sample sizes.

Sharing is linked to architecture: Egalitarian sharing, maintained by mutual surveillance, is found where structures are flimsy and people's lives

are largely open to view (Endicott 1988:117; Wilson 1988). With substantial houses, family life is hidden from others, so that they can conceal
food stores and avoid sharing. Peter Wilson also suggests that this privacy
leads to suspicion, tensions, and witchcraft accusations. Ethnoarchaeology has refined this architectural link, noting that hearths and huts are
located closer to each other when the inhabitants share extensively, providing an indication of the structure of ancient sharing networks through
spatial analysis (Cohen 1961; Gargett and Hayden 1991; O'Connell
1987). Sharing and storage are alternative strategies to smooth out variations in food acquisition and to use large game effectively (Woodburn
1998). Richard Gould (1981) attributes foragers' choices between these
two approaches to features of the local environment. Where resources
are relatively abundant and reliable, storage will be favored, but sharing works better where major environmental perturbations such as long
droughts occur.

Based on the principle that storage and sharing are alternative strategies, Gideon Shelach (2006) has taken the presence of household storage
facilities to indicate the lack of sharing. However, ethnography shows
that although groups may emphasize sharing or storage as a primary risk-
avoidance strategy, those who store also share to some degree (Waguues-
pack 2002), as Shelach acknowledges. In another simple approach, a
Later Stone Age mass kill of springbok in South Africa is taken as evidence of the presence of sharing, because there would be too much
meat for a small band. Additionally, ethnographically known groups in
the area practice extensive sharing (Dewar et al. 2006). Mass kills in
general cannot be assumed to indicate sharing, however. They certainly
imply cooperative hunting, and there would need to be some mechanism
to assign ownership of the animals killed. Yet having claimed their animals, the hunters could in principle consume them entirely within their
own household or store them. Mass kills potentially provide sufficient
food for each household, so that sharing is less necessary than with the
uneven results of individual hunting (although we have seen earlier that
the game from communal hunts is frequently shared out). McGuire and
Hildebrandt (2005) argue that an increase in large game hunting in the
Middle Archaic of the Great Basin supports a costly signaling model of
meat sharing, with men targeting animals that they can share out for
greater social benefit rather than following the strategy that will yield

the most food. They suggest that this occurs specifically in the Middle Archaic because settlements become more aggregated at this time, thereby providing a sufficient audience for such display to be effective. The sharing, however, is assumed rather than demonstrated.

Zooarchaeologists have an advantage in that the parts of animal bodies can be distinguished, making it easier to trace their circulation. Of course, as is apparent from ethnoarchaeological studies, there are many influences on body part patterning, but spatial analysis combined with taphonomic awareness holds considerable promise (Enloe 2004). Paul Parmalee and Walter Klippel (1983:286) investigated meat sharing at the protohistoric Kickapoo Rhoads site. They looked for variation in body part distribution of the white-tailed deer that dominate the assemblage among the pits that yielded the majority of the faunal remains, but failed to find it. Even if we assume that the assemblage from a pit represents a single or small number of households consistently depositing their waste in the same place, however, body part differences are likely to be apparent only if the site is a very short-term occupation or if sharing is asymmetrical so that given body parts flow to particular households. If sharing is egalitarian, body parts will tend to even out over time.

I took a similar approach at Opovo, using correlation matrices to examine the tendency of taxa and body parts to cluster. For taxa, I assumed that symmetrical sharing should produce an even distribution across the pits; clustering of some taxa would result either from asymmetrical sharing or from a lack of sharing (thus revealing interhousehold differences in hunting success and herding practices). I assumed that sharing would produce a tendency for adjacent bones to cluster in pits, as joints of meat circulated; lack of sharing would show no patterning because the whole animal, minus the effects of attritional processes, would be deposited in a single pit. Likewise, sharing might produce lower correlations between right and left sides of a given body part, because they are likely to circulate separately. At Opovo, taxa are quite evenly distributed among the pits, suggesting symmetrical sharing. Left/right correlations are high for roe deer, but lower for the larger animals. Moreover, they vary differently through the body for the various taxa, suggesting that red deer hindlimbs were more likely to be shared than forelimbs, whereas pig/boar forelimbs and upper hindlimbs circulated more often. Correlations among adjacent bones also indicated that roe deer were shared less than larger taxa, and there were differing patterns of division into joints for sharing among the various taxa. Overall, animal size appeared to be the major factor in meat sharing (or division for sharing, at any rate; it is possible that entire roe deer were distributed). Contrary to my expectations, wild animals do not seem to have been shared more than domestic animals, although they were divided somewhat differently (Russell 2000).

Based on her ethnoarchaeological work with the Aka in Central Africa, Jean Hudson proposes measuring the degree to which body parts of animals are spread around settlements through a redistribution value statistic: $\Sigma$(household MNI)/site MNI. Zooarchaeologists will recognize that this statistic capitalizes on what is usually a deficiency of the minimum number of individuals (MNI) as a quantitative measure: Values vary depending on the units within which they are calculated and are nonadditive (J. Watson 1979). There are a number of variants on MNI, but the basic approach is to calculate the value of the most frequent body part in an assemblage that cannot be repeated in a single individual (e.g., the left distal humerus). Where household assemblages can be unambiguously identified and taphonomic processes have removed no bone, Hudson's redistribution value will equal 1 if there is no sharing, because the remains of individual animals will stay entirely within the assemblages of the household that acquired them, and in this case adding them will equate to the MNI for the site. These conditions will never wholly apply archaeologically, but where pit or hearth assemblages can be reasonably assigned to households, the degree to which the redistribution value exceeds 1 can provide an indication of the amount of interhousehold sharing (Hudson 1990, as cited in Enloe 2003).

A more direct, but labor-intensive, approach to identifying the circulation of body parts is through conjoining or refitting studies. George Frison (1971) pioneered this approach at the Eden-Farson site, a single-component, short-term Shoshonean site in Wyoming. Frison attempted to conjoin bones from pits associated with lodges, and he found that bones conjoined within pits but not between them. He concluded that meat was divided as whole animals after a mass kill of pronghorns, and each family processed its own.

Enloe has applied a technique developed by Lawrence Todd (Todd and Frison 1992) to the study of meat sharing. Todd's innovation is to use measurements to reduce the work of conjoining in large assemblages by honing in on likely articulations. The measurements can also be used to identify likely right/left matches. Enloe's study of conjoining reindeer bones at Upper Paleolithic Pincevent in northern France has demonstrated movement of body parts among hearth groups. Moreover, it is the meaty parts that circulated (Enloe 1994, 2003; Enloe and David 1989, 1992; Enloe et al. 1994). Enloe (2003) compared the results of conjoining with Hudson's redistribution value and concluded that in this archaeological situation, albeit one with unusually good resolution, Hudson's technique revealed some sharing, but not the degree attested by conjoining.

Melinda Zeder and Susan Arter (1996) combined conjoining and body part distribution at the Mississippian Snodgrass site in Missouri to examine meat sharing. Using bones from pits and structures, they were able to identify sharing groups of multiple structures. Despite the stratified structure of Mississippian society, sharing appears to have been egalitarian at this site.

Nicole Waguespack (2002) also used a combination of body part distribution and conjoining at the Palangana site in Alaska. Occupied in the late 19th century, Binford (1978) recorded the site as part of his Nunamiut ethnoarchaeological work, along with oral history about its residents. The portion excavated included the structures and discard of two households, headed by a renowned hunter and a skilled stone and bone artisan (but less expert hunter). Waguespack modeled three scenarios: tolerated theft (asymmetrical) sharing, where the flow would be primarily from the better hunter to the poorer one; variance reduction, where meat would flow evenly between the households; and no sharing. For tolerated theft she predicted that the household of the better hunter would have a larger faunal assemblage with more internal refits and more meaty body parts. Variance reduction should show similar assemblages for the two households in terms of size and body part composition, with refits across them. If no sharing occurred, there should be no refits across the assemblages, and they should be similar in composition. At Palangana the pattern conforms to the tolerated theft model. As Waguespack points out, "tolerated theft" may be an inappropriate term because the meat may have been repaid in another currency, here likely to be stone and bone artifacts.

An interesting feature of the Palangana study is that body part patterning indicates that the pelvis and scapula were most likely to be shared, and these elements are also the ones that show the most damage from dog gnawing. Waguespack proposes that much of the sharing may have been motivated by a need to feed dogs rather than humans. Lucien Jourdan and Jean-François Le Mouel (1987) make a similar point with respect to a Dorset site where patterns of cut marks and digestion show that seal hind flippers were segmented and fed to dogs. They argue that this type of feeding should be seen as sharing meat with dogs, enlarging the sharing network beyond humans.

Further application of conjoining and other techniques to trace actual meat sharing should help sort out and refine sharing models. It is already apparent that a single model is inadequate to explain all meat sharing, and in fact more than one model may well operate in a single settlement.


## Feasting

Feasting is one way to share food, but it is worth separating from the sharing out of uncooked meat discussed in the previous section because the commensality involved creates particular social and political opportunities. Feasting and sharing probably occur in all societies, but in a rough sense meat sharing predominates in generalized foraging groups, whereas feasting is more common among agriculturalists and complex foragers (Wiessner 1996). Much as Garfinkel (2003) claims for dancing, Hayden (2001a) argues that feasting is of greatest importance in transegalitarian groups: those between egalitarian foragers and complex chiefdoms, or roughly what would be called tribes in the classic sense (Service 1962). In these societies without rigid governmental institutions, feasts provide a key political arena. Further, Ingold (1980:184) states that feasting is a feature of milch pastoralism (based on keeping herds for dairy products), but not carnivorous pastoralism (based on using animals only for meat), because the carnivorous pastoralist could not afford the destruction of wealth.

Definitions of what makes a meal a feast have focused on different aspects. Some stress the nature of the food served, as distinct from ordinary meals (Hayden 2001a). Others emphasize ritualization as the factor that sets feasts apart (Clarke 2001; Dietler 2001; Hamilakis 2008 Powdermaker 1932; Wright 2004). My own preference is to base the definition on scale: meals attended by guests beyond the household (Wiessner 2001). Many feasts exhibit all these traits, and some definitions require a combination of special foods and larger scale (Caplan 1994), or special foods and ritualization (Steel 2004). Katheryn Twiss (2008:419) defines feasts as "occasions consciously distinguished from everyday meals" by any of these three aspects. Cross-culturally, large amounts of meat are a frequent feature of feasts, and sometimes a feast is the only context in which meat or the meat of certain animals is eaten (Bloch 1985), making feasts a prime concern for zooarchaeology.

Feasting has become a hot topic in archaeology in recent years, and there is a vast ethnographic literature on the topic. Therefore I do not attempt a comprehensive discussion, but instead point to some of the key issues. Feasting is a particularly visible aspect of what Chris Gregory (1982) has termed "gift economies." Present in some spheres even in modern capitalist societies (Hyde 1983), gift economies dominate in societies not centered on markets and commodities, and they are especially important in transegalitarian societies. The currency of the gift economy is prestige, and therefore its logic is the inverse of that of the market economy: Whereas capitalists seek to maximize profits by minimizing costs, givers seek to maximize prestige by maximizing costs. Generosity is highly valued, and givers seek renown by making their gifts as costly as possible, often accompanied by display and performance to enhance the occasion (Mauss 1967).

Crucially, like bridewealth, this impulse to excel in generosity provides a motivation for intensification that is otherwise lacking in the domestic mode of production (Bender 1989; Dietler 2001; Ellen 1996; Friedman and Rowlands 1977; Hayden 1990, 1996a, 2001a; Sahlins 1972; Spielmann 2002). Polly Wiessner (2001) provides a particularly interesting example from oral history work in New Guinea, where big-men deliberately encouraged feasting as a way to valorize pigs so that people would be incentivized to raise more of them, which the big-men could use to build their reputations and power. Barbara Bender (1978) and especially Brian Hayden (1990, 1992, 1995a, 2003, 2009; cf. Keeley 1995) have argued that agriculture is the result of an intensification of production driven by feasting and gift exchange (see Chapter 6, *Models of Origins*). Hayden adds the requirement that the environment must be rich enough to support such intensification, and in particular the resources targeted for feasting must be resistant to overexploitation. In addition to food production, feasting also builds demand for special serving vessels and other items related to food preparation and consumption, for valuable items given or exchanged in the feasting context (jewelry, textiles, etc.), and for paraphernalia (costumes, musical instruments, emblems) associated with the performative aspect of feasts (Blanton and Taylor 1995; Hayden 1995c, 1998, 2001a). Thus the origins of pottery have also been linked to feasting (Rice 1999), and whether or not feasting motivated the creation of pottery, it has certainly stimulated its elaboration (Mills 2007; Smith et al. 2003).

Particularly as feasts become more elaborate, staging one demands considerable organizational skills. The host must persuade his or her family, friends, and relations or followers to invest extra labor in the necessary surplus production. He or she must orchestrate exchanges to produce debts that can be called in at the right moment, and the host must direct others in the preparation, display, and serving of large amounts of food and drink, as well as the music, singing, and dancing that typically accompany feasts. Ritual specialists may need to be hired (Adams 2004; Holmberg 1989). Hosts normally spend years preparing for major feasts in transegalitarian societies (Blanton and Taylor 1995; DeBoer 2001; Oliver 1955; Reay 1984). The distribution of meat and other food at feasts constructs social relationships and can be as tense as the sharing out of game (see the previous section, *Meat Sharing*). For these reasons, feasts are at the center of political life in such societies, and they are an important path to power, in the form of the authority that comes from prestige. Hayden and others see feasting as a major factor in increasing inequality (Bender 1989; Hayden 1995b, 1996b, 2001b, 2002). In more stratified societies, feasts serve other ends: as a forum for the redistribution of goods or their concentration in elite hands (Hayden 2001a; Kelly 2001) or as a way to distinguish elite from commoners (Caplan 1994; Dietler 1996, 2001; Van der Veen 2003).

However, not all of the politics of feasting is about inequality. All feasts also create a sense of community and solidarity among the participants, and in some cases this aspect predominates. Indeed, the bonding effect of commensality helps give feasts their power to work in other ways (Dietler 1996; Jones 2007). The potential of feasts to create solidarity is enhanced by their frequent association with ritual and performance; singing and dancing together are also powerful bonding experiences (Garfinkel 2003), and singing and dancing for others mark social distinctions (Campbell 2008). As noted in Chapter 3, sacrifices usually involve feasting, and sometimes the feasting may be the dominant aspect (Bloch

1992:37). Animal sacrifice is one performative aspect of feasting, often the central one.

Hamilakis notes that feasts produce strong memories by disrupting the routine temporality created by the rhythm of daily meals: "It is the memory of the distinctive event, of the performances, of the processions, of the violence and sensory effects produced by the sacrificing and killing of animals, of distinctive participants with their elaborate garments, their perfumed bodies and their rare and exotic drinking vessels, of the substances consumed with their psychoactive effects, and so on" (Hamilakis 2008:16). All the senses are involved, particularly the powerfully mnemonic senses of taste and smell. Hamilakis argues that feasts draw their special power in comparison to other ceremonies from the act of incorporation in a collective setting, equating the body with the body politic. He also points out that whereas a successful feast can make the reputation of the host, unfavorable comparison with the memory of a past feast can damage that reputation.

There is typically a gendered aspect to the production of feasts. In most cases the hosts are primarily male, but women usually provide the majority of the labor to produce and prepare the food and drink (Bevan 1997:85; Evans-Pritchard 1951; Gero 1992; Hendon 1996:50; Watson 1977). Often a substantial portion of this female labor is devoted to brewing beer or other alcoholic beverages; along with meat, alcohol is a highlight of many feasts (Arnold 1999; Arthur 2003; Bendall 2004; Bruman 2000; Dietler 2006; Sherratt 1986; Vencl 1994; Washburne 1961; Woolf and Eldridge 1994). Ambitious hosts are therefore highly dependent on their female relatives, and women's labor is generally the limiting factor for transegalitarian feasts (Jennings 2004). The desire to host impressive feasts is therefore a major motivation for polygyny (which, via bridewealth, can further drive intensification of production; see Chapter 8). Of course, gender is also one of the distinctions that may be marked at the feast itself, by such devices as differential access to food and drink; who serves, sings, and dances; and where men and women sit (Dietler 2001; Lokuruka 2006; Powdermaker 1932).

Ethnography reveals a dizzying array of occasions that may be marked with feasts. Sometimes feasts follow the successful hunting of a large animal (Bodenhorn 2000; Hovelsrud-Broda 2000; Tanner 1979), although more often this meat is shared out (see the earlier section, *Meat Sharing*). Feasts may mark calendrical events and recur on a regular schedule,

as with harvest festivals and other annual events (Tanner 1979). Even
if feasts observe other occasions, they tend to be scheduled around the
harvest or the season of greatest wild food abundance, for obvious reasons. Among the Tamang, during the dry season after harvest "a typical
household engages in as many as ten to fifteen memorial death feasts,
five or more tonsure ceremonies, exchanges in association with marriage,
pilgrimages, and festivals" (Holmberg 1989:112). Ceremonies including feasting often mark major life-cycle events: birth, puberty/initiation,
marriage, and death (Hovelsrud-Broda 2000; Kahn 1986; Powdermaker
1932; Schneider 1957; Tanner 1979). Funerary and memorial feasts are
often given particular importance, as occasions when wealth and position can be displayed and redistributed (Lindström 1988; Raharijaona
and Kus 2001). Additionally, funerary feasts may seek to construct an
ancestor from the deceased, who will subsequently aid the living (Nelson
2003:65–6). Feasts may celebrate victories in warfare and other suc-
cesses or the host's accession to a new position (Hoskins 1993; Powdermaker 1932). Some feasts act as fines exacted on the host for antisocial
behavior (Schneider 1957). When feasting follows sacrifice, any occasion for a sacrifice is also an occasion for a feast (Evans-Pritchard 1956).
Although organizing a feast involves marshaling and channeling substantial amounts of labor in itself, feasts may also serve as an incentive for
collective labor in large agricultural or construction tasks, among others
(Kahn 1986). Perhaps feasts held to prepare for warfare fall into this
category (Powdermaker 1932).

Because the precise occasion for a feast is difficult to discern archaeologically, archaeologists have tended to categorize feasts according to
their function. Hayden (2001a) has produced a rather elaborate typology, sorted into three main categories: alliance and cooperation feasts,
economic feasts, and diacritical feasts. James Perodie (2001) largely follows Hayden, but groups the types into no-return feasts (the host does
not expect a reciprocal invitation), equal-return feasts (reciprocity is
expected), and greater-return feasts (the host expects to receive more
than he provides at future feasts).

I find Michael Dietler's (2001) approach most useful, with its emphasis on the political aspects of feasts. His three groups are empowering,
patron-role, and diacritical feasts. Formerly known as entrepreneurial
feasts (Dietler 1996), empowering feasts serve to enhance the host's
prestige and, sometimes, wealth. Some are overtly competitive, but even

if perceived as leveling devices to redistribute accumulated wealth, the feast thereby converts economic to symbolic capital. This category also includes work-party feasts to marshal labor for large projects. Empowering feasts frequently impoverish the host in the short term, although, if successful, they pay dividends in the longer term. Patron-role feasts are redistributive, maintaining and legitimizing an existing hierarchy. Like empowering feasts, they are based on the notion of reciprocity and the debt created by a gift, but here the host does not expect a return in kind. Rather, the loyalty and labor of the followers are earned by the generosity of the leader/host. Diacritical feasts are all about marking off an elite group. The emphasis is not on quantity but on quality, with special (rare, exotic, labor-intensive) food and paraphernalia that are not accessible to commoners. This is the realm of cuisine and discriminating taste signaling elite status (see the earlier section, *Cooking and Consumption*).

Clearly these types have a rough correspondence with the sociopolitical structure, as noted by both Dietler and Hayden, although they also stress that the correspondence is imperfect. Moreover, a given feast may have elements of more than one type, especially in Hayden's more elaborate typology. Hamilakis (2008:17) feels that the great variability in feasts and the overlap of aspects of the ideal types present in most actual feasts obviate the utility of such typologies. Rather, he suggests analyzing, for example, the cooperative or diacritical features of particular feasts.

The historical literature is full of accounts of the diacritical feasts found in states (e.g., Hammond 1993; Strong 2002), but empowering feasts are best known from ethnography. In particular, competitive feasting such as the pig feasts of Melanesia and the potlatch of the northwest coast of North America have provoked enduring discussion in an effort to understand why people would invest so much labor to build up wealth, only to give it away or destroy it (Codere 1950; Mauss 1967; Rappaport 1968; Walens 1982). To capitalist eyes this is strange behavior, although it makes perfect sense in a gift economy. In this kind of highly competitive feast, the idiom of reciprocity is used to gain prestige and position by staging large, elaborate feasts, accompanied by gifts of food and nonfood and sometimes the conspicuous destruction of property. Not only do these events demonstrate the wealth and generosity of the host but they also indebt the guests and thereby place them in an inferior position. This can be reversed only by reciprocating with an even more sumptuous feast, leading to a cycle of increasing production driven by spiraling consumption, until one side is defeated (unable to reciprocate).

The roots of such feasts in both areas, as well as similar events in South-east Asia (Adams 2004; Durrenberger 1976; Hoskins 1993), extend into prehistory, but there are indications of relatively recent changes that may have intensified them. In Melanesia, the arrival of the sweet potato (*Ipomoea batatas*) a few hundred years ago enabled much more inten-sive pig raising than was previously possible; the result has been termed the Ipomoean Revolution (Watson 1977). A similar effect may have occurred with the introduction of new foods and trade goods in the Pacific Northwest with European contact (Birket-Smith 1964). In both regions, before colonial pacification there were two realms for prestige competition, often seen as explicitly parallel: warfare and feasting (Codere 1950; Young 1971). Competitive feasting has probably intensified as the military avenue to glory was closed off. In any case, it is quite likely that, in the absence of colonial control, where there is strongly competitive feasting there is also likely to be low-level warfare (raiding), and perhaps vice versa.

In sum, feasting is likely to occur in all societies, but it plays different roles. It is probably least important for generalized foragers, but is clearly documented. For instance, Tanner (1979:163) describes numerous occa-sions for feasting among the Mistassini Cree: calendrical events, life-cycle events, the first kill of a member of a major taxon for the season, a par-ticularly successful hunt, or the killing of an adult bear. Although some feasts may celebrate a bonanza from a good hunt, in other cases hunting is intensified in the preceding days to enable a feast to be held (e.g., Descola 1994:244). The communal, solidarity-building aspect is usually ascendant in these groups. Feasting plays a central role in the politics of transegalitarian societies. Generosity is highly valued in both foraging and transegalitarian farming societies. Yet whereas generalized foragers enact generosity on a daily basis through meat sharing, for herders it is more episodic, practiced mainly in feasts that are a contrast to the hoarding of their animals that is necessary most of the time to maintain their herds. In stratified societies, feasts are more restricted in scope and more elaborate in content, at least among the elite.

## THE ARCHAEOLOGY OF FEASTING

Given the great variability in the form of feasts, there can be no simple archaeological signature to identify feasting. However, because feasts are by definition set apart from ordinary meals (by quantity, quality, and/or ritualization, and possibly spatially), it should be possible to detect feasting remains where there is relatively good archaeological resolution. It is particularly easy to find remains of diacritical feasts, because hosts expend great effort to distinguish them from everyday meals. Yet even less ostentatious events are often visible through careful contextual analysis. As always, textual information or direct historical analogy is useful where available and can give clues about the nature of feasts in a particular culture. In deeper prehistory, we usually must rely on contrasts with the more general pattern of consumption. In all cases, it behooves us to draw on as many lines of evidence as possible, taking into account food preparation facilities and fancy serving ware, for example. Hayden (2001a) provides a fairly thorough list of the kinds of nonfaunal indicators one might seek for feasting, and Twiss (2008) covers both faunal and other material signatures. Here I focus on zooarchaeological approaches, although they always work in conjunction with other evidence. Because the zooarchaeological study of feasting has burgeoned in recent years, I can only scratch the surface.

A wide variety of material evidence, sometimes contradictory, has been advanced to argue for the occurrence of past feasting. It is important to realize that contradictory criteria may both be correct, because feasting is best understood in the context of the overall commensal practices of each society. Thus, rather than developing a feasting index that can be applied universally, zooarchaeologists need to build arguments for feasting in each case. However, comparison to other feasting remains and to ethnographic and ethnoarchaeological accounts can guide us toward the kinds of features that may help build the case. Zooarchaeological feasting evidence can be roughly classified into three categories: spatial and contextual associations; selection of feasting foods; and treatment of the carcass, including disposal.

### Spatial and contextual associations

Because feasts are often linked to larger ceremonies, association with ceremonial places or structures is a clue that faunal remains may derive from feasts. As discussed in Chapter 3, animal remains that show signs of consumption and are associated with temples may provide evidence for both sacrifice and the feasting that typically follows; indeed they more directly attest feasting in a religious context than sacrifice (Kolb 1999; Lev-Tov and McGeough 2007). Monuments such as the megalithic constructions of Neolithic northwest Europe are also considered to be the loci of ceremonies, and animal bones found in these locations are usually judged to be feasting remains (McOmish 1996; Thomas 1991; Whittle and Pollard 1999). The same would seem to apply to sites like Göbekli Tepe. Interestingly, however, its analysts have interpreted the associated faunal and other materials not as feasting remains, but midden from undiscovered settlement(s) at an unknown distance, hauled in to fill the ceremonial structures (Peters and Schmidt 2004). If one were instead to regard this midden material as redeposited remains of meals consumed at this ceremonial aggregation site for surrounding communities – hence probably feasts – these meals do not seem to differ much from ordinary meals except in their spatial and social context. Hayden (2001a) suggests such lack of differentiation is likely to characterize solidarity feasts in egalitarian contexts. Feasting is proposed for other, roughly contemporary, ceremonial sites in the Near East (Twiss 2008), as well as those from other times and places (Crabtree 2004).

More subtly, open areas or plazas within settlements are prime locations for public rituals, and associated animal bone deposits are likely to be feasting remains (Rosenberg and Redding 1998); Vernon Knight (2001) argues that Woodland period platform mounds in southeastern North America formed a similar public space for ceremonies including feasting. Association with palaces, elite dwellings, or ceremonial structures also puts faunal remains into a public realm that may imply feasting (Hockett 1998; Kelly 2001; Lucas and McGovern 2007; Masson 1999; Muir and Driver 2004). Occasionally, as at the Classic Mayan village of Cerén in El Salvador, we may be able to identify buildings used to store food and ritual paraphernalia for feasts/ceremonies (Brown 2001). Yet another architectural association pointing to feasting is the association of food remains with construction phases of buildings, whether public structures (Vega-Centeno Sara-Lafosse 2007) or private houses (Russell in press-b; Russell et al. 2009). These deposits are likely to indicate work-party feasts.

Association with human remains or burials is also a marker of ceremonial context. The "Death Pit" at Halafian Domuztepe, with its mingled, disarticulated, human and animal remains, is one striking example (Kansa and Campbell 2004). Uruk period pit 88 at El Kowm-Caracol in Syria is a similar, smaller scale instance from another Ceramic Neolithic Near Eastern site (Vila 1991). In other cases, the faunal remains are deposited near human graves or charnel structures, and they are considered to derive from associated ceremonies (Chaix 1989; Goring-Morris and Horwitz 2007; Munro and Grosman 2010; Seeman 1979). Most of these feasts are presumably funerary (and thus, as noted earlier, particularly likely to be competitive or redistributive in nature). Similarly, offerings of food in burials, although obviously not consumed themselves, may be indicators of funerary feasts shared with the deceased (e.g., Anthony 1998; Auxiette 1995; Clarke 2001; Crabtree 1995; Crubézy et al. 1996; Kim 1994; Nelson 2003).

In addition to associations with architectural and other features, internal associations within a deposit may be indicative of feasting. Most basically, if a deposit can be shown to result from a single event or a short period of time, an unusually high density or large quantity of faunal remains suggests feasting (Becker 2002; Chaix 1989; Davis and Payne 1993; Goring-Morris and Horwitz 2007; Halstead and Isaakidou 2004; Hockett 1998; Lentacker et al. 2004; McOmish 1996; Munro and Grosman 2010; Pappa et al. 2004; Rosenberg and Redding 1998). The case is stronger if the deposit contains other items associated with feasting. As well as nonfaunal artifacts such as serving vessels and alcohol containers, animal bones apart from the remains of meals may signal a ceremonial occasion. Such bones might include costume paraphernalia (Brown 2001) or knucklebones for divination, often a part of ceremonies linked to feasts (Lev-Tov and McGeough 2007; Steel 2004).

### Selection of feasting foods

Feasts are often marked by foods that differ from everyday fare, so faunal assemblages that are notably different in composition from ordinary food waste may flag feasting activities. Some foods, notably large animals (Dabney et al. 2004; Dean 2001; Goring-Morris and Horwitz 2007; Halstead 2007; Junker 2001; Kelly 2001; V. Knight 2001; Masson 1999; Munro and Grosman 2010; Serjeantson 2006) or those obtained in mass kills (Dewar et al. 2006; Vila 1991), are both particularly suitable for feasting and yield such quantities of meat that they necessitate a feast in the absence of viable storage technology. Where domestic herd animals provide the bulk of the meat diet, greater taxonomic diversity has been taken as an indicator of feasting (Lev-Tov and McGeough 2007; Moseley et al. 2005). In contrast, where the ordinary diet is broad spectrum in nature, as was true for much of prehistoric North America, lower diversity may mark feasting foods (Kelly 2001). In general, a balance of taxa that differs from that typically found is often used to argue for feasting, especially if the putative feasting deposit is weighted toward taxa seen as higher value or symbolically linked to the context (e.g., Blitz 1993; Kansa and Campbell 2004; Lentacker et al. 2004; Muir and Driver 2004; Munro and Grosman 2010, Wilson and Rathje 2001). A refinement of this approach identifies a mismatch between a concentration of a particular taxon and its small role in the diet as indicated by stable isotope studies of the human remains (Fornander et al. 2008). Although there are ethnographic cases where domestic animals are consumed only in the context of feasts (Adams 2004; Blanton and Taylor 1995; Hayden 2003), zooarchaeologists rarely are so bold as to suggest this, although Twiss (2008:430) tentatively raises the issue for the Pre-Pottery Neolithic B of the Levant.

Within taxa, animals chosen for feasting may differ in age or sex from those consumed at quotidian meals. Most often, zooarchaeologists argue that a bias to adults may be indicative of feasting, because these are more valuable animals and because for larger taxa the decision to raise them to full size means choosing to produce animals larger than a household can eat on its own (Grant 1991; Halstead 2007; Kansa and Campbell 2004; Lev-Tov and McGeough 2007). However, Pam Crabtree (2004) suggests that where dairy is important and cows will not let down their milk except in the presence of their calves, a bias to infantile cattle displays extravagance. Some have also suggested that male animals are more likely to be selected for feasting, because they are more expendable (Maltby 1985) or have higher prestige value (Lev-Tov and McGeough 2007; Steel 2004). Males are likely to be selected for culling for ordinary meals as well, however, to preserve the breeding stock. The key point may rather be that males are raised to full size (making them possible to sex) for feasting, rather than slaughtered young. Animals raised for feasting may be fattened on special diets, which may be detectable isotopically or from dental microwear (Kirch 2001; Mainland and Halstead 2005; White et al. 2001).

Although this will not always be the case, some feasting deposits may be marked by limited body part distributions, particularly if meat is brought to the feast from a distance as joints (Albarella and Serjeantson 2002; Blitz 1993; Halstead and Isaakidou 2004; V. Knight 2001; Lev-Tov and McGeough 2007; Marciniak 2005a; Masson 1999). In contrast, Finbar McCormick (2002) argues that where elites would normally be provisioned with only choice cuts, to find all body parts in an elite context indicates that they hosted a feast to which commoners were invited. Certain body parts, especially skulls and horns, may be displayed as trophies to materialize the memory of the feast (Adams 2004; Bogaard et al. 2009; Chaix 1989; Clarke 2001; Davis and Payne 1993; Junker 2001; Lucas and McGovern 2007; Raharijaona and Kus 2001; Simoons 1968; Steel 2004; Twiss 2008). Trophy display, indicating the prestige that feasts bring to the hosts, shows that there is a competitive element to these events.

### Treatment of the carcass and remains

Meat and waste from feasts are likely to be treated differently in various ways, both to make the meal special and because the larger scale poses particular problems. With domestic animals, the slaughter itself may take place in a ritualized context, whether or not it is a sacrifice, and so distinctive methods may be used. Unfortunately, given the lack of soft parts and subsequent processing, zooarchaeologists can rarely identify the slaughter technique. However, at Durrington Walls four bones have broken bits of flint embedded in them; one is clearly the tip of an arrowhead. The analysts suggest that domestic cattle and pigs may have been killed by shooting them in a ritualized "hunt," a dramatic performance in this ceremonial space – or else that the animals ranged half-wild and had to be hunted for the feasts (Albarella and Serjeantson 2002).

In butchery, Stephanie Knight (2001) suggests that fewer dismemberment marks, indicating that the carcass was broken down into larger pieces than usual, might indicate feasting, specifically feasting of a relatively egalitarian nature with broad participation. Halstead (2007), concerned with distinguishing among feasting, wastage, and storage as alternate ways of managing the consumption of animals too large for a single household to eat, argues that a higher rate of fillet marks on the bones of large animals supports (although it does not demonstrate) drying for storage and thus may mean feasting did not occur. Similarly, Halstead suggests that less processed large animal bones – that is, wastage of marrow and perhaps bits of attached meat – could mean that the owners chose not to share these carcasses in a feast. However, most analysts, drawing on ethnography, see less processed bones (wastage) that nevertheless show signs of meat consumption as indicative of feasting, when meat is plentiful (Albarella and Serjeantson 2002; Kansa and Campbell

2004; Kelly 2001; Potter 2000; Russell 1999; Russell and Martin in press; Serjeantson 2006; Thomas 1991; Twiss 2008). Conspicuous wastage is more likely to occur in competitive feasts such as potlatches, whereas feasts emphasizing solidarity have fewer motives for excess.

Feasts may be marked by special cooking methods, which may add value to the food through display (as in the public roasting of whole animals), through increased labor investment in more elaborate preparations, or simply through being different from quotidian meals. Some have suggested that, because boiling meat on the bone extracts nutrients most thoroughly, the more wasteful methods of roasting or pit roasting are particularly likely to be associated with feasting. In addition to burning and fragmentation patterns that may give clues to cooking methods, carnivore gnawing on bones may indicate that meat was either roasted or stripped from the bones before cooking, because boiling removes the grease that attracts dogs (Albarella and Serjeantson 2002; Kolb 1999; Needham and Bowman 2005; Russell 1999; Russell and Martin in press; Serjeantson 2006). However, cooking methods for feasts must always be evaluated in the context of daily cooking practices; roasting is not a straightforward feasting signature because some feasts will use other methods and roasting may also be used for daily meals. For example, alternative feasting practices in Bronze Age western Europe were based on boiling in large cauldrons or roasting; these are attested by flesh-hooks (to retrieve boiled meat from the cauldrons) vs. spits, with the spits and flesh-hooks showing mutually exclusive distributions (Needham and Bowman 2005).

Many of the special deposits described in Chapter 3 are likely to have derived from animals consumed at feasts; for instance, the reconstructed pregnant cow at Basta and the Çatalhöyük commemorative deposits (Becker 2002; Russell et al. 2009). Such carefully placed deposits indicate that the animal remains retained special power that needed to be harnessed or contained; thus there was probably more to the ceremony than the feast alone. More prosaic considerations may also shape discard patterns of feasting material. Where meat is normally shared out, finding most of a large mammal in a midden or pit associated with a single household suggests feasting remains (Clarke 2001; Marshall 1994). However, if portions of feasting food are distributed for home consumption, as is attested in some ethnographic cases (Blackwood 1981; Clarke 2001; Evans-Pritchard 1951; Hoskins 1993; Kahn 1986; Potter 2000; Raharijaona and Kus 2001; Stevenson 1937), butchery waste is likely to be found at the host's house or the ceremonial space, with the meaty parts dispersed, quite possibly beyond the settlement (Dabney et al. 2004; Halstead 2007).

In many cases, the bone waste from daily meals is simply dumped nearby or tossed to the dogs. However, the quantity of (before long) smelly bones from a feast, their propensity to attract scavengers and flies (Kramer 1982:42), and perhaps the residual power inherent in ceremonial remains (Davenport 1986) may incline people to dispose of these remains more formally. These measures may include rapid burial (Dabney et al. 2004; V. Knight 2001; Russell and Martin 2005; Steel 2004), burial in pits (Kelly 2001; Lentacker et al. 2004; Maltby 1985; Marciniak 2005a; Pappa et al. 2004; Russell 1999) or ditches (Albarella and Serjeantson 2002; Thomas 1991; Whittle and Pollard 1999), or trash fires (Clarke 2001; Russell 1999). Other feasting remains and paraphernalia are likely to be included in these deposits, and the combination of rapid burial (hence less disturbance) and less processing means that they often contain articulated sets of bones (Goring-Morris and Horwitz 2007; Munro and Grosman 2010; Rosenberg and Redding 1998; Serjeantson 2006; Steel 2004).

### Understanding ancient feasts

Recent work has identified remains of feasts in most parts of the world and through many periods. Nevertheless, archaeologists surely underestimate past feasting for a variety of reasons. We may simply miss the evidence if we are not attuned to the possibility. Crabtree's (2004) reanalysis of her own work at medieval Irish Dún Ailinne illustrates the difference that outlook can make to interpretation. Despite the ceremonial nature of the site, in her earlier work she had approached the animal remains as reflecting general subsistence practices. Returning to the material more recently, she now understands the assemblage as shaped by the demand of the elite for costly foods for diacritical feasts. Sometimes older reports contain hints of deposits we might now see as feasting remains; for example, the so-called butcher shop at PPNB Beidha with its dense deposit of large pieces of large animals, some articulated, and a nearby room with a concentration of ground-stone tools that may be associated with plant food preparation (Kirkbride 1968). Likewise the deposit at Early Bronze Age Arslantepe in Turkey – with a narrower range of taxa than usual at the site, including wild animals, and a bias to meaty body parts and subadult or adult animals – is described as a sacrificial deposit, but seems more likely to be feasting remains (Bökönyi 1983).

Even when we evaluate faunal and other archaeological data with feasting in mind, it will not always be visible. We will not always be able to establish the daily meal pattern against which we can distinguish feasting. If meat or the meat of domestic animals is only eaten at feasts, this pattern will be difficult to detect. In such cases, as Priscilla Keswani (1994) has suggested for Chalcolithic and Bronze Age Cyprus, faunal assemblages consist largely of feasting remains, and the requirements of feasts and ceremonies drive herding practices as reflected in mortality profiles. Rebecca Dean (2001) has made a similar argument for large mammal hunting in the Puebloan American Southwest.

Beyond simply identifying the presence of feasting, archaeologists are increasingly examining the nature of past feasts. I indicated earlier some of the ways that faunal evidence can be used in this endeavor. Archaeology is particularly well placed to investigate changes in feasting practices through time, in concert with social and political change. For example, in the southern Levant Twiss (2008) traces feasting through the Pre-Pottery Neolithic. Feasting appears to be present in a small way in the PPNA, peaks in the PPNB (a time of aggregation), and drops off in the PPNC as settlement becomes more dispersed. The scale of feasts also appears to be largest in the PPNB. She suggests that, although there were both competitive and integrative aspects throughout the PPN, feasting may have been one of the few arenas for competition in the PPNA, whereas the more differentiated households in the PPNB brought a greater need for the integrative function of feasting, at the same time that the competitive side contributed to the household differentiation.

In Neolithic Europe, Hodder (1990) argues that where the domus (roughly household) is central in southeast Europe and the earlier Neolithic of central Europe, feasting is competitive; as the foris (community) becomes dominant in central and western Europe, feasting becomes more communal, tied to public places and monuments. Similarly, in the American Southwest James Potter (2000) sees feasting starting on a small scale in Pueblo I, primarily communal and integrative. It then becomes more competitive and larger in scale (although less so than in areas famous for their competitive feasts, such as the Pacific Northwest) in Pueblo II and III. However, in the Pueblo IV period, despite larger and more complex settlements, feasting again becomes more communal in nature, associated with central plazas where inclusive rituals are performed, in contrast to the earlier more dispersed rituals and feasts. He also draws on zooarchaeological, ceramic, architectural, and other evidence to counter Hayden's model in this case. The intensity of feasting does not seem to be associated with more productive environments, nor does it lead to inequality. Potter suggests that, on the contrary, feasting does not drive sociopolitical change but follows it, particularly changing religion and ritual.

The growing literature on feasting, and increasing attention to forms of commensality more generally, will continue to illuminate the workings of ancient societies. Gross statements may be possible on the basis of sitewide information such as the proportions of taxa, but understanding the operation of social and political processes enacted in the commensal sphere requires contextual analysis and the integration of multiple lines of evidence in addition to animal remains.

## Medicinal uses

We tend to think of the health value of meat in terms of protein, calories, and fat. However, for many cultures, quite aside from the medicinal use of assorted animal body parts (in traditional Chinese medicine, for instance) or the sacrifice of animals as part of a curing ceremony, certain meats have therapeutic value in the treatment of illness. In modern western culture we see this in the reputed efficacy of chicken soup for minor ailments. Ethnographically and historically we can find many other examples, although plants are more frequently the source of medicines.

Although many meats may be eaten medicinally, the flesh of nonstaple animals carries particular medicinal value. Not surprisingly, animals that are not normally considered edible or only marginally so have greater therapeutic power; often this means the strong-tasting flesh of carnivores. So, for example, in northern Thailand the field rat and chameleon, which are unclassified in the local schema opposing domestic and bush taxa because they are found in the village but are not domestic, are eaten medicinally (Tambiah 1969:449). So are raptor eggs by the Nage in Indonesia (Forth 2004:0). Eduardo Corona (2005) presents ethnohistorical evidence for Mesoamerican medicinal use of many body parts and some meat of a variety of birds. Raptors feature here as well, but turkey, quail, doves, grackles, and hummingbirds also have applications. What we might regard as typical food animals can have medicinal uses: The Assyrians used pork to treat chest ailments or to hasten a slow labor (for which purpose tortoise and fox meat were also considered efficacious); other pig body parts were also used medicinally (Levy et al. 2006).

Primates, with their resemblance to humans, are widely used medicinally, mainly as particular body parts. However, orangutan flesh is reportedly eaten as an aphrodisiac, and in India some eat rhesus macaques to treat epidemic diseases (cholera, malaria, typhoid, etc.), and the brains of both rhesus and Assam macaques are consumed to relieve rheumatism (Alves et al. 2010). Like primates, dogs are typically seen as particularly close to humans. This makes them good medicine, attested for a number of ailments in Nigeria (Ojoade 1990:219), ethnohistorically in Mesoamerica (White et al. 2001), and in classical Greece and Rome (Gilhus 2006; Trantalidou 2006). In Malawi, people possessed by animal spirits are treated by hunting or capturing an animal of that species. The patient drinks the blood mixed with herbs, and the participants in the healing ceremony eat the meat mixed with maize porridge (Morris 2000:247–8).

Medicinal use is not easy to detect archaeologically, and there have been few attempts. Schmidt (2000:225) argues that beaver mandibles in a Mesolithic burial at Oleneostrovski mogilnik in Karelia, Russia, mark the deceased as a shaman, because they adorn some shamans' costumes and are seen as having medicinal power by many boreal groups. Drawing on textual sources, Vila (2002) raises the possibility that a cache of gazelle horn cores at Early Bronze Age Tell Chuera in Syria might represent the use of the horns for magical/medicinal purposes, although craft use is an alternative. I have tentatively suggested that the microfaunal remains of carnivore scat in a few burials at Çatalhöyük might have been collected for medicinal use (Russell and Meece 2006). Without ethnographic or historical evidence, it will be difficult to guess what might have been considered medicinal, but we might at least consider the possibility for rare taxa in an assemblage, especially ones that are not considered prime meat sources or are strongly flavored, such as many carnivores. As Corona suggests, some deposits of particular body parts that we tend to interpret as evidence of ritual may more specifically be remains of medicinal practices. More subtle medicinal uses, as in systems based on humors in which foods (and other things) are categorized as hot or cold, or as some larger number of categories that must be kept in balance, are still harder to detect. Such systems are widely attested in the present and recent past, however (E. Anderson 2004). It is possible that such beliefs might account for some variation in household faunal assemblages, if the state of health of the inhabitants inclines them to eat some animals and avoid others.

## Meaty topics

In this chapter I have tried to sketch some of the ways in which meat acts in its social form as food. Meat forms social relations in many ways and in differing contexts. This is true of all food, but the special value given to meat and the advantage that bone waste provides in tracing it mean that it is particularly amenable to archaeological study. We have seen through this chapter that most of the tools in the zooarchaeologist's arsenal are relevant here, such as balance of taxa, mortality profiles, body part distribution, conjoining, and stable isotope studies. The key is modeling that takes the social aspects of meat into account (O'Connor 1992b). In addition, in most cases, contextual analysis is critical to detecting the flows of meat that construct social relations.

10

# Studying human–animal relations

> One ironic implication of post-processual developments is the increased need for better middle range theory. Middle range theory developed in the context of processual archaeology when it became clear that the quality of reconstructions of past behaviour was inadequate to fulfill the goals set by the processualists. Middle range theory has been developed through experimental, ethnoarchaeological and cross-cultural studies in order to provide tested links between archaeological data and past behaviour. Post-processual archaeology demands greater attention to the particular contexts in which past behaviours and actions occurred; consequently, post-processual approaches require better reconstruction of the past and place greater reliance on the development of middle range theory. (Driver 1997:81)

Having covered a lot of ground in the preceding chapters, a full summary would be difficult and probably not particularly useful. Rather I seek here to draw some general lessons from the topics examined for the practice of social zooarchaeology. What does it mean for our methods if we take seriously the social and symbolic aspects of animals and meat?

## Some lessons

If nothing else, this review has yielded an abundance of cautionary tales for those seeking to model hunting and herding strategies. In addition to nutritional and economic factors, the balance of taxa and mortality profiles are quite likely to be influenced by the prestige or wealth value of the animal; by bridewealth, sacrificial, or feasting requirements; and by taboos and ethnic or other food preferences. Binford (1978) famously defined a number of utility indices (e.g., meat, marrow, and grease utility indices; general utility index) to aid in interpreting body part distributions, and others have added their own versions (Friesen 2001; Friesen et al. 2001; Garvey 2010; Jones and Metcalfe 1988; Lyman et al. 1992; Madrigal 2004; Metcalfe and Jones 1988; Monks 2004; Morin 2007; Olivera and Nasti 2001; Outram and Rowley-Conwy 1998; Rowley-Conwy et al. 2002; Savelle and Friesen 1996; Savelle et al. 1996). For the most part, these indices treat utility in nutritional terms, although James Savelle (1997) has offered an architectural utility index for whale remains. However, in addition to forces of attrition that affect body part distributions, which have been extensively studied by Binford and others, human selection of bones for trophies, special deposits, hunting shrines, respectful disposal, divination, and other uses may shape our assemblages. Skulls and horns, generally rated as low-utility body parts, are particularly likely to be transported, curated, and displayed to commemorate hunts, sacrifices, or feasts (e.g., Russell and Martin 2005).

Zooarchaeologists have long struggled with equifinality (e.g., Bonnichsen 1989; Gifford-Gonzalez 1991; Halstead 1998; Lyman 2004; Rogers 2000), so in part I am just adding more factors to the mix. Yet my hope is that through awareness and more sophisticated modeling we can actually distinguish among the possibilities. Doing so will usually require bringing multiple lines of evidence to bear; the mortality profile or utility index is only a starting point. In recent years, an increasing number of analyses have incorporated these social considerations; I have referred to many of them in earlier chapters. This effort extends well beyond the boundaries of postprocessual archaeology (if this term retains any salience). Note the recent surge in costly signaling models. Although human behavioral ecology previously manifested itself in zooarchaeology and ethnographic studies of hunting chiefly through optimal foraging models of prey choice, the current fashion is to invoke costly signaling (performing under a handicap to signal the high quality of one's genes to prospective mates) to account for what we might otherwise ascribe to prestige: nonoptimal choices to hunt large, dangerous animals or to herd instead of hunting, for example (e.g., Aldenderfer 2006; Bliege Bird and Smith 2005; Hawkes and Bliege Bird 2002).

Another lesson we might take is that rare taxa can be important. This depends, of course, on how importance is measured. I plead guilty to the common practice of largely limiting discussion to the major taxa (in quantitative terms), which are surely the most significant in terms of diet and probably for herding strategies. Yet numerically minor taxa may have major social significance. These may be the animals that were taboo (often because of their strong symbolic value) or those important for divinatory or medicinal purposes. It is instructive to note that prehistoric people took the trouble to capture and transport animals of minor dietary importance to islands along with or instead of their staple meat sources (see Chapter 7, *Island Introductions*). This may be one of the clearest indicators of what animals were important to these ancient people.

## Animal pathologies

Although I have given them limited attention in the preceding chapters, pathologies, in the broad sense, provide one of the most direct windows on human–animal relationships. Osteological traces of hunting wounds have been used to reconstruct hunting methods, sometimes with great specificity (Bratlund 1996; Noe-Nygaard 1975). Pathologies have played a major role in arguments for animal herding in the Upper Paleolithic of western Europe (Bahn 1980, 1984; Munro 1902), both as cribbing wear on horse teeth and as healed fractures that would have disabled the animal. These claims are, of course, hotly disputed (Rogers and Rogers 1988; Rowley-Conwy 1990; White 1989), and it is apparent from the wildlife literature and my own observations of modern skeletons that wild animals can survive horrendous fractures without human care long enough for them to heal and leave them hobbling on three legs, in many cases, as long as they are still able to eat and predation pressure is not too intense, and depending on the body part (Bartosiewicz 2008b; Kistner 1982; McDiarmid 1987; Middleton 1975; Rowley-Conwy 1990; Spinage 1971). In contrast, set fractures are a clear sign of human care.

In my experience, pathologies in wild animals tend to derive from trauma (fractures, ossified hematomas, etc.), whereas those in early domestic animals are more often the indirect result of poor nutrition (caries and dental abscesses, infections), suggesting that Neolithic herders did not always provide their flocks with optimal care. Signs of trauma are found particularly on dogs among the domestic animals, a reminder that they were very often not pampered pets (Bartosiewicz 2008b; Russell 1993). Further clues to the conditions of ancient herding may be found in pathologies such as penning elbow in sheep that result from crowding (Baker and Brothwell 1980). Use of animals for traction (Baker 1984; Bartosiewicz 2008a; de Cupere et al. 2000; Fabiš 2005; Higham et al. 1981; Johannsen 2005) or riding may also produce characteristic pathologies (Anthony and Brown 1989; Bendrey 2007; Daugnora and

Thomas 2005; Pluskowski et al. 2010). In light of the recent trend to
see domestication in terms of care rather than domination (Clark 2007;
Oma 2007; Orton 2010a), paleopathological evidence may provide useful evidence of the nature of human–animal relations.

## Taphonomy beyond attrition

As discussed in Chapter 1, taphonomy has had a huge and salutary impact
on zooarchaeology. Many of these excellent studies have been phrased as
cautionary tales warning of the biases introduced by dogs and other scavengers, burrowing animals, soil processes, butchering, and bone grease
preparation, to name a few factors. In many versions of a classic diagram
first published by Meadow (1980:67), zooarchaeologists have shown
how various processes progressively reduce the living assemblage of animals in a landscape to the death assemblage at a site, from this to the
bones actually buried, still further to those that survive until excavation,
to the proportion of these actually recovered by the archaeologists, and
finally to the studied assemblage recorded by the zooarchaeologist (Davis
1987; Reitz and Wing 1999).

As Meadow outlines, the death assemblage is rarely the same as the
living assemblage, because of factors such as high infant mortality that
lead to a younger age profile in the death than the living assemblage,
and biases created by selective hunting or culling strategies. The death
assemblage is transformed by human butchering, cooking, and disposal
practices, and then by scavengers and soil conditions. All of these affect
some bones more than others, generally tending to remove the softer
bones of the skeleton and the bones of younger animals at higher rates,
so that mortality profiles and body part distributions will be altered.
Archaeologists often excavate only part of a site; spatial differentiation
in the faunal remains may result in a skewed sample. Even where they
do excavate, they will not recover everything. Smaller bones will be lost
to varying degrees depending on whether the sediments are screened,
the size of the screen's mesh, and how much flotation is used. Finally,
zooarchaeologists make decisions about what they record and how hard
they will try to identify fragmentary specimens.

All in all, it paints a bleak picture of assemblages that reach the analyst
already riddled with systematic biases, most of them beyond our control.
However, although it is certainly important that we be aware of all these

factors and understand their workings as thoroughly as possible, the situation is not so hopeless as it might seem. Rarely are we, as archaeologists, primarily interested in reconstructing the living assemblage of animals in a region. We are, on the contrary, interested in the behavior of ancient humans. Because many of the alterations to the assemblages result from the actions of these very humans of interest, they can be regarded not as biases, but as sources of information. Taphonomic information has been put to good use in addressing questions related to early hominid hunting and scavenging (e.g., Bunn 1991; Domínguez-Rodrigo et al. 2010). There is considerable room for expansion in the issues approached through taphonomic information. Even taphonomic forces that seem to have less to do with human behavior can tell us much about the depositional history of the context from which the bone is recovered; they are thus a rich source of information about human behavior less directly related to animals and meat, such as discard and construction practices, child's play (and hence the nature of childhood), and the places to which dogs had access (Marciniak 2005a, 2005b; Murray 2000; Orton 2010b; Russell and Martin 2000; Russell and Twiss in press; Serjeantson 2000). Let us mine this taphonomic information to its full potential.

## Contextual zooarchaeology

Above all, the discussions in the preceding chapters illustrate the need for a contextual approach to zooarchaeology. Meadow (1975, 1978) issued an early call for attention to context to avoid bias in interpretation of subsistence strategies; he later pioneered the use of contextual analysis to understand depositional processes (Meadow 1991). Just as an earlier generation of zooarchaeologists called for screening and systematic recovery of faunal samples (e.g., Maltby 1985; Meadow 1980; Payne 1972; Shaffer 1992), so must we now advocate for the collection and retention of contextual information for faunal remains and for its use in zooarchaeological analysis (Crabtree 1990). Happily, this is becoming far more frequent, but it is still common to see studies that cry out for the use of contextual data addressed only at the level of the sitewide assemblage.

Questions should be studied at an appropriate scale, and for some analyses the scale of sitewide or even regional assemblages may be appropriate. However, for the most part, to address social questions adequately, we must work with units closer to the scale of lived experience. Of course, smaller units raise sample size issues, and we will often need to move back and forth among various scales, but sometimes a smaller sample size is actually helpful (Locock 1999; Lupo 2001).

In addition to the archaeological context, animal remains need to be understood in their broader social contexts. This means considering other materials and our understanding of the workings of the ancient society in question. I will confess to my discomfort about the many places in this book where I have made quite generalized arguments for the consideration of various social factors in zooarchaeology. My intent is not to provide cookie-cutter solutions, along the lines of a sacrificial utility index that could be applied to any assemblage, but rather to bring these social aspects into our collective archaeological consciousness. We must always be attentive to the particularities of the sites we study, and we must employ as many lines of evidence as possible to build robust interpretations through rigorous methods. Yet we should also be bold enough to seek ways to study the plethora of past human–animal relations that we know must have existed.

# References

Aaris-Sørensen, Kim 1981 A zoological analysis of the osteological material from the sacrificial layer at the Maussolleion at Halikarnassos. In *The Maussolleion at Halikarnassos I: The Sacrificial Deposit*. Pp. 91–110. Jutland Archaeological Society Publications. Copenhagen: Nordisk Forlag.

Abbink, Jon 1993 Reading the entrails: Analysis of an African divination discourse. *Man* 28(4):705–26.

Abbink, Jon 2003 Love and death of cattle: The paradox in Suri attitudes toward livestock. *Ethnos* 68(3):341–64.

Abrams, H. Leon, Jr. 1987 The preferences for animal protein and fat: A cross-cultural survey. In *Food and Evolution: Toward a Theory of Human Food Habits*. M. Harris and E. B. Ross, eds. Pp. 207–23. Philadelphia: Temple University Press.

Adams, Carol J. 1990 *The Sexual Politics of Meat*. New York: Continuum.

Adams, Ron L. 2004 An ethnoarchaeological study of feasting in Sulawesi, Indonesia. *Journal of Anthropological Archaeology* 23(1):56–78.

Adán, Gema E., Diego Álvarez-Lao, Pablo Turrero, Miguel Arbizu, and Eva García-Vázquez 2009 Fish as diet resource in North Spain during the Upper Paleolithic. *Journal of Archaeological Science* 36(3):895–9.

Adovasio, James M., and Jeffrey S. Illingworth 2003 Basketry and textile impressions. In *Prehistoric Sitagroi: Excavations in Northeast Greece 1968–1970*. E. S. Elster and A. C. Renfrew, eds. Pp. 252–7. Vol. 2: The Final Report. Los Angeles: Cotsen Institute of Archaeology, University of California, Los Angeles.

Adovasio, James M., and Robert F. Maslowski 1988 Textile impressions on ceramic vessels at Divostin. In *Divostin and the Neolithic of Central Serbia*. A. McPherron and D. Srejović, eds. Pp. 345–54. Pittsburgh: University of Pittsburgh, Ethnology Monographs.

Adovasio, James M., Olga Soffer, and Bohuslav Klíma 1996 Upper Palaeolithic fibre technology: Interlaced woven finds from Pavlov I, Czech Republic, *c.* 26,000 years ago. *Antiquity* 70(269):526–34.

Agenbroad, Larry D. 2001 Columbian mammoths (*M. columbi*) and pygmy mammoths (*M. exilis*): A comparison. In *Proceedings of the International Conference on Mammoth Site Studies*. D. L. West, ed. Pp. 137–42. University of Kansas Publications in Anthropology. Lawrence, KS: University of Kansas Department of Anthropology.

Albarella, Umberto, Keith M. Dobney, and Peter A. Rowley-Conwy 2006a The domestication of the pig (*Sus scrofa*): New challenges and approaches. In *Documenting Domestication: New Genetic and Archaeological Paradigms*. M. A. Zeder, D. G. Bradley, E. Emshwiller, and B. D. Smith, eds. Pp. 209–27. Berkeley: University of California Press.

Albarella, Umberto, Filippo Manconi, Peter A. Rowley-Conwy, and Jean-Denis Vigne 2006b Pigs of Corsica and Sardinia: A biometrical re-evaluation of their status and history. In *Archaeozoological Studies in Honour of Alfredo Riedel*. U. Tecchiati and B. Sala, eds. Pp. 285–302. Bolzano: Province of Bolzano.

Albarella, Umberto, and Dale Serjeantson 2002 A passion for pork: Meat consumption at the British Late Neolithic site of Durrington Walls. In *Consuming Passions and Patterns of Consumption*. P. T. Miracle and N. Milner, eds. Pp. 33–49. Cambridge: McDonald Institute for Archaeological Research.

Alcover, Josep Antoni 2008 The first Mallorcans: Prehistoric colonization in the western Mediterranean. *Journal of World Prehistory* 21(1):19–84.

Alcover, Josep Antoni, Antonia Sans, and Miquel Palmer 1998 The extent of extinctions of mammals on islands. *Journal of Biogeography* 25(5):913–18.

Alcover, Josep Antoni, Bartomeu Seguí, and Pere Bover 1999 Extinctions and local disappearances of vertebrates in the western Mediterranean islands. In *Extinctions in Near Time: Causes, Contexts, and Consequences*. R. D. E. MacPhee, ed. Pp. 165–88. New York: Kluwer Academic/Plenum Publishers.

Aldenderfer, Mark S. 2006 Costly signaling, the sexual division of labor, and animal domestication in the Andean highlands. In *Behavioral Ecology and the Transition to Agriculture*. D. J. Kennett and B. Winterhalder, eds. Pp. 167–96. Berkeley: University of California Press.

Alexander, Bobby C. 1997 Ritual and current studies of ritual: Overview. In *Anthropology of Religion: A Handbook*. S. D. Glazier, ed. Pp. 139–60. Westport, CT: Greenwood Press.

Algaze, Guillermo 2001 Initial social complexity in southwestern Asia: The Mesopotamian advantage. *Current Anthropology* 42(2):199–233.

Alger, Janet M., and Steven F. Alger 2003 *Cat Culture: The Social World of a Cat Shelter*. Philadelphia: Temple University Press.

Allen, Glover M. 1920 Dogs of the American aborigines. *Bulletin of the Museum of Comparative Zoology* 63:429–517.

Allsen, Thomas T. 2006 *The Royal Hunt in Eurasian History*. Philadelphia: University of Pennsylvania Press.

Alroy, John 1999 Putting North America's end-Pleistocene megafaunal extinction in context: Large-scale analyses of spatial patterns, extinction rates, and size distributions. In *Extinctions in Near Time: Causes, Contexts, and Consequences.* R. D. E. MacPhee, ed. Pp. 105–43. New York: Kluwer Academic/Plenum Publishers.

Alroy, John 2001 A multispecies overkill simulation of the end-Pleistocene megafaunal mass extinction. *Science* 292(5523):1893–6.

Altman, Jon, and Nicolas Peterson 1988 Rights to game and rights to cash among Australian hunter-gatherers. In *Hunters and Gatherers 2: Property, Power and Ideology.* T. Ingold, D. Riches, and J. Woodburn, eds. Pp. 75–94. New York: Berg.

Altuna, Jesús 1983 On the relationship between archaeofaunas and parietal art in the caves of the Cantabrian region. In *Animals and Archaeology: 1. Hunters and their Prey.* J. Clutton-Brock and C. Grigson, eds. Pp. 227–38. British Archaeological Reports, International Series. Oxford: Archaeopress.

Altuna, Jesús, Anne Eastham, Koro Mariezkurrena, Arthur E. Spiess, and Lawrence G. Straus 1991 Magdalenian and Azilian hunting at the Abri Dufaure, SW France. *ArchaeoZoologia* 4(2):87–108.

Alvard, Michael S. 2001 Mutualistic hunting. In *Meat-Eating and Human Evolution.* C. B. Stanford and H. T. Bunn, eds. Pp. 261–78. Oxford: Oxford University Press.

Alvarez, Ticul, and Aurelio Ocaña 1991 Restos óseos de vertebrados terrestres de las ofrendas del Templo Mayor, ciudad de México. In *La Fauna en el Templo Mayor.* O. J. Polaco, ed. Pp. 105–57. Mexico City: Instituto Nacional de Antropología e Historia.

Alves, Rômulo R. N., Wedson M. S. Souto, and Raynner R. D. Barboza 2010 Primates in traditional folk medicine: A world overview. *Mammal Review* 40(2):155–80.

Amandry, Pierre 1984 Os et coquilles. In *L'Antre Corycien II.* P. Amandry, ed. Pp. 347–80. Bulletin de Correspondance Hellénique, Supplément. Paris: École Française d'Athènes.

Ammerman, Albert J., and L. Luca Cavalli-Sforza 1971 Measuring the rate of spread of early farming in Europe. *Man* 6(4):674–88.

Ammerman, Albert J., and L. Luca Cavalli-Sforza 1984 *The Neolithic Transition and the Genetics of Populations in Europe.* Princeton: Princeton University Press.

Amoroso, Emmanuel C., and Peter A. Jewell 1963 The exploitation of the milk ejection reflex by primitive peoples. In *Man and Cattle.* A. E. Mourant and F. E. Zeuner, eds. Pp. 126–37. Royal Anthropological Institute Occasional Papers. London: Royal Anthropological Institute of Great Britain and Ireland.

Andersen, Johs 1953 Analysis of a Danish roe-deer population (*Capreolus capreolus* (L.)) based upon the extermination of the total stock. *Danish Review of Game Biology* 2:131–55.

Anderson, Atholl J. 1989a Mechanics of overkill in the extinction of New Zealand moas. *Journal of Archaeological Science* 16(2):137–51.

Anderson, Atholl J. 1989b *Prodigious Birds: Moas and Moa-Hunting in Prehistoric New Zealand.* Cambridge: Cambridge University Press.

Anderson, Atholl J. 2001 No meat on that beautiful shore: The prehistoric abandonment of subtropical Polynesian islands. *International Journal of Osteoarchaeology* 11(1–2):14–23.

Anderson, Eugene N. 2004 *Everyone Eats: Understanding Food and Culture.* New York: New York University Press.

Anderson, Virginia D. 2004 *Creatures of Empire: How Domestic Animals Transformed Early America.* New York: Oxford University Press.

Andree, Richard 1906 Scapulimantia. In *Boas Anniversary Volume: Anthropological Papers Written in Honor of Franz Boas.* B. Laufer and H. A. Andrews, eds. New York: G. E. Stechert & Co.

Andrews, Charles W. 1915 A description of the skull and skeleton of a peculiarly modified rupicaprine antelope (*Myotragus balearicus*, Bate), with a notice of a new variety, *M. balearicus* var. *major. Philosophical Transactions of the Royal Society of London. Series B, Biological Sciences* 206:281–305.

Andrews, Peter 1990 *Owls, Caves and Fossils: Predation, Preservation, and Accumulation of Small Mammal Bones in Caves, with an Analysis of the Pleistocene Cave Faunas from Westbury-sub-Mendip, Somerset, UK.* Chicago: University of Chicago Press.

Andrews, Peter, Theya I. Molleson, and Başak Boz 2005 The human burials at Çatalhöyük. In *Inhabiting Çatalhöyük: Reports from the 1995–1999 Seasons.* I. Hodder, ed. Pp. 261–78. McDonald Institute Monographs. Cambridge: McDonald Institute for Archaeological Research.

Angel, J. Lawrence 1971 Early neolithic skeletons from Çatal Hüyük: Demography and pathology. *Anatolian Studies* 21:77–98.

Anthony, David W. 1986 The 'Kurgan Culture,' Indo-European origins, and the domestication of the horse: A reconsideration. *Current Anthropology* 27(4):291–314.

Anthony, David W. 1991 The domestication of the horse. In *Equids in the Ancient World.* R. H. Meadow and H.-P. Uerpmann, eds. Pp. 250–77. Tübinger Atlas des Vorderen Orients, Reihe A, Naturwissenschaften. Wiesbaden: Dr. Ludwig Reichert Verlag.

Anthony, David W. 1994 The earliest horseback riders and Indo-European origins: New evidence from the steppes. In *Die Indogermanen und das Pferd: Akten des Internationalen Interdisziplinären Kolloquiums Freie Universität Berlin, 1.-3. Juli 1992.* B. Hänsel and S. Zimmer, eds. Pp. 185–95. Budapest: Archaeolingua Alapítvány.

Anthony, David W. 1995 Horse, wagon & chariot: Indo-European languages and archaeology. *Antiquity* 69(264):554–65.

Anthony, David W. 1997 Bridling horse power: The history of domestication. In *Horses through Time.* S. L. Olsen, ed. Pp. 59–82. Pittsburgh: Carnegie Museum of Natural History.

Anthony, David W. 1998 The opening of the Eurasian steppe at 2000 BCE. In *The Bronze Age and Early Iron Age Peoples of Eastern Central Asia*. V. H. Mair, ed. Pp. 94–113. Vol. 1. Washington, DC: Institute for the Study of Man.

Anthony, David W. 2007 *The Horse, the Wheel and Language: How Bronze-Age Riders from the Eurasian Steppes Shaped the Modern World*. Princeton: Princeton University Press.

Anthony, David W., and Dorcas R. Brown 1989 Looking a gift horse in the mouth: Identification of the earliest bitted equids and the microscopic analysis of wear. In *Early Animal Domestication and its Cultural Context*. P. J. Crabtree, D. V. Campana, and K. Ryan, eds. Pp. 98–116. MASCA Research Papers in Science and Archaeology. Philadelphia: University of Pennsylvania.

Anthony, David W., and Dorcas R. Brown 1991 The origins of horseback riding. *Antiquity* 65:22–38.

Anthony, David W., and Dorcas R. Brown 2000 Eneolithic horse exploitation in the Eurasian steppes: Diet, ritual and riding. *Antiquity* 74(283):75–86.

Anthony, David W. *et al.* 2005 The Samara Valley Project: Late Bronze Age economy and ritual in the Russian steppes. *Eurasia Antiqua* 11:395–417.

Anthony, David W., Dimitri Telegin, and Dorcas R. Brown 1991 The origin of horseback riding. *Scientific American* 265(6):94–100.

Anthony, David W., and Nikolai B. Vinogradov 1995 Birth of the chariot. *Archaeology* 48(2):36–41.

Antikas, Theo 2006 Symbols of heroism: Horse burials in royal and common Macedonian tombs. In *Equids in Time and Space*. M. Mashkour, ed. Pp. 203–9. Oxford: Oxbow.

Arbogast, Rose-Marie, Vincent Blouet, Jean Desloges, and Christine Guillaume 1989 Le cerf et le chien dans les pratiques funéraires de la seconde moitié du Néolithique du nord de la France. In *L'Animal dans les Pratiques Religieuses: Les Manifestations Matérielles*. J.-D. Vigne, ed. Pp. 37–42. Anthropozoologica. Paris: Éditions du Centre National de la Recherche Scientifique.

Arbogast, Rose-Marie, Jean Desloges, and Antoine Chancerel 2002 Sauvages et domestiques: Les restes animaux dans les sépultures monumentales normandes du néolithique. *Anthropozoologica* 35:17–27.

Arbuckle, Benjamin S., Aliye Öztan, and Sevil Gülçur 2009 The evolution of sheep and goat husbandry in central Anatolia. In *Zooarchaeology and the Reconstruction of Cultural Systems: Case Studies from the Old World*. B. S. Arbuckle, C. A. Makarewicz, and A. L. Atici, eds. Pp. 129–57. Anthropozoologica, Vol. 44. Paris: L'Homme et l'Animal, Société de Recherche Interdisciplinaire.

Ardrey, Robert 1966 *The Territorial Imperative: A Personal Inquiry into the Animal Origins of Property and Nations*. New York: Atheneum.

Argent, Gala 2010 Do the clothes make the horse? Relationality, roles and statuses in Iron Age Inner Asia. *World Archaeology* 42(2):157–74.

Arias, Pablo 1999 The origins of the Neolithic along the Atlantic coast of continental Europe: A survey. *Journal of World Prehistory* 13(4):403–64.

Arluke, Arnold 1988 Sacrificial symbolism in animal experimentation: Object or pet? *Anthrozoös* 2(2):98–117.

Armelagos, George J., Alan H. Goodman, and Kenneth H. Jacobs 1991 The origins of agriculture: Population growth during a period of declining health. *Population and Environment* 13(1):9–22.

Armit, Ian, and William D. Finlayson 1992 Hunter-gatherers transformed: The transition to agriculture in northern and western Europe. *Antiquity* 66: 664–76.

Armitage, Philip L. 1986 Domestication of animals. In *Bioindustrial Ecosystems.* D. J. A. Cole and G. C. Brander, eds. Pp. 5–30. Amsterdam: Elsevier.

Armitage, Philip L. 1994 Unwelcome companions: Ancient rats reviewed. *Antiquity* 68(259):231–40.

Arndt, Allan, Wim Van Neer, Bart Hellemans, Johan Robben, Filip Volckaert, and Marc Waelkens 2003 Roman trade relationships at Sagalassos (Turkey) elucidated by ancient DNA of fish remains. *Journal of Archaeological Science* 30(9):1095–105.

Arnold, Bettina 1999 'Drinking the feast': Alcohol and the legitimation of power in Celtic Europe. *Cambridge Archaeological Journal* 9(1):71–93.

Arnold, David 1996 *The Problem of Nature: Environment, Culture and European Expansion.* Oxford: Blackwell.

Arnold, Elizabeth R. 2008 A consideration of livestock exploitation during the Early Iron Age in the Thukela Valley, KwaZulu-Natal. In *Animals and People: Archaeozoological Papers in Honour of Ina Plug.* S. Badenhorst, P. J. Mitchell, and J. C. Driver, eds. Pp. 152–68. British Archaeological Reports, International Series. Oxford: Archaeopress.

Arnott, W. Geoffrey 1993 Bull-leaping as initiation. *Liverpool Classical Monthly* 18(8):114–16.

Arthur, John 2003 Brewing beer: Status, wealth and ceramic use alteration among the Gamo of south-western Ethiopia. *World Archaeology* 34(3):516–28.

Asquith, Pamela J. 1997 Why anthropomorphism is not metaphor: Crossing concepts and cultures in animal behavior studies. In *Anthropomorphism, Anecdotes, and Animals.* R. W. Mitchell, N. S. Thompson, and H. L. Miles, eds. Pp. 22–34. Albany: State University of New York Press.

Atalay, Sonya 2006 Domesticating clay: The role of clay balls, mini balls and geometric objects in daily life at Çatalhöyük. In *Changing Materialities at Çatalhöyük: Reports from the 1995–99 Seasons.* I. Hodder, ed. Pp. 139–68. McDonald Institute Monographs. Cambridge: McDonald Institute for Archaeological Research.

Aunger, Robert, Jr. 1994 Are food avoidances maladaptive in the Ituri Forest of Zaire? *Journal of Anthropological Research* 50(3):277–310.

Aura Tortosa, J. Emili, V. Villaverde Bonilla, Manuel Pérez Ripoll, R. Martínez Valle, and P. Guillem Calatayud 2002 Big game and small prey: Paleolithic and Epipaleolithic economy from Valencia (Spain). *Journal of Archaeological Method and Theory* 9(3):215–68.

Austin, C. C. 1999 Lizards took express train to Polynesia. *Nature* 397:113–14.

Auxiette, Ginette 1995 L'évolution du rituel funéraire à travers les offrandes animales des nécropoles Gauloises de Bucy-le-Long (450/100 avant J.-C.). *Anthropozoologica* 21:245–52.

Axelrod, D. I. 1967 Quaternary extinctions of large mammals. *University of California Publications in Geological Science* 74:1–42.

Baal, Jan Van 1976 Offering, sacrifice and gift. *NUMEN – International Review for the History of Religions* 23(3):161–78.

Badenhorst, Shaw, and Ina Plug 2002 Appendix: Animal remains from recent excavations at a Late Iron Age site, Simunye, Swaziland. *Southern African Humanities* 14:45–50.

Baglione, Vittorio, Daniela Canestrari, José M. Marcos, and Jan Ekman 2006 Experimentally increased food resources in the natal territory promote off-spring philopatry and helping in cooperatively breeding carrion crows. *Proceedings of the Royal Society of London, Series B* 273(1593):1529–35.

Bahn, Paul G. 1977 Seasonal migration in South-west France during the late glacial period. *Journal of Archaeological Science* 4(3):245–57.

Bahn, Paul G. 1980 Crib-biting: Tethered horses in the Palaeolithic? *World Archaeology* 12(2):212–17.

Bahn, Paul G. 1984 Preneolithic control of animals in western Europe: The faunal evidence. In *Animals and Archaeology: 4. Husbandry in Europe*. C. Grigson and J. Clutton-Brock, eds. Pp. 27–34. British Archaeological Reports, International Series. Oxford: Archaeopress.

Bahn, Paul G., and Jean Vertut 1997 *Journey through the Ice Age*. Berkeley: University of California Press.

Bahti, Mark T. 1990 Animals in Hopi duality. In *Signifying Animals: Human Meaning in the Natural World*. R. Willis, ed. Pp. 134–9. London: Unwin Hyman.

Bahuchet, Serge 1990 Food sharing among the Pygmies of Central Africa. *African Study Monographs* 11:27–53.

Baird, Douglas 2009 The Boncuklu project: Investigating the beginnings of agriculture, sedentism and herding in central Anatolia. *Anatolian Archaeology* 15:9–10.

Baker, John R. 1984 The study of animal diseases with regard to agricultural practices and man's attitudes to his animals. In *Animals and Archaeology: 4. Husbandry in Europe*. C. Grigson and J. Clutton-Brock, eds. Pp. 253–57. British Archaeological Reports, International Series. Oxford: Archaeopress.

Baker, John R., and Don R. Brothwell 1980 *Animal Diseases in Archaeology*. New York: Academic Press.

Baker, Steve 1993 *Picturing the Beast: Animals, Identity and Representation*. Manchester: Manchester University Press.

Bakker, Jan Albert, Janusz Kruk, Albert E. Lanting, and Sarunas Milisauskas
1999 The earliest evidence of wheeled vehicles in Europe and the Near East.
*Antiquity* 73(282):778–90.

Baldick, Julian 2000 *Animal and Shaman: Ancient Religions of Central Asia.*
London: I. B. Tauris.

Balzer, Marjorie M. 1996 Flights of the sacred: Symbolism and theory in Siberian
shamanism. *American Anthropologist* 98(2):305–18.

Bamforth, Douglas B. 2002 High-tech foragers? Folsom and later Paleoindian
technology on the Great Plains. *Journal of World Prehistory* 16(1):55–98.

Bammer, Anton, Friedrich Brein, and Petra Wolff 1978 Das Tieropfer am
Artemisaltar von Ephesos. In *Studien zur Religion und Kultur Kleinasiens.*
S. Şahin, E. Schwertheim, and J. Wagner, eds. Pp. 107–15. Leiden: E. J. Brill.

Bar-El, Theodora, and Eitan Tchernov 2001 Lagomorph remains at prehistoric
sites in Israel and southern Sinai. *Paléorient* 26(1):93–109.

Bar-Oz, Guy 2001 An inscribed astragalus with dedication to Hermes. *Near
Eastern Archaeology* 64(4):211–13.

Bar-Yosef, Ofer, and Daniella E. Bar-Yosef Mayer 2002 Early Neolithic tribes
in the Levant. In *The Archaeology of Tribal Societies.* W. A. Parkinson, ed.
Pp. 340–71. Archaeological Series. Ann Arbor: International Monographs in
Prehistory.

Bar-Yosef, Ofer, and Anna Belfer-Cohen 1989 The origins of sedentism and
farming communities in the Levant. *Journal of World Prehistory* 3(4):447–98.

Bar-Yosef, Ofer, and Richard H. Meadow 1995 The origins of agriculture in the
Near East. In *Last Hunters–First Farmers: New Perspectives on the Prehistoric
Transition to Agriculture.* T. D. Price and A. B. Gebauer, eds. Pp. 39–94.
Santa Fe: School of American Research Press.

Barber, B., and D. Bowsher 2000 *The Eastern Cemetery of Roman London: Excavations 1983–90.* MoLAS Monograph, No. 4. London: Museum of London
Archaeology Service.

Barber, Elizabeth W. 1994 *Prehistoric Textiles: The Development of Cloth in the
Neolithic and Bronze Ages.* Princeton: Princeton University Press.

Barbujani, Guido, and Giorgio Bertorelle 2001 Genetics and the population
history of Europe. *Proceedings of the National Academy of Sciences* 98(1):
22–5.

Baring, Anne, and Jules Cashford 1991 *The Myth of the Goddess.* New York:
Viking Press.

Barker, Graeme W. W. 1989 Animals, ritual and power in ancient Samnium. In
*L'Animal dans les Pratiques Religieuses: Les Manifestations Materielles.* J.-D.
Vigne, ed. Pp. 111–17. Anthropozoologica. Paris: Éditions du Centre National
de la Recherche Scientifique.

Barker, Gracme W. W. 1992 Animals as wealth in the African Iron Age: The
origins of status. In *Animals and Their Products in Trade and Exchange.*
A. Grant, ed. Pp. 47–52. Anthropozoologica. Paris: Anthropozoologica.

Barker, Graeme W. W., and Clive S. Gamble 1985 Beyond domestication: A strategy for investigating the process and consequence of social complexity. In *Beyond Domestication in Prehistoric Europe: Investigations in Subsistence Archaeology and Social Complexity*. G. W. W. Barker and C. S. Gamble, eds. Pp. 1–31. New York: Academic Press.

Barnes, Robert H. 1980 Marriage, exchange and the meaning of corporations in eastern Indonesia. In *The Meaning of Marriage Payments*. J. L. Comaroff, ed. Pp. 93–124. New York: Academic Press.

Barnett, William K. 2000 Cardial pottery and the agricultural transition in Mediterranean Europe. In *Europe's First Farmers*. T. D. Price, ed. Pp. 93–116. Cambridge: Cambridge University Press.

Barnosky, Anthony D., and Emily L. Lindsey 2010 Timing of Quaternary megafaunal extinction in South America in relation to human arrival and climate change. *Quaternary International* 217(1–2):10–29.

Barrett, James H. *et al.* 2008 Detecting the medieval cod trade: A new method and first results. *Journal of Archaeological Science* 35(4):850–61.

Barrett, John C. 1991 Towards an archaeology of ritual. In *Sacred and Profane: Proceedings of a Conference on Archaeology, Ritual and Religion*. P. Garwood, D. Jennings, R. Skeates, and J. Toms, eds. Pp. 1–9. Oxford University Committee for Archaeology Monograph. Oxford: Oxford University Committee for Archaeology.

Barrett, Louise, Peter Henzi, and Drew Rendall 2007 Social brains, simple minds: Does social complexity really require cognitive complexity? *Philosophical Transactions of the Royal Society of London. Series B, Biological Sciences* 362(1480):561–75.

Barry, John 1999 *Environment and Social Theory*. London: Routledge.

Barsh, Russell L., J. Megan Jones, and Wayne Suttles 2006 History, ethnography, and archaeology of the Coastal Salish woolly-dog. In *Dogs and People in Social, Working, Economic or Symbolic Interaction*. L. M. Snyder and E. A. Moore, eds. Pp. 1–11. Oxford: Oxbow.

Barstow, Anne 1978 The uses of archaeology for women's history: James Mellaart's work on the Neolithic goddess at Çatal Hüyük. *Feminist Studies* 4(3):7–18.

Bartelle, Barney G. *et al.* 2010 Trauma and pathology of a buried dog from San Nicolas Island, California, U.S.A. *Journal of Archaeological Science* 37(11):2721–34.

Barton, Loukas, Seth D. Newsome, Fa-Hu Chen, Hui Wang, Thomas P. Guilderson, and Robert L. Bettinger 2009 Agricultural origins and the isotopic identity of domestication in northern China. *Proceedings of the National Academy of Sciences* 106(14):5523–8.

Bartosiewicz, László 1990 Species interferences and the interpretation of Neolithic animal exploitation. *Acta Archaeologica Academiae Scientiarum Hungaricae* 42:287–92.

Bartosiewicz, László 1993 Metapodial asymmetry in draft cattle. *International Journal of Osteoarchaeology* 3(2):69–75.

Bartosiewicz, László 2000a Cattle offering from the temple of Montuhotep, Sankhkara (Thebes, Egypt). In *Archaeozoology of the Near East IVB: Proceedings of the Fourth International Symposium on the Archaeozoology of Southwestern Asia and Adjacent Areas.* M. Mashkour, A. M. Choyke, H. Buitenhuis, and F. Poplin, eds. Pp. 164–76. ARC – Publicatie. Groningen: Center for Archeological Research and Consultancy.

Bartosiewicz, László 2000b Metric variability in Roman period dogs in Pannonia province and the Barbaricum (Hungary). In *Dogs through Time: An Archaeological Perspective.* S. J. Crockford, ed. Pp. 181–9. British Archaeological Reports, International Series. Oxford: Archaeopress.

Bartosiewicz, László 2008a Bone structure and function in draft cattle. In *Limping Together through the Ages: Joint Afflictions and Bone Infections.* G. Grupe, G. McGlynn, and J. Peters, eds. Pp. 153–64. Documenta Archaeobiologiae. Rahden: Verlag Marie Leidorf.

Bartosiewicz, László 2008b Description, diagnosis and the use of published data in animal palaeopathology: A case study using fractures. *Veterinarija ir Zootechnika* 41(63):12–24.

Bartosiewicz, László, and Gábor Bartosiewicz 2002 'Bamboo spine' in a Migration Period horse from Hungary. *Journal of Archaeological Science* 29(8):819–30.

Bartosiewicz, László, Wim Van Neer, and An Lentacker 1997 *Draught Cattle: Their Osteological Identification and History.* Annales Sciences Zoologiques, No. 281. Tervuren: Musée Royale de l'Afrique Centrale.

Baryshnikov, Gennady F., John F. Hoffecker, and Robin L. Burgess 1996 Palaeontology and zooarchaeology of Mezmaiskaya Cave (northwestern Caucasus, Russia). *Journal of Archaeological Science* 23(3):313–35.

Batchelor, John 1908 Ainus. In *Encyclopaedia of Religion and Ethics.* J. Hastings, ed. Pp. 239–52. Vol. I. New York: Charles Scribner's Sons.

Bate, Dorothea M. 1909 A new artiodactyl from Majorca. *Geological Magazine* 5–6:385–8.

Bäumler, Hans 1921 Die morphologischen Veränderungen des Schweineschädels unter dem Einfluss der Domestikation. *Archiv für Naturgeschichte* 87(12):140–78.

Baxter, Ian L. 2006 A dwarf hound skeleton from a Romano-British grave at York Road, Leicester, England, U.K., with a discussion of other Roman small dog types and speculation regarding their respective aetiologies. In *Dogs and People in Social, Working, Economic or Symbolic Interaction.* L. M. Snyder and E. A. Moore, eds. Pp. 12–23. Oxford: Oxbow.

Beal, Richard 2002 Hittite oracles. In *Magic and Divination in the Ancient World.* L. J. Ciraolo and J. L. Seidel, eds. Pp. 57–81. Leiden: E. J. Brill.

Beavitt, Paul 1989 The ethnoarchaeology of sacrifice: Some comments on the visible and invisible with respect to human contacts with the spirit world in

Borneo. In *L'Animal dans les Pratiques Religieuses: Les Manifestations Materielles*. J.-D. Vigne, ed. Pp. 173–80. Anthropozoologica. Paris: Éditions du Centre National de la Recherche Scientifique.

Beck, Michael W. 1996 On discerning the cause of Late Pleistocene megafaunal extinctions. *Paleobiology* 22(1):91–103.

Becker, Cornelia 2002 Nothing to do with indigenous domestication? Cattle from Late PPNB Basta. In *Archaeozoology of the Near East V: Proceedings of the Fifth International Symposium on the Archaeozoology of Southwestern Asia and Adjacent Areas*. H. Buitenhuis, A. M. Choyke, M. Mashkour, and A. H. Al-Shiyab, eds. Pp. 112–37. ARC – Publicatie. Groningen: Center for Archeological Research and Consultancy.

Bégouën, Henri, and Henri Breuil 1958 *Les cavernes du Volp*. Paris: Arts et Métiers Graphiques.

Behrensmeyer, Anna K. 1978 Taphonomic and ecologic information from bone weathering. *Paleobiology* 4(2):150–62.

Behrensmeyer, Anna K., and Andrew P. Hill, eds. 1980 *Fossils in the Making: Vertebrate Taphonomy and Paleoecology*. Chicago: University of Chicago Press.

Beidelman, Thomas O. 1966 The ox and Nuer sacrifice. *Man* 1:453–67.

Bekoff, Marc 2004 Wild justice and fair play: Cooperation, forgiveness, and morality in animals. *Biology and Philosophy* 19(4):489–520.

Belfer-Cohen, Anna 1995 Rethinking social stratification in the Natufian culture: The evidence from burials. In *The Archaeology of Death in the Ancient Near East*. S. Campbell and A. Green, eds. Pp. 9–16. Oxbow Monographs. Oxford: Oxbow.

Belfer-Cohen, Anna, and Ofer Bar-Yosef 2000 Early sedentism in the Near East: A bumpy ride to village life. In *Life in Neolithic Farming Communities: Social Organization, Identity, and Differentiation*. I. Kuijt, ed. Pp. 19–37. Dordrecht: Kluwer Academic Publishers.

Bell, Catherine M. 1992 *Ritual Theory, Ritual Practice*. Oxford: Oxford University Press.

Bell, Catherine M. 1997 *Ritual: Perspectives and Dimensions*. New York: Oxford University Press.

Bellier, Claire, Saskia Bott, Pierre Cattelain, Carole Fritz, and Ivan Jadin 1999 La rondelle au mammouth de Chaleux. In *Préhistoire d'Os: Receuil d'Études sur l'Industrie Osseuse Préhistorique Offert à Henriette Camps-Fabrer*. M. Julien, A. Averbouh, D. Ramseyer, C. Bellier, D. Buisson, P. Cattelain, M. Patou-Mathis, and N. Provenzano, eds. Pp. 97–121. Aix-en-Provence: Université de Provence.

Bellomo, Randy V. 1994 Methods of determining early hominid behavioral activities associated with the controlled use of fire at FxJj20 Main, Koobi Fora, Kenya. *Journal of Human Evolution* 27:173–95.

Bement, Leland C. 1999 *Bison Hunting at Cooper Site: Where Lightning Bolts Drew Thundering Herds*. Norman: University of Oklahoma Press.

Bendall, Lisa 2004 Fit for a king? Hierarchy, exclusion, aspiration and desire in the social structure of Mycenaean banqueting. In *Food, Cuisine and Society in Prehistoric Greece.* P. L. J. Halstead and J. C. Barrett, eds. Pp. 105–35. Oxford: Oxbow.

Bender, Barbara 1978 Gatherer-hunter to farmer: A social perspective. *World Archaeology* 10(2):204–22.

Bender, Barbara 1985 Prehistoric developments in the American midcontinent and in Brittany, northwest France. In *Prehistoric Hunter-Gatherers: The Emergence of Cultural Complexity.* T. D. Price and J. A. Brown, eds. Pp. 21–57. New York: Academic Press.

Bender, Barbara 1989 The roots of inequality. In *Domination and Resistance.* D. Miller, M. J. Rowlands, and C. Tilley, eds. Pp. 83–95. London: Unwin Hyman.

Bendrey, Robin 2007 New methods for the identification of evidence for bitting on horse remains from archaeological sites. *Journal of Archaeological Science* 34(7):1036–50.

Benecke, Norbert 1994 *Archäozoologische Studien zur Entwicklung der Haustierhaltung in Mitteleuropa und Südskandinavien von den Anfängen bis zum ausgehenden Mittelalter.* Berlin: Akademie Verlag.

Benecke, Norbert 2006 Animal sacrifice at the Late Archaic Artemision of Olympia: The archaeozoological evidence. In *Archaeozoological Studies in Honour of Alfredo Riedel.* U. Tecchiati and B. Sala, eds. Pp. 153–60. Bolzano: Province of Bolzano.

Benecke, Norbert, and Angela von den Driesch 2003 Horse exploitation in the Kazakh steppes during the Eneolithic and Bronze Age. In *Prehistoric Steppe Adaptation and the Horse.* M. A. Levine, A. C. Renfrew, and K. V. Boyle, eds. Pp. 69–82. McDonald Institute Monographs. Cambridge: McDonald Institute for Archaeological Research.

Bennett, Keith D., W. D. Simonson, and S. M. Peglar 1990 Fire and man in post-glacial woodlands of eastern England. *Journal of Archaeological Science* 17:635–42.

Benzi, Valerio, Laura Abbazzi, Paolo Bartolomei, Massimo Esposito, Cecilia Fasso, Ornella Fonzo, Roberto Giampieri, Francesco Murgia, and Jean-Louis Reyss 2007 Radiocarbon and U-series dating of the endemic deer *Praemegaceros cazioti* (Deperet) from "Grotta Juntu," Sardinia. *Journal of Archaeological Science* 34(5):790–4.

Berger, Joel, Jon E. Swenson, and Inga-Lill Persson 2001 Recolonizing carnivores and naive prey: Conservation lessons from Pleistocene extinctions. *Science* 291(5506):1036–9.

Bergquist, Birgitta 1988 The archaeology of sacrifice: Minoan-Mycenaean versus Greek. In *Early Greek Cult Practice.* R. Hägg, N. Marinatos, and G. Nordquist, eds. Pp. 21–34. Skrifter Utgivna av Svenska Institutet i Athen. Stockholm: Svenska Institutet i Athen.

Bernabeu Auban, Joan, C. Michael Barton, and Manuel Perez Ripoll 2001 A taphonomic perspective on Neolithic beginnings: Theory, interpretation, and empirical data in the western Mediterranean. *Journal of Archaeological Science* 28(6):597–612.

Bestor, Theodore C. 2001 Supply-side sushi: Commodity, market, and the global city. *American Anthropologist* 103(1):76 95.

Beteille, André 1981 The idea of natural inequality. In *Social Inequality*. G. D. Berreman, ed. Pp. 59–80. New York: Academic Press.

Betzig, Laura L. 2008 Hunting kings. *Cross-Cultural Research* 42(3):270–89.

Betzig, Laura L., and Paul W. Turke 1986 Food sharing on Ifaluk. *Current Anthropology* 27(4):397–400.

Bevan, Lynne 1997 Skin scrapers and pottery makers? 'Invisible' women in prehistory. In *Invisible People and Processes: Writing Gender and Childhood into European Archaeology*. J. Moore and E. Scott, eds. Pp. 81–7. London: Leicester University Press.

Bicho, Nuno F., Bryan S. Hockett, Jonathan Haws, and William R. Belcher 2000 Hunter-gatherer subsistence at the end of the Pleistocene: Preliminary results from Picareiro Cave, central Portugal. *Antiquity* 74(285):500–6.

Bickerton, Derek 2000 Resolving discontinuity: A minimalist distinction between human and non-human minds. *American Zoologist* 40(6):862–73.

Bienert, Hans-Dieter 1991 Skull cult in the prehistoric Near East. *Journal of Prehistoric Religion* 5:9–23.

Biesele, Megan 1993 *Women Like Meat: The Folklore and Foraging Ideology of the Kalahari Ju/'hoan*. Bloomington: Indiana University Press.

Bietak, Manfred 1994 Die Wandmalereien aus Tell el-Dab'a/'Ezbet Helmi: Erste Eindrücke. *Ägypten und Levante* 4:44–58.

Binder, Didier 2000 Mesolithic and Neolithic interaction in southern France and northern Italy: New data and current hypotheses. In *Europe's First Farmers*. T. D. Price, ed. Pp. 117–43. Cambridge: Cambridge University Press.

Binford, Lewis R. 1978 *Nunamiut Ethnoarchaeology*. New York: Academic Press.

Binford, Lewis R. 1981 *Bones: Ancient Men and Modern Myths*. New York: Academic Press.

Binford, Lewis R. 1984a Butchering, sharing, and the archaeological record. *Journal of Anthropological Archaeology* 3:235–57.

Binford, Lewis R. 1984b *Faunal Remains from Klasies River Mouth*. New York: Academic Press.

Binford, Lewis R. 1985 Human ancestors: Changing views of their behavior. *Journal of Anthropological Archaeology* 4:292–327.

Binford, Lewis R. 1987 Were there elephant hunters at Torralba? In *The Evolution of Human Hunting*. M. H. Nitecki and D. V. Nitecki, eds. Pp. 47–105. New York: Plenum.

Binford, Lewis R., and Jack B. Bertram 1977 Bone frequencies – and attritional processes. In *For Theory Building in Archaeology*. L. R. Binford, ed. Pp. 77–153. New York: Academic Press.

Binford, Lewis R., M. Gus L. Mills, and Nancy M. Stone 1988 Hyena scavenging behavior and its implications for the interpretation of faunal assemblages from FLK 22 (the Zinj floor) at Olduvai Gorge. *Journal of Anthropological Archaeology* 7(2):99–135.

Binford, Lewis R., and Nancy M. Stone 1986 Zhoukoudian: A closer look. *Current Anthropology* 27(5):453–76.

Bird-David, Nurit H. 1990 The giving environment: Another perspective on the economic system of gatherer-hunters. *Current Anthropology* 31(2):189–95.

Bird-David, Nurit H. 1993 Tribal metaphorization of human-nature relatedness: A comparative analysis. In *Environmentalism: The View from Anthropology*. K. Milton, ed. Pp. 112–25. ASA Monograph. London: Routledge.

Bird-David, Nurit H. 1999 "Animism" revisited: Personhood, environment, and relational epistemology. *Current Anthropology* 40(Supplement):S67–S91.

Birke, Lynda I. A. 1995 Exploring boundaries: Feminism, animals, and science. In *Animals and Women: Feminist Theoretical Explorations*. C. J. Adams and J. Donovan, eds. Pp. 32–54. Durham: Duke University Press.

Birket-Smith, Kaj 1964 An analysis of the potlatch institution of North America. *Folk* 6(2):5–13.

Birtalan, Ágnes 2003 Ritualistic use of livestock bones in the Mongolian belief system and customs. In *Proceedings of the 45th Permanent International Altaistic Conference (PIAC), Budapest, Hungary, June 23–28*, 2002. A. Sárközi and A. Rákos, eds. Pp. 33–62. Altaica Budapestinensia. Budapest: Research Group for Altaic Studies, Hungarian Academy of Sciences.

Bischoff, Damien 2002 Symbolic worlds of Central and Southeast Anatolia in the Neolithic. In *The Neolithic of Central Anatolia: Internal Developments and External Relations during the 9th–6th Millennia cal BC*. F. Gérard and L. Thissen, eds. Pp. 237–51. Istanbul: Ege Yayınları.

Blackburn, Tim M., Phillip Cassey, Richard P. Duncan, Karl L. Evans, and Kevin J. Gaston 2004 Avian extinction and mammalian introductions on Oceanic islands. *Science* 305(5692):1955–7.

Blackwood, Peter 1981 Rank, exchange and leadership in four Vanuatu societies. In *Vanuatu: Politics, Economics, and Ritual in Island Melanesia*. M. R. Allen, ed. Pp. 35–84. New York: Academic Press.

Blanton, Richard E., and Jody Taylor 1995 Patterns of exchange and the social production of pigs in highland New Guinea: Their relevance to questions about the origins and evolution of agriculture. *Journal of Archaeological Research* 3(2):113–46.

Bliege Bird, Rebecca L. 1999 Cooperation and conflict: The behavioral ecology of the sexual division of labor. *Evolutionary Anthropology* 8(2):65–75.

Bliege Bird, Rebecca L., and Douglas W. Bird 1997 Delayed reciprocity and tolerated theft: The behavioral ecology of food-sharing strategies. *Current Anthropology* 38(1):49–78.

Bliege Bird, Rebecca L., and Douglas W. Bird 2008 Why women hunt: Risk and contemporary foraging in a Western Desert Aboriginal community. *Current Anthropology* 49(4):655–93.

Bliege Bird, Rebecca L., Douglas W. Bird, Brian F. Codding, Christopher H. Parker, and James H. Jones 2008 The "fire stick farming" hypothesis: Australian Aboriginal foraging strategies, biodiversity, and anthropogenic fire mosaics. *Proceedings of the National Academy of Sciences* 105(39):14796–801.

Bliege Bird, Rebecca L., and Eric A. Smith 2005 Signaling theory, strategic interaction, and symbolic capital. *Current Anthropology* 46(2):221–48.

Blitz, John H. 1993 Big pots for big shots: Feasting and storage in a Mississippian community. *American Antiquity* 58(1):80–96.

Bloch, Maurice 1985 Almost eating the ancestors. *Man* 20(4):631–46.

Bloch, Maurice 1992 *Prey into Hunter: The Politics of Religious Experience*. Cambridge: Cambridge University Press.

Bloedow, Edmund F. 1996 Notes on animal sacrifices in Minoan religion. *Journal of Prehistoric Religion* 10:31–44.

Blumenschine, Robert J. 1986a Carcass consumption sequences and the archaeological distinction of scavenging and hunting. *Journal of Human Evolution* 15:639–59.

Blumenschine, Robert J. 1986b *Early Hominid Scavenging Opportunities: Implications of Carcass Availability in the Serengeti and Ngorongoro Ecosystems*. British Archaeological Reports, International Series, No. 283. Oxford: Archaeopress.

Blumenschine, Robert J. 1987 Characteristics of an early hominid scavenging niche. *Current Anthropology* 28(4):383–407.

Blumenschine, Robert J. 1989 A landscape taphonomic model of the scale of prehistoric scavenging opportunities. *Journal of Human Evolution* 18:345–71.

Blumenschine, Robert J. 1991a Breakfast at Olorgesailie: The natural history approach to Early Stone Age archaeology. *Journal of Human Evolution* 21:307–21.

Blumenschine, Robert J. 1991b Hominid carnivory and foraging strategies, and the socio-economic function of early archaeological sites. *Philosophical Transactions of the Royal Society, London B* 334:211–21.

Blumenschine, Robert J. 1991c Prey size and age models of prehistoric hominid scavenging: Test cases from the Serengeti. In *Human Predators and Prey Mortality*. M. C. Stiner, ed. Pp. 121–47. Boulder: Westview.

Blumenschine, Robert J. 1995 Percussion marks, tooth marks, and experimental determinations of the timing of hominid and carnivore access to long bones at FLK *Zinjanthropus*, Olduvai Gorge, Tanzania. *Journal of Human Evolution* 29:21–51.

Blumenschine, Robert J., and John A. Cavallo 1992 Scavenging and human evolution. *Scientific American* 267:90–6.

Blumenschine, Robert J., John A. Cavallo, and Salvatore D. Capaldo 1994 Competition for carcasses and early hominid behavioral ecology: A case study and conceptual framework. *Journal of Human Evolution* 27(1/2/3):197–213.

Blumenschine, Robert J., and T. Cregg Madrigal 1993 Variability in long bone marrow yields of East African ungulates and its zooarchaeological implications. *Journal of Archaeological Science* 20:555–87.

Blurton-Jones, Nicholas G. 1984 A selfish origin for human food sharing: Tolerated theft. *Ethnology and Sociobiology* 4:145–7.

Bocheński, Zbigniew M., Teresa Tomek, Jaroslaw Wilczynski, Jiří Svoboda, Krzysztof Wertz, and Piotr Wojtal 2009 Fowling during the Gravettian: The avifauna of Pavlov I, the Czech Republic. *Journal of Archaeological Science* 36(12):2655–65.

Bocquet-Appel, Jean-Pierre, Stephan Naji, Marc Vander Linden, and Janusz K. Kozłowski 2009 Detection of diffusion and contact zones of early farming in Europe from the space-time distribution of 14C dates. *Journal of Archaeological Science* 36(3):807–20.

Bodenhorn, Barbara 2000 It's good to know who your relatives are but we were taught to share with everybody: Shares and sharing among Inupiaq households. In *The Social Economy of Sharing: Resource Allocation and Modern Hunter-Gatherers*. G. W. Wenzel, G. K. Hovelsrud-Broda, and N. Kishigami, eds. Pp. 27–60. Senri Ethnological Studies. Osaka: National Museum of Ethnology.

Boesch, Christophe, and Michael Tomasello 1998 Chimpanzee and human cultures. *Current Anthropology* 39(5):591–614.

Boessneck, Joachim 1994 Zooarchäologische Ergebnisse an den Tierknochen- und Molluskenfunden. In *Haus und Stadt im Klassischen Griechenland*. W. Hoepfner and E.-L. Schwandner, eds. Pp. 175–9. München: Deutscher Kunstverlag.

Boessneck, Joachim, Angela von den Driesch, and Nils-Gustaf Gejvall 1967 *The Archaeology of Skedemosse. 3. Die Knochenfunde von Säugetieren und vom Menschen*. Stockholm: Almqvist & Wiksell.

Boessneck, Joachim, Jean-Pierre Jéquier, and Hans R. Stampfli 1963 *Seeberg Burgäschisee-Süd. Die Tierreste*. Acta Bernensia, No. II, Teil 3. Bern: Stampfli.

Bogaard, Amy *et al.* 2009 Private pantries and celebrated surplus: Saving and sharing food at Neolithic Çatalhöyük, Central Anatolia. *Antiquity* 83(321):649–68.

Bogan, Arthur E. 1983 Evidence for faunal resource partitioning in an Eastern North American chiefdom. In *Animals and Archaeology: 1. Hunters and their Prey*. J. Clutton-Brock and C. Grigson, eds. Pp. 305–24. British Archaeological Reports, International Series. Oxford: Archaeopress.

Bogucki, Peter I. 1984 Linear Pottery ceramic sieves and their economic implications. *Oxford Journal of Archaeology* 3(1):15–30.

Bogucki, Peter I. 1988 *Forest Farmers and Stockherders: Early Agriculture and its Consequences in North-Central Europe*. Cambridge: Cambridge University Press.

Bogucki, Peter I. 1989 The exploitation of domestic animals in Neolithic Central Europe. In *Early Animal Domestication and its Cultural Context*. P. J. Crabtree, D. V. Campana, and K. Ryan, eds. Pp. 118–34. MASCA Research Papers in Science and Archaeology. Philadelphia: University of Pennsylvania University Museum.

Bogucki, Peter I. 1993 Animal traction and household economies in neolithic Europe. *Antiquity* 67(256):492–503.

Bogucki, Peter I. 1995 Prelude to agriculture in north-central Europe. In *Before Farming: Hunter-Gatherer Society and Subsistence*. D. V. Campana, ed. Pp. 105–16. MASCA Research Papers in Science and Archaeology. Philadelphia: University of Pennsylvania, University Museum.

Bogucki, Peter I. 1996 The spread of early farming in Europe. *American Scientist* 84:242–53.

Bogucki, Peter I. 2000 How agriculture came to north-central Europe. In *Europe's First Farmers*. T. D. Price, ed. Pp. 197–218. Cambridge: Cambridge University Press.

Bogucki, Peter I., and Ryszard Grygiel 1983 Early farmers of the North European Plain. *Scientific American* 248(4):104–12.

Bogucki, Peter I., and Ryszard Grygiel 1993 The first farmers of Central Europe: A survey article. *Journal of Field Archaeology* 20(4):399–426.

Bökönyi, Sándor 1969 Archaeological problems and methods of recognizing animal domestication. In *The Domestication and Exploitation of Plants and Animals*. P. J. Ucko and G. W. Dimbleby, eds. Pp. 219–29. London: Duckworth.

Bökönyi, Sándor 1970 A new method for the determination of the number of individuals in animal bone material. *American Journal of Archaeology* 74(2):291–2.

Bökönyi, Sándor 1974 *History of Domestic Mammals in Central and Eastern Europe*. L. Halápy, transl. Budapest: Akadémiai Kiadó.

Bökönyi, Sándor 1983 Late Chalcolithic and Early Bronze I animal remains from Arslantepe (Malatya), Turkey, a preliminary report. In *Perspectives on Proto-urbanization in Eastern Anatolia: Arslantepe (Malatya): An Interim Report on 1975–1983 Campaigns*. M. Frangipane and A. Palmieri, eds. Pp. 581–98. Origini. Roma: Università di Roma "La Sapienza," Dipartimento di Scienze Storiche Archeologiche e Antropologiche dell'Antichità.

Bökönyi, Sándor 1984 *Animal Husbandry and Hunting in Tác-Gorsium: The Vertebrate Fauna of a Roman Town in Pannonia*. Budapest: Akadémiai Kiadó.

Bökönyi, Sándor 1989 Definitions of animal domestication. In *The Walking Larder: Patterns of Domestication, Pastoralism, and Predation*. J. Clutton-Brock, ed. Pp. 22–7. London: Unwin Hyman.

Bökönyi, Sándor 1993 Interactions between hunting and economic, social and cultural relations in two large prehistoric sites of southwest Asia. *Exploitation des Animaux Sauvages à travers les Temps: IVe Colloque International de l'Homme et l'Animal.* J. Desse and F. Audoin-Rouzeau, eds. Pp. 125–35. Juan-les-Pins: Éditions APCDA-CNRS.

Bolin, Hans 2000 Animal magic: The mythological significance of elks, boats and humans in north Swedish rock art. *Journal of Material Culture* 5(2):153–76.

Bond, Julie M., and Fay L. Worley 2006 Companions in death: The roles of animals in Anglo-Saxon and Viking cremation rituals in Britain. In *Social Archaeology of Funerary Remains.* R. L. Gowland and C. J. Knüsel, eds. Pp. 89–98. Oxford: Oxbow.

Bonnichsen, Robson 1989 Constructing taphonomic models: Theory, assumptions, and procedures. In *Bone Modification.* R. Bonnichsen and M. H. Sorg, eds. Pp. 515–23. Orono, ME: Center for the Study of the First Americans.

Bonogofsky, Michelle 2005 A bioarchaeological study of plastered skulls from Anatolia: New discoveries and interpretations. *International Journal of Osteoarchaeology* 15(2):124–35.

Bonte, Pierre 1995 Du sacrifice au capital: De l'animal comme valeur. *Anthropozoologica* 21:231–8.

Bonte, Pierre, and John G. Galaty 1991 Introduction. In *Herders, Warriors, and Traders: Pastoralism in Africa.* J. G. Galaty and P. Bonte, eds. Pp. 2–30. Boulder: Westview.

Booth, Paul, Kate M. Clark, and Adrienne Powell 1996 A dog skin from Asthall. *International Journal of Osteoarchaeology* 6(4):382–7.

Borić, Dušan, and Sofija Stefanović 2004 Birth and death: Infant burials from Vlasac and Lepenski Vir. *Antiquity* 78(301):526–46.

Borowski, Oded 2002 Animals in the religions of Syria-Palestine. In *A History of the Animal World in the Ancient Near East.* B. J. Collins, ed. Pp. 405–23. Leiden: E. J. Brill.

Borrero, Luís A. 1995 The archaeology of the far south of America – Patagonia and Tierra del Fuego. In *Ancient Peoples and Landscapes.* E. Johnson, ed. Pp. 207–15. Lubbock, TX: Museum of Texas Tech University.

Borrero, Luís A. 1999 The faunas of the Pleistocene/Holocene boundary in the Seno de la Ultima Esperanza, Chile. In *Zooarchaeology of the Pleistocene/ Holocene Boundary.* J. C. Driver, ed. Pp. 59–62. British Archaeological Reports, International Series. Oxford: Archaeopress.

Borrero, Luis A., and Fabiana M. Martin 2008 A reinterpretation of the Pleistocene human and faunal association at Las Buitreras Cave, Santa Cruz, Argentina. *Quaternary Science Reviews* 27(27–28):2509–15.

Bouchud, Jean 1953 Paléolithique utilisaient-ils les plumes? *Bulletin de la Société Préhistorique Française* 50:556–60.

Bourdieu, Pierre 1977 *Outline of a Theory of Practice.* R. Nice, transl. Cambridge: Cambridge University Press.

Bourget, Steve 2001 Children and ancestors: Ritual practices at the Moche site of Huaca de la Luna, north coast of Peru. In *Ritual Sacrifice in Ancient Peru.* E. P. Benson and A. G. Cook, eds. Pp. 93–118. Austin: University of Texas Press.

Boursot, P., J.-C. Auffray, J. Britton-Davidian, and F. Bonhomme 1993 The evolution of house mice. *Annual Review of Ecology and Systematics* 24:119–52.

Bover, Pere, and Josep Antoni Alcover 2008 Extinction of the autochthonous small mammals of Mallorca (Gymnesic Islands, Western Mediterranean) and its ecological consequences. *Journal of Biogeography* 35(6):1112–22.

Bover, Pere, Josep Quintana, and Josep Antoni Alcover 2008 Three islands, three worlds: Paleogeography and evolution of the vertebrate fauna from the Balearic Islands. *Quaternary International* 182(1):135–44.

Bowles, Samuel 2011 Cultivation of cereals by the first farmers was not more productive than foraging. *Proceedings of the National Academy of Sciences* 108(12):4760–5.

Bowman, David M. J. S., Brett P. Murphy, and Clive R. McMahon 2010 Using carbon isotope analysis of the diet of two introduced Australian megaherbivores to understand Pleistocene megafaunal extinctions. *Journal of Biogeography* 37(3):499–505.

Boyce, Mary 1993 Corpse, disposal of, in Zoroastrianism. In *Encyclopaedia Iranica.* E. Yarshater, ed. Pp. 279–86. Vol. 6. London: Routledge & Kegan Paul.

Bradley, Richard 1990 *The Passage of Arms: An Archaeological Analysis of Prehistoric Hoards and Votive Deposits.* Cambridge: Cambridge University Press.

Bradley, Richard 2000 *An Archaeology of Natural Places.* London: Routledge.

Bradley, Richard 2001 Humans, animals and the domestication of visual images. *Cambridge Archaeological Journal* 11(2):261–3.

Bradley, Richard 2005 *Ritual and Domestic Life in Prehistoric Europe.* London: Routledge.

Brain, Charles K. 1969 The contribution of the Namib Desert Hottentots to an understanding of australopithecine bone accumulations. *Scientific Papers of the Namib Desert Research Station* 39:13–22.

Brain, Charles K. 1981 *The Hunters or the Hunted?: An Introduction to African Cave Taphonomy.* Chicago: University of Chicago Press.

Brain, Charles K., and Andrew Sillen 1988 Evidence from the Swartkrans cave for the earliest use of fire. *Nature* 336(6198):464–6.

Bramanti, B. *et al.* 2009 Genetic discontinuity between local hunter-gatherers and Central Europe's first farmers. *Science* 326(5949):137–40.

Brantingham, P. Jeffrey 1998 Mobility, competition, and Plio-Pleistocene hominid foraging groups. *Journal of Archaeological Method and Theory* 5(1):57–98.

Brasser, Ted J. 1982 The tipi as an element in the emergence of historic Plains Indian nomadism. *Plains Anthropologist* 27(98):309–21.

Bratlund, Bodil 1991 A study of hunting lesions containing flint fragments in reindeer bones at Stellmoor, Schleswig-Holstein, Germany. In *The Late Glacial in North-West Europe: Human Adaptation and Environmental Change at the End of the Pleistocene.* N. Barton, A. J. Roberts, and D. A. Roe, eds. Pp. 193–207. Council for British Archaeology Research Report. London: Council for British Archaeology.

Bratlund, Bodil 1992 Die spätglazialen 'Opfertiere' von Meiendorf und Stellmoor, Kreis Stormarn. Neue Ansätze zur Interpretation alter Funde. *Offa* 48:41–73.

Bratlund, Bodil 1996 Hunting strategies in the Late Glacial of northern Europe: A survey of the faunal evidence. *Journal of World Prehistory* 10(1):1–48.

Breitburg, Emanuel, John B. Broster, Arthur L. Reesman, and Richard G. Strearns 1996 The Coats-Hines site: Tennessee's first Paleoindian-mastodon association. *Current Research in the Pleistocene* 13:6–8.

Breland, Keller, and Marian Breland 1966 *Animal Behavior.* New York: Macmillan.

Breuil, Henri, and Raymond Lantier 1951 *Les Hommes de la Pierre Ancienne: Paléolithique et Mésolithique.* Paris: Payot.

Brewster, Paul 1960 A sampling of games from Turkey. *East and West* 11:15–23.

Briard, Jacques 1987 *Mythes et Symboles de l'Europe Préceltique: Les Religions de l'Age du Bronze (2500–800 av. J.C.).* Paris: Éditions Errance.

Bridault, Anne 1992 The status of elk during the Mesolithic. In *Animals and Their Products in Trade and Exchange.* A. Grant, ed. Pp. 151–60. Anthropozoologica. Paris: Éditions du Centre National de la Recherche Scientifique.

Brightman, Robert A. 1993 *Grateful Prey: Rock Cree Human-Animal Relationships.* Berkeley: University of California Press.

Brightman, Robert A. 1996 The sexual division of foraging labor: Biology, taboo, and gender politics. *Comparative Studies in Society and History* 38(4):687–729.

Brink, John W. 1997 Fat content in leg bones of *Bison bison*, and applications to archaeology. *Journal of Archaeological Science* 24(3):259–74.

Brizinski, Morris J., and Howard G. Savage 1983 Dog sacrifices among the Algonkian Indians: An example from the Frank Bay site. *Ontario Archaeology* 39:33–40.

Broadhurst, Peter L. 1963 *The Science of Animal Behaviour.* Baltimore: Penguin.

Bronner, Simon J. 2008 *Killing Tradition: Inside Hunting and Animal Rights Controversies.* Lexington, KY: University Press of Kentucky.

Broodbank, Cyprian, and Thomas F. Strasser 1991 Migrant farmers and the Neolithic colonization of Crete. *Antiquity* 65(247):233–45.

Brook, Barry W., and David M. J. S. Bowman 2004 The uncertain blitzkrieg of Pleistocene megafauna. *Journal of Biogeography* 31(4):517–23.

Brotherston, Gordon 1989 Andean pastoralism and Inca ideology. In *The Walking Larder: Patterns of Domestication, Pastoralism, and Predation.* J. Clutton-Brock, ed. Pp. 240–55. London: Unwin Hyman.

Brothwell, Don R. 1981 The Pleistocene and Holocene archaeology of the house mouse and related species. In *Biology of the House Mouse*. R. J. Berry, ed. Pp. 1–13. London: Academic Press.

Brothwell, Don R. 1986 *The Bog Man and the Archaeology of People*. London: British Museum Publications.

Broughton, Jack M., David A. Byers, Reid A. Bryson, William Eckerle, and David B. Madsen 2008 Did climatic seasonality control late Quaternary artiodactyl densities in western North America? *Quaternary Science Reviews* 27(19–20):1916–37.

Browman, David L. 1989 Origins and development of Andean pastoralism: An overview of the past 6000 years. In *The Walking Larder: Patterns of Domestication, Pastoralism, and Predation*. J. Clutton-Brock, ed. Pp. 256–68. London: Unwin Hyman.

Brown, Dorcas R., and David W. Anthony 1998 Bit wear, horseback riding and the Botai Site in Kazakstan. *Journal of Archaeological Science* 25(4):331–47.

Brown, Linda A. 2001 Feasting on the periphery: The production of ritual feasting and village festivals at the Cerén site, El Salvador. In *Feasts: Archaeological and Ethnographic Perspectives on Food, Politics, and Power*. M. Dietler and B. Hayden, eds. Pp. 368–90. Washington, DC: Smithsonian Institution Press.

Brown, Linda A. 2005 Planting the bones: Hunting ceremonialism at contemporary and nineteenth-century shrines in the Guatemalan Highlands. *Latin American Antiquity* 16(2):131–46.

Brown, Linda A., and Kitty F. Emery 2008 Negotiations with the animate forest: Hunting shrines in the Guatemalan highlands. *Journal of Archaeological Method and Theory* 15(4):300–37.

Brück, Joanna 1999 Ritual and rationality: Some problems of interpretation in European archaeology. *European Journal of Archaeology* 2(3):313–44.

Bruman, Henry J. 2000 *Alcohol in Ancient Mexico*. Salt Lake City: University of Utah Press.

Brumbach, Hetty Jo, and Robert Jarvenpa 1997 Woman the hunter: Ethnoarchaeological lessons from Chipewyan life-cycle dynamics. In *Women in Prehistory: North America and Mesoamerica*. C. P. Claassen and A. A. Joyce, eds. Pp. 17–32. Philadelphia: University of Pennsylvania Press.

Bryan, Alan L., Rodolfo M. Casamiquela, José M. Cruxent, Ruth Gruhn, and Claudio Ochsenius 1978 An El Jobo mastodon kill at Taima-taima, Venezuela. *Science* 200:1275–7.

Bryden, M. M., Sue O'Connor, and Rhys Jones 1999 Archaeological evidence for the extinction of a breeding population of elephant seals in Tasmania in prehistoric times. *International Journal of Osteoarchaeology* 9:430–7.

Bubenik, Anton B. 1982 Physiology. In *Elk of North America: Ecology and Management*. J. W. Thomas and D. E. Toweill, eds. Pp. 125–79. Harrisburg: Stackpole.

Buchanan, Briggs, Mark Collard, and Kevan Edinborough 2008 Paleoindian demography and the extraterrestrial impact hypothesis. *Proceedings of the National Academy of Sciences* 105(33):11651–4.

Budiansky, Stephen 1992 *The Covenant of the Wild: Why Animals Chose Domestication.* New York: William Morrow & Company.

Buitenhuis, Hijlke 2002 The transition from foraging to farming: The archaeozoological perspective in Anatolia. In *The Dawn of Farming in the Near East.* R. T. J. Cappers and S. Bottema, eds. Pp. 183–9. Studies in Early Near Eastern Production, Subsistence, and Environment. Berlin: Ex Oriente.

Bulliet, Richard W. 1990 *The Camel and the Wheel.* Reprint edition. New York: Columbia University Press.

Bulmer, Ralph 1967 Why is the cassowary not a bird? A problem of zoological taxonomy among the Karam of the New Guinea highlands. *Man* n.s. 2:5–25.

Bulmer, Ralph 1976 Selectivity in hunting and in disposal of animal bone by the Kalam of the New Guinea Highlands. In *Problems in Economic and Social Archaeology.* G. d. G. Sieveking, I. H. Longworth, and K. E. Wilson, eds. Pp. 169–86. London: Duckworth.

Bunimovitz, Shlomo, and Ran Barkai 1996 Ancient bones and modern myths: Ninth millennium BC hippopotamus hunters at Akrotiri *Aetokremnos,* Cyprus? *Journal of Mediterranean Archaeology* 9(1):85–96.

Bunn, Henry T. 1981 Archaeological evidence for meat-eating by Plio-Pleistocene hominids from Koobi Fora and Olduvai Gorge. *Nature* 291:574–77.

Bunn, Henry T. 1982 *Meat-Eating and Human Evolution: Studies on the Diet and Subsistence Patterns of Plio-Pleistocene Hominids in East Africa.* Unpublished Ph.D. thesis, University of California, Berkeley.

Bunn, Henry T. 1983 Evidence on the diet and subsistence patterns of Plio-Pleistocene hominids at Koobi Fora, Kenya, and Olduvai Gorge, Tanzania. In *Animals and Archaeology: 1. Hunters and their Prey.* J. Clutton-Brock and C. Grigson, eds. Pp. 21–30. British Archaeological Reports, International Series. Oxford: Archaeopress.

Bunn, Henry T. 1989 Diagnosing Plio-Pleistocene hominid activity with bone fracture evidence. In *Bone Modification.* R. Bonnichsen and M. H. Sorg, eds. Pp. 299–315. Orono, ME: Center for the Study of the First Americans.

Bunn, Henry T. 1991 A taphonomic perspective on the archaeology of human origins. *Annual Review of Anthropology* 20:433–67.

Bunn, Henry T. 2001 Hunting, power scavenging, and butchering by Hadza foragers and by Plio-Pleistocene *Homo.* In *Meat-Eating and Human Evolution.* C. B. Stanford and H. T. Bunn, eds. Pp. 199–218. Oxford: Oxford University Press.

Bunn, Henry T., Laurence E. Bartram, Jr., and Ellen M. Kroll 1988 Variability in bone assemblage formation from Hadza hunting, scavenging, and carcass processing. *Journal of Anthropological Archaeology* 7:412–57.

Bunn, Henry T., and Joseph A. Ezzo 1993 Hunting and scavenging by Plio-Pleistocene hominids: Nutritional constraints, archaeological patterns, and behavioural implications. *Journal of Archaeological Science* 20(4):365–98.

Bunn, Henry T., John W. K. Harris, Glynn Ll. Isaac, Zefe Kaufulu, Ellen M. Kroll, Kathy D. Schick, Nicholas Toth, and Anna K. Behrensmeyer 1980 FxJj50: An Early Pleistocene site in northern Kenya. *World Archaeology* 12(2):109–36.

Bunn, Henry T., and Ellen M. Kroll 1986 Systematic butchery by Plio/Pleistocene hominids at Olduvai Gorge, Tanzania. *Current Anthropology* 27(5):431–52.

Burch, Ernest S., Jr. 1972 The caribou/wild reindeer as a human resource. *American Antiquity* 37(3):339–68.

Burger, Joachim, M. Kirchner, B. Bramanti, W. Haak, and M. G. Thomas 2007 Absence of the lactase-persistence-associated allele in early Neolithic Europeans. *Proceedings of the National Academy of Sciences* 104(10):3736–41.

Burke, Ariane M. 1993 Applied skeletochronology: The horse as human prey during the Pleniglacial in southwestern France. In *Hunting and Animal Exploitation in the Later Palaeolithic and Mesolithic of Eurasia*. G. L. Peterkin, H. M. Bricker, and P. A. Mellars, eds. Pp. 145–50. Archaeological Papers of the American Anthropological Association. Washington, DC: American Anthropological Association.

Burkert, Walter 1983 *Homo Necans: The Anthropology of Ancient Greek Sacrificial Ritual and Myth*. P. Bing, transl. Berkeley: University of California Press.

Burkert, Walter 1987 The problem of ritual killing. In *Violent Origins: Ritual Killing and Cultural Formation*. R. G. Hamerton-Kelly, ed. Pp. 149–88. Stanford: Stanford University Press.

Burleigh, Richard, and Don R. Brothwell 1978 Studies on Amerindian dogs, 1: Carbon isotopes in relation to maize in the diet of domestic dogs from early Peru and Ecuador. *Journal of Archaeological Science* 5:355–62.

Burleigh, Richard, and Juliet Clutton-Brock 1980 The survival of *Myotragus balearicus* Bate, 1909, into the Neolithic on Mallorca. *Journal of Archaeological Science* 7(4):385–8.

Burney, David A. 1997 Theories and facts regarding Holocene environmental change before and after human colonization. In *Natural Change and Human Impact in Madagascar*. S. M. Goodman and B. D. Patterson, eds. Pp. 75–89. Washington, DC: Smithsonian Institution Press.

Burney, David A. 1999 Rates, patterns, and processes of landscape transformation and extinction in Madagascar. In *Extinctions in Near Time: Causes, Contexts, and Consequences*. R. D. E. MacPhee, ed. Pp. 145–64. New York: Kluwer Academic/Plenum Publishers.

Burney, David A., Helen F. James, Frederick V. Grady, Jean-Gervais Rafamantanantsoa, Ramilisonina, Henry T. Wright, and James B. Cowart 1997 Environmental change, extinction and human activity: Evidence from caves in NW Madagascar. *Journal of Biogeography* 24(6):755–67.

Burney, David A., Guy S. Robinson, and Lida P. Burney 2003 *Sporormiella* and the late Holocene extinctions in Madagascar. *Proceedings of the National Academy of Sciences* 100(19):10800–5.

Burnham, Harold B. 1965 Çatal Hüyük – The textiles and twine fabrics. *Anatolian Studies* 15:169–74.

Burton, Robert K., J. Josh Snodgrass, Diane P. Gifford-Gonzalez, Tom Guilderson, Tom Brown, and Paul L. Koch 2001 Holocene changes in the ecology of northern fur seals: Insights from stable isotopes and archaeofauna. *Oecologia* 128(1):107–15.

Butler, James R. A. 1998 *The Ecology of Domestic Dogs* Canis familiaris *in the Communal Lands of Zimbabwe.* Unpublished Ph.D. thesis, University of Zimbabwe.

Butler, James R. A., and John Bingham 2000 Demography and dog-human relationships of the dog population in Zimbabwean communal lands. *The Veterinary Record* 147:442–6.

Butler, James R. A., and Johan T. du Toit 2002 Diet of free-ranging domestic dogs (*Canis familiaris*) in rural Zimbabwe: Implications for wild scavengers on the periphery of wildlife reserves. *Animal Conservation* 5(1):29–37.

Butler, James R. A., Johan T. du Toit, and John Bingham 2004 Free-ranging domestic dogs (*Canis familiaris*) as predators and prey in rural Zimbabwe: Threats of competition and disease to large wild carnivores. *Biological Conservation* 115:369–78.

Byers, David A., and Andrew Ugan 2005 Should we expect large game specialization in the late Pleistocene? An optimal foraging perspective on early Paleoindian prey choice. *Journal of Archaeological Science* 32(11):1624–40.

Byrd, Brian F. 2005 Reassessing the emergence of village life in the Near East. *Journal of Archaeological Research* 13(3):231–90.

Byrd, Brian F., and Christopher M. Monahan 1995 Death, mortuary ritual, and Natufian social structure. *Journal of Anthropological Archaeology* 14(3):251–87.

Byrne, Roger 1987 Climatic change and the origins of agriculture. In *Studies in the Neolithic and Urban Revolutions: The V. Gordon Childe Colloquium.* L. Manzanilla, ed. Pp. 21–34. British Archaeological Reports, International Series. Oxford: British Archaeological Reports.

Cachel, Susan 1997 Dietary shifts and the European Upper Palaeolithic transition. *Current Anthropology* 38(4):579–603.

Cachel, Susan 2000 Subsistence among Arctic peoples and the reconstruction of social organization from prehistoric human diet. In *Animal Bones, Human Societies.* P. A. Rowley-Conwy, ed. Pp. 39–48. Oxford: Oxbow.

Cameron, Dorothy O. 1981 *Symbols of Birth and of Death in the Neolithic Era.* London: Kenyon-Deane.

Campbell, Stuart 2008 Feasting and dancing: Gendered representation and pottery in later Mesopotamian prehistory. In *Gender through Time in the Ancient Near East.* D. L. Bolger, ed. Pp. 53–76. Lanham, MD: AltaMira Press.

Campbell, Stuart, and Douglas Baird 1990 Excavations at Ginnig, the Aceramic to early Ceramic Neolithic sequence in north Iraq. *Paléorient* 16(2):65–78.

Canestrari, Daniela, Jose M. Marcos, and Vittorio Baglione 2008 Reproductive success increases with group size in cooperative carrion crows, *Corvus corone corone*. *Animal Behaviour* 75(2):403–16.

Cannon, Aubrey, Henry P. Schwarcz, and Martin Knyf 1999 Marine-based subsistence trends and the stable isotope analysis of dog bones from Namu, British Columbia. *Journal of Archaeological Science* 26:399–407.

Cannon, Michael D., and David J. Meltzer 2008 Explaining variability in Early Paleoindian foraging. *Quaternary International* 191(1):5–17.

Caplan, Pat 1994 *Feasts, Fasts, Famine: Food for Thought*. Berg Occasional Papers in Anthropology, No. 2. New York: Berg.

Carmody, Rachel N., and Richard W. Wrangham 2009 The energetic significance of cooking. *Journal of Human Evolution* 57(4):379–91.

Caro, Tim, and Paul Sherman 2009 Rewilding can cause rather than solve ecological problems. *Nature* 462(7276):985.

Carter, George F. 1977 A hypothesis suggesting a single origin of agriculture. In *Origins of Agriculture*. C. A. Reed, ed. Pp. 89–133. The Hague: Mouton.

Carter, Tristan 2007 Of blanks and burials: Hoarding obsidian at Neolithic Çatalhöyük. In *Technical Systems and Near Eastern PPN Communities: Proceedings of the 5th International Workshop, Fréjus, 2004*. L. Astruc, D. Binder, and F. Briois, eds. Pp. 344–55. Antibes: Éditions APDCA-CNRS.

Cartmill, Matt 1993 *A View to a Death in the Morning: Hunting and Nature through History*. Cambridge: Harvard University Press.

Cartmill, Matt 1999 Hunting and humanity in western thought. In *Humans and Other Animals*. A. Mack, ed. Pp. 365–78. Columbus, OH: Ohio State University Press.

Cartmill, Matt 2000 Animal consciousness: Some philosophical, methodological, and evolutionary problems. *American Zoologist* 40(6):835–46.

Cartmill, Matt 2001 Taxonomic revolutions and the animal-human boundary. In *Ape, Man, Apeman: Changing Views since 1600*. R. Corbey and B. Theunissen, eds. Pp. 97–106. Leiden: Department of Prehistory, Leiden University.

Cassidy, Rebecca 2002 *The Sport of Kings: Kinship, Class, and Thoroughbred Breeding in Newmarket*. Cambridge: Cambridge University Press.

Casteel, Richard W. 1978 Faunal assemblages and the "Wiegemethode" or weight method. *Journal of Field Archaeology* 5(1):71–7.

Cauvin, Jacques 1972 *Religions Néolithiques de Syro-Palestine*. Publications du Centre de Recherches d'Écologie et de Préhistoire, No. 1. Paris: J. Maisonneuve.

Cauvin, Jacques 1994 *Naissance des Divinités, Naissance de l'Agriculture: La Révolution des Symboles au Néolithique*. Paris: Éditions du Centre National de la Recherche Scientifique.

Cauvin, Jacques 2000a *The Birth of the Gods and the Origins of Agriculture: A Symbolic Interpretation*. T. Watkins, transl. Cambridge: Cambridge University Press.

Cauvin, Jacques 2000b The symbolic foundations of the Neolithic Revolution in the Near East. In *Life in Neolithic Farming Communities: Social Organization, Identity, and Differentiation*. I. Kuijt, ed. Pp. 235–51. Dordrecht: Kluwer Academic Publishers.

Cavalli-Sforza, L. Luca 1996 The spread of agriculture and nomadic pastoralism: Insights from genetics, linguistics and archaeology. In *The Origins and Spread of Agriculture and Pastoralism in Eurasia*. D. R. Harris, ed. Pp. 51–69. London: UCL Press.

Cavallo, Chiara 1997 Animal remains enclosed in oval clay objects from the 'burnt village' of Tell Sabi Abyad, northern Syria. *Anthropozoologica* 25/26:663–70.

Çelik, Bahattin 2000 A new Early Neolithic site, Karahan Tepe. *Neo-Lithics* 2(3):6–8.

Çelik, Bahattin 2005 A new statue of the early Pre-Pottery Neolithic period from Gaziantep, southeastern Turkey. *Neo-Lithics* 1/05:28–9.

Chaix, Louis 1989 Animaux et sépultures, deux exemples: Le dolmen M XI à Sion (Suisse) et la nécropole de Kerma (Soudan). In *L'Animal dans les Pratiques Religieuses: Les Manifestations Materielles*. J.-D. Vigne, ed. Pp. 43–51. Anthropozoologica. Paris: Éditions du Centre National de la Recherche Scientifique.

Chaix, Louis, Anne Bridault, and Régis Picavet 1997 A tamed brown bear (*Ursus arctos* L.) of the late Mesolithic from La Grande-Rivoire (Isère, France)? *Journal of Archaeological Science* 24(12):1067–74.

Chamberlain, Andrew T., and Stephen T. Forbes 2005 A preliminary study of microscopic evidence for lactation in cattle. In *The Zooarchaeology of Fats, Oils, Milk and Dairying*. J. Mulville and A. K. Outram, eds. Pp. 44–9. Oxford: Oxbow.

Chang, Kwang-Chih 1983 *Art, Myth, and Ritual: The Path to Political Authority in Ancient China*. Cambridge, MA: Harvard University Press.

Chaplin, Raymond E. 1969 The use of non-morphological criteria in the study of animal domestication from bones found on archaeological sites. In *The Domestication and Exploitation of Plants and Animals*. P. J. Ucko and G. W. Dimbleby, eds. Pp. 231–45. London: Duckworth.

Chaplin, Raymond E. 1975 The ecology and behaviour of deer in relation to their impact on the environment of prehistoric Britain. In *The Effect of Man on the Landscape: The Highland Zone*. J. G. Evans, S. Limbrey, and H. Cleere, eds. Pp. 40–2. Council for British Archaeology, Research Report. London: Council for British Archaeology.

Chapman, John C. 1981 *The Vinča Culture of South-East Europe*. British Archaeological Reports International Series, No. 117. Oxford: British Archaeological Reports.

Chapman, John C. 1997 Changing gender relations in the later prehistory of Eastern Hungary. In *Invisible People and Processes: Writing Gender and Childhood into European Archaeology*. J. Moore and E. Scott, eds. Pp. 131–49. London: Leicester University Press.

Chase, Philip G., Dominique Armand, André Debénath, Harold L. Dibble, and Arthur J. Jelinek 1994 Taphonomy and zooarchaeology of a Mousterian faunal assemblage from La Quina, Charente, France. *Journal of Field Archaeology* 21(3):289–305.

Chauvet, Jean-Marie, Eliette Brunel Deschamps, and Christian Hillaire 1996 *Chauvet Cave: The Discovery of the World's Oldest Paintings*. London: Thames & Hudson.

Chebykin, Eugene P., David N. Edgington, Mikhail A. Grachev, Tatyana O. Zheleznyakova, Svetlana S. Vorobyova, Natalia S. Kulikova, Irina N. Azarova, Oleg M. Khlystov, and Evgeny L. Goldberg 2002 Abrupt increase in precipitation and weathering of soils in East Siberia coincident with the end of the last glaciation (15 cal kyr BP). *Earth and Planetary Science Letters* 200(1–2):167–75.

Chenal-Vélardé, Isabelle, and Jacqueline Studer 2003 Archaeozoology in a ritual context: The case of a sacrificial altar in Geometric Eretria. In *Zooarchaeology in Greece: Recent Advances*. E. Kotjabopoulou, Y. Hamilakis, P. L. J. Halstead, C. S. Gamble, and P. Elefanti, eds. Pp. 215–20. Vol. 9. Athens: British School at Athens.

Cherry, John F. 1990 The first colonization of the Mediterranean islands: A review of recent research. *Journal of Mediterranean Archaeology* 3:145–221.

Cherryson, Annia Kristina 2002 The identification of archaeological evidence for hawking in medieval England. *Acta Zoologica Cracoviensia* 45(special issue):307–14.

Chikhi, Lounès, Richard A. Nichols, Guido Barbujani, and Mark A. Beaumont 2002 Y genetic data support the Neolithic demic diffusion model. *Proceedings of the National Academy of Sciences* 99(17):11008–13.

Childe, V. Gordon 1951 *Man Makes Himself*. New York: New American Library.

Choquenot, David, and D. M. J. S. Bowman 1998 Marsupial megafauna, Aborigines and the overkill hypothesis: Application of predator-prey models to the question of Pleistocene extinction in Australia. *Global Ecology and Biogeography Letters* 7(3):167–80.

Choyke, Alice M. 1987 The exploitation of Red Deer in the Hungarian Bronze Age. *ArchaeoZoologia* 1(1):109–16.

Choyke, Alice M., and László Bartosiewicz 1984 Interactions between game biology, environment and human behaviour in patterns of deer hunting: Analysis of a Precolumbian site in Pennsylvania, USA. *Mitteilungen des Archäologischen Instituts der Ungarischen Akademie der Wissenschaften* 12/13:253–62.

Christensen, Marianne 1999 *Technologie de l'Ivoire au Paléolithique Supérieur: Caractérisation Physico-Chimique du Matériau et Analyse Fonctionelle des*

*Outils de Transformation.* British Archaeological Reports, International Series, No. 751. Oxford: British Archaeological Reports.

Chun, Myung Sun 2005 *Ŭng Kol Pang,* a 14th century Korean treatise on falconry. In *Feathers, Grit and Symbolism: Birds and Humans in the Ancient Old and New Worlds.* G. Grupe and J. Peters, eds. Pp. 287–94. Documenta Archaeobiologiae. Rahden: Verlag Marie Leidorf.

Clark, Caven P. 1990 A dog burial from Isle Royal, Lake Superior: An example of household ritual sacrifice in the terminal Woodland period. *Midcontinental Journal of Archaeology* 15:265–78.

Clark, Kate M. 1995 The later prehistoric and protohistoric Dog: The emergence of canine diversity. *ArchaeoZoologia* 7(2):9–32.

Clark, Kate M. 2000 Dogged persistence: The phenomenon of canine skeletal uniformity in British prehistory. In *Dogs through Time: An Archaeological Perspective.* S. J. Crockford, ed. Pp. 163–9. British Archaeological Reports, International Series. Oxford: Archaeopress.

Clark, Nigel 2007 Animal interface: The generosity of domestication. In *Where the Wild Things Are Now: Domestication Reconsidered.* R. Cassidy and M. H. Mullin, eds. Pp. 49–70. Oxford: Berg.

Clarke, Michael J. 2001 Akha feasting: An ethnoarchaeological perspective. In *Feasts: Archaeological and Ethnographic Perspectives on Food, Politics, and Power.* M. Dietler and B. D. Hayden, eds. Pp. 144–67. Washington, DC: Smithsonian Institution Press.

Clason, Anneke T. 1989/90 The Bouqras bird frieze. *Anatolica* 16:209–13.

Clottes, Jean 1995 *Les Cavernes de Niaux.* Paris: Éditions du Seuil.

Clottes, Jean, ed. 2003 *Chauvet Cave: The Art of Earliest Times.* Salt Lake City: University of Utah Press.

Clottes, Jean, and Jean Courtin 1996 *The Cave beneath the Sea: Paleolithic Images at Cosquer.* M. Garner, transl. New York: Harry N. Abrams.

Clottes, Jean, and J. David Lewis-Williams 1998 *The Shamans of Prehistory: Trance and Magic in the Painted Caves.* S. Hawkes, transl. New York: Harry N. Abrams.

Clutton-Brock, Juliet 1992 The process of domestication. *Mammal Review* 22(2):79–85.

Clutton-Brock, Juliet 1994 The unnatural world: Behavioural aspects of humans and animals in the process of domestication. In *Animals and Human Society: Changing Perspectives.* A. Manning and J. A. Serpell, eds. Pp. 23–35. London: Routledge.

Clutton-Brock, Juliet 1995 Origins of the dog: Domestication and early history. In *The Domestic Dog: Its Evolution, Behavior, and Interactions with People.* J. A. Serpell, ed. Pp. 7–20. Cambridge: Cambridge University Press.

Clutton-Brock, Juliet 1999 Aristotle, the Scale of Nature, and modern attitudes to animals. In *Humans and Other Animals.* A. Mack, ed. Pp. 5–24. Columbus, OH: Ohio State University Press.

Clutton-Brock, Juliet 2001 Ritual burial of a dog and six domestic donkeys. In *Excavations at Tell Brak, Volume 2: Nagar in the Third Millennium BC.* D. Oates, J. Oates, and H. McDonald, eds. Pp. 327–38. London: British School of Archaeology in Iraq.

Clutton-Brock, Juliet, and Richard Burleigh 1991 The mandible of a Mesolithic horse from Seamer Carr, Yorkshire, England. In *Equids in the Ancient World.* R. H. Meadow and H.-P. Uerpmann, eds. Pp. 238–41. Tübinger Atlas des Vorderen Orients, Reihe A, Naturwissenschaften. Wiesbaden: Dr. Ludwig Reichert Verlag.

Clutton-Brock, Juliet, and Norman Hammond 1994 Hot dogs: Comestible canids in Preclassic Maya culture at Cuello, Belize. *Journal of Archaeological Science* 21:819–26.

Clutton-Brock, Juliet, and Nanna Noe-Nygaard 1990 New osteological and C-isotope evidence on Mesolithic dogs: Companions to hunters and fishers at Star Carr, Seamer Carr and Kongemose. *Journal of Archaeological Science* 17:643–53.

Clutton-Brock, Timothy H., and S. D. Albon 1989 *Red Deer in the Highlands.* Oxford: BSP Professional Books.

Clutton-Brock, Timothy H., F. E. Guinness, and S. D. Albon 1982 *Red Deer: Behavior and Ecology of Two Sexes.* Chicago: University of Chicago Press.

Codding, Brian F., Judith F. Porcasi, and Terry L. Jones 2010 Explaining prehistoric variation in the abundance of large prey: A zooarchaeological analysis of deer and rabbit hunting along the Pecho Coast of Central California. *Journal of Anthropological Archaeology* 29(1):47–61.

Codere, H. 1950 *Fighting with Property: A Study of Kwakiutl Potlatching and Warfare, 1792–1930.* Seattle: University of Washington Press.

Cohen, Yehudi A. 1961 Food and its vicissitudes: A cross-cultural study of sharing and nonsharing. In *Social Structure and Personality: A Casebook.* Y. A. Cohen, ed. Pp. 312–50. New York: Holt, Rinehart & Winston.

Cole, Jennifer 2001 *Forget Colonialism?: Sacrifice and the Art of Memory in Madagascar.* Berkeley: University of California Press.

Collard, Mark, Kevan Edinborough, Stephen J. Shennan, and Mark G. Thomas 2010 Radiocarbon evidence indicates that migrants introduced farming to Britain. *Journal of Archaeological Science* 37(4):866–70.

Collier, Stephen, and J. Peter White 1976 Get them young? Age and sex inferences on animal domestication in archaeology. *American Antiquity* 41(1):96–102.

Collins, Derek 2008 Mapping the entrails: The practice of Greek hepatoscopy. *American Journal of Philology* 129(3):319–45.

Collins, Paul W. 1991a Interaction between island foxes (*Urocyon littoralis*) and Indians on islands off the coast of southern California: I. Morphologic and archaeological evidence of human assisted dispersal. *Journal of Ethnobiology* 11(1):51–81.

Collins, Paul W. 1991b Interaction between island foxes (*Urocyon littoralis*) and Native Americans on islands off the coast of southern California: II. Ethnographic, archaeological, and historic evidence. *Journal of Ethnobiology* 11(2):205–29.

Collon, Dominique 1994 Bull-leaping in Syria. *Ägypten und Levante* 4:81–8.

Comaroff, Jean, and John L. Comaroff 1991 "How beasts lost their legs": Cattle in Tswana economy and society. In *Herders, Warriors, and Traders: Pastoralism in Africa*. J. G. Galaty and P. Bonte, eds. Pp. 33–61. Boulder: Westview.

Comba, Enrico 1991 Wolf warriors and dog feasts: Animal metaphors in Plains military socieities. *European Review of Native American Studies* 5(2):41–8.

Conkey, Margaret W. 1987 New approaches in the search for meaning? A review of research in "Paleolithic art." *Journal of Field Archaeology* 14(4):413–30.

Conkey, Margaret W. 1989 The structural analysis of Paleolithic art. In *Archaeological Thought in America*. C. C. Lamberg-Karlovsky, ed. Pp. 135–54. Cambridge: Cambridge University Press.

Conkey, Margaret W., and Janet D. Spector 1984 Archaeology and the study of gender. In *Advances in Archaeological Method and Theory*. M. B. Schiffer, ed. Pp. 1–38. Vol. 7. New York: Academic Press.

Conolly, James 1999 *The Çatalhöyük Flint and Obsidian Industry: Technology and Typology in Context*. British Archaeological Reports, International Series, No. 787. Oxford: Archaeopress.

Conolly, James, Susan M. Colledge, Keith M. Dobney, Jean-Denis Vigne, Joris Peters, Barbara Stopp, Kate Manning, and Stephen J. Shennan 2011 Meta-analysis of zooarchaeological data from SW Asia and SE Europe provides insight into the origins and spread of animal husbandry. *Journal of Archaeological Science* 38(3):538–45.

Conrad, Jack R. 1957 *The Horn and the Sword: The History of the Bull as Symbol of Power and Fertility*. New York: Dutton.

Cooper, Zarine 2001 The enigma of gender in the archaeological record of the Andaman Islands. In *In Pursuit of Gender: Worldwide Archaeological Approaches*. S. M. Nelson and M. Rosen-Ayalon, eds. Pp. 173–85. Walnut Creek, CA: Altamira Press.

Copet-Rougier, Elisabeth 1988 Le jeu de l'entre-deux: Le chien chez les Mkako (Est-Cameroun). *Homme* 28(4):108–21.

Coppinger, Raymond, and Lorna Coppinger 2001 *Dogs: A Startling New Understanding of Canine Origin, Behavior, and Evolution*. New York: Scribner.

Corbey, Raymond 2005 *The Metaphysics of Apes: Negotiating the Animal-Human Boundary*. Cambridge: Cambridge University Press.

Corona M., Eduardo 2005 Archaeozoology and the role of birds in the traditional medicine of pre-Hispanic Mexico. In *Feathers, Grit and Symbolism: Birds and Humans in the Ancient Old and New Worlds*. G. Grupe and J. Peters, eds. Pp. 295–301. Documenta Archaeobiologiae. Rahden: Verlag Marie Leidorf.

Corrado, André, Anthony Bonanno, and Nicholas C. Vella 2004 Bones and bowls: A preliminary interpretation of the faunal remains from the Punic levels in Area B, at the temple of Tas-Silg, Malta. In *Behaviour behind Bones: The Zooarchaeology of Ritual, Religion, Status and Identity.* S. J. O'Day, W. Van Neer, and A. Ervynck, eds. Pp. 47–53. Oxford: Oxbow.

Cosgrove, Richard *et al.* 2010 Overdone overkill – the archaeological perspective on Tasmanian megafaunal extinctions. *Journal of Archaeological Science* 37(10):2486–503.

Coutts, Peter J. F., and Mark Jurisich 1973 Canine passengers in Maori canoes. *World Archaeology* 5:72–85.

Crabtree, Donald E. 1939 Mastodon bone with artifacts in California. *American Antiquity* 5:148–9.

Crabtree, Pam J. 1990 Zooarchaeology and complex societies: Some uses of faunal analysis for the study of trade, social status, and ethnicity. In *Archaeological Method and Theory.* M. B. Schiffer, ed. Pp. 155–205. Vol. 2. Tucson: University of Arizona Press.

Crabtree, Pam J. 1993 Early animal domestication in the Middle East and Europe. In *Archaeological Method and Theory.* M. B. Schiffer, ed. Pp. 201–45. Vol. 5. Tucson: University of Arizona Press.

Crabtree, Pam J. 1995 The symbolic role of animals in Anglo-Saxon England: Evidence from burials and cremations. In *The Symbolic Role of Animals in Archaeology.* K. Ryan and P. J. Crabtree, eds. Pp. 20–6. MASCA Research Papers in Science and Archaeology. Philadelphia: University of Pennsylvania, University Museum.

Crabtree, Pam J. 2004 Ritual feasting in the Irish Iron Age: Re-examining the fauna from Dún Ailinne in light of contemporary archaeological theory. In *Behaviour behind Bones: The Zooarchaeology of Ritual, Religion, Status and Identity.* S. J. O'Day, W. Van Neer, and A. Ervynck, eds. Pp. 62–5. Oxford: Oxbow.

Crabtree, Pam J., and Douglas V. Campana 1987 A new model for the domestication of the dog. *MASCA Journal* 4(3):98–102.

Crabtree, Pam J., and J. M. Monge 1987 The faunal remains from the sanctuary of Demeter and Persephone at Cyrene, Libya. *MASCA Journal* 4(3):139–43.

Craig, Oliver E., M. D. Forster, S. H. Andersen, Eva Koch, P. Crombe, N. J. Milner, B. Stern, Geoffrey N. Bailey, and Carl P. Heron 2007 Molecular and isotopic demonstration of the processing of aquatic products in northern European prehistoric pottery. *Archaeometry* 49(1):135–52.

Craig, Oliver E., Jacqui Mulville, Michael Parker Pearson, Robert J. Sokol, Keith Gelsthorpe, Rebecca Stacey, and Matthew J. Collins 2000 Detecting milk proteins in ancient pots. *Nature* 408(6810):312.

Cram, Leslie 2000 Varieties of dogs in Roman Britain. In *Dogs through Time: An Archaeological Perspective.* S. J. Crockford, ed. Pp. 171–80. British Archaeological Reports, International Series. Oxford: Archaeopress.

Cranstone, Bryan A. L. 1969 Animal husbandry: The evidence from ethnography. In *The Domestication and Exploitation of Plants and Animals.* P. J. Ucko and G. W. Dimbleby, eds. Pp. 247–63. London: Duckworth.

Creel, Darrell, and Charmion McKusick 1994 Prehistoric macaws and parrots in the Mimbres area, New Mexico. *American Antiquity* 59(3):510–24.

Cribb, Roger L. D. 1984 Computer simulation of herding systems as an interpretive and heuristic device in the study of kill-off strategies. In *Animals and Archaeology: 3. Early Herders and their Flocks*. J. Clutton-Brock and C. Grigson, eds. Pp. 161–70. British Archaeological Reports, International Series. Oxford: British Archaeological Reports.

Cribb, Roger L. D. 1985 The analysis of ancient herding systems: An application of computer simulation in faunal studies. In *Beyond Domestication in Prehistoric Europe*. G. W. W. Barker and C. S. Gamble, eds. Pp. 75–106. New York: Academic Press.

Cribb, Roger L. D. 1987 The logic of the herd: A computer simulation of archaeological herd structure. *Journal of Anthropological Archaeology* 6:376–415.

Crist, Eileen 1999 *Images of Animals: Anthropomorphism and Animal Mind*. Philadelphia: Temple University Press.

Crockford, Susan J. 2000 Dog evolution: A role for thyroid hormone physiology in domestication changes. In *Dogs through Time: An Archaeological Perspective*. S. J. Crockford, ed. Pp. 11–20. British Archaeological Reports, International Series. Oxford: Archaeopress.

Croft, Paul 2003 The animal bones. In *The Colonisation and Settlement of Cyprus: Investigations at Kissonerga-Mylouthkia, 1976–1996*. E. J. Peltenburg and D. L. Bolger, eds. Pp. 49–58. Studies in Mediterranean Archaeology. Göteborg: Paul Åströms.

Cromarty, Robert J. 2008 *Burning Bulls, Broken Bones: Sacrificial Ritual in the Context of Palace Period Minoan Religion*. British Archaeological Reports, International Series, No. 1792. Oxford: Archaeopress.

Cronk, Lee 1989 From hunters to herders: Subsistence change as a reproductive strategy among the Mukogodo. *Current Anthropology* 30(2):224–34.

Cronk, Lee 1991 Wealth, status, and reproductive success among the Mukagodo of Kenya. *American Anthropologist* 93(2):345–60.

Cronk, Lee 2004 *From Mukogodo to Maasai: Ethnicity and Cultural Change in Kenya*. Boulder: Westview.

Cronon, William, ed. 1995 *Uncommon Ground: Toward Reinventing Nature*. New York: W. W. Norton & Co.

Crowley, Brooke E. 2010 A refined chronology of prehistoric Madagascar and the demise of the megafauna. *Quaternary Science Reviews* 29(19–20):2591–603.

Crubézy, Eric, H. Martin, P.-H. Giscard, Z. Batsaikhan, S. Erdenebaatar, J. P. Verdier, and Bruno Maureille 1996 Funeral practices and animal sacrifices in Mongolia at the Uigur period: Archaeological and ethno-historical study of a *kurgan* in the Egyin Gol valley (Baikal region). *Antiquity* 70(270):891–9.

Cucchi, Thomas, A. Hulme-Beaman, Jing Yuan, and Keith M. Dobney 2011 Early Neolithic pig domestication at Jiahu, Henan Province, China: Clues from molar shape analyses using geometric morphometric approaches. *Journal of Archaeological Science* 38(1):11–22.

Cucchi, Thomas, and Jean-Denis Vigne 2006 Origin and diffusion of the house mouse in the Mediterranean. *Human Evolution* 21(2):95–106.

Cucchi, Thomas, Jean-Denis Vigne, Jean-Christophe Auffray, Paul Croft, and Edgar J. Peltenburg 2002 Introduction involontaire de la souris domestique (*Mus musculus domesticus*) à Chypre dès le Néolithique précéramique ancien (fin IX eet VIII emillénaires av. J.-C.). *Comptes Rendus Palevol* 1(4):235–41.

Cucchiari, Salvatore 1981 The gender revolution and the transition from bisexual horde to patrilocal band: The origins of gender hierarchy. In *Sexual Meanings: The Cultural Construction of Gender and Sexuality*. S. B. Ortner and H. Whitehead, eds. Pp. 31–79. Cambridge: Cambridge University Press.

Cunliffe, Barry W. 1992 Pits, preconceptions and propitiation in the British Iron Age. *Oxford Journal of Archaeology* 11:69–84.

Cupper, Matthew L., and Jacqui Duncan 2006 Last glacial megafaunal death assemblage and early human occupation at Lake Menindee, southeastern Australia. *Quaternary Research* 66(2):332–41.

Currie, Elizabeth J. 2001 Manteño ceremony and symbolism: Mortuary practices and ritual activities at López Viejo, Manabí, Ecuador. In *Mortuary Practices and Ritual Associations: Shamanic Elements in Prehistoric Funerary Contexts in South America*. J. E. Staller and E. J. Currie, eds. Pp. 67–91. Vol. 982. Oxford: Archaeopress.

d'Errico, Francesco, Marian Vanhaeren, and Lyn Wadley 2008 Possible shell beads from the Middle Stone Age layers of Sibudu Cave, South Africa. *Journal of Archaeological Science* 35(10):2675–85.

Dabney, Mary K., Paul L. J. Halstead, and Patrick Thomas 2004 Mycenaean feasting on Tsoungiza at ancient Nemea. In *The Mycenaean Feast*. J. C. Wright, ed. Pp. 77–95. Hesperia. Princeton: American School of Classical Studies.

Dahl, Gudrun 1981 Production in pastoral societies. *The Future of Pastoral Peoples*. Pp. 200–9. Commission on Nomadic Peoples, International Union of Anthropological and Ethnological Sciences. Ottawa: International Development Research Centre.

Dalton, George 1966 "Bridewealth" vs. "Brideprice." *American Anthropologist* 68(3):732–7.

Dandoy, Jeremiah 1996 Astragali, the ubiquitous gaming pieces. *Expedition* 38(1):51–8.

Dandoy, Jeremiah R. 2006 Astragali through time. In *Integrating Zooarchaeology*. J. M. Maltby, ed. Pp. 131–7. Oxford: Oxbow.

Dart, Raymond A. 1957 *The Osteodontokeratic Culture of Australopithecus prometheus*. Memoir of the Transvaal Museum, No. 10. Pretoria: Transvaal Museum.

Daston, Lorraine, and Gregg Mitman, eds. 2005 *Thinking with Animals: New Perspectives on Anthropomorphism*. New York: Columbia University Press.

Daugnora, Linas, and Richard Thomas 2005 Horse burials from Middle Lithuania: A palaeopathological investigation. In *Diet and Health in Past Animal Populations: Current Research and Future Directions*. J. J. Davies, M. Fabiš, I. L. Mainland, M. P. Richards, and R. Thomas, eds. Pp. 68–74. Oxford: Oxbow.

Davenport, William H. 1986 Two kinds of value in the Eastern Solomon Islands. In *The Social Life of Things: Commodities in Cultural Perspective*. A. Appadurai, ed. Pp. 95–109. Cambridge: Cambridge University Press.

David, Florence N. 1962 *Games, Gods and Gambling: The Origins and History of Probability and Statistical Ideas from the Earliest Times to the Newtonian Era*. London: C. Griffin.

Davidson, Janet M. 1985 New Zealand prehistory. In *Advances in World Archaeology*. F. Wendorf and A. E. Close, eds. Pp. 239–91. Vol. 4. New York: Academic Press.

Davis, Simon J. M. 1981 The effects of temperature change and domestication on the body size of Late Pleistocene to Holocene mammals of Israel. *Paleobiology* 7(1):101–14.

Davis, Simon J. M. 1984a Khirokitia and its mammal remains: A Neolithic Noah's Ark. In *Fouilles Récentes à Khirokitia (Chypre) 1977–1981*. A. Le Brun, ed. Pp. 147–79. Paris: ADPF, Éditions Recherche sur les Civilisations.

Davis, Simon J. M. 1984b The advent of milk and wool production in western Iran: Some speculations. In *Animals and Archaeology: 3. Early Herders and their Flocks*. J. Clutton-Brock and C. Grigson, eds. Pp. 265–78. British Archaeological Reports, International Series. Oxford: Archaeopress.

Davis, Simon J. M. 1987 *The Archaeology of Animals*. London: Batsford.

Davis, Simon J. M. 1989 Some more animal remains from the Aceramic Neolithic of Cyprus. In *Fouilles Récentes à Khirokitia (Chypre) 1983–1986*. A. Le Brun, ed. Pp. 189–221. Paris: ADPF, Éditions Recherche sur les Civilisations.

Davis, Simon J. M. 1991 When and why did prehistoric people domesticate animals? Some evidence from Israel and Cyprus. In *The Natufian Culture in the Levant*. O. Bar-Yosef and F. R. Valla, eds. Pp. 381–90. International Monographs in Prehistory. Ann Arbor: International Monographs in Prehistory.

Davis, Simon J. M. 1995 Even more bones from Khirokitia: The 1988–1991 excavations. In *Fouilles Récentes à Khirokitia (Chypre) 1988–1991*. A. Le Brun, ed. Pp. 305–33. Paris: ADPF, Éditions Recherche sur les Civilisations.

Davis, Simon J. M. 1996 Animal sacrifices. In *The Sanctuary of Apollo Hylates at Kourion: Excavations in the Archaic Precinct*. D. Buitron-Oliver, ed. Pp. 181–2. Studies in Mediterranean Archaeology. Jonsered: Paul Åström.

Davis, Simon J. M. 2002 The mammals and birds from the Gruta do Caldeirão, Portugal. *Revista Portuguesa de Arqueologia* 5(2):29–98.

Davis, Simon J. M. 2004 The zoo-archaeology of Khirokitia (Neolithic Cyprus) including a view from the mainland. In *Le Néolithique de Chypre: Actes du Colloque International Organisé par le Département des Antiquités de Chypre et l'École Française d'Athènes, Nicosie, 17–19 M 2001.* J. Guilaine, A. Le Brun, and O. Daune-Le Brun, eds. Pp. 253–8. Athens: École Française d'Athènes.

Davis, Simon J. M., and Sebastian Payne 1993 A barrow full of cattle skulls. *Antiquity* 67(254):12–22.

Davis, Simon J. M., and François R. Valla 1978 Evidence for domestication of the dog 12,000 years ago in the Natufian of Israel. *Nature* 276:608–10.

Davis, Whitney 1992 The deconstruction of intentionality in archaeology. *Antiquity* 66:334–47.

Dawkins, Richard 1976 *The Selfish Gene.* Oxford: Oxford University Press.

Day, Leslie P. 1984 Dog burials in the Greek world. *American Journal of Archaeology* 88:21–32.

Day, S. P. 1996 Dogs, deer and diet at Star Carr: A reconsideration of C-isotope evidence from early Mesolithic dog remains from the Vale of Pickering, Yorkshire, England. *Journal of Archaeological Science* 23:783–7.

de Cupere, Beatrice, An Lentacker, Wim Van Neer, Marc Waelkens, and Laurent Verslype 2000 Osteological evidence for the draught exploitation of cattle: First applications of a new methodology. *International Journal of Osteoarchaeology* 10(4):286–309.

De Grossi Mazzorin, Jacopo, and Claudia Minniti 2006 Dog sacrifice in the ancient world: A ritual passage? In *Dogs and People in Social, Working, Economic or Symbolic Interaction.* L. M. Snyder and E. A. Moore, eds. Pp. 62–6. Oxford: Oxbow.

De Grossi Mazzorin, Jacopo, and Antonio Tagliacozzo 1997 Dog remains in Italy from the Neolithic to the Roman period. *Anthropozoologica* 25/26:429–40.

De Grossi Mazzorin, Jacopo, and Antonio Tagliacozzo 2000 Morphological and osteological changes in the dog from the Neolithic to the Roman period in Italy. In *Dogs through Time: An Archaeological Perspective.* S. J. Crockford, ed. Pp. 141–61. British Archaeological Reports, International Series. Oxford: Archaeopress.

de Sales, Anne 1980 Deux conceptions de l'alliance à travers la fête de l'ours en Sibérie. *Études Mongoles* 11:147–213.

de Vos, John 1996 Taxonomy, ancestry, and speciation of the endemic Pleistocene deer of Crete compared with the taxonomy, ancestry, and speciation of Darwin's finches. In *The Pleistocene and Holocene Fauna of Crete and its First Settlers.* D. S. Reese, ed. Pp. 111–24. Monographs in World Archaeology. Madison: Prehistory Press.

de Vries, Danny, Paul W. Leslie, and J. Terrence McCabe 2006 Livestock acquisitions dynamics in nomadic pastoralist herd demography: A case study among Ngisonyoka herders of south Turkana, Kenya. *Human Ecology* 34(1):1–25.

de Waal, Franz 1989 Food sharing and reciprocal obligations among chimpanzees. *Journal of Human Evolution* 18:433–59.

de Waal, Franz 2001 *The Ape and the Sushi Master: Cultural Reflections by a Primatologist.* New York: Basic Books.

Dean, Rebecca M. 2001 Social change and hunting during the Pueblo III to Pueblo IV transition, east-central Arizona. *Journal of Field Archaeology* 28(3/4):271–85.

DeBoer, Warren R. 2001 The big drink: Feast and forum in the upper Amazon. In *Feasts: Archaeological and Ethnographic Perspectives on Food, Politics, and Power*. M. Dietler and B. Hayden, eds. Pp. 215–39. Washington, DC: Smithsonian Institution Press.

Delluc, Brigitte, and Gilles Delluc 1989 La place des representations animales dans le dispositif parietal des grottes ornées magdaléniennes du Haut Périgord: Grottes de Villars, La Croix, Teyjat, Fronsac et La Font Bargeix, Dordogne. In *L'Animal dans les Pratiques Religieuses: Les Manifestations Materielles*. J.-D. Vigne, ed. Pp. 27–36. Anthropozoologica. Paris: Éditions du Centre National de la Recherche Scientifique.

Denèfle, Michelle, Anne-Marie Lézine, Eric Fouache, and Jean-Jacques Dufaure 2000 A 12,000-year pollen record from Lake Maliq, Albania. *Quaternary Research* 54(3):423–32.

Dennell, Robin W. 1992 The origins of crop agriculture in Europe. In *The Origins of Agriculture: An International Perspective*. C. W. Cowan and P. J. Watson, eds. Pp. 71–100. Washington, DC: Smithsonian Institution Press.

Dennett, Daniel C. 1999 Animal consciousness: What matters and why. In *Humans and Other Animals*. A. Mack, ed. Pp. 281–300. Columbus, OH: Ohio State University Press.

Descola, Philippe 1994 *In the Society of Nature: A Native Ecology in Amazonia*. Cambridge: Cambridge University Press.

Detienne, Marcel 1979 Pratiques culinaires et esprit de sacrifice. In *La Cuisine du Sacrifice en Pays Grec*. M. Detienne and J.-P. Vernant, eds. Pp. 7–35. Paris: Gallimard.

Detry, Cleia, and João Luís Cardoso 2010 On some remains of dog (*Canis familiaris*) from the Mesolithic shell-middens of Muge, Portugal. *Journal of Archaeological Science* 37(11):2762–74.

DeVore, Irven, and Sherwood L. Washburn 1968 Baboon ecology and human evolution. In *Man in Adaptation: The Biosocial Background*. Y. A. Cohen, ed. Pp. 93–108. Chicago: Aldine.

Dewar, Genevieve, David Halkett, Timothy Hart, Jayson Orton, and Judith C. Sealy 2006 Implications of a mass kill site of springbok (*Antidorcas marsupialis*) in South Africa: Hunting practices, gender relations, and sharing in the Later Stone Age. *Journal of Archaeological Science* 33(9):1266–75.

Dewar, Robert E. 1997 Were people responsible for the extinction of Madagascar's subfossils, and how will we ever know? In *Natural Change and Human Impact in Madagascar*. S. M. Goodman and B. D. Patterson, eds. Pp. 364–77. Washington, DC: Smithsonian Institution Press.

Dewez, Michel C. 1974 New hypotheses concerning two engraved bones from La Grotte de Remouchamps, Belgium. *World Archaeology* 5:337–45.

Diamond, Jared M. 1989a Quaternary megafaunal extinctions: Variations on a theme by Paganini. *Journal of Archaeological Science* 16(2):167–75.

Diamond, Jared M. 1989b The present, past and future of human-caused extinctions. *Philosophical Transactions of the Royal Society of London. Series B, Biological Sciences* 325(1228):469–76.

Diamond, Jared M. 1997 *Guns, Germs, and Steel: The Fates of Human Societies*. New York: W. W. Norton & Co.

Diener, Paul, D. Nonini, and Eugene E. Robkin 1978 The dialectics of sacred cow: Ecological adaptation versus political appropriation in the origins of India's sacred cattle complex. *Dialectical Anthropology* 3:221–41.

Diener, Paul, and Eugene E. Robkin 1978 Ecology, evolution, and the search for cultural origins: The question of Islamic pig prohibition. *Current Anthropology* 19:493–540.

Dietler, Michael 1996 Feasts and commensal politics in the political economy: Food, power and status in prehistoric Europe. In *Food and the Status Quest: An Interdisciplinary Perspective*. P. Wiessner and W. Schiefenhövel, eds. Pp. 87–125. Providence: Berghahn Books.

Dietler, Michael 2001 Theorizing the feast: Rituals of consumption, commensal politics, and power in African contexts. In *Feasts: Archaeological and Ethnographic Perspectives on Food, Politics, and Power*. M. Dietler and B. Hayden, eds. Pp. 65–114. Washington, DC: Smithsonian Institution Press.

Dietler, Michael 2006 Alcohol: Anthropological/archaeological perspectives. *Annual Review of Anthropology* 35:229–49.

Digard, Jean-Pierre 1980 Chiens de campement et chiens de troupeau chez les nomades Baxtyâri d'Iran. *Studia Iranica* 9(1):131–9.

Digard, Jean-Pierre 1990 *L'Homme et les Animaux Domestiques: Anthropologie d'une Passion*. Paris: Fayard.

di Lernia, Savino 2006 Building monuments, creating identity: Cattle cult as a social response to rapid environmental changes in the Holocene Sahara. *Quaternary International* 151(1):50–62.

Dillehay, Tom D. 1989 *Monte Verde, a Late Pleistocene Settlement in Chile*. Washington, DC: Smithsonian Institution Press.

Dillehay, Tom D., Gerardo Ardila Calderón, Gustavo G. Politis, and Maria da Conceicao de Moraes Coutinho Beltrão 1992 Earliest hunters and gatherers of South America. *Journal of World Prehistory* 6(2):145–204.

Dillehay, Tom D., C. Ramírez, M. Pino, M. B. Collins, Jack Rossen, and J. D. Pino-Navarro 2008 Monte Verde: Seaweed, food, medicine, and the peopling of South America. *Science* 320(5877):784–6.

Dimitrijević, Vesna 2000 The Lepenski Vir fauna: Bones in houses and between houses. *Documenta Praehistorica* 27:101–17.

Dobkin, Marlene 1969 Fortune's malice: Divination, psychotherapy, and folk medicine in Peru. *Journal of American Folklore* 82(324):132–41.

Dobney, Keith M. 2002 Flying a kite at the end of the Ice Age: The possible significance of raptor remains from proto- and early Neolithic sites of the Middle East. In *Archaeozoology of the Near East V: Proceedings of the Fifth International Symposium on the Archaeozoology of Southwestern Asia and Adjacent Areas*. H. Buitenhuis, A. M. Choyke, M. Mashkour, and A. H. Al-Shiyab, eds. Pp. 74–84. ARC – Publicatie. Groningen: Center for Archeological Research and Consultancy.

Dobney, Keith M., Mark Beech, and Deborah Jaques 1999 Hunting the broad spectrum revolution: The characterisation of early Neolithic animal exploitation at Qermez Dere, northern Mesopotamia. In *Zooarchaeology of the Pleistocene/Holocene Boundary*. J. C. Driver, ed. Pp. 47–57. British Archaeological Reports, International Series. Oxford: Archaeopress.

Dobney, Keith M., and Deborah Jaques 2002 Avian signatures for identity and status in Anglo-Saxon England. *Acta Zoologica Cracoviensia* 45(special issue):7–21.

Dobney, Keith M., and Greger Larson 2006 Genetics and animal domestication: New windows on an elusive process. *Journal of Zoology* 269(2):261–71.

Dobrowolski, Kazimierz A. 1990 Sculpted bird heads from Nemrik (tentative ornithological expertise). In *Nemrik 9: Pre-Pottery Neolithic Site in Iraq (General Report – Seasons 1985–1986)*. S. K. Kozłowski, ed. Pp. 181–3. Warsaw: Wydawnictwa Uniwersytetu Warszawskiego.

Dods, Roberta R. 2002 The death of Smokey Bear: The ecodisaster myth and forest management practices in prehistoric North America. *World Archaeology* 33(3):475–87.

Döhle, Hans-Jürgen 1999 Pferdenachweise aus dem Mesolithikum und Neolithikum in Deutschland. In *Historia Animalium ex Ossibus: Festschrift für Angela von den Driesch*. C. Becker, H. Manhart, J. Peters, and J. Schibler, eds. Pp. 149–59. Rahden: Verlag Marie Leidorf.

Döhle, Hans-Jürgen, and Heribert Stahlhofen 1985 Neolithischen Rindergraber auf dem "Löwenberg" bei Derenburg, Kr. Wernigerode. *Jahresschrift für Mitteldeutsche Vorgeschichte* 68:157–77.

Dombrowski, Kirk 1993 Some considerations for the understanding of small herd dynamics in East African arid zones: The long-term consequences of bridewealth exchange networks. *Human Ecology* 21(1):23–50.

Domínguez-Rodrigo, Manuel 2002 Hunting and scavenging by early humans: The state of the debate. *Journal of World Prehistory* 16(1):1–54.

Domínguez-Rodrigo, Manuel *et al.* 2010 Disentangling hominin and carnivore activities near a spring at FLK North (Olduvai Gorge, Tanzania). *Quaternary Research* 74(3):363–75.

Donnan, Christopher B. 1997 Deer hunting and combat: Parallel activities in the Moche world. In *The Spirit of Ancient Peru: Treasures from the Museo Arqueológico Rafael Larco Herrera*. K. Berrin, ed. Pp. 51–9. New York: Thames & Hudson.

Douglas, Mary 1966 *Purity and Danger: An Analysis of Concepts of Pollution.* New York: Praeger.

Douglas, Mary, ed. 1984 *Food in the Social Order.* New York: Russell Sage Foundation.

Douglas, Mary 1990 The pangolin revisited: A new approach to animal symbolism. In *Signifying Animals: Human Meaning in the Natural World.* R. Willis, ed. Pp. 25–36. London: Unwin Hyman.

Douglass, Carrie B. 1997 *Bulls, Bullfighting, and Spanish Identities.* Tucson: University of Arizona Press.

Dowling, John H. 1968 Individual ownership and the sharing of game in hunting societies. *American Anthropologist* 70(3):502–7.

Downs, James F. 1960 Domestication: An examination of the changing social relationships between man and animals. *Kroeber Anthropological Society Papers* 20:18–67.

Drake, Abby G., and Christian P. Klingenberg 2010 Large-scale diversification of skull shape in domestic dogs: Disparity and modularity. *American Naturalist* 175(3):289–301.

Driver, Jonathan C. 1997 Zooarchaeology and social organization in non-state societies. *Anthropozoologica* 25/26:79 84.

Driver, Jonathan C. 1999 Raven skeletons from Paleoindian contexts, Charlie Lake Cave, British Columbia. *American Antiquity* 64(2):289–98.

Dronfield, Jeremy 1995 Subjective vision and the source of Irish megalithic art. *Antiquity* 69(264):539–49.

Ducos, Pierre 1966 Los huesos de animales. In *Excavaciones en la Terraza de 'El-Khiam' (Jordania) II. Los Nivelos Meso-Neolíticos, Estudia de la Fauna, Flora y Analisis de las tierras del Yacimiento.* J. González Echegaray, ed. Pp. 155–64. Bibliotheca Praehistorica Hispana. Madrid: Consejo Superior de Investigaciones Científicas.

Ducos, Pierre 1978 "Domestication" defined and methodological approaches to its recognition in faunal assemblages. In *Approaches to Faunal Analysis in the Middle East.* R. H. Meadow and M. A. Zeder, eds. Pp. 53–6. Peabody Museum Bulletins. Cambridge: Peabody Museum, Harvard University.

Ducos, Pierre 1988 *Archaeozoologie quantitative – Les valeurs numériques immediates à Çatal Hüyük.* Les Cahiers du Quaternaire, No. 12. Paris: Éditions du Centre National de la Recherche Scientifique.

Ducos, Pierre 1989 Defining domestication: A clarification. In *The Walking Larder: Patterns of Domestication, Pastoralism, and Predation.* J. Clutton-Brock, ed. Pp. 28–30. London: Unwin Hyman.

Ducos, Pierre 1993 Fawns, kids and lambs. In *Skeletons in her Cupboard: Festschrift for Juliet Clutton-Brock.* A. T. Clason, S. Payne, and H.-P. Uerpmann, eds. Pp. 85–90. Oxbow Monograph. Oxford: Oxbow.

Ducos, Pierre 1997 A re-evaluation of the fauna from the Neolithic levels of El-Khiam. *Mitekufat Haeven* 27:75–81.

Ducos, Pierre 2000 The introduction of animals by man in Cyprus: An alternative to the Noah's Ark model. In *Archaeozoology of the Near East IVA: Proceedings of the Fourth International Symposium on the Archaeozoology of Southwestern Asia and Adjacent Areas*. M. Mashkour, A. M. Choyke, H. Buitenhuis, and F. Poplin, eds. Pp. 74–82. ARC – Publicatie. Groningen: Center for Archeological Research and Consultancy.

Dudd, Stephanie N., and Richard P. Evershed 1998 Direct demonstration of milk as an element of archaeological economies. *Science* 282(5393):1478–81.

Dunayer, Joan 1995 Sexist words, speciesist roots. In *Animals and Women: Feminist Theoretical Explorations*. C. J. Adams and J. Donovan, eds. Pp. 11–31. Durham: Duke University Press.

Dunayer, Joan 2001 *Animal Equality: Language and Liberation*. Derwood, MD: Ryce Publishing.

Dunbar, Robin I. M. 1996 *Grooming, Gossip, and the Evolution of Language*. Cambridge, MA: Harvard University Press.

Duncan, Richard P., Tim M. Blackburn, and Trevor H. Worthy 2002 Prehistoric bird extinctions and human hunting. *Proceedings of the Royal Society of London, Series B* 269(1490):517–21.

Durand, Jean-Louis 1987 Sacrifice et découpe en Grèce ancienne. In *La Découpe et le Partage du Corps à travers le Temps et L'Espace*. J.-D. Vigne, ed. Pp. 59–65. Anthropozoologica. Paris: Éditions du Centre National de la Recherche Scientifique.

Durkheim, Emile, and Marcel Mauss 1963 *Primitive Classification*. R. Needham, transl. Chicago: University of Chicago Press.

Durrenberger, E. Paul 1976 The economy of a Lisu village. *American Ethnologist* 3(4):633–44.

Dwyer, Peter D. 1985 A hunt in New Guinea: Some difficulties for optimal foraging theory. *Man* 20:243–53.

Dwyer, Peter D. 1996 The invention of nature. In *Redefining Nature: Ecology, Culture and Domestication*. R. F. Ellen and K. Fukui, eds. Pp. 157–86. Oxford: Berg.

Eddy, Timothy J., Gordon G. Gallup, Jr., and Daniel J. Povinelli 1993 Attribution of cognitive states to animals: Anthropomorphism in comparative perspective. *Journal of Social Issues* 49:87–101.

Ehrenberg, Margaret 1989 *Women in Prehistory*. London: British Museum Publications.

Eiseley, Loren 1945 The mastodon and early man in America. *Science* 102(2640):108–10.

Eisenberg, Leslie E. 1989 On gaming pieces and culture contact. *Current Anthropology* 30(3):345.

Eisler, Riane 1987 *The Chalice and the Blade*. San Francisco: Harper & Row.

Ekvall, Robert B. 1963 Role of the dog in Tibetan nomadic society. *Central Asiatic Journal* 8:163–73.

Elder, William H. 1965 Primeval deer hunting pressures revealed by remains from American Indian middens. *Journal of Wildlife Management* 29(2):366–70.

Eldredge, Niles 1999 Cretaceous meteor showers, the human ecological "niche," and the sixth extinction. In *Extinctions in Near Time: Causes, Contexts, and Consequences.* R. D. E. MacPhee, ed. Pp. 1–15. New York: Kluwer Academic/ Plenum Publishers.

Elias, Scott A. 1995 A paleoenvironmental setting for early Paleoindians in western North America. In *Ancient Peoples and Landscapes.* E. Johnson, ed. Pp. 255–72. Lubbock, TX: Museum of Texas Tech University.

Ellen, Roy F. 1996 Individual strategy and cultural regulation in Nuaulu hunting. In *Redefining Nature: Ecology, Culture and Domestication.* R. F. Ellen and K. Fukui, eds. Pp. 597–635. Oxford: Berg.

Ellenberg, Hermann 1978 *Zur Populationsökologie des Rehes (Capreolus capreolus L., Cervidae) in Mitteleuropa.* Spixiana, supplement, No. 2. Munich: Pfeil Verlag.

Emery, Kitty F. 2004 Animals from the Maya underworld: Reconstructing elite Maya ritual at the Cueva de los Quetzales, Guatemala. In *Behaviour behind Bones: The Zooarchaeology of Ritual, Religion, Status and Identity.* S. J. O'Day, W. Van Neer, and A. Ervynck, eds. Pp. 101–13. Oxford: Oxbow.

Emery, Nathan J. 2006 Cognitive ornithology: The evolution of avian intelligence. *Philosophical Transactions of the Royal Society of London. Series B, Biological Sciences* 361(1465):23–43.

Endicott, Kirk 1988 Property, power and conflict among the Batek of Malaysia. In *Hunters and Gatherers 2: Property, Power and Ideology.* T. Ingold, D. Riches, and J. Woodburn, eds. Pp. 110–27. New York: Berg.

Engels, Frederick 1972 *The Origin of the Family, Private Property and the State.* A. West, transl. New York: International Publishers.

Enloe, James G. 1994 Comparaison entre les troupeaux de rennes de Pincevent et de Verberie. In *Environnements et Habitats Magdaléniens dans le Centre du Bassin Parisien.* Y. Taborin, ed. Pp. 115–17. Documents d'Archéologie Française. Paris: Éditions de la Maison des Sciences de l'Homme.

Enloe, James G. 2003 Food sharing past and present: Archaeological evidence for economic and social interactions. *Before Farming* 2(1):29–46.

Enloe, James G. 2004 Equifinality, assemblage integrity and behavioral inferences at Verberie. *Journal of Taphonomy* 2.

Enloe, James G., and Francine David 1989 Le remontage des os par individus: Le partage du renne chez les Magdaléniens de Pincevent (La Grande Paroisse, Seine-et-Marne). *Bulletin de la Société Préhistorique Française* 86(9):275–81.

Enloe, James G., and Francine David 1992 Food sharing in the Paleolithic: Carcass refitting at Pincevent. In *Piecing Together the Past: Applications of Refitting Studies in Archaeology.* J. L. Hofman and J. G. Enloe, eds. Pp. 296–315. British Archaeological Reports, International Series. Oxford: Tempus Reparatum.

Enloe, James G., Francine David, and Timothy S. Hare 1994 Patterns of faunal processing at Section 27 of Pincevent: The use of spatial analysis and ethnoarchaeological data in the interpretation of archaeological site structure. *Journal of Anthropological Archaeology* 13(2):105–24.

Ericson, Per G. P. 1997 The earliest record of house sparrows (*Passer domesticus*) in northern Europe. *Journal of Archaeological Science* 24:183–90.

Eriksson, Gunilla, Anna Linderholm, Elin Fornander, Marie Kanstrup, Pia Schoultz, Hanna Olofsson, and Kerstin Lidén 2008 Same island, different diet: Cultural evolution of food practice on Öland, Sweden, from the Mesolithic to the Roman Period. *Journal of Anthropological Archaeology* 27(4):520–43.

Escobar, Arturo 1999 After nature: Steps to an anti-essentialist political ecology. *Current Anthropology* 40(1):1–30.

Estioko-Griffin, Agnes, and P. Bion Griffin 1981 Woman the hunter: The Agta. In *Woman the Gatherer*. F. Dahlberg, ed. Pp. 121–51. New Haven: Yale University Press.

Evans, John D. 1963 Cretan cattle-cults and sports. In *Man and Cattle*. A. E. Mourant and F. E. Zeuner, eds. Pp. 138–43. Royal Anthropological Institute Occasional Papers. London: Royal Anthropological Institute of Great Britain and Ireland.

Evans-Pritchard, Edward E. 1931 An alternative term for "bride-price." *Man* 31:36–9.

Evans-Pritchard, Edward E. 1940 *The Nuer: A Description of the Modes of Livelihood and Political Institutions of a Nilotic People.* Oxford: Oxford University Press.

Evans-Pritchard, Edward E. 1951 *Kinship and Marriage among the Nuer.* Oxford: Clarendon.

Evans-Pritchard, Edward E. 1954 The meaning of sacrifice among the Nuer. *Journal of the Royal Anthropological Institute* 84(1/2):21–33.

Evans-Pritchard, Edward E. 1956 *Nuer Religion.* Oxford: Clarendon.

Evernden, Neil 1992 *The Social Creation of Nature.* Baltimore: Johns Hopkins University Press.

Evershed, Richard P. *et al.* 2008 Earliest date for milk use in the Near East and southeastern Europe linked to cattle herding. *Nature* 455(7212):528–31.

Evins, M. A. 1982 The fauna from Shanidar Cave: Mousterian wild goat exploitation in northeastern Iraq. *Paléorient* 8(1):37–58.

Ewers, John C. 1955 *The Horse in Blackfoot Indian Culture, with Comparative Material from Other Western Tribes.* Washington, DC: U.S. Government Printing Office.

Fabiš, Marian 2005 Pathological alteration of cattle skeletons – evidence for the draught exploitation of animals? In *Diet and Health in Past Animal Populations: Current Research and Future Directions.* J. J. Davies, M. Fabiš, I. L. Mainland, M. P. Richards, and R. Thomas, eds. Pp. 58–62. Oxford: Oxbow.

Facciolo, Alessandra, and Antonio Tagliacozzo 2006 Animal burials from via S. Eufemia in the Paleovenetian contexts – Padova (Italia). In *Archaeozoological*

*Studies in Honour of Alfredo Riedel.* U. Tecchiati and B. Sala, eds. Pp. 143–52. Bolzano: Province of Bolzano.

Fairén, Sara 2004 Rock-art and the transition to farming: The Neolithic Landscape of the central Mediterranean coast of Spain. *Oxford Journal of Archaeology* 23(1):1–19.

Falk, Dean 1997 Brain evolution in females: An answer to Mr Lovejoy. In *Women in Human Evolution.* L. D. Hager, ed. Pp. 114–36. London: Routledge.

Faraday, L. Winifred 1904 *The Cattle-Raid of Cualnge (Tain bo Cuailnge).* London: Nutt.

Farkas, Dénes, and Sándor Csányi 1990 Current problems of roe deer (*Capreolus capreolus*) management in Hungary. *Folia Zoologica* 39(1):37–46.

Faure, Eric, and Andrew C. Kitchener 2009 An archaeological and historical review of the relationships between felids and people. *Anthrozoös* 22(3):221–38.

Fausto, Carlos 2007 Feasting on people: Eating animals and humans in Amazonia. *Current Anthropology* 48(4):497–530.

Fedele, Francesco G. 1993 Zoo-archéologie sans os: Hypothèses sur la chasse épipaléolithique d'altitude dans les Alpes. *Exploitation des Animaux Sauvages à travers les Temps: IVe Colloque International de l'Homme et l'Animal.* J. Desse and F. Audoin-Rouzeau, eds. Pp. 183–99. Juan-les-Pins: Éditions APCDA-CNRS.

Fedigan, Linda M. 1986 The changing role of women in models of human evolution. *Annual Review of Anthropology* 15:25–66.

Feinman, Gary M., Linda M. Nicholas, and Edward F. Maher 2008 Domestic offerings at El Palmillo. *Ancient Mesoamerica* 19(2):175–94.

Feinman, Saul 1979 An evolutionary theory of food-sharing. *Social Science Information* 18(4–5):695–726.

Fenton, William N. 1978 Northern Iroquoian culture patterns. In *Handbook of North American Indians.* B. G. Trigger, ed. Pp. 296–321. Vol. 15. Washington, DC: Smithsonian Institution Press.

Ferguson, James 1985 The bovine mystique: Power, property and livestock in rural Lesotho. *Man* 20:647–74.

Fiałkowski, Konrad R. 1986 A mechanism for the origin of the human brain: A hypothesis. *Current Anthropology* 27(3):288–90.

Fiddes, Nick 1991 *Meat: A Natural Symbol.* London: Routledge.

Fiedel, Stuart J. 1999 Older than we thought: Implications of corrected dates for Paleoindians. *American Antiquity* 64(1):95–115.

Field, Judith H., Richard L. K. Fullagar, and Garry Lord 2001 A large area archaeological excavation at Cuddie Springs. *Antiquity* 75(290):696–702.

Fillios, Melanie, Judith H. Field, and Bethan Charles 2010 Investigating human and megafauna co-occurrence in Australian prehistory: Mode and causality in fossil accumulations at Cuddie Springs. *Quaternary International* 211(1–2):123–43.

Finet, André 1966 La place du devin dans la société de Mari. In *La Divination en Mésopotamie Ancienne et dans les Régions Voisines*. F. Wendel, ed. Pp. 87–94. Paris: Presses Universitaires de France.

Firestone, R. B. *et al.* 2007 Evidence for an extraterrestrial impact 12,900 years ago that contributed to the megafaunal extinctions and the Younger Dryas cooling. *Proceedings of the National Academy of Sciences* 104(41):16016–21.

Firth, Raymond 1963 Offering and sacrifice: Problems of organization. *Journal of the Anthropological Institute of Great Britain and Ireland* 93(1):12–24.

Fischer, Anders 1982 Trade in Danubian shaft-hole axes and the introduction of neolithic economy in Denmark. *Journal of Danish Archaeology* 1:7–12.

Fisher, Daniel C. 1984a Mastodon butchery by North American Paleo-Indians. *Nature* 308:271–2.

Fisher, Daniel C. 1984b Taphonomic analysis of late Pleistocene mastodon occurrences: Evidence of butchery by North American Paleo-Indians. *Paleobiology* 10:338–57.

Fisher, Daniel C. 1987 Mastodont procurement by Paleoindians of the Great Lakes region: Hunting or scavenging? In *The Evolution of Human Hunting*. M. H. Nitecki and D. V. Nitecki, eds. Pp. 309–421. New York: Plenum.

Fisher, John W., Jr. 1995 Bone surface modifications in zooarchaeology. *Journal of Archaeological Method and Theory* 2(1):7–68.

Fisher, John W., Jr. 2001 Elephant butchery practices in the Ituri Forest, Democratic Republic of Congo, and their relevance for interpreting human activities at proboscidean sites. In *Proceedings of the International Conference on Mammoth Site Studies*. D. L. West, ed. Pp. 1–10. University of Kansas Publications in Anthropology. Lawrence, KS: University of Kansas Department of Anthropology.

Fiskesjö, N. Magnus 2001 Rising from blood-stained fields: Royal hunting and state formation in Shang Dynasty China. *The Museum of Far Eastern Antiquities Bulletin* 73:48–191.

Flad, Rowan K. 2008 Divination and power: A multiregional view of the development of oracle bone divination in early China. *Current Anthropology* 49(3):403–37.

Flannery, Kent V. 1969 Origins and ecological effects of early domestication in Iran and the Near East. In *The Domestication and Exploitation of Plants and Animals*. P. J. Ucko and G. W. Dimbleby, eds. Pp. 73–100. London: Duckworth.

Flannery, Timothy F., and Richard G. Roberts 1999 Late Quaternary extinctions in Australasia: An overview. In *Extinctions in Near Time: Causes, Contexts, and Consequences*. R. D. E. MacPhee, ed. Pp. 239–55. New York: Kluwer Academic/Plenum Publishers.

Fleisher, Michael L., and Garth J. Holloway 2004 The problem with boys: Bridewealth accumulation, sibling gender, and the propensity to participate in cattle raiding among the Kuria of Tanzania. *Current Anthropology* 45(2):284–8.

Fletcher, Michael-Shaen, and Ian Thomas 2010 The origin and temporal development of an ancient cultural landscape. *Journal of Biogeography* 37(11):2183–96.

Flores, Diane V. 2003 *Funerary Sacrifice of Animals in the Egyptian Predynastic Period*. British Archaeological Reports, International Series, No. 1153. Oxford: Archaeopress.

Fogelin, Lars 2007 The archaeology of religious ritual. *Annual Review of Anthropology* 36(1):55–71.

Foley, Robert A. 2001 The evolutionary consequences of increased carnivory in hominids. In *Meat-Eating and Human Evolution*. C. B. Stanford and H. T. Bunn, eds. Pp. 305–31. Oxford: Oxford University Press.

Forde, C. Darryl 1963 *Habitat, Economy and Society: A Geographical Introduction to Ethnology*. New York: E. P. Dutton.

Foreman, Dave 2004 *Rewilding North America: A Vision for Conservation in the 21st Century*. Washington: Island Press.

Forest, Jean-Daniel 1993 Çatal Hüyük et son décor: Pour le déchiffrement d'un code symbolique. *Anatolia Antiqua* 2:1–42.

Fornander, Elin, Gunilla Eriksson, and Kerstin Lidén 2008 Wild at heart: Approaching Pitted Ware identity, economy and cosmology through stable isotopes in skeletal material from the Neolithic site Korsnäs in Eastern Central Sweden. *Journal of Anthropological Archaeology* 27(3):281–97.

Forstenpointner, Gerhard 2003 Promethean legacy: Investigations into the ritual procedure of 'Olympian' sacrifice. In *Zooarchaeology in Greece: Recent Advances*. E. Kotjabopoulou, Y. Hamilakis, P. L. J. Halstead, C. S. Gamble, and P. Elefanti, eds. Pp. 203–13. Vol. 9. Athens: British School at Athens.

Forstenpointner, Gerhard, Rita Krachler, and Bernadette Schildorfer 1999 Archäozoologische Untersuchungen zu den Formen des Tieropfers im Artemision von Ephesos. In *100 Jahre Österreichische Forschungen in Ephesos*. H. Friesinger and F. Krinzinger, eds. Pp. 225–32. Vienna: Verlag der Österreichischen Akademie der Wissenschaften.

Forth, Gregory L. 2004 *Nage Birds: Classification and Symbolism among an Eastern Indonesian People*. London: Routledge.

Fox, John W., Calvin B. Smith, and Kenneth T. Wilkins, eds. 1992 *Proboscidean and Paleoindian Interactions*. Waco, TX: Markham Press Fund of Baylor University Press.

Fox, Michael W. 1978 Man, wolf, and dog. In *Wolf and Man: Evolution in Parallel*. R. L. Hall and H. S. Sharp, eds. Pp. 19–30. New York: Academic Press.

Franklin, Adrian 1999 *Animals and Modern Cultures: A Sociology of Human-Animal Relations in Modernity*. London: Sage Publications.

Fraser, Francis C., and Judith E. King 1954 Faunal remains. In *Excavations at Star Carr*. J. G. D. Clark, ed. Pp. 70–95. Cambridge: Cambridge University Press.

Fraser, K. L. 2001 Variation in tuna fish catches in Pacific prehistory. *International Journal of Osteoarchaeology* 11(1–2):127–35.

Frazer, James G. 1935 *The Golden Bough: A Study in Magic and Religion*. Third edition. New York: Macmillan.

Freud, Sigmund 1918 *Totem and Taboo: Resemblances between the Psychic Lives of Savages and Neurotics*. New York: Moffat, Yard and Company.

Friedman, Jonathan, and Michael J. Rowlands 1977 Notes toward an epigenetic model of the evolution of 'civilisation'. In *The Evolution of Social Systems*. J. Friedman and M. J. Rowlands, eds. Pp. 201–76. London: Duckworth.

Friesen, T. Max 2001 A zooarchaeological signature for meat storage: Rethinking the drying utility index. *American Antiquity* 66(2):315–31.

Friesen, T. Max, James M. Savelle, and Mark C. Diab 2001 A consideration of the inter-specific application of food utility indices, with reference to five species in the order Pinnipedia. In *People and Wildlife in Northern North America*. S. C. Gerlach and M. S. Murray, eds. Pp. 275–284. British Archaeological Reports, International Series, S944. Oxford: Archaeopress.

Frison, George C. 1971 Shoshonean antelope procurement in the Upper Green River Basin, Wyoming. *Plains Anthropologist* 16(54):258–84.

Frison, George C. 1989 Experimental use of Clovis weaponry and tools on African elephants. *American Antiquity* 54(4):766–84.

Frison, George C. 2004 *Survival by Hunting: Prehistoric Human Predators and Animal Prey*. Berkeley: University of California Press.

Frison, George C., and Lawrence C. Todd 1986 *The Colby Mammoth Site: Taphonomy and Archaeology of a Clovis Kill in Northern Wyoming*. Albuquerque: University of New Mexico Press.

Frison, George C., and Lawrence C. Todd 2001 The Colby Mammoth Kill site 48WA322: Hunting mammoths; and experiments with Clovis tools and weaponry. In *Proceedings of the International Conference on Mammoth Site Studies*. D. L. West, ed. Pp. 11–26. University of Kansas Publications in Anthropology. Lawrence, KS: University of Kansas Department of Anthropology.

Fuentes, Agustin 2006 The humanity of animals and the animality of humans: A view from biological anthropology inspired by J. M. Coetzee's *Elizabeth Costello*. *American Anthropologist* 108(1):124–32.

Fulford, Michael 2001 Links with the past: Pervasive 'ritual' behaviour in Roman Britain. *Britannia* 32:199–218.

Fuller, Dorian Q., Emma Harvey, and Ling Qin 2007 Presumed domestication? Evidence for wild rice cultivation and domestication in the fifth millennium BC of the Lower Yangtze region. *Antiquity* 81(312):316–31.

Fuller, Dorian Q., and Ling Qin 2010 Declining oaks, increasing artistry, and cultivating rice: The environmental and social context of the emergence of farming in the Lower Yangtze Region. *Environmental Archaeology* 15(2):139–59.

Fuller, Errol 2001 *Extinct Birds*. Revised edition. Ithaca: Comstock Publishing Associates.

Funabiki, Takeo 1981 On pigs of the Mbotgote in Malekula. In *Vanuatu: Politics, Economics, and Ritual in Island Melanesia*. M. R. Allen, ed. Pp. 173–88. New York: Academic Press.

Fürer-Haimendorf, Christoph von 1963 The social background of cattle domestication in India. In *Man and Cattle*. A. E. Mourant and F. E. Zeuner, eds. Pp. 144–9. Royal Anthropological Institute Occasional Papers. London: Royal Anthropological Institute of Great Britain and Ireland.

Furst, Peter T. 1991 Crowns of power: Bird and feather symbolism in Amazonian shamanism. In *The Gift of Birds: Featherwork of Native South American Peoples*. R. E. Reina and K. M. Kensinger, eds. Pp. 92–109. University Museum Monograph. Philadelphia: University of Pennsylvania, University Museum.

Gadd, Cyril J. 1966 Some Babylonian divinatory methods, and their interrelations. In *La Divination en Mésopotamie Ancienne et dans les Régions Voisines*. F. Wendel, ed. Pp. 21–34. Paris: Presses Universitaires de France.

Galaty, John G. 1989 Cattle and cognition: Aspects of Maasai practical reasoning. In *The Walking Larder: Patterns of Domestication, Pastoralism, and Predation*. J. Clutton-Brock, ed. Pp. 215–30. London: Unwin Hyman.

Galaty, John G., and Douglas L. Johnson 1990 Introduction: Pastoral systems in global perspective. In *The World of Pastoralism: Herding Systems in Comparative Perspective*. J. G. Galaty and D. L. Johnson, eds. Pp. 1–31. New York: Guilford.

Galik, Alfred 2000 Dog remains from the late Hallstatt period of the chimney cave Durezza, near Villach (Carinthia, Austria). In *Dogs through Time: An Archaeological Perspective*. S. J. Crockford, ed. Pp. 129–37. British Archaeological Reports, International Series. Oxford: Archaeopress.

Galik, Alfred 2004 An Iron Age bone assemblage from Durezza Cave, Carinthia, Austria: Detecting ritual behaviour through archaeozoological and taphonomical analyses. In *Behaviour behind Bones: The Zooarchaeology of Ritual, Religion, Status and Identity*. S. J. O'Day, W. Van Neer, and A. Ervynck, eds. Pp. 54–61. Oxford: Oxbow.

Galloway, Patricia 1997 Where have all the menstrual huts gone? The invisibility of menstrual seclusion in the late prehistoric Southeast. In *Women in Prehistory: North America and Mesoamerica*. C. P. Claassen and R. A. Joyce, eds. Pp. 47–62. Philadelphia: University of Pennsylvania Press.

Gallup, Gordon G., Jr., James L. Boren, Gregg J. Gagliardi, and Larry B. Wallnau 1977 A mirror for the mind of man, or will the chimpanzee create an identity crisis for *Homo sapiens*? *Journal of Human Evolution* 6(3):303–13.

Gamble, Clive S. 1985 Formation processes and the animal bones from the sanctuary at Phylakopi. In *The Archaeology of Cult: The Sanctuary at Phylakopi*. A. C. Renfrew, ed. Pp. 479–83. British School of Archaeology at Athens, Supplemental Volume. London: Thames & Hudson.

Gamble, Clive S., John A. J. Gowlett, and Robin I. M. Dunbar 2011 The social brain and the shape of the Palaeolithic. *Cambridge Archaeological Journal* 21(1):115–36.

Garfinkel, Yosef 1987 Burnt lime products and social implications in the Pre-Pottery Neolithic B villages of the Near East. *Paléorient* 13(1):69–76.

Garfinkel, Yosef 2003 *Dancing at the Dawn of Agriculture.* Austin: University of Texas Press.

Gargett, Robert H. 1996 *Cave Bears and Modern Human Origins: The Spatial Taphonomy of Pod Hradem Cave, Czech Republic.* Lanham, MD: University Press of America.

Gargett, Robert H., and Brian D. Hayden 1991 Site structure, kinship, and sharing in aboriginal Australia. In *The Interpretation of Archaeological Spatial Patterning.* E. M. Kroll and T. D. Price, eds. Pp. 11–32. New York: Plenum.

Garrard, Andrew N. 1984 The selection of South-West Asian animal domesticates. In *Animals and Archaeology: 3. Early Herders and their Flocks.* J. Clutton-Brock and C. Grigson, eds. Pp. 117–32. British Archaeological Reports, International Series. Oxford: Archaeopress.

Garvey, Jillian 2010 Economic anatomy of the Bennett's wallaby (*Macropus rufogriseus*): Implications for understanding human hunting strategies in late Pleistocene Tasmania. *Quaternary International* 211(1–2):144–56.

Gaudzinski, Sabine 2000 On the variability of Middle Palaeolithic procurement tactics: The case of Salzgitter Lebenstedt, northern Germany. *International Journal of Osteoarchaeology* 10(5):396–406.

Gauthier-Pilters, Hilde, and Anne I. Dagg 1981 *The Camel: Its Evolution, Ecology, Behavior, and Relationship to Man.* Chicago: University of Chicago Press.

Gebre Mariam, Ayele 1980 The collection and interpretation of quantitative data on pastoral societies: Reflections on case studies from Ethiopia. In *The Future of Pastoral Peoples, Nairobi, 1980,* pp. 359–69. Commission on Nomadic Peoples, International Union of Anthropological and Ethnological Sciences. Ottawa: International Development Research Centre.

Geddes, David S. 1985 Mesolithic domestic sheep in west Mediterranean Europe. *Journal of Archaeological Science* 12:25–48.

Geist, Valerius 1982 Adaptive behavioral strategies. In *Elk of North America: Ecology and Management.* J. W. Thomas and D. E. Toweill, eds. Pp. 219–77. Harrisburg: Stackpole.

Gejvall, Nils-Gustaf 1969 *Lerna: The Fauna.* Princeton: American School of Classical Studies.

Gero, Joan M. 1991 Genderlithics: Women's roles in stone tool production. In *Engendering Archaeology: Women and Prehistory.* J. M. Gero and M. W. Conkey, eds. Pp. 163–93. Oxford: Basil Blackwell.

Gero, Joan M. 1992 Feasts and females: Political meals in the Andes. *Norwegian Archaeological Review* 25(1):15–30.

Gibbs, Liv 1987 Identifying gender representation in the archaeological record: A contextual study. In *The Archaeology of Contextual Meanings.* I. Hodder, ed. Pp. 79–89. Cambridge: Cambridge University Press.

Gibson, Kathleen 2002 Customs and cultures in animals and humans: Neuro-biological and evolutionary considerations. *Anthropological Theory* 2(3):323–40.

Gibson, Thomas 1988 Meat sharing as a political ritual: Forms of transaction versus modes of subsistence. In *Hunters and Gatherers 2: Property, Power and Ideology*. T. Ingold, D. Riches, and J. Woodburn, eds. Pp. 165–79. New York: Berg.

Giddens, Anthony 1979 *Central Problems in Social Theory: Action, Structure and Contradiction in Social Analysis*. Berkeley: University of California Press.

Gifford, Diane P. 1981 Taphonomy and paleoecology: A critical review of archae-ology's sister disciplines. In *Advances in Archaeological Method and Theory*. M. B. Schiffer, ed. Pp. 365–438. Vol. 4. New York: Academic Press.

Gifford-Gonzalez, Diane P. 1989 Ethnographic analogues for interpreting mod-ified bones: Some cases from East Africa. In *Bone Modification*. R. Bonnichsen and M. H. Sorg, eds. Pp. 179–246. Orono, ME: Center for the Study of the First Americans.

Gifford-Gonzalez, Diane P. 1991 Bones are not enough: Analogues, knowl-edge, and interpretive strategies in zooarchaeology. *Journal of Anthropological Archaeology* 10(3):215–54.

Gifford-Gonzalez, Diane P. 1993 Gaps in the zooarchaeological analysis of butchery: Is gender an issue? In *From Bones to Behavior: Ethnoarchaeologi-cal and Experimental Contributions to the Interpretation of Faunal Remains*. J. Hudson, ed. Pp. 181–99. Southern Illinois University, Center for Archaeolog-ical Investigations, Occasional Papers. Carbondale: Center for Archaeological Investigations, Southern Illinois University at Carbondale.

Gifford-Gonzalez, Diane P. 2007 Thoughts on a method for zooarchaeological study of quotidian life. *Treballs d'Arqueologia* 13:5–27.

Gilbert, Allan S., and Paul Steinfeld 1977 Faunal remains from Dinkha Tepe, northwestern Iran. *Journal of Field Archaeology* 4(3):329–51.

Gilbert, M. Thomas P. *et al.* 2008 DNA from pre-Clovis human coprolites in Oregon, North America. *Science* 320(5877):786–9.

Gilby, Ian C. 2006 Meat sharing among the Gombe chimpanzees: Harassment and reciprocal exchange. *Animal Behaviour* 71(4):953–63.

Gilhus, Ingvild Sælid 2006 *Animals, Gods and Humans: Changing Attitudes to Animals in Greek, Roman and Early Christian Ideas*. London: Routledge.

Gillespie, Richard 2008 Updating Martin's global extinction model. *Quaternary Science Reviews* 27(27–28):2522–9.

Gilmore, Melvin R. 1933 The Arikara method of preparing a dog for a feast. *Papers of the Michigan Academy of Science, Arts and Letters* 19:37–8.

Gilmour, G. H. 1997 The nature and function of astragalus bones from archae-ological contexts in the Levant and eastern Mediterranean. *Oxford Journal of Archaeology* 16(2):167–75.

Gimbutas, Marija A. 1977 Gold treasure at Varna. *Archaeology* 30:44–51.

Gimbutas, Marija A. 1982 *The Goddesses and Gods of Old Europe 6500–3500 BC.* Second edition. Berkeley: University of California Press.

Gimbutas, Marija A. 1989 *The Language of the Goddess.* San Francisco: Harper & Row.

Gimbutas, Marija A. 1991 *The Civilization of the Goddess: The World of Old Europe.* San Francisco: Harper & Row.

Gimbutas, Marija A. 1999 *The Living Goddesses.* Berkeley: University of California Press.

Girard, René 1972 *La Violence et le Sacré.* Paris: B. Grasset.

Gladkih, Mikhail I., Ninelj L. Kornietz, and Olga Soffer 1984 Mammoth-bone dwellings on the Russian plain. *Scientific American* 251(5):164–75.

Glickman, Stephen E. 1999 The spotted hyena from Aristotle to the Lion King: Reputation is everything. In *Humans and Other Animals.* A. Mack, ed. Pp. 87–123. Columbus, OH: Ohio State University Press.

Glob, Peter V. 1988 *The Bog People: Iron-Age Man Preserved.* R. Bruce-Mitford, transl. Ithaca: Cornell University Press.

Gluckman, Max 1950 Kinship and marriage among the Lozi of northern Rhodesia and the Zulu of Natal. In *African Systems of Kinship and Marriage.* A. R. Radcliffe-Brown and C. D. Forde, eds. Oxford: Oxford University Press.

Gluckman, Max 1953 Bridewealth and the stability of marriage. *Man* 53:141–3.

Godelier, Maurice 1999 *The Enigma of the Gift.* N. Scott, transl. Chicago: University of Chicago Press.

Godfrey, Laurie R., William L. Jungers, Kaye E. Reed, Elwyn L. Simons, and Prithijit S. Chatrath 1997 Subfossil lemurs: Inferences about past and present primate communities in Madagascar. In *Natural Change and Human Impact in Madagascar.* S. M. Goodman and B. D. Patterson, eds. Pp. 218–56. Washington, DC: Smithsonian Institution Press.

Gomes, Cristina M., Roger Mundry, and Christophe Boesch 2009 Long-term reciprocation of grooming in wild West African chimpanzees. *Proceedings of the Royal Society of London, Series B* 276(1657):699–706.

Good, Kenneth R. 1987 Limiting factors in Amazonian ecology. In *Food and Evolution: Toward a Theory of Human Food Habits.* M. Harris and E. B. Ross, eds. Pp. 407–21. Philadelphia: Temple University Press.

Goodall, Jane 1971 *In the Shadow of Man.* Boston: Houghton Mifflin.

Goodall, Jane 1990 *Through a Window: My Thirty Years with the Chimpanzees of Gombe.* Boston: Houghton Mifflin.

Goodman, Steven M., and Lucien M. A. Rakotozafy 1997 Subfossil birds from coastal sites in western and southwestern Madagascar: A paleoenvironmental reconstruction. In *Natural Change and Human Impact in Madagascar.* S. M. Goodman and B. D. Patterson, eds. Pp. 257–79. Washington, DC: Smithsonian Institution Press.

Goody, Jack 1973 Bridewealth and dowry in Africa and Eurasia. In *Bridewealth and Dowry.* J. Goody and S. J. Tambiah, eds. Pp. 1–58. Cambridge Papers in Social Anthropology. Cambridge: Cambridge University Press.

Goody, Jack 1976 *Production and Reproduction: A Comparative Study of the Domestic Domain*. Cambridge: Cambridge University Press.

Goody, Jack 1982 *Cooking, Cuisine, and Class: A Study in Comparative Sociology*. Cambridge: Cambridge University Press.

Goren-Inbar, Naama, Nira Alperson, Mordechai E. Kislev, Orit Simchoni, Yoel Melamed, Adi Ben-Nun, and Ella Werker 2004 Evidence of hominin control of fire at Gesher Benot Ya'aqov, Israel. *Science* 304(5671):725–7.

Goring-Morris, A. Nigel, and Liora R. K. Horwitz 2007 Funerals and feasts during the Pre-Pottery Neolithic B of the Near East. *Antiquity* 81(314):902–19.

Gosden, Christopher 1995 Arboriculture and agriculture in coastal Papua New Guinea. *Antiquity* 69(265):807–17.

Gottlieb, Alma 1998 Do infants have religion? The spiritual lives of Beng babies. *American Anthropologist* 100(1):122–35.

Gottlieb, Alma 2004 *The Afterlife Is Where We Come From: The Culture of Infancy in West Africa*. Chicago: University of Chicago Press.

Gould, Richard A. 1967 Notes on hunting, butchering, and sharing of game among the Ngatatjara and their neighbors in the West Australian Desert. *Kroeber Anthropological Society Papers* 36:41–66.

Gould, Richard A. 1981 Comparative ecology of food sharing in Australia and northwest California. In *Omnivorous Primates: Gathering and Hunting in Human Evolution*. R. S. O. Harding and G. Teleki, eds. Pp. 422–54. New York: Columbia University Press.

Gowlett, John A. J. 2009 Artefacts of apes, humans, and others: Towards comparative assessment and analysis. *Journal of Human Evolution* 57(4):401–10.

Grahn, Judy 1993 *Blood, Bread, and Roses: How Menstruation Created the World*. Boston: Beacon Press.

Grandin, Barbara E. 1988 Wealth and pastoral dairy production: A case study from Maasailand. *Human Ecology* 16(1):1–21.

Grant, Annie 1984 Survival or sacrifice? A critical appraisal of animal burials in Britain in the Iron Age. In *Animals and Archaeology: 4. Husbandry in Europe*. C. Grigson and J. Clutton-Brock, eds. Pp. 221–7. British Archaeological Reports, International Series. Oxford: Archaeopress.

Grant, Annie 1989 Animals and ritual in early Britain: The visible and the invisible. In *L'Animal dans les Pratiques Religieuses: Les Manifestations Materielles*. J.-D. Vigne, ed. Pp. 341–55. Anthropozoologica, Vol. 3. Paris: Éditions du Centre National de la Recherche Scientifique.

Grant, Annie 1991 Economic or symbolic? Animals and ritual behaviour. In *Sacred and Profane: Proceedings of a Conference on Archaeology, Ritual and Religion*. P. Garwood, D. Jennings, R. Skeates, and J. Toms, eds. Pp. 109–14. Oxford University Committee for Archaeology Monograph. Oxford: Oxford University Committee for Archaeology.

Grantham, Bill 1995 Dinner in Buqata: The symbolic nature of food animals and meal sharing in a Druze village. In *The Symbolic Role of Animals in*

*Archaeology.* K. Ryan and P. J. Crabtree, eds. Pp. 73–8. MASCA Research Papers in Science and Archaeology. Philadelphia: University of Pennsylvania, University Museum.

Grayson, Donald K. 1973 On the methodology of faunal analysis. *American Antiquity* 38(4):432–9.

Grayson, Donald K. 1977 Pleistocene avifaunas and the overkill hypothesis. *Science* 195(4279):691–3.

Grayson, Donald K. 1979 On the quantification of vertebrate archaeofaunas. In *Advances in Archaeological Method and Theory.* M. B. Schiffer, ed. Pp. 199–237. Vol. 2. New York: Academic Press.

Grayson, Donald K. 1987 An analysis of the chronology of late Pleistocene mammalian extinctions in North America. *Quaternary Research* 28:281–9.

Grayson, Donald K. 1989 The chronology of North American Late Pleistocene extinctions. *Journal of Archaeological Science* 16(2):153–65.

Grayson, Donald K. 1991 Late Pleistocene mammalian extinctions in North America: Taxonomy, chronology, and explanations. *Journal of World Prehistory* 5(3):193–231.

Grayson, Donald K. 2001 The archaeological record of human impacts on animal populations. *Journal of World Prehistory* 15(1):1–68.

Grayson, Donald K., and Françoise Delpech 1994 The evidence for Middle Palaeolithic scavenging from Couche VIII, Grotte Vaufrey (Dordogne, France). *Journal of Archaeological Science* 21:359–75.

Grayson, Donald K., and Françoise Delpech 2002 Specialized Early Upper Palaeolithic hunters in southwestern France? *Journal of Archaeological Science* 29(12):1439–49.

Grayson, Donald K., and Françoise Delpech 2003 Ungulates and the Middle-to-Upper Paleolithic transition at Grotte XVI (Dordogne, France). *Journal of Archaeological Science* 30(12):1633–48.

Grayson, Donald K., and Françoise Delpech 2008 The large mammals of Roc de Combe (Lot, France): The Châtelperronian and Aurignacian assemblages. *Journal of Anthropological Archaeology* 27(3):338–62.

Grayson, Donald K., Françoise Delpech, Jean-Philippe Rigaud, and Jan F. Simek 2001 Explaining the development of dietary dominance by a single ungulate taxon at Grotte XVI, Dordogne, France. *Journal of Archaeological Science* 28(2):115–25.

Grayson, Donald K., and David J. Meltzer 2002 Clovis hunting and large mammal extinction: A critical review of the evidence. *Journal of World Prehistory* 16(4):313–59.

Grayson, Donald K., and David J. Meltzer 2003 A requiem for North American overkill. *Journal of Archaeological Science* 30(5):585–93.

Green, Miranda J. 1992 *Animals in Celtic Life and Myth.* London: Routledge.

Green, Miranda J. 1997 Images in opposition: Polarity, ambivalence and liminality in cult representation. *Antiquity* 71(274):898–911.

Green, Miranda J. 1998 Crossing the boundaries: Triple horns and emblematic transference. *European Journal of Archaeology* 1(2):219–40.

Green, Miranda J. 2001 Cosmovision and metaphor: Monsters and shamans in Gallo-British cult-expression. *European Journal of Archaeology* 4(2):203–31.

Green, Roger C., and Marshall I. Weisler 2004 Prehistoric transfer and extinction of animals in Mangareva, southeast Polynesia. *Archaeology in Oceania* 39:34–41.

Greenfield, Haskel J. 1984 A model of changing animal exploitation strategies during the later prehistory of the Central Balkans. In *Animals and Archaeology: 4. Husbandry in Europe*. C. Grigson and J. Clutton-Brock, eds. Pp. 45–56. British Archaeological Reports, International Series. Oxford: Archaeopress.

Greenfield, Haskel J. 1988 The origins of milk and wool production in the Old World. *Current Anthropology* 29(4):573–93.

Greenfield, Haskel J. 1989 Zooarchaeology and aspects of the secondary products revolution: A central Balkan perspective. *ArchaeoZoologia* 3(1–2):191–200.

Greenfield, Haskel J. 1999 The advent of transhumant pastoralism in the temperate southeast Europe: A zooarchaeological perspective from the Central Balkans. In *Transhumant Pastoralism in Southern Europe: Recent Perspectives from Archaeology, History and Ethnology*. L. Bartosiewicz and H. J. Greenfield, eds. Pp. 15–36. Budapest: Archaeolingua Alapítvány.

Greenfield, Haskel J. 2005 A reconsideration of the Secondary Products Revolution in south-eastern Europe: On the origins and use of domestic animals for milk, wool, and traction in the central Balkans. In *The Zooarchaeology of Fats, Oils, Milk and Dairying*. J. Mulville and A. K. Outram, eds. Pp. 14–31. Oxford: Oxbow.

Greenfield, Haskel J. 2010 The Secondary Products Revolution: The past, the present and the future. *World Archaeology* 42(1):29–54.

Greenfield, Haskel J., and Leonard O. van Schalkwyk 2006 Spatial models of intra-settlement spatial organization in the EIA of southern Africa: A view from Ndondondwane on the Central Cattle Pattern. In *Space and Spatial Analysis in Archaeology*. E. C. Robertson, J. D. Seibert, D. C. Fernandez, and M. U. Zender, eds. Pp. 61–8. Calgary: University of Calgary Press.

Gregory, Chris A. 1980 Gifts to men and gifts to gods: Gift exchange and capital accumulation in contemporary Papua. *Man* (n.s.) 15:626–52.

Gregory, Chris A. 1982 *Gifts and Commodities*. New York: Academic Press.

Gregory, Chris A. 1997 *Savage Money: The Anthropology and Politics of Commodity Exchange*. Amsterdam: Harwood Academic Publishers.

Greig, James R. A., and Peter Warren 1974 Early Bronze Age agriculture in western Crete. *Antiquity* 48:130–2.

Griffin, Donald R. 2001 *Animal Minds: Beyond Cognition to Consciousness*. Chicago: University of Chicago Press.

Griffin, P. Bion 1998 An ethnographic view of the pig in selected traditional Southeast Asian societies. In *Ancestors for the Pigs: Pigs in Prehistory*. S. M.

Nelson, ed. Pp. 27–37. MASCA Research Papers in Science and Archaeology. Philadelphia: University of Pennsylvania, University Museum.

Grigson, Caroline 1969 The uses and limitations of differences in absolute size in the distinction between the bones of aurochs (*Bos primigenius*) and domestic cattle (*Bos taurus*). In *The Domestication and Exploitation of Plants and Animals*. P. J. Ucko and G. W. Dimbleby, eds. Pp. 277–94. London: Duckworth.

Grigson, Caroline 1984 The domestic animals of the earlier Neolithic in Britain. In *Der Beginn der Haustierhaltung in der "Alten Welt"*. G. Nobis, ed. Pp. 205–20. Köln: Bohlau.

Grigson, Caroline 2000 The secondary products revolution? Changes in animal management from the fourth to the fifth millennium, at Arjoune, Syria. In *Archaeozoology of the Near East IVB: Proceedings of the Fourth International Symposium on the Archaeozoology of Southwestern Asia and Adjacent Areas*. M. Mashkour, A. M. Choyke, H. Buitenhuis, and F. Poplin, eds. Pp. 12–28. ARC – Publicatie. Groningen: Center for Archeological Research and Consultancy.

Grigson, Caroline 2006 Farming? Feasting? Herding? Large mammals from the Chalcolithic of Gilat. In *Archaeology, Anthropology and Cult: The Sanctuary at Gilat, Israel*. T. E. Levy, ed. Pp. 215–319. London: Equinox.

Grosman, Leore, Natalie D. Munro, and Anna Belfer-Cohen 2008 A 12,000-year-old Shaman burial from the southern Levant (Israel). *Proceedings of the National Academy of Sciences* 105(46):17665–9.

Gross, Daniel R. 1975 Protein capture and cultural development in the Amazon Basin. *American Anthropologist* 77:526–49.

Groves, Colin P. 1984 Of mice and men and pigs in the Indo-Australian archipelago. *Canberra Anthropology* 7(1–2):1–19.

Groves, Colin P. 1989 Feral mammals of the Mediterranean islands: Documents of early domestication. In *The Walking Larder: Patterns of Domestication, Pastoralism, and Predation*. J. Clutton-Brock, ed. Pp. 46–58. London: Unwin Hyman.

Grün, Rainer, Stephen Eggins, Maxime Aubert, Nigel A. Spooner, Alistair W. G. Pike, and Wolfgang Müller 2010 ESR and U-series analyses of faunal material from Cuddie Springs, NSW, Australia: Implications for the timing of the extinction of the Australian megafauna. *Quaternary Science Reviews* 29(5–6):596–610.

Guenther, Mathias J. 1988 Animals in Bushman thought, myth and art. In *Hunters and Gatherers 2: Property, Power and Ideology*. T. Ingold, D. Riches, and J. Woodburn, eds. Pp. 192–202. New York: Berg.

Guilday, John E. 1977 Animal remains from archeological excavations at Fort Ligonier. In *Experimental Archeology*. D. W. Ingersoll, Jr., J. E. Yellen, and W. MacDonald, eds. Pp. 121–32. New York: Columbia University Press.

Guillén, Ann C. 1998 Women, rituals, and social dynamics at ancient Chalcatzingo. In *Reader in Gender Archaeology*. K. Hays-Gilpin and D. S. Whitley, eds. Pp. 269–89. London: Routledge.

Gunnerson, James H. 1997 Mountain lions and Pueblo shrines in the American Southwest. In *Icons of Power: Feline Symbolism in the Americas.* N. J. Saunders, ed. Pp. 228–57. London: Routledge.

Gurven, Michael 2004 To give and to give not: The behavioral ecology of human food transfers. *Behavioral and Brain Sciences* 27(4):543–59.

Gurven, Michael, and Kim Hill 2009 Why do men hunt? A reevaluation of 'Man the Hunter' and the sexual division of labor. *Current Anthropology* 50(1):51–74.

Guthrie, R. Dale 2001 Origin and causes of the mammoth steppe: A story of cloud cover, woolly mammal tooth pits, buckles, and inside-out Beringia. *Quaternary Science Reviews* 20(1–3):549–74.

Guthrie, Stewart E. 1993 *Faces in the Clouds: A New Theory of Religion.* New York: Oxford University Press.

Guthrie, Stewart E. 1997 Anthropomorphism: A definition and a theory. In *Anthropomorphism, Anecdotes, and Animals.* R. W. Mitchell, N. S. Thompson, and H. L. Miles, eds. Pp. 50–8. Albany: State University of New York Press.

Haak, Wolfgang *et al.* 2005 Ancient DNA from the first European farmers in 7500-year-old Neolithic sites. *Science* 310(5750):1016–18.

Haak, Wolfgang *et al.* 2008 Ancient DNA, strontium isotopes, and osteological analyses shed light on social and kinship organization of the Later Stone Age. *Proceedings of the National Academy of Sciences* 105(47):18226–31.

Haak, Wolfgang *et al.* 2010 Ancient DNA from European Early Neolithic farmers reveals their Near Eastern affinities. *PLoS Biology* 8(11):e1000536.

Hagberg, Ulf Erik 1967 The Archaeology of Skedemosse. Volume II: *The Votive Deposits in the Skedemosse Fen and their Relation to the Iron-Age Settlement on Öland, Sweden.* Stockholm: Almqvist & Wiksell.

Hagen, James M. 1999 The good behind the gift: Morality and exchange among the Maneo of eastern Indonesia. *Journal of the Royal Anthropological Institute* 5(3):361–76.

Hager, Lori D. 1997 Sex and gender in paleoanthropology. In *Women in Human Evolution.* L. D. Hager, ed. Pp. 1–28. London: Routledge.

Hahn, Eduard 1896 *Die Haustiere und ihre Beziehungen zur Wirtschaft des Menschen.* Leipzig: Duncker & Humblot.

Hakansson, N. Thomas 1994 Grain, cattle, and power: Social processes of intensive cultivation and exchange in precolonial western Kenya. *Journal of Anthropological Research* 50(3):249–76.

Hakker-Orion, Dalia 1984 The rôle of the camel in Israel's early history. In *Animals and Archaeology: 3. Early Herders and their Flocks.* J. Clutton-Brock and C. Grigson, eds. Pp. 207–12. British Archaeological Reports, International Series. Oxford: Archaeopress.

Hallam, Sylvia J. 1979 *Fire and Hearth: A Study of Aboriginal Usage and European Usurpation in South-Western Australia.* Australian Aboriginal Studies, No. 58.

Halliday, Tim 1978 *Vanishing Birds: Their Natural History and Conservation.* London: Sidgwick & Jackson.

Halliday, William R. 1913 *Greek Divination: A Study of its Methods and Principles.* London: Macmillan.

Halstead, Paul L. J. 1981a Counting sheep in Neolithic and Bronze Age Greece. In *Pattern of the Past: Studies in Honour of David Clarke.* I. Hodder, G. L. Isaac, and N. Hammond, eds. Pp. 307–39. Cambridge: Cambridge University Press.

Halstead, Paul L. J. 1981b From determinism to uncertainty: Social storage and the rise of the Minoan palace. In *Economic Archaeology: Towards an Integration of Ecological and Social Approaches.* A. Sheridan and G. N. Bailey, eds. Pp. 187–213. British Archaeological Reports, International Series. Oxford: British Archaeological Reports.

Halstead, Paul L. J. 1987 Man and other animals in later Greek prehistory. *Annual of the British School at Athens* 82:71–83.

Halstead, Paul L. J. 1992 Dimini and the 'DMP': Faunal remains and animal exploitation in Late Neolithic Thessaly. *Annual of the British School at Athens* 87:29–59.

Halstead, Paul L. J. 1996 The development of agriculture and pastoralism in Greece: When, how, who and what? In *The Origins and Spread of Agriculture and Pastoralism in Eurasia.* D. R. Harris, ed. Pp. 296–309. London: UCL Press.

Halstead, Paul L. J. 1998 Mortality models and milking: Problems of uniformitarianism, optimality and equifinality reconsidered. *Anthropozoologica* 27: 3–20.

Halstead, Paul L. J. 2007 Carcasses and commensality: Investigating the social context of meat consumption in Neolithic and Early Bronze Age Greece. In *Cooking up the Past: Food and Culinary Practices in the Neolithic and Bronze Age Aegean.* C. B. Mee and J. Renard, eds. Pp. 25–48. Oxford: Oxbow.

Halstead, Paul L. J., and John C. Barrett, eds. 2004 *Food, Cuisine and Society in Prehistoric Greece.* Oxford: Oxbow.

Halstead, Paul L. J., and Valasia Isaakidou 2004 Faunal evidence for feasting: Burnt offerings from the Palace of Nestor at Pylos. In *Food, Cuisine and Society in Prehistoric Greece.* P. L. J. Halstead and J. C. Barrett, eds. Pp. 136–54. Oxford: Oxbow.

Halverson, John 1976 Animal categories and terms of abuse. *Man* 11:505–16.

Ham, Jennifer, and Matthew Senior, eds. 1997 *Animal Acts: Configuring the Human in Western History.* London: Routledge.

Hamayon, Roberte N. 1990 *La Chasse à l'Âme. Esquisse d'une Théorie du Chamanisme Sibérien.* Nanterre: Société d'Ethnologie.

Hamell, George R. 1997 Long-Tail: The panther in Huron-Wyandot and Seneca myth, ritual, and material culture. In *Icons of Power: Feline Symbolism in the Americas.* N. J. Saunders, ed. Pp. 258–91. London: Routledge.

Hames, Raymond 1990 Sharing among the Yanomamö: Part I, the effects of risk. In *Risk and Uncertainty in Tribal and Peasant Economies*. E. A. Cashdan, ed. Pp. 89–105. Boulder: Westview.

Hamilakis, Yannis 2008 Time, performance, and the production of a mnemonic record: From feasting to an archaeology of eating and drinking. In *Dais: The Aegean Feast*. L. A. Hitchcock, R. Laffineur, and J. Crowley, eds. Pp. 3–20. Liège: Université de Liège.

Hamilakis, Yannis, and Eleni Konsolaki 2004 Pigs for the gods: Burnt animal sacrifices as embodied rituals at a Mycenaean sanctuary. *Oxford Journal of Archaeology* 23(2):135–51.

Hamilton, Annette 1972 Aboriginal man's best friend? *Mankind* 8:287–95.

Hamilton, Marcus J., and Briggs Buchanan 2007 Spatial gradients in Clovis-age radiocarbon dates across North America suggest rapid colonization from the north. *Proceedings of the National Academy of Sciences* 104(40):15625–30.

Hamilton-Dyer, Sheila 2002 The bird resources of Medieval Novgorod, Russia. *Acta Zoologica Cracoviensia* 45(special issue):99–107.

Hammond, P. W. 1993 *Food and Feast in Medieval England*. Stroud: Sutton Publishing.

Handley, Brent M. 2000 Preliminary results in determining dog types from prehistoric sites in the northeastern United States. In *Dogs through Time: An Archaeological Perspective*. S. J. Crockford, ed. Pp. 205–15. British Archaeological Reports, International Series. Oxford: Archaeopress.

Hanks, Bryan K. 2010 Archaeology of the Eurasian steppes and Mongolia. *Annual Review of Anthropology* 39(1):469–86.

Hanson, C. Bruce 1980a Fluvial taphonomic processes: Models and experiments. In *Fossils in the Making: Vertebrate Taphonomy and Paleoecology*. A. K. Behrensmeyer and A. P. Hill, eds. Pp. 156–81. Chicago: University of Chicago Press.

Hanson, Jeffery R. 1980b Structure and complexity of medicine bundle systems of selected Plains Indian tribes. *Plains Anthropologist* 25(89):199–216.

Haraway, Donna J. 1991 *Simians, Cyborgs, and Women: The Reinvention of Nature*. London: Routledge.

Harris, David R. 1996 Domesticatory relationships of people, plants and animals. In *Redefining Nature: Ecology, Culture and Domestication*. R. F. Ellen and K. Fukui, eds. Pp. 437–63. Oxford: Berg.

Harris, David R. 1998 The origins of agriculture in southwest Asia. *The Review of Archaeology* 19(2):5–11.

Harris, Marvin 1966 The cultural ecology of India's sacred cattle. *Current Anthropology* 7(1).

Harris, Marvin 1985 *Good to Eat: Riddles of Food and Culture*. New York: Simon and Schuster.

Harrod, Howard 2000 *The Animals Came Dancing: Native American Sacred Ecology and Animal Kinship*. Tucson: University of Arizona Press.

Hart, Keith, and Louise Sperling 1987 Cattle as capital. *Ethnos* 52(3–4):324–38.

Harwood, Alan 1970 *Witchcraft, Sorcery, and Social Categories among the Safwa*. London: International African Institute.

Hasegawa, Toshikazu, Mariko Hiraiwa, Toshisada Nishida, and Hiroyuki Takasaki 1983 New evidence on scavenging behavior in wild chimpanzees. *Current Anthropology* 24(2):231–2.

Haudricourt, André G. 1962 Domestication des animaux, culture des plantes et traitement d'autrui. *Homme* 2(1):40–50.

Haudricourt, André G. 1977 Note d'ethnozoologie. Le rôle des excrétats dans la domestication. *Homme* 17(2–3):125–6.

Hauptmann, Harald 1999 The Urfa region. In *Neolithic in Turkey: The Cradle of Civilization – New Discoveries*. N. Başgelen and M. Özdoğan, eds. Pp. 65–86. Istanbul: Arkeoloji ve Sanat Yayınları.

Hawkes, Kristen 1993 Why hunter-gatherers work: An ancient version of the problem of public goods. *Current Anthropology* 34(4):341–61.

Hawkes, Kristen 2001 Is meat the hunter's property? Big game, ownership, and explanations of hunting and sharing. In *Meat-Eating and Human Evolution*. C. B. Stanford and H. T. Bunn, eds. Pp. 219–36. Oxford: Oxford University Press.

Hawkes, Kristen, and Rebecca L. Bliege Bird 2002 Showing off, handicap signaling, and the evolution of men's work. *Evolutionary Anthropology* 11(2):58–67.

Hayden, Brian D. 1975 Dingoes: Pets and producers? *Mankind* 10(1):11–15.

Hayden, Brian D. 1990 Nimrods, piscators, pluckers, and planters: The emergence of food production. *Journal of Anthropological Archaeology* 9(1):31–69.

Hayden, Brian D. 1992 Models of domestication. In *Transitions to Agriculture in Prehistory*. A. B. Gebauer and T. D. Price, eds. Pp. 11–19. Monographs in World Archaeology (Prehistory Press). Madison: Prehistory Press.

Hayden, Brian D. 1995a A new overview of domestication. In *Last Hunters–First Farmers: New Perspectives on the Prehistoric Transition to Agriculture*. T. D. Price and A. B. Gebauer, eds. Pp. 273–99. Santa Fe: School of American Research Press.

Hayden, Brian D. 1995b Pathways to power: Principles for creating socioeconomic inequalities. In *Foundations of Social Inequality*. T. D. Price and G. M. Feinman, eds. Pp. 15–86. New York: Plenum.

Hayden, Brian D. 1995c The emergence of prestige technologies and pottery. In *The Emergence of Pottery: Technology and Innovation in Ancient Societies*. W. K. Barnett and J. W. Hoopes, eds. Pp. 257–65. Washington, DC: Smithsonian Institution Press.

Hayden, Brian D. 1996a Feasting in prehistoric and traditional societies. In *Food and the Status Quest: An Interdisciplinary Perspective*. P. Wiessner and W. Schiefenhövel, eds. Pp. 127–47. Providence: Berghahn Books.

Hayden, Brian D. 1996b Thresholds of power in emergent complex societies. In *Emergent Complexity: The Evolution of Intermediate Societies*. J. E. Arnold, ed. Pp. 50–8. Archaeological Series. Ann Arbor: International Monographs in Prehistory.

Hayden, Brian D. 1998 Practical and prestige technologies: The evolution of material systems. *Journal of Archaeological Method and Theory* 5(1):1–55.

Hayden, Brian D. 2001a Fabulous feasts: A prolegomenon to the importance of feasting. In *Feasts: Archaeological and Ethnographic Perspectives on Food, Politics, and Power*. M. Dietler and B. D. Hayden, eds. Pp. 23–64. Washington, DC: Smithsonian Institution Press.

Hayden, Brian D. 2001b The dynamics of wealth and poverty in the Transegalitarian societies of Southeast Asia. *Antiquity* 75(289):571–81.

Hayden, Brian D. 2002 Hunting and feasting: Health and demographic consequences. *Before Farming* 1(3–4).

Hayden, Brian D. 2003 Were luxury foods the first domesticates? Ethnoarchaeological perspectives from Southeast Asia. *World Archaeology* 34(3):458–69.

Hayden, Brian D. 2009 The proof is in the pudding: Feasting and the origins of domestication. *Current Anthropology* 50(5):597–601.

Haynes, C. Vance, Jr., J. Boerner, K. Domanik, D. Lauretta, J. Ballenger, and J. Goreva 2010 The Murray Springs Clovis site, Pleistocene extinction, and the question of extraterrestrial impact. *Proceedings of the National Academy of Sciences* 107(9):4010–15.

Haynes, Gary 1989 Late Pleistocene mammoth utilization in northern Eurasia and North America. *ArchaeoZoologia* 3(1–2):81–108.

Haynes, Gary 1990 Taphonomy: Science and folklore. In *Problem Solving in Taphonomy: Archaeological and Palaeontological Studies from Europe, Africa and Oceania*. S. Solomon, I. Davidson, and D. Watson, eds. Pp. 7–17. Tempus. St. Lucia: University of Queensland Anthropology Museum.

Haynes, Gary 1991 *Mammoths, Mastodonts, and Elephants: Biology, Behavior, and the Fossil Record*. Cambridge: Cambridge University Press.

Haynes, Gary 1995 Pre-Clovis and Clovis megamammals: A comparison of carcass disturbance, age profiles, and other characteristics in light of recent actualistic studies. In *Ancient Peoples and Landscapes*. E. Johnson, ed. Pp. 9–27. Lubbock, TX: Museum of Texas Tech University.

Haynes, Gary, and B. Sunday Eiselt 1999 The power of Pleistocene hunter-gatherers: Forward and backward searching for evidence about mammoth extinction. In *Extinctions in Near Time: Causes, Contexts, and Consequences*. R. D. E. MacPhee, ed. Pp. 71–93. New York: Kluwer Academic/Plenum Publishers.

Hays, Kelley Ann 1993 When is a symbol archaeologically meaningful? Meaning, function, and prehistoric visual arts. In *Archaeological Theory: Who Sets the Agenda?* N. Yoffee and A. G. Sherratt, eds. Pp. 81–92. Cambridge: Cambridge University Press.

Hazelwood, Lee, and James Steele 2004 Spatial dynamics of human dispersals: Constraints on modelling and archaeological validation. *Journal of Archaeological Science* 31(6):669–79.

Hecker, Howard M. 1982 Domestication revisited: Its implications for faunal analysis. *Journal of Field Archaeology* 9(2):217–36.

Hecker, Howard M. 1984 A new look at Childe's oasis-propinquity theory. In *Animals and Archaeology: 3. Early Herders and their Flocks.* J. Clutton-Brock and C. Grigson, eds. Pp. 133–43. British Archaeological Reports, International Series. Oxford: Archaeopress.

Hedges, Robert E. M. 2004 Isotopes and red herrings: Comments on Milner *et al.* and Lidén *et al. Antiquity* 78(299):34–7.

Heeßel, Nils 2010 The calculation of the stipulated term in extispicy. In *Divination and Interpretation of Signs in the Ancient World.* A. Annus, ed. Pp. 163–75. Chicago: Oriental Institute of the University of Chicago.

Heesterman, J. C. 1993 *The Broken World of Sacrifice: An Essay in Ancient Indian Ritual.* Chicago: University of Chicago Press.

Hegmon, Michelle 1991 The risks of sharing and sharing as risk reduction: Inter-household sharing in egalitarian societies. In *Between Bands and States.* S. A. Gregg, ed. Pp. 309–29. Southern Illinois University, Center for Archaeological Investigations, Occasional Papers. Carbondale: Center for Archaeological Investigations, Southern Illinois University at Carbondale.

Heinrich, Bernd 1999 *Mind of the Raven: Investigations and Adventures with Wolf-Birds.* New York: Cliff Street Books.

Heinrich, Bernd, and John Marzluff 1995 Why ravens share. *American Scientist* 83(4):342–9.

Heinrich, Dirk 1997 Some remarks on the occurrence of buzzard (*Buteo buteo*) and goshawk (*Accipiter gentilis*) in Europe. *Anthropozoologica* 25/26:465–77.

Heizer, Robert F., and Gordon W. Hewes 1940 Animal ceremonialism in central California in the light of archaeology. *American Anthropologist* 42:587–603.

Helbaek, Hans 1963 Textiles from Çatal Hüyük. *Archaeology* Spring 1963:39–46.

Hell, Bertrand 1996 Enraged hunters: The domain of the wild in northwestern Europe. In *Nature and Society: Anthropological Perspectives.* P. Descola and G. Pálsson, eds. Pp. 205–17. London: Routledge.

Helmer, Daniel, Lionel Gourichon, Hervé Monchot, Joris Peters, and Maria Saña Seguí 2005 Identifying early domestic cattle from Pre-Pottery Neolithic sites on the Middle Euphrates using sexual dimorphism. In *The First Steps of Animal Domestication.* J.-D. Vigne, J. Peters, and D. Helmer, eds. Pp. 86–95. Oxford: Oxbow.

Helmer, Daniel, Lionel Gourichon, and Danielle Stordeur 2004 A l'aube de la domestication animale: Imaginaire et symbolisme animal dans les premières sociétés néolithiques du nord du Proche-Orient. *Anthropozoologica* 39:143–63.

Helmer, Daniel, Lionel Gourichon, and Emmanuelle Vila 2007 The development of the exploitation of products from *Capra* and *Ovis* (meat, milk and fleece) from the PPNB to the Early Bronze in the northern Near East (8700 to 2000 BC cal.). *Anthropozoologica* 42(2):41–70.

Helvenston, Patricia A., Paul G. Bahn, John L. Bradshaw, and Christopher Chippindale 2003 Testing the 'three stages of trance' model. *Cambridge Archaeological Journal* 13(2):213–24.

Hemmer, Helmut 1990 *Domestication: The Decline of Environmental Appreciation*. Second edition. N. Beckhaus, transl. Cambridge: Cambridge University Press.

Hendon, Julia A. 1996 Archaeological approaches to the organization of domestic labor: Household practice and domestic relations. *Annual Review of Anthropology* 25:45–61.

Henry, Donald O. 1989 *From Foraging to Agriculture: The Levant at the End of the Ice Age*. Philadelphia: University of Pennsylvania Press.

Henry, Jules 1951 The economics of Pilagá food distribution. *American Anthropologist* 53:187–219.

Herskovits, Melville J. 1926 The cattle complex in East Africa. *American Anthropologist* 28:230–72, 361–80, 494–528, 633–64.

Herva, Vesa-Pekka 2005 The life of buildings: Minoan building deposits in an ecological perspective. *Oxford Journal of Archaeology* 24(3):215–28.

Hesse, Brian C. 1982 Slaughter patterns and domestication: The beginnings of pastoralism in western Iran. *Man* (n.s.) 17:403–17.

Hesse, Brian C. 1984 These are our goats: The origins of herding in west central Iran. In *Animals and Archaeology: 3. Early Herders and their Flocks*. J. Clutton-Brock and C. Grigson, eds. Pp. 243–64. British Archaeological Reports, International Series. Oxford: British Archaeological Reports.

Hesse, Brian C. 1986 Buffer resources and animal domestication in prehistoric northern Chile. *ArchaeoZoologia* Mélanges:73–85.

Hesse, Brian C. 1989 Paleolithic faunal remains from Ghar-i-Khar, western Iran. In *Early Animal Domestication and its Cultural Context*. P. J. Crabtree, D. V. Campana, and K. Ryan, eds. Pp. 37–45. MASCA Research Papers in Science and Archaeology. Philadelphia: University of Pennsylvania, University Museum.

Hesse, Brian C. 1993 Carnivorous pastoralism: Part of the origins of domestication or a secondary product revolution? In *Culture and Environment: A Fragile Coexistence*. R. W. Jamieson, S. Abonyi, and N. A. Mirau, eds. Pp. 99–109. Calgary: University of Calgary.

Hesse, Brian C., and Paula Wapnish 1998 Pig use and abuse in the ancient Levant: Ethnoreligious boundary-building with swine. In *Ancestors for the Pigs: Pigs in Prehistory*. S. M. Nelson, ed. Pp. 123–35. MASCA Research Papers in Science and Archaeology. Philadelphia: University of Pennsylvania, University Museum.

Hesse, Brian C., and Paula Wapnish 2002 An archaeozoological perspective on the cultural use of mammals in the Levant. In *A History of the Animal World in the Ancient Near East*. B. J. Collins, ed. Pp. 457–91. Leiden: E. J. Brill.

Heusch, Luc de 1985 *Sacrifice in Africa: A Structuralist Approach*. L. O'Brien and A. Morton, transl. Bloomington: Indiana University Press.

Higgs, Eric S., and Michael R. Jarman 1972 The origins of animal and plant husbandry. In *Papers in Economic Prehistory: Studies by Members and*

*Associates of the British Academy Major Research Project in the Early History of Agriculture.* E. S. Higgs, ed. Pp. 3–13. Cambridge: Cambridge University Press.

Higham, Charles F. W. 1968 Faunal sampling and economic prehistory. *Zeitschrift für Säugetierkunde* 33(5):297–305.

Higham, Charles F. W., Amphan Kijngam, Bryan F. J. Manly, and S. J. E. Moore 1981 The bovid third phalanx and prehistoric ploughing. *Journal of Archaeological Science* 8(4):353–65.

Hildebrandt, William R., and Kelly R. McGuire 2002 The ascendance of hunting during the California Middle Archaic: An evolutionary perspective. *American Antiquity* 67(2):231–56.

Hill, Andrew P. 1979 Butchery and natural disarticulation: An investigatory technique. *American Antiquity* 44(4):739–44.

Hill, Erica 2000 The contextual analysis of animal interments and ritual practice in southwestern North America. *Kiva* 65(4):361–98.

Hill, Jeremy D. 1995 *Ritual and Rubbish in the Iron Age of Wessex: A Study on the Formation of a Specific Archaeological Record.* British Archaeological Reports, British Series, No. 242. Oxford: Tempus Reparatum.

Hill, Jeremy D. 1996 The identification of ritual deposits of animal bones. A general perspective from a specific study of 'special animal deposits' from the southern English Iron Age. In *Ritual Treatment of Human and Animal Remains: Proceedings of the First Meeting of the Osteoarchaeological Research Group Held in Cambridge on 8th October 1994.* S. Anderson and K. V. Boyle, eds. Pp. 17–32. Oxford: Oxbow.

Hill, Kim, and Hillard Kaplan 1993 On why male foragers hunt and share food. *Current Anthropology* 34(5):701–6.

Hill, Kim, and Keith W. Kintigh 2009 Can anthropologists distinguish good and poor hunters? Implications for hunting hypotheses, sharing conventions, and cultural transmission. *Current Anthropology* 50(3):369–78.

Hill, Matthew E., Jr. 2007 A moveable feast: Variation in faunal resource use among central and western North American Paleoindian sites. *American Antiquity* 72(3):417–38.

Hill, Matthew E., Jr. 2008 Variation in Paleoindian fauna use on the Great Plains and Rocky Mountains of North America. *Quaternary International* 191(1):34–52.

Hjort, Anders 1980 Herds, trade, and grain: Pastoralism in a regional perspective. *The Future of Pastoral Peoples, Nairobi, Kenya, 1980.* Pp. 135–43. Commission on Nomadic Peoples, International Union of Anthropological and Ethnological Sciences. Ottawa: International Development Research Centre.

Hobsbawm, Eric J., ed. 1964 *Karl Marx: Pre-Capitalist Economic Formations.* New York: International Publishers.

Hockett, Bryan S. 1998 Sociopolitical meaning of faunal remains from Baker Village. *American Antiquity* 63(2):289–302.

Hockett, Bryan S., and Nuno F. Bicho 2000 The rabbits of Picareiro Cave: Small mammal hunting during the late Upper Palaeolithic in the Portuguese Estremadura. *Journal of Archaeological Science* 27(8):715–23.

Hockett, Bryan S., and Jonathan A. Haws 2009 Continuity in animal resource diversity in the Late Pleistocene human diet of Central Portugal. *Before Farming* 2009(2).

Hodder, Ian 1987 Contextual archaeology: An interpretation of Çatal Hüyük and a discussion of the origins of agriculture. *Bulletin of the Institute of Archaeology (London)* 24:43–56.

Hodder, Ian 1990 *The Domestication of Europe: Structure and Contingency in Neolithic Societies.* Oxford: Basil Blackwell.

Hodder, Ian 1991 Gender representation and social reality. In *The Archaeology of Gender.* D. Walde and N. D. Willows, eds. Pp. 11–16. Calgary: Archaeological Association of the University of Calgary.

Hodder, Ian 2006 *The Leopard's Tale: Revealing the Mysteries of Çatalhöyük.* London: Thames & Hudson.

Hodder, Ian, with a note on building complexity by Tim Ritchey 1996 Re-opening Çatalhöyük. In *On the Surface: Çatalhöyük 1993–95.* I. Hodder, ed. Pp. 1–18. British Institute of Archaeology at Ankara Monographs. Cambridge: McDonald Institute for Archaeological Research.

Hoffecker, John F., and Naomi E. Cleghorn 2000 Mousterian hunting patterns in the northwestern Caucasus and the ecology of the Neanderthals. *International Journal of Osteoarchaeology* 10(5):368–78.

Hofman, Jack L. 2001 Mehl's dilemma: Paleomortology and interpretation of the Clovis-mammoth association at Domebo, Oklahoma. In *Proceedings of the International Conference on Mammoth Site Studies.* D. L. West, ed. Pp. 95–103. University of Kansas Publications in Anthropology. Lawrence, KS: University of Kansas Department of Anthropology.

Hogue, S. Homes 2006 Carbon isotope and microwear analysis of dog burials: Evidence for maize agriculture at a small Mississippian/protohistoric site. In *Integrating Zooarchaeology.* J. M. Maltby, ed. Pp. 123–30. Oxford: Oxbow.

Hohmann, Gottfried, and Barbara Fruth 1996 Food sharing and status in unprovisioned bonobos. In *Food and the Status Quest: An Interdisciplinary Perspective.* P. Wiessner and W. Schiefenhövel, eds. Pp. 47–67. Providence: Berghahn Books.

Højlund, Flemming 1981 The deposit of sacrificed animals at the entrance to the tomb chamber. In *The Maussolleion at Halikarnassos I: The Sacrificial Deposit.* Pp. 23–89. Jutland Archaeological Society Publications. Copenhagen: Nordisk Forlag.

Højlund, Flemming 1983 The Mausselleion sacrifice. *American Journal of Archaeology* 87(2):145–52.

Holdaway, Richard N. 1999 Introduced predators and avifaunal extinction in New Zealand. In *Extinctions in Near Time: Causes, Contexts, and Consequences.*

R. D. E. MacPhee, ed. Pp. 189–238. New York: Kluwer Academic/Plenum Publishers.

Holdaway, Richard N., and C. Jacomb 2000 Rapid extinction of the moas (Aves: Dinornithiformes): Model, test, and implications. *Science* 287(5461):2250–4.

Holden, Clare J., and Ruth Mace 2003 Spread of cattle led to the loss of matrilineal descent in Africa: A coevolutionary analysis. *Proceedings of the Royal Society of London, Series B* 270(1532):2425–33.

Hole, Frank 1996 The context of caprine domestication in the Zagros region. In *The Origins and Spread of Agriculture and Pastoralism in Eurasia*. D. R. Harris, ed. Pp. 263–81. London: UCL Press.

Holmberg, David H. 1989 *Order in Paradox: Myth, Ritual, and Exchange among Nepal's Tamang*. Ithaca: Cornell University Press.

Holt, Julie Z. 1996 Beyond optimization: Alternative ways of examining animal exploitation. *World Archaeology* 28(1):89–109.

Holzhaider, Jenny C., M. D. Sibley, A. H. Taylor, P. J. Singh, Russell D. Gray, and Gavin R. Hunt 2011 The social structure of New Caledonian crows. *Animal Behaviour* 81(1):83–92.

Horard-Herbin, Marie-Pierre 2000 Dog management and use in the late Iron Age: The evidence from the Gallic site of Levroux (France). In *Dogs through Time: An Archaeological Perspective*. S. J. Crockford, ed. Pp. 115–21. British Archaeological Reports, International Series. Oxford: Archaeopress.

Horigan, Stephen 1988 *Nature and Culture in Western Discourses*. London: Routledge.

Horner, Victoria, Andrew Whiten, Emma Flynn, and Franz B. M. de Waal 2006 Faithful replication of foraging techniques along cultural transmission chains by chimpanzees and children. *Proceedings of the National Academy of Sciences* 103(37):13878–83.

Horwitz, Liora R. K. 2001 Animal offerings in the Middle Bronze Age: Food for the gods, food for thought. *Palestine Exploration Quarterly* 133:78–90.

Horwitz, Liora R. K., and A. Nigel Goring-Morris 2004 Animals and ritual during the Levantine PPNB: A case study from the site of Kfar Hahoresh, Israel. *Anthropozoologica* 39:165–78.

Horwitz, Liora R. K., and Gila Kahila Bar-Gal 2006 The origin and genetic status of insular caprines in the eastern Mediterranean: A case study of free-ranging goats (*Capra aegagrus cretica*) on Crete. *Human Evolution* 21(2):123–38.

Horwitz, Liora R. K., and Patricia Smith 1990 A radiographic study of the extent of variation in cortical bone thickness in Soay sheep. *Journal of Archaeological Science* 17:655–64.

Horwitz, Liora R. K., and Patricia Smith 1991 A study of diachronic change in bone mass of sheep and goats Jericho (Tel-Es Sultan). *ArchaeoZoologia* 4(1):29–38.

Horwitz, Liora R. K., Eitan Tchernov, Pierre Ducos, Cornelia Becker, Angela von den Driesch, Louise Martin, and Andrew N. Garrard 1999 Animal domestication in the southern Levant. *Paléorient* 25(2):63–80.

Hoskins, Janet 1993 Violence, sacrifice, and divination: Giving and taking life in eastern Indonesia. *American Ethnologist* 20(1):159–78.

Houston, David C. 1983 The adaptive radiation of the griffon vultures. In *Vulture Biology and Management*. S. R. Wilbur and J. A. Jackson, eds. Pp. 135–52. Berkeley: University of California Press.

Hovelsrud-Broda, Grete K. 2000 'Sharing', transfers and the concept of generalized reciprocity. In *The Social Economy of Sharing: Resource Allocation and Modern Hunter-Gatherers*. G. W. Wenzel, G. K. Hovelsrud-Broda, and N. Kishigami, eds. Pp. 193–214. Senri Ethnological Studies. Osaka: National Museum of Ethnology.

Howell, Signe 1996 Nature in culture or culture in nature? Chewong ideas of 'humans' and other species. In *Nature and Society: Anthropological Perspectives*. P. Descola and G. Pálsson, eds. Pp. 127–44. London: Routledge.

Hrdy, Sarah B. 1999 *The Woman that Never Evolved*. Revised edition. Cambridge: Harvard University Press.

Hubert, Henri, and Marcel Mauss 1964 *Sacrifice: Its Nature and Function*. W. D. Halls, transl. Chicago: University of Chicago Press.

Hudson, Jean 1990 Identifying food sharing archaeologically: An ethnoarchaeological study among the Aka. Paper presented at the *6th International Conference on Hunting and Gathering Societies*. Fairbanks, AL.

Huffman, Thomas N. 1990 Broederstroom and the origins of cattle-keeping in southern Africa. *African Studies* 49(2):1–12.

Hugh-Jones, Christine 1996a Houses in the Neolithic imagination: An Amazonian example. In *Neolithic Houses in Northwest Europe and Beyond*. T. Darvill and J. S. Thomas, eds. Pp. 185–93. Oxbow Monographs. Oxford: Oxbow.

Hugh-Jones, Stephen 1996b Bonnes raisons ou mauvaise conscience? De l'ambivalence de certains amazoniens envers la consommation de viande. *Terrain* 26:123–48.

Humphrey, Caroline, and James Laidlaw 2007 Sacrifice and ritualization. In *The Archaeology of Ritual*. E. Kyriakidis, ed. Pp. 255–76. Cotsen Advanced Seminars. Los Angeles: Cotsen Institute of Archaeology, University of California, Los Angeles.

Hunt, Gavin R., Michael C. Corballis, and Russell D. Gray 2006a Design complexity and strength of laterality are correlated in New Caledonian crows' pandanus tool manufacture. *Proceedings of the Royal Society of London, Series B* 273(1590):1127–33.

Hunt, Gavin R., Robb B. Rutledge, and Russell D. Gray 2006b The right tool for the job: What strategies do wild New Caledonian crows use? *Animal Cognition* 9(4):307–16.

Hunt, Terry L. 2007 Rethinking Easter Island's ecological catastrophe. *Journal of Archaeological Science* 34(3):485–502.

Hutson, Scott R., Travis W. Stanton, Aline Magnoni, Richard Terry, and Jason Craner 2007 Beyond the buildings: Formation processes of ancient Maya houselots and methods for the study of non-architectural space. *Journal of Anthropological Archaeology* 26(3):442–73.

Hutten, Louisa 2008 Symbolic animal burials from the Venda region in the Limpopo Province, South Africa. In *Animals and People: Archaeozoological Papers in Honour of Ina Plug*. S. Badenhorst, P. J. Mitchell, and J. C. Driver, eds. Pp. 186–99. British Archaeological Reports, International Series. Oxford: Archaeopress.

Hyde, Lewis 1983 *The Gift: Imagination and the Erotic Life of Property*. New York: Vintage Books.

Iakovleva, Liudmila, and François Djindjian 2001 Epigravettian settlement models in the Dniepr Basin in the light of the new excavations of the Gontsy site (Ukraine). In *Proceedings of the International Conference on Mammoth Site Studies*. D. L. West, ed. Pp. 85–94. University of Kansas Publications in Anthropology. Lawrence, KS: University of Kansas Department of Anthropology.

Iakovleva, Liudmila, and François Djindjian 2005 New data on Mammoth bone settlements of Eastern Europe in the light of the new excavations of the Gontsy site (Ukraine). *Quaternary International* 126–128:195–207.

Ikram, Salima 2004 Typhonic bones: A ritual deposit from Saqqara? In *Behaviour Behind Bones: The Zooarchaeology of Ritual, Religion, Status and Identity*. S. J. O'Day, W. Van Neer, and A. Ervynck, eds. Pp. 41–6. Oxford: Oxbow.

Ingold, Tim 1980 *Hunters, Pastoralists, and Ranchers: Reindeer Economies and their Transformations*. Cambridge: Cambridge University Press.

Ingold, Tim 1984 Time, social relationships and the exploitation of animals: Anthropological reflections on prehistory. In *Animals and Archaeology: 3. Early Herders and their Flocks*. J. Clutton-Brock and C. Grigson, eds. Pp. 3–12. British Archaeological Reports, International Series. Oxford: British Archaeological Reports.

Ingold, Tim 1987 *The Appropriation of Nature: Essays on Human Ecology and Social Relations*. Iowa City: University of Iowa Press.

Ingold, Tim 1988 The animal in the study of humanity. In *What is an Animal?* T. Ingold, ed. Pp. 84–99. London: Unwin Hyman.

Ingold, Tim 1994 From trust to domination: An alternative history of human-animal relations. In *Animals and Human Society: Changing Perspectives*. A. Manning and J. A. Serpell, eds. Pp. 1–22. London: Routledge.

Ingold, Tim 1996a Growing plants and raising animals: An anthropological perspective on domestication. In *The Origins and Spread of Agriculture and Pastoralism in Eurasia*. D. R. Harris, ed. Pp. 12–24. London: UCL Press.

Ingold, Tim 1996b The optimal forager and economic man. In *Nature and Society: Anthropological Perspectives*. P. Descola and G. Pálsson, eds. Pp. 25–44. London: Routledge.

Insoll, Timothy 2010 Talensi animal sacrifice and its archaeological implications. *World Archaeology* 42(2):231–44.

Isaac, Erich 1971 On the domestication of cattle. In *Prehistoric Agriculture*. S. Struever, ed. Pp. 451–70. Garden City, NY: Natural History Press.

Isaac, Glynn Ll. 1978 The food-sharing behavior of protohuman hominids. *Scientific American* 238(4):90–108.

Isaac, Glynn Ll., and Diana C. Crader 1981 To what extent were early hominids carnivorous? An archaeological perspective. In *Omnivorous Primates: Gathering and Hunting in Human Evolution*. R. S. O. Harding and G. Teleki, eds. Pp. 37–103. New York: Columbia University Press.

Isaakidou, Valasia 2006 Ploughing with cows: Knossos and the Secondary Products Revolution. In *Animals in the Neolithic of Britain and Europe*. D. Serjeantson and D. Field, eds. Pp. 95–112. Neolithic Studies Group Seminar Papers. Oxford: Oxbow.

Isaakidou, Valasia 2007 Cooking in the Labyrinth: Exploring 'cuisine' at Bronze Age Knossos. In *Cooking up the Past: Food and Culinary Practices in the Neolithic and Bronze Age Aegean*. C. B. Mee and J. Renard, eds. Pp. 5–24. Oxford: Oxbow.

Isaakidou, Valasia, Paul L. J. Halstead, Jack Davis, and Sharon Stocker 2002 Burnt animal sacrifice at the Mycenaean 'Palace of Nestor', Pylos. *Antiquity* 76(291):86–92.

Jameson, Michael H. 1988 Sacrifice and animal husbandry in Classical Greece. In *Pastoral Economies in Classical Antiquity*. C. R. Whittaker, ed. Pp. 87–119. Cambridge Philological Society, Supplementary Volume. Cambridge: Cambridge Philological Society.

Jankuhn, Herbert 1967 Archaeologische Beobachtungen zu Tier- und Menschenopfern bei den Germanen in der Römischen Kaiserzeit. *Nachrichten der Akademie der Wissenschaften in Göttingen, I. Philologisch-historische Klasse* 6:117–47.

Jarman, Michael R. 1972 European deer economies and the advent of the Neolithic. In *Papers in Economic Prehistory: Studies by Members and Associates of the British Academy Major Research Project in the Early History of Agriculture*. E. S. Higgs, ed. Pp. 125–47. Cambridge: Cambridge University Press.

Jarman, Michael R. 1973 Preliminary report on the animal bones. In *Knossos: The Sanctuary of Demeter*. J. N. Coldstream, ed. Pp. 177–9. British School of Archaeology at Athens, Supplemental Volume. London: Thames & Hudson.

Jarman, Michael R. 1977 Early animal husbandry. In *The Early History of Agriculture*. J. Hutchinson, J. G. D. Clark, E. M. Jope, and R. Riley, eds. Pp. 85–94. Oxford: Oxford University Press.

Jarman, Michael R. 1996 Human influence in the development of the Cretan mammalian fauna. In *The Pleistocene and Holocene Fauna of Crete and its First Settlers*. D. S. Reese, ed. Pp. 211–30. Monographs in World Archaeology. Madison: Prehistory Press.

Jarman, Michael R., and Paul F. Wilkinson 1972 Criteria of animal domestication. In *Papers in Economic Prehistory: Studies by Members and Associates of the British*

*Academy Major Research Project in the Early History of Agriculture.* E. S. Higgs, ed. Pp. 83–96. Cambridge: Cambridge University Press.

Jarvenpa, Robert, and Hetty Jo Brumbach 1983 Ethnoarchaeological perspectives on an Athapaskan moose kill. *Arctic* 36:174–84.

Jay, Nancy B. 1992 *Throughout your Generations Forever: Sacrifice, Religion, and Paternity.* Chicago: University of Chicago Press.

Jennings, Justin 2004 La chichera y el patrón: Chicha and the energetics of feasting in the prehistoric Andes. In *Foundations of Power in the Prehispanic Andes.* K. J. Vaughn, D. Ogburn, and C. A. Conlee, eds. Pp. 241–59. Archeological Papers of the American Anthropological Association. Arlington, VA: American Anthropological Association.

Jensen, Adolf E. 1963 *Myth and Cult among Primitive Peoples.* M. T. Choldin and W. Weissleder, transl. Chicago: University of Chicago Press.

Jerome, Norge W. 1980 An ecological approach to nutritional anthropology. In *Nutritional Anthropology: Contemporary Approaches to Diet & Culture.* N. W. Jerome, R. F. Kandel, and G. H. Pelto, eds. Pp. 13–45. Pleasantville, NY: Redgrave.

Jiang, Leping, and Li Liu 2006 New evidence for the origins of sedentism and rice domestication in the Lower Yangzi River, China. *Antiquity* 80(308):355–61.

Jing, Yuan, and Rowan K. Flad 2002 Pig domestication in ancient China. *Antiquity* 76(293):724–32.

Johannsen, Niels N. 2005 Palaeopathology and Neolithic cattle traction: Methodological issues and archaeological perspectives. In *Diet and Health in Past Animal Populations: Current Research and Future Directions.* J. J. Davies, M. Fabiš, I. L. Mainland, M. P. Richards, and R. Thomas, eds. Pp. 39–51. Oxford: Oxbow.

Johnson, Christopher N. 2005 What can the data on late survival of Australian megafauna tell us about the cause of their extinction? *Quaternary Science Reviews* 24(20–21):2167–72.

Johnson, Donald L. 1980 Problems in the land vertebrate zoogeography of certain islands and the swimming powers of elephants. *Journal of Biogeography* 7(4):383–98.

Johnson, Gregory A. 1982 Organizational structure and scalar stress. In *Theory and Explanation in Archaeology: The Southampton Conference.* A. C. Renfrew, M. J. Rowlands, and B. Segraves, eds. Pp. 389–421. New York: Academic Press.

Jolly, Margaret 1984 The anatomy of pig love: Substance, spirit and gender in South Pentecost, Vanuatu. *Canberra Anthropology* 7(1–2):78–108.

Jones, Andrew 1998 Where eagles dare: Landscape, animals and the Neolithic of Orkney. *Journal of Material Culture* 3(3):301–24.

Jones, Kevin T., and Duncan Metcalfe 1988 Bare bones archaeology: Bone marrow indices and efficiency. *Journal of Archaeological Science* 15(4):415–23.

Jones, Martin K. 2007 *Feast: Why Humans Share Food*. Oxford: Oxford University Press.

Jones, Terry L., Judith F. Porcasi, Jon M. Erlandson, H. Dallas, Jr., Thomas A. Wake, and R. Schwaderer 2008 The protracted Holocene extinction of California's flightless sea duck (*Chendytes lawi*) and its implications for the Pleistocene overkill hypothesis. *Proceedings of the National Academy of Sciences* 105(11):4105–8.

Joukowsky, Martha S. 1986 *Prehistoric Aphrodisias: An Account of the Excavations and Artifact Studies. Volume I: Excavations and Artifact Studies*. Archaeologia Transatlantica, No. 3. Providence: Brown University, Center for Old World Archaeology and Art.

Jourdan, Lucien, and Jean-François Le Mouel 1987 Découpe de phoque: Partage entre l'Homme et l'Animal. In *La Découpe et le Partage du Corps à travers le Temps et L'Espace*. J.-D. Vigne, ed. Pp. 31–8. Anthropozoologica. Paris: Éditions du Centre National de la Recherche Scientifique.

Jovanović, Borislav 1972 The autochthonous and the migrational components of the Early Neolithic in the Iron Gates. *Balcanica* 3:49–58.

Junker, Laura L. 2001 The evolution of ritual feasting systems in prehispanic Philippine chiefdoms. In *Feasts: Archaeological and Ethnographic Perspectives on Food, Politics, and Power*. M. Dietler and B. D. Hayden, eds. Pp. 267–310. Washington, DC: Smithsonian Institution Press.

Kadletz, Edward 1976 *Animal Sacrifice in Greek and Roman Religion*. Unpublished Ph.D. thesis, University of Washington.

Kahila Bar-Gal, Gila, Patricia Smith, Eitan Tchernov, Charles Greenblatt, Pierre Ducos, Armelle Gardeisen, and Liora R. K. Horwitz 2002 Genetic evidence for the origin of the agrimi goat (*Capra aegagrus cretica*). *Journal of Zoology* 256(3):369–77.

Kahn, Miriam 1986 *Always Hungry, Never Greedy*. Cambridge: Cambridge University Press.

Kalof, Linda, Amy Fitzgerald, and Lori Baralt 2004 Animals, women, and weapons: Blurred sexual boundaries in the discourse of sport hunting. *Society and Animals* 12(3):237–51.

Kansa, Sarah W., and Stuart Campbell 2004 Feasting with the dead? – A ritual bone deposit at Domuztepe, south eastern Turkey (*c.* 5550 cal BC). In *Behaviour behind Bones: The Zooarchaeology of Ritual, Religion, Status and Identity*. S. J. O'Day, W. Van Neer, and A. Ervynck, eds. Pp. 2–13. Oxford: Oxbow.

Kaplan, Hillard, and Kim Hill 1985 Hunting ability and reproductive success among male Ache foragers: Preliminary results. *Current Anthropology* 26(1):131–3.

Kaplan, Hillard, Kim Hill, Kristen Hawkes, and Ana M. Hurtado 1984 Food sharing among Ache hunter-gatherers of eastern Paraguay. *Current Anthropology* 25(1):113–15.

Keeley, Brian L. 2004 Anthropomorphism, primatomorphism, mammalomorphism: Understanding cross-species comparisons. *Biology and Philosophy* 19(4):521–40.

Keeley, Lawrence H. 1995 Protoagricultural practices among hunter-gatherers: A cross-cultural survey. In *Last Hunters–First Farmers: New Perspectives on the Prehistoric Transition to Agriculture*. T. D. Price and A. B. Gebauer, eds. Pp. 243–72. Santa Fe: School of American Research Press.

Keeley, Lawrence H., and Nicholas Toth 1981 Microwear polishes on early stone tools from Koobi Fora, Kenya. *Nature* 293(5382):464–5.

Kehoe, Alice B. 1991 The weaver's wraith. In *The Archaeology of Gender*. D. Walde and N. D. Willows, eds. Pp. 430–5. Calgary: Archaeological Association of the University of Calgary.

Kehoe, Alice B. 2000 *Shamans and Religion: An Anthropological Exploration in Critical Thinking*. Prospect Heights, IL: Waveland.

Kellert, Stephen R. 1993 The biological basis for human values of nature. In *The Biophilia Hypothesis*. S. R. Kellert and E. O. Wilson, eds. Pp. 42–69. Washington, DC: Island Press.

Kelly, Lucretia S. 2001 A case of ritual feasting at the Cahokia site. In *Feasts: Archaeological and Ethnographic Perspectives on Food, Politics, and Power*. M. Dietler and B. D. Hayden, eds. Pp. 334–67. Washington, DC: Smithsonian Institution Press.

Kelly, Raymond C. 1985 *The Nuer Conquest: The Structure and Development of an Expansionist System*. Ann Arbor: University of Michigan Press.

Kelly, Robert L. 1995 *The Foraging Spectrum: Diversity in Hunter-Gatherer Lifeways*. Washington, DC: Smithsonian Institution Press.

Kenady, Stephen M., Michael C. Wilson, Randall F. Schalk, and Robert R. Mierendorf 2011 Late Pleistocene butchered *Bison antiquus* from Ayer Pond, Orcas Island, Pacific Northwest: Age confirmation and taphonomy. *Quaternary International* 233(2):130–41.

Kennedy, John S. 1992 *The New Anthropomorphism*. Cambridge: Cambridge University Press.

Kenrick, Justin 2002 Anthropology and anthropocentrism: Images of hunter-gatherers, westerners and the environment. In *Self- and Other-Images of Hunter-Gatherers*. H. Stewart, A. Barnard, and K. Omura, eds. Pp. 191–213. Osaka: National Museum of Ethnology.

Kensinger, Kenneth M. 1989 Hunting and male domination in Cashinahua society. In *Farmers as Hunters: The Implications of Sedentism*. S. Kent, ed. Pp. 18–26. Cambridge: Cambridge University Press.

Kent, Susan 1989 Cross-cultural perceptions of farmers as hunters and the value of meat. In *Farmers as Hunters: The Implications of Sedentism*. S. Kent, ed. Pp. 1–17. Cambridge: Cambridge University Press.

Kent, Susan 1993a Sharing in an egalitarian Kalahari community. *Man* (n.s.) 28:479–514.

Kent, Susan 1993b Variability in faunal assemblages: The influence of hunting skill, sharing, dogs, and mode of cooking on faunal remains at a sedentary Kalahari community. *Journal of Anthropological Archaeology* 12(4):323–85.

Kenward, Ben, Christian Rutz, Alex A. S. Weir, and Alex Kacelnik 2006 Development of tool use in New Caledonian crows: Inherited action patterns and social influences. *Animal Behaviour* 72(6):1329–43.

Kershaw, A. P. 1986 Climatic change and Aboriginal burning in north-east Australia during the last two glacial/interglacial cycles. *Nature* 322:47–9.

Keswani, Priscilla S. 1994 The social context of animal husbandry in early agricultural societies: Ethnographic insights and an archaeological example from Cyprus. *Journal of Anthropological Archaeology* 13(3):255–77.

Khazanov, Anatoly M. 1994 *Nomads and the Outside World*. Second edition. Madison: University of Wisconsin Press.

Kim, Seung-Og 1994 Burials, pigs, and political prestige in Neolithic China. *Current Anthropology* 35(2):119–42.

Kirch, Patrick V. 1982 Advances in Polynesian prehistory: Three decades in review. In *Advances in World Archaeology*. F. Wendorf and A. E. Close, eds. Pp. 51–97. Vol. 1. New York: Academic Press.

Kirch, Patrick V. 1997 Microcosmic histories: Island perspective on 'global' change. *American Anthropologist* 99(1):30–42.

Kirch, Patrick V. 2001 Polynesian feasting in ethnohistoric, ethnographic, and archaeological contexts: A comparison of three societies. In *Feasts: Archaeological and Ethnographic Perspectives on Food, Politics, and Power*. M. Dietler and B. D. Hayden, eds. Pp. 168–84. Washington, DC: Smithsonian Institution Press.

Kirkbride, Diana 1968 Beidha: Early Neolithic life south of the Dead Sea. *Antiquity* 42:263–74.

Kislev, Mordechai E. 1999 Agriculture in the Near East in the seventh millennium BC. In *Prehistory of Agriculture: New Experimental and Ethnographic Approaches*. P. C. Anderson, ed. Pp. 51–5. Monograph. Los Angeles: UCLA Institute of Archaeology.

Kistner, T. P. 1982 Diseases and parasites. In *Elk of North America: Ecology and Management*. J. W. Thomas and D. E. Toweill, eds. Pp. 181–217. Harrisburg: Stackpole.

Kitanishi, Koichi 2000 The Aka and the Baka: Food sharing among two central African hunter-gatherer groups. In *The Social Economy of Sharing: Resource Allocation and Modern Hunter-Gatherers*. G. W. Wenzel, G. K. Hovelsrud-Broda, and N. Kishigami, eds. Pp. 149–69. Senri Ethnological Studies. Osaka: National Museum of Ethnology.

Klein, Cecilia F., Eulogio Guzmán, Elisa C. Mandell, and Maya Stanfield-Mazzi 2002 The role of shamanism in Mesoamerican art: A reassessment. *Current Anthropology* 43(3):383–419.

Klein, Richard G. 1982 Age (mortality) profiles as a means of distinguishing hunted species from scavenged ones in Stone Age archaeological sites. *Paleobiology* 8(2):151–8.

Klippel, Walter E., and Lynn M. Snyder 1999 Harvest profiles, domestic ovicaprids, and Bronze Age Crete. In *The Practical Impact of Science on Near Eastern and Aegean Archaeology*. S. Pike and S. Gitin, eds. Pp. 53–61. Wiener Laboratory Monograph. London: Archetype Publications.

Knauer, Elfriede R. 1998 *The Camel's Load in Life and Death*. Zürich: Akanthvs.

Knauft, Bruce M. 1991 Violence and sociality in human evolution. *Current Anthropology* 32(4):391–428.

Knight, Stephanie 2001 Beasts and burial in the interpretation of ritual space: A case study from Danebury. In *Holy Ground: Theoretical Issues Relating to the Landscape and Material Culture of Ritual Space Objects*. A. T. Smith and A. Brookes, eds. Pp. 49–59. British Archaeological Reports, International Series. Oxford: Archaeopress.

Knight, Vernon J. 2001 Feasting and the emergence of platform mound ceremonialism in eastern North America. In *Feasts: Archaeological and Ethnographic Perspectives on Food, Politics, and Power*. M. Dietler and B. D. Hayden, eds. Pp. 311–33. Washington, DC: Smithsonian Institution Press.

Koerper, Henry C., and Nancy A. Whitney-Desautels 1999 Astragalus bones: Artifacts or ecofacts? *Pacific Coast Archaeological Society Quarterly* 35(2–3):69–80.

Köhler, Ilse 1984 The dromedary in modern pastoralist societies and implications for its process of domestication. In *Animals and Archaeology: 3. Early Herders and their Flocks*. J. Clutton-Brock and C. Grigson, eds. Pp. 201–6. British Archaeological Reports, International Series. Oxford: British Archaeological Reports.

Köhler, Meike, and Salvador Moyà-Solà 2001 Phalangeal adaptations in the fossil insular goat *Myotragus*. *Journal of Vertebrate Paleontology* 21(3):621–4.

Köhler-Rollefson, Ilse 1996 The one-humped camel in Asia: Origin, utilization and mechanisms of dispersal. In *The Origins and Spread of Agriculture and Pastoralism in Eurasia*. D. R. Harris, ed. Pp. 282–94. London: UCL Press.

Köhler-Rollefson, Ilse, and Gary O. Rollefson 2002 Brooding about breeding: Social implications for the process of animal domestication. In *The Dawn of Farming in the Near East*. R. T. J. Cappers and S. Bottema, eds. Pp. 177–81. Studies in Early Near Eastern Production, Subsistence, and Environment. Berlin: Ex Oriente.

Kohn, Eduardo O. 2007 How dogs dream: Amazonian natures and the politics of transspecies engagement. *American Ethnologist* 34(1):3–24.

Köksal-Schmidt, Çiğdem, and Klaus Schmidt 2010 The Göbekli Tepe 'totem pole': A first discussion of an autumn 2010 discovery (PPN, southeastern Turkey). *Neo-Lithics* 2010(1):74–6.

Kolb, Michael J. 1999 Staple finance, ritual pig sacrifice, and ideological power in ancient Hawai'i. In *Complex Polities in the Ancient Tropical World*. E. A.

Bacus and L. J. Lucero, eds. Pp. 89–107. Archeological Papers of the American Anthropological Association. Arlington, VA: American Anthropological Association, Archeology Section.

König, Claus 1983 Interspecific and intraspecific competition for food among Old World vultures. In *Vulture Biology and Management*. S. R. Wilbur and J. A. Jackson, eds. Pp. 153–71. Berkeley: University of California Press.

Kornfeld, Marcel 1996 The big-game focus: Reinterpreting the archaeological record of Cantabrian Upper Paleolithic economy. *Current Anthropology* 37(4):629–57.

Kortlandt, Adriaan 1980 How might early hominids have defended themselves against large predators and food competitors? *Journal of Human Evolution* 9:79–112.

Kosmetatou, Elizabeth 1993 Horse sacrifices in Greece and Cyprus. *Journal of Prehistoric Religion* 7:31–41.

Kovacik, Joseph J. 2000 A faunal perspective on the spatial structuring of Anasazi everyday life in Chaco Canyon, New Mexico, U.S.A. In *Animal Bones, Human Societies*. P. A. Rowley-Conwy, ed. Pp. 133–41. Oxford: Oxbow.

Kowalski, Gary 1991 *The Souls of Animals*. Walpole, NH: Stillpoint.

Kozłowski, Janusz K., and Anta Montet-White 2001 The hunting-butchering tool-kit from Krakow-Spadzista: A Gravettian site in southern Poland. In *Proceedings of the International Conference on Mammoth Site Studies*. D. L. West, ed. Pp. 109–16. University of Kansas Publications in Anthropology. Lawrence, KS: University of Kansas Department of Anthropology.

Kramer, Carol 1982 *Village Ethnoarchaeology: Rural Iran in Archaeological Perspective*. New York: Academic Press.

Krantz, Grover S. 1968 A new method of counting mammal bones. *American Journal of Archaeology* 72:285–8.

Krasnokutsky, G. E. 1996 *Bison Hunting and Human Adaptation: A Case of Comparative Study of the Upper Palaeolithic of Southern Ukraine*. Odessa: Polis Press.

Krech, Shepard, III, ed. 1981 *Indians, Animals, and the Fur Trade: A Critique of Keepers of the Game*. Athens, GA: University of Georgia Press.

Krech, Shepard, III 1999 *The Ecological Indian: Myth and History*. New York: W. W. Norton & Co.

Kruuk, Hans 1972 *The Spotted Hyena: A Study of Predation and Social Behavior*. Chicago: University of Chicago Press.

Küchler, Susanne 2002 *Malanggan: Art, Memory and Sacrifice*. Oxford: Berg.

Kuhn, Steven L., and Catherine Sarther 2000 Food, lies, and paleoanthropology: Social theory and the evolution of sharing in humans. In *Social Theory in Archaeology*. M. B. Schiffer, ed. Pp. 79–96. Salt Lake City: University of Utah Press.

Kuijt, Ian 1994 Pre-Pottery Neolithic A settlement variability: Evidence for sociopolitical developments in the Southern Levant. *Journal of Mediterranean Archaeology* 7(2):41–68.

Kuijt, Ian 1996 Negotiating equality through ritual: A consideration of Late Natufian and Prepottery Neolithic A period mortuary practices. *Journal of Anthropological Archaeology* 15(4):313–36.

Kummer, Hans, and Fred Kurt 1968 Social units of a free-living population of hamadryas baboons. In *Man in Adaptation: The Biosocial Background*. Y. A. Cohen, ed. Pp. 115–21. Chicago: Aldine.

Kuper, Adam 1982 *Wives for Cattle: Bridewealth and Marriage in Southern Africa*. Boston: Routledge & Kegan Paul.

Kuznetsov, Pavel F. 2006 The emergence of Bronze Age chariots in eastern Europe. *Antiquity* 80(309):638–45.

Kvavadze, Eliso, Ofer Bar-Yosef, Anna Belfer-Cohen, Elisabetta Boaretto, Nino Jakeli, Zinovi Matskevich, and Tengiz Meshveliani 2009 30,000-year-old wild flax fibers. *Science* 325(5946):1359.

LaCapra, Dominick 2009 *History and its Limits: Human, Animal, Violence*. Ithaca: Cornell University Press.

LaMotta, Vincent M., and Michael B. Schiffer 1999 Formation processes of house floor assemblages. In *The Archaeology of Household Activities: Dwelling in the Past*. P. M. Allison, ed. Pp. 19–29. London: Routledge.

Laroulandie, Véronique 2005 Bird exploitation pattern: The case of Ptarmigan *Lagopus* sp. in the Upper Magdalenian site of La Vache (Ariège, France). In *Feathers, Grit and Symbolism: Birds and Humans in the Ancient Old and New Worlds*. G. Grupe and J. Peters, eds. Pp. 165–78. Documenta Archaeobiologiae. Rahden: Verlag Marie Leidorf.

Larsen, Clark S. 2006 The agricultural revolution as environmental catastrophe: Implications for health and lifestyle in the Holocene. *Quaternary International* 150(1):12–20.

Larson, Greger *et al.* 2010 Patterns of East Asian pig domestication, migration, and turnover revealed by modern and ancient DNA. *Proceedings of the National Academy of Sciences* 107(17):7686–91.

Lascu, Cristian, Florian Baciu, Mihai Gligan, and Serban Sarbu 1996 A Mousterian cave bear worship site in Transylvania, Roumania. *Journal of Prehistoric Religion* 10:17–30.

Laub, Richard S., and Gary Haynes 1998 Fluted points, mastodons, and evidence of Late-Pleistocene drought at the Hiscock site, western New York State. *Current Research in the Pleistocene* 15:32–4.

Laughlin, William S. 1968 Hunting: An integrating biobehavior system and its evolutionary importance. In *Man the Hunter*. R. B. Lee and I. DeVore, eds. Pp. 304–20. New York: Aldine.

Lauwerier, Roel C. G. M. 2004 The economic and non-economic animal: Roman depositions and offerings. In *Behaviour behind Bones: The Zooarchaeology of Ritual, Religion, Status and Identity*. S. J. O'Day, W. Van Neer, and A. Ervynck, eds. Pp. 66–72. Oxford: Oxbow.

Lawick-Goodall, Jane van, and Hugo van Lawick 1966 Use of tools by the Egyptian vulture (*Neophron percnopterus*). *Nature* 212(5069):1468–9.

Layard, John 1942 *Stone Men of Malekula*. London: Chatto & Windus.

Layton, Robert 2000 Shamanism, totemism and rock art: *Les Chamanes de la Préhistoire* in the context of rock art research. *Cambridge Archaeological Journal* 10:169–86.

Lazarovici, Georghe 1989 Das neolithische Heiligtum von Parţa. In *Neolithic of Southeastern Europe and its Near Eastern Connections*. S. Bökönyi, ed. Pp. 149–74. Varia Archaeologica Hungarica. Budapest: Institute of Archaeology of the Hungarian Academy of Sciences.

Leach, Edmund R. 1953 Bridewealth and the stability of marriage. *Man* 53:179–80.

Leach, Edmund R. 1964 Anthropological aspects of language: Animal categories and verbal abuse. In *New Directions in the Study of Language*. E. H. Lenneberg, ed. Pp. 23–63. Cambridge, MA: MIT Press.

Lechevallier, Monique, Richard H. Meadow, and Gonzague Quivron 1982 Dépôts d'animaux dans les sépultures néolithiques de Mehrgarh, Pakistan. *Paléorient* 8(1):99–106.

Lee, Richard B. 1968 What hunters do for a living, or, how to make out on scarce resources. In *Man the Hunter*. R. B. Lee and I. DeVore, eds. Pp. 30–48. New York: Aldine.

Lee, Richard B. 1993 *The Dobe Ju/'hoansi*. Second edition. Fort Worth: Harcourt Brace College Publishers.

Lee, Richard B., and Irven DeVore, eds. 1968 *Man the Hunter*. New York: Aldine.

Lee-Thorp, Julia A., Matt Sponheimer, and Nikolaas J. van der Merwe 2003 What do stable isotopes tell us about hominid dietary and ecological niches in the Pliocene? *International Journal of Osteoarchaeology* 13(1–2):104–13.

Lee-Thorp, Julia A., J. Francis Thackeray, and Nikolaas J. van der Merwe 2000 The hunters and the hunted revisited. *Journal of Human Evolution* 39(6):565–76.

Legge, Anthony J. 1972 Prehistoric exploitation of the gazelle in Palestine. In *Papers in Economic Prehistory: Studies by Members and Associates of the British Academy Major Research Project in the Early History of Agriculture*. E. S. Higgs, ed. Pp. 119–24. Cambridge: Cambridge University Press.

Legge, Anthony J. 1989 Milking the evidence: A reply to Entwistle and Grant. In *The Beginnings of Agriculture*. A. Milles, D. Williams, and N. Gardner, eds. Pp. 217–42. British Archaeological Reports, International Series. Oxford: Archaeopress.

Legge, Anthony J. 1996 The beginning of caprine domestication in Southwest Asia. In *The Origins and Spread of Agriculture and Pastoralism in Eurasia*. D. R. Harris, ed. Pp. 238–62. London: UCL Press.

Legge, Anthony J. 2005 Milk use in prehistory: The osteological evidence. In *The Zooarchaeology of Fats, Oils, Milk and Dairying*. J. Mulville and A. K. Outram, eds. Pp. 8–13. Oxford: Oxbow.

Legge, Anthony J., and Peter A. Rowley-Conwy 1988 *Star Carr Revisited: A Re-analysis of the Large Mammals.* London: University of London, Centre for Extra-Mural Studies.

Legge, Anthony J., John Williams, and Phoebe Williams 2000 Lambs to the slaughter: Sacrifice at two Roman temples in southern England. In *Animal Bones, Human Societies.* P. A. Rowley-Conwy, ed. Pp. 152–7. Oxford: Oxbow.

LeMoine, Genevieve M., James W. Helmer, and Don Hanna 1995 Altered states: Human-animal transformational images in Dorset art. In *The Symbolic Role of Animals in Archaeology.* K. Ryan and P. J. Crabtree, eds. Pp. 38–49. MASCA Research Papers in Science and Archaeology. Philadelphia: University of Pennsylvania, University Museum.

Lemonnier, Pierre 1993 Pigs as ordinary wealth: Technical logic, exchange and leadership in New Guinea. In *Technological Choices: Transformations in Material Cultures since the Neolithic.* P. Lemonnier, ed. Pp. 126–56. London: Routledge.

Lempert, Bernard 2000 *Critique de la Pensée Sacrificielle.* Paris: Seuil.

Lengerken, H. van 1955 *Ur, Hausrind und Mensch.* Wissenschaftliche Abhandlungen, No. 14. Berlin: Deutsche Akademie der Landwirtschaftswissenschaften.

Lentacker, An, Anton Ervynck, and Wim Van Neer 2004 Gastronomy or religion? The animal remains from the *mithraeum* at Tienen (Belgium). In *Behaviour behind Bones: The Zooarchaeology of Ritual, Religion, Status and Identity.* S. J. O'Day, W. Van Neer, and A. Ervynck, eds. Pp. 77–94. Oxford: Oxbow.

Leroi-Gourhan, André 1964 *Les Religions de la Préhistoire (Paléolithique).* Paris: Presses Universitaires de France.

Leroi-Gourhan, André 1965 *Préhistoire de l'Art Occidental.* Paris: Éditions d'art L. Mazenod.

Leroi-Gourhan, André 1966 Réflexions de méthode sur l'art páleolithique. *Bulletin de la Société Préhistorique Française* 63(1):35–49.

Leroi-Gourhan, André 1968 The evolution of Paleolithic art. *Scientific American* 218(2):58–70.

Leroi-Gourhan, André 1982 *The Dawn of European Art: An Introduction to Palaeolithic Cave Painting.* S. Champion, transl. Cambridge: Cambridge University Press.

Lev-Tov, Justin S. E. 2000 Late prehistoric faunal remains from new excavations at Tel Ali (northern Israel). In *Archaeozoology of the Near East IVA: Proceedings of the Fourth International Symposium on the Archaeozoology of Southwestern Asia and Adjacent Areas.* M. Mashkour, A. M. Choyke, H. Buitenhuis, and F. Poplin, eds. Pp. 208–17. ARC – Publicatie. Groningen: Center for Archeological Research and Consultancy.

Lev-Tov, Justin S. E., and Kevin McGeough 2007 Examining feasting in Late Bronze Age Syro-Palestine through ancient texts and bones. In *The Archaeology of Food and Identity.* K. C. Twiss, ed. Pp. 85–111. Center for Archaeological

Investigations Occasional Paper. Carbondale: Center for Archaeological Investigations, Southern Illinois University at Carbondale.

Lev-Yadun, Simcha, Avi Gopher, and Shahal Abbo 2000 The cradle of agriculture. *Science* 288(5471):1602–3.

Lévi-Strauss, Claude 1963 *Totemism*. R. Needham, transl. Boston: Beacon Press.

Lévi-Strauss, Claude 1965 Le triangle culinaire. *L'Arc* 26:19–29.

Lévi-Strauss, Claude 1988 *The Origin of Table Manners*. New York: Harper & Row.

Levy, Jacques, Annie Attia, and Gilles Buisson 2006 L'usage médical des cochons. In *De la Domestication au Tabou: Le Cas des Suidés au Proche-Orient Ancien*. B. Lion and C. Michel, eds. Pp. 195–203. Paris: De Boccard.

Lewis, Henry T. 1972 The role of fire in the domestication of plants and animals. *Man* 7(2):195–222.

Lewis, Krista 2007 Fields and tables of Sheba: Food, identity, and politics in early historic southern Arabia. In *The Archaeology of Food and Identity*. K. C. Twiss, ed. Pp. 192–217. Center for Archaeological Investigations Occasional Paper. Carbondale: Center for Archaeological Investigations, Southern Illinois University at Carbondale.

Lewis, Patrick J., María A. Gutierrez, and Eileen Johnson 2000 *Ondatra zibethicus* (Arvicolinae, Rodentia) dental microwear patterns as a potential tool for palaeoenvironmental reconstruction. *Journal of Archaeological Science* 27(9):789–98.

Lewis, R. Barry 1988 Old World dice in the protohistoric southern United States. *Current Anthropology* 29(5):759–67.

Lewis-Williams, J. David 1984 Ideological continuities in prehistoric southern Africa: The evidence of rock art. In *Past and Present in Hunter Gatherer Studies*. C. Schrire, ed. Pp. 225–52. New York: Academic Press.

Lewis-Williams, J. David 1988 "People of the eland": An archaeo-linguistic crux. In *Hunters and Gatherers 2: Property, Power and Ideology*. T. Ingold, D. Riches, and J. Woodburn, eds. Pp. 203–11. New York: Berg.

Lewis-Williams, J. David 1997 Agency, art and altered consciousness: A motif in French (Quercy) Upper Palaeolithic parietal art. *Antiquity* 71(274):810–30.

Lewis-Williams, J. David 1998 Wrestling with analogy: A methodological dilemma in Upper Palaeolithic art research. In *Reader in Archaeological Theory: Post-Processual and Cognitive Approaches*. D. S. Whitley, ed. Pp. 157–75. London: Routledge.

Lewis-Williams, J. David 2002 *The Mind in the Cave: Consciousness and the Origins of Art*. London: Thames & Hudson.

Lewis-Williams, J. David 2004 Constructing a cosmos: Architecture, power and domestication at Çatalhöyük. *Journal of Social Archaeology* 4(1):28–59.

Lewis-Williams, J. David, and Thomas A. Dowson 1988 The signs of all times: Entoptic phenomena in Upper Palaeolithic art. *Current Anthropology* 29(2):201–46.

Lewis-Williams, J. David, and Thomas A. Dowson 1993 On vision and power in the Neolithic: Evidence from the decorated monuments. *Current Anthropology* 34(1):55–65.

Lewis-Williams, J. David, and David C. Pearce 2005 *Inside the Neolithic Mind: Consciousness, Cosmos and the Realm of the Gods*. London: Thames & Hudson.

Li, Guoqiang 2007 Sacrifices et domestication des bovins dans la Chine antique sous les Shang postérieurs (vers 1300 à 1046 avant J.-C.). *Anthropozoologica* 42(1):19–46.

Lichter, Clemens 2001 *Untersuchungen zu den Bestattungssitten des Südosteuropäischen Neolithikums und Chalkolithikums*. Monographien (Internationale Interakademische Kommission für die Erforschung der Vorgeschichte des Balkans), No. 5. Mainz am Rhein: Verlag Philipp von Zabern.

Lidén, Kerstin, Gunilla Eriksson, Bengt Nordqvist, Anders Götherström, and Erik Bendixen 2004 "The wet and the wild followed by the dry and the tame" – or did they occur at the same time? Diet in Mesolithic-Neolithic southern Sweden. *Antiquity* 78(299):23–33.

Lieberman, Daniel E. 1993 Variability in hunter-gatherer seasonal mobility in the southern Levant: From the Mousterian to the Natufian. In *Hunting and Animal Exploitation in the Later Palaeolithic and Mesolithic of Eurasia*. G. L. Peterkin, H. M. Bricker, and P. A. Mellars, eds. Pp. 207–19. Archaeological Papers of the American Anthropological Association. Arlington, VA: American Anthropological Association.

Lieberman, Daniel E., and John J. Shea 1994 Behavioral differences between archaic and modern humans in the Levantine Mousterian. *American Anthropologist* 96(2):300–32.

Lienhardt, R. G. 1961 *Divinity and Experience: The Religion of the Dinka*. Oxford: Clarendon.

Linares, Olga F. 1976 Animals that were bad to eat were good to compete with: An analysis of the Conte style from ancient Panama. In *Ritual and Symbol in Native Central America*. P. Young and J. Howe, eds. Pp. 1–20. University of Oregon Anthropological Papers. Eugene: University of Oregon, Department of Anthropology.

Lindström, Jan 1988 The monopolization of a spirit: Livestock prestations during an Iramba funeral. In *On the Meaning of Death: Essays on Mortuary Rituals and Eschatological Beliefs*. S. Cederroth, C. Corlin, and J. Lindström, eds. Pp. 169–83. Uppsala Studies in Cultural Anthropology. Stockholm: Acta Universitatis Upsaliensis.

Lion, Brigitte, and Cécile Michel 2006 Les chasses royales néo-assyriennes: Textes et images. In *La Chasse: Pratiques Sociales et Symboliques*. I. Sidéra, E. Vila, and P. Erikson, eds. Pp. 217–33. Paris: De Boccard.

Llewelyn-Davies, Melissa 1981 Women, warriors, and patriarchs. In *Sexual Meanings: The Cultural Construction of Gender and Sexuality*. S. B. Ortner and H. Whitehead, eds. Pp. 330–58. Cambridge: Cambridge University Press.

Lloyd, Seton 1967 *Early Highland Peoples of Anatolia*. New York: McGraw-Hill.

Lobban, Richard A. 1998 Pigs in ancient Egypt. In *Ancestors for the Pigs: Pigs in Prehistory*. S. M. Nelson, ed. Pp. 137–48. MASCA Research Papers in Science and Archaeology. Philadelphia: University of Pennsylvania, University Museum.

Lockwood, Randall 1989 Anthropomorphism is not a four letter word. In *Perceptions of Animals in American Culture*. R. J. Hoage, ed. Pp. 41–56. Washington, DC: Smithsonian Institution Press.

Locock, Martin 1999 The analysis of historical bone assemblages: Is big beautiful? In *Current and Recent Research in Osteoarchaeology 2*. S. Anderson, ed. Pp. 8–11. Oxford: Oxbow.

Lohmann, Roger I. 2005 The afterlife of Asabano corpses: Relationships with the deceased in Papua New Guinea. *Ethnology* 44(2):189–206.

Lokuruka, Michael N. I. 2006 Meat is the meal and status is by meat: Recognition of rank, wealth, and respect through meat in Turkana culture. *Food and Foodways* 14(3–4):201–29.

Lorenz, Konrad 1966 *On Aggression*. M. K. Wilson, transl. New York: Bantam.

Louys, Julien, Darren Curnoe, and Haowen Tong 2007 Characteristics of Pleistocene megafauna extinctions in Southeast Asia. *Palaeogeography, Palaeoclimatology, Palaeoecology* 243(1–2):152–73.

Lovejoy, C. Owen 1981 The origin of man. *Science* 211(4480):341–50.

Lovett, E., M. Longworth Dames, D. F. de l'Hoste Ranking, C. Violet Turner, E. Linder, and E. C. Sykes 1901 The ancient and modern game of astragals. *Folklore* 12(3):280–93.

Loy, Thomas H., and Andrée R. Wood 1989 Blood residue analysis at Çayönü Tepesi, Turkey. *Journal of Field Archaeology* 16(4):451–60.

Lucas, Gavin M., and Thomas H. McGovern 2007 Bloody slaughter: Ritual decapitation and display at the Viking settlement of Hofstaðir, Iceland. *European Journal of Archaeology* 10(1):7–30.

Lucy, Sam J. 2000 *The Anglo-Saxon Way of Death: Burial Rites in Early England*. Thrupp, Stroud, Gloucestershire: Sutton.

Luff, Rosemary M. 1996 The 'bare bones' of identifying ritual behaviour in the archaeological record. In *Ritual Treatment of Human and Animal Remains: Proceedings of the First Meeting of the Osteoarchaeological Research Group Held in Cambridge on 8th October 1994*. S. Anderson and K. V. Boyle, eds. Pp. 1–10. Oxford: Oxbow.

Lundelius, Ernest L., Jr. 1989 The implications of disharmonious assemblages for Pleistocene extinctions. *Journal of Archaeological Science* 16(4):407–17.

Lupo, Karen D. 1998 Experimentally derived extraction rates for marrow: Implications for body part exploitation strategies of Plio-Pleistocene hominid scavengers. *Journal of Archaeological Science* 25(7):657–75.

Lupo, Karen D. 2001 Archaeological skeletal part profiles and differential transport: An ethnoarchaeological example from Hadza bone assemblages. *Journal of Anthropological Archaeology* 20(3):361–78.

Luxereau, Anne 1989 Animaux des hommes, animaux des dieux, animaux-dieux (région de Maradi, Niger). In *L'Animal dans les Pratiques Religieuses: Les Manifestations Materielles.* J.-D. Vigne, ed. Pp. 149–56. Anthropozoologica. Paris: Éditions du Centre National de la Recherche Scientifique.

Lyman, R. Lee 1984 Bone density and differential survivorship of fossil classes. *Journal of Anthropological Archaeology* 3:259–99.

Lyman, R. Lee 1987 On the analysis of vertebrate mortality profiles: Sample size, mortality type, and hunting pressure. *American Antiquity* 52(1):125–42.

Lyman, R. Lee 1994 *Vertebrate Taphonomy.* Cambridge: Cambridge University Press.

Lyman, R. Lee 2004 The concept of equifinality in taphonomy. *Journal of Taphonomy* 2(1).

Lyman, R. Lee, James M. Savelle, and Peter Whitridge 1992 Derivation and application of a meat utility index for Phocid Seals. *Journal of Archaeological Science* 19(5):531–55.

Lynch, Michael E. 1988 Sacrifice and the transformation of the animal body into a scientific object: Laboratory culture and ritual practice in the neurosciences. *Social Studies of Science* 18(2):265–89.

MacArthur, Robert H., and Edward O. Wilson 1967 *The Theory of Island Biogeography.* Princeton: Princeton University Press.

Mace, Ruth 1993 Transitions between cultivation and pastoralism in sub-Saharan Africa. *Current Anthropology* 34(4):363–82.

Mace, Ruth, and Alasdair Houston 1989 Pastoralist strategies for survival in unpredictable environments: A model of herd composition that maximises household viability. *Agricultural Systems* 31(2):185–204.

MacEachern, A. Scott, Claire Bourges, and Maureen Reeves 2001 Early horse remains from northern Cameroon. *Antiquity* 75(287):62–7.

MacIntyre, Martha 1984 The problem of the semi-alienable pig. *Canberra Anthropology* 7(1–2):109–22.

MacKinnon, Michael 2006 Supplying exotic animals for the Roman amphitheatre games: New reconstructions combining archaeological, ancient textual, historical and ethnographic data. *Mouseion* 6:137–61.

MacKinnon, Michael 2010 "Sick as a dog": Zooarchaeological evidence for pet dog health and welfare in the Roman world. *World Archaeology* 42(2):290–309.

MacKinnon, Michael, and Kyle Belanger 2006 In sickness and in health: Care for an arthritic Maltese dog from the Roman cemetery of Yasmina, Carthage, Tunisia. In *Dogs and People in Social, Working, Economic or Symbolic Interaction.* L. M. Snyder and E. A. Moore, eds. Pp. 38–43. Oxford: Oxbow.

MacPhee, Ross D. E., and Clare Flemming 1999 Requiem æternam: The last five hundred years of mammalian species extinctions. In *Extinctions in Near Time: Causes, Contexts, and Consequences.* R. D. E. MacPhee, ed. Pp. 333–71. New York: Kluwer Academic/Plenum Publishers.

MacPhee, Ross D. E., and P. A. Marx 1997 The 40,000-year plague: Humans, hyperdisease, and first-contact extinctions. In *Natural Change and Human Impact in Madagascar*. S. M. Goodman and B. D. Patterson, eds. Pp. 169–217. Washington, DC: Smithsonian Institution Press.

MacPhee, Ross D. E., Alexei N. Tikhonov, Dick Mol, Christian de Marliave, Hans van der Plicht, Alex D. Greenwood, Clare Flemming, and Larry D. Agenbroad 2002 Radiocarbon chronologies and extinction dynamics of the Late Quaternary mammalian megafauna of the Taimyr Peninsula, Russian Federation. *Journal of Archaeological Science* 29(9):1017–42.

MacQueen, J. G. 1978 Secondary burial at Çatal Hüyük. *NUMEN – International Review for the History of Religions* 25(3):226–39.

Madrigal, T. Cregg 2004 The derivation and application of white-tailed deer utility indices and return rates. *Journal of Taphonomy* 2.

Maher, Lisa A., Jay T. Stock, Sarah Finney, James J. N. Heywood, Preston T. Miracle, and Edward B. Banning 2011 A unique human-fox burial from a pre-Natufian cemetery in the Levant (Jordan). *PloS One* 6(1): e15815.

Mainland, Ingrid L., and Paul L. J. Halstead 2005 The diet and management of domestic sheep and goats at Neolithic Makriyalos. In *Diet and Health in Past Animal Populations: Current Research and Future Directions*. J. J. Davies, M. Fabiš, I. L. Mainland, M. P. Richards, and R. Thomas, eds. Pp. 104–12. Oxford: Oxbow.

Makarewicz, Cheryl A. 2009 Complex caprine harvesting practices and diversified hunting strategies: Integrated animal exploitation systems at Late Pre-Pottery Neolithic B 'Ain Jamman. In *Zooarchaeology and the Reconstruction of Cultural Systems: Case Studies from the Old World*. B. S. Arbuckle, C. A. Makarewicz, and A. L. Atici, eds. Pp. 79–101. Anthropozoologica, Vol. 44. Paris: L'Homme et l'Animal, Société de Recherche Interdisciplinaire.

Makkay, János 2001 *Textile Impressions and Related Finds of the Early Neolithic Körös Culture in Hungary*. Budapest: János Makkay.

Mallowan, Max E. L. 1946 Excavations in the Balih Valley, 1938. *Iraq* 8:111–59.

Maltby, J. Mark 1985 Patterns in faunal assemblage variability. In *Beyond Domestication in Prehistoric Europe*. G. W. W. Barker and C. S. Gamble, eds. Pp. 33–74. New York: Academic Press.

Manaseryan, Nina H. 2006 The stature of horses in Armenian Bronze and Early Iron Age burials. In *Horses and Humans: The Evolution of Human-Equine Relationships*. S. L. Olsen, S. Grant, A. M. Choyke, and L. Bartosiewicz, eds. Pp. 271–74. British Archeological Reports, International Series. Oxford: Archaeopress.

Manaseryan, Nina H., and L. Antonian 2000 Dogs of Armenia. In *Dogs through Time: An Archaeological Perspective*. S. J. Crockford, ed. Pp. 227–35. British Archaeological Reports, International Series. Oxford: Archaeopress.

Manhart, Henriette, and Katrin Vagedes 1999 Eine Hasendeponierung der Münchshöfener Kulturgruppe in Murr, Lkr. Freising/Oberbayern. In *Historia Animalium ex Ossibus: Festschrift für Angela von den Driesch.* C. Becker, H. Manhart, J. Peters, and J. Schibler, eds. Pp. 265–8. Rahden: Verlag Marie Leidorf.

Mannermaa, Kristiina 2008 Birds and burials at Ajvide (Gotland, Sweden) and Zvejnieki (Latvia) about 8000–3900 BP. *Journal of Anthropological Archaeology* 27(2):201–25.

Manwell, Clyde, and C. M. Ann Baker 1984 Domestication of the dog: Hunter, food, bed-warmer, or emotional object? *Zeitschrift für Tierzuchtung und Zuchtungsbiologie* 101:241–56.

March, Kathryn S. 1980 Deer, bears, and blood: A note on nonhuman animal response to menstrual odor. *American Anthropologist* 82(1):125–7.

Marciniak, Arkadiusz 2005a *Placing Animals in the Neolithic: Social Zooarchaeology of Prehistoric Farming Communities.* London: UCL Press.

Marciniak, Arkadiusz 2005b Social changes in the early European Neolithic: A taphonomy perspective. In *Biosphere to Lithosphere: New Studies in Vertebrate Taphonomy.* T. P. O'Connor, ed. Pp. 146–54. Oxford: Oxbow.

Marean, Curtis W. 1989 Sabertooth cats and their relevance for early hominid diet and evolution. *Journal of Human Evolution* 18:559–82.

Marean, Curtis W. 1997 Hunter-gatherer foraging strategies in tropical grasslands: Model building and testing in the East African Middle and Later Stone Age. *Journal of Anthropological Archaeology* 16(3):189–225.

Marean, Curtis W. *et al.* 2007 Early human use of marine resources and pigment in South Africa during the Middle Pleistocene. *Nature* 449(7164): 905–8.

Marean, Curtis W., and Celeste L. Ehrhardt 1995 Paleoanthropological and paleoecological implications of the taphonomy of a sabertooth's den. *Journal of Human Evolution* 29(6):515–47.

Marín Arroyo, Ana Belén 2011 Palaeolithic human subsistence in Mount Carmel (Israel). A taphonomic assessment of Middle and Early Upper Palaeolithic faunal remains from Tabun, Skhul and el-Wad. *International Journal of Osteoarchaeology* 21(2).

Marinatos, Nanno 1988 The imagery of sacrifice: Minoan and Greek. In *Early Greek Cult Practice.* R. Hägg, N. Marinatos, and G. Nordquist, eds. Pp. 9–20. Skrifter Utgivna av Svenska Institutet i Athen. Stockholm: Svenska Institutet i Athen.

Marinatos, Nanno 1989 The bull as an adversary: Some observations on bull-hunting and bull-leaping. *Ariadne* 5:23–32.

Marinelli, M. 1995 The bone artifacts of Ilıpınar. In *The Ilıpınar Excavations I.* J. J. Roodenberg, ed. Pp. 121–42. Istanbul: Nederlands Historisch-Archaeologisch Instituut.

Maringer, Johannes 1960 *The Gods of Prehistoric Man.* First American edition. M. Ilford, transl. New York: Knopf.

Marshall, Fiona 1993 Food sharing and the faunal record. In *From Bones to Behavior: Ethnoarchaeological and Experimental Contributions to the Interpretation of Faunal Remains.* J. Hudson, ed. Pp. 228–46. Carbondale, IL: Southern Illinois University, Center for Archaeological Investigations, Occasional Papers.

Marshall, Fiona 1994 Food sharing and body part representation in Okiek faunal assemblages. *Journal of Archaeological Science* 21(1):65–77.

Martin, Calvin 1978 *Keepers of the Game: Indian-Animal Relationships and the Fur Trade.* Berkeley: University of California Press.

Martin, Larry D., Virginia L. Naples, and H. Todd Wheeler 2001 Did mammoths have nonhuman predators? In *Proceedings of the International Conference on Mammoth Site Studies.* D. L. West, ed. Pp. 27–34. University of Kansas Publications in Anthropology. Lawrence, KS: University of Kansas Department of Anthropology.

Martin, Louise, and Nerissa Russell 2006 The equid remains from Neolithic Çatalhöyük, central Anatolia: A preliminary report. In *Horses and Humans: The Evolution of Human-Equine Relationships.* S. L. Olsen, S. Grant, A. M. Choyke, and L. Bartosiewicz, eds. Pp. 115–26. British Archeological Reports, International Series. Oxford: Archaeopress.

Martin, Louise, Nerissa Russell, and Denise Carruthers 2002 Animal remains from the central Anatolian Neolithic. In *The Neolithic of Central Anatolia: Internal Developments and External Relations during the 9th–6th Millennia cal BC.* F. Gérard and L. Thissen, eds. Pp. 193-206. Istanbul: Ege Yayınları.

Martin, Paul S. 1967 Prehistoric overkill. In *Pleistocene Extinctions: The Search for a Cause.* P. S. Martin and H. E. Wright, Jr., eds. Pp. 75–120. New Haven: Yale University Press.

Martin, Paul S. 2005 *Twilight of the Mammoths: Ice Age Extinctions and the Rewilding of America.* Berkeley: University of California Press.

Martin, Paul S., and David W. Steadman 1999 Prehistoric extinctions on islands and continents. In *Extinctions in Near Time: Causes, Contexts, and Consequences.* R. D. E. MacPhee, ed. Pp. 17–52. New York: Kluwer Academic/Plenum Publishers.

Martinez-Lira, Patricia, Eduardo Corona M., Joaquin Arroyo-Cabrales, and John P. Carpenter 2005 Bird bundles from La Playa, Sonora, Mexico. In *Feathers, Grit and Symbolism: Birds and Humans in the Ancient Old and New Worlds.* G. Grupe and J. Peters, eds. Pp. 201–6. Documenta Archaeobiologiae. Rahden: Verlag Marie Leidorf.

Marvin, Garry 1994 *Bullfight.* Urbana: University of Illinois Press.

Marx, Karl 1936[1890] *Capital: A Critique of Political Economy.* New York: Random House.

Marzluff, John M., and Tony Angell 2005 *In the Company of Crows and Ravens.* New Haven: Yale University Press.

Mashkour, Marjan, Olivier Lecomte, and Véra Eisenmann 1998 Animal sacrifice at the temple of E. babbar at Larsa (Iraq) in the Hellenistic period: The evidence from bones. *Anthropozoologica* 27:51–66.

Mason, Otis T. 1966[1895] *The Origin of Invention: A Study of Industry Among Primitive Peoples.* Cambridge, MA: MIT Press.

Mason, Sarah L. R. 2000 Fire and Mesolithic subsistence – Managing oaks for acorns in northwest Europe? *Palaeogeography, Palaeoclimatology, Palaeoecology* 164(1–4):139–50.

Masseti, Marco 2009 The wild goats *Capra aegagrus* Erxleben, 1777 of the Mediterranean Sea and the Eastern Atlantic Ocean islands. *Mammal Review* 39(2):141–57.

Masseti, Marco, Alberto Cavallaro, Elena Pecchioli, and Cristiano Vernesi 2006 Artificial occurrence of the fallow deer, *Dama dama dama* (L., 1758), on the island of Rhodes (Greece): Insight from mtDNA analysis. *Human Evolution* 21(2):167–75.

Masseti, Marco, and Anna Maria De Marinis 2008 Prehistoric and historic artificial dispersal of lagomorphs on the Mediterranean islands. In *Lagomorph Biology: Evolution, Ecology, and Conservation.* P. C. Alves, N. Ferrand, and K. Hackländer, eds. Pp. 13–25. Berlin: Springer.

Masson, Marilyn A. 1999 Animal resource manipulation in ritual and domestic contexts at Postclassic Maya communities. *World Archaeology* 31(1):93–120.

Mateescu, Corneliu 1975 Remarks on cattle breeding and agriculture in the Middle and Late Neolithic on the Lower Danube. *Dacia* 19:13–18.

Mauss, Marcel 1967 *The Gift: Forms and Functions of Exchange in Archaic Societies.* I. Cunnison, transl. New York: W. W. Norton & Co.

Maxwell, H. A. 1967 Red deer and forestry with special reference to the Highlands of Scotland. *Forestry* (supplement):37–43.

McBrearty, Sally, and Alison S. Brooks 2000 The revolution that wasn't: A new interpretation of the origin of modern human behavior. *Journal of Human Evolution* 39(5):453–563.

McBrearty, Sally, and Marc Moniz 1991 Prostitutes or providers? Hunting, tool use and sex roles in earliest *Homo.* In *The Archaeology of Gender.* D. Walde and N. D. Willows, eds. Pp. 71–82. Calgary: Archaeological Association of the University of Calgary.

McCabe, Richard E. 1982 Elk and Indian: Historical values and perspectives. In *Elk of North America: Ecology and Management.* J. W. Thomas and D. E. Toweill, eds. Pp. 61–123. Harrisburg: Stackpole.

McCall, Grant S. 2007 Add shamans and stir? A critical review of the shamanism model of forager rock art production. *Journal of Anthropological Archaeology* 26(2):224–33.

McCarthy, Frederick D., and Margaret McArthur 1960 Food consumption and dietary levels of groups of Aborigines living on naturally occurring foods. In *Records of the American-Australian Scientific Expedition to Arnhem Land.* C. P. Mountford, ed. Pp. 90–135. Vol. 2. Melbourne: Melbourne University Press.

McCaughey, Martha 2007 *The Caveman Mystique: Pop-Darwinism and the Debates over Sex, Violence, and Science.* London: Routledge.

McClenon, James 2001 *Wondrous Healing: Shamanism, Human Evolution, and the Origin of Religion*. DeKalb: Northern Illinois University Press.

McCormick, Finbar 1992 Early faunal evidence for dairying. *Oxford Journal of Archaeology* 11(2):201–9.

McCormick, Finbar 2002 The distribution of meat in a hierarchical society: The Irish evidence. In *Consuming Passions and Patterns of Consumption*. P. T. Miracle and N. Milner, eds. Pp. 25–31. Cambridge: McDonald Institute for Archaeological Research.

McCorriston, Joy 1997 The fiber revolution: Textile extensification, alienation, and social stratification in ancient Mesopotamia. *Current Anthropology* 38(4):517–49.

McCorriston, Joy, and Frank Hole 1991 The ecology of seasonal stress and the origins of agriculture in the Near East. *American Anthropologist* 93(1):46–69.

McCracken, Robert D. 1971 Lactase deficiency: An example of dietary evolution. *Current Anthropology* 12(4/5):479–517.

McDiarmid, Archibald 1987 Some disorders of red deer (*Cervus elaphus*) in Scotland. In *Wild Deer: Culling, Conservation and Management*. A. J. d. Nahlik, ed. Pp. 224–9. Southampton: Ashford Press.

McDonaugh, Christian 1997 Breaking the rules: Changes in food acceptability among the Tharu of Nepal. In *Food Preferences and Taste: Continuity and Change*. H. Macbeth, ed. Pp. 155–66. Providence: Berghahn Books.

McFarlane, Donald A. 1999 A comparison of methods for the probabilistic determination of vertebrate extinction chronologies. In *Extinctions in Near Time: Causes, Contexts, and Consequences*. R. D. E. MacPhee, ed. Pp. 95–103. New York: Kluwer Academic/Plenum Publishers.

McGovern, Patrick E. 2003 *Ancient Wine: The Search for the Origins of Viniculture*. Princeton: Princeton University Press.

McGowan, Kevin J. 1996 Family lives of the uncommon American crow. *Cornell Plantations* 51(1):1–4.

McGrew, William C. 1981 The female chimpanzee as a human evolutionary prototype. In *Woman the Gatherer*. F. Dahlberg, ed. Pp. 35–73. New Haven: Yale University Press.

McGrew, William C. 1996 Dominance status, food sharing, and reproductive success in chimpanzees. In *Food and the Status Quest: An Interdisciplinary Perspective*. P. Wiessner and W. Schiefenhövel, eds. Pp. 39–45. Providence: Berghahn Books.

McGuire, Kelly R., and William R. Hildebrandt 2005 Re-thinking Great Basin foragers: Prestige hunting and costly signaling during the Middle Archaic period. *American Antiquity* 70(4):695–712.

McKell, Sheila M. 1998 An axe to grind: More ripping yarns from Australian prehistory. In *Reader in Gender Archaeology*. K. Hays-Gilpin and D. S. Whitley, eds. Pp. 107–14. London: Routledge.

McNiven, Ian J., and Ricky Feldman 2003 Ritually orchestrated seascapes: Hunting magic and dugong bone mounds in Torres Strait, NE Australia. *Cambridge Archaeological Journal* 13(2):169–94.

McOmish, David 1996 East Chisenbury: Ritual and rubbish at the British Bronze Age-Iron Age transition. *Antiquity* 70(267):68–76.

Meadow, Richard H. 1975 Mammal remains from Hajji Firuz: A study in methodology. In *Archaeozoological Studies.* A. T. Clason, ed. Pp. 265–83. Amsterdam: North Holland.

Meadow, Richard H. 1978 Effects of context on the interpretation of faunal remains: A case study. In *Approaches to Faunal Analysis in the Middle East.* R. H. Meadow and M. A. Zeder, eds. Pp. 169–80. Peabody Museum Bulletin. Cambridge: Peabody Museum, Harvard University.

Meadow, Richard H. 1980 Animal bones: Problems for the archaeologist together with some possible solutions. *Paléorient* 6:65–77.

Meadow, Richard H. 1984 A camel skeleton from Wheeler's excavations at Mohenjo-Daro. In *Frontiers of the Indus Civilization: Sir Mortimer Wheeler Memorial Volume.* B. B. Lal and S. P. Gupta, eds. Pp. 133–9. Delhi: Books and Books.

Meadow, Richard H. 1989 Osteological evidence for the process of animal domestication. In *The Walking Larder: Patterns of Domestication, Pastoralism, and Predation.* J. Clutton-Brock, ed. Pp. 80–90. London: Unwin Hyman.

Meadow, Richard H. 1991 Faunal remains and urbanism at Harappa. In *Harappa Excavations 1986–1990: A Multidisciplinary Approach to Third Millennium Urbanism.* R. H. Meadow, ed. Pp. 89–106. Monographs in World Archaeology. Madison, WI: Prehistory Press.

Meadow, Richard H. 1993 Animal domestication in the Middle East: A revised view from the eastern margin. In *Harappan Civilization.* G. L. Possehl, ed. Pp. 295–320. New Delhi: Oxford & IBH.

Meadow, Richard H. 1996 The origins and spread of agriculture and pastoralism in northwestern South Asia. In *The Origins and Spread of Agriculture and Pastoralism in Eurasia.* D. R. Harris, ed. Pp. 390–412. London: UCL Press.

Mech, L. David, L. D. Frenzel, P. D. Karns, and D. W. Kuehen 1970 Mandibular dental anomalies in white tailed deer from Minnesota. *Journal of Mammalogy* 51:804–6.

Médard, Fabienne 2006 *Les Activités de Filage au Néolithique sur le Plateau Suisse: Analyse Technique, Économique et Sociale.* CRA-Monographies, No. Paris: Éditions du Centre National de la Recherche Scientifique.

Meggitt, Mervyn J. 1965 The association between Australian Aborigines and dingoes. In *Man, Culture, and Animals: The Role of Animals in Human Ecological Adjustments.* A. Leeds and A. P. Vayda, eds. Pp. 7–26. Washington, DC: American Association for the Advancement of Science.

Melamed, Yoel, Uzi Plitmann, and Mordechai E. Kislev 2008 *Vicia peregrina*: An edible early Neolithic legume. *Vegetation History and Archaeobotany* 17(1):29–34.

Mellaart, James 1962 Excavations at Çatal Hüyük, 1961: First preliminary report. *Anatolian Studies* 12:41–65.

Mellaart, James 1963 Excavations at Çatal Hüyük, 1962: Second preliminary report. *Anatolian Studies* 13:43–103.

Mellaart, James 1964 Excavations at Çatal Hüyük, 1963: Third preliminary report. *Anatolian Studies* 14:39–119.

Mellaart, James 1966a Chatal Huyuk: The world's oldest city. *The Illustrated London News* May 28, 1966:26–7.

Mellaart, James 1966b Excavations at Çatal Hüyük, 1965: Fourth preliminary report. *Anatolian Studies* 16:165–91.

Mellaart, James 1967 *Çatal Hüyük: A Neolithic Town in Anatolia*. London: Thames & Hudson.

Mellaart, James 1970 *Excavations at Hacılar*. Edinburgh: Edinburgh University Press.

Mellaart, James 1984 Animals in the Neolithic art of Çatal Hüyük and Hacılar and their religious significance. In *L'Animal, l'Homme, le Dieu dans le Proche-Orient Ancien: Actes du Colloque de Cartigny* 1981. P. Borgeaud, Y. Christie, and I. Urio, eds. Pp. 39–46. Les Cahiers du CEPOA. Leuven: Peeters.

Mellars, Paul A. 1976 Fire ecology, animal populations, and man: A study of some ecological relationships. *Proceedings of the Prehistoric Society* 42:15–46.

Mellars, Paul A. 2004 Reindeer specialization in the early Upper Palaeolithic: The evidence from south west France. *Journal of Archaeological Science* 31(5):613–17.

Mellars, Paul A. 2006 Why did modern human populations disperse from Africa ca. 60,000 years ago? A new model. *Proceedings of the National Academy of Sciences* 103(25):9381–6.

Mellink, Machteld J. 1956 *A Hittite Cemetery at Gordion*. University Museum Monograph. Philadelphia: University of Pennsylvania, University Museum.

Meltzer, David J. 1995 Clocking the first Americans. *Annual Review of Anthropology* 24:21–45.

Meltzer, David J. 2006 *Folsom: New Archaeological Investigations of a Classic Paleoindian Bison Kill*. Berkeley: University of California Press.

Meltzer, David J., Donald K. Grayson, Gerardo Ardila, Alex W. Barker, Dena F. Dincauze, C. Vance Haynes, Jr., Francisco Mena, Lautaro Núñez, and Dennis J. Stanford 1997 On the Pleistocene antiquity of Monte Verde, southern Chile. *American Antiquity* 62(4):659–63.

Meltzer, David J., Lawrence C. Todd, and Vance T. Holliday 2002 The Folsom (Paleoindian) type site: Past investigations, current studies. *American Antiquity* 67(1):5–36.

Mengoni-Goñalons, Guillermo L. 2008 Camelids in ancient Andean societies: A review of the zooarchaeological evidence. *Quaternary International* 185(1):59–68.

Méniel, Patrice 1989 Les animaux dans les pratiques religieuses des Gaulois. In *L'Animal dans les Pratiques Religieuses: Les Manifestations Materielles*. J.-D. Vigne, ed. Pp. 87–97. Anthropozoologica. Paris: Éditions du Centre National de la Recherche Scientifique.

Méniel, Patrice 1992 *Les Sacrifices d'Animaux chez les Gaulois*. Paris: Éditions Errance.

Merchant, Carolyn 1980 *The Death of Nature: Women, Ecology, and the Scientific Revolution*. San Francisco: Harper & Row.

Merrifield, Ralph 1987 *The Archaeology of Ritual and Magic*. London: Batsford.

Méry, Sophie, Vincent Charpentier, Ginette Auxiette, and E. Pelle 2009 A dugong bone mound: The Neolithic ritual site on Akab in Umm al-Quwain, United Arab Emirates. *Antiquity* 83(321):696–708.

Metailie, Jean-Paul 1981 *Le Feu Pastoral dans les Pyrénées Centrales (Barousse, Oueil, Larboust)*. Paris: Éditions du Centre National de la Recherche Scientifique.

Metcalfe, Duncan, and Kevin T. Jones 1988 A reconsideration of animal body-part utility indices. *American Antiquity* 53(3):486–504.

Meyer, Melissa 2005 *Thicker than Water: The Origins of Blood as Ritual and Symbol*. London: Routledge.

Michell, E. B. 1900 *The Art and Practice of Hawking*. London: Methuen.

Middleton, H. S. 1975 Two pathological conditions in the Muntjac deer (*Muntiacus reevesi*). *Journal of Zoology* 176:271–95.

Mignon-Grasteau, Sandrine *et al.* 2005 Genetics of adaptation and domestication in livestock. *Livestock Production Science* 93(1):3–14.

Milisauskas, Sarunas, and Janusz Kruk 1991 Utilization of cattle for traction during the later Neolithic in southeastern Poland. *Antiquity* 65:562–6.

Miller, George R., and Richard L. Burger 1995 Our father the cayman, our dinner the llama: Animal utilization at Chavín de Huántar, Peru. *American Antiquity* 60(3):421–58.

Miller, Gifford H., Marilyn L. Fogel, John W. Magee, Michael K. Gagan, Simon J. Clarke, and Beverly J. Johnson 2005 Ecosystem collapse in Pleistocene Australia and a human role in megafaunal extinction. *Science* 309(5732):287–90.

Miller, Gifford H., John W. Magee, Beverly J. Johnson, Marilyn L. Fogel, Nigel A. Spooner, Malcolm T. McCulloch, and Linda K. Ayliffe 1999 Pleistocene extinction of *Genyornis newtoni*: Human impact on Australian megafauna. *Science* 283(5399):205–8.

Miller, Susanne J. 1983 Osteo-archaeology of the mammoth-bison assemblage at Owl Cave, the Wasden Site, Idaho. In *Carnivores, Human Scavengers & Predators: A Question of Bone Technology*. G. M. LeMoine and A. S.

MacEachern, eds. Pp. 39–53. Calgary: Archaeological Association of the University of Calgary.

Mills, Barbara J. 2007 Performing the feast: Visual display and suprahousehold commensalism in the Puebloan Southwest. *American Antiquity* 72(2):210–39.

Milner, Nicky 2002 Oysters, cockles and kitchenmiddens: Changing practices at the Mesolithic/Neolithic transition. In *Consuming Passions and Patterns of Consumption*. P. T. Miracle and N. Milner, eds. Pp. 89–96. McDonald Institute Monographs. Cambridge: McDonald Institute for Archaeological Research.

Milner, Nicky, Oliver E. Craig, Geoffrey N. Bailey, K. Pedersen, and S. H. Andersen 2004 Something fishy in the Neolithic? A re-evaluation of stable isotope analysis of Mesolithic and Neolithic coastal populations. *Antiquity* 78(299):9–22.

Milo, Richard G. 1998 Evidence for hominid predation at Klasies River Mouth, South Africa, and its implications for the behaviour of early modern humans. *Journal of Archaeological Science* 25:99–133.

Milton, Kay 2005 Anthropomorphism or egomorphism? The perception of non-human persons by human ones. In *Animals in Person: Cultural Perspectives on Human-Animal Intimacy*. J. Knight, ed. Pp. 255–71. Oxford: Berg.

Minnegal, Monica 1997 Consumption and production: Sharing and the social construction of use-value. *Current Anthropology* 38(1):25–48.

Miracle, Preston T. 2005 Late Mousterian subsistence and cave use in Dalmatia: The zooarchaeology of Mujina Pećina, Croatia. *International Journal of Osteoarchaeology* 15(2):84–105.

Miracle, Preston T., and Stašo Forenbaher 2005 Neolithic and Bronze Age herders of Pupićina Cave, Croatia. *Journal of Field Archaeology* 30(3):255–81.

Mitani, John C., and David P. Watts 1999 Demographic influences on the hunting behavior of chimpanzees. *American Journal of Physical Anthropology* 109:439–54.

Mitani, John C., and David P. Watts 2001 Why do chimpanzees hunt and share meat? *Animal Behaviour* 61(5):915–24.

Mitchell, Brian, William Grant, and John Cubby 1981 Notes on the performance of Red deer, *Cervus elaphus*, in a woodland habitat. *Journal of Zoology* 194(2):279–84.

Mitchell, Brian, Brian W. Staines, and David Welch 1977 *Ecology of Red Deer: A Research Review Relevant to their Management in Scotland*. Banchory: Institute of Terrestrial Ecology.

Mithen, Steven J. 1988 To hunt or to paint: Animals and art in the Upper Palaeolithic. *Man* 23(4):671–95.

Mithen, Steven J. 1993 Simulating mammoth hunting and extinction: Implications for the late Pleistocene of the Central Russian Plain. In *Hunting and*

*Animal Exploitation in the Later Palaeolithic and Mesolithic of Eurasia.* G. L. Peterkin, H. M. Bricker, and P. A. Mellars, eds. Pp. 163–78. Archaeological Papers of the American Anthropological Association. Washington, DC: American Anthropological Association.

Mithen, Steven J. 1997 Simulating mammoth hunting and extinctions: Implications for North America. In *Time, Process, and Structured Transformation in Archaeology.* S. E. van der Leeuw and J. McGlade, eds. Pp. 176–215. London: Routledge.

Mithen, Steven J. 2007 Did farming arise from a misapplication of social intelligence? *Philosophical Transactions of the Royal Society of London. Series B, Biological Sciences* 362(1480):705–18.

Moholy-Nagy, Hattula 2004 Vertebrates in Tikal burials and caches. In *Maya Zooarchaeology: New Directions in Method and Theory.* K. F. Emery, ed. Pp. 193–205. Los Angeles: Cotsen Institute of Archaeology, University of California, Los Angeles.

Monks, Gregory G. 2004 An oil utility index for whale bones. In *The Exploitation and Cultural Importance of Sea Mammals.* G. G. Monks, ed. Pp. 138–53. Oxford: Oxbow.

Monks of New Skete 2002 *How to Be Your Dog's Best Friend: The Classic Training Manual for Dog Owners.* Second edition. Boston: Little, Brown.

Montagna, William 1965 The skin. *Scientific American* 212(2):56–66.

Moore, Henrietta L. 1982 The interpretation of spatial patterning in settlement residues. In *Symbolic and Structural Archaeology.* I. Hodder, ed. Pp. 74–9. Cambridge: Cambridge University Press.

Moore, Omar Khayyam 1957 Divination: A new perspective. *American Anthropologist* 59(1):69–74.

Morales, Edmundo 1995 *The Guinea Pig: Healing, Food, and Ritual in the Andes.* Tucson: University of Arizona Press.

Morales Muñiz, Lola C., and Arturo Morales Muñiz 1995 The Spanish bullfight: Some historical aspects, traditional interpretations, and comments of archaeozoological interest for the study of the ritual slaughter. In *The Symbolic Role of Animals in Archaeology.* K. Ryan and P. J. Crabtree, eds. Pp. 91–105. MASCA Research Papers in Science and Archaeology. Philadelphia: University of Pennsylvania, University Museum.

Morelli, Laura, Daniela Contu, Federico Santoni, Michael B. Whalen, Paolo Francalacci, and Francesco Cucca 2010 A comparison of Y-chromosome variation in Sardinia and Anatolia is more consistent with cultural rather than demic diffusion of agriculture. *PloS One* 5(4):1–10.

Morey, Darcy F. 1992 Size, shape and development in the evolution of the domestic dog. *Journal of Archaeological Science* 19:181–204.

Morey, Darcy F. 1994 The early evolution of the domestic dog. *American Scientist* 82:336–47.

Morey, Darcy F. 2006 Burying key evidence: The social bond between dogs and people. *Journal of Archaeological Science* 33(2):158–75.

Morey, Darcy F. 2010 *Dogs: Domestication and the Development of a Social Bond*. New York: Cambridge University Press.

Morey, Darcy F., and Michael D. Wiant 1992 Early Holocene domestic dog burials from the North American Midwest. *Current Anthropology* 33(2): 224–9.

Morgan, Elaine 1972 *The Descent of Woman*. New York: Stein and Day.

Morgan, Elaine 1982 *The Aquatic Ape*. New York: Stein and Day.

Morgan, Gary S., and Charles A. Woods 1986 Extinction and the zoogeography of West Indian land mammals. *Biological Journal of the Linnean Society* 28:167–203.

Morin, Eugène 2007 Fat composition and Nunamiut decision-making: A new look at the marrow and bone grease indices. *Journal of Archaeological Science* 34(1):69–82.

Morris, Brian 1998 *The Power of Animals: An Ethnography*. Oxford: Berg.

Morris, Brian 2000 *Animals and Ancestors: An Ethnography*. Oxford: Berg.

Morris, Brian 2004 *Insects and Human Life*. English edition. Oxford: Berg.

Morris, Desmond 1967 *The Naked Ape*. New York: McGraw-Hill.

Morris, Desmond 2002 *Dogs: The Ultimate Dictionary of over 1,000 Dog Breeds*. North Pomfret, VT: Trafalgar Square.

Morter, Jon, and John E. Robb 1998 Space, gender and architecture in the southern Italian Neolithic. In *Gender and Italian Archaeology: Challenging the Stereotypes*. R. D. Whitehouse, ed. Pp. 83–94. Accordia Specialist Studies on Italy. London: Accordia Research Institute, University of London.

Moseley, Michael E., Donna J. Nash, Patrick J. Williams, Susan D. deFrance, Ana Miranda, and Mario Ruales 2005 Burning down the brewery: Establishing and evacuating an ancient imperial colony at Cerro Baúl, Peru. *Proceedings of the National Academy of Sciences* 102(48):17264–71.

Moses, Sharon K. 2008 Çatalhöyük's foundation burials: Ritual child sacrifice or convenient deaths? In *Babies Reborn: Infant/Child Burials in Pre- and Protohistory*. K. Bacvarov, ed. Pp. 45–52. British Archaeological Reports, International Series. Oxford: Archaeopress.

Moulherat, Christophe, Margareta Tengberg, Jérôme-F. Haquet, and Benoît Mille 2002 First evidence of cotton at Neolithic Mehrgarh, Pakistan: Analysis of mineralized fibres from a copper bead. *Journal of Archaeological Science* 29(12):1393–401.

Muir, Robert J., and Jonathan C. Driver 2004 Identifying ritual use of animals in the northern American Southwest. In *Behaviour behind Bones: The Zooarchaeology of Ritual, Religion, Status and Identity*. S. J. O'Day, W. Van Neer, and A. Ervynck, eds. Pp. 128–43. Oxford: Oxbow.

Müller, Hanns-Hermann 1984 Zoological and historical interpretation of bones from food and sacrifices in early Medieval times. In *Animals and Archaeology: 4. Husbandry in Europe*. C. Grigson and J. Clutton-Brock, eds. Pp. 187–93. British Archaeological Reports, International Series. Oxford: British Archaeological Reports.

Müller, Hanns-Hermann 1993 Falconry in central Europe in the Middle Ages. *Exploitation des Animaux Sauvages à travers le Temps: IVe Colloque International de l'Homme et l'Animal.* J. Desse and F. Audoin-Rouzeau, eds. Pp. 431–7. Juan-les-Pins: Éditions APCDA-CNRS.

Müller, Hanns-Hermann, and Ralf-Jürgen Prilloff 2006 Zur Geschichte der Avifauna in Sachsen-Anhalt auf Grund subfossiler Nachweise. In *Archaeozoological Studies in Honour of Alfredo Riedel.* U. Tecchiati and B. Sala, eds. Pp. 99–110. Bolzano: Province of Bolzano.

Mullin, Molly H. 1999 Mirrors and windows: Sociocultural studies of human-animal relationships. *Annual Review of Anthropology* 28:201–24.

Mullin, Molly H. 2007 Feeding the animals. In *Where the Wild Things Are Now: Domestication Reconsidered.* R. Cassidy and M. H. Mullin, eds. Pp. 277–303. Oxford: Berg.

Mundy, Peter J., Duncan Butchart, John Ledger, and Steven Piper 1992 *The Vultures of Africa.* London: Academic Press.

Munro, Natalie D., and Leore Grosman 2010 Early evidence (ca. 12,000 B.P.) for feasting at a burial cave in Israel. *Proceedings of the National Academy of Sciences* 107(35):15362–6.

Munro, Robert 1902 On the prehistoric horses of Europe and their supposed domestication in Paleolithic times. *Archaeological Journal* 59:109–43.

Munson, Patrick J. 2000 Age-correlated differential destruction of bones and its effect on archaeological mortality profiles of domestic sheep and goats. *Journal of Archaeological Science* 27(5):391–407.

Munson, Patrick J., and Rexford C. Garniewicz 2003 Age-mediated survivorship of ungulate mandibles and teeth in canid-ravaged faunal assemblages. *Journal of Archaeological Science* 30(4):405–16.

Murphy, Kimmarie A. 2010 A meal on the hoof or wealth in the kraal? Stable isotopes at Kgaswe and Taukome in eastern Botswana. *International Journal of Osteoarchaeology.*

Murray, Maribeth 2000 A zooarchaeological approach to Arctic prehistory. In *Animal Bones, Human Societies.* P. A. Rowley-Conwy, ed. Pp. 58–64. Oxford: Oxbow.

Musil, Rudolf 2000 Evidence for the domestication of wolves in Central European Magdalenian sites. In *Dogs through Time: An Archaeological Perspective.* S. J. Crockford, ed. Pp. 21–8. British Archaeological Reports, International Series. Oxford: Archaeopress.

Nadasdy, Paul 2003 *Hunters and Bureaucrats: Power, Knowledge, and Aboriginal-State Relations in the Southwest Yukon.* Vancouver: UBC Press.

Nadasdy, Paul 2007 The gift in the animal: The ontology of hunting and human-animal sociality. *American Ethnologist* 34(1):25–43.

Nadel, Dani, Avinoam Danin, Ella Werker, Tamar Schick, Mordechai E. Kislev, and K. Stewart 1994 19,000-year-old twisted fibers from Ohalo II. *Current Anthropology* 35(4):451–8.

Nagaoka, Lisa 2001 Using diversity indices to measure changes in prey choice at the Shag River Mouth site, southern New Zealand. *International Journal of Osteoarchaeology* 11(1–2):101–11.

Nagaoka, Lisa 2005 Declining foraging efficiency and moa carcass exploitation in southern New Zealand. *Journal of Archaeological Science* 32(9):1328–38.

Nahlik, Andrew J. de 1987 *Wild Deer: Culling, Conservation and Management.* Second edition. Southampton: Ashford Press.

Nair, K. Narayanan 1987 Animal protein consumption and the sacred cow complex in India. In *Food and Evolution: Toward a Theory of Human Food Habits.* M. Harris and E. B. Ross, eds. Pp. 445–54. Philadelphia: Temple University Press.

Nakhai, Beth A. 2001 *Archaeology and the Religions of Canaan and Israel.* ASOR Books, No. 7. Boston: American Schools of Oriental Research.

Neck, Raymond W. 1995 Extirpation of Quaternary molluscs of the southern High Plains – An ecological model of favorable activity periods. In *Ancient Peoples and Landscapes.* E. Johnson, ed. Pp. 283–7. Lubbock, TX: Museum of Texas Tech University.

Needham, Stuart P., and Sheridan Bowman 2005 Flesh-hooks, technological complexity and the Atlantic Bronze Age feasting complex. *European Journal of Archaeology* 8(2):93–136.

Negahban, Ezat O. 1979 A brief report on the painted building of Zaghe (late 7th-early 6th millennium B.C.). *Paléorient* 5:239–50.

Nelson, Richard K. 1993 Searching for the lost arrow: Physical and spiritual ecology in the hunter's world. In *The Biophilia Hypothesis.* S. R. Kellert and E. O. Wilson, eds. Pp. 201–28. Washington, DC: Island Press.

Nelson, Richard K. 1997 *Heart and Blood: Living with Deer in America.* New York: Alfred A. Knopf.

Nelson, Sarah M. 2002 Performing power in early China: Examples from the Shang dynasty and the Hongshan culture. In *The Dynamics of Power.* M. O'Donovan, ed. Pp. 151–67. Occasional Paper. Carbondale: Center for Archaeological Investigations, Southern Illinois University at Carbondale.

Nelson, Sarah M. 2003 Feasting the ancestors in early China. In *The Archaeology and Politics of Food and Feasting in Early States and Empires.* T. L. Bray, ed. Pp. 65–89. New York: Kluwer Academic/Plenum Publishers.

Nesbitt, R. Mark 2002 When and where did domesticated cereals first occur in southwest Asia? In *The Dawn of Farming in the Near East.* R. T. J. Cappers and S. Bottema, eds. Pp. 113–32. Studies in Early Near Eastern Production, Subsistence, and Environment. Berlin: Ex Oriente.

Nikolandić, Đuro 1968 Ekološke karakteristike populacije srna na Belju. *Jelen* 7:73–95.

Nilsson, Martin P. 1927 *The Minoan-Mycenaean Religion and its Survival in Greek Religion.* Lund: C. W. K. Gleerup.

Nissen, Hans J. 1988 *The Early History of the Ancient Near East, 9000–2000 B.C.* E. Lutzeier, transl. Chicago: University of Chicago Press.

Nobis, Günter 1988 Die Haus- und Wildtiere aus dem Bergheiligtum Kato Syme/SO Kreta – Grabungen 1972 bis 1984. *Tier und Museum* 1(2):29–60.

Nobis, Günter 1990 Der 'Minotaurus' von Knossos auf Kreta – im Lichte moderner archäozoologischer Forschung. *Tier und Museum* 2(1):15–19.

Nobis, Günter 1993 Zur antiken Wild- und Haustierfauna Kretas – nach Studien an Tierresten aus den archäologischen Grabungen Poros bei Iraklion und Eléftherna bei Arkhadi. *Tier und Museum* 3(4):109–20.

Nobis, Günter 1996 Der Aurochse oder Ur (*Bos primigenius*) auf Kreta. In *The Pleistocene and Holocene Fauna of Crete and its First Settlers*. D. S. Reese, ed. Pp. 263–72. Monographs in World Archaeology. Madison: Prehistory Press.

Nobis, Günter 1997 Tieropfer aus einem Heroen- und Demeterheiligtum des antiken Messene (SW-Peloponnes, Griechenland) – Grabungen 1992 bis 1996. *Tier und Museum* 5(4):97–111.

Noe-Nygaard, Nanna 1975 Bone injuries caused by human weapons in Mesolithic Denmark. In *Archaeozoological Studies*. A. T. Clason, ed. Pp. 151–9. Amsterdam: North Holland.

Noe-Nygaard, Nanna, T. Douglas Price, and Signe U. Hede 2005 Diet of aurochs and early cattle in southern Scandinavia: Evidence from 15 N and 13 C stable isotopes. *Journal of Archaeological Science* 32(6):855–71.

Noe-Nygaard, Nanna, and Jane Richter 1990 Seventeen wild boar mandibles from Sludegårds Sømose: Offal or sacrifice? In *Experimentation and Reconstruction in Environmental Archaeology*. D. E. Robinson, ed. Pp. 175–89. Oxford: Oxbow.

Norton, Mark R., John B. Broster, and Emanuel Breitburg 1998 The Trull site (40PY276): A Paleoindian-mastodon association in Tennessee. *Current Research in the Pleistocene* 15:50–1.

Nowak, Marek 2001 The second phase of Neolithization in east-central Europe. *Antiquity* 75(289):582–92.

O'Connell, James F. 1987 Alyawara site structure and its archaeological implications. *American Antiquity* 52(1):74–108.

O'Connell, James F., and Jim Allen 1998 When did humans first arrive in greater Australia and why is it important to know? *Evolutionary Anthropology* 6(4):132–46.

O'Connell, James F., and Jim Allen 2004 Dating the colonization of Sahul (Pleistocene Australia-New Guinea): A review of recent research. *Journal of Archaeological Science* 31(6):835–53.

O'Connell, James F., Kristen Hawkes, and Nicholas G. Blurton-Jones 1988 Hadza scavenging: Implications for Plio/Pleistocene hominid subsistence. *Current Anthropology* 29(2):356–63.

O'Connell, James F., Kristen Hawkes, Karen D. Lupo, and Nicholas G. Blurton-Jones 2002 Male strategies and Plio-Pleistocene archaeology. *Journal of Human Evolution* 43(6):831–72.

O'Connor, Terence P. 1992a Pets and pests in Roman and medieval Britain. *Mammal Review* 22(2):107–13.

O'Connor, Terence P. 1992b Provisioning urban communities: A topic in search of a model. *Anthropozoologica* 16:101–6.

O'Connor, Terence P. 1994 A horse skeleton from Sutton Hoo, Suffolk, U.K. *ArchaeoZoologia* 6(2):29–37.

O'Connor, Terence P. 1997 Working at relationships: Another look at animal domestication. *Antiquity* 71(271):149–56.

O'Connor, Terence P. 1998 On the difficulty of detecting seasonal slaughtering of sheep. *Environmental Archaeology* 3:5–11.

Oates, Joan, Theya I. Molleson, and Arkadiusz Sokysia 2008 Equids and an acrobat: Closure rituals at Tell Brak. *Antiquity* 82(316):390–400.

Oberholtzer, Cath 2002 Fleshing out the evidence: From Archaic dog burials to historic dog feasts. *Ontario Archaeology* 73:3–14.

Oelschlaeger, Max 1991 *The Idea of Wilderness: From Prehistory to the Age of Ecology*. New Haven: Yale University Press.

Ojoade, J. Olowo 1990 Nigerian cultural attitudes to the dog. In *Signifying Animals: Human Meaning in the Natural World*. R. Willis, ed. Pp. 215–21. London: Unwin Hyman.

Oliveira-Santos, Luiz G. R., and Fernando A. S. Fernandez 2010 Pleistocene rewilding, Frankenstein ecosystems, and an alternative conservation agenda. *Conservation Biology* 24(1):4–5.

Oliver, Douglas L. 1955 *A Solomon Island Society: Kinship and Leadership among the Siuai of Bougainville*. Cambridge, MA: Harvard University Press.

Oliver, Symmes C. 1962 *Ecology and Cultural Continuity as Contributing Factors in the Social Organization of the Plains Indians*. University of California Publications in American Archaeology and Ethnology, No. 48(1). Berkeley: University of California Press.

Olivera, Daniel E., and Atilio Nasti 2001 Processing and economic yield in *Lama glama*. In *Ethnoarchaeology of Andean South America: Contributions to Archaeological Method and Theory*. L. A. Kuznar, ed. Pp. 296–309. International Monographs in Prehistory, Archaeological Series. Ann Arbor: Prehistory Press.

Olsen, Sandra L. 1995 Pleistocene horse-hunting at Solutré: Why bison jump analogies fail. In *Ancient Peoples and Landscapes*. E. Johnson, ed. Pp. 65–75. Lubbock, TX: Museum of Texas Tech University.

Olsen, Sandra L. 2000 The secular and sacred roles of dogs at Botai, north Kazakhstan. In *Dogs Through Time: An Archaeological Perspective*. S. J. Crockford, ed. Pp. 71–92. British Archaeological Reports, International Series. Oxford: Archaeopress.

Olsen, Sandra L. 2003 The exploitation of horses at Botai, Kazakhstan. In *Prehistoric Steppe Adaptation and the Horse*. M. A. Levine, A. C. Renfrew, and K. V. Boyle, eds. Pp. 83–103. McDonald Institute Monographs. Cambridge: McDonald Institute for Archaeological Research.

Olsen, Sandra L. 2006 Early horse domestication on the Eurasian steppe. In *Documenting Domestication: New Genetic and Archaeological Paradigms*. M. A. Zeder, D. G. Bradley, E. Emshwiller, and B. D. Smith, eds. Pp. 245–69. Berkeley: University of California Press.

Olson, Storrs L., and Helen F. James 1982 Fossil birds from the Hawaiian Islands: Evidence for wholesale extinction by man before Western contact. *Science* 217:633–5.

Oma, Kristin A. 2007 *Human-Animal Relationships: Mutual Becomings in Scandinavian and Sicilian Households 900–500 BC*. Oslo Arkeologiske Serie, No. 9. Oslo: Unipub.

Onar, Vedat, Altan Armutak, Oktay Belli, and Erkan Konyar 2002 Skeletal remains of dogs unearthed from the Van-Yoncatepe necropolises. *International Journal of Osteoarchaeology* 12(5):317–34.

Orton, David 2010a Both subject and object: Herding, inalienability and sentient property in prehistory. *World Archaeology* 42(2):188–200.

Orton, David C. 2010b Taphonomy and interpretation: An analytical framework for social zooarchaeology. *International Journal of Osteoarchaeology*.

Outram, Alan K. 2000 Hunting meat and scavenging marrow? A seasonal explanation for Middle Stone Age subsistence strategies at Klasies River Mouth. In *Animal Bones, Human Societies*. P. A. Rowley-Conwy, ed. Pp. 20–7. Oxford: Oxbow.

Outram, Alan K. 2001 Economic anatomy, element abundance and optimality: A new way of examining hunters' bone transportation choices. In *Archaeological Sciences '97*. A. Millard, ed. Pp. 117–26. British Archaeological Reports, International Series. Oxford: Archaeopress.

Outram, Alan K., and Peter A. Rowley-Conwy 1998 Meat and marrow utility indices for horse (*Equus*). *Journal of Archaeological Science* 25:839–49.

Outram, Alan K., Natalie A. Stear, Robin Bendrey, Sandra L. Olsen, Alexei K. Kasparov, Victor Zaibert, Nick Thorpe, and Richard P. Evershed 2009 The earliest horse harnessing and milking. *Science* 323(5919):1332–5.

Owen-Smith, Norman 1999 The interaction of humans, megaherbivores, and habitats in the Late Pleistocene extinction event. In *Extinctions in Near Time: Causes, Contexts, and Consequences*. R. D. E. MacPhee, ed. Pp. 57–69. New York: Kluwer Academic/Plenum Publishers.

Owens, D'Ann, and Brian D. Hayden 1997 Prehistoric rites of passage: A comparative study of transegalitarian hunter-gatherers. *Journal of Anthropological Archaeology* 16(2):121–61.

Özdoğan, Aslı 1999 Çayönü. In *Neolithic in Turkey: The Cradle of Civilization – New Discoveries*. N. Başgelen and M. Özdoğan, eds. Pp. 35–63. Istanbul: Arkeoloji ve Sanat Yayınları.

Paine, Robert 1971 Animals as capital: Comparisons among northern nomadic herders and hunters. *Anthropological Quarterly* 44(3):157–72.

Pappa, Maria, Paul L. J. Halstead, Kostas Kotsakis, and Dushka Urem-Kotsou 2004 Evidence for large-scale feasting at Late Neolithic Makriyalos, northern Greece. In *Food, Cuisine and Society in Prehistoric Greece*. P. L. J. Halstead and J. C. Barrett, eds. Pp. 16–44. Oxford: Oxbow.

Paris, François 1998 Les inhumations de *Bos* au Sahara méridional au Néolithique. In *Animals and People in the Holocene of North Africa*. A. Gautier, ed. Pp. 113–21. ArchaeoZoologia. Grenoble: La Pensée Sauvage.

Paris, François 2000 African livestock remains from Saharan mortuary contexts. In *The Origins and Development of African Livestock: Archaeology, Genetics, Linguistics and Ethnography*. R. M. Blench and K. C. MacDonald, eds. Pp. 111–26. London: UCL Press.

Park, Robert W. 1987 Dog remains from Devon Island, N.W.T.: Archaeological and osteological evidence for domestic dog use in the Thule Culture. *Arctic* 40(3):184–90.

Parker, Heidi G. *et al.* 2004 Genetic structure of the purebred domestic dog. *Science* 304(5674):1160–4.

Parker Pearson, Michael 1999 Food, sex and death: Cosmologies in the British Iron Age with particular reference to east Yorkshire. *Cambridge Archaeological Journal* 9(1):43–69.

Parker Pearson, Michael 2000 Eating money: A study in the ethnoarchaeology of food. *Archaeological Dialogues* 7(2):217–32.

Parkes, Peter 1987 Livestock symbolism and pastoral ideology among the Kafirs of the Hindu Kush. *Man* 22(4):637–60.

Parkin, David 1980 Kind bridewealth and hard cash: Eventing a structure. In *The Meaning of Marriage Payments*. J. L. Comaroff, ed. Pp. 197–220. New York: Academic Press.

Parkin, David 1992 Ritual as spatial direction and bodily division. In *Understanding Rituals*. D. de Coppet, ed. Pp. 11–25. London: Routledge.

Parkington, John E. 2003 Eland and therianthropes in southern African rock art: When is a person an animal? *African Archaeological Review* 20(3):135–47.

Parmalee, Paul W. 1959 Use of mammalian skulls and mandibles by prehistoric Indians of Illinois. *Illinois Academy of Sciences, Transactions* 52:85–95.

Parmalee, Paul W., and Walter E. Klippel 1983 The role of native animals in the food economy of the historic Kickapoo in central Illinois. In *Lulu Linear Punctated: Essays in Honor of George Irving Quimby*. R. C. Dunnell and D. K. Grayson, eds. Pp. 253–324. Anthropological Papers. Ann Arbor: University of Michigan Museum of Anthropology.

Parmalee, Paul W., and D. Stephens 1972 A wolf mask and other carnivore skull artifacts from the Palestine site, Illinois. *Pennsylvania Archaeologist* 42:71–5.

Patou, Marylène 1987 Les marmottes: Animaux intrusifs ou gibiers des préhistoriques du Paléolithique. *ArchaeoZoologia* 1(1):93–107.

Patou-Mathis, Marylène 2000 Neanderthal subsistence behaviours in Europe. *International Journal of Osteoarchaeology* 10(5):379–95.

Patou-Mathis, Marylène 2009 *Mangeurs de Viande: De la Préhistoire à nos Jours.* Paris: Perrin.

Patton, Mark A. 1990 On entoptic images in context: Art, monuments, and society in Neolithic Brittany. *Current Anthropology* 31(5): 554–8.

Pauketat, Timothy R. 2001 Practice and history in archaeology: An emerging paradigm. *Anthropological Theory* 1(1):73–98.

Payne, Sebastian 1972 Partial recovery and sample bias: The results of some sieving experiments. In *Papers in Economic Prehistory: Studies by Members and Associates of the British Academy Major Research Project in the Early History of Agriculture.* E. S. Higgs, ed. Pp. 49–64. Cambridge: Cambridge University Press.

Payne, Sebastian 1973 Kill-off patterns in sheep and goats: The mandibles from Aşvan Kale. *Anatolian Studies* 23:281–303.

Payne, Sebastian 1995 The small mammals. In *Kommos I(1): The Kommos Region and Houses of the Minoan Town.* J. W. Shaw and M. C. Shaw, eds. Pp. 278–91. Princeton: Princeton University Press.

Pegge, Samuel 1773 A dissertation on the crane, as a dish served up at great tables in England. *Archaeologia* 2:171–6.

Pendlebury, J. D. S. 1939 *The Archaeology of Crete, an Introduction.* London: Methuen.

Pepperberg, Irene M. 1999 *The Alex Studies: Cognitive and Communicative Abilities of Grey Parrots.* Cambridge, MA: Harvard University Press.

Perez, Ventura R., Laurie R. Godfrey, Malgosia Nowak-Kemp, David A. Burney, Jonah Ratsimbazafy, and Natalia Vasey 2005 Evidence of early butchery of giant lemurs in Madagascar. *Journal of Human Evolution* 49(6):722–42.

Perkins, Dexter, Jr. 1964 Prehistoric fauna from Shanidar, Iraq. *Science* 144(3626):1565–6.

Perkins, Dexter, Jr. 1969 Fauna of Çatal Hüyük: Evidence for early cattle domestication in Anatolia. *Science* 164(3876):177–9.

Perkins, Dexter, Jr. 1973a A critique on the methods of quantifying faunal remains from archaeological sites. In *Domestikationsforschung und Geschichte der Haustiere: Internationales Symposion in Budapest,* 1971. J. Matolcsi, ed. Pp. 367–9. Budapest: Akadémiai Kiadó.

Perkins, Dexter, Jr. 1973b The beginnings of animal domestication in the Near East. *American Journal of Archaeology* 77(3):279–82.

Perodie, James R. 2001 Feasting for prosperity: A study of southern Northwest Coast feasting. In *Feasts: Archaeological and Ethnographic Perspectives on Food, Politics, and Power.* M. Dietler and B. D. Hayden, eds. Pp. 185–214. Washington, DC: Smithsonian Institution Press.

Perri, Angela 2010 Holocene climate change, hunting adaptations and dog burials. Paper presented at the meetings of the International Council for Archaeozoology, Paris.

Peters, Charles R., and John C. Vogel 2005 Africa's wild C4 plant foods and possible early hominid diets. *Journal of Human Evolution* 48(3):219–36.

Peters, Emrys L. 1980 Aspects of Bedouin bridewealth among camel herders in Cyrenaica. In *The Meaning of Marriage Payments*. J. L. Comaroff, ed. Pp. 125–60. New York: Academic Press.

Peters, Joris 1993 Archaic Milet: Daily life and religious customs from an archaeozoological perspective. In *Archaeozoology of the Near East: Proceedings of the First International Symposium on the Archaeozoology of Southwestern Asia and Adjacent Areas.* H. Buitenhuis and A. T. Clason, eds. Pp. 88–96. Leiden: Universal Book Services.

Peters, Joris, and Klaus Schmidt 2004 Animals in the symbolic world of Pre-Pottery Neolithic Göbekli Tepe, south-eastern Turkey: A preliminary assessment. *Anthropozoologica* 39:179–218.

Peterson, Nicolas 1993 Demand sharing: Reciprocity and the pressure for generosity among foragers. *American Anthropologist* 95(4):860–74.

Petit, Jean-Paul 1989 Bliesbruck et les grands ensembles de puits et de fosses cultuels de la Gaule romaine: Aspect d'un rituel où l'animal occupe une place prédominante. In *L'Animal dans les Pratiques Religieuses: Les Manifestations Materielles*. J.-D. Vigne, ed. Pp. 99–110. Anthropozoologica. Paris: Éditions du Centre National de la Recherche Scientifique.

Petrasch, Jörg 2004 Von Menschen und Hunden: Befunde aus Kreisgrabenanlagen der Oberlauterbacher Gruppe und der Lengyel-Kultur und deren Interpretationen. In *Zwischen Karpaten und Ägäis: Neolithikum und ältere Bronzezeit. Gedenkschrift für Viera Němejcová-Pavúková*. B. Hänsel and E. Studeníková, eds. Pp. 295–308. Internationale Archäologie. Studia Honoraria. Rahden: Verlag Marie Leidorf.

Pétrequin, Pierre, Rose-Marie Arbogast, Anne-Marie Pétrequin, Samuel van Willigen, and Maxence Bailly 2006 *Premiers Chariots, Premiers Araires: La Diffusion de la Traction Animale en Europe pendant les IVe et IIIe Millénaires avant notre ère*. CRA Monographies, No. 29. Paris: Éditions du Centre National de la Recherche Scientifique.

Pidoplichko, Ivan G. 1998 *Upper Palaeolithic Dwellings of Mammoth Bones in the Ukraine: Kiev-Kirillovskii, Gontsy, Dobranichevka, Mezin and Mezhirich*. British Archaeological Reports, International Series, No. 712. Oxford: Archaeopress.

Piggott, Stuart 1962 Heads and hoofs. *Antiquity* 36:110–18.

Piggott, Stuart 1979 The beginnings of wheeled transport. In *Civilization: Readings from Scientific American*. B. M. Fagan, ed. Pp. 65–73. San Francisco: W. H. Freeman.

Piggott, Stuart 1983 *The Earliest Wheeled Transport: From the Atlantic Coast to the Caspian Sea*. Ithaca: Cornell University Press.

Pike-Tay, Anne 1991 *Red Deer Hunting in the Upper Paleolithic of South-West France: A Study in Seasonality*. British Archaeological Reports International Series, No. 569. Oxford: Archaeopress.

Pinhasi, Ron, and Noreen von Cramon-Taubadel 2009 Craniometric data supports demic diffusion model for the spread of agriculture into Europe. *PloS One* 4(8).

Pinsent, J. 1983 Bull-leaping. In *Minoan Society: Proceedings of the Cambridge Colloquium, 1981*. O. Krzyszkowska and L. Nixon, eds. Pp. 259–71. Bristol: Bristol Classical Press.

Pinter, Nicholas, Stuart J. Fiedel, and Jon E. Keeley 2011 Fire and vegetation shifts in the Americas at the vanguard of Paleoindian migration. *Quaternary Science Reviews* 30(3–4):269–72.

Piperno, Dolores R., and Deborah M. Pearsall 1998 *The Origins of Agriculture in the Lowland Neotropics*. New York: Academic Press.

Pitt-Rivers, Julian A. 1993 The Spanish bull-fight and kindred activities. *Anthropology Today* 9(4):11–15.

Planhol, Xavier de 1969 Le chien de berger: Développement et signification géographique d'une technique pastorale. *Bulletin de l'Association des Géographes Français* 370:355–68.

Pluciennik, Mark 1996 A perilous but necessary search: Archaeology and European identities. In *Nationalism and Archaeology: Scottish Archaeological Forum*. J. A. Atkinson, I. Banks, and J. O'Sullivan, eds. Pp. 35–58. Glasgow: Cruithne Press.

Pluskowski, Aleksander G., Krish Seetah, and J. Mark Maltby 2010 Potential osteoarchaeological evidence for riding and the military use of horses at Malbork Castle, Poland. *International Journal of Osteoarchaeology* 20(3):335–43.

Pohl, Mary E. D. 1991 Women, animal rearing, and social status: The case of the Formative period Maya of Central America. In *The Archaeology of Gender*. D. Walde and N. D. Willows, eds. Pp. 392–9. Calgary: Archaeological Association of the University of Calgary.

Pohl, Mary E. D., and Lawrence H. Feldman 1982 The traditional role of women and animals in lowland Maya economy. In *Maya Subsistence: Studies in Memory of Dennis E. Puleston*. K. V. Flannery, ed. Pp. 295–311. New York: Academic Press.

Pohlhausen, H. 1953 Zum Motiv der Rentierversenkung der Hamburger und Ahrensburger Stufe des niederdeutschen Flachlandmagdalénien. *Anthropos* 48:987–90.

Politis, Gustavo G., and Pablo G. Messineo 2008 The Campo Laborde site: New evidence for the Holocene survival of Pleistocene megafauna in the Argentine Pampas. *Quaternary International* 191(1):98–114.

Politis, Gustavo G., Jose L. Prado, and Roelf P. Beukens 1995 The human impact in Pleistocene-Holocene extinctions in South America. In *Ancient Peoples and Landscapes*. E. Johnson, ed. Pp. 187–205. Lubbock, TX: Museum of Texas Tech University.

Politis, Gustavo G., and Nicholas J. Saunders 2002 Archaeological correlates of ideological activity: Food taboos and spirit-animals in an Amazonian hunter-gatherer society. In *Consuming Passions and Patterns of Consumption*.

P. T. Miracle and N. Milner, eds. Pp. 113–30. McDonald Institute Monographs. Cambridge: McDonald Institute for Archaeological Research.

Pollex, Axel 1999 Comments on the interpretation of the so-called cattle burials of Neolithic Central Europe. *Antiquity* 73(281):542–50.

Pollock, Donald K. 1998 Food and sexual identity among the Culina. In *Food and Gender: Identity and Power*. C. M. Counihan and S. L. Kaplan, eds. Pp. 11–27. Amsterdam: Harwood Academic Publishers.

Poplin, François 1979 Origine du Mouton de Corse dans une nouvelle perspective paléontologique: Par marronage. *Annales de Génétique et de Sélection Animales* 11:133–43.

Poplin, François 1984 Contributions ostéo-archéologique à la connaissance des astragales de l'Antre Corycien. In *L'Antre Corycien II*. P. Amandry, ed. Pp. 381–93. Bulletin de Correspondance Hellénique, Supplément. Paris: École Française d'Athènes.

Poplin, François 1986 Le problème des fonctions du chien au Néolithique. In *Le Néolithique de la France*. J.-P. Demoule and J. Guilaine, eds. Pp. 46–9. Paris: Picard.

Poplin, François 1990 La vraie chasse et l'animal vrai. *Anthropozoologica* 13:45–7.

Porcasi, Judith F., Terry L. Jones, and L. Mark Raab 2000 Trans-Holocene marine mammal exploitation on San Clemente Island, California: A tragedy of the commons revisited. *Journal of Anthropological Archaeology* 19(2):200–20.

Porr, M., and Kurt W. Alt 2006 The burial of Bad Dürrenberg, Central Germany: Osteopathology and osteoarchaeology of a Late Mesolithic shaman's grave. *International Journal of Osteoarchaeology* 16(5):395–406.

Postgate, J. Nicholas, Tao Wang, and Toby Wilkinson 1995 The evidence for early writing: Utilitarian or ceremonial? *Antiquity* 69(264):459–80.

Potter, James M. 1997 Communal ritual and faunal remains: An example from the Dolores Anasazi. *Journal of Field Archaeology* 24(3):353–64.

Potter, James M. 2000 Pots, parties, and politics: Communal feasting in the American Southwest. *American Antiquity* 65(3):471–92.

Potts, Richard, and Pat Shipman 1981 Cutmarks made by stone tools on bones from Olduvai Gorge, Tanzania. *Nature* 291:577–80.

Powdermaker, Hortense 1932 Feasts in New Ireland: The social function of eating. *American Anthropologist* 34:236–47.

Powell, Joseph F., and D. Gentry Steele 1994 Diet and health of Paleoindians: An examination of early Holocene human dental remains. In *Paleonutrition: The Diet and Health of Prehistoric Americans*. K. D. Sobolik, ed. Pp. 178–94. Southern Illinois University, Center for Archaeological Investigations, Occasional Papers.

Power, Camilla, and Leslie Aiello 1997 Female proto-symbolic strategies. In *Women in Human Evolution*. L. D. Hager, ed. Pp. 153–71. London: Routledge.

Powers, William K., and Marla M. N. Powers 1984 Metaphysical aspects of an Oglala food system. In *Food in the Social Order: Studies of Food and Festivities in*

*Three American Communities*. M. Douglas, ed. Pp. 40–96. New York: Russell Sage Foundation.

Prentice, Guy 1986 Origins of plant domestication in the eastern United States: Promoting the individual in archaeological theory. *Southeastern Archaeology* 5:103–19.

Preston, Richard J. 1964 Ritual hangings: An aboriginal 'survival' in a northern North American trapping community. *Man* LXIV:142–4.

Price, Edward O. 2002 *Animal Domestication and Behavior*. New York: CAB International.

Price, Gilbert J., Gregory E. Webb, Jian-xin Zhao, Yue-xing Feng, Andrew S. Murray, Bernard N. Cooke, Scott A. Hocknull, and Ian H. Sobbe 2011 Dating megafaunal extinction on the Pleistocene Darling Downs, eastern Australia: The promise and pitfalls of dating as a test of extinction hypotheses. *Quaternary Science Reviews* 30(7–8):899–914.

Price, J. A. 1975 Sharing: The integration of intimate economics. *Anthropologica* 17:3–27.

Price, T. Douglas 1995 Social inequality at the origins of agriculture. In *Foundations of Social Inequality*. T. D. Price and G. M. Feinman, eds. Pp. 129–51. New York: Plenum.

Price, T. Douglas 2000 The introduction of farming in northern Europe. In *Europe's First Farmers*. T. D. Price, ed. Pp. 260–300. Cambridge: Cambridge University Press.

Price, T. Douglas, R. Alexander Bentley, Jens Lüning, Detlef Gronenborn, and Joachim Wahl 2001 Prehistoric human migration in the *Linearbandkeramik* of Central Europe. *Antiquity* 75(289):593–603.

Price, T. Douglas, Anne Birgitte Gebauer, and Lawrence H. Keeley 1995 The spread of farming into Europe north of the Alps. In *Last Hunters–First Farmers: New Perspectives on the Prehistoric Transition to Agriculture*. T. D. Price and A. B. Gebauer, eds. Pp. 95–126. Santa Fe: School of American Research Press.

Prideaux, Gavin J. *et al.* 2010 Timing and dynamics of Late Pleistocene mammal extinctions in southwestern Australia. *Proceedings of the National Academy of Sciences* 107(51):22157–62.

Prummel, Wietske 1997 Evidence of hawking (falconry) from bird and mammal bones. *International Journal of Osteoarchaeology* 7(4):333–8.

Prummel, Wietske 2003 Animal remains from the Hellenistic town of New Halos in the Almirós plain, Thessaly. In *Zooarchaeology in Greece: Recent Advances*. E. Kotjabopoulou, Y. Hamilakis, P. L. J. Halstead, C. S. Gamble, and P. Elefanti, eds. Pp. 153–9. Vol. 9. Athens: British School at Athens.

Prummel, Wietske 2006 Bronze Age dogs from graves in Borger (Netherlands) and Dimini (Greece). In *Dogs and People in Social, Working, Economic or Symbolic Interaction*. L. M. Snyder and E. A. Moore, eds. Pp. 67–76. Oxford: Oxbow.

Prummel, Wietske, and Jelle W. Bouma 1997 Animal offerings at Borgo le Ferriere (Latium, Italy). *Anthropozoologica* 25/26:531–7.

Pushkina, Diana, and Pasquale Raia 2008 Human influence on distribution and extinctions of the late Pleistocene Eurasian megafauna. *Journal of Human Evolution* 54(6):769–82.

Quinn, Daniel 1999 *Beyond Civilization: Humanity's Next Great Adventure.* New York: Harmony Books.

Rabenold, Patricia P. 1983 The communal roost in Black and Turkey Vultures – An information center? In *Vulture Biology and Management.* S. R. Wilbur and J. A. Jackson, eds. Pp. 303–21. Berkeley: University of California Press.

Rabinovich, Rivka 1998 'Drowning in numbers' – Gazelles dominance and body size groups in the archaeozoological record. In *Archaeozoology of the Near East III: Proceedings of the Third International Symposium on the Archaeozoology of Southwestern Asia and Adjacent Areas.* H. Buitenhuis, L. Bartosiewicz, and A. M. Choyke, eds. Pp. 45–71. Groningen: Groninger Institute for Archaeology.

Radovanović, Ivana 2000 Houses and burials at Lepenski Vir. *European Journal of Archaeology* 3(3):330–49.

Radovanović, Ivana 2006 Further notes on Mesolithic-Neolithic contacts in the Iron Gates Region and the Central Balkans. *Documenta Praehistorica* XXXIII:107–124.

Raduncheva, Ana, Velichka Matsanova, Ivan Gatsov, Georgi Kovachev, Georgi I. Georgiev, Elena Chakalova, and Elisabeta Bozhilova 2002 *Neolitno Selishte do Grad Rakitovo.* Razkopki i Prouchvaniya, No. 29. Sofia: Gal-Iko.

Rafferty, Sean M. 2008 Evidence of ritual practices at the Pethick site, Schoharie County, New York. *The Bulletin: Journal of the New York State Archaeological Association* 124:47–55.

Raharijaona, Victor, and Susan M. Kus 2001 Matters of life and death: Mortuary rituals as part of a larger whole among the Betsileo of Madagascar. In *Social Memory, Identity, and Death: Anthropological Perspectives on Mortuary Rituals.* M. S. Chesson, ed. Pp. 56–68. Archeological Papers of the American Anthropological Association. Washington, DC: American Anthropological Association.

Rainbird, Paul 1993 Prehistory in the northwest tropical Pacific: The Caroline, Mariana, and Marshall Islands. *Journal of World Prehistory* 8(3):293–349.

Ramble, Charles 1982 Status and death: Mortuary rites and attitudes to the body in a Tibetan village. *Kailash* 9(4):333–59.

Ramenofsky, Ann F., Alicia K. Wilbur, and Anne C. Stone 2003 Native American disease history: Past, present and future directions. *World Archaeology* 35(2):241–57.

Ramis, Damià, and Pere Bover 2001 A review of the evidence for domestication of *Myotragus balearicus* Bate 1909 (Artiodactyla, Caprinae) in the Balearic Islands. *Journal of Archaeological Science* 28(3):265–82.

Rappaport, Roy A. 1968 *Pigs for the Ancestors: Ritual in the Ecology of a New Guinea People.* New Haven: Yale University Press.

Rawlings, Tiffany A., and Jonathan C. Driver 2010 Paleodiet of domestic turkey, Shields Pueblo (5MT3807), Colorado: Isotopic analysis and its implications for care of a household domesticate. *Journal of Archaeological Science* 37(10):2433–41.

Ray, Keith, and Julian S. Thomas 2003 In the kinship of cows: The social centrality of cattle in the earlier Neolithic of southern Britain. In *Food, Culture and Identity in the Neolithic and Early Bronze Age*. M. Parker Pearson, ed. Pp. 37–51. British Archaeological Reports, International Series. Oxford: Archaeopress.

Reay, Marie 1984 A high pig culture of the New Guinea highlands. *Canberra Anthropology* 7(1–2):71–7.

Redding, Richard W. 1984 Theoretical determinants of a herder's decisions: Modeling variation in the sheep/goat ratio. In *Animals and Archaeology: 3. Early Herders and their Flocks*. J. Clutton-Brock and C. Grigson, eds. Pp. 223–41. British Archaeological Reports, International Series. Oxford: British Archaeological Reports.

Redding, Richard W., and Michael Rosenberg 1998 Ancestral pigs: A New (Guinea) model for pig domestication in the Middle East. In *Ancestors for the Pigs: Pigs in Prehistory*. S. M. Nelson, ed. Pp. 65–76. MASCA Research Papers in Science and Archaeology. Philadelphia: University of Pennsylvania, University Museum.

Redman, Charles L. 1999 *Human Impact on Ancient Environments*. Tucson: University of Arizona Press.

Reed, Charles A. 1977 A model for the origin of agriculture in the Near East. In *Origins of Agriculture*. C. A. Reed, ed. Pp. 543–67. The Hague: Mouton.

Reese, David S. 1985 Appendix VIII.C: The Kition astragali. In *Excavations at Kition V*. V. Karageorghis, ed. Pp. 382–91. Nicosia: Department of Antiquities.

Reese, David S. 1989 Faunal remains from the altar of Aphrodite Ourania, Athens. *Hesperia* 58(1):63–70.

Reese, David S. 1994 Recent work in Greek zooarchaeology. In *Beyond the Site: Regional Studies in the Aegean Area*. P. N. Kardulias, ed. Pp. 191–221. Lanham, MD: University Press of America.

Reese, David S. 1995 Equid sacrifices/burials in Greece and Cyprus: An addendum. *Journal of Prehistoric Religion* 9:35–42.

Reese, David S. 1996 Cypriot hippo hunters no myth. *Journal of Mediterranean Archaeology* 9(1):107–12.

Reese, David S. 2001 Some comments on the Akrotiri *Aetokremnos* fauna. In *The Earliest Prehistory of Cyprus from Colonization to Exploitation*. S. Swiny, ed. Pp. 19–36. American Schools of Oriental Research Archaeological Reports. Boston: American Schools of Oriental Research.

Reese, David S. 2002 On the incised cattle scapulae from the East Mediterranean and Near East. *Bonner Zoologische Beiträge* 50(3):183–98.

Reichel-Dolmatoff, Gerardo 1985 Tapir avoidance in the Colombian northwest Amazon. In *Animal Myths and Metaphors in South America*. G. Urton, ed. Pp. 107–43. Salt Lake City: University of Utah Press.

Reid, Andrew 1996 Cattle herds and the redistribution of cattle resources. *World Archaeology* 28(1):43–57.

Reid, Anthony 1988 *Southeast Asia in the Age of Commerce*, 1450–1680. Volume 1. New Haven: Yale University Press.

Reitz, Elizabeth J., and Elizabeth S. Wing 1999 *Zooarchaeology*. Cambridge: Cambridge University Press.

Rendu, William 2010 Hunting behavior and Neanderthal adaptability in the Late Pleistocene site of Pech-de-l'Azé I. *Journal of Archaeological Science* 37(8):1798–1810.

Renfrew, A. Colin 1986 Varna and the emergence of wealth in prehistoric Europe. In *The Social Life of Things: Commodities in Cultural Perspective*. A. Appadurai, ed. Pp. 141–68. Cambridge: Cambridge University Press.

Renfrew, A. Colin 1996 Language families and the spread of farming. In *The Origins and Spread of Agriculture and Pastoralism in Eurasia*. D. R. Harris, ed. Pp. 70–92. London: UCL Press.

Renouf, Priscilla 2000 Symbolism and subsistence: Seals and caribou at Port au Choix, northwestern Newfoundland. In *Animal Bones, Human Societies*. P. A. Rowley-Conwy, ed. Pp. 65–73. Oxford: Oxbow.

Rheubottom, David B. 1980 Dowry and wedding celebrations in Yugoslav Macedonia. In *The Meaning of Marriage Payments*. J. L. Comaroff, ed. Pp. 221–49. New York: Academic Press.

Rice, Michael 1997 *The Power of the Bull*. London: Routledge.

Rice, Michael 2006 *Swifter than the Arrow: The Golden Hunting Hounds of Ancient Egypt*. London: I. B. Tauris.

Rice, Patricia C., and Ann L. Paterson 1985 Cave art and bones: Exploring the interrelationships. *American Anthropologist* 87:94–100.

Rice, Patricia C., and Ann L. Paterson 1986 Validating the cave art-archeofaunal relationship in Cantabrian Spain. *American Anthropologist* 88(3):658–67.

Rice, Prudence M. 1999 On the origins of pottery. *Journal of Archaeological Method and Theory* 6(1):1–54.

Richards, Colin C., and Julian S. Thomas 1984 Ritual activity and structured deposition in later Neolithic Wessex. In *Neolithic Studies: A Review of Some Current Research*. R. Bradley and J. Gardiner, eds. Pp. 189–218. British Archaeological Reports, British Series. Oxford: British Archaeological Reports.

Richards, Martin B. 2003 The Neolithic invasion of Europe. *Annual Review of Anthropology* 32:135–62.

Richards, Michael P., T. Douglas Price, and Eva Koch 2003 Mesolithic and Neolithic subsistence in Denmark: New stable isotope data. *Current Anthropology* 44(2):288–95.

Richards, Michael P., and Rick J. Schulting 2006 Touch not the fish: The Mesolithic-Neolithic change of diet and its significance. *Antiquity* 80(308):444–58.

Richards, Michael P., Rick J. Schulting, and Robert E. M. Hedges 2003b Sharp shift in diet at onset of Neolithic. *Nature* 6956:366.

Richardson, Seth F. C. 2010 On seeing and believing: Liver divination and the Era of Warring States (II). In *Divination and Interpretation of Signs in the Ancient World*. A. Annus, ed. Pp. 225–66. Chicago: Oriental Institute of the University of Chicago.

Rick, Torben C., Jon M. Erlandson, René L. Vellanoweth, Todd J. Braje, Paul W. Collins, Daniel A. Guthrie, and Thomas W. Stafford, Jr. 2009 Origins and antiquity of the island fox (*Urocyon littoralis*) on California's Channel Islands. *Quaternary Research* 71(2):93–8.

*The Rig Veda*. 1981 W. D. O'Flaherty, transl. Harmondsworth, Middlesex: Penguin.

Rindos, David 1984 *The Origins of Agriculture: An Evolutionary Perspective*. New York: Academic Press.

Rindos, David 1989 Darwinism and its role in the explanation of domestication. In *Foraging and Farming: The Evolution of Plant Exploitation*. D. R. Harris and G. C. Hillman, eds. Pp. 27–41. London: Unwin Hyman.

Ringrose, T. J. 1993 Bone counts and statistics: A critique. *Journal of Archaeological Science* 20(2):121–57.

Ritvo, Harriet 1999 Border trouble: Shifting the line between people and other animals. In *Humans and Other Animals*. A. Mack, ed. Pp. 67–86. Columbus, OH: Ohio State University Press.

Robb, John E. 1999 Secret agents: Culture, economy, and social reproduction. In *Material Symbols: Culture and Economy in Prehistory*. J. E. Robb, ed. Pp. 3–15. Southern Illinois University, Center for Archaeological Investigations, Occasional Papers. Carbondale: Center for Archaeological Investigations, Southern Illinois University at Carbondale.

Robb, John E. 2007 *The Early Mediterranean Village: Agency, Material Culture, and Social Change in Neolithic Italy*. Cambridge: Cambridge University Press.

Robb, John E., and Preston T. Miracle 2007 Beyond 'migration' versus 'acculturation': New models for the spread of agriculture. In *Going Over: The Mesolithic–Neolithic Transition in Western Europe*. A. Whittle, ed. Pp. 90–113. Proceedings of the British Academy. London: British Academy.

Robbins, Paul 1998 Shrines and butchers: Animals as deities, capital, and meat in contemporary north India. In *Animal Geographies: Place, Politics, and Identity in the Nature-Culture Borderlands*. J. R. Wolch and J. Emel, eds. Pp. 218–40. London: Verso.

Roberts, C. Neil 2002 Did prehistoric landscape management retard the postglacial spread of woodland in Southwest Asia? *Antiquity* 76(294):1002–10.

Roberts, Richard G. *et al.* 2001 New ages for the last Australian megafauna: Continent-wide extinction about 46,000 years ago. *Science* 292(5523):1888–92.

Robertson-Mackay, M. E. 1980 A 'head and hooves' burial beneath a round barrow, with other Neolithic and Bronze Age sites on Hemp Knoll, near Avebury, Wiltshire. *Proceedings of the Prehistoric Society* 46:123–76.

Rodríguez, Iokiñe 2007 Pemon perspectives of fire management in Canaima National Park, southeastern Venezuela. *Human Ecology* 35(3):331–43.

Rodríguez Loredo de March, Cecilia 1993 La chasse de rapaces diurnes pour l'obtention de plumes dans le site inca 'Potrero-Chaquiago' (Argentine). *Exploitation des Animaux Sauvages à travers les Temps: IVe Colloque International de l'Homme et l'Animal.* J. Desse and F. Audoin-Rouzeau, eds. Pp. 517–21. Juan-les-Pins: Éditions APCDA-CNRS.

Roe, Peter G. 1997 Paragon or peril? The jaguar in Amazonian Indian society. In *Icons of Power: Feline Symbolism in the Americas.* N. J. Saunders, ed. Pp. 171–202. London: Routledge.

Rofes, Juan 2004 Prehispanic guinea pig sacrifices in southern Perú, the case of El Yaral. In *Behaviour behind Bones: The Zooarchaeology of Ritual, Religion, Status and Identity.* S. J. O'Day, W. Van Neer, and A. Ervynck, eds. Pp. 95–100. Oxford: Oxbow.

Rogers, Alan R. 2000 On equifinality in faunal assemblages. *American Antiquity* 65(4):709–23.

Rogers, Richard A., and Laurine A. Rogers 1988 Notching and anterior beveling on fossil horse incisors: Indicators of domestication? *Quaternary Research* 29(1):72–4.

Rolett, Barry V. 1992 Faunal extinctions and depletions linked with prehistory and environmental change in the Marquesas Islands (French Polynesia). *Journal of the Polynesian Society* 101:86–94.

Ronen, Avraham 2004 Why was the dog domesticated? In *The Last Hunter-Gatherers in the Near East.* C. Delage, ed. Pp. 153–60. British Archaeological Reports, International Series. Oxford: Archaeopress.

Rose, Lisa M., and Fiona Marshall 1996 Meat eating, hominid sociality, and home bases revisited. *Current Anthropology* 37(2):307–37.

Rosenberg, Michael, R. Mark Nesbitt, Richard W. Redding, and Brian L. Peasnall 1998 Hallan Çemi, pig husbandry, and post-Pleistocene adaptations along the Taurus-Zagros arc (Turkey). *Paléorient* 24(1):25–41.

Rosenberg, Michael, R. Mark Nesbitt, Richard W. Redding, and Thomas F. Strasser 1995 Hallan Çemi Tepesi: Some preliminary observations concerning early Neolithic subsistence behaviors in eastern Anatolia. *Anatolica* 21:1–12.

Rosenberg, Michael, and Richard W. Redding 1998 Early pig husbandry in southwestern Asia and its implications for modeling the origins of food production. In *Ancestors for the Pigs: Pigs in Prehistory.* S. M. Nelson, ed. Pp. 55–64.

MASCA Research Papers in Science and Archaeology. Philadelphia: University of Pennsylvania, University Museum.

Rosman, Abraham, and Paula G. Rubel 1971 *Feasting with Mine Enemy: Rank and Exchange among Northwest Coast Societies*. New York: Columbia University Press.

Rosman, Abraham, and Paula G. Rubel 1989 Stalking the wild pig: Hunting and horticulture in Papua New Guinea. In *Farmers as Hunters: The Implications of Sedentism*. S. Kent, ed. Pp. 27–36. Cambridge: Cambridge University Press.

Ross, Eric B. 1978 Food taboos, diet, and hunting strategy: The adaptation to animals in Amazon cultural ecology. *Current Anthropology* 19(1):1–36.

Ross, Eric B. 1987 An overview of trends in dietary variation from hunter-gatherer to modern capitalist societies. In *Food and Evolution: Toward a Theory of Human Food Habits*. M. Harris and E. B. Ross, eds. Pp. 7–55. Philadelphia: Temple University Press.

Rossel, Stine, Fiona Marshall, Joris Peters, Tom Pilgram, Matthew D. Adams, and David O'Connor 2008 Domestication of the donkey: Timing, processes, and indicators. *Proceedings of the National Academy of Sciences* 105(10):3715–20.

Rowley-Conwy, Peter A. 1987 The interpretation of ard marks. *Antiquity* 61(232):263–6.

Rowley-Conwy, Peter A. 1990 On the osteological evidence for Palaeolithic domestication: Barking up the wrong tree. *Current Anthropology* 31(5):543–7.

Rowley-Conwy, Peter A. 2000 Milking caprines, hunting pigs: The Neolithic economy of Arene Candide in its West Mediterranean context. In *Animal Bones, Human Societies*. P. A. Rowley-Conwy, ed. Pp. 124–32. Oxford: Oxbow.

Rowley-Conwy, Peter A. 2004 How the West was lost: A reconsideration of agricultural origins in Britain, Ireland, and southern Scandinavia. *Current Anthropology* 45(Supplement):S83-S113.

Rowley-Conwy, Peter A., Paul L. J. Halstead, and Patricia Collins 2002 Derivation and application of a food utility index (FUI) for European wild boar (*Sus scrofa* L.). *Environmental Archaeology* 7:77–87.

Roy, James 2007 The consumption of dog-meat in classical Greece. In *Cooking up the Past: Food and Culinary Practices in the Neolithic and Bronze Age Aegean*. C. B. Mee and J. Renard, eds. Pp. 342–53. Oxford: Oxbow.

Ruel, Malcolm 1990 Non-sacrificial ritual killing. *Man* 25(2):323–35.

Runnels, Curtis N., and Tjeerd H. van Andel 1988 Trade and the origins of agriculture in the eastern Mediterranean. *Journal of Mediterranean Archaeology* 1(1):83–109.

Russell, Kenneth W. 1988 *After Eden: The Behavioural Ecology of Early Food Production in the Near East and North Africa*. British Archaeological Reports, International Series, No. 391. Oxford: British Archaeological Reports.

Russell, Nerissa 1990 The bone tools. In *Selevac: A Neolithic Village in Yugoslavia*. R. E. Tringham and D. Krstić, eds. Pp. 521–48. Los Angeles: UCLA Institute of Archaeology.

Russell, Nerissa 1993 *Hunting, Herding and Feasting: Human Use of Animals in Neolithic Southeast Europe*. Unpublished Ph.D. thesis, University of California, Berkeley.

Russell, Nerissa 1995 The bone tool industry at Mehrgarh and Sibri. In *Mehrgarh: Field Reports 1974–1985 – From Neolithic Times to the Indus Civilization*. C. Jarrige, J.-F. Jarrige, R. H. Meadow, and G. Quivron, eds. Pp. 583–613. Karachi: Department of Culture and Tourism, Government of Sindh, Pakistan.

Russell, Nerissa 1999 Symbolic dimensions of animals and meat at Opovo, Yugoslavia. In *Material Symbols: Culture and Economy in Prehistory*. J. E. Robb, ed. Pp. 153–72. Southern Illinois University, Center for Archaeological Investigations, Occasional Papers. Carbondale: Center for Archaeological Investigations, Southern Illinois University at Carbondale.

Russell, Nerissa 2000 Household variation and meat sharing in Neolithic: Spatial dimensions of the faunal remains from Opovo, Yugoslavia. In *Technology, Style and Society: Contributions to the Innovations between the Alps and the Black Sea in Prehistory*. L. Nikolova, ed. Pp. 41–50. British Archaeological Reports, International Series. Oxford: Archaeopress.

Russell, Nerissa 2006 Çatalhöyük worked bone. In *Changing Materialities at Çatalhöyük: Reports from the 1995–99 Seasons*. I. Hodder, ed. Pp. 339–67. McDonald Institute Monographs. Cambridge: McDonald Institute for Archaeological Research.

Russell, Nerissa 2010 Navigating the human-animal boundary. *Reviews in Anthropology* 39(1):1–22.

Russell, Nerissa in press-a Hunting sacrifice at Neolithic Çatalhöyük. In *Social Aspects of Human and Animal Sacrifice in the Ancient Near East*. G. M. Schwartz and A. Porter, eds. Warsaw, IN: Eisenbrauns.

Russell, Nerissa in press-b Mammals from the BACH Area at Çatalhöyük. In *The Last House on the Hill: Excavation of Building 3 at Çatalhöyük, Turkey*. R. E. Tringham and M. Stevanović, eds. Monumenta Archaeologica. Los Angeles: Cotsen Institute of Archaeology UCLA.

Russell, Nerissa, and Bleda S. Düring 2006 Worthy is the lamb: A double burial at Neolithic Çatalhöyük (Turkey). *Paléorient* 32(1):73–84.

Russell, Nerissa, and Louise Martin 2000 Histories written in bone. Presented at Society for American Archaeology, Philadelphia.

Russell, Nerissa, and Louise Martin 2005 The Çatalhöyük mammal remains. In *Inhabiting Çatalhöyük: Reports from the 1995–1999 Seasons*. I. Hodder, ed. Pp. 33–98. McDonald Institute Monographs. Cambridge: McDonald Institute for Archaeological Research.

Russell, Nerissa, and Louise Martin in press Cooking meat and bones at Neolithic Çatalhöyük, Turkey. In *The Menial Art of Cooking: Archaeological Studies of*

*Cooking and Food Preparation.* S. R. Graff and E. Rodríguez-Alegría, eds. Boulder: University Press of Colorado.

Russell, Nerissa, Louise Martin, and Katheryn C. Twiss 2009 Building memories: Commemorative deposits at Çatalhöyük. In *Zooarchaeology and the Reconstruction of Cultural Systems: Case Studies from the Old World.* B. S. Arbuckle, C. A. Makarewicz, and A. L. Atici, eds. Pp. 103–25. Anthropozoologica. Paris: L'Homme et l'Animal, Société de Recherche Interdisciplinaire.

Russell, Nerissa, and Kevin J. McGowan 2003 Dance of the cranes: Crane symbolism at Çatalhöyük and beyond. *Antiquity* 77(297):445–55.

Russell, Nerissa, and Kevin J. McGowan 2005 The Çatalhöyük bird bones. In *Inhabiting Çatalhöyük: Reports from the 1995–1999 Seasons.* I. Hodder, ed. Pp. 99–110. McDonald Institute Monographs. Cambridge: McDonald Institute for Archaeological Research.

Russell, Nerissa, and Stephanie Meece 2006 Animal representations and animal remains at Çatalhöyük. In *Çatalhöyük Perspectives: Reports from the 1995–99 Seasons.* I. Hodder, ed. Pp. 209–30. McDonald Institute Monographs. Cambridge: McDonald Institute for Archaeological Research.

Russell, Nerissa, Mirjana Stevanović, Philippa Ryan, Marina Milić, and Dragana Filipović 2008 Bringing down the house: House closing and abandonment deposits at Neolithic Çatalhöyük, Turkey. Presented at Society for American Archaeology, Vancouver.

Russell, Nerissa, and Katheryn C. Twiss in press Digesting the data: Dogs as taphonomic agents at Neolithic Çatalhöyük, Turkey. In *Archaeozoology of the Near East IX: Proceedings of the Ninth International Symposium on the Archaeozoology of Southwestern Asia and Adjacent Areas.* M. Mashkour and M. Beech, eds. Oxford: Oxbow.

Rutledge, Robb, and Gavin R. Hunt 2004 Lateralized tool use in wild New Caledonian crows. *Animal Behaviour* 67(2):327–32.

Ryan, Kathleen, Karega Munene, Samuel M. Kahinju, and Paul N. Kunoni 2000 Ethnographic perspectives on cattle management in semi-arid environments: A case study from Maasailand. In *The Origins and Development of African Livestock: Archaeology, Genetics, Linguistics and Ethnography.* R. M. Blench and K. C. MacDonald, eds. Pp. 462–77. London: UCL Press.

Ryder, Michael L. 1965 Report of textiles from Çatal Hüyük. *Anatolian Studies* 15:175–6.

Ryder, Michael L. 1973 The use of the skin and coat in studies of changes following domestication. In *Domestikationsforschung und Geschichte der Haustiere: Internationales Symposion in Budapest,* 1971. J. Matolcsi, ed. Pp. 163–8. Budapest: Akadémiai Kiadó.

Ryder, Michael L. 1984 Sheep representations, written records and wool measurements. In *Animals and Archaeology: 3. Early Herders and their Flocks.* J. Clutton-Brock and C. Grigson, eds. Pp. 69–82. British Archaeological Reports, International Series. Oxford: British Archaeological Reports.

Ryder, Michael L. 1994 New thoughts on the pig meat taboo. *Journal of the Anthropological Society of Oxford* XXV(3):272–5.

Ryder, Michael L., and Thea Gabra-Sanders 1985 The application of microscopy to textile history. *Textile History* 16(2):123–40.

Ryder, Richard 2000 *Animal Revolution: Changing Attitudes towards Speciesism*. Oxford: Berg.

Sacks, Karen 1975 Engels revisited: Women, the organization of production, and private property. In *Toward an Anthropology of Women*. R. R. Reiter, ed. Pp. 211–34. New York: Monthly Review Press.

Sahlins, Marshall D. 1972 *Stone Age Economics*. Chicago: Aldine-Atherton.

Sakellarakis, Yannis 1971 Das Kuppelgrab A von Archanes und das Kretisch-mycenische Tieropferritual. *Prähistorische Zeitschrift* 45:135–219.

Sakellaridis, Margaret 1979 *The Economic Exploitation of the Swiss Area in the Mesolithic and Neolithic Periods*. British Archaeological Reports, International Series, No. 67. Oxford: British Archaeological Reports.

Salisbury, Joyce E. 1994 *The Beast Within: Animals in the Middle Ages*. New York: Routledge.

Salzman, Philip C. 1999 Is inequality universal? *Current Anthropology* 40(1):31–61.

Sampietro, M. L., O. Lao, David Caramelli, Martina Lari, R. Pou, M. Martí, Jaume Bertranpetit, and Carles Lalueza Fox 2007 Palaeogenetic evidence supports a dual model of Neolithic spreading into Europe. *Proceedings of the Royal Society of London, Series B* 274(1622):2161–7.

Sanden, Wijnand Van Der 1996 *Through Nature to Eternity: The Bog Bodies of Northwest Europe*. S. J. Mellor, transl. Amsterdam: Batavian Lion International.

Sandweiss, Daniel H., and Elizabeth S. Wing 1997 Ritual rodents: The guinea pigs of Chincha, Peru. *Journal of Field Archaeology* 24(1):47–58.

SAPPO 2007 Sixteen years of archaeological investigations in the Euphrates Valley and the Djezireh: Tell Halula, Tell Amarna, and Chagar Bazar. *Neo-Lithics* 1/07:9–13.

Sasson, Aharon 2007 Corpus of 694 Astragali (knucklebones) from Stratum II at Tel Beer-Sheba. *Tel Aviv* 34(2):171–81.

Sauer, Carl O. 1969 *Agricultural Origins and Dispersals: The Domestication of Animals and Foodstuffs*. Second edition. Cambridge, MA: MIT Press.

Saunders, Nicholas J. 1997 Architecture of symbolism: The feline image. In *Icons of Power: Feline Symbolism in the Americas*. N. J. Saunders, ed. Pp. 12–52. London: Routledge.

Savelle, James M. 1997 The role of architectural utility in the formation of zooarchaeological whale bone assemblages. *Journal of Archaeological Science* 24(10):869–85.

Savelle, James M., and T. Max Friesen 1996 An odontocete (Cetacea) meat utility index. *Journal of Archaeological Science* 23:713–21.

Savelle, James M., T. Max Friesen, and R. Lee Lyman 1996 Derivation and application of an otariid utility index. *Journal of Archaeological Science* 23:705–12.

Sayers, Ken, and C. Owen Lovejoy 2008 The chimpanzee has no clothes: A critical examination of *Pan troglodytes* in models of human evolution. *Current Anthropology* 49(1):87–114.

Schaller, George B. 1972 *The Serengeti Lion: A Study of Predator-Prey Relations.* Chicago: University of Chicago Press.

Schaller, George B., and G. B. Lowther 1969 The relevance of carnivore behavior to the study of early hominids. *Southwestern Journal of Anthropology* 25:307–41.

Schefold, Reimar 2002 Visions of the wilderness on Siberut in a comparative Southeast Asian perspective. In *Tribal Communities in the Malay World: Historical, Cultural and Social Perspectives.* G. Benjamin and C. Chou, eds. Pp. 422–38. Leiden: Curzon Press.

Scheid, Christelle, Judith Schmidt, and Ronald Noë 2008 Distinct patterns of food offering and co-feeding in rooks. *Animal Behaviour* 76(5):1701–7.

Scheinsohn, Vivian 2003 Hunter-gatherer archaeology in South America. *Annual Review of Anthropology* 32:339–61.

Schiffer, Michael B. 1972 Archaeological context and systemic context. *American Antiquity* 37(2):156–65.

Schleidt, Wolfgang M. 1999 Apes, wolves, and the trek to humanity: Did wolves show us the way? *Discovering Archaeology* 1(2):8–10.

Schliemann, Heinrich 1884 *Troja.* New York: Harper & Bros.

Schloegl, Christian, Kurt Kotrschal, and Thomas Bugnyar 2007 Gaze following in common ravens, *Corvus corax*: Ontogeny and habituation. *Animal Behaviour* 74(4):769–78.

Schmandt-Besserat, Denise 1983 The earliest precursor of writing. In *Prehistoric Times: Readings from Scientific American.* B. M. Fagan, ed. Pp. 194–203. New York: W. H. Freeman.

Schmandt-Besserat, Denise 1992 *Before Writing, Volume I: From Counting to Cuneiform.* Austin: University of Texas Press.

Schmandt-Besserat, Denise 1996 *How Writing Came About.* Austin: University of Texas Press.

Schmidt, Klaus 1999 Frühe Tier- und Menschenbilder vom Göbekli Tepe. *Istanbuler Mitteilungen des Deutschen Archäologischen Instituts* 49:5–21.

Schmidt, Klaus 2001 Göbekli Tepe, southeastern Turkey: A preliminary report on the 1995–1999 excavations. *Paléorient* 26(1):45–54.

Schmidt, Klaus 2003 The 2003 campaign at Göbekli Tepe (southeastern Turkey). *Neo-Lithics* 2003(2):3–8.

Schmidt, Klaus 2006 Animals and a headless man at Göbekli Tepe. *Neo-Lithics* 2006(2):38–40.

Schmidt, Klaus 2008 Göbekli Tepe – Enclosure C. *Neo-Lithics* 2008(2):27–32.

Schmidt, Robert A. 2000 Shamans and northern cosmology: The direct historical approach to Mesolithic sexuality. In *Archaeologies of Sexuality*. R. A. Schmidt and B. L. Voss, eds. Pp. 220–35. London: Routledge.

Schneider, Harold K. 1957 The subsistence role of cattle among the Pakot and in East Africa. *American Anthropologist* 59(2):278–300.

Schneider, Harold K. 1979 *Livestock and Equality in East Africa: The Economic Basis for Social Structure*. Bloomington: Indiana University Press.

Schneider, Harold K. 1980 Livestock as food and money. *The Future of Pastoral Peoples*. Pp. 210–23. Commission on Nomadic Peoples, International Union of Anthropological and Ethnological Sciences. Ottawa: International Development Research Centre.

Schüle, Wilhelm 1993 Mammals, vegetation and the initial human settlement of the Mediterranean islands: A palaeoecological approach. *Journal of Biogeography* 20(4):399–412.

Schulting, Rick J., and Michael P. Richards 2002 The wet, the wild and the domesticated: The Mesolithic-Neolithic transition on the west coast of Scotland. *European Journal of Archaeology* 5(2):147–90.

Schüz, Ernst, and Claus König 1983 Old World vultures and man. In *Vulture Biology and Management*. S. R. Wilbur and J. A. Jackson, eds. Pp. 461–9. Berkeley: University of California Press.

Schwab, Christine, Thomas Bugnyar, Christian Schloegl, and Kurt Kotrschal 2008 Enhanced social learning between siblings in common ravens, Corvus corax. *Animal Behaviour* 75(2):501–8.

Schwabe, Calvin W. 1994 Animals in the ancient world. In *Animals and Human Society: Changing Perspectives*. A. Manning and J. A. Serpell, eds. Pp. 36–58. London: Routledge.

Schwartz, Jeffrey H. 1973 The paleozoology of Cyprus: A preliminary report on recently analysed sites. *World Archaeology* 5:215–20.

Schwartz, Marion 1997 *A History of Dogs in the Early Americas*. New Haven: Yale University Press.

Scott, Eleanor 1991 Animal and infant burials in Romano-British villas: A revitalization movement. In *Sacred and Profane: Proceedings of a Conference on Archaeology, Ritual and Religion*. P. Garwood, D. Jennings, R. Skeates, and J. Toms, eds. Pp. 115–21. Oxford University Committee for Archaeology Monograph. Oxford: Oxford University Committee for Archaeology.

Scott, Susan L., and H. Edwin Jackson 1996 Early Caddo ritual and patterns of animal use: An analysis of faunal remains from the Crenshaw site (3MI6), southwestern Arkansas. *Arkansas Archeologist* 37:1–37.

Scurlock, JoAnn 2002 Animal sacrifice in ancient Mesopotamian religion. In *A History of the Animal World in the Ancient Near East*. B. J. Collins, ed. Pp. 389–403. Leiden: E. J. Brill.

Sebeok, Thomas A. 1988 'Animal' in biological and semiotic perspective. In *What Is an Animal?* T. Ingold, ed. Pp. 63–76. London: Unwin Hyman.

Seeman, Mark F. 1979 Feasting with the dead: Ohio Hopewell charnel house ritual as a context for redistribution. In *Hopewell Archaeology: The Chillicothe Conference*. D. S. Brose and N. Greber, eds. Pp. 39–46. Kent, OH: Kent State University Press.

Séfériadès, Michel 1992 L'os et le bois de cervidé. In *Dikili Tash, Village Préhistorique de Macédoine Orientale I/1*. R. Treuil, ed. Pp. 99–112. BCH Supplément. Paris: École Française d'Athènes.

Segobye, Alinah 1998 Daughters of cattle: The significance of herding in the growth of complex societies in southern Africa between the 10th and 15th centuries AD. In *Gender in African Prehistory*. S. Kent, ed. Pp. 227–33. Walnut Creek, CA: Altamira Press.

Selvaggio, Marie M. 1998a Evidence for a three-stage sequence of hominid and carnivore involvement with long bones at FLK *Zinjanthropus*, Olduvai Gorge, Tanzania. *Journal of Archaeological Science* 25(3):191–202.

Selvaggio, Marie M. 1998b The archaeological implications of water-cached hyena kills. *Current Anthropology* 39(3):381–3.

Semonin, Paul 2000 *American Monster: How the Nation's First Prehistoric Creature Became a Symbol of National Identity*. New York: New York University Press.

Sept, Jeanne M. 1992 Was there no place like home? A new perspective on early hominid archaeological sites from the mapping of chimpanzee nests. *Current Anthropology* 33(2):187–207.

Sered, Susan 2002 Towards a gendered typology of sacrifice: Women & feasting, men & death in an Okinawan village. In *Sacrifice in Religious Experience*. A. I. Baumgarten, ed. Pp. 13–38. Boston: E. J. Brill.

Serjeantson, Dale 1990 The introduction of mammals to the Outer Hebrides and the role of boats in stock management. *Anthropozoologica* 13:7–18.

Serjeantson, Dale 2000 Good to eat *and* good to think with: Classifying animals from complex sites. In *Animal Bones, Human Societies*. P. A. Rowley-Conwy, ed. Pp. 179–89. Oxford: Oxbow.

Serjeantson, Dale 2001 The great auk and the gannet: A prehistoric perspective on the extinction of the great auk. *International Journal of Osteoarchaeology* 11(1–2):43–55.

Serjeantson, Dale 2006 Food or feast at Neolithic Runnymede. In *Animals in the Neolithic of Britain and Europe*. D. Serjeantson and D. Field, eds. Pp. 113–34. Neolithic Studies Group Seminar Papers. Oxford: Oxbow.

Serjeantson, Dale, and James T. Morris 2011 Ravens and crows in Iron Age and Roman Britain. *Oxford Journal of Archaeology* 30(1):85–107.

Serpell, James A. 1986 *In the Company of Animals: A Study of Human-Animal Relationships*. Oxford: Basil Blackwell.

Serpell, James A. 1989 Pet-keeping and animal domestication: A reappraisal. In *The Walking Larder: Patterns of Domestication, Pastoralism, and Predation*. J. Clutton-Brock, ed. Pp. 10–21. London: Unwin Hyman.

Serpell, James A. 1995 From paragon to pariah: Some reflections on human attitudes to dogs. In *The Domestic Dog: Its Evolution, Behavior, and Interactions with People.* J. A. Serpell, ed. Pp. 245–56. Cambridge: Cambridge University Press.

Serpell, James A. 2002 Anthropomorphism and anthropomorphic selection – Beyond the "cute response." *Society and Animals* 10(4):437–54.

Serrano Espinosa, Manuel 1998 Acerca de los orígenes de la tauromaquia cretense. *Gerión* 16:39–48.

Service, Elman R. 1962 *Primitive Social Organization: An Evolutionary Perspective.* New York: Random House.

Shaffer, Brian S. 1992 Quarter-inch screening: Understanding biases in recovery of vertebrate faunal remains. *American Antiquity* 57(1):129–36.

Shanklin, Eugenia 1983 Ritual and social uses of goats in Kom. In *The Keeping of Animals: Adaptation and Social Relations in Livestock Producing Communities.* R. Berleant-Schiller and E. Shanklin, eds. Pp. 11–36. Totowa, NJ: Allenheld, Osmun.

Sharp, Henry S. 1976 Man: wolf: woman: dog. *Arctic Anthropology* 13:25–34.

Sharp, Henry S. 1988 Dry meat and gender: The absence of Chipewyan ritual for the regulation of hunting and animal numbers. In *Hunters and Gatherers 2: Property, Power and Ideology.* T. Ingold, D. Riches, and J. Woodburn, eds. Pp. 183–91. New York: Berg.

Shea, John J. 1993 Lithic use-wear evidence for hunting by Neandertals and early modern humans from the Levantine Mousterian. In *Hunting and Animal Exploitation in the Later Palaeolithic and Mesolithic of Eurasia.* G. L. Peterkin, H. M. Bricker, and P. A. Mellars, eds. Pp. 189–97. Archaeological Papers of the American Anthropological Association. Washington, DC: American Anthropological Association.

Shea, John J. 1998 Neandertal and early modern human behavioral variability: A regional-scale approach to lithic evidence for hunting in the Levantine Mousterian. *Current Anthropology* 39(supplement):S45–S78.

Shelach, Gideon 2006 Economic adaptation, community structure, and sharing strategies of households at early sedentary communities in northeast China. *Journal of Anthropological Archaeology* 25(3):318–45.

Shell, Marc 1986 The family pet. *Representations* 15:121–53.

Shepard, Paul 1993 On animal friends. In *The Biophilia Hypothesis.* S. R. Kellert and E. O. Wilson, eds. Pp. 275–300. Washington, DC: Island Press.

Sherratt, Andrew G. 1981 Plough and pastoralism: Aspects of the Secondary Products Revolution. In *Pattern of the Past: Studies in Honour of David Clarke.* I. Hodder, G. L. Isaac, and N. Hammond, eds. Pp. 261–306. Cambridge: Cambridge University Press.

Sherratt, Andrew G. 1982 Mobile resources: Settlement and exchange in early agricultural Europe. In *Ranking, Resource and Exchange: Aspects of the*

*Archaeology of Early European Society.* A. C. Renfrew and S. J. Shennan, eds. Pp. 13–26. Cambridge: Cambridge University Press.

Sherratt, Andrew G. 1983 The secondary exploitation of animals in the Old World. *World Archaeology* 15(1):90–104.

Sherratt, Andrew G. 1986 Cups that cheered. In *Bell Beakers of the Western Mediterranean.* W. H. Waldren and R. C. Kennard, eds. Pp. 81–114. British Archaeological Reports, International Series. Oxford: British Archaeological Reports.

Sherratt, Andrew G. 1995 Reviving the grand narrative: Archaeology and long-term change. *Journal of European Archaeology* 3(1):1–32.

Sherratt, Andrew G. 2003 The horse and the wheel: The dialectics of change in the circum-Pontic region and adjacent areas, 4500–1500 BC. In *Prehistoric Steppe Adaptation and the Horse.* M. A. Levine, A. C. Renfrew, and K. V. Boyle, eds. Pp. 233–52. McDonald Institute Monographs. Cambridge: McDonald Institute for Archaeological Research.

Shigehara, Nobuo, and Hitomi Hongo 2000 Ancient remains of Jomon dogs from Neolithic sites in Japan. In *Dogs through Time: An Archaeological Perspective.* S. J. Crockford, ed. Pp. 61–7. British Archaeological Reports, International Series. Oxford: Archaeopress.

Shipman, Pat 1981 *Life History of a Fossil: An Introduction to Taphonomy and Paleoecology.* Cambridge: Harvard University Press.

Shipman, Pat 1983 Early hominid lifestyle: Hunting and gathering or foraging and scavenging? In *Animals and Archaeology: 1. Hunters and Their Prey.* J. Clutton-Brock and C. Grigson, eds. Pp. 31–49. British Archaeological Reports, International Series. Oxford: British Archaeological Reports.

Shipman, Pat 1986a Scavenging or hunting in early hominids: Theoretical framework and tests. *American Anthropologist* 88(1):27–43.

Shipman, Pat 1986b Studies of hominid-faunal interactions at Olduvai Gorge. *Journal of Human Evolution* 15:691–706.

Shipman, Pat 1989 Altered bones from Olduvai Gorge, Tanzania: Techniques, problems, and implications of their recognition. In *Bone Modification.* R. Bonnichsen and M. H. Sorg, eds. Pp. 317–34. Orono, ME: Center for the Study of the First Americans.

Sidell, Elizabeth J., and Claire Scudder 2005 The eggshell from Çatalhöyük: A pilot study. In *Inhabiting Çatalhöyük: Reports from the 1995–1999 Seasons.* I. Hodder, ed. Pp. 117–21. McDonald Institute Monographs. Cambridge: McDonald Institute for Archaeological Research.

Sidoff, Phillip G. 1977 An ethnohistorical investigation of the Medicine Bundle Complex among selected tribes of the Great Plains. *Wisconsin Archeologist* 58(3):173–204.

Sillitoe, Paul 2001 Hunting for conservation in the Papua New Guinea highlands. *Ethnos* 66(3):365–93.

Simmons, Alan H. 1988 Extinct pygmy hippopotamus and early man in Cyprus. *Nature* 333(6173):554–7.

Simmons, Alan H. 1991a Humans, island colonization, and Pleistocene extinctions in the Mediterranean: The view from Akrotiri *Aetokremnos*, Cyprus. *Antiquity* 65(249):857–69.

Simmons, Alan H. 1991b One flew over the hippo's nest: Extinct Pleistocene fauna, early man, and conservative archaeology in Cyprus. In *Perspectives on the Past: Theoretical Biases in Mediterranean Hunter-Gatherer Research*. G. A. Clark, ed. Pp. 282–304. Philadelphia: University of Pennsylvania Press.

Simmons, Alan H. 1996 Whose myth? Archaeological data, interpretations, and implications for the human association with extinct Pleistocene fauna at Akrotiri *Aetokremnos*, Cyprus. *Journal of Mediterranean Archaeology* 9(1):97–105.

Simmons, Alan H. 1999 *Faunal Extinction in an Island Society: Pygmy Hippopotamus Hunters of Cyprus*. Dordrecht: Kluwer Academic Publishers.

Simmons, Alan H. 2001 The first humans and last pygmy hippopotami of Cyprus. In *The Earliest Prehistory of Cyprus from Colonization to Exploitation*. S. Swiny, ed. Pp. 1–18. American Schools of Oriental Research Archaeological Reports. Boston: American Schools of Oriental Research.

Simmons, Alan H., and Mohammad Najjar 2006 Ghwair I: A small, complex Neolithic community in southern Jordan. *Journal of Field Archaeology* 31(1):77–95.

Simons, Dwight D. 1983 Interactions between California Condors and humans in prehistoric far western North America. In *Vulture Biology and Management*. S. R. Wilbur and J. A. Jackson, eds. Pp. 470–94. Berkeley: University of California Press.

Simoons, Frederick J. 1968 *A Ceremonial Ox of India: The Mithan in Nature, Culture, and History*. Madison: University of Wisconsin Press.

Simoons, Frederick J. 1979 Questions in the sacred-cow controversy. *Current Anthropology* 20(3):467–93.

Simoons, Frederick J., and Deryck O. Lodrick 1981 Background to understanding the cattle situation of India: The sacred cow concept in Hindu religion and folk culture. *Zeitschrift für Ethnologie* 106(1–2):121–37.

Singh, Purushottam 1974 *Neolithic Cultures of Western Asia*. London: Seminar Press.

Sipahi, Tunç 2001 New evidence from Anatolia regarding bull-leaping scenes in the art of the Aegean and the Near East. *Anatolica* 27:107–25.

Sîrbu, Valeriu 1993 Sacrificii rituale de animale la traco-geto-daci, dacii liberi şi daco-romani/secolele XI î de H. – III d.H. *Arheologia Moldovei* 16:87–120.

Skak-Nielsen, Niels V. 2009 Flint and metal daggers in Scandinavia and other parts of Europe: A re-interpretation of their function in the Late Neolithic and Early Copper and Bronze Age. *Antiquity* 83(320):349–58.

Skinner, J. O. 1904 The house sparrow. *Annual Report of the Board of Regents of the Smithsonian Institution*. 1904:423–8.

Skybreak, Ardea 1984 *Of Primeval Steps and Future Leaps: An Essay on the Emergence of Human Beings, the Source of Women's Oppression, and the Road to Emancipation.* Chicago: Banner Press.

Sloan, R. E., and M. A. Duncan 1978 Zooarchaeology of Nichoria. In *Excavations at Nichoria in Southwest Greece I: Site, Environs and Techniques.* G. Rapp, Jr. and S. E. Aschenbrenner, eds. Pp. 60–77. Minneapolis: University of Minnesota Press.

Smith, Andrew B. 1990a On becoming herders: Khoikhoi and San ethnicity in southern Africa. *African Studies* 49(2):51–73.

Smith, Andrew B. 2000 The origins of the domesticated animals of southern Africa. In *The Origins and Development of African Livestock: Archaeology, Genetics, Linguistics and Ethnography.* R. M. Blench and K. C. MacDonald, eds. Pp. 222–38. London: UCL Press.

Smith, Eric A. 2004 Why do good hunters have higher reproductive success? *Human Nature* 15(4):343–64.

Smith, Jonathan Z. 1987 The domestication of sacrifice. In *Violent Origins: Ritual Killing and Cultural Formation.* R. G. Hamerton-Kelly, ed. Pp. 191–235. Stanford: Stanford University Press.

Smith, Kate 2006 *Guides, Guards and Gifts to the Gods: Domesticated Dogs in the Art and Archaeology of Iron Age and Roman Britain.* British Archaeological Reports, British Series, No. 422. Oxford: Archaeopress.

Smith, Michael E., Jennifer B. Wharton, and Jan Marie Olson 2003 Aztec feasts, rituals, and markets: Political uses of ceramic vessels in a commercial economy. In *The Archaeology and Politics of Food and Feasting in Early States and Empires.* T. L. Bray, ed. Pp. 235–68. New York: Kluwer Academic/Plenum Publishers.

Smith, Patricia, and Liora R. K. Horwitz 1984 Radiographic evidence for changing patterns of animal exploitation in the southern Levant. *Journal of Archaeological Science* 11(6):467–75.

Smith, Patricia R., and Michael T. Wilson 2001 Blood residues in archaeology. In *Handbook of Archaeological Sciences.* D. R. Brothwell and A. M. Pollard, eds. Pp. 313–22. London: John Wiley & Sons.

Smith, Philip E. L. 1976 *Food Production and its Consequences.* Menlo Park: Cummings.

Smith, Philip E. L. 1990b Architectural innovation and experimentation at Ganj Dareh, Iran. *World Archaeology* 21(3):323–35.

Snyder, Lynn M. 1991 Barking mutton: Ethnohistoric, archaeological and nutritional evidence pertaining to the domestic dog as a Native American food resource on the Plains. *Illinois State Museum Scientific Papers* 23:359–78.

Sobania, Neal 1991 Feasts, famines and friends: Nineteenth century exchange and ethnicity in the eastern Lake Turkana region. In *Herders, Warriors, and Traders: Pastoralism in Africa.* J. G. Galaty and P. Bonte, eds. Pp. 118–42. Boulder: Westview.

Soffer, Olga, James M. Adovasio, and David C. Hyland 2000 The well-dressed 'Venus': Women's wear ca. 27,000 BP. *Archaeology, Ethnology & Anthropology of Eurasia* 1(1):37–47.

Soffer, Olga, Valery Yu. Suntsov, and Ninelj L. Kornietz 2001 Thinking mammoth in domesticating late Pleistocene landscapes. In *Proceedings of the International Conference on Mammoth Site Studies*. D. L. West, ed. Pp. 143–51. University of Kansas Publications in Anthropology. Lawrence, KS: University of Kansas Department of Anthropology.

Solecki, Rose L., and Thomas H. McGovern 1980 Predatory birds and prehistoric man. In *Theory and Practice: Essays Presented to Gene Weltfish*. S. Diamond, ed. Pp. 79–95. The Hague: Mouton.

Sondaar, Paul Y., and Sandra A. E. van der Geer 2000 Mesolithic environment and animal exploitation on Cyprus and Sardinia/Corsica. In *Archaeozoology of the Near East IVA: Proceedings of the Fourth International Symposium on the Archaeozoology of Southwestern Asia and Adjacent Areas*. M. Mashkour, A. M. Choyke, H. Buitenhuis, and F. Poplin, eds. Pp. 67–73. ARC – Publicatie. Groningen: Center for Archeological Research and Consultancy.

Song, Hoon 2010 *Pigeon Trouble: Bestiary Biopolitics in a Deindustrialized America*. Philadelphia: University of Pennsylvania Press.

Sorrentino, Claudio 1989 Il *Sus scrofa* L. come offerta funebre: La sua distribuzione nelle tombe della necropoli romana del 'Cantone' a Collelongo (L'Aquila, Abruzzo, Italia). In *L'Animal dans les Pratiques Religieuses: Les Manifestations Materielles*. J.-D. Vigne, ed. Pp. 119–26. Anthropozoologica. Paris: Éditions du Centre National de la Recherche Scientifique.

Speller, Camilla F., Brian M. Kemp, Scott D. Wyatt, Cara Monroe, William D. Lipe, Ursula M. Arndt, and Dongya Y. Yang 2010 Ancient mitochondrial DNA analysis reveals complexity of indigenous North American turkey domestication. *Proceedings of the National Academy of Sciences* 107(7):2807–12.

Speth, John D. 1983 *Bison Kills and Bone Counts: Decision Making by Ancient Hunters*. Chicago: University of Chicago Press.

Speth, John D. 1990 Seasonality, resource stress, and food sharing in so-called 'egalitarian' foraging societies. *Journal of Anthropological Archaeology* 9(2):148–88.

Speth, John D. 1991 Taphonomy and early hominid behavior: Problems in distinguishing cultural from non-cultural agents. In *Human Predators and Prey Mortality*. M. C. Stiner, ed. Pp. 31–40. Boulder: Westview.

Speth, John D., and Katherine A. Spielmann 1983 Energy source, protein metabolism, and hunter-gatherer subsistence strategies. *Journal of Anthropological Archaeology* 2(1):1–31.

Speth, John D., and Eitan Tchernov 2001 Neandertal hunting and meat-processing in the Near East: Evidence from Kebara Cave (Israel). In *Meat-Eating and Human Evolution*. C. B. Stanford and H. T. Bunn, eds. Pp. 52–72. Oxford: Oxford University Press.

Speth, John D., and Eitan Tchernov 2002 Middle Paleolithic tortoise use at Kebara Cave (Israel). *Journal of Archaeological Science* 29(5):471–83.

Spielmann, Katherine A. 1989 A review: Dietary restrictions on hunter-gatherer women and the implications for fertility and infant mortality. *Human Ecology* 17(3):321–35.

Spielmann, Katherine A. 2002 Feasting, craft specialization, and the ritual mode of production in small-scale societies. *American Anthropologist* 104(1):195–207.

Spiess, Arthur E. 1979 *Reindeer and Caribou Hunters: An Archaeological Study*. New York: Academic Press.

Spinage, Clive A. 1971 Two records of pathological conditions in the Impala (*Aepyceros melampus*). *Journal of Zoology* 164:269–70.

Sponheimer, Matt, Julia A. Lee-Thorp, Darryl J. de Ruiter, Daryl Codron, Jacqui Codron, Alexander T. Baugh, and J. Francis Thackeray 2005 Hominins, sedges, and termites: New carbon isotope data from the Sterkfontein valley and Kruger National Park. *Journal of Human Evolution* 48(3):301–12.

Sponheimer, Matt, Benjamin H. Passey, Darryl J. de Ruiter, Debbie Guatelli-Steinberg, Thure E. Cerling, and Julia A. Lee-Thorp 2006 Isotopic evidence for dietary variability in the early hominin *Paranthropus robustus*. *Science* 314(5801):980–2.

Spotorno, Angel E., J. C. Marín, G. Manríquez, J. P. Valladares, E. Rico, and C. Rivas 2006 Ancient and modern steps during the domestication of guinea pigs (*Cavia porcellus* L.). *Journal of Zoology* 270(1):57–62.

Spriggs, Matthew 1996 Early agriculture and what went before in island Melanesia: Continuity or intrusion? In *The Origins and Spread of Agriculture and Pastoralism in Eurasia*. D. R. Harris, ed. Pp. 524–37. London: UCL Press.

Srejović, Dragoslav 1972 *Europe's First Monumental Sculpture: New Discoveries at Lepenski Vir*. L. F. Edwards, transl. New York: Stein and Day.

St. John, H. C. 1873 The Ainos: Aborigines of Yeso. *Journal of the Anthropological Institute of Great Britain and Ireland* 2(2):248–54.

Stahl, Ann B. 1984 Hominid dietary selection before fire. *Current Anthropology* 25(2):151–68.

Stallibrass, Sue 1996 Sacred cows from Solway: Bog bodies on the Anglo-Scottish border. In *Ritual Treatment of Human and Animal Remains: Proceedings of the First Meeting of the Osteoarchaeological Research Group Held in Cambridge on 8th October 1994*. S. Anderson and K. V. Boyle, eds. Pp. 35–43. Oxford: Oxbow.

Stanc, Simina, and Luminiţa Bejenaru 2004 Animal offerings found in necropoleis belonging to Santana of Mureş-Cerniahov culture from the east and the south extra-Carpathian zones of Romania. In *Behaviour behind Bones: The Zooarchaeology of Ritual, Religion, Status and Identity*. S. J. O'Day, W. Van Neer, and A. Ervynck, eds. Pp. 14–19. Oxford: Oxbow.

Stanford, Craig B. 1996 The hunting ecology of wild chimpanzees: Implications for the evolutionary ecology of Pliocene hominids. *American Anthropologist* 98(1):96–113.

Stanford, Craig B. 1999 *The Hunting Apes: Meat Eating and the Origins of Human Behavior*. Princeton: Princeton University Press.

Stanford, Craig B. 2001 A comparison of social meat-foraging by chimpanzees and human foragers. In *Meat-Eating and Human Evolution*. C. B. Stanford and H. T. Bunn, eds. Pp. 122–40. Oxford: Oxford University Press.

Starhawk 1989 *The Spiral Dance: A Rebirth of the Ancient Religion of the Great Goddess*. Tenth anniversary edition. San Francisco: HarperSan Francisco.

Steadman, David W. 1989 Extinction of birds in eastern Polynesia: A review of the record, and comparisons with other Pacific island groups. *Journal of Archaeological Science* 16(2):177–205.

Steadman, David W. 1995 Prehistoric extinctions of Pacific Island birds: Biodiversity meets zooarchaeology. *Science* 267(5201):1123–31.

Steadman, David W. 2006 *Extinction and Biogeography of Tropical Pacific Birds*. Chicago: University of Chicago Press.

Steadman, David W., Paul S. Martin, Ross D. E. MacPhee, A. J. T. Jull, H. Gregory McDonald, Charles A. Woods, Manuel Iturralde-Vinent, and Gregory W. L. Hodgins 2005 Asynchronous extinction of late Quaternary sloths on continents and islands. *Proceedings of the National Academy of Sciences* 102(33):11763–68.

Steadman, David W., Gregory K. Pregill, and Storrs L. Olson 1984 Fossil vertebrates from Antigua, Lesser Antilles: Evidence for Late Holocene human-caused extinctions in the West Indies. *Proceedings of the National Academy of Sciences* 81(14):4448–51.

Steadman, David W., and Barry V. Rolett 1996 A chronostratigraphic analysis of landbird extinction on Tahuata, Marquesas Islands. *Journal of Archaeological Science* 23:81–94.

Steadman, David W., J. Peter White, and Jim Allen 1999 Prehistoric birds from New Ireland, Papua New Guinea: Extinctions on a large Melanesian island. *Proceedings of the National Academy of Sciences* 96(5):2563–8.

Steadman, Sharon R. 2000 Spatial patterning and social complexity on prehistoric Anatolian tell sites: Models for mounds. *Journal of Anthropological Archaeology* 19(2):164–99.

Steel, Louise 2004 A goodly feast . . . a cup of mellow wine: Feasting in Bronze Age Cyprus. In *The Mycenaean Feast*. J. C. Wright, ed. Pp. 161–80. Hesperia. Princeton: American School of Classical Studies.

Steensma, Karel J., and David S. Reese 1999 Genet. In *Faunal Extinction in an Island Society: Pygmy Hippopotamus Hunters of Cyprus*. A. H. Simmons, ed. Pp. 167–9. Dordrecht: Kluwer Academic Publishers.

Stein, Gil J. 1989 Strategies of risk reduction in herding and hunting systems of Neolithic southeast Anatolia. In *Early Animal Domestication and its*

*Cultural Context.* P. J. Crabtree, D. V. Campana, and K. Ryan, eds. Pp. 87–97. MASCA Research Papers in Science and Archaeology. Philadelphia: University of Pennsylvania, University Museum.

Steppan, Karlheinz 2006 The Neolithic human impact and wild horses in Germany and Switzerland: Horse size variability and the chrono-ecological context. In *Horses and Humans: The Evolution of Human-Equine Relationships.* S. L. Olsen, S. Grant, A. M. Choyke, and L. Bartosiewicz, eds. Pp. 209–20. British Archeological Reports, International Series. Oxford: Archaeopress.

Stevens, Jeffrey R. 2004 The selfish nature of generosity: Harassment and food sharing in primates. *Proceedings of the Royal Society of London, Series B* 271(1538):451–6.

Stevenson, Henry M., and Bruce H. Anderson 1994 *Birdlife of Florida.* Gainesville: University Press of Florida.

Stevenson, Henry N. C. 1937 Feasting and meat division among the Zahau Chins of Burma; a preliminary analysis. *Journal of the Royal Anthropological Institute* 47:15–32.

Stiner, Mary C. 1990 The use of mortality patterns in archaeological studies of hominid predatory adaptations. *Journal of Anthropological Archaeology* 9:305–51.

Stiner, Mary C. 1991a An interspecific perspective on the emergence of the modern human predatory niche. In *Human Predators and Prey Mortality.* M. C. Stiner, ed. Pp. 149–85. Boulder: Westview.

Stiner, Mary C. 1991b Food procurement and transport by human and non-human predators. *Journal of Archaeological Science* 18(4):455–82.

Stiner, Mary C. 1993a Modern human origins – Faunal perspectives. *Annual Review of Anthropology* 22:55–82.

Stiner, Mary C. 1993b Small animal exploitation and its relation to hunting, scavenging, and gathering in the Italian Mousterian. In *Hunting and Animal Exploitation in the Later Palaeolithic and Mesolithic of Eurasia.* G. L. Peterkin, H. M. Bricker, and P. A. Mellars, eds. Pp. 107–25. Archaeological Papers of the American Anthropological Association. Washington, DC: American Anthropological Association.

Stiner, Mary C. 1993c The place of hominids among predators: Interspecific comparisons of food procurement and transport. In *From Bones to Behavior: Ethnoarchaeological and Experimental Contributions to the Interpretation of Faunal Remains.* J. Hudson, ed. Pp. 38–61. Carbondale: Southern Illinois University, Center for Archaeological Investigations, Occasional Papers.

Stiner, Mary C. 1994 *Honor among Thieves: A Zooarchaeological Study of Neandertal Ecology.* Princeton: Princeton University Press.

Stiner, Mary C. 1999 Palaeolithic mollusc exploitation at Riparo Mochi (Balzi Rossi, Italy): Food and ornaments from the Aurignacian through Epigravettian. *Antiquity* 282(73):735–54.

Stiner, Mary C. 2009 Prey choice, site occupation intensity & economic diversity in the Middle – early Upper Palaeolithic at the Üçağızlı Caves, Turkey. *Before Farming* 2009(3).

Stiner, Mary C., Ran Barkai, and Avi Gopher 2009 Cooperative hunting and meat sharing 400, 200 kya at Qesem Cave, Israel. *Proceedings of the National Academy of Sciences* 106(32):13207–12.

Stiner, Mary C., and Steven L. Kuhn 1992 Subsistence, technology, and adaptive variation in Middle Paleolithic Italy. *American Anthropologist* 94(2):306–39.

Stiner, Mary C., and Natalie D. Munro 2002 Approaches to prehistoric diet breadth, demography, and prey ranking systems in time and space. *Journal of Archaeological Method and Theory* 9(2):181–214.

Stiner, Mary C., Natalie D. Munro, and Todd A. Surovell 2000 The tortoise and the hare: Small-game use, the broad-spectrum revolution, and paleolithic demography. *Current Anthropology* 41(1):39–73.

Stocker, Sharon R., and Jack L. Davis 2004 Animal sacrifice, archives, and feasting at the Palace of Nestor. In *The Mycenaean Feast.* J. C. Wright, ed. Pp. 59–75. Hesperia. Princeton: American School of Classical Studies.

Stone, Richard 2001 The cold zone. *Discover* 22(2):58–65.

Storr, Anthony 1968 *Human Aggression.* New York: Bantam.

Strasser, Thomas F. 1996 Archaeological myths and the overkill hypothesis in Cypriot prehistory. *Journal of Mediterranean Archaeology* 9(1):113–16.

Strathern, Andrew J. 1971 Pig complex and cattle complex: Some comparisons and counterpoints. *Mankind* 8(2):129–36.

Strathern, Andrew J. 1980 The central and the contingent: Bridewealth among the Melpa and the Wiru. In *The Meaning of Marriage Payments.* J. L. Comaroff, ed. Pp. 49–66. New York: Academic Press.

Strong, Roy 2002 *Feast: A History of Grand Eating.* London: Jonathan Cape.

Stuart, Anthony J. 1999 Late Pleistocene megafaunal extinctions: A European perspective. In *Extinctions in Near Time: Causes, Contexts, and Consequences.* R. D. E. MacPhee, ed. Pp. 257–69. New York: Kluwer Academic/Plenum Publishers.

Stuart, Anthony J. 2005 The extinction of woolly mammoth (*Mammuthus primigenius*) and straight-tusked elephant (*Palaeoloxodon antiquus*) in Europe. *Quaternary International* 126–128:171–7.

Stuart, Anthony J., Pavel A. Kosintsev, Thomas F. G. Higham, and Adrian M. Lister 2004 Pleistocene to Holocene extinction dynamics in giant deer and woolly mammoth. *Nature* 431(7009):684–9.

Studer, Jacqueline 1988 Entre Chien et Homme au Bronze Final. *ArchaeoZoologia* 2(1–2):269–80.

Sturdy, Derek A. 1975 Some reindeer economies in prehistoric Europe. In *Palaeoeconomy.* E. S. Higgs, ed. Pp. 55–95. Cambridge: Cambridge University Press.

Suchentrunk, Franz, H. Ben Slimen, C. Stamatis, H. Sert, M. Scandura, Marco Apollonio, and Z. Mamuris 2006 Molecular approaches revealing prehistoric, historic, or recent translocations and introductions of hares (genus *Lepus*) by humans. *Human Evolution* 21(2):151–65.

Surovell, Todd A. 1999 Modeling occupation intensity and small game use in the Levant. In *Zooarchaeology of the Pleistocene/Holocene Boundary*. J. C. Driver, ed. Pp. 31–6. British Archaeological Reports, International Series. Oxford: Archaeopress.

Surovell, Todd A., Vance T. Holliday, Joseph A. M. Gingerich, Caroline Ketron, C. Vance Haynes, Jr., Ilene Hilman, Daniel P. Wagner, Eileen Johnson, and Philippe Claeys 2009 An independent evaluation of the Younger Dryas extraterrestrial impact hypothesis. *Proceedings of the National Academy of Sciences* 106(43):18155–8.

Surovell, Todd A., and Nicole M. Waguespack 2008 How many elephant kills are 14?: Clovis mammoth and mastodon kills in context. *Quaternary International* 191(1):82–97.

Surovell, Todd A., Nicole M. Waguespack, and P. Jeffrey Brantingham 2005 Global archaeological evidence for proboscidean overkill. *Proceedings of the National Academy of Sciences* 102(17):6231–6.

Sutter, John W. 1987 Cattle and inequality: Herd size differences and pastoral production among the Fulani of northeastern Senegal. *Africa* 57(2):196–218.

Svoboda, Jiří 2001 Seeing mammoths and using mammoths: Evidence from Upper Paleolithic Moravia. In *Proceedings of the International Conference on Mammoth Site Studies*. D. L. West, ed. Pp. 153–61. University of Kansas Publications in Anthropology. Lawrence, KS: University of Kansas Department of Anthropology.

Sykes, Naomi J. 2005 Hunting for the Anglo-Normans: Zooarchaeological evidence for medieval identity. In *Just Skin and Bones? New Perspectives on Human-Animal Relations in the Historical Past*. A. G. Pluskowski, ed. Pp. 73–80. British Archeological Reports, International Series. Oxford: Archaeopress.

Szuter, Christine R. 2001 Gender and animals: Hunting technology, ritual, and subsistence in the greater Southwest. In *Women and Men in the Prehispanic Southwest: Labor, Power, and Prestige*. P. L. Crown, ed. Pp. 197–220. Santa Fe: School of American Research Press.

Szynkiewicz, Slawoj 1990 Sheep bone as a sign of human descent: Tibial symbolism among the Mongols. In *Signifying Animals: Human Meaning in the Natural World*. R. Willis, ed. Pp. 74–84. London: Unwin Hyman.

Tambiah, Stanley J. 1969 Animals are good to think and good to prohibit. *Ethnology* 8:423–59.

Tambiah, Stanley J. 1973 Dowry and bridewealth, and the property rights of women in South Asia. In *Bridewealth and Dowry*. J. Goody and S. J. Tambiah, eds. Pp. 59–169. Cambridge Papers in Social Anthropology.

Tani, Yutaka 1996 Domestic animal as serf: Ideologies of nature in the Mediterranean and the Middle East. In *Redefining Nature: Ecology, Culture and Domestication*. R. F. Ellen and K. Fukui, eds. Pp. 387–415. Oxford: Berg.

Tankersley, Kenneth B., Michael R. Waters, and Thomas W. Stafford, Jr. 2009 Clovis and the American mastodon at Big Bone Lick, Kentucky. *American Antiquity* 74(2):558–67.

Tannen, Deborah 1990 *You Just Don't Understand: Women and Men in Conversation*. New York: Ballantine Books.

Tanner, Adrian 1979 *Bringing Home Animals: Religious Ideology and Mode of Production of the Mistassini Cree Hunters*. New York: St. Martin's Press.

Tanner, Nancy Makepeace 1981 *On Becoming Human*. Cambridge: Cambridge University Press.

Tappen, Martha 1995 Savanna ecology and natural bone deposition: Implications for early hominid site formation, hunting, and scavenging. *Current Anthropology* 36(2):223–60.

Tapper, Richard 1988 Animality, humanity, morality, society. In *What Is an Animal?* T. Ingold, ed. Pp. 47–62. London: Unwin Hyman.

Tarcan, Carmen, Jean-Marie Cordy, Luminita Bejenaru, and Mircea Şt. Udrescu 2000 Consommation de la viande de chien: Le *vicus* de Braives (Belgique) et les sites géto-daces et romains de Roumanie. In *Dogs through Time: An Archaeological Perspective*. S. J. Crockford, ed. Pp. 123–8. British Archaeological Reports, International Series. Oxford: Archaeopress.

Taylor, A. H., Gavin R. Hunt, F. S. Medina, and Russell D. Gray 2009 Do New Caledonian crows solve physical problems through causal reasoning? *Proceedings of the Royal Society of London, Series B* 276(1655):247–54.

Taylor, Kenneth I. 1974 *Sanumá Fauna: Prohibitions and Classifications*. Caracas: Fundación La Salle de Ciencias Naturales.

Tchernov, Eitan 1984 Commensal animals and human sedentism in the Middle East. In *Animals and Archaeology: 3. Early Herders and their Flocks*. J. Clutton-Brock and C. Grigson, eds. Pp. 91–115. British Archaeological Reports, International Series. Oxford: British Archaeological Reports.

Tchernov, Eitan 1991 Biological evidence for human sedentism in southwest Asia during the Natufian. In *The Natufian Culture in the Levant*. O. Bar-Yosef and F. R. Valla, eds. Pp. 315–40. International Monographs in Prehistory. Ann Arbor: International Monographs in Prehistory.

Tchernov, Eitan 1993 From sedentism to domestication – A preliminary review for the southern Levant. In *Skeletons in Her Cupboard: Festschrift for Juliet Clutton-Brock*. A. T. Clason, S. Payne, and H.-P. Uerpmann, eds. Pp. 189–233. Oxbow Monograph.

Tchernov, Eitan, and Liora R. K. Horwitz 1991 Body size diminution under domestication: Unconscious selection in primeval domesticates. *Journal of Anthropological Archaeology* 10(1):54–75.

Tebbich, Sabine, Amanda M. Seed, Nathan J. Emery, and Nicola S. Clayton 2007 Non-tool-using rooks, *Corvus frugilegus*, solve the trap-tube problem. *Animal Cognition* 10(2):225–31.

Tedlock, Barbara 2001 Divination as a way of knowing: Embodiment, visualisation, narrative, and interpretation. *Folklore* 112(2):189–97.

Tegner, Henry S. 1951 *The Roe Deer: Their History, Habits and Pursuit*. London: Batchworth.

ten Raa, Eric 1986 The acquisition of cattle by hunter-gatherers: A traumatic experience in cultural change. *Sprache und Geschichte in Afrika* 7(2):361–74.

Testart, Alain 1986 *Essais sur les fondements de la division sexuelle du travail chez les chasseurs-cueilleurs*. Cahiers de l'Homme, Nouvelle Série, No. 25. Paris: Éditions de l'École des Hautes Études en Sciences Sociales.

Testart, Alain 1987 Game sharing systems and kinship systems among hunter-gatherers. *Man* 22(2):287–304.

Testart, Alain 2006 Interprétation symbolique et interprétation religieuse en archéologie: L'exemple du taureau à Çatal Höyük. *Paléorient* 32(2):23–57.

Thomas, Chad R., Christopher Carr, and Cynthia Keller 2005 Animal-totemic clans of Ohio Hopewellian peoples. In *Gathering Hopewell: Society, Ritual and Ritual Interaction*. C. Carr and D. T. Case, eds. Pp. 339–85. New York: Springer.

Thomas, David H. 1971 On distinguishing natural from cultural bone in archaeological sites. *American Antiquity* 36:366–71.

Thomas, Julian S. 1991 *Rethinking the Neolithic*. Cambridge: Cambridge University Press.

Thomas, Julian S. 1996 The cultural context of the first use of domesticates in continental Central and Northwest Europe. In *The Origins and Spread of Agriculture and Pastoralism in Eurasia*. D. R. Harris, ed. Pp. 310–22. London: UCL Press.

Thomas, Julian S. 1999 *Understanding the Neolithic*. London: Routledge.

Thomas, Julian S. 2003 Thoughts on the 'repacked' Neolithic Revolution. *Antiquity* 77(295):67–74.

Thomas, Keith 1983 *Man and the Natural World: A History of the Modern Sensibility*. New York: Pantheon.

Thomas, Nicholas, and Caroline Humphrey, eds. 1994 *Shamanism, History, and the State*. Ann Arbor: University of Michigan Press.

Thomas, Richard M. 2005 Perceptions versus reality: Changing attitudes towards pets in medieval and postmedieval England. In *Just Skin and Bones? New Perspectives on Human-Animal Relations in the Historical Past*. A. G. Pluskowski, ed. Pp. 95–104. British Archeological Reports, International Series. Oxford: Archaeopress.

Tilley, Christopher 1999 *Metaphor and Material Culture*. Oxford: Blackwell.

Todd, Lawrence C., and George C. Frison 1992 Reassembly of bison skeletons from the Horner site: A study in anatomical refitting. In *Piecing Together the*

*Past: Applications of Refitting Studies in Archaeology.* J. L. Hofman and J. G. Enloe, eds. Pp. 63–82. British Archaeological Reports, International Series.

Todd, Lawrence C., Jack L. Hofman, and C. Bertrand Schultz 1990 Seasonality of the Scottsbluff and Lipscomb bison bonebeds: Implications for modeling Paleoindian subsistence. *American Antiquity* 55(4):813–27.

Tooker, Elisabeth 1965 The Iroquois white dog sacrifice in the latter part of the 18th century. *Ethnohistory* 12:129–40.

Trantalidou, Katerina 2006 Companions from the oldest times: Dogs in ancient Greek literature, iconography and osteological testimony. In *Dogs and People in Social, Working, Economic or Symbolic Interaction.* L. M. Snyder and E. A. Moore, eds. Pp. 96–120. Oxford: Oxbow.

Tresset, Anne, and Jean-Denis Vigne 2006 Le dépôt d'animaux de la structure e4: Une illustration de la symbolique des bovins à la charnière du Mésolithique et du Néolithiques bretons? In *Monuments Mégalithiques à Locmariaquer (Morbihan): Le Long Tumulus d'Er Grah dans son Environnement.* C.-T. Le Roux, ed. Pp. 123–45. Gallia Préhistoire Supplements. Paris: Éditions du Centre National de la Recherche Scientifique.

Trigger, Bruce G. 1990 *The Huron: Farmers of the North.* Fort Worth: Holt, Rinehart & Winston.

Trigger, Bruce G. 1995 Expanding middle-range theory. *Antiquity* 69(264): 449–58.

Tringham, Ruth E., Bogdan Brukner, Timothy M. Kaiser, Ksenija Borojević, Ljubomir Bukvić, Petar Šteli, Nerissa Russell, Mirjana Stevanović, and Barbara A. Voytek 1992 Excavations at Opovo, 1985–1987: Socioeconomic change in the Balkan Neolithic. *Journal of Field Archaeology* 19(3):351–86.

Tringham, Ruth E., and Dušan Krstić 1990 Conclusion: Selevac in the wider context of European prehistory. In *Selevac: A Neolithic Village in Yugoslavia.* R. E. Tringham and D. Krstić, eds. Pp. 567–616. Los Angeles: UCLA Institute of Archaeology.

Trinkaus, Erik 1987 Bodies, brawn, brains and noses: Human ancestors and human predation. In *The Evolution of Human Hunting.* M. H. Nitecki and D. V. Nitecki, eds. Pp. 107–45. New York: Plenum.

Trolle-Lassen, Tine 1987 Human exploitation of fur animals in Mesolithic Denmark – A case study. *ArchaeoZoologia* 1(2):85–102.

Trueman, Clive N. G., Judith H. Field, Joe Dortch, Bethan Charles, and Stephen Wroe 2005 Prolonged coexistence of humans and megafauna in Pleistocene Australia. *Proceedings of the National Academy of Sciences* 102(23):8381–5.

Trut, Lyudmila N. 1999 Early canid domestication: The fox-farm experiment. *American Scientist* 87:160–9.

Tsonev, Tsoni 1996 Neolithisation – A monotonic or catastrophic model for the transition to early farming? *Journal of European Archaeology* 4:87–97.

Tsuneki, Akira 2002 A Neolithic foundation deposit at Tell 'Ain el-Kerkh. In *Magic Practices and Ritual in the Near Eastern Neolithic: Proceedings of a*

*Workshop Held at the 2nd ICAANE, Copenhagen University, May 2000.* H. G. K. Gebel, B. D. Hermansen, and C. Hoffmann Jensen, eds. Pp. 133–43. Berlin: Ex Oriente.

Tuan, Yi-fu 1984 *Dominance and Affection: The Making of Pets.* New Haven: Yale University Press.

Tudge, Colin 1999 *Neanderthals, Bandits and Farmers: How Agriculture Really Began.* New Haven: Yale University Press.

Türkcan, Ali Umut 2007 Is it goddess or bear? The role of Catalhöyük animal seals in Neolithic symbolism. *Documenta Praehistorica* 34:257–66.

Turner, Rick C., and Robert G. Scaife, eds. 1995 *Bog Bodies: New Discoveries and New Perspectives.* London: British Museum Publications.

Turner, Terence S. 1985 Animal symbolism, totemism and the structure of myth. In *Animal Myths and Metaphors in South America.* G. Urton, ed. Pp. 49–106. Salt Lake City: University of Utah Press.

Turner, Terence S. 2006 Structure, process, form. In *Theorizing Ritual.* J. Kreinath, J. Snoek, and M. Stausberg, eds. Pp. 207–46. Leiden: Brill.

Turner, Victor W. 1969 *The Ritual Process: Structure and Anti-Structure.* Chicago: Aldine.

Turney, Chris S. M. *et al.* 2008 Late-surviving megafauna in Tasmania, Australia, implicate human involvement in their extinction. *Proceedings of the National Academy of Sciences* 105(34):12150–3.

Turton, David 1980 The economics of Mursi bridewealth: A comparative perspective. In *The Meaning of Marriage Payments.* J. L. Comaroff, ed. Pp. 67–92. New York: Academic Press.

Twiss, Katheryn C., ed. 2007 *The Archaeology of Food and Identity.* Carbondale: Center for Archaeological Investigations, Southern Illinois University at Carbondale.

Twiss, Katheryn C. 2008 Transformations in an early agricultural society: Feasting in the southern Levantine Pre-Pottery Neolithic. *Journal of Anthropological Archaeology* 27(4):418–42.

Twiss, Katheryn C. *et al.* 2008 Arson or accident? The burning of a Neolithic house at Çatalhöyük, Turkey. *Journal of Field Archaeology* 33(1):41–57.

Twiss, Katheryn C., Amy Bogaard, Michael P. Charles, Jennifer Henecke, Nerissa Russell, Louise Martin, and Glynis Jones 2009 Plants and animals together: Interpreting organic remains from Building 52 at Çatalhöyük. *Current Anthropology* 50(6):885–95.

Twiss, Katheryn C., and Nerissa Russell 2009 Taking the bull by the horns: Cattle horns at Neolithic Çatalhöyük, Turkey. *Paléorient* 35(2):19–32.

Tylor, Edward B. 1964 *Researches into the Early History of Mankind and the Development of Civilization.* Chicago: University of Chicago Press.

Tyrberg, Tommy 2002 The archaeological record of domesticated and tamed birds in Sweden. *Acta Zoologica Cracoviensia* 45(special issue):215–31.

Ubelaker, Douglas H., and Waldo R. Wedel 1975 Bird bones, burials, and bundles in Plains archaeology. *American Antiquity* 40:444–52.

Uerpmann, Hans-Peter 1973 Ein Beitrag zur Methodik der wirtschafthistorischen Auswertung von Tierknochenfunden aus Siedlungen. In *Domestikationsforschung und Geschichte der Haustiere: Internationales Symposion in Budapest, 1971.* J. Matolcsi, ed. Pp. 391–5. Budapest: Akadémiai Kiadó.

Uerpmann, Hans-Peter 1979 *Probleme der Neolithisierung des Mittelmeerraums.* Beihefte zum Tübinger Atlas des vorderen Oriente, Reihe B, No. 28. Wiesbaden: Dr. Ludwig Reichert Verlag.

Uerpmann, Hans-Peter 1990 Die Domestikation des Pferdes im Chalkolithikum West- und Mitteleuropas. *Madrider Mitteilungen* 31:109–53.

Uerpmann, Hans-Peter 1996 Animal domestication – accident or intention? In *The Origins and Spread of Agriculture and Pastoralism in Eurasia.* D. R. Harris, ed. Pp. 227–37. London: UCL Press.

Ugan, Andrew, and David A. Byers 2008 A global perspective on the spatiotemporal pattern of the Late Pleistocene human and woolly mammoth radiocarbon record. *Quaternary International* 191(1):69–81.

Ullén, Inga 1994 The power of case studies. Interpretation of a late-Bronze-Age settlement in central Sweden. *Journal of European Archaeology* 2(2):249–62.

Valeri, Valerio 1994 Wild victims: Hunting as sacrifice and sacrifice as hunting in Huaulu. *History of Religions* 34(2):101–31.

van Andel, Tjeerd H., and Curtis N. Runnels 1995 The earliest farmers in Europe. *Antiquity* 69(264):481–500.

Van der Veen, Marijke 2003 When is food a luxury? *World Archaeology* 34(3):405–27.

Van Neer, Wim, Omri Lernau, Renée F. Friedman, G. Mumford, J. Poblome, and Marc Waelkens 2004 Fish remains from archaeological sites as indicators of former trade connections in the Eastern Mediterranean. *Paléorient* 30(1):101–48.

Van Straten, Folkert T. 1988 The god's portion in Greek sacrificial representations: Is the tail doing nicely? In *Early Greek Cult Practice.* R. Hägg, N. Marinatos, and G. Nordquist, eds. Pp. 51–68. Skrifter Utgivna av Svenska Institutet i Athen. Stockholm: Svenska Institutet i Athen.

Van Straten, Folkert T. 1995 *Hierà Kalá: Images of Animal Sacrifice in Archaic and Classical Greece.* Religions in the Graeco-Roman World, No. 127. Leiden: E. J. Brill.

Van Tilburg, Jo Anne 1994 *Easter Island: Archaeology, Ecology, and Culture.* Washington, DC: Smithsonian Institution Press.

Vartanyan, Sergey L., Khikmat A. Arslanov, Juha A. Karhu, Göran Possnert, and Leopold D. Sulerzhitsky 2008 Collection of radiocarbon dates on the mammoths (*Mammuthus primigenius*) and other genera of Wrangel Island, northeast Siberia, Russia. *Quaternary Research* 70(1):51–9.

Vassas, Claudine 2006 Questions anthropologiques autour de l'interdit du porc dans le judaïsme et de son élection par le christianisme. In *De la Domestication au Tabou: Le Cas des Suidés au Proche-Orient Ancien.* B. Lion and C. Michel, eds. Pp. 227–32. Paris: De Boccard.

Vega-Centeno Sara-Lafosse, Rafael 2007 Construction, labor organization, and feasting during the Late Archaic Period in the Central Andes. *Journal of Anthropological Archaeology* 26(2):150–71.

Vellanoweth, René L., Barney G. Bartelle, Amira F. Ainis, Amanda C. Cannon, and Steven J. Schwartz 2008 A double dog burial from San Nicolas Island, California, USA: Osteology, context, and significance. *Journal of Archaeological Science* 35(12):3111–23.

Veltre, Douglas W., David R. Yesner, Kristine J. Crossen, Russell W. Graham, and Joan B. Coltrain 2008 Patterns of faunal extinction and paleoclimatic change from mid-Holocene mammoth and polar bear remains, Pribilof Islands, Alaska. *Quaternary Research* 70(1):40–50.

Vencl, Slavomil 1994 The archaeology of thirst. *Journal of European Archaeology* 2(2):299–326.

Venturi, Fabrizio 2006 Deux dépôts de fondation d'astragales à Tell Afis (Syrie). *Orient Express* 2006(1):27 – 9.

Verhoeven, Marc 2000 Death, fire and abandonment: Ritual practice at Neolithic Tell Sabi Abyad, Syria. *Archaeological Dialogues* 7(1):46–83.

Verhoeven, Marc 2002a Ritual and ideology in the Pre-Pottery Neolithic B of the Levant and southeast Anatolia. *Cambridge Archaeological Journal* 12(2):233–58.

Verhoeven, Marc 2002b Ritual and its investigation in prehistory. In *Magic Practices and Ritual in the Near Eastern Neolithic: Proceedings of a Workshop Held at the 2nd ICAANE, Copenhagen University, May 2000.* H. G. K. Gebel, B. D. Hermansen, and C. Hoffmann Jensen, eds. Pp. 5–40. Berlin: Ex Oriente.

Verhoeven, Marc 2004 Beyond boundaries: Nature, culture and a holistic approach to domestication in the Levant. *Journal of World Prehistory* 18(3):179–282.

Vigne, Jean-Denis 1988 *Les Mammifères Post-Glaciaires de Corse: Étude Archéozoologique.* Gallia Préhistoire, Supplément, No. 26. Paris: Éditions du Centre National de la Recherche Scientifique.

Vigne, Jean-Denis 1992 Zooarchaeology and the biogeographical history of the mammals of Corsica and Sardinia since the last ice age. *Mammal Review* 22(2):87–96.

Vigne, Jean-Denis 1993 Domestication ou appropriation pour la chasse: Histoire d'un choix socio-culturel depuis le Néolithique. L'exemple des cerfs (*Cervus*). *Exploitation des Animaux Sauvages à travers les Temps: IVe Colloque International de l'Homme et l'Animal.* Pp. 201-220. Juan-les-Pins: Éditions APCDA-CNRS.

Vigne, Jean-Denis 1996 Did man provoke extinctions of endemic large mammals on the Mediterranean islands? The view from Corsica. *Journal of Mediterranean Archaeology* 9(1):117–20.

Vigne, Jean-Denis 1999 The large 'true' Mediterranean islands as a model for the Holocene human impact on the European vertebrate fauna? Recent data and new reflections. In *The Holocene History of the European Vertebrate Fauna: Modern Aspects of Research*. N. Benecke, ed. Pp. 295–322. Archäologie in Eurasien. Rahden: Verlag Marie Leidorf.

Vigne, Jean-Denis 2001 Large mammals of early Aceramic Neolithic Cyprus: Preliminary results from Parekklisha *Shillourokambos*. In *The Earliest Prehistory of Cyprus from Colonization to Exploitation*. S. Swiny, ed. Pp. 55–60. American Schools of Oriental Research Archaeological Reports. Boston: American Schools of Oriental Research.

Vigne, Jean-Denis 2008 Zooarchaeological aspects of the Neolithic diet transition in the Near East and Europe, and their putative relationships with the Neolithic demographic transition. In *The Neolithic Demographic Transition and its Consequences*. J.-P. Bocquet-Appel and O. Bar-Yosef, eds. Pp. 179–205. Berlin: Springer.

Vigne, Jean-Denis, Isabelle Carrère, and Jean Guilaine 2004a Unstable status of early domestic ungulates in the Near East: The example of Shillourokambos (Cyprus, 9–8th millennia cal. BC). In *Le Néolithique de Chypre: Actes du Colloque International Organisé par le Département des Antiquités de Chypre et l'École Française d'Athènes, Nicosie, 17–19 M 2001*. J. Guilaine, A. Le Brun, and O. Daune-Le Brun, eds. Pp. 295–311. Athens: École Française d'Athènes.

Vigne, Jean-Denis, Isabelle Carrère, Jean-François Saliége, Alain Person, Hervé Bocherens, Jean Guilaine, and François Briois 2000 Predomestic cattle, sheep, goat and pig during the late 9th and the 8th millennium cal. BC on Cyprus: Preliminary results of Shillourokambos (Parekklisha, Limassol). In *Archaeozoology of the Near East IVA: Proceedings of the Fourth International Symposium on the Archaeozoology of Southwestern Asia and Adjacent Areas*. M. Mashkour, A. M. Choyke, H. Buitenhuis, and F. Poplin, eds. Pp. 83–106. ARC – Publicatie. Groningen: Center for Archeological Research and Consultancy.

Vigne, Jean-Denis, and Jean Guilaine 2004 Les premiers animaux de compagnie, 8500 ans avant notre ère? . . . ou comment j'ai mangé mon chat, mon chien et mon renard. *Anthropozoologica* 39:249–73.

Vigne, Jean-Denis, Jean Guilaine, K. Debue, L. Haye, and P. Gérard 2004b Early taming of the cat in Cyprus. *Science* 304(5668):259.

Vigne, Jean-Denis, and Daniel Helmer 2007 Was milk a "secondary product" in the Old World Neolithisation process? Its role in the domestication of cattle, sheep and goats. *Anthropozoologica* 42(2):9–40.

Vigne, Jean-Denis, Antoine Zazzo, Jean-François Saliége, François Poplin, Jean Guilaine, and Alan H. Simmons 2009 Pre-Neolithic wild boar management and introduction to Cyprus more than 11,400 years ago. *Proceedings of the National Academy of Sciences* 106(38):16135–8.

Vila, Emmanuelle 1991 Note sur un dépôt de gazelles dans une fosse Uruk d'El Kowm 2 – Caracol (Syrie). *Cahiers de l'Euphrate* 5–6:55–60.

Vila, Emmanuelle 2000 Bone remains from sacrificial places: The temples of Athena Alea at Tegea and of Asea on Agios Elias (the Peleponnese, Greece). In *Archaeozoology of the Near East IVB: Proceedings of the Fourth International Symposium on the Archaeozoology of Southwestern Asia and Adjacent Areas.* M. Mashkour, A. M. Choyke, H. Buitenhuis, and F. Poplin, eds. Pp. 197–205. ARC – Publicatie. Groningen: Center for Archeological Research and Consultancy.

Vila, Emmanuelle 2002 Les vestiges de chevilles osseuses de gazelles du secteur F à Tell Chuera (Syrie, bronze ancien). In *Archaeozoology of the Near East V: Proceedings of the Fifth International Symposium on the Archaeozoology of Southwestern Asia and Adjacent Areas.* H. Buitenhuis, A. M. Choyke, M. Mashkour, and A. H. Al-Shiyab, eds. Pp. 241–50. ARC – Publicatie. Groningen: Center for Archeological Research and Consultancy.

Vila, Emmanuelle, and Anne-Sophie Dalix 2004 Alimentation et idéologie: La place du sanglier et du porc à l'Âge du Bronze sur la côte levantine. *Anthropozoologica* 39:219–36.

Villari, Pietro 1991 The faunal remains in the Bothros at Eolo (Lipari). *Archaeo-Zoologia* 4(2):109–26.

Vinnicombe, Patricia 1976 *People of the Eland: Rock Paintings of the Drakensberg Bushmen as a Reflection of Their Life and Thought.* Pietermaritzburg: University of Natal Press.

Virah-Sawmy, Malika, Katherine J. Willis, and Lindsey Gillson 2010 Evidence for drought and forest declines during the recent megafaunal extinctions in Madagascar. *Journal of Biogeography* 37(3):506–19.

Voigt, Elizabeth A. 1984 Iron Age herders of the northern Transvaal, South Africa, in the First Millennium A.D. In *Animals and Archaeology: 3. Early Herders and their Flocks.* J. Clutton-Brock and C. Grigson, eds. Pp. 371–93. British Archaeological Reports, International Series. Oxford: British Archaeological Reports.

Vonk, Jennifer, Sarah F. Brosnan, Joan B. Silk, Joseph Henrich, Amanda S. Richardson, Susan P. Lambeth, Steven J. Schapiro, and Daniel J. Povinelli 2008 Chimpanzees do not take advantage of very low cost opportunities to deliver food to unrelated group members. *Animal Behaviour* 75(5):1757–70.

Voytek, Barbara A., and Ruth E. Tringham 1988 Rethinking the Mesolithic: The case of southeast Europe. In *The Mesolithic in Europe.* C. Bonsall, ed. Pp. 492–9. Edinburgh: University of Edinburgh Press.

Vucetich, John A., Rolf. O. Peterson, and Thomas A. Waite 2004 Raven scavenging favours group foraging in wolves. *Animal Behaviour* 67(6):1117–26.

Waguespack, Nicole M. 2002 Caribou sharing and storage: Refitting the Palangana site. *Journal of Anthropological Archaeology* 21(3):396–417.

Waldren, William H. 1974 Evidence of the extinction of the *Myotragus balearicus*. In *Prehistoria y Arqueología de las Islas Baleares: VI Simposium de Prehistoria Peninsular.* Pp. 31–8. Instituto del Arqueología y Prehistoria, Publicaciones Eventuales. Barcelona: Universidad de Barcelona.

Waldren, William H. 1982 *Balearic Prehistoric Ecology and Culture: The Excavation of Certain Caves, Rock Shelters and Settlements.* British Archaeological Reports, International Series, No. 149. Oxford: British Archaeological Reports.

Walens, Stanley J. 1982 The weight of my name is a mountain of blankets: Potlatch ceremonies. In *Celebration: Studies in Festivity and Ritual.* V. W. Turner, ed. Pp. 178–89. Washington, DC: Smithsonian Institution Press.

Walsh, Kathleen D. 1989 *Cattle of the Moon: Religion and Ritual in the Domestication and Early History of* Bos primigenius *in the Mediterranean Region.* Unpublished Ph.D. thesis, University of California, Berkeley.

Walter, Hartmut S. 2004 The mismeasure of islands: Implications for biogeographical theory and the conservation of nature. *Journal of Biogeography* 31(2):177–98.

Wang, Weiming, Jin-Long Ding, Junwu Shu, and Wei Chen 2010 Exploration of early rice farming in China. *Quaternary International* 227(1):22–8.

Wapnish, Paula, and Brian C. Hesse 1993 Pampered pooches or plain pariahs? The Ashkelon dog burials. *Biblical Archaeologist* 56(2):55–80.

Ward, Anne 1968 The Cretan bull-sports. *Antiquity* 42(166):117–22.

Warman, Sylvia 2004 Predynastic Egyptian bovid burial in the elite cemetery at Hieronkonpolis. In *Behaviour behind Bones: The Zooarchaeology of Ritual, Religion, Status and Identity.* S. J. O'Day, W. Van Neer, and A. Ervynck, eds. Pp. 34–40. Oxford: Oxbow.

Warren, Diane M. 2000 Palaeopathology of Archaic period dogs from the North American Southeast. In *Dogs through Time: An Archaeological Perspective.* S. J. Crockford, ed. Pp. 105–14. British Archaeological Reports, International Series. Oxford: Archaeopress.

Washburn, Sherwood L., and Virginia Avis 1958 Evolution of human behavior. In *Behavior and Evolution.* A. Roe and G. G. Simpson, eds. Pp. 421–436. New Haven: Yale University Press.

Washburn, Sherwood L., and Chesley S. Lancaster 1968 The evolution of hunting. In *Man the Hunter.* R. B. Lee and I. DeVore, eds. Pp. 293–303. New York: Aldine.

Washburne, Chandler 1961 *Primitive Drinking: A Study of the Uses and Functions of Alcohol in Preliterate Societies.* New York: College and University Press.

Waters, Michael R. *et al.* 2011 The Buttermilk Creek Complex and the origins of Clovis at the Debra L. Friedkin site, Texas. *Science* 331(6024):1599–1603.

Waters, Michael R., and Thomas W. Stafford, Jr. 2007 Redefining the age of Clovis: Implications for the peopling of the Americas. *Science* 315(5815):1122–6.

Watson, James B. 1977 Pigs, fodder, and the Jones Effect in Postipomoean New Guinea. *Ethnology* 16(1):57–70.

Watson, John P. N. 1979 The estimation of the relative frequencies of mammalian species: Khirokitia 1972. *Journal of Archaeological Science* 6:127–37.

Watson, Patty Jo 1979 *Archaeological Ethnography in Western Iran*. Viking Fund Publications in Anthropology, No. 57. Tucson: University of Arizona Press.

Webb, R. Esmée 1998 Megamarsupial extinction: The carrying capacity argument. *Antiquity* 72(275):46–55.

Webb, S. David, ed. 2006 *First Floridians and Last Mastodons: The Page-Ladson Site in the Aucilla River*. New York: Springer.

Webb, S. David, and C. Andrew Hemmings 2006 Last horses and first humans in North America. In *Horses and Humans: The Evolution of Human-Equine Relationships*. S. L. Olsen, S. Grant, A. M. Choyke, and L. Bartosiewicz, eds. Pp. 11–23. British Archeological Reports, International Series. Oxford: Archaeopress.

Webb, S. David, Jerald T. Milanich, Roger C. Alexon, and James S. Dunbar 1984 A *Bison antiquus* kill site, Wacissa River, Jefferson County, Florida. *American Antiquity* 49(2):384–92.

Webb, William S., and Raymond S. Baby 1957 *The Adena People: No. 2*. Columbus: Ohio Historical Society.

Weiner, Annette B. 1992 *Inalienable Possessions: The Paradox of Keeping-while-Giving*. Berkeley: University of California Press.

Weinstock, Jaco 2002 Reindeer hunting in the Upper Palaeolithic: Sex ratios as a reflection of different procurement strategies. *Journal of Archaeological Science* 29(4):365–77.

Weir, Alex A. S., Jackie Chappell, and Alex Kacelnik 2002 Shaping of hooks in New Caledonian crows. *Science* 297(5583):981.

Weir, Alex A. S., and Alex Kacelnik 2006 A New Caledonian crow (*Corvus moneduloides*) creatively re-designs tools by bending or unbending aluminium strips. *Animal Cognition* 9(4):317–34.

Weissbrod, Lior, and Guy Bar-Oz 2004 Caprines and toads: Taphonomic patterning of animal offering practices in a Late Bronze Age burial assemblage. In *Behaviour behind Bones: The Zooarchaeology of Ritual, Religion, Status and Identity*. S. J. O'Day, W. Van Neer, and A. Ervynck, eds. Pp. 20–4. Oxford: Oxbow.

Wells, Neil A., and Benjamin R. Andriamihaja 1997 Extreme gully erosion in Madagascar and its natural and anthropogenic causes. In *Natural Change and Human Impact in Madagascar*. S. M. Goodman and B. D. Patterson, eds. Pp. 44–74. Washington, DC: Smithsonian Institution Press.

Wengrow, David 1998 'The changing face of clay': Continuity and change in the transition from village to urban life in the Near East. *Antiquity* 72(278):783–95.

West, Dixie L. 1997 *Hunting Strategies in Central Europe during the Last Glacial Maximum.* British Archaeological Reports, International Series, No. 672. Oxford: British Archaeological Reports.

West, Dixie L. 2001 Mammoth hunting or scavenging during the Upper Paleolithic? In *Proceedings of the International Conference on Mammoth Site Studies.* D. L. West, ed. Pp. 57–67. University of Kansas Publications in Anthropology. Lawrence, KS: University of Kansas Department of Anthropology.

West, Dixie L. 2006 Horse hunting in Central Europe at the end of the Pleistocene. In *Horses and Humans: The Evolution of Human-Equine Relationships.* S. L. Olsen, S. Grant, A. M. Choyke, and L. Bartosiewicz, eds. Pp. 25–47. British Archeological Reports, International Series. Oxford: Archaeopress.

West, Terry L. 1983 Family herds – individual owners: Livestock ritual and inheritance among the Aymara of Bolivia. In *The Keeping of Animals: Adaptation and Social Relations in Livestock Producing Communities.* R. Berleant-Schiller and E. Shanklin, eds. Pp. 93–106. Totowa, NJ: Allenheld, Osmun.

Wheat, Joe Ben 1972 *The Olsen-Chubbuck Site: A Paleoindian Bison Kill.* Society for American Archaeology Memoirs, No. 26. Washington, DC: Society for American Archaeology.

Whitcher, Sarah E., Caroline Grigson, and Thomas E. Levy 1998 Recent faunal analyses at Shiqmim, Israel: A preliminary analysis of the 1993 assemblage. In *Archaeozoology of the Near East III: Proceedings of the Third International Symposium on the Archaeozoology of Southwestern Asia and Adjacent Areas.* H. Buitenhuis, L. Bartosiewicz, and A. M. Choyke, eds. Pp. 103–16. Groningen: Groninger Institute for Archaeology.

White, Arthur W., Trevor H. Worthy, Stuart Hawkins, Stuart Bedford, and Matthew Spriggs 2010 Megafaunal meiolaniid horned turtles survived until early human settlement in Vanuatu, Southwest Pacific. *Proceedings of the National Academy of Sciences* 107(35):15512–16.

White, Christine D., Mary E. D. Pohl, Henry P. Schwarcz, and Fred J. Longstaffe 2001 Isotopic evidence for Maya patterns of deer and dog use at Preclassic Colha. *Journal of Archaeological Science* 28(1):89–107.

White, Christine D., Mary E. D. Pohl, Henry P. Schwarcz, and Fred J. Longstaffe 2004 Feast, field, and forest: Deer and dog diets at Lagartero, Tikal, and Copán. In *Maya Zooarchaeology: New Directions in Method and Theory.* K. F. Emery, ed. Pp. 141–58. Los Angeles: Cotsen Institute of Archaeology, University of California, Los Angeles.

White, Elwyn Brooks 1952 *Charlotte's Web.* New York: Harper & Bros.

White, Randall 1989 Husbandry and herd control in the Upper Paleolithic: A critical review of the evidence. *Current Anthropology* 30(5):609–32.

White, Theodore E. 1952 Observations on the butchering technique of some aboriginal peoples. I. *American Antiquity* 17(4):337–8.

White, Theodore E. 1953a A method of calculating the dietary percentage of various food animals utilized by aboriginal peoples. *American Antiquity* 18(4):396–8.

White, Theodore E. 1953b Observations on the butchering technique of some aboriginal peoples. No. 2. *American Antiquity* 19:160–4.

White, Theodore E. 1954 Observations on the butchering technique of some aboriginal peoples. Nos. 3, 4, 5, and 6. *American Antiquity* 19(3):254–64.

White, Theodore E. 1955 Observations on the butchering technique of some aboriginal peoples. Nos. 7, 8, and 9. *American Antiquity* 20:170–8.

Whitehead, Harriet 2000 *Food Rules: Hunting, Sharing, and Tabooing Game in Papua New Guinea*. Ann Arbor: University of Michigan Press.

Whiten, Andrew, and Carel P. van Schaik 2007 The evolution of animal 'cultures' and social intelligence. *Philosophical Transactions of the Royal Society of London. Series B, Biological Sciences* 362(1480):603–20.

Whitley, David S. 1992 Prehistory and post-positivist science: A prolegomenon to cognitive archaeology. In *Archaeological Method and Theory*. M. B. Schiffer, ed. Pp. 57–100. Vol. 4. Tucson: University of Arizona Press.

Whitley, David S. 1998 Cognitive neuroscience, shamanism and rock art of native California. *Anthropology of Consciousness* 9(1):22–37.

Whittle, Alasdair, and Joshua Pollard 1999 The harmony of symbols: Wider meanings. In *The Harmony of Symbols: The Windmill Hill Causewayed Enclosure*. A. Whittle, J. Pollard, and C. Grigson, eds. Pp. 381–90. Oxford: Oxbow.

Wiessner, Polly 1983 Style and social information in Kalahari San projectile points. *American Antiquity* 48(2):253–76.

Wiessner, Polly 1996 Leveling the hunter: Constraints on the status quest in foraging societies. In *Food and the Status Quest: An Interdisciplinary Perspective*. P. Wiessner and W. Schiefenhövel, eds. Pp. 171–91. Providence: Berghahn Books.

Wiessner, Polly 2001 Of feasting and value: Enga feasts in a historical perspective (Papua New Guinea). In *Feasts: Archaeological and Ethnographic Perspectives on Food, Politics, and Power*. M. Dietler and B. D. Hayden, eds. Pp. 115–43. Washington, DC: Smithsonian Institution Press.

Wilken, G. A. 1883 *Over de Verwantschap en het Huwelijksen Erfrecht bij de Volken van den Indischen Archipel: Beschouwd uit het Oogpunt van de Nieuwere Leerstellingen op het Gebied der Maatschappelijke Ontwikkelingsgeschiedenis*. Leiden: E. J. Brill.

Wilkens, Barbara 1996 The fauna from Italian excavations on Crete. In *The Pleistocene and Holocene Fauna of Crete and its First Settlers*. D. S. Reese, ed. Pp. 241–62. Monographs in World Archaeology. Madison: Prehistory Press.

Wilkens, Barbara 1997 Restes de chiens provenant d'un puits de l'Age du Fer à Lavello, Potenza (Italie). *Anthropozoologica* 25/26:799–801.

Wilkens, Barbara 2004 Roman *suovitaurilia* and its predecessors. In *Behaviour behind Bones: The Zooarchaeology of Ritual, Religion, Status and Identity*. S. J. O'Day, W. Van Neer, and A. Ervynck, eds. Pp. 73–6. Oxford: Oxbow.

Wilkens, Barbara 2006 The sacrifice of dogs in ancient Italy. In *Dogs and People in Social, Working, Economic or Symbolic Interaction*. L. M. Snyder and E. A. Moore, eds. Pp. 132–7. Oxford: Oxbow.

Willcox, George H., Sandra Fornite, and Linda Herveux 2008 Early Holocene cultivation before domestication in northern Syria. *Vegetation History and Archaeobotany* 17(3):313–25.

Willerslev, Rane 2007 *Soul Hunters: Hunting, Animism, and Personhood among the Siberian Yukaghirs*. Berkeley: University of California Press.

Williams, Mike 2002 Tales from the dead: Remembering the bog bodies in the Iron Age of north-western Europe. In *Archaeologies of Remembrance: Death and Memory in Past Societies*. H. Williams, ed. Pp. 89–112. Dordrecht: Kluwer Academic Publishers.

Willis, Katherine J., and Keith D. Bennett 1994 The Neolithic transition – Fact or fiction? Palaeoecological evidence from the Balkans. *The Holocene* 4(3):326–30.

Willoughby, Pamela R. 1991 Human origins and the sexual division of labour: An archaeological perspective. In *The Archaeology of Gender*. D. Walde and N. D. Willows, eds. Pp. 284–91. Calgary: Archaeological Association of the University of Calgary.

Wilmshurst, Janet M., Atholl J. Anderson, Thomas F. G. Higham, and Trevor H. Worthy 2008 Dating the late prehistoric dispersal of Polynesians to New Zealand using the commensal Pacific rat. *Proceedings of the National Academy of Sciences* 105(22):7676–80.

Wilson, Bob 1992 Considerations for the identification of ritual deposits of animal bones in Iron Age pits. *International Journal of Osteoarchaeology* 2:341–9.

Wilson, Bob 1996 Aspects of the literature on the theory and identification of ritual. In *Ritual Treatment of Human and Animal Remains: Proceedings of the First Meeting of the Osteoarchaeological Research Group Held in Cambridge on 8th October 1994*. S. Anderson and K. V. Boyle, eds. Pp. 11–15. Oxford: Oxbow.

Wilson, Daniel 1862 *Prehistoric Man: Researches into the Origin of Civilisation in the Old and the New World*. Cambridge: Macmillan.

Wilson, Don E., and DeeAnn M. Reeder, eds. 2005 *Mammal Species of the World: A Taxonomic and Geographic Reference*. Third edition. Baltimore: Johns Hopkins University Press.

Wilson, Douglas C., and William L. Rathje 2001 Garbage and the modern American feast. In *Feasts: Archaeological and Ethnographic Perspectives on Food, Politics, and Power*. M. Dietler and B. D. Hayden, eds. Pp. 404–21. Washington, DC: Smithsonian Institution Press.

Wilson, Edward O. 1975 *Sociobiology: The New Synthesis.* Cambridge: Harvard University Press.

Wilson, Edward O. 1984 *Biophilia.* Cambridge: Harvard University Press.

Wilson, Edward O. 1993 Biophilia and the conservation ethic. In *The Biophilia Hypothesis.* S. R. Kellert and E. O. Wilson, eds. Pp. 31–41. Washington, DC: Island Press.

Wilson, Peter J. 1988 *The Domestication of the Human Species.* New Haven: Yale University Press.

Winder, Nicholas P. 1991 How many bones make five? The art and science of guesstimation in archaeozoology. *International Journal of Osteoarchaeology* 1(2):111–26.

Wing, Elizabeth S. 1977 Animal domestication in the Andes. In *Origins of Agriculture.* C. A. Reed, ed. Pp. 837–59. The Hague: Mouton.

Wing, Elizabeth S. 1978 Use of dogs for food: An adaptation to the coastal environment. In *Prehistoric Coastal Adaptations: The Economy and Ecology of Maritime Middle America.* B. L. Stark and B. Voorhies, eds. Pp. 29–41. New York: Academic Press.

Wing, Elizabeth S. 1984 Use and abuse of dogs. In *Contributions in Quaternary Vertebrate Paleontology.* H. H. Genoways and M. R. Dawson, eds. Pp. 228–32. Carnegie Museum of Natural History Special Publications.

Wing, Elizabeth S. 1993 The realm between wild and domestic. In *Skeletons in Her Cupboard: Festschrift for Juliet Clutton-Brock.* A. T. Clason, S. Payne, and H.-P. Uerpmann, eds. Pp. 243–50. Oxbow Monograph. Oxford: Oxbow.

Winkelman, Michael 2002 Shamanism and cognitive evolution. *Cambridge Archaeological Journal* 12(1):71–101.

Winkelman, Michael 2010 The shamanic paradigm: Evidence from ethnology, neuropsychology and ethology. *Time and Mind* 3:159–82.

Winterhalder, Bruce 1986 Diet choice, risk, and food sharing in a stochastic environment. *Journal of Anthropological Archaeology* 5:369–92.

Wobber, Victoria, Brian Hare, and Richard W. Wrangham 2008 Great apes prefer cooked food. *Journal of Human Evolution* 55(2):340–8.

Wojtal, Piotr, and Krzysztof Sobczyk 2005 Man and woolly mammoth at the Kraków Spadzista Street (B) – taphonomy of the site. *Journal of Archaeological Science* 32(2):193–206.

Wolverton, Steve 2010 The North American Pleistocene overkill hypothesis and the re-wilding debate. *Diversity and Distributions* 16(5):874–6.

Wood, Brian, and Kim Hill 2000 A test of the 'showing-off' hypothesis with Ache hunters. *Current Anthropology* 41(1):124–5.

Woodburn, James 1968 An introduction to Hadza ecology. In *Man the Hunter.* R. B. Lee and I. DeVore, eds. Pp. 49–55. New York: Aldine.

Woodburn, James 1982 Egalitarian societies. *Man* (n.s.) 17(3):431–51.

Woodburn, James 1998 'Sharing is not a form of exchange': Property-sharing in immediate-return hunter-gatherer societies. In *Property Relations:*

*Renewing the Anthropological Tradition.* C. M. Hann, ed. Pp. 48–63. Cambridge: Cambridge University Press.

Woolf, Alex, and Roy Eldridge 1994 Sharing a drink with Marcel Mauss: The uses and abuses of alcohol in early medieval Europe. *Journal of European Archaeology* 2(2):327–40.

Worthy, Trevor H., and Richard N. Holdaway 2002 *The Lost World of the Moa: Prehistoric Life of New Zealand.* Bloomington: Indiana University Press.

Wragg, G. M., and Marshall I. Weisler 1994 Extinctions and new records of birds from Henderson Island, Pitcairn Group, South Pacific Ocean. *Notornis* 41:61–70.

Wrangham, Richard W. 2009 *Catching Fire: How Cooking Made Us Human.* New York: Basic Books.

Wrangham, Richard W., James H. Jones, Greg Laden, David Pilbeam, and NancyLou Conklin-Brittain 1999 The raw and the stolen: Cooking and the ecology of human origins. *Current Anthropology* 40(5):567–94.

Wrangham, Richard W., and Dale Peterson 1996 *Demonic Males: Apes and the Origins of Human Violence.* Boston: Houghton Mifflin.

Wright, Gary A. 1978 Social differentiation in the early Natufian. In *Social Archeology: Beyond Subsistence and Dating.* C. L. Redman, M. J. Berman, E. V. Curtin, W. T. Langhorne, N. M. Versaggi, and J. C. Wanser, eds. Pp. 201–23. New York: Academic Press.

Wright, James C. 2004 A survey of evidence for feasting in Mycenaean society. In *The Mycenaean Feast.* J. C. Wright, ed. Pp. 13–58. Hesperia. Princeton: American School of Classical Studies.

Wright, Katherine I. 2000 The social origins of cooking and dining in early villages of western Asia. *Proceedings of the Prehistoric Society* 66:89–121.

Wroe, Stephen, and Judith H. Field 2006 A review of the evidence for a human role in the extinction of Australian megafauna and an alternative interpretation. *Quaternary Science Reviews* 25(21–22):2692–703.

Wylie, Turrell 1964–1965 Mortuary customs at Sa-skya, Tibet. *Harvard Journal of Asiatic Studies* 25:229–42.

Yartah, Thaer 2005 Les bâtiments communitaires de Tell 'Abr 3 (PPNA, Syrie). *Neo-Lithics* 1/05:3–9.

Yellen, John E. 1977 Cultural patterning in faunal remains: Evidence from the !Kung Bushmen. In *Experimental Archeology.* D. W. Ingersoll, Jr., J. E. Yellen, and W. MacDonald, eds. Pp. 271–331. New York: Columbia University Press.

Yen, Douglas E. 1989 The domestication of environment. In *Foraging and Farming: The Evolution of Plant Exploitation.* D. R. Harris and G. C. Hillman, eds. Pp. 55–75. London: Unwin Hyman.

Yohe, Robert M., II, and Max G. Pavesic 2000 Early Archaic domestic dogs from western Idaho, USA. In *Dogs through Time: An Archaeological Perspective.* S. J. Crockford, ed. Pp. 93–104. British Archaeological Reports, International Series. Oxford: Archaeopress.

Yorzinski, Jessica L., Sandra L. Vehrencamp, Anne B. Clark, and Kevin J. McGowan 2006 The inflected alarm caw of the American Crow: Differences in acoustic structure among individuals and sexes. *Condor* 108(3):518–29.

Young, Michael W. 1971 *Fighting with Food: Leadership, Values and Social Control in a Massim Society*. Cambridge: Cambridge University Press.

Younger, John G. 1976 Bronze Age representations of Aegean bull-leaping. *American Journal of Archaeology* 80(2):125–37.

Yuan, Jing, and Rowan K. Flad 2005 New zooarchaeological evidence for changes in Shang Dynasty animal sacrifice. *Journal of Anthropological Archaeology* 24(3):252–70.

Yuan, Jing, Rowan K. Flad, and Yunbing Luo 2008 Meat-acquisition patterns in the Neolithic Yangzi river valley, China. *Antiquity* 82(316):351–66.

Zachrisson, Inger, and Elisabeth Iregren 1974 *Lappish Bear Graves in Northern Sweden: An Archaeological and Osteological Study*. Early Norrland, No. 5. Stockholm: Kungl. Vitterhets Historie och Antikvitets Akademien.

Zalai-Gaál, István 1998 Das Rindergrab von Endröd 130: Neue Angaben zum Tierkult der mitteleuropäischen Kupferzeit. In *Man and the Animal World: Studies in Archaeozoology, Archaeology, Anthropology and Palaeolinguistics in Memoriam Sandor Bökönyi*. P. P. Anreiter, L. Bartosiewicz, E. Jerem, and W. Meid, eds. Pp. 545–68. Budapest: Archaeolingua Alapítvány.

Zarins, Juris 1986 Equids associated with human burials in third millennium B.C. Mesopotamia: Two complementary facets. In *Equids in the Ancient World*. R. H. Meadow and H.-P. Uerpmann, eds. Pp. 164–93. Tübinger Atlas des Vorderen Orients, Reihe A, Naturwissenschaften. Wiesbaden: Dr. Ludwig Reichert Verlag.

Zarur, Elizabeth N. C. 1991 Social and spiritual languages of feather art: The Bororo of central Brazil. In *The Gift of Birds: Featherwork of Native South American Peoples*. R. E. Reina and K. M. Kensinger, eds. Pp. 26–39. University Museum Monograph. Philadelphia: University of Pennsylvania, University Museum.

Zeder, Melinda A. 1991 *Feeding Cities: Specialized Animal Economy in the Ancient Near East*. Washington, DC: Smithsonian Institution Press.

Zeder, Melinda A. 1998 Pigs and emergent complexity in the ancient Near East. In *Ancestors for the Pigs: Pigs in Prehistory*. S. M. Nelson, ed. Pp. 109–22. MASCA Research Papers in Science and Archaeology. Philadelphia: University of Pennsylvania, University Museum.

Zeder, Melinda A. 2001 A metrical analysis of a collection of modern goats (*Capra hircus aegagrus* and *C. h. hircus*) from Iran and Iraq: Implications for the study of caprine domestication. *Journal of Archaeological Science* 28(1):61–79.

Zeder, Melinda A. 2008 Domestication and early agriculture in the Mediterranean Basin: Origins, diffusion, and impact. *Proceedings of the National Academy of Sciences* 105(33):11597–604.

Zeder, Melinda A., and Susan R. Arter 1996 Meat consumption and bone use in a Mississippian village. In *Case Studies in Environmental Archaeology*. E. J. Reitz, L. A. Newsom, and S. J. Scudder, eds. Pp. 319–38. New York: Plenum.

Zeder, Melinda A., and Brian C. Hesse 2000 The initial domestication of goats (*Capra hircus*) in the Zagros Mountains 10,000 years ago. *Science* 287(5461):2254–7.

Zeuner, Frederick E. 1953 The colour of the wild cattle of Lascaux. *Man* 53:68–9.

Zeuner, Frederick E. 1958 Animal remains from a Late Bronze Age sanctuary on Cyprus, and the problem of the domestication of fallow deer. *Journal of the Palaeontological Society of India* 3:131–5.

Zeuner, Frederick E. 1963 *A History of Domesticated Animals*. New York: Harper & Row.

Zihlman, Adrienne L. 1981 Women as shapers of the human adaptation. In *Woman the Gatherer*. F. Dahlberg, ed. Pp. 75–120. New Haven: Yale University Press.

Zihlman, Adrienne L. 1991 Did the australopithecines have a division of labor? In *The Archaeology of Gender*. D. Walde and N. D. Willows, eds. Pp. 64–70. Calgary: Archaeological Association of the University of Calgary.

Zihlman, Adrienne L. 1997 The Paleolithic glass ceiling: Women in human evolution. In *Women in Human Evolution*. L. D. Hager, ed. Pp. 91–113. London: Routledge.

Zihlman, Adrienne L., and Nancy Makepeace Tanner 1978 Gathering and the hominid adaptation. In *Female Hierarchies*. L. Tiger and H. Fowler, eds. Pp. 163–94. Chicago: Beresford Book Service.

Zohary, Daniel 1999 Domestication of the Neolithic Near Eastern crop assemblage. In *Prehistory of Agriculture: New Experimental and Ethnographic Approaches*. P. C. Anderson, ed. Pp. 42–50. Monograph. Los Angeles: UCLA Institute of Archaeology.

Zohary, Daniel, and Maria Hopf 2000 *Domestication of Plants in the Old World: The Origin and Spread of Cultivated Plants in West Asia, Europe, and the Nile Valley*. Third edition. Oxford: Oxford University Press.

Zohary, Daniel, Eitan Tchernov, and Liora R. K. Horwitz 1998 The role of unconscious selection in the domestication of sheep and goats. *Journal of Zoology* 245:129–35.

Zvelebil, Marek 1986 Mesolithic societies and the transition to farming: Problems of time, scale and organisation. In *Hunters in Transition: Mesolithic Societies of Temperate Eurasia and their Transition to Farming*. M. Zvelebil, ed. Pp. 167–88. Cambridge: Cambridge University Press.

Zvelebil, Marek 1996 The agricultural frontier and the transition to farming in the circum-Baltic region. In *The Origins and Spread of Agriculture and Pastoralism in Eurasia*. D. R. Harris, ed. Pp. 323–45. London: UCL Press.

Zvelebil, Marek 2000 Fat is a feminist issue: On ideology, diet and health in hunter-gatherer societies. In *Gender and Material Culture in Archaeological Perspective*. M. Donald and L. Hurcombe, eds. Pp. 209–21. New York: St. Martin's Press.

Zvelebil, Marek, and Malcolm C. Lillie 2000 Transition to agriculture in eastern Europe. In *Europe's First Farmers*. T. D. Price, ed. Pp. 57–92. Cambridge: Cambridge University Press.

# Index